Neoliberalism or Developmentalism

Studies in Critical Social Sciences Book Series

Haymarket Books is proud to be working with Brill Academic Publishers (www.brill.nl) to republish the *Studies in Critical Social Sciences* book series in paperback editions. This peer-reviewed book series offers insights into our current reality by exploring the content and consequences of power relationships under capitalism, and by considering the spaces of opposition and resistance to these changes that have been defining our new age. Our full catalog of *SCSS* volumes can be viewed at https://www.haymarketbooks .org/series_collections/4-studies-in-critical-social-sciences.

NEOLIBERALISM OR DEVELOPMENTALISM

The PT Governments in the Eye of the Storm

EDITED BY

ALFREDO SAAD-FILHO
ANA PAULA FREGNANI COLOMBI
JUAN GRIGERA

Haymarket Books
Chicago, IL

First published in 2022 by Brill Academic Publishers, The Netherlands
© 2022 Koninklijke Brill NV, Leiden, The Netherlands

Published in paperback in 2023 by
Haymarket Books
P.O. Box 180165
Chicago, IL 60618
773-583-7884
www.haymarketbooks.org

ISBN: 978-1-64259-8100

Distributed to the trade in the US through Consortium Book Sales and
Distribution (www.cbsd.com) and internationally through Ingram Publisher
Services International (www.ingramcontent.com).

This book was published with the generous support of Lannan Foundation and
Wallace Action Fund.

Special discounts are available for bulk purchases by organizations and
institutions. Please call 773-583-7884 or email info@haymarketbooks.org for more
information.

Cover design by Jamie Kerry and Ragina Johnson.

Printed in the United States.

10 9 8 7 6 5 4 3 2 1

Library of Congress Cataloging-in-Publication data is available.

Contents

Acknowledgements

We are grateful to the journal *Latin American Perspectives* (LAP) for their permission to include in this collection updated versions of essays originally published in LAP 47 (1) and 47 (2), 2020, and to Patrícia Fierro, Luis Fierro and Sean Purdy for their translations of several contributions to *Latin American Perspectives*.

Figures and Tables

Figures

Tables

Abbreviations

ABAG	Associação Brasileira do Agronegócio (Brazilian Agribusiness Association)
ALADI	Associação Latino-Americana de Integração (Latin American Integration Association)
BCB	Banco Central do Brasil (Central Bank of Brazil)
BNDES	Banco Nacional de Desenvolvimento Econômico e Social (Brazilian Development Bank)
BPC	Benefício de Prestação Continuada (Continued Assistance Programme)
BRICS	Brazil, Russia, India, China and South Africa
CB	Cross-border
CBIC	Câmara Brasileira da Indústria da Construção (Brazilian Chamber of the Construction Industry)
CCTs	Conditional Cash Transfers
CELAC	Comunidade de Estados Latino-Americanos e Caribenhos (Community of Stades Latin Americans and Caribbean)
CEO	Chief Executive Officer
CGTB	Central Geral dos Trabalhadores do Brasil
CII	*Coeficiente* de Insumo Industrial Importado (Imported Industrial Input Coefficient)
CLAS	Centre of Latin American Studies
CNI	Confederação Nacional da Indústria (National Confederation of Industry)
CODACE	Comitê de Datação de Ciclos Econômicos (Brazilian Business Cycle Dating Committee)
CSP	Central Sindical e Popular
CTB	Central de Trabalhadores e Trabalhadoras do Brasil
CUT	Central Única dos Trabalhadores
CX	Coefficient of Exports
DIEESE	Departamento Intersindical de Estatística e Estudos Socioeconômicos (Inter-union Department of Statistics and Socioeconomic Studies)
EC95	Emenda Constitucional 95 (Constitutional Amendment 95)
ECLAC	Economic Commission for Latin America and the Caribbean
FEBRABAN	Federação Brasileira de Bancos (Brazilian Federation of Banks)
FGTS	Fundo de Garantia Por Tempo de Serviço (Severance Indemnity Fund for employee)
FHC	Fernando Henrique Cardoso
FIES	Fundo de Financiamento Estudantil (Student Financing Fund)

FIESP	Federação das Indústrias do Estado de São Paulo (Federation of Industries of the State of São Paulo)
FIFA	Fédération Internationale de Football Association
FS	Força Sindical
FTAA	Free Trade Area of the Americas
GDP	Gross Domestic Product
HEI	Higher Education Institutions
IBGE	Instituto Brasileiro de Geografia e Estatística (Brazilian Institute of Geography and Statistics)
IBSA	India–Brazil–South-Africa
IDEB	Índice de Desenvolvimento da Educação Básica (Basic Education Development Index)
IEDI	Instituto de Estudos para o Desenvolvimento Industrial (Institute of Study for Industrial Development)
IGP-DI	Índice Geral de Preços (General Price Index)
ILO	Interntional Labor Organization
IMF	International Monetary Fund
INPC	Índice Nacional de Preços ao Consumidor (National Price Index for Consumers)
IPCA	Índice Nacional de Preços ao Consumidor Amplo (Extended National Price Index for Consumers)
IPEA	Instituto de Pesquisa Econômica Aplicada (Institute for Applied Economic Research)
ISI	Import Substituting Industrialisation
LAP	Latin American Perspectives
LP	Labour Power
MAV	Manufacturing Value Added
MCMV	Minha Casa, Minha Vida (My House, My Life)
MERCOSUR	Mercado Comum do Sul (Southern Economic Market)
MWS	Minimum Wages
NEM	New Economic Matrix
NFP	National Fascist Party
NGO	Non-governmental Organization
NHS	British National Health Service
NPRD	National Policy for Regional Development
OECD	Organisation for Economic Co-operation and Development
PAC	Programa de Aceleração do Crescimento (Growth Acceleration Programme)
PBF	Programa Bolsa Família (Family Allowance Programme)

PEC	Proposta de Emenda Constitucional (Constitutional Amendment Proposal)
PMDB	Partido Movimento Brasileiro (Brazilian Democratic Movement Party)
PNAD	Pesquisa Nacional por Amostra de Domicílios (Continuous National Household Survey)
PPA	Pluri(Multi) Annual Plan
PPE	Programa de Proteção ao Emprego (Employment Protection Program)
PREVIC	Superintendência Nacional de Previdência Complementar (National Office of Supplementary Social Security)
ProUni	Programa Universidade para Todos (University for Everyone Programme)
PSDB	Partido da Social Democracia Brasileira (Brazilian Social Democratic Party)
PSOL	Partido Socialismo e Liberdade (Socialism and Freedom Party)
PSTU	Partido Socialista dos Trabalhadores Unificado (Unified Workers' Socialist Party)
PT	Partido dos Trabalhadores (Brazilian Workers' Party)
QE2	Second Wave of Quantitative Easing
RAIS	Relação Anual de Informações Sociais (Annual List of Social Information)
REUNI	Programa de Apoio a Planos de Reestruturação e Expansão das Universidades Federais (University Restructuring and Expansion)
SELIC	Basic Interest Rate
SoA	System of Accumulation
STF	Supremo Tribunal Federal (Supreme Court)
SUS	Sistema Único de Saúde (Universal Healthcare System)
TCU	Tribunal de Contas da União (Brazilian Federal Court of Auditors)
TLP	Taxa de Longo Prazo (long-term rate)
TPP	Trans-Pacific Partnership
TTIP	Transatlantic Trade and Investment Partnership
UGT	União Geral dos Trabalhadores
UNASUR	União de Nações Sul-Americanas (Union of South American Nations)
UNCTAD	United Nations Conference on Trade and Development
WTO	World Trade Organization

Notes on Contributors

Lucas Salvador Andrietta
is a post-doctoral researcher at the Faculty of Medicine of the University of São Paulo, and holds a Ph.D. in Economic Development from the University of Campinas (UNICAMP). His work focuses on health policy and systems, public health, and political economy.

Marcelo Arend
is professor of economics and international relations at the Federal University of Santa Catarina and holds a postdoctoral fellowship from the Autonomous University of Madrid. His research focuses on political economy, structural change and economic development, with emphasis on industrial development and technological and institutional change.

Pedro Paulo Zahluth Bastos
is professor at the Institute of Economics, University of Campinas (UNICAMP), and was a visiting scholar at UC Berkeley (2017–2018). He is former President of Brazilian Society of Economic History (ABPHE, 2009–2011) and head of the Department of Political Economy and Economic History at UNICAMP (2008–2012). His research interests include the development of capitalism in Brazil, the political economy of economic policy, and short-term macroeconomic analysis.

Armando Boito Jr.
is professor of political science at the University of Campinas (UNICAMP), and editor of the journal Crítica Marxista.

Ruy Braga
is professor at the Department of Sociology of the University of São Paulo and a Research Associate at Society, Work and Politics Institute (SWOP), University of Witwatersrand. He specialises in the sociology of work, focusing on classes and social movements. His book *The politics of the precariat: from populism to Lulista hegemony* (Brill, 2018) was a finalist for the Jabuti award (the most prestigious award in Brazilian literature).

Soraia Aparecida Cardozo
is professor of economics at the Federal University of Uberlândia. Her main areas of interest are regional development and regional development policies.

Ana Paula Fregnani Colombi
is professor at the Federal University of Espírito Santo and a researcher at the Brazilian Centre of Studies in Trade Unionism and Labor Economics, at the University of Campinas (UNICAMP). Her main areas of interest are labor economics and trade unionism.

Luiz Fernando de Paula
is professor of economics at the Institute of Economics of the Federal University of Rio de Janeiro, and at the Institute of Social and Political Studies at the State University of Rio de Janeiro, and researcher at CNPq and FAPERJ. His work focuses on monetary economics and development, financial systems, currency hierarchy, financialization, Post-Keynesian economics and Latin American development, especially in Brazil.

Eduardo Fagnani
is professor at the Institute of Economics, University of Campinas (UNICAMP), researcher the Brazilian Centre of Studies in Trade Unionism and Labor Economics, and coordinator of its Social Policy Platform.

Cristhiane Falchetti
holds a Ph.D. in Sociology from University of São Paulo on a scholarship from the Brazilian National Council for Scientific and Technological Development. She is a lecturer at the School of Sociology and Politics of São Paulo and works on State theory and public management.

Luiz Filgueiras
is professor of economics at the Federal University of Bahia. He works in the fields of political economy, capitalist development and the contemporary Brazilian economy, focusing on the patterns of capitalist development, international insertion and economic policy. He is the author of *História do Plano Real* (2000); with Reinaldo Gonçalves, *A Economia Política do Governo Lula* (2007) and with Graça Druck, *O Brasil nas Trevas (2013–2020): do golpe neoliberal ao neofascismo* (2020).

Pedro Cezar Dutra Fonseca
is professor of economics and international relations at the Federal University of Rio Grande do Sul, co-ordinator of the Brazilian Economic Development Teaching Network, and a member of the Economics Committee of the National Council for Scientific and Technological Development and of the

board of directors of the Celso Furtado International Centre. His areas of interest include the economic development of Brazil and the history of economic thought.

Gustavo Codas Friedmann

(d. August 12, 2019) was professor at the Perseu Abramo Foundation. He was born in Paraguay and was exiled to Brazil for his political views. He was instrumental in the agreement that established the Itaipú Binacional hydroelectric dam and served as its l director general in 2010–11.

Barbara Fritz

is professor of economics for Latin America at the Freie Universität Berlin. Her work focuses on monetary economics and development, with publications on regional monetary cooperation among developing countries, macroeconomics and inequality, and Latin American development, especially in Brazil.

Andréia Galvão

is professor of political science at the University of Campinas (UNICAMP) and editor of the journal *Crítica Marxista*. Her main areas of interest are labour relations, unionism and social movements.

Denise Gentil

is professor at the Institute of Economics, Federal University of Rio de Janeiro, and her work focuses on pension reform, financialization and fiscal policy.

Juan Grigera

is lecturer at the Department of International Development, King's College London. His research interests include structural transformation, social conflict, and technological innovation.

Glaison Augusto Guerrero

is professor of economics and international relations at the Federal University of Rio Grande do Sul.

Célio Hiratuka

is professor in the Institute of Economics of the University of Campinas (UNICAMP). His research focuses on the international trade, transnational companies, foreign direct investment, industrial development and Brazil–China relations.

Cecilia Hoff

is professor in the Pontifical Catholic University of Rio Grande do Sul and a researcher in the Statistical and Economics Department of Rio Grande Sul. Her research focuses on the macroeconomics, Brazilian economy and the economy of Rio Grande do Sul.

José Dari Krein

is professor in the Institute of Economics of the University of Campinas (UNICAMP). His main research interests are on labour economics and trade unionism.

Lena Lavinas

is professor of Welfare Economics at the Institute of Economics, Federal University of Rio de Janeiro. Her current research addresses the relationship between financialization and social policy.

Patrícia Rocha Lemos

is a researcher at the Brazilian Center of Studies in Trade Unionism and Labor Economics of the University of Campinas (UNICAMP). Her main areas of interest are labour regimes in global production networks and labour movements.

Pedro Mendes Loureiro

is lecturer in Latin American Studies at the Centre of Latin American Studies (CLAS) and the Department of Politics and International Studies (POLIS), University of Cambridge, and Fellow of Fitzwilliam College. His research focuses on the dynamics of inequalities and on the critique of development strategies in Latin America.

Paula Marcelino

is professor of sociology at the University of São Paulo (USP) and editor of the journal Crítica Marxista. She works on labour and worker organisation, trade unionism, productive restructuring, gender relations at work, and the impact of neoliberalism on workers.

Adalmir Antonio Marquetti
is professor of economics and researcher in the postgraduate programme in economic development at the Pontifical Catholic University of Rio Grande do Sul.

Humberto Martins
is professor at the Institute of Economics and International Relations at the Federal University of Uberlândia. His main research interests include regional economics and economic development.

Guilherme Mello
is professor at the Institute of Economics of the University of Campinas (UNICAMP) and co-ordinator of its graduate programme in economic development. His current research addresses the styles of development of the Brazilian economy, fiscal and monetary policy.

Alessandro Miebach
is professor of economics and researcher in the postgraduate programme in economics at the Federal University of Rio Grande do Sul.

Rafael Moura
is a post-doctoral researcher at the National Institute of Science and Technology in Public Policies, Strategies and Development (INCT-PPED) and assistant secretary at the Latin American Political Science Association (ALACIP). His research interests include political economy; state capabilities for development; national innovation systems; the Chinese economy, and state-market relations in East Asian industrial policy.

Daniela Magalhães Prates
is a senior economic affairs officer at UNCTAD and associate professor of economics at the University of Campinas (UNICAMP). Her main areas of research are international economics and open macroeconomics, with focus on developing countries.

Claudio A. Castelo Branco Puty
is professor of economics at the Federal University of Pará and at the University of International Business and Economics (Beijing). He was a PT deputy in Congress from 2011 to 2015.

Pedro Rossi

is professor in the Institute of Economics of the University of Campinas (IE-UNICAMP). His work focuses on macroeconomic development in Brazil, the social impact of fiscal policy, and exchange rate policies.

Alfredo Saad-Filho

is professor and Head of Department, Department of International Development, King's College London. His main research interests include heterodox economic policy, strategies of industrial development, inflation and stabilisation, and the labour theory of value and its applications.

Fabiano Santos

is professor of political science at the Institute of Social and Political Studies at the State University of Rio de Janeiro (IESP/UERJ), and researcher at CNPq and FAPERJ.

Fabio Luis Barbosa dos Santos

is professor of Latin American studies at the Federal University of São Paulo (Unifesp), and a research associate at the Society, Work and Politics Institute (SWOP) at the University of Witwatersrand.

André Singer

is professor of political science at the University of São Paulo (USP). His research interests include Brazilian politics, the PT governments and political authoritarianism.

Introduction

Alfredo Saad-Filho, Ana Paula Fregnani Colombi and Juan Grigera

In a global context dominated by an aggressive neoliberalism, Brazil was a poster child for social democracy during the federal administrations led by the Workers' Party (*Partido dos Trabalhadores*, PT), between 2003 and 2016. Under the leadership of Presidents Luiz Inácio Lula da Silva (2003–6, 2007–10) and Dilma Rousseff (2011–14, 2015–16), Brazil achieved significant improvements in the measures of poverty, inequality, health, education, and social provision more generally, together with the acceleration of the rate of growth of GDP. These achievements were widely attributed to the drive and determination of the PT, and the political acumen of its leadership, especially President Lula.

The PT emerged in the late 1970s, out of a cycle of struggles against the military dictatorship (1964–85), and bringing together some of the most important strands of the 'new' (militant and confrontational, but not socialist in the traditional sense of the word) labour movement, left intellectuals, the powerful Liberation Theology wing of the Catholic Church, a wide range of small revolutionary left-wing organisations, many NGOs and progressive organisations, movements and individuals. The PT and its leader, Lula, gained popularity over time, but Lula only managed to win a presidential election, at his fourth attempt, when he bent over decisively towards the political centre, accommodated neoliberal economic policies, and built a broad coalition of forces in support of his administration. This rickety alliance would provide conditional support to his initiatives, and Lula would eventually achieve extraordinarily high approval rates in most opinion polls. Lula's handpicked successor, Dilma Rousseff, would not be so fortunate. She did not have Lula's charisma or his talent to bring together conflicting political forces; Rousseff also had to face a much harsher economic and political environment.

Lula's government could enjoy the favourable winds of the commodity boom and explore unprecedented spaces in global diplomacy, in order to implement neo-developmentalist policies within a broader neoliberal framework. In contrast, Rousseff had to contend both with the Global Financial Crisis (that started in 2008, but only hit Brazil after the end of the commodity boom, in 2011) and a much more assertive US foreign policy, after years of distraction in the Middle East. The cracks in the political architecture of the PT governments soon started to appear. The political coalition fractured; the neoliberal lobby of finance, business, the mainstream media, right-wing politicians and orthodox economists raised the ante, US foreign policy moved into outright sabotage, and the political right gained a mass base among the country's elite. These forces converged around allegations of corruption that encircled the federal government. Even though corruption has always been part of the political environment in Brazil, and there was nothing new or culpable in most decisions taken by the PT administrations, their alleged trespasses were weaponised by a conspiracy of elites sponsored by the US government. Large right-wing demonstrations emerged for the first time in decades, and they included increasingly radical slogans against the left, the PT, and Rousseff. The judiciary and the Federal Police joined the conspiracy and launched a wide-ranging investigation about the state-owned oil company, Petrobras (operation *lava jato*, or car wash), from which evidence was gathered to convict businesspeople and politicians linked to the PT; similar attacks were launched against Lula himself. Even though Rousseff was re-elected in 2014, the circle was becoming tighter. She was charged with fiscal malpractice (*pedaladas fiscais*, a poorly defined term that, in its vagueness, helped to provide a political smokescreen for the conspiracy) and impeached by a rebellious Congress in 2016.

This was not the end. Rousseff's Vice-President, Michel Temer – himself implicated in countless (substantiated) corruption scandals, led an authoritarian neoliberal administration that attacked labour rights, social security and all manner of achievements of the PT administrations. In the meantime, the leadership of the PT was disabled by a relentless succession of judicial attacks that would culminate with the imprisonment of former President Lula.

Despite their best efforts, the centre-right could never stabilise its own political hegemony after the impeachment. Its potential leaders were invariably implicated in glaring scandals involving public resources or worse, and their political project failed to enthuse the right-wing masses that, by then, were driving the radicalisation of the political environment. These forces coalesced around the candidacy of Federal Deputy Jair Bolsonaro in the 2018 elections. Previously a marginalised and somewhat comical political figure, Bolsonaro managed to capture growing support from business and the media, while his rivals on the moderate right fell by the wayside, one by one. At the end of a tumultuous campaign, Bolsonaro was left to confront PT candidate Fernando Haddad in the second round of the elections. While Haddad offered intelligence, flair, experience and moderation, Bolsonaro offered a fascist discourse: coarse, misogynistic, without clear policy content, and peppered with threats against his opponents. Not even one mainstream media outlet or businessperson of any significance supported Haddad, and Bolsonaro won the second round of the elections with an advantage of 10 percentage points.

Bolsonaro's administration proceeded with gusto to dismantle even more pillars of Brazil's emerging welfare state, focusing on the labour market, social security provision, the environment, and the remaining state-owned enterprises, invariably in the name of 'fiscal probity', 'credibility' and 'development'. In the meantime, Bolsonaro escalated his attacks against the left, women, minorities and Venezuela (which he offered to attack on behalf of the USA, until he was stopped by his own Armed Forces), populated his government with military officers, and brought *lava jato* into the heart of government by appointing the head of the operation, Judge Sergio Moro, as his Minister of Justice (Moro would not last long in this role, but the damage was already done).

The political storm was intensified by the deepest economic crisis in Brazilian history which, despite promises, the coup against Rousseff failed to address. On top of these entangled crises came the COVID-19 pandemic. The magnitude of the catastrophe surpassed all expectations, and it was driven entirely by Bolsonaro's obsession with 'herd immunity' – that is, resisting as much as possible any effective policies to protect public health and address the pandemic. As the death toll rose, Bolsonaro sabotaged his own Health Ministry (and went through four Ministers in the first year of the health emergency), undermined Mayors and State Governors, stood against any form of lockdown, movement restriction and even mask use, refused to support the development of vaccines in Brazil, delayed vaccine imports as much as possible, and so on, showing a determination to sabotage public health without parallel in any major country. Inevitably, given the poverty and entrenched inequalities in Brazil, the death toll from COVID-19 climbed relentlessly, leaving the country to face a catastrophe unmatched in its history.

At the time of writing, the storm due to the convergence of the political, economic and health crises threatens to engulf Bolsonaro's administration. In the meantime, Lula was released from prison and his convictions were suspended by the Supreme Court. Moro, who left the Ministry of Justice in order to pursue an independent political career, saw his hopes dashed when the Supreme Court declared him 'suspect' of being partial when leading the *lava jato* operation. The political turmoil continues. In the meantime, the economic crisis deepened because of the pandemic. This conflagration is also unprecedented.

The breathtaking sequence of tragedies overtaking Brazil has its roots in the PT administrations. It poses several puzzles which this book addresses in 19 chapters.

The first set of analyses opens with Chapter 1 by Alfredo Saad Filho. Starting from a conceptualisation of neoliberalism as a system of accumulation, or as the contemporary mode of existence of capitalism, this chapter identifies the varieties of neoliberalism in Brazil. Two varieties of this system of accumulation are identified during the period of the PT administrations: inclusive neoliberalism (2003–6), and developmental neoliberalism (2006–13). This is followed by Luiz Filgueiras, who develops in Chapter 2 the concept of patterns of capitalist development and argues that the 'liberal-peripheric' pattern is the mode of existence of neoliberalism in Brazil. This chapter also argues that, from this perspective, the administrations between Fernando Collor de Mello (1990–92) and Dilma Rousseff are fundamentally identical, while the developmentalist literature focuses on the (relatively less significant) differences between them. Chapter 3, by Daniela Prates, Barbara Fritz, and Luiz Fernando de Paula, outlines the different types of developmentalism in the literature, and use this framework to review the macroeconomic, industrial and social policies of the PT administrations, while also considering the external constraints afflicting all peripheral economies. This chapter shows that, while the PT administrations deployed different types of developmentalism, they were always attached to mainstream economic policies. In Chapter 4, Pedro Cezar Dutra Fonseca, Marcelo Arendt and Glaison Guerreiro argue that the PT was never truly developmentalist, because the party did not have a strategy to reverse Brazil's deindustrialisation. It follows that, even though the economic policies of Lula and Rousseff gradually moved away from neoliberalism, they cannot be considered developmentalist because they did not embody a national development project and were never supported by an articulation of classes that could make that project hegemonic. Chapter 5, by Gustavo Friedmann and Claudio Puty, examines the PT's politics in the context of the Latin American 'Pink Tide', and identify far more continuity than conflict between them. In the case of Brazil, their analysis of the trajectory of the PT administrations focuses on the interaction of the key economic and social policies with the interests of the ruling classes. They conclude that the PT administrations were defined by a progressive programme bounded by low conflict intensity; in other words, the attempt to promote social inclusion and improve the conditions of life and work of the majority of the population was constrained by the need to avoid tensions with the traditional ruling classes.

The following two chapters stress macroeconomic policy issues. Chapter 6, by Pedro Rossi, Guilherme Melo and Pedro Paulo Zahluth Bastos, reviews the PT's experience in the light of Celso Furtado's notion of ideal types of growth, to show how this model failed to deliver structural changes in Brazil. The difficulty confronted by the PT was how to reconcile poverty alleviation with policies promoting mass consumption, while keeping them closely articulated with the expansion of manufacturing output and productivity growth. Sadly, this proved to be impossible. Adalmir Marquetti, Cecilia Hoff and Alessandro Miebach probe, in Chapter 7, the dynamics of profitability during the first years of the PT and after the 2008 crisis. From this angle, they argue that PT governments did not confront neoliberalism; instead, rising profitability allowed neoliberal economic policies to coexist with developmentalism and facilitated a political accommodation between capitalists and workers. These favourable conditions lasted until the Global Financial Crisis eroded profitability and undermined the class alliance that had underpinned Lula's administration.

The following section turns to the Brazilian political dynamics. Armando Boito, in Chapter 8, reviews the concept of fascism, and advances the notion of neo-fascism as a way to understand the government of Jair Bolsonaro. In Chapter 9, André Singer examines the political reasons explaining the defeat of developmentalism in Brazil. This chapter suggests that the limitations and mixed fortunes of 'Lulismo' offer a valuable angle to review the failure of Dilma Rousseff's developmentalist programme. Ruy Braga and Fabio Barbosa dos Santos focus, in Chapter 10, on the accumulation strategies promoted by the PT administrations, and review the forms of political legitimacy during that period. They suggest that President Rousseff's impeachment should be understood as part of the crisis of the 'Lulista' mode of regulation of social conflicts, at which point the PT administrations lost functionality from the point of view of preserving the established order.

The following chapters focus on detailed analyses of the policies implemented by the PT governments, examining its macroeconomic, industrial, regional, labour and social policies, and the role of the trade union movement. Chapter 11, by Luiz Fernando de Paula, Fabiano Santos and Rafael Moura examines the economic and political context of the PT administrations, especially the relationship between domestic policy choices and the external constraints limiting the PT's redistributive efforts. The chapter claims that these governments shared a project close to social-developmentalism and, consequently, distinct from centrist liberalism of the previous administrations. Chapter 12, by Pedro Paulo Zahluth Bastos and Celio Hiratuka, probes the external policies of President Rousseff, emphasising their continuities with Lula's, despite the adverse shifts in the global context. Ana Paula Colombi and José Dari Krein, in Chapter 13, review the labour market policies of the PT governments, showing that, despite improved employment indicators, 'flexible' forms of labour expanded continuously during that period. Chapter 14, by Pedro Mendes Loureiro, investigates Brazil's social structure and the distributive policies of the PT administrations; the chapter argues that these policies can best be described as representing a poverty-reducing variety of neoliberalism. Andreia Galvão and Paula Marcelino, in Chapter 15, examine the trade unions, and argue that they became a subordinate force under the PT.

The final chapters turns to social policies. In Chapter 16, Lena Lavinas and Denise Gentil offer a detailed examination of the social policies in Brazil, both before and after President Rousseff's impeachment. They argue that, during the PT administrations, social inclusion was driven primarily by consumption, which carried the implication that large strata of an impoverished population must accumulate high levels of debt. At a later stage, after the coup, the provision of social services in Brazil would be defined by a logic of wholesale privatisation. Lucas Andrietta, Patrícia Rocha Lemos and Eduardo Fagnani focus on social security in Chapter 17. They claim that, despite their rhetorical differences with previous (unquestionably neoliberal) administrations, the policies of the PT governments did not change the tendency of commodification of social provision in Brazil. In Chapter 18, Cristhiane Falchetti reviews Brazil's housing policies, and highlight why and how the policies pursued by the PT have intensified the commodification of social policies in general and housing policies specifically. Finally, Chapter 19, by Soraia Cardozo and Humberto Martins, examines the regional policies under the PT, showing that they were sufficient to promote the development of poorer regions, but lacked coherence and depth to reverse regional inequalities, or to address the legacy of deprivation in the poorer areas in the country.

The essays included in this collection offer a comprehensive and penetrating review of multiple aspects of the experience of the PT in government. We hope that they will serve as a record of the achievements and shortcomings of these administrations, and support critical analyses of the economic, social, political and health storms engulfing Brazil for years to come.

CHAPTER 1

Shades of Neoliberalism: Brazil under the Workers' Party (2003–2020)

Alfredo Saad-Filho

1 Introduction[1]

On 31 August 2016, a judicial-parliamentary coup removed the fourth democratically elected federal administration led by the Brazilian Workers' Party (PT).[2] This chapter examines the achievements, limitations and collapse of the administrations led by Presidents Luís Inácio Lula da Silva (2003–6, 2007–10) and Dilma Rousseff (2011–14, 2015–16), from the point of view of the tensions and contradictions in the dominant system of accumulation (SoA) in Brazil: neoliberalism. This SoA had two varieties during the period in office of the PT, *inclusive neoliberalism* (2003–6) and *developmental neoliberalism* (2006–13) (the years 2013–16 are undefined, because economic policy became incoherent, and output and employment collapsed). They were followed by *authoritarian neoliberalism* (2016–present) after Rousseff's impeachment.

Identification of the SoA and its varieties is complex, for three reasons. First, SoAs are determined by the dominant modality of production of the material conditions of social reproduction and, at a more concrete level, by the historically specific constraints imposed upon the mode of production by the balance of payments, availability of labour and finance, the institutional framework and the political system, which must be managed by economic, industrial, social and other policies. These overlapping, shifting, and potentially contradictory determinations can make it difficult to identify the SoA and its varieties. Second, while in government, the PT had to rely on unwieldy and unstable political alliances that limited the scope for coherent policymaking. Third, the social base of support for the PT changed during their period in office, as part of the contradictions in the Party's programme and its implementation.

---

1 A previous version of this chapter was published as 'Varieties of Neoliberalism in Brazil (2003–2019)', *Latin American Perspectives* 47 (1) (2020), pp. 9–27. Extensively revised and updated for this volume.

2 For detailed accounts, see, *inter alia*, Gentili (2016), Rousseff (2017), Saad-Filho and Boito (2017), Saad-Filho and Morais (2018, chs. 7–9), Souza (2017) and Snider (2017).

Despite these limitations, examination of the social relations and patterns of accumulation, forms of political representation and policymaking between 2003 and 2016 and in the subsequent period suggests that the main (systemic) feature of this period is *the continuity of neoliberalism*.[3] This is demonstrated by the enduring grip of the macroeconomic policy framework encapsulated in the 'policy tripod' during the PT administrations and beyond. The tripod was introduced in 1999 by the unquestionably neoliberal administration led by Fernando Henrique Cardoso, of the Brazilian Social Democratic Party (*Partido da Social Democracia Brasileira*, PSDB), traditionally the PT's main rival. The tripod enforced economic policies typically associated with neoliberalism: inflation targeting and the operational independence of the Central Bank; floating exchange rates with largely unregulated international flows of capital; and contractionary monetary and fiscal policies, buttressed by the Fiscal Responsibility Law of May 2000.[4]

Even though the PT administrations implemented the tripod with increasing flexibility, those neoliberal policies and institutions – grounded in the Constitution and in law –constrained significantly the formulation, implementation and monitoring of economic policy. In addition, the ideological hegemony of neoliberalism ensured that the tripod itself was rarely the subject of debate in the media or in Congress: dissenting voices were systematically marginalised. In this way, the PT governments accepted that their industrial, financial, wage and welfare policies would be bounded by the reproduction of neoliberalism. This would inevitably limit any potential gains in redistribution and in output and employment growth. Finally, the PT neither sought nor achieved significant changes in the patterns of ownership or control of property, finance, production, technology, employment or international integration. In summary, *the PT administrations were neoliberal*, because they were constrained by global neoliberalism, supported its reproduction domestically, and reaffirmed it ideologically.

As a SoA, neoliberalism is both historically specific and inherently variegated (see Brenner, Peck and Theodore 2010; and Fine and Saad-Filho 2017). The specificity of neoliberalism under the PT derives from the Party's tepid commitment to social inclusion and developmental outcomes: it was for faster economic growth (within the limits imposed by the macroeconomic policy tripod), industrial policy (without compulsion, clear targets or much guidance of private capital), redistribution (at the margin, because of the imperatives to

---

3 For a similar approach despite its distinct focus, see Ban (2013).

4 For an overview of typically neoliberal policies, see Dardot and Laval (2013), Lemke (2001), Mirowski and Plehwe (2009) and Saad-Filho (2018). The 'tripod' is examined below.

preserve the existing distribution of assets and secure large fiscal surpluses), employment creation (limited by the continuing processes of deindustriali- sation and reprimarisation of the economy) and the promotion of citizenship (limited by Brazil's profound inequalities). It follows that social inclusion and developmental goals were only secondary features in the *essentially* neoliberal administrations led by the PT.

This chapter includes four sections. This introduction is the first. The second describes the concept of SoA, outlines the main SoAs in Brazil, and examines the distinguishing features of neoliberalism and neodevelopmentalism. The third reviews the transition to neoliberalism in Brazil, the varieties of neolib- eralism during the PT administrations (inclusive neoliberalism, and develop- mental neoliberalism), and the imposition of authoritarian neoliberalism after Rousseff's impeachment. The fourth section concludes.

2   From Modes of Production to Systems of Accumulation

The capitalist mode of production is a concrete universal distinguished by a narrow set of abstract features, including the commodification of social exchanges, the generalisation of the production of commodities for profit, and the transformation of waged work into the social form of labour (Ilyenkov 1982; Saad-Filho 2002, chs. 1–4). In turn, the SoA is the instantiation, configura- tion or mode of existence of capitalism in a particular historical context; thus, SoAs are both historically specific and intrinsically variegated. They are deter- mined by, first, the manner in which class relations are embedded in the mode of extraction, accumulation and distribution of (surplus) value. Second, the material and institutional structures through which those classes reproduce themselves, including the state, law, forms of property, technology, money, credit, labour and commodity markets, and the relationships between domes- tic accumulation, the natural environment and the rest of the world. Third, the ideologies legitimising those social relations and institutional forms, and the structures of representation of conflicting interests.

In any SoA, the process of accumulation is bounded by *constraints* express- ingthe form of appearance of the contradictions of the mode of production, and the ensuing limitations to the expanded reproduction of capital. The constraints are contingent and historically specific, rather than permanent or logically necessary; they must be identified empirically, and are normally addressed by public policy.

Identification of the constraints to accumulation can start from the circuit of industrial capital as it was described by Karl Marx, that is: $M - C < \dfrac{MP}{LP} \cdots P \cdots C' - M'$, where M is money, C is commodities of two

types: MP, or the means of production (land, buildings, machines, material inputs, and so on), and LP, or labour power. In sequence, ... P ... is production, and M' is a greater sum of money, or M' > M. Typical constraints might include the availability and discipline of the workforce, the cost of finance, the allocation of resources, the balance of payments, and the institutional setting, for example, the property structure, the mode of competition, and the role of the state. In other words, the constraints encapsulate the key features *and* limitations of the SoA.

Although it is widely recognised that accumulation is always subject to constraints, these are often examined in isolation, as if they were assorted hindrances to the (otherwise unproblematic) expansion of the capitalist economy. This is misguided, since the constraints are embedded within, and define, the SoA and its varieties. Finally, the *accumulation strategy* is the spectrum of policies and strategies securing the reproduction of the SoA, regulating the restructuring of capital, and managing, dislocating or transforming the constraints.

3   The Main SoAs in Brazil

Brazil has experienced three SoAs since independence, in 1822. First, primary export-driven growth with an oligarchic state, lasting until 1930. Second, import-substituting industrialisation (ISI) with a developmental state and a wide variety of political regimes between 1930 and 1980 (see Saes 2001). Third, after a decade-long transition, neoliberalism with political democracy until the present time.

In general, the economic and political shifts *within* these SoAs were driven by domestic imperatives; in contrast, transitions *between* SoAs tended to follow major transformations in global capitalism. Global shifts would generally tighten up the constraints to the Brazilian SoA, usually starting from the balance of payments, which would reduce policymaking capacity (that, in Brazil, was rarely coherent, see below), and undermine economic performance for long periods. The ensuing crisis would spread across the political-economy divide, rendering unviable the traditional modalities of economic and social reproduction.

Across the SoAs described above, the Brazilian state invariably had two contradictory roles. Its *conservative role* is due to the imperative to maintain social order in order to secure the mode of exploitation and reproduce the inequalities of income, wealth and privilege in the country, regardless of economic performance. Attempts to challenge these imperatives of the state have always triggered political instability, for example, in 1922–30, 1953–55, 1961–64, and 2013–16. The *transformative role* of the state is due to the need to deploy public policy in order to drive the expansion of capital(ism), steer accumulation and hothouse a capitalist class drawing, in succession, upon commodity exports, manufacturing, and finance, and manage the links between Brazilian and international capital. In doing this, the Brazilian state has influenced decisively the class structure, social reproduction, labour markets, wages, the distribution of income and wealth, the patterns of consumption, and the scope for social mobility; that is, it has both shaped the SoA and, within limits, addressed its constraints.

Tensions between these conservative and transformative roles help to explain why the Brazilian state has generally been strong 'vertically', vigorously addressing the labour constraint and enforcing the subordination of the working population including, over time, slaves, poor immigrants, peasants, wage workers and the 'unruly masses' in general. In contrast, because of its fragmented social and political composition, the state has tended to be weak 'horizontally', always having difficulty managing conflicts between elite groups. These groups include foreign capital, the internationalised bourgeoisie, large and medium-sized internal capital (especially in manufacturing and finance, as well as agricultural exporters and traders), large landlords, regional and local political chiefs, the technocracy, top civil servants, military officers, the Catholic church and, more recently, large evangelical sects, the media and their intellectual and political hangers-on. Their interests have generally been accommodated through deal-making, the deployment of public funds, patronage, corruption, manipulation of the law, fraud, targeted violence, and the redistribution of power at the margin.

Because of these tensions and the imperative to maintain political stability, the institutions of the Brazilian state have tended to develop unsystematically, and pursue policies determined by improvisation, deal-making and minimum common denominators. Despite these limitations, the Brazilian economy has thrived for long periods, largely through the plunder of nature and the ruthless exploitation of the working population.

4   The Case of Neoliberalism

Neoliberalism is the current phase, stage, or mode of existence of capitalism (Saad-Filho 2017). This SoA has five key features. First, the financialisation of production, exchange and social reproduction, that is, the penetration of interest-bearing capital into ever more areas of economic and social life. Second, the international integration of production ('globalisation') at the level of individual firms and circuits of accumulation. Third, under neoliberalism, transnationalised and financialised capital has gained a central role in accumulation and balance of payments stability. This has facilitated the introduction of new technologies, patterns of production and modes of international specialisation, which have transformed the economy and the society and delivered higher rates of exploitation than were possible under previous SoAs (Keynesianism, different forms of developmentalism, and Soviet-style socialism). Fourth, in legal, institutional and policy terms, neoliberalism includes widespread privatisations, capital-friendly forms of regulation of profitability, and the diffusion of managerialism. Fifth, neoliberalism demands contractionary ('prudent', 'austere') fiscal and monetary policies, Central Bank independence, inflation targeting, (distinct modalities of) trade and financial liberalisation, and neoliberal social policies.[5] They are enforced by a nominally independent Judiciary, and buttressed by political, academic and media discourses stressing the imperatives of 'competition', 'efficiency', 'productivity growth' and 'inflation control' (Ayers and Saad-Filho 2014; Fine and Saad-Filho 2017; Saad-Filho 2018).

The first (transition or shock) phase of neoliberalism generally includes forceful state intervention to change laws and reform institutions, promote the transnational integration of capital and finance, privatise public property, contain labour and disorganise the left. This is normally followed by a second (mature) phase which aims to stabilise the social relations imposed in the earlier period, consolidate the new role of finance in economic and social reproduction, manage the new mode of international integration, and introduce specifically neoliberal social policies to manage the deprivation created in the previous phase. This has been followed by a third phase, after the Global Financial Crisis, driven by the imposition of an uncompromising variety of neoliberalism, presumably justified by the imperative of 'fiscal austerity', buttressed by political authoritarianism. Inevitably, these phases of neoliberalism are more logical than chronological, as they can be sequenced, delayed, accelerated, or even overlain in specific ways depending on country, region and economic and political circumstances (Fine and Saad-Filho 2014).

Across its specific configurations, the neoliberal SoA is limited, first, by class conflict, although in most circumstances this can be contained by ideological

---

5   The social policies typical of neoliberalism are examined in Saad-Filho (2015).

hegemony, promotion of consumerism, unemployment and different forms of repression. Second, accumulation is constrained by the instabilities created by an enlarged, transnationalised and ideologically hegemonic finance, that can move capital in and out of the economy, into competing circuits of production, or into purely financial speculation increasingly easily, often undermining or destabilising productive activity. Third, the neoliberal SoA is limited by the (financialised) balance of payments constraint that neoliberalism itself has imposed. For example, in Brazil, the contractionary monetary policies typical of neoliberalism have tended to overvalue the currency, hollow out manufacturing, induce current account deficits and foster the reprimarisation of the economy; all of them require regular inflows of foreign capital. In sum, because of its distinguishing features and constraints, and the ways in which they have been addressed by public policy, neoliberalism has both expanded the power of capital *and* created an income-concentrating dynamic of accumulation that can be limited, but not reversed, by marginal interventions. Here, too, the Brazilian experience provides a good illustration.

5   The Neodevelopmentalist Alternative

Neodevelopmentalism emerged in Latin America in the 2000s, presumably as an alternative to neoliberalism. There are multiple versions of neodevelopmentalism, drawing upon different combinations of Latin American structuralism, Keynesianism, evolutionary political economy and other heterodox schools of thought. They argued that traditional Latin American developmentalism, associated with ISI, failed because it unwittingly concentrated income and wealth and was unable to internalise new technologies and the sources of productivity growth. The neodevelopmentalists aimed to build a new SoA drawing upon strong linkages between the state and the private sector, and between investment and consumption. The goals of this proposed SoA included enhanced national economic independence by rebuilding the production chains hollowed out by neoliberalism, the revitalisation of manufacturing, export diversification and the rollback of financialisation, plus redistribution of income and greater social mobility.

To achieve these goals, the state should reduce uncertainty, secure macroeconomic stability and support private investment. This would require intertemporal fiscal balance, low inflation, low interest rates and a sustainable balance of payments, through an appropriate (relatively undervalued) exchange rate and controls on international flows of capital. In some versions of neodevelopmentalism, the state should also implement industrial policies, promote competition and employment creation and nurture domestic firms.[6] These policies can be supported by higher lending for consumption and investment, and the redistribution of income. The outcome should be a self-sustaining growth process based on the expansion of domestic demand.

A neodevelopmentalist SoA would need to address economic vulnerabilities due to the (initial) lack of 'credibility' of its policies with domestic and international capital; it would also have to manage conflicts between rival fractions of capital. These limitations could become severe if the neodevelopmentalist policies were conditional on political 'deals' between the state and elite groups, unsupported by mass mobilisations. These arrangements could become even more fragile if the (potential) mass base of support for neodevelopmentalism were demobilised in order to 'reassure' capital that its political hegemony would remain unchallenged. In this case, neodevelopmentalist policies could become hostage to the political humour and short-term interests of competing capital(ists). Once again, events in Brazil can provide useful illustrations.

6   Neoliberalism in Brazil

6.1   *The Economic Transition to Neoliberalism*

The political transition from military dictatorship to democracy in Brazil took place between the mid-1970s and the late 1980s. It was followed by an economic transition from an increasingly dysfunctional ISI into neoliberalism, between the late 1980s and the mid-1990s (Saad-Filho and Morais 2018, chs. 2–4). The Brazilian transition to neoliberalism came relatively late and advanced slowly when compared with most other countries. This was due, in part, to the vigorous resistance offered by the political left that had emerged during the democratic transition.

In the 1980s, most analysts came to accept that Brazilian ISI faced irresolvable challenges, which explained the country's disappointing economic performance, rising inflation and external vulnerability. They included a shallow and inefficient financial system; insufficient access to foreign savings, investment, technology and markets; a weak national system of innovation; excessive diversification and lack of scale in the manufacturing sector; lack of foreign

---

6   See, for example, Bresser-Pereira (2003b; 2005) and Sicsú, Paula and Michel (2005). For a review of diverse interpretations of neodevelopmentalism (new, post-Keynesian, and social developmentalism), see Amado and Mollo (2015), Fritz, Paula and Prates (2017) and Mollo and Fonseca (2013).

competition due to protectionism; and chronic fiscal deficits due to 'economic populism', distributive conflicts and the indexation of wages and prices. Supposedly, these obstacles could be overcome by a transition to neoliberalism. This view was supported by the US government, international financial institutions, the mainstream media, foreign capital and the Brazilian internationalised bourgeoisie, and it was validated by claims of success elsewhere.[7]

These views were deceptive at three levels. First, ISI was intrinsically limited, structurally fragile and socially and distributionally regressive, but the crisis of the 1980s was only partly due to its shortcomings; it also derived from external processes that peripheral countries could not realistically influence. Second, it would soon become clear that neoliberalism could neither address the flaws of ISI, nor match the country's growth performance under the previous SoA. Third, the examples of successful 'reforms' were both partial and misleading.[8]

The administration led by José Sarney relaxed controls on the exchange rate and international capital flows in 1988. The transition to neoliberalism was validated politically by the presidential election in 1989, when Fernando Collor's neoliberal programme narrowly defeated Lula's left-wing campaign (see Valença 2002). The domestic financial system was reformed, and the country started a unilateral process of import liberalisation. Average tariffs fell from 58 per cent in 1987 to 14 per cent in 1993, and 11 per cent in 2004, and non-tariff barriers were slashed (Kume, Piani, and Souza 2003; Paula 2011; Squeff 2015). Since this was not accompanied by a devaluation of the currency, support for domestic producers or anti-dumping measures, the country's import bill shot up, while the manufacturing sector contracted sharply. Finally, Brazil renegotiated its foreign debt through the Brady Plan in 1994, as part of a strategy of financial internationalisation. The emerging SoA was secured by the 1994 Real inflation stabilisation plan, implemented by Presidents Itamar Franco (1992–94) and Fernando Henrique Cardoso (1995–98, 1999–2002) (Saad-Filho and Morais 2018, chs. 3–4).

The transition to neoliberalism imposed an economic stabilisation-speculation trap, including chronic loss of competitivity, continuing deindustrialisation, falling rates of savings, investment and GDP growth, intractable infrastructure and productivity gaps vis-à-vis the advanced economies in the OECD, and a tight balance of payments constraint that required continuing

---

7   See Bresser-Pereira (1996), Franco (1995) and Kormann (2015, part III). For a critique, see
    Bianchi (2004) and Machado (2002).
8   See, for example, Chang and Yoo (2000) for the case of South Korea, Felder (2013) for
    Argentina, and Valle Baeza and Martínez González (2011) for Mexico.

inflows of foreign capital which, in turn, integrated Brazilian production and finance increasingly tightly into global circuits of accumulation. However, when those inflows were insufficient the economy would stall. Neoliberalism also created a pattern of employment centred on low productivity, informal and low-paid jobs in urban services, while manufacturing and the public sector lost millions of posts (see Saad-Filho and Morais 2018, ch. 4). As a result, under neoliberalism Brazil remained an unequal, dependent and poverty-generating economy, but it also became an internationalised and financialised *low growth* economy, where economic performance was tightly constrained by balance of payments and exchange rate instability.[9] The exchange rate crisis in January 1999 closed the transition phase to neoliberalism and inaugurated the mature phase of the SoA. This shift was marked by the imposition of the macroconomic policy tripod.[10]

6.2   *Inclusive Neoliberalism*

The currency crisis, in 1999, demoralised Cardoso's administration and sapped the political hegemony of neoliberalism, opening the space for Lula's election to the Presidency in 2002, after three consecutive defeats. Lula's election was, then, partly a reaction against the perceived insufficiencies of the neoliberal SoA; Lula's PT also offered a fresh image, seemingly uncontaminated by the corruption, incompetence and self-serving policies and practices of Cardoso's PSDB and its allies.

In order to secure Lula's election and maintain political stability within the 'rules of the game', the PT committed itself to neoliberalism in general, and to the policy tripod specifically. The administration's attachment to neoliberalism was tempered, first, by a shift in the social composition of the state, as the PT appointed hundreds of trade unionists and left activists to positions of power,[11] and, second, by the expansion of the government's social programmes across health, education, pensions and benefits, improvements in

---

9   The average rate of GDP growth in the 1990s was only 1.8 per cent per annum, the lowest in the century. In contrast, between 1933 and 1980 the economy expanded, on average, 6.4 per cent per annum. GDP growth in the first decade of neoliberalism was even lower than in the so-called 'lost decade' of the 1980s (2.6 per cent per annum) (all macroeconomic data are from www.ipeadata.gov.br, unless stated otherwise).

10   For an overview, see Arestis, Paula and Ferrari-Filho (2009), Paula and Saraiva (2015) and Saad-Filho and Morais (2018, ch. 3).

11   The President, a former metalworker, appointed five working-class ministers; over 100 trade unionists took high-level posts in the administration and the SOEs, and they appointed hundreds of lower-level colleagues; Marcelino (2017, p. 11) suggests that 1,300 trade unionists were appointed to government posts.

the minimum wage, and the expansion of personal credit.[12] The variety of the SoA in Lula's first administration can be termed *inclusive neoliberalism*. While this is an oxymoron, since the dominant tendency in neoliberalism is the generation of inequality, poverty, precarious employment and social exclusion, Lula's first administration introduced important countertendencies to those trends.[13]

Inclusive neoliberalism in Brazil was underpinned by global economic prosperity, the beginnings of the so-called 'commodity supercycle', and abundant inflows of capital. They relaxed the constraints on the balance of payments and the fiscal budget, boosted aggregate demand and employment, and generated an unprecedented growth dynamic under neoliberalism. Simultaneously, the government expanded its social programmes and promoted the formalisation of employment, which protected millions of workers, at the same time as it raised tax revenues and social security contributions. Public spending and GDP growth picked up while inflation fell and the government met stringent fiscal targets.

This virtuous arrangement was limited and unstable, because it never sought transformative outcomes; it was also conditional on a relaxed balance of payments constraint (which Brazil influenced only marginally), and on political alliances predicated on Lula's political acumen. While these conditions lasted, it became possible to achieve slightly higher growth rates, redistribution at the margin, limited social integration, and political stability, depite the hegemony of neoliberalism.

Yet, Lula's administration found itself in a cul-de-sac after only two years. Realising Lula's vulnerability, the neoliberal elite, including the financial bourgeoisie, the mainstream media and most of the upper middle class launched a vicious attack, in 2005, focusing on allegations that the PT was buying votes in Congress with monthly cash payments (the grotesque *mensalão* scandal) (see Martuscelli 2015, pp. 214–216; Saad-Filho and Morais 2018, chs. 5–6, and Singer 2009). The scandal almost brought down Lula, and it claimed the scalps of his likely successor, Finance Minister Antonio Palocci, Lula's Chief of Staff (and the PT's leading strategist) José Dirceu, the president and the treasurer of the PT, and several other influential members and close allies of the PT.

---

12   For a detailed analysis of Lula's first administration, see Saad-Filho and Morais (2018, ch. 5).

13   Lula's second administration intensified the inclusive countertendencies introduced in this period (see below), as part of a fuller neodevelopmentalist inflection in the neoliberal SoA. Nevertheless, the first administration can be aptly described through its policies limiting the adverse social implications of neoliberalism.

Lula realised that he could not count on the support of the radical left or the formal-sector workers, who were disappointed with his attachment to neoliberalism and the slow turnaround of the economy, nor could he rely on most of the elite for his political survival. He retreated to the urban peripheries and the poorest regions in Brazil, where his social programmes made him popular. He also strengthened his commitment to the internal bourgeoisie that, by and large, continued to support his administration (for a detailed analysis, see Boito 2012).

6.3   Developmental Neoliberalism under Lula

Neodevelopmentalist ideas gained influence in academic, NGO and policy circles during Lula's first administration, driven by the strength of heterodox economics in Brazil, growing disappointment with the government's attachment to neoliberalism, and perceptions of economic underperformance. The neodevelopmentalists had limited ambitions, merely hoping that activist fiscal, monetary, credit and industrial policies could nudge GDP growth 'one or two per centage points above the rates expected by the supporters of the neoliberal view' (Barbosa and Souza 2010, p. 11). This reinforces the view that they were willing to compromise with neoliberalism in order to secure political stability.

After Lula's re-election, in 2006, neodevelopmentalist policymakers were brought into the Ministries of Finance, Planning, and Strategic Affairs, but the staunchly neoliberal Central Bank was left untouched. The administration introduced several neodevelopmentalist policies, which would later be strengthened by Dilma Rousseff. These policies did not replace the neoliberal policy framework; instead, they were juxtaposed to it, creating a variety of the SoA that can be called *developmental neoliberalism*.

Given the relaxation of the balance of payments constraint (at least until the global economic crisis), and the extraordinary levels of support for Lula,[14] developmental neoliberalism could achieve positive outcomes in terms of GDP growth, the expansion of state and private enterprises, redistribution and poverty reduction. The country could also implement an independent foreign policy that would have been unthinkable only a few years before. State activism centred on public investment and the reduction of inequality at two levels. First, through the Growth Acceleration Programme (*Programa de Aceleração do Crescimento*, PAC) based on state-led investments in infrastructure, energy and transport. Second, through the expansion of consumption through

---

14   Lula's approval ratings rose from around 40 per cent, during the *mensalão*, to 50 per cent at the start of his second administration, and over 80 per cent in 2010 (see CNT/MDA 2018, pp. 43–44).

transfer programmes, personal loans and faster growth of the minimum wage, that rose 70 per cent between 2003 and 2010, triggering automatic increases in federal transfers to pensioners, the unemployed and disabled.[15] Finally, the government promoted the expansion of selected (large) domestic companies, the 'national champions'.

These measures drove a virtuous circle of growth based on domestic investment and mass consumption. Employment growth in the country's main metropolitan areas increased from 150,000 jobs per year under Cardoso to 500,000 per year under Lula. In the 2000s, 21 million jobs were created, in contrast with only 11 million during the 1990s. Around 80 per cent of those new jobs were in the formal sector.[16] Significantly, 90 per cent paid less than 1.5 times the minimum wage (in contrast with 51 per cent in the 1990s). Unemployment declined steadily, especially in the lower segments of the labour market. The Gini coefficient fell from 0.57 in 1995 to 0.52 in 2008, and absolute poverty declined from 35.8 per cent of households in 2003, to 21.4 per cent in 2009.[17]

The strengths of developmental neoliberalism were further demonstrated after the global financial crisis. Similarly, to other developing countries, led by China, the Brazilian government confronted the downturn with aggressive fiscal and monetary policies. They raised the nominal fiscal deficit from 1.9 per cent of GDP, at the end of 2008, to 4.1 per cent, in 2009, while the domestic public debt rose from 40.5 per cent of GDP to 43.0 per cent. However, the economy rebounded rapidly, and GDP expanded by 7.5 per cent in 2010 – faster than at any time since the mid-1980s – with further gains in income distribution, despite the continuing overvaluation of the *real*.

6.4   *Developmental Neoliberalism under Dilma Rousseff*

Dilma Rousseff's administration was even more deeply committed to developmental neoliberalism than Lula's. Her government expanded further the federal programmes of social assistance, and it was determined to tackle Brazil's lagging productivity, creeping deindustrialisation and rising current account deficit. In order to address these challenges, the government designed a 'new economic matrix' (NEM), which was so closely aligned with the demands of the internal bourgeoisie that it became known as the 'FIESP programme', after the country's most powerful business organisation (see FIESP et al. 2011; and

---

15 The Constitution of 1988 determines that social security and unemployment benefits cannot be lower than the minimum wage.

16 See Pomar (2013, p. 42) and www.ibge.gov.br, monthly employment survey.

17 Source: Pesquisa Nacional por Amostra de Domicílios, http://www.ibge.gov.br/home/ estatistica/populacao/trabalhoerendimento/pnad2004/default.shtm.

Singer 2015, pp. 43–45, 55–56). NEM aimed to reduce production costs across finance (through lower interest rates and subsidised loans), imported inputs (via controls on capital inflows and the devaluation of the real exchange rate), energy (lower tariffs and better infrastructure) and transport (cheaper tolls and an improved road network), and a tax reform (for an overview, see Barbosa 2013; and Souza 2015).

In August 2011, the Central Bank started reducing base (SELIC) rates, marking a significant departure from the contractionary policies in the previous two decades. The base rate fell from 12.4 per cent to 7.16 per cent, in early 2013, when real interest rates reached only 2 per cent. However, it soon became clear that lower interest rates and the devaluation of the currency would not induce a growth cycle driven by private investment. In 2011 the global economy entered another downturn, commodity prices fell, and global trade slowed down. The devaluation of the real was undermined by the inflows of capital driven by the second wave of quantitative easing (QE2) in the advanced economies, launched after the Eurozone crisis. Brazil's GDP growth rates plummeted from 7.5 per cent, in 2010, to only 3.8 per cent.

The government responded with more aggressive credit policies, in line with neodevelopmentalism. In 2012, the state-owned banks expanded their loans by 20 per cent, and the Brazilian Development Bank (BNDES) by 16 per cent. In order to neutralise the expansionary impact of these policies, the government tightened up fiscal policy, reducing and postponing expenditures. The administration also introduced controls on capital inflows, but they were too marginal and came too late. In the meantime, the earlier devaluation of the *real* pushed inflation above the ceiling of the Central Bank's target range (6.5 per cent per annum). GDP growth fell to only 1.9 per cent, because of the government's mildly contractionary fiscal policy and the stagnation of investment.

QE2, rising inflation and declining GDP growth rates changed business expectations: it became widely accepted that they required contractionary fiscal and monetary policies. Under intense pressure from finance, the media and the opposition, the Central Bank abandoned its developmentalist experiment in March 2013. Interest rates started rising, signalling the renewed policy dominance of the tripod. In the meantime, the administration continued to stress its developmental and social policy ambitions and refused to align fiscal policy with the new monetary policy stance. The disconnect between the Ministry of Finance and the Central Bank damaged the reputation of the government and triggered a further deterioration of expectations (see Singer 2015, pp. 39–49). The consequence was another round of contraction of investment and output, and a spiralling current account deficit, peaking at 4.3 per cent of GDP, in 2014.

The economic strategy reached an impasse. Attempts to control inflation through high interest rates and an overvalued exchange rate worsened the current account deficit and reduced GDP growth; however, trying to control inflation by containing wages, transfers and public investment would stall the improvements in competitivity and distribution and, again, undermine economic growth.

Having failed to improve competitivity through the relaxation of fiscal as well as monetary policy, the government shifted its focus to infrastructure and the costs of energy and transport. However, in these areas too Rousseff's policies were rejected by large segments of capital, and could never be implemented.[18] Foreign capital and the Brazilian elite increasingly claimed that the government's neodevelopmentalist inclinations made it 'populist', interventionist, and unsympathetic to business (see Rovai 2013).

Finally, the administration attempted an ambitious tax reform. However, by 2013 this had become politically impossible, and the reform fizzled out into a mélange of subsidies and tax rebates, initially targeting the export industries but, later, sprawling into all manner of sectors because the government was too weak to resist special pleading. Those transfers to capital were provided without conditions: they were simply incorporated into profits and brought no macroeconomic gains. Alarmingly, many beneficiaries would soon forget the government's generosity and join the plot to overthrow Dilma Rousseff.

The economic slowdown and the subsidies and tax rebates triggered a steep deterioration of the fiscal balance. In the meantime, the ideological shift of the internal bourgeoisie, and their economic losses due to the recession and foreign competition pushed this group towards the opposition. The government was confronted by a perfect storm, across deteriorating terms of trade, rising inflation, plummeting demand, falling investment, political paralysis and even water scarcity, because of an untimely drought. Then, in 2014, the Federal Police and the Attorney General's Office launched the *lava jato* anti-corruption investigation, targeting the PT and its allies both in the state and in the 'business community' (see Lassance 2017; and Saad-Filho 2018, ch. 9).

Dilma Rousseff was re-elected in late 2014, after a bitter campaign that pitted her own reformist programme against the overtly neoliberal programme of her main opponent, from the PSDB. She won in the second round by 52–48 per cent, despite media hostility, the *lava jato* investigations, and the collapse of her parliamentary base with the election of the most right-wing Congress in decades.

---

18   For a detailed analysis, see Saad-Filho and Morais (2018, ch. 7).

Politically isolated and with the economy in freefall, Rousseff attempted to buy policy space by abandoning her developmental aspirations and electoral commitments and turning towards neoliberalism. She dismissed the neodevelopmentalist Guido Mantega and appointed to the Ministry of Finance a banker chosen by Bradesco, one of Brazil's largest financial conglomerates. Joaquim Levy was tasked with implementing a contractionary adjustment while, at the same time, preserving most social rights, entitlements and programmes. However, it was impossible for the government to cut its way to growth, and its policies were insufficient to gain any major constituency.[19] Every policy was rejected by the media and the neoliberal elite, and every initiative was either blocked in Congress or undermined by the passive resistance of the PT and the left.

The political base of support of Rousseff's government fragmented until its remnants were overwhelmed by the opposition. The government alienated the organised workers because of the worsening economic situation, corruption scandals, policy turn to neoliberalism, and failure to address key demands of the working class: the reduction of the working week, limitation of subcontracting, and improvements in pensions. Although Rousseff's support held better among the informal workers, many were alienated for the same reasons. The government was never supported by the internationalised bourgeoisie, finance and the media, especially after its attempt to reduce interest rates. The administration lost the internal bourgeoisie because of the economic slowdown, perceptions that the President was excessively 'autonomous', disagreements over public policy, and the pressure of *lava jato*. The upper middle class was alienated by its own relative losses, given the gains of the rich as well as the poor (see Loureiro and Saad-Filho 2019), and perceptions of generalised corruption. The administration also earned the hostility of Congress because of its unwillingness or inability to dish out targeted favours. These groups coalesced around claims that the state was 'out of control', the economy was in irreversible decline, the fiscal deficit was ballooning, inflation would soon explode, and the PT was corrupt.

Despite these converging threats, the PT and the left reacted only weakly. Most social movements had long been captured by the PT administrations and demobilised as part of the PT's effort to win elections and govern by the established rules, and the party was crippled by fear, shame and confusion. The far left remained small, scattered and hostile. Finally, the media had campaigned

---

19   For a review of economic policy during this period, see Belluzzo and Bastos (2016) and Rossi and Mello (2017).

implacably against the government since 2013, making it hard to mobilise the population in support of Rousseff's mandate. She lost an impeachment vote in the Chamber of Deputies by 367–137 votes on 17 April 2016 and had to step down 'provisionally'. She lost in the Senate by 61–20 votes on 31 August and was removed from office.

6.5   *Authoritarian Neoliberalism*

The impeachment of Dilma Rousseff was not merely the tortured end of a flawed administration or the outcome of a savage attack on the PT, but the party was largely disabled in the process: its base of support dissolved and the PT suffered severe losses in the local elections in October 2016.

The mediocrity, incompetence and mendacity of the coup plotters was soon revealed, but the administration led by former Vice-President Michel Temer could always count on the support of the elite and most of the Legislature, the party system, the Judiciary and other state institutions, which allowed it to rule despite its own staggering unpopularity.[20] Under the pretence of fighting corruption, Temer undermined the Constitution, normalised a state of exception, brought the Armed Forces back into politics, protected gangster-politicians, and imposed an accumulation strategy based on an unprecedentedly exclusionary, authoritarian and internationalised variety of neoliberalism.

Key initiatives included, first, the change in oil exploration contracts to benefit transnational capital at the expense of state-owned Petrobras, and the partial break-up and denationalisation of the company (October 2016). Second, a constitutional amendment freezing primary fiscal spending (excluding interest payments on the domestic public debt) in real terms for 20 years (December 2016). Third, a legal reform drastically liberalising the labour market (July 2017). Fourth, a determined attempt to reform pensions and social security, that fizzled out but was revived under Temer's successor, Jair Bolsonaro. In the meantime, Lula was found guilty of corruption under the flimsiest pretexts and sent to jail for 12 years (he ended up serving a little over a year and a half).

Many of the income and employment gains achieved under the PT evaporated. Output contracted between 2014 and 2016, and then stagnated. The fiscal deficit remained large, and the domestic public debt continued to grow. Several 'national champions' were weakened or sold off to the highest (foreign)

---

20   Temer's approval ratings rarely exceeded 10 per cent, and often went as low as 3 per cent, while negative perceptions of his administration exceeded 80 per cent; see, for example, CNT-MDA (2018, pp. 4–7).

bidder. Petrobras and the oil chain were extensively dismantled, and there were escalating repression against social movements and the left. The far right recovered a mass base among the upper middle class for the first time since the early 1960s. To cap it all, former Army Captain Jair Bolsonaro, a coarse ultra-right winger, was elected President in October 2018.

Bolsonaro was supported by an assortment of small parties and neophyte politicians. His campaign was based on four themes. First, denunciations of 'corruption' against everyone else, drawing upon Bolsonaro's purported status as a political outsider. Second, conservative moral values and the rollback of citizenship. The candidate attacked social movements and the left because they are 'corrupt', 'communist' and 'godless', and advocated the restoration of 'lost' cultural values by deathly violence. Third, public security and easier access to weapons, a slogan with a strong appeal in a country enduring over 60,000 murders per year. Fourth, a neoliberal economic programme, drawing upon the intuitively appealing notion of reducing bureaucracy and the dead-weight of a corrupt state.

While the political side of Bolsonaro's administration was marked by unrelenting confusion, as the government pushed against citizenship and social and labour rights as and when the opportunity arose, the economic side was dominated by Finance Minister Paulo Guedes, a minor 'Chicago Boy' in General Pinochet's Chile, and a banker and occasional academic in Brazil, whose goals focused on public spending cuts and the privatisation 'of everything'.

Guedes's firm hand may be the main reason why capital and the upper middle class tolerate Bolsonaro, despite his antics and likely involvement in criminal syndicates in his home state of Rio de Janeiro. However, the political dynamics changed dramatically with the COVID-19 pandemic in early 2020, in which Bolsonaro demonstrated a degree of recklessness and incompetence unmatched anywhere else. Hundreds of thousands of deaths followed, while the President focused on his own criminal problems and those of his sons, changed ministers repeatedly (including in the critically important Ministry of Health), and displayed a shocking lack of empathy with the tragedy engulfing Brazilian households. In the meantime, Bolsonaro continued to plot his way to a coup in order to amass even more power.

Under authoritarian neoliberalism, Brazil's economy, society and political system are a perillous state; the democratic 1988 Constitution is frayed if not mortally wounded, and there is no clear path back to economic growth and democratic stability. Curiously, the right-wing movement itself is bereft of leadership, in contrast with similar processes in Hungary, India, Turkey and elsewhere. An 'ordinary' electoral defeat will not suffice to roll back these destructive processes but, in any case, the left is far from being in a position to drive a new federal administration with a programme grounded on human values. Brazil has submerged into a swamp of authoritarianism and political disintegration for a long time to come.

7 Conclusion

This chapter reviewed the varieties of the neoliberal system of accumulation under the PT administrations led by Luís Inácio Lula da Silva and Dilma Rousseff, in order to identify and classify the stages of the SoA, and the drivers of its evolution over time. In doing this, it offers an original interpretation not only of the structure and dynamics of neoliberalism in Brazil, but also a framework to examine its phases, vulnerabilities and evolution, culminating with the growing incompatibility between neoliberalism and democracy, through the imposition of an authoritarian variety of neoliberalism in the country.

When examining the administrations led by the PT, it was shown that, under favourable external circumstances, these administrations could deliver rising GDP growth, political stability, incremental democratisation of the state and social integration through inclusive and, later, developmental neoliberalism. It appeared that the more the accumulation strategy moved away from neoliberalism, the faster was the economy's growth rate and the greater were the economic and social gains for the majority.

However, these achievements were bounded by the stability of the neoliberal SoA, including the tripod as the foundation of macroeconomic policy. They enforced high interest rates, an overvalued currency and a low investment rate, the deindustrialisation and reprimarisation of the economy, current account deficits, and the creeping privatisation of public services, justified by the limits on public spending. Neoliberalism externalised the drivers of growth through the integration of accumulation into transnational circuits and made the balance of payments increasingly dependent on foreign capital flows; it also created a regressive pattern of employment with adverse implications for Brazil's social structure and political dynamic.

The PT governments were unable or unwilling to confront these constraints through the transformation of the fields of politics, media or class relations. The Party accepted the laws and institutions of neoliberalism and introduced only minimalist reforms. Despite their achievements, the social policies of the PT governments were bound by neoliberalism, and fostered the marketisation and financialisation of daily life, instead of limiting the commodification of social reproduction.[21]

Since the PT was committed to the 'rules of the game' in order to stabilise a fragmented and decentralised political system, its governments had to rely on unwieldy alliances and case-by-case negotiations. They could deliver the PT's goals only if the party had a mobilised base of support outside Congress – but the PT chose to disarm itself instead, making itimpossible to implement a systemic alternative to neoliberalism. The PT also behaved as if the accretion of incremental changes would eventually weaken the foundations of neoliberalism; instead, it merely exposed the roots of the elite's power: the patterns of ownership and economic reproduction, the structure of the political system, the monopoly of the media, and so on.

The collapse of the PT's transformative project was due to its attachment to neoliberalism. The party's administrations collapsed because of their pragmatism even when it had become counterproductive, and because of the PT's dogged triangulation towards a political centre that was collapsing into the far right.

The political crisis in Brazil and the impeachment of Dilma Rousseff expressed the limitations of developmental neoliberalism and the contradictions of the political project of the PT. They showed, in particular, that what was lasting in the experience of the federal administrations led by the PT was their neoliberal economic base, and what was untenable was the distributional policy superimposed upon the SoA. In the end, the PT's dalliance with neoliberalism opened political space for the far right, propelled Rousseff's impeachment, and supported the reversal of the economic, distributive and social advances of the 2000s.

References

Amado, A., and Mollo, M.L.R. (2015). The 'Developmentalism' Debate in Brazil: Some Economic and Political Issues. *Review of Keynesian Economics* 3(1): 77–89.

Arestis, P., Paula, L.F., and Ferrari-Filho, F. (2009). A Nova Política Monetária: Uma Análise do Regime de Metas de Inflação no Brasil. *Economia e Sociedade* 18(1): 1–30.

Ayers, A., and Saad-Filho, A. (2014). Democracy Against Neoliberalism: Paradoxes, Limitations, Transcendence. *Critical Sociology* 41(4–5): 597–618.

---

21   For a detailed analysis, see Lavinas (2017) and Saad-Filho (2015).

Ban, C. (2013). Brazil's Liberal Neo-Developmentalism: New Paradigm or Edited Orthodoxy?. *Review of International Political Economy* 20(2): 298–331.

Barbosa, N. (2013). Dez Anos de Política Econômica. In: E. Sader (ed.), *10 Anos de Governos Pós-Neoliberais no Brasil: Lula e Dilma*. São Paulo: Boitempo (Kindle edition).

Barbosa, N., and Souza, J.A.P. (2010). A Inflexão do Governo Lula: Política Econômica, Crescimento e Distribuição de Renda. In: Sader, E., and Garcia, M.A. (eds.), *Brasil Entre o Passado e o Futuro*. São Paulo: Boitempo.

Belluzzo, L.G., and Bastos, P.P.Z. (eds.). (2016). *Austeridade para Quem? Balanço e Perspectivas do Governo Dilma Rousseff*. São Paulo: Carta Maior.

Bianchi, A. (2004). *O Ministério dos Industriais: A Federação das Indústrias do Estado de São Paulo na Crise das Décadas de 1980 e 1990*. Ph.D. thesis, IFCH-UNICAMP.

Boito, A. (2012). Governos Lula: a Nova Burguesia Nacional no Poder. In: Boito, A., and Galvão, A. (eds.), *Política e Classes Sociais no Brasil dos Anos 2000*. São Paulo: Alameda.

Brenner, N., Peck, Jamie, and Theodore, N. (2010). Variegated Neoliberalization: Geographies, Modalities, Pathways. *Global Networks* 10(2): 1–41.

Bresser-Pereira, L.C. (1996). *Economic Crisis and State Reform in Brazil*. Boulder, CO: Lynne Rienner.

Bresser-Pereira, L.C. (2003). Macroeconomia do Brasil pós-1994. *Análise Econômica* 21(40): 7–38.

Bresser-Pereira, L.C. (2005). Macroeconomia Pós-Plano Real: As Relações Básicas. In: Sicsú, J., Paula, L.F., and Michel, R. (eds.), *Novo-Desenvolvimentismo: um Projeto Nacional de Crescimento com Eqüidade Social*. Rio de Janeiro: Fundação Konrad Adenauer.

Chang, H.-J., and Yoo, C.G. (2000). The Triumph of the Rentiers? *Challenge* 43(1): 105–124.

CNT/MDA. (2018). *Pesquisa CND/MDA: Relatório Síntese*, Rodada 135, 28 de fevereiro a 03 de março.

Dardot, P., and Laval, C. (2013). *The New Way of the World: On Neoliberal Society*. London: Verso.

Felder, R.S. (2013). *Neoliberal Reforms, Crisis and Recovery in Argentina (1990s-2000s)*, Ph.D. Thesis, Department of Political Science, York University, Toronto.

FIESP, CUT, Sindicato dos Metalúrgicos do ABC, Força Sindical, and Sindicato dos Metalúrgicos de São Paulo e Mogi das Cruzes. (2011). *Brasil do Diálogo, da Produção e do Emprego*, www.fiesp.com.br/brasil-do-dialogo-pela-producao-e-emprego/ (accessed 15 November 2020).

Fine, B., and Saad-Filho, A. (2014). Politics of Neoliberal Development: Washington Consensus and post-Washington Consensus. In: H. Weber (ed.), *The Politics of Development: A Survey*. London: Routledge.

Fine, B., and Saad-Filho, A. (2017). Thirteen Things You Need to Know About Neoliberalism. *Critical Sociology* 43(4–5): 685–706.

Franco, G.H.B. (1995). *O Plano Real e Outros Ensaios*. Rio de Janeiro: Francisco Alves.

Fritz, B., Paula, L.F., and Prates, D. (2017). Developmentalism at the Periphery: Can Productive Change and Income Distribution be Compatible with Global Financial Asymmetries?. *DesiguALdades.net Working Paper No.101*, https://www.researchgate.net/publication/316998112_desiguALdadesnet_Working_Paper_Series_Developmentalism_at_the_Periphery_Can_Productive_Change_and_Income_Redistribution_be_Compatible_with_Global_Financial_Asymmetries_Developmentalism_at_the_Peripher (accessed 15 November 2020).

Gentili, P. (ed.). (2016). *Golpe en Brasil: Genealogía de Una Farsa*. Buenos Aires: CLACSO.

Ilyenkov, E.V. (1982). *The Dialectics of the Abstract and the Concrete in Marx's Capital*. Moscow: Progress Publishers.

Kormann, L.F. (2015). *Big Business and Brazil's Economic Reforms*. London: Routledge.

Kume, H., Piani, G., and Souza, C.F.B. (2003). A Política Brasileira de Importação no Período 1987–1998: Descrição e Avaliação. In: Corseuil, C.H., and Kume, H. (eds.), *A Abertura Comercial Brasileira nos Anos 1990: Impactos Sobre Emprego e Salário*. Brasília. MTE/IPEA.

Lassance, A. (2017). Para Entender a Lógica e o Timing da Lava Jato. http://www.cartamaior.com.br/?/Editoria/Politica/Para-entender-a-logica-e-o-timing-da-Lava-Jato/4/38135 (accessed 15 November 2020).

Lavinas, L. (2017). *The Brazilian Paradox: The Takeover of Social Policy by Financialization*. London: Palgrave.

Lemke, T. (2001). The Birth of Bio-Politics: Michel Foucaults Lecture at the Collège De France on Neo-Liberal Governmentality. *Economy & Society* 30(2): 190–207.

Loureiro, P., and Saad-Filho, A. (2019). The Limits of Pragmatism: The Rise and Fall of the Brazilian Workers Party (2002–2016). *Latin American Perspectives* 46(1) (2019): 66–84.

Machado, G.V. (2002). *A Burguesia Brasileira e a Incorporação da Agenda Liberal nos Anos 90*. M.Sc. dissertation, Instituto de Economia, UNICAMP.

Marcelino, P. (2017). Sindicalismo e Neodesenvolvimentismo: Analisando as Greves entre 2003 e 2013 no Brasil. *Tempo Social* 29(3): 201–227.

Martuscell, D.E. (2015). *Crises Políticas e Capitalismo Neoliberal no Brasil*. Curitiba: Editora CRV.

Mirowski, P., and Plehwe, D. (eds.). (2009). *The Road from Mont Pèlerin: The Making of the Neoliberal Thought Collective*. Cambridge, MA: Harvard University Press.

Mollo, M.L.R., and Fonseca, P.C.D. (2013). Desenvolvimentismo e Novo-Desenvolvimentismo: Raízes Teóricas e Precisões Conceituais. *Revista de Economia Política* 33(2) 131: 222–239.

Paula, L.F. (2011). *Financial Liberalization and Economic Performance: Brazil at the Crossroads*. London: Routledge.

Paula, L.F., and Saraiva, P.J. (2015). Novo Consenso Macroeconômico e Regime de Metas de Inflação: Algumas Implicações para o Brasil. *Revista Paranaense de Desenvolvimento* 36(128): 19–32.

Pomar, V. (2013). *Debatendo Classes e Luta de Classes no Brasil.* https://www.scribd.com/document/116459858/Caderno-SRI-Debatendo-Classes-e-Luta-de-Classes-No-Brasil (accessed 15 November 2020).

Rossi, P., and Mello, G. (2017). Choque Recessivo e a Maior Crise da História: A Economia Brasileira em Marcha à Ré. *Nota do Cecon, I.E.-UNICAMP*, No. 1, http://brasildebate.com.br/wp-content/uploads/NotaCecon1_Choque-recessivo-2.pdf (accessed 15 November 2020).

Rousseff, D. (2017). Entrevista exclusiva: Dilma Rousseff sem censura, ou quase. https://jornalggn.com.br/noticia/entrevista-exclusiva-dilma-rousseff-sem-censura-ou-quase/ (accessed 15 November 2020).

Rovai, R. (2013). Jantar com empresários: Campos percebeu que o ponto fraco do governo Dilma é a boca. https://revistaforum.com.br/blogs/blogdorovai/bblogdorovai-jantar-com-empresarios-campos-percebeu-que-o-ponto-fraco-do-governo-dilma-e-a-boca/ (accessed 15 November 2020).

Saad-Filho, A. (2002). *The Value of Marx*. London: Routledge.

Saad-Filho, A. (2015). Social Policy for Neoliberalism: The Bolsa Família Programme in Brazil. *Development and Change* 46(6): 1227–1252.

Saad-Filho, A. (2017). Neoliberalism. In: Brennan, D.M., Kristjanson-Gural, D., Mulder, C., and Olsen, E. (eds.), *The Routledge Handbook of Marxian Economics*. London: Routledge.

Saad-Filho, A. (2018). Monetary Policy and Neoliberalism. In: Cahill, D., Cooper, M., and Konings, M. (eds.), *SAGE Handbook of Neoliberalism*. London: Sage.

Saad-Filho, A., and Boito, A. (2017). Brazil's Crisis of Hegemony. https://www.jacobinmag.com/2017/05/temer-corruption-impeachment-pt-jbs-lava-jato (accessed 15 November 2020).

Saad-Filho, A., and Morais, L. (2018). *Brazil: Neoliberalism versus Democracy*. London: Pluto Press.

Saes, D. (2001). *República do Capital: Capitalismo e Processo Político no Brasil*. São Paulo: Boitempo.

Sicsú, J., Paula, L.F., and Renault, M. (eds.). (2005). *Novo-Desenvolvimentismo: um Projeto Nacional de Crescimento com Eqüidade Social*. Rio de Janeiro: Fundação Konrad Adenauer.

Singer, A. (2009). Raízes Sociais e Ideológicas do Lulismo. *Novos Estudos* 85: 83–102.

Singer, A. (2015). Cutucando Onças Com Varas Curtas: O Ensaio Desenvolvimentista no Primeiro Mandato de Dilma Rousseff (2011–2014). *Novos Estudos* 102: 43–71.

Souza, F.E.P. (2015). Por Que a Indústria Parou? In: Barbosa, N., Marconi, N., Pinheiro, M.C., and Carvalho, L. (eds.), *Indústria e Desenvolvimento Produtivo no Brasil*. Rio de Janeiro: FGV.

Souza, J. (2017). *A Elite do Atraso*. Rio de Janeiro: Leya.

Squeff, G.C. (2015). Rigidez Produtiva e Importações no Brasil: 1995–2009. In: *Dinâmica Macrossetorial Brasileira*. Brasília: IPEA.

Valença, M.M. (2002). The Politics of Giving in Brazil: The Rise and Demise of Collor (1990–1992). *Latin American Perspectives* 29(1): 115–152.

Valle Baeza, A., and Martínez González, G. (2011). *México, Otro Capitalismo Fallido*. Buenos Aires: Ediciones RyR.

CHAPTER 2

Capitalist Development Pattern and Macroeconomic Policy Regimes in Brazil since 1994

Luiz Filgueiras

1 Introduction[1]

The debate about the nature of the governments of the Partido dos Trabalhadores (Workers' Party – PT) tends to contrast two diametrically opposite views: that they constituted a total rupture with the neoliberalism of the previous period (the governments of Fernando Collor de Mello/Itamar Franco and Fernando Henrique Cardoso) and that they simply continued the political-economic model of the past, creating, at best, a sort of social liberalism. These different views are accompanied by positions that emphasize the ambiguous or hybrid nature of the PT governments and therefore are situated between the two poles. With the unfolding of the debate, the various responses have been reduced to the opposition between neoliberalism and developmentalism (the latter with nuances). Normally, the arguments presented to defend the different points of view use the comparison of the performance (macroeconomic and social) of the Brazilian economy during the PT governments vis-à-vis the previous governments (Collor de Mello / Itamar Franco and Fernando Henrique Cardoso), and the identification (existence or otherwise) of a set of economic and social reforms and policies, the content of which, together with a greater or lesser economic activism of the state, would define a neoliberal or a developmental government (Neo, New or Social).

The problem is that, despite the importance of the aspects considered, this approach does not unequivocally distinguish the structural dimension, which determines the deeper characteristics of the Brazilian capitalist development pattern established at the beginning of the 1990s, from the macroeconomic policy regimes that have conditioned and limited the actions of Brazil's governments for the past three decades. In addition, the opposing views (neoliberal and developmentalist) are generally either fundamentally economic or essentially political in character, and even when advocates consider both of

---

1 An earlier version of the arguments in this chapter appeared in Filgueiras (2020).

these dimensions of the Brazilian capitalist development pattern, they cannot adequately articulate them. By fragmenting these dimensions or weakly articulating them they lose sight of the whole and make it difficult to understand how the material, social, and political interests of classes and class fractions intersect and determine each other, producing a long-term trend around which fluctuations and inflections (economic and political) occur, or how that pattern might be altered.

Employing the (transdisciplinary) concept of the capitalist development pattern (Filgueiras 2013) and identifying the particular form it has assumed in Brazil since the 1990s, this chapter seeks to overcome the lack of hierarchization between structure and context and the separation (or weak articulation) between economics and politics. The proposal defended here is that, from the point of view of the capitalist development pattern, the governments of Collor de Mello, Cardoso, and Temer, on the one hand, and Lula da Silva and Dilma Rousseff, on the other, are similar: the former are actively promoting it and the seconds accepting it as irreversible, the limit of the possible, and adapting to it. They differed, however, in the macroeconomic policy regimes they adopted.

The understanding of neoliberalism adopted here is as a political-ideological doctrine systematized shortly after World War II by Hayek and Friedman, among others, out of a critique of the welfare state and socialism – a regressive update of liberalism (Anderson 1995). In addition, accepting the conception of Dardot and Laval (2016), neoliberalism, rather than an ideology, is a global political rationale drawn from commercial competition whose logic tends to spread to all social spheres and all political subjects. Its political-practical marriage with big financial capital after the crisis of capitalism in the 1970s was expressed in a general political-economic program that can be summarized as privatization, deregulation, and liberalization. However, this program and its policies were implemented according to the specificities of the various socio-economic formations – distinguished, above all, by their condition of center or periphery but not only by this, because neither the center nor the periphery is homogeneous. Therefore, there is more than one capitalist development pattern associated with neoliberalism. What is referred to here as the peripheral-liberal pattern is the form assumed by neoliberalism in Brazil, shaped by the country's previous economic and social structure and the disputes between different fractions of its bourgeoisie and between these and the working classes. In short, neoliberalism is a doctrine and a general political-economic program, but the capitalist development patterns associated with it are more or less differentiated from one country to another according to their economic and social formations.

This chapter, in addition to this introduction and the conclusion, has four sections. In the first, based on the literature, I summarize the debate about the nature of the PT governments that has intensified since the end of the first Lula da Silva government with the flexibilization of the macroeconomic tripod inherited from the second Cardoso government. In this sequence, the dependent character of Brazilian capitalism stands out, along with the *unavoidable* historical-structural conditioning that accompanies all the development patterns through which the country has passed since its political independence. Subsequently I consider the origin, nature, characteristics, and inflections of the current peripheral-liberal capitalist development pattern established in Brazil since the 1990s. Finally, I review the different macroeconomic policy regimes that the country has experienced within this pattern of development and associate them with the inflections that occurred in the power bloc.

2   Interpretations of the PT Governments

The following list of some of the main interpretations of the PT governments is intended simply to locate the main aspects of the problem in the interest of a better understanding of the alternative interpretation defended here – which, although different, uses countless contributions present in this debate.

2.1   *The Developmental Rupture (or Inflection) of the Lula da Silva*
         Government
From the perspective of those who participated in the governments of Lula da Silva, Barbosa and Souza (2010) argue that around 2006–2007 there was the transition from a neoliberal economic model to a new developmentalist model in which economic growth driven by the domestic market leads to the distribution of income. Despite having benefited from a very favorable international economic environment, this transition was mainly the result of a choice by the government. From a macroeconomic point of view, it required the flexibility of the tripod inherited from the second Cardoso government. Reducing the primary fiscal surplus, maintaining the inflation target of 4.5 percent, and managing the exchange rate, along with the expansion and diversification of Brazilian exports (destination and nature of products), allowed the accumulation of international reserves and the reduction of the country's vulnerability. According to Barbosa and Souza, this change of course relied above all on the return of the state to guidance and planning of the development process with the resumption of public investment (the Growth Acceleration Program) and fiscal incentives and credit for private investment (financing, through the

Brazilian Development Bank, of large national groups to allow them to expand and internationalize their activities) and for consumption (consigned credit). In addition, two other policies were decisive because they were at the center of the "new model": social policy (especially the Bolsa Família program, which significantly reduced absolute poverty) and the policy of real wage growth, which, in addition to reducing poverty and inequality, boosted economic growth.

From the same perspective but political, Singer (2012) identifies the emergence of a new phenomenon called "Lulismo" that resulted partly from the socioeconomic transformations pointed to by Barbosa and Souza. Lulismo expressed a long-term political tendency toward the replacement of the traditional confrontation between capital and labor with the opposition between rich and poor. This change was a consequence, on the one hand, of the removal of the middle class from the Lula da Silva government because of the so-called *mensalão* (purchase of senators) and, on the other hand, the support for the government of the subproletariat (the poor) because of economic and social policies that led to the expansion of the labor market, with growth in formal employment and higher wages – the reduction of absolute poverty, access to durable consumer goods, and improvement in the income distribution.

The favorable international environment (the commodities boom) helped to create Lulism, but the decisive factor may have been the government decisions that led to the reduction of poverty. In Singer's view, Lula's government was guided by a "weak reformism" that was sufficient to discourage conflict but focused on the poorest without confronting the rest. For this reason, the subproletariat, which was politically and morally conservative, identified with Lula and his policies, and this helped him to improve their lives. Moreover, and more important, because it was a fragmented and disorganized social segment and was unable to express itself independently in the political arena, the subproletariat identified Lula as its representative.

The Lulist project, according to Singer, divided society into a productivist coalition (factory owners and workers) and a rentier coalition (national and international financial capital and perhaps agribusiness and the traditional middle class, which supported it massively). Lulism (a kind of "Bonapartism") balanced these interests with the support of the subproletariat, aiming to meet its aspirations and reduce absolute poverty. While the productivist coalition program sought to control the flow of foreign capital, reduce interest rates, manage exchange rates with devaluation of the real, make public investments in infrastructure, reduce inequality, and protect the industry against the "Dutch disease"; the rentier coalition advocated high interest rates, the free flow of foreign capital, the maintenance of the appreciated real, and the reduction of the tax burden. Although Singer does not believe, as do the previous writers, that there has been a break with neoliberalism, he seems to point more to an ill-defined hybrid situation characterized by neoliberal elements and other components opposed to neoliberalism.

2.2   *A Hybrid Economic Policy*

Starting from a broader concept of economic policy that incorporates policies other than the macroeconomic, Morais and Saad-Filho (2011) also point to the improved performance of the Brazilian economy from 2006–2007 on and the aforementioned changes, especially the partial adoption of economic policies defended by the so-called new developmentalism. However, since these were accompanied by neoliberal macroeconomic policies (inflation targets, primary fiscal surpluses, and floating exchange rates), they constituted not a fully coherent new development policy but a hybrid one that was both neoliberal and developmentalist. Thus, while they agree that, as of 2006, the economic policy of Lula's government underwent an inflection with the flexibilization of the macroeconomic tripod and the introduction of other economic policies, they do not consider the new situation a replacement of previous policies. Although they call the new policies "developmentalist", they emphasize their similarities to New Developmentalism.

Also identifying the Lula da Silva governments as hybrid and indefinite, Fonseca, Cunha, and Bichara (2012), analyzing the performance and recent policies of the Brazilian economy and comparing them with those of the "era of developmentalism" (1930–1980), conclude that, despite the resumption of growth, "good macroeconomic fundamentals", and increased consumption by the poorest, it was not unequivocally a matter of the resumption of development as the guiding ideology of a new phase of the Brazilian economy and society. Adopting the same perspective as Morais and Saad-Filho, they defend the coexistence of rupture and continuity with the previous neoliberal period. Accordingly, they argue, no clear project or classes and social segments to support it can be identified. Finally, they say that Lula da Silva's government was close to the classic Keynesian-inspired post-World War II European social-democratic standard, with the adoption of policies to stimulate demand, public investment, and social protection.

2.3   *Social Developmentalism*

In defense of the governments of Lula da Silva and Dilma Rousseff and identifying with both is the formulation called "social developmentalist" or "left developmentalist" associated with the second generation of the Campinas school (Costa 2012). This current of thought coincides with Barbosa and Morais's, although the date of the transition (second half of 2004) to a new pattern of growth is different. According to this idea, investment began to increase above GDP, indicating that the new growth cycle would have greater depth than the previous ones (Carneiro 2011).

In the beginning (in 2003) this cycle was "pulled" by external demand associated with the international commodities price cycle and the new role played by China, but in the following two years exports lost importance compared with the domestic market. As of 2008, the external sector became a factor in the reduction of aggregate demand due to the negative current-account balance. The significant change in the Brazilian export agenda, coupled with the growth of industrial or agricultural commodities (18 of the 20 main export products), brought about few changes in the industrial structure of the economy with regard to its technological intensity. Thus, although it evidences a process of "regressive specialization" in the profile of Brazilian exports, deindustrialization and exchange rate policy do not seem to be the main concern of this view. In this it differs from new-developmentalist thinking, which emphasizes exchange-rate overvaluation as a fundamental determinant of deindustrialization and, consequently, of low economic growth. In this new pattern of growth, investment was initially induced by exports (mining, steel, pulp and paper, oil and gas) and then by consumption, failing to move on to a pattern driven by autonomous investment. The increase in consumption was through credit and improved income distribution – the latter stemming from the increase in formal employment, minimum-wage adjustments, and government transfers (an increase in the social security benefit and the Bolsa Família program). Economic growth and low inflation recovered the economy's average real wage after mid-2004.

Despite the positive evaluation of this new pattern expansion, which allowed the return of growth accompanied by a better income distribution, the social-developmentalist current acknowledged that it could not continue indefinitely (Costa 2012). Thus, dynamically, this pattern would give way to a new one in which growth would be controlled by autonomous investment and not by exports, as proposed by the new developmentalism. Net exports cannot constitute "a relevant and permanent source of growth increase in Brazil" (Carneiro 2011: 16) for two reasons. First, the high-income elasticity of imports due to the regressive specialization that occurred in the 1990s increased the significance of imports in meeting domestic demand. Second, the exchange rate and the difference between domestic and external growth rates combined would increase the current-account deficit.

2.4   *The New Developmentalism*

In contrast to the "old" developmentalism, the new developmentalism, adopting a post-Keynesian and neostructuralist (ECLAC 1998) approach, holds that exports "pull" development, the state ceases to invest and returns to promoting private investment, industrial policy becomes less important, public finances must be balanced or generate a surplus, and monetary stability must be constantly pursued (Bresser-Pereira and Gala 2010). As did the old structuralist theory, it conceives (structural) underdevelopment as a counterpart of development, admits the existence of a tendency of the terms of trade to deteriorate, identifies a tendency of wages to increase less than productivity (because of the unlimited supply of labor), and considers promotion by the state strategic for development.

From this perspective, Oreiro (2011) identifies three macroeconomic policy regimes since the implementation of the Real Plan in 1994: (1) the anchored exchange rate (1995–1998), (2) the macroeconomic tripod (inflation targets, primary fiscal surpluses, and a floating exchange rate) (1999–2005), and (3) inconsistent development originating in the flexibilization of the tripod that began in 2006–2007 (2008–2014). According to Oreiro, the inconsistency of the last regime derives from the impossibility of simultaneously achieving its various objectives: stabilizing the real exchange rate, increasing the proportion of wages in the national income, controlling the rate of inflation in the long term, promoting a significant increase in actual output, and enabling a strong increase in domestic aggregate demand through an accelerated growth of primary government spending. As a consequence of the abandonment of one of its objectives, the stabilization of the real exchange rate, there was a tendency toward deterioration of the current-account balance of payments and the deepening of deindustrialization. In short, the inconsistent development regime typical of the governments of Lula da Silva and Dilma Rousseff was unsustainable in that it tended to revive the vulnerability of the Brazilian economy.

Thus, the growth of the Brazilian economy in the period analyzed was wage-led. In other words, economic growth was "pulled" by the growth of wages faster than the increase in labor productivity. As a consequence, the proportion of wages in the national income and the proportion of consumption in the GDP tended to increase over time, leading to a loss of export competitiveness and then to balance-of-payments problems and eventually an exchange-rate crisis. Under this regime, the tendency was toward reduction of the rate of economic growth in the medium and long term and the return of the economy to the primary-export condition.

2.5   Neoliberal Neodevelopmentalism

Finally, in an interpretation, like Singer's, verging on political science, Boito Jr. (2012) argues that the PT's "model of development", although it had undergone reform, remained neoliberal in nature – identifying, as an expression of this reform in the 2000s, the adoption of a neodevelopmentalist economic policy and social policies that moderated the negative effects of the model. According to Boito Jr., neodevelopmentalism "is the development policy possible within the limits of the neoliberal capitalist model". From the political point of view, neodevelopmentalism rests on a political front of very heterogeneous classes and class fractions that strengthened the "Brazilian internal big bourgeoisie" and secondarily addressed some of the interests of the popular classes. Economic growth and some income distribution converged to unite this front. This developmentalist front had the participation of the great internal bourgeoisie: mining, heavy construction, the top of agribusiness, the manufacturing industry, and to some extent the large state-owned and privately owned banks. Unified by the favoring and protection of the state through trade surplus policies, financing from the National Bank for Economic and Social Development (BNDES), state purchases and large state-owned enterprises, and foreign policy – which ruled out the Free Trade Area of the Americas and prioritized the Southern Economic Market (MERCOSUR).

In the area of the dominated classes, the front had the (organized) participation of the urban working class and the lower middle class (recovery of employment, the policy of minimum-wage adjustment, and union organization and struggle). The peasantry also participated in the front in an organized way, benefiting from the financing of family agriculture and government purchase of its products. The poor peasantry of the Landless Workers' Movement was the most fragile segment of the front and received no tangible benefit. The front also included unemployed and underemployed workers, organized in part by popular protest movements (who benefited from the housing program called My House, My Life). Its socially marginalized segment, a politically disorganized and passive electoral social base, was the beneficiary of the social assistance policy. Among the programs were the Bolsa Família (a kind of minimum-income policy aimed at families with incomes below the poverty line) and the Continuous Benefit programs (the payment of a monthly minimum wage for people with disabilities and/ or over 65 whose family has per capita income less than a quarter of the minimum wage).

3   Dependency and the Capitalist Development Pattern

3.1   *The International Division of Labor and Dependency*

The fundamental characteristic of the economies of the underdeveloped or developing countries is dependency. These are capitalist economies whose dynamics and trajectories are heavily conditioned and constrained by capital accumulation on the world stage, which imposes on them the need to adapt their productive structures to the demands of the dominant countries. They are, therefore, subordinate economies with very little autonomy that transfer income and wealth to the central countries of the world capitalist system. They are the national economies of countries that, since their emergence in the mid-nineteenth century, have occupied a subordinate position in the international division of labor established under British hegemony and reconfigured several times by capitalism as it developed. The forms of this dependency, always involving the transfer of income and wealth (surplus) to the central countries, have changed throughout history, reflecting the modifications that have occurred in the international division of labor. From the 1970s on, with the distinct but articulated world processes of prodctive restructuring, globalization of capital, and financialization under neoliberal ideology and policies, a new form of dependency emerged and became consolidated in the 1990s.

This new technological and financial dependency redefined the incorporation of the peripheral countries into the international division of labor, deepening and radicalizing their dependency. It transformed them into a platform for the accumulation of international financial capital through the securitization and financing of public debt and the payment of rents derived from the monopoly of knowledge and information. For those that, like Brazil, had industrialized in the previous period, it brought back the condition of exporters of agricultural commodities (soy and meat), minerals (iron), and manufactured goods of low added value and low technological intensity and made them consumers but not producers of the typical products of the third and fourth technological revolutions. The major consequences of this new dependency were the almost complete loss of autonomy with regard to the development of socioeconomic policy and a long and painful process of deindustrialization – a decline in the proportion of industry, particularly manufacturing, in the GDP and employment with the country's growing distance from the frontier of technological innovation.

In short, Brazil is a technologically and financially dependent country. On the one hand, with rare exceptions it does not endogenously generate its own technology and is increasingly moving away from the forefront of knowledge. Additionally, along with all other peripheral countries, it has no internationally convertible currency, which means that its international role is conditional upon access to the currencies of the central countries (the dollar and the euro).

3.2   *The Capitalist Development Pattern*

A capitalist development pattern is defined by a set of attributes – economic-social and political – that structures, organizes, and delimits the dynamics of capital accumulation and the socioeconomic relations that exist in a given national state (space) during a certain historical period (Filgueiras 2013). The attribute that both expresses and delimits all the others is the configuration of the bloc in power (Poulantzas 1975; 1977). It is composed in each case of distinct classes or class fractions one of which assumes the position of leadership and hegemony. This hegemony (Gramsci 2002; Liguori and Voza 2017) expresses the dominance and leadership of a certain fraction of capital in the accumulation in progress, and it is characterized by its capacity to unify and direct, politically and ideologically, the other fractions of capital in terms of its own interests and theirs. When this hegemony incorporates, to a greater or lesser degree, the interests of the subordinate classes or some of its fractions, it extends beyond the bloc in power to encompass the whole of society. The identification of the different fractions of the bourgeoisie and of capital and of which fraction assumes the leadership of the process of accumulation and hegemony within the bloc in power is fundamental for characterizing this bloc and describing the dominant dynamics and interests of the capitalist development pattern in force. These interests are expressed, above all, in the economic and political performance of the state and in macroeconomic, social, and other policies.

The other main defining attributes of a development pattern, which are closely associated with the bloc in power, are the nature and type of regulation of the capital–labor relationship, the nature of intercapitalist relations, the state's relationship to the process of accumulation, the process of incorporation of technical progress (the endogenous capacity to generate innovations and whether there is an industrial and technological policy), the method of financing accumulation (public or private and/or external), the structure of ownership and distribution of income and wealth and the content of social policies, the country's international role, and the types of organization and political representation of the distinct classes and class fractions.

In Brazil, dependency has been associated throughout its history with three distinct patterns of capitalist development that have tracked the reconfigurations of the international division of labor: the capitalist-exporter, the import-substitution, and the peripheral-liberal.

In capitalist-exporter development (1850–1930), the hegemonic fraction of the bourgeoisie in the bloc in power was big coffee capital, combining the functions of producer, trader, financier, and exporter. In the interior, regional oligarchies made up of big landowners were established. Strictly speaking, from the point of view of the capital-labor relationship, two distinct moments can be identified during the period of predominance of this pattern, one based on slave labor and one on free wage labor. This change in the labor relationship had an important impact on the development of the productive forces and the expansion of capital accumulation, but it did not change the commercial-financial nature of the dependency characteristic of the period or modify the reflexive dynamics of the economy. It was basically driven by the world market because of the decisive importance of its exports of coffee to the economy as a whole.

In the pattern of import-substitution development (1930–1990), the bloc in power was constituted until the mid-1950s by big industrial capital (national and state) and agrarian oligarchies under the hegemony of the industrial bourgeoisie. From then on, with foreign direct investment and therefore the internalization of its interests, multinational industrial capital was incorporated into the bloc in power, occupying a hegemonic position along with the portion of the big national capital associated with it and state capital. Thus, the national-developmentalism of the early stages of industrialization became associated-dependent developmentalism, with the central economic decisions being externalized, and a cosmopolitan bourgeois fraction and an upper middle class identified with it emerged. In this pattern, with the implementation of the durable consumer goods and capital goods segments, industrialization began, and the cycle of capital and accumulation was largely internalized, with the resulting expansion of the internal market. This market became more important than the external market for the country's production. The interests of the cosmopolitan bourgeoisie and its mode of reproduction as a social class have long been strongly associated and interwoven with foreign capital, financial capital, and imperialism, and its political-ideological hegemony has been expressed unequivocally in the Congress, the judicial branch, and the mass media.[2]

---

2 The cosmopolitan bourgeoisie can be recognized in Brazil mainly in the following sectors: financial activities and markets (banks, investment and pension funds, financial advisory and consulting firms, insurance companies, brokerages, health insurance); suppliers and service providers established or associated with multinationals in various types of business; the top management of multinational companies in industry and agribusiness; large marketing and communication groups; large law and auditing firms; and, more recently, large private universities, many of them already owned by foreign capital.

Finally, the current pattern of capitalist development in Brazil (1990–2019), here called the peripheral-liberal, established in the 1990s under the Collor de Mello government, configured what was already a reality at the global level, a new hegemony. This one was led by financial capital, which subordinated productive logic to its own volatile and short-term logic. This pattern deepened during the governments of Cardoso and consolidated during the governments of Lula da Silva and Dilma Rousseff.

4 The Peripheral-Liberal Pattern of Capitalist Development

The fundamental structural characteristics of the peripheral-liberal pattern of capitalist development can be summarized as follows (Filgueiras 2013; 2006):

> Capital/labor asymmetry favored the former because of the restructuring of production and trade liberalization, which led to an increase in structural unemployment, informal work, outsourcing, and lack of job security. As a result, the capacity for union organizing, mobilization, and negotiation was reduced (although it has recovered since the end of the first Lula government, when the economy resumed growth and formal employment increased).

As a result of the commercial-financial opening and privatizations, intercapitalist relations were redefined, changing the positions and the relative importance of the various fractions of capital in the process of accumulation and macroeconomic dynamics. Financial capital (national and international) came to occupy a dominant position, displacing industrial capital, state capital lost relevance in favor of foreign capital, and large national economic groups producing/exporting commodities (Brasil Foods, JBS, Gerdau, Votorantim) and agribusiness were strengthened.

The country's position in the new international division of labor changed for the worse, increasing its structural vulnerability. On the one hand, the export agenda of the country once again included primary products (products with low added value and limited technological intensity, whose surplus trade balance compensated for the deficits observed in the medium-high- and high-technology segments) and deepened the deindustrialization begun in the 1980s. On the other hand, its financial dependency dramatically increased, weakening the state and greatly reducing its ability to develop macroeconomic policy. All this was due to the commercial-financial opening that also fueled deindustrialization and an increase in public debt (currently R$5.4 trillion, almost 80 percent of GDP and, as in other peripheral countries, an accumulation platform for international financial capital).

The role of the state in accumulation and macroeconomic dynamics changed with privatization and financial opening. Despite its momentous rescue by the governments of Lula da Silva and Dilma Rousseff, the state became financially fragile and lost its ability to regulate the economy and operationalize macroeconomic and production support policies.

Finally, because of all these changes and at the same time reinforcing them, a new power bloc was established under the hegemony, at first, of financial capital (national and foreign) and the cosmopolitan bourgeoisie associated directly or indirectly with foreign capital, which imposed fundamental state monetary, fiscal, exchange-rate, industrial, and foreign trade policies. Subsequently, as a condition of the survival of peripheral-liberal development itself, the importance of agribusiness and commodity-producing industry grew, along with the role of the internal bourgeoisie.

In sum, the pattern was liberal because it was based on the commercial and financial opening, privatization, and deregulation of the economy under the clear hegemony of financial capital, and it was peripheral because neoliberalism assumed specific characteristics in dependent capitalist countries, becoming even more regressive than it was in the central ones (Filgueiras and Gonçalves 2007).

From the point of view of macroeconomic dynamics, the fundamental characteristic of this capitalist development pattern, which structurally deepened the country's technological and financial dependency, was expressed in its extreme instability and great structural vulnerability, closely following the cyclical changes in the international economy (the increase in liquidity since the early 1990s, China's entry into the World Trade Organization at the beginning of the following decade, the global crisis of capitalism that occurred in 2007–2008, and the slowdown in postcrisis global growth). This pattern of development has characterized all Brazilian governments since 1990.

In its constitution and development, the peripheral-liberal pattern has gone through five phases since the beginning of the 1990s:

1. A rather turbulent rupture with the import-substitution pattern and the implementation of the first concrete actions of a neoliberal nature (commercial opening and privatization). In this phase there was resistance from many industrial sectors (capital goods and nondurable consumer goods) and trade liberalization.

2. Expansion and consolidation of the new socioeconomic order with the implementation of the Real Plan and deepening of neoliberal reforms (commercial and financial opening, privatizations, and a first reform of

social security) in which the hegemony of the interests of financial capital was expanded and consolidated within the bloc in power (the first Cardoso government) with the occupation of the ministries related to the economy (Finance, Planning) and the Central Bank.

3.   The end of the exchange-rate anchor and the adoption of the macroeconomic tripod (in January 1999), in which commodity-producing capital (especially agribusiness) was strengthened, expanding in importance in the power bloc (Ministries of Agriculture, Industry, and Foreign Trade) because it was vital for reducing the instability of the model (the second Cardoso government and the first government of Lula da Silva).

4.   Increased presence of the internal big bourgeoisie[3] within the bloc in power in articulation with the state. The latter started to play an active and more direct role in the economic process, especially in the structuring of the oil production chain, the internationalization of large national economic groups, the financing of the country's infrastructure through increased public investment, and the arbitration of the interests of the various fractions of capital (the second government of Lula da Silva and the government of Dilma Rousseff).

5.   Reestablishment of the hegemony of financial capital and the cosmopolitan bourgeoisie (Ministries of Finance, Industry, and Mines and Energy, Central Bank) with a new wave of neoliberal reforms (privatizations, disruption of the oil-production chain, change in the Pre-Salt exploitation regime, unrestricted outsourcing, and labor and pension reforms) and the return of the macroeconomic tripod in its rigid version (the governments of Michel Temer and Jair Bolsonaro).

In the course of these five phases, the pattern underwent three inflections that, in addition to partially reconfiguring the bloc in power, led to changes in its dynamics through the adoption of different macroeconomic policy regimes that were directly related to changes in the international economic environment.

---

3   The internal big bourgeoisie, a concept coined by Nicolas Poulantzas (1974; 1977), is not synonymous with the national bourgeoisie. In contrast to the latter, which has not existed in Brazil for decades, it has no contradictions with foreign capital and imperialism, since it is not nationalist. It does, however, an approach to the reproduction of capital that does not necessarily involve an alliance with outsiders, and therefore it differs from the cosmopolitan bourgeoisie associated, politically and objectively, with imperialism. It can be identified in various branches of industry (textiles, food, beverages, and capital goods, among others), in the petroleum production chain, in heavy civil construction, in agricultural and mineral commodity production, and in segments of large retail and agribusiness.

5   The Peripheral-Liberal Pattern and Its Macroeconomic Policy Regimes

The policy regimes in question, whose terms depended decisively on the international situation and that reflected different priorities and advantages with regard to the different fractions of capital, always imply some accommodation by the bloc in power. Therefore, they differentiate the governments of Cardoso and Temer, on the one hand, from those of Lula da Silva and Dilma Rousseff, on the other. Thus, the hegemony of financial capital in Brazil was undeniable until the beginning of the second Cardoso government (in 1999), when the Real Plan economic policy centered on the so-called exchange-rate anchor and combined with passive monetary and fiscal policies, produced the overvaluation of the real and a devastating currency crisis that forced a change in macroeconomic policy. The power bloc undertook an adaptation of the correlation of internal forces with the strengthening of its export capital fractions (mineral extractive industry and agribusiness) – a crucial condition for reducing the country's external conjunctural vulnerability. Alongside the devaluation of the exchange rate, monetary (inflation targeting) and fiscal (obtaining primary fiscal surpluses) policies established the so-called macroeconomic tripod.

Later, during the transition from the first to the second Lula da Silva government, the bloc in power accomplished a second accommodation. Capital fractions such as large contractors and large retail chains increased in importance in the wake of the resumption of state investment, with the BNDES playing a fundamental role in the centralization and internationalization of large national economic groups. In addition, a monetary policy was adopted to stimulate consumption. There were reductions of interest rates and credit expansions, along with a new wave of exchange-rate appreciation and real increases in the minimum wage. From a fiscal point of view, primary fiscal surpluses were reduced, and, after the 2008 crisis, a policy of tax relief was implemented, with problematic consequences for public accounts that were made explicit in the second Dilma government. Her response, early on, was to adopt a "fiscal adjustment" policy that pushed the economy into a brutal recession.

Finally, starting with the Temer government, financial capital and the cosmopolitan bourgeoisie recovered their hegemony within the bloc in power (Filgueiras 2017). The interest rate continued to rise rapidly and the BNDES withdrew its support for the large national economic groups and the development of the oil production chain. In addition, the failure of the "fiscal adjustment" (with cuts in primary public spending) further deepened the recession, and there was a new devaluation of the exchange rate.

Throughout this period, the hegemony of financial capital was never questioned (despite its being forced to share power with other fractions of capital), and this was expressed during the second Lula da Silva government in the relaxation of the macroeconomic policy tripod. This flexibilization produced a reduction of the interest rate and the primary fiscal surplus and interventions in the foreign exchange-rate market for the accumulation of reserves. The international economic boom of the 2000s, interrupted only by the global crisis that began in 2008, allowed the flexibility of the macroeconomic tripod to be reduced because of the reduction of the country's economic vulnerability. Along with other policies adopted since the end of the first Lula government – the Bolsa Família, the real increase of the minimum wage, and a popular housing program – this led to an increase of the country's growth rates, the reduction of unemployment rates, the reduction of absolute poverty, and a small decrease in the concentration of income.

The improvement of these and other indicators was accompanied by an inflection of the bloc in power in which financial capital underwent a shift in its hegemony with the increasing influence in state management of other fractions of capital: agribusiness, commodity-producing and exporting capital, large contractors, and large groups in retail trade. In short, the so-called internal bourgeoisie became a priority target of state policies, especially through the BNDES, the Banco do Brasil, the Caixa Econômica Federal, and Petrobrás.

This particular moment of the peripheral-liberal pattern, brought about by a favorable international conjuncture and characterized by a macroeconomic policy regime that flexibilized the tripod and rearranged the different fractions of capital within the bloc in power, allowing them to analyze certain popular demands. This circumstance, which brought to the forefront the establishment of an informal alliance between the internal bourgeoisie and segments of the working class that propitiated the passive incorporation of the latter via the market, was interpreted, in the heat of the political struggle, as a new development pattern called new developmentalism (development with income distribution and social inclusion). It was believed that this had at least partially superseded the peripheral-liberal pattern characteristic of the governments of Collor de Mello and Cardoso. However, the global crisis of capitalism that began in 2008 and the impeachment of Dilma Rousseff and the resumption of neoliberal counter reforms categorically belied this illusion. The crisis initially hindered and ultimately made it impossible to continue the flexibilization of the macroeconomic tripod and reconcile the divergent interests of different fractions of capital and diverse sectors of the population.

With the persistence of the international crisis, the countercyclical policy adopted by Lula's second government lost its effectiveness during the Dilma

Rousseff government. In particular, the policy of tax exemptions failed to induce private investment and, what is worse, disrupted public finances. With this, financial capital once again had a more active role and demanded a return to the strict application of the macroeconomic tripod as a permanent state economic policy. The ensuing dispute between the cosmopolitan bourgeoisie and the internal big bourgeoisie for the leadership of the state ended in the defeat of the latter impelled by the impeachment of the president and the return, already in the Temer government, of the neoliberal agenda in its most radical form.

6   Conclusion

The fundamental argument presented here has been that, despite the differences between the macroeconomic policy regimes adopted since the beginning of the 1990s and some inflections in the ruling bloc, the essential characteristics of the Brazilian capitalist development pattern (the peripheral-liberal) did not change. This pattern is a concrete form of expression of the neoliberal doctrine and program in Brazil, and therefore it is a particular historical variety of neoliberalism just as neoliberalism is a product of the economic-social formation that incorporates it.

From the structural point of view, the peripheral-liberal pattern has updated some of the fundamental characteristics of the Brazilian socio-economic formation: technological and financial dependency, with significant income transfer abroad; passive and subaltern participation in the international division of labor with enormous concentration of income, downgrading of the status of worker, promiscuity and illegal favoritism in public–private relations; and, as a product of the loss of hegemony of the bourgeoisie, centralization and displacement of real political power from formal political institutions and, more recently, the "judicialization" of politics, deterioration of formal democracy, and the gradual construction of a state of exception.

Throughout the trajectory of the peripheral-liberal pattern, there has been consensus among the various fractions of big capital, unified by financial logic despite the different positions they occupied in the process of capitalist accumulation, on the following points:

1.   The commercial and financial opening of the economy and its consequent internationalization (implemented starting with the Collor government and initially contested by industrial capital) is a prerequisite for the country's participation in the new order dominated by financial

capital (although there are still different views as to the pace and intensity at which this should occur).

2.   The dominance of financial capital and the financialization of the economy is essentially unquestionable – hence the limitation that it imposes
on the development and implementation of macroeconomic policy.
The decline in interest rates, for example, during the first Dilma government was strongly opposed by financial capital and was quickly reversed
even before the start of the second government. Another example is the
repeated attempts at pension reform, the latest version of which (that
of the Bolsonaro government) has as its fundamental axis the creation
of a system of capitalization, the usual aspiration of financial capital.
Therefore, adaptation to the new capitalist order under the hegemony
of financial accumulation is considered the only approach for individual
capitals.

3.   Privatization, with the consequent reduction of the state in the productive sphere, must continue both through the privatization of new
investments in the country's infrastructure area (public–private partnerships) and through the sale of the remaining public enterprises. This is a
long-standing consensus, actually forged under the Sarney government
even before the neoliberal wave of the 1990s. Although varying in form,
pace, scope, and sectors affected, there was no interruption of it in the
PT governments, although the process was accelerated in the Temer government and, more recently, the Bolsonaro (with Petrobrás, the Pre-Salt
project, and Eletrobrás).

4.   The deregulation of the labor market and the flexibilization of labor law
must be deepened in line with the "primacy of the negotiated over the
legislated" – hence the unrestricted support expressed by all fractions of
capital and their associations for the labor reform passed by the Temer
government as an essential condition for leveraging the competitiveness
of the Brazilian economy.

The neoliberal reforms once again on the agenda and the reduction of social
policy to a minimum are defended as preconditions for the reduction of the
"Brazil cost" and the development of Brazilian capitalism. The dismantling of
these policies and the radicality of the pension reform proposed by the Temer
and Bolsonaro governments are not criticized or resisted by any fraction of
big capital. Thus, given the absolute inability of the Brazilian bourgeoisie to
express and incorporate, economically and politically, the differentiated interests of the whole of Brazilian society, especially of the working classes, there is
no possibility of a capitalist national project to be directed by any fraction of it.
In particular, its dominant fraction, the dependent cosmopolitan bourgeoisie,

cannot achieve and cannot cope with a better distribution of income. The need for the overexploitation of labor is historically entrenched as part of its character and of the subjectivity of its members (Souza 2017; 2015).

References

Anderson, P. (1995). Balanço do neoliberalismo. In: Emir Sader and Pablo Gentile (eds.), *Pós-neoliberalismo: As políticas sociais e o estado democrático*, pp. 9–23. Rio de Janeiro: Paz e Terra.

Barbosa, N., and Souza, J. (2010). A inflexão do governo Lula: política econômica, crescimento e distribuição de renda. In: Emir Sader and Marco Aurélio Garcia (eds.), *Brasil entre o passado e o futuro*, pp. 57–110. São Paulo: Boitempo Editorial.

Boito Jr., A. (2012). As bases políticas do neodesenvolvimentismo. Paper presented at the Ninth Economics Forum of the Fundação Getúlio Vargas, São Paulo.

Bresser-Pereira, L.C., and Gala, P. (2010). Macroeconomia estruturalista do desenvolvimento e novo-desenvolvimentismo. *Revista de Economia Política* 30: 663–684.

Carneiro, R., Mariutti, E., Bastos, P.P.Z., Sarti, F., Hiratuka, C., Maciel, C., Brandão, C., Biancareli, A., Lopreato, F., Baltar, P., Santos, A., Costa, F.N., and Belik, W. (2012). O desenvolvimento brasileiro: temas estratégicos. In: *Rede Desenvolvimentista*, Textos para Discussão, n. 1. Disponível em: http://reded.net.br/?option=com_jdownloads&Itemid=419&view=finish&cid=160&catid=14&lang=pt.

Carneiro, R.M. (2011). Desafios do desenvolvimento brasileiro. In: Ricardo de Medeiros Carneiro and Milko Matijascic (eds.), *Desafios do desenvolvimento brasileiro*, pp. 15–28. Brasília: IPEA.

Costa, F.N. (2012). *Desenvolvimento do desenvolvimentismo: Do socialismo utópico ao social-desenvolvimentismo*. Texto para Discussão 2005.

Dardot, P., and Laval, C. (2016). *A nova razão do mundo: Ensaio sobre a sociedade neoliberal*. São Paulo: Boitempo.

Filgueiras, L. (2006). O neoliberalismo no Brasil: estrutura, dinâmica e ajuste do modelo econômico. In: Eduardo M. Basualdo and Enrique Arceo (eds.), *Neoliberalismo y sectores dominantes: tendências globales y experiências nacionales*, pp. 179–206. Buenos Aires: CLACSO.

Filgueiras, L. (2013). A natureza do atual padrão de desenvolvimento brasileiro e o processo de desindustrialização. In: Inez Sílvia Batista Castro (ed.), *Novas interpretações desenvolvimentistas*. Rio de Janeiro: Centro Internacional Celso Furtado.

Filgueiras, L. (2017). Política, economia e corrupção: a reconfiguração do bloco no poder no Brasil. https://www.analisepoliticaemsaude.org/oaps/pensamentos/5be24078b400ab6191da0e8afa8c38f3/1/ (accessed April 26, 2017).

Filgueiras, L. (2020). The Governments of the Workers' Party: Capitalist Development Pattern and Macroeconomic Policy Regimes. *Latin American Perspectives*, Issue 230, Vol. 47 No. 1, January, 45–64.

Filgueiras, L., and Reinaldo, G. (2007). *A economia política do governo Lula*. Rio de Janeiro: Contraponto.

Fonseca, P.C.D., Cunha, A.M., and Bichara, J.S. (2012). O Brasil na era Lula: retorno ao desenvolvimentismo? *Nova Economia* vol.23, n. 2, (Belo Horizonte Maio/ Agosto. 2013), pp. 403–427.

Gramsci, A. (2002). *Cadernos do cárcere*. Translated and edited by Carlos Nelson Coutinho, Marco Aurélio Nogueira, and Luiz Sérgio Henriques. Rio de Janeiro: Civilização Brasileira.

Liguori, G., and Voza, P. (eds.). (2017). *Dicionário Gramsciano (1926–1937)*. São Paulo: Boitempo.

Morais, L., and Saad-Filho, A. (2011). Da economia política a política econômica: o novo-desenvolvimentismo e o governo Lula. *Revista de Economia Política* 31: 507–527.

Oreiro, J.L. (2011). Crescimento e regimes de política macroeconômica: teoria e aplicação ao caso brasileiro (1999–2011). Paper presented at the Eighth Economics Forum of the Fundação Getúlio Vargas, São Paulo.

Poulantzas, N. (1974). *As classes sociais no capitalismo de hoje*. Rio de Janeiro: Zahar.

Poulantzas, N. (1977). *Poder político e classes sociais*. São Paulo: Martins Fontes.

Singer, A. (2012). *Os sentidos do lulismo: Reforma gradual e pacto conservador*. São Paulo: Companhia das Letras.

Souza, J. (2015). *A tolice da inteligência brasileira: Ou como o país se deixa manipular pela elite*. São Paulo: Leya.

Souza, J. (2017). *A elite do atraso: da escravidão à Lava Jato*. Rio de Janeiro: Leya.

CHAPTER 3

Varieties of Developmentalism: A Critical Assessment of the PT Governments

Daniela Magalhães Prates, Barbara Fritz and Luiz Fernando de Paula

1 Introduction[1]

Brazil received considerable attention in the 2000s for combining growth with equity, but its deep crisis in recent years has raised the question whether both this success and its implosion were the result of a deliberate strategy or of changes in the international context (mainly the boom-and-bust of commodities prices and capital flows) or domestic policy failures. This debate involves supporters and opponents of the strategy adopted by successive Brazilian governments led by the Partido dos Trabalhadores (Workers' Party – PT) over more than a decade, which many have labeled (though with different prefixes) "developmentalist" (Ban 2012; Bielschowsky 2015) or (by analogy with "varieties of capitalism")[2] "varieties of neoliberalism" (Saad-Filho in this volume).[3] Following Fonseca (2014), the concept of developmentalism is ambiguous by definition, nurtured both by theory and by experiences with economic policy. Indeed, a common denominator for academics and the Brazilian governments of this period (Ministério de Planejamento 2003) was the aim of combining sustained economic growth with the restructuring of production and income distribution by giving the state an active role.

We ask whether and to what extent the PT governments (2003 to mid-2016) adopted a developmentalist approach and, if so, what kind. We also address the

---

1 This is an updated version of the paper published in *Latin American Perspectives* 47(1) (2020): 45–64, which extends the analysis to the Temer government of 2016–18.

2 This concept has been proposed by Hall and Soskice (2001) to describe different forms of capitalism with regard to diverging forms of institutional complementarity and coordination of economic systems; the French regulationists also refer to this concept in a different theoretical framework (e.g., Boyer 2002).

3 According to some authors (e.g., Carvalho 2014), "neoliberalism" refers to a general paradigm that gives economic policies general guidance for economic liberalization and reduction of state intervention without establishing a well-defined set of policies to be adopted. Conversely, following a Marxist approach, Saad-Filho (2017) calls the current system of accumulation of global capitalism "neoliberalism".

question what policies the subsequent Temer government (2016–18) adopted, and if these helped to reduce or reinforced the economic crisis underway. To address our research question, we offer three main hypotheses: (1) that there is a set of conceptual approaches that can be labeled "developmentalist"; (2) that the policies developed during this period represented different kinds of developmentalism and even encompassed elements that we classify as "orthodox"; and (3) that the significant changes of the policy mix over time were conditioned both by the international context and by domestic factors. With this we address a lacuna in the literature on the Brazilian case by attempting to shed light on the policies applied, also to bring out the differences between the PT governments and the starkly orthodox government of President Michel Temer, who took office with the impeachment of President Dilma Rousseff in August 2016.

The chapter is divided in five sections, besides this Introduction. Section 2 presents the different varieties of developmentalism. Section 3 presents stylized facts of the external context and summarizes the macroeconomic features of the Brazilian economy in the period under review. Section 4 lists the economic and social policies applied from 2003 to 2018, while section 5 proposes a periodization and typology of economic policies in this period in terms of the distinction between different developmentalist and other approaches. The final section offers conclusions.

2   Varieties of Developmentalism

"Developmentalism" involves two intertwined perspectives, that of a phenomenon of the material world (economic practices) and that of a phenomenon of the world of ideas (concepts or views of the world). The former is also expressed as political discourse, while the latter seeks to form a school of thought (Fonseca 2014: 30). Developmentalism emerged from the development studies of the 1950s and the Latin American structuralist approach, which sought to understand the specificities of underdevelopment and how to overcome it. Classic developmentalism departed from the idea that the typical division of labor between developed and developing economies created a structural balance-of-payments constraint and impaired domestic growth. As a phenomenon of the material world, it translated into national-developmentalist strategies for promoting industrial development on the assumption that it was the most efficient way of achieving an increase in productivity and in national income. It used the "center-periphery" metaphor to translate the productive and technological asymmetries of the international order and saw industrialization as the only way for the peripheral economies to gain access to some of the technical progress of the developed economies and gradually raise living standards (Prebisch 1950; Ocampo 2001).

The current debate has been intertwined with policy discourse and policy making, especially in the many Latin American countries where until recently leftist parties dominated governments. Updated concepts of developmentalism attracted attention in semimature economies of the continent such as those of Argentina and Brazil,[4] which featured more diversified structures of production and ran the risk of premature deindustrialization, because of profound discontent with orthodox policies based on the neoliberal recommendations of the so-called Washington Consensus. Indeed, the region with the most economic inequality in the world experienced stagnation or even worsening of inequality throughout the period of liberalization. In the course of a critical assessment of the neoliberal agenda of domestic market liberalization, trade and financial openness, and reduction of the role of the state, income distribution emerged at the center of debate.

Within this renewed and multidisciplinary debate in Brazil, we identify two new concepts in the economic field, social developmentalism and new developmentalism,[5] the updated classic developmentalism and added new dimensions. Both rejected the neoclassical idea of welfare maximization by specializing in comparative advantage at the global level (much as did classic developmentalism), seeing structural external constraints caused by incorporation of peripheral economies into the global market as the cause of the lack of economic dynamism at the domestic level. Thus, they supported a national strategy of economic development with the state playing an active role in promoting structural change toward (re-)industrialization, resulting in social transformation (Fonseca 2014: 41; Bielschowsky 2015). While the concept of new developmentalism is rather well developed and clearly defined in paradigmatic terms in various papers mainly by Bresser-Pereira (2011; 2015), social developmentalism is treated less coherently by a number of writers. Although the two are rather similar in their policy aims, seeking to achieve change in

---

4   According to some authors (e.g., Cunha and Ferrari 2009), this strategy was also adopted in Argentina during the government of President Néstor Kirchner (2003–2007).

5   The debate has also flourished among political scientists. For instance, Boito and Berringer (2014) analyse the political coalition supporting the PT governments' strategy, which they call "neodevelopmentalism". Singer (2015), in turn, examines the establishment and dissolution of the political coalition of the first Rousseff term, which he calls a "developmentalist experiment".

production with income redistribution, they clearly differ regarding most of their targets and tools.

Social developmentalism is closer to the classic developmentalist approach, continuing to focus on the shortage of domestic demand to push investment into productive diversification, but it gives the aim of equal income distribution a more prominent role and stresses increasing domestic mass consumption to drive economic growth and increase production. The structural balance-of-payments constraint is expected to be mitigated by export growth induced by scale effects and industrialization and by domestic demand, given the complementarity of the domestic and foreign markets. Growth may also be supplemented, at least temporarily, by the expansion of the natural-resource-intensive sector and its supply chains (Bielschowsky 2012; Biancarelli 2017). New developmentalism takes a predominantly macroeconomic approach inspired by the development path of the emerging Asian markets, with their strategy of export surplus. It sees two obstacles to development: the tendency toward currency overvaluation as a result, mainly, of specialization in commodities exports (the "Dutch disease") and the net flows of foreign capital stimulated by the policy of growth-cum-foreign savings and the tendency of wages to increase less than productivity because of the unlimited supply of labor. Here the aim of (re-)industrialization is directly linked to the target of an export surplus of manufactured goods, pushing for further investment in this sector that will enable the country to avoid incurring foreign debt. In this view, the exchange rate plays the key role in influencing both imports and exports. Improvement in income distribution will result from (formal) job creation in the manufacturing sector and increases in wages alongside productivity gains (Bresser-Pereira 2011).

Regarding the policy tools attached to each of these approaches, Carneiro (2012) notes that reflections on social developmentalism are rather fragmented, especially in the first generation of papers (Bastos 2012; Bielschowsky 2012; Carneiro 2012), in which the focus is on policies oriented toward redistribution and shifting production patterns, as follows: (1) wage policies, being the minimum wage a powerful policy instrument to foster wage increases in real terms especially in the lower income range; (2) income transfers targeted at the poor; (3) consumer credit and subsidized financing by public banks; (4) public investment, especially in infrastructure, seen as crucial for creating demand but especially as an incentive for private investment; and (5) industrial policies to stimulate private investment.

Macroeconomic considerations appear mainly in the second generation of publications. Rossi (2014) argues that macroeconomic policy consistent with social developmentalism should maintain economic growth through countercyclical fiscal policies. Fostering investment in production would require low interest rates and a nonappreciated and nonvolatile exchange rate, which could be pursued along with a more flexible execution of the current orthodox framework, the so-called macroeconomic tripod of inflation targeting, a floating exchange rate, and a primary-surplus target. He does not explain, however, how to make these macroeconomic tools compatible with the main pillar of social developmentalist policies, wage increases in real terms, without jeopardizing price stability or a competitive exchange rate.

For new developmentalism, Bresser-Pereira (2011) describes the necessary tools: currency devaluation (if necessary, supported by capital controls) and the subsequent maintenance of the exchange rate at a level where domestic industry becomes internationally competitive; other macroeconomic instruments for maintaining price stability, supported by the combination of a low interest rate and a balanced public budget with room for countercyclical fiscal policies over the cycle (meaning an austerity bias during a boom); and industrial policy that is secondary and targeted at exports until the economy catches up with the advanced economies. Wages may lose purchasing power in the short term as a consequence of currency devaluation, but in the medium term they should grow along with productivity to prevent their spurring inflation. Income redistribution is expected to stem from additional job creation in the manufacturing sector. Redistributive policies are included as an addendum in later publications (Bresser-Pereira 2015), reacting to the heated debate around redistributional issues' not being vital to the new developmentalist strategy.

Thus, the new varieties of developmentalism substantially diverge in terms of the priority given to targets and tools (Table 3.1). This results in sharply different modes of policy coordination.[6]

To facilitate the analysis of policy coordination, we analytically disaggregate the two varieties of developmentalism into three different layers of policy aims, targets and tools. We also refer in this table to the orthodox approach, to sharpen the understanding of the differences between the body of developmentalist concepts and the orthodox approach that has globally dominated the formulation of development strategies at least since the 1990s. For our purposes, we find the label 'orthodox' more precise to differentiate macroeconomic and social policies than the more general label 'neoliberal'. Yet, as the orthodox concept is well established, in the following we only detail the two developmentalist approaches.

---

6   For an extended comparative analysis to the two recent developmentalist concepts, see Fritz, Paula, and Prates (2017).

TABLE 3.1   Varieties of developmentalism and the orthodox approach compared

	Orthodox approach	Social developmentalism	New developmentalism
Aims	Increase of total factor productivity	Productive change with broad income redistribution Industrialization pushed by domestic market growth	Productive change with moderate income redistribution (Re-)industrialization
Targets	Price stability Reduced state intervention Private investment International competitiveness based on comparative advantage	Increase of domestic demand Industrial production Reduction of Gini index Balanced trade account	Export surplus (manufactured) Industrial production Moderate reduction of Gini index
Tools	Inflation targeting Fiscal neutrality Floating exchange rate Privatization Commercial and financial opening Labor market flexibilization Targeted social policies	Wage policy: real increases Social policies: income transfers Active fiscal policies: public investment Industrial policies Financial policies: public banks, consumer credit Monetary policies: low interest rates	Exchange rate policy: competitive exchange rate Monetary policy: low interest rate Fiscal policy: anticyclical with austerity bias Wage policy: real increases along with productivity Capital controls: limiting external debt and net capital flows

3   Macroeconomic Features: The Brazilian Economy

Over the period under consideration, the international context underwent important changes. Four phases can be identified: (1) from 2003 to the global financial crisis,, which was benign for emerging economies in terms of trade (high commodities prices and external demand) and capital flows; (2) from September 2008 to 2010, including the crisis, the rapid recovery, and the new "twin boom" of commodities prices and capital flows; and (3) from 2011 to mid-2016, characterized by a deterioration of international conditions; (4) from midst of 2016 to 2018, global growth, capital flows and commodity prices slowly recovered (Figure 3.1; for details, see Biancarelli, Rosa, and Vergnharini 2017).

During the first phase (specifically, from 2004 to mid-2008), the Brazilian economy experienced unprecedented growth compared with the 1980s and 1990s, an average of 4.8 percent per year. During this pre-crisis boom, the main engine of growth was household consumption (around 60 percent of the GDP). Another novelty of this period was the continuous growth of credit to households and firms. In line with the situations of other emerging economies, the recession caused by the contagion effect of the global financial crisis was brief, mainly because household consumption mitigated the adverse effects of the crisis. The economy recovered quickly, and in 2010 GDP recorded a growth rate

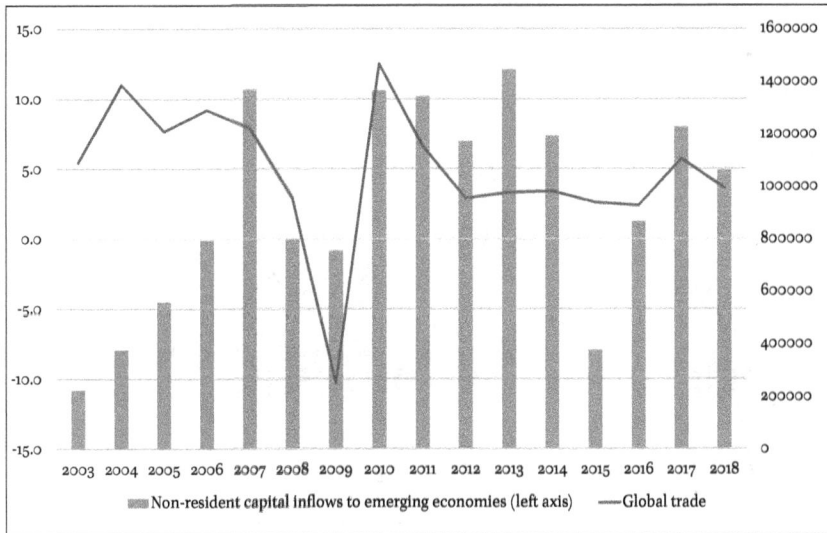

FIGURE 3.1   World trade (annual change in percent) and capital flows (US$ billion), 2003–2016

DATA FROM IMF, 2020

of 7.5 percent; both consumption and investment contributed to that healthy
recovery.

Growth began to slow down again in late 2010, however, further decelerat-
ing in 2012 and turning into the worst economic recession since at least that of
the 1930s (Banco Central do Brasil 2017). A set of shocks contributed to this crisis, among them a deterioration of the terms of trade, accelerated inflation due
to a de-freezing of monitored service prices and strong currency devaluation,
plus a water shortage crisis. The recession, fuelled by a tightening of monetary
and fiscal policies from 2015 on, produced declining wages and profits, and this
caused a huge slowdown in the supply of credit (Figure 3.2) and a deterioration of the financial situation of nonfinancial corporations, further delaying
the recovery of the economy (Paula and Pires 2017). This recovery started in a
very slow mode in 2017, with growth of only 1.6% p.a. on average in 2017 and
2018, but with investment contracting, from 19.9% of GDP in 2014 to around
15% in 2016–2018 (see Table 3.3).

Economic growth in 2003–2013 was accompanied by a sharp reduction in
the unemployment rate, from 12.4 percent in 2003 to 5.1 percent in 2013 (this
rate increased to 8 percent in 2015 because of the recession). The combination
of low unemployment and real wage increases contributed to an improvement
in social indicators, especially economic inequality – a trend also observed in
other Latin America countries (Fritz and Lavinas 2015). In the case of Brazil,

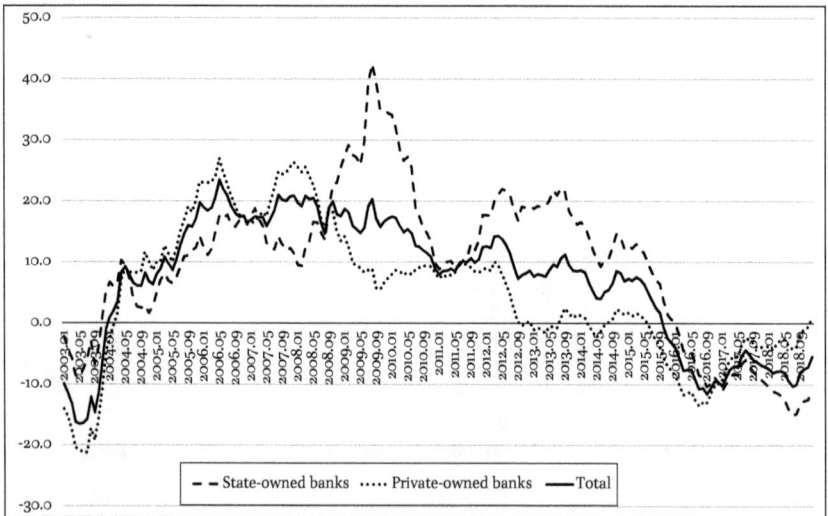

FIGURE 3.2 Credit supply by ownership (growth rate in percent compared with previous year
         in real values deflated by general price index – IGP-DI), 2003–2018
         DATA FROM BANCO CENTRAL DO BRASIL, 2020

the poverty rate fell sharply, from 35.8 percent in 2003 to 13.3 percent in 2014 (IPEADATA 2020). The process of income redistribution encompassed both the personal dimension, with a reduction of the Gini index, and the functional one, with an increase of the wage share of total income.

However, studies using personal income tax records (e.g., Gobetti and Orair 2015; Morgan 2017) show a different picture of Brazilian personal inequality, revealing that the Gini index, which is based on household survey data, overestimates the improvements in the personal income distribution under the PT governments mainly because of the underestimation of the level of incomes at the top of the distribution. These studies confirm that poverty and inequality of income from labor registered a decline, but the exceptionally large concentration of income at the top did not change. As a result, the bottom made gains at the expense of the "squeezed middle" of income earners.[7] According to Carvalho (2018, p. 50): "(...) even though wages were less concentrated in the 2000s thanks to accelerated income growth for workers at the bottom of the pyramid – the result of the policy of raising the minimum wage and the expansion of labor-intensive sectors with low skills, capital income grew even more and remained highly concentrated in the hands of the most richest." The even more contractionary stance of monetary policy over 2015–2017, the implementation of some liberal reforms (such as labor reform) and the rise in unemployment during the recession intensified this trend. As a result, the Gini index promptly increased from 0.518 in 2014 to 0.545 in 2018, returning to the same level of 10 years ago (see Table 3.3). Besides growth and income redistribution, the third aim of developmentalism is to achieve a reallocation of productive resources from the traditional sector (especially agriculture) to the manufacturing sector (mainly its higher-tech segments), but in 2008–2016 the decline of this sector's share of the GDP gained momentum (Figure 3.3).

Moreover, this descending trajectory was accompanied by increasing deficits in balance of trade in manufacturing goods, certainly fostered by the appreciation of the currency in real terms until 2012, only compensated partially by the surplus in commodities favoured by the increasing terms of trade (Figure 3.4). As a result, de-industrialization, underway since the 1990s, was reinforced in a context of exchange rate appreciation and global structural changes (the formation of global production chains and competition from China). In 2015–2016, this trajectory was abruptly reversed by the sharp contraction in imports

---

7 According to Morgan (2017), in 2001–2015 the average income of the richest 1 percent grew 31.4 percent, while that of the poorest 50 percent (favored by the policy of real increase in the minimum wage) grew 28.7 percent, and that of the middle class (the middle 40 percent, with an average annual income of US$15,760 [PPP] in 2015) grew only 11.5 percent.

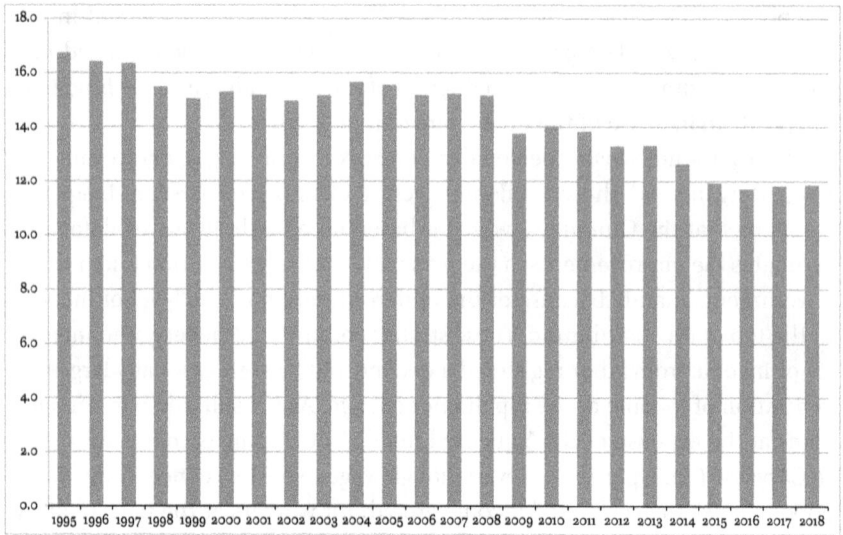

FIGURE 3.3   Manufacturing sector (% of GDP), 1994–2018
                  IBGE, 2020

and a partial recuperation of exports, mainly due to the recession. As domestic demand continued below the pre-crisis level until 2018, and the terms of trade improved, the trade surplus increased in 2017–2018.

Even with a subsequent reverse in the appreciation trend, the profitability of exports increased only slightly. In this setting, industrial output first stagnated and, from 2013, began to fall. Meanwhile, retail sales and the import coefficient of industry inputs kept growing, indicating a replacement of domestic production by imports both in final and intermediary manufacturing goods (Paula, Modenesi, and Pires 2015).

The negative results regarding structural change were apparent in a deterioration of external solvency in the medium and long term, since the growth rate of net foreign debt was higher than that of exports. The situation was worse with regard to exports of manufactured products, which are characterized by lower price volatility and higher income-elasticity than commodities. From this perspective, the country's capacity for generating foreign currency to serve its foreign debt decreased during the period under analysis (see the performance of the indicator "net external liability/manufacturing exports" in Table 3.3 in Appendix). Only in 2017/2018 debt indicators in relation to trade stabilized, due to higher exports, including manufactured goods (see Table 3.3).

In contrast, external liquidity – vulnerability in the short term – improved during the boom years not only because of the policy of accumulating foreign

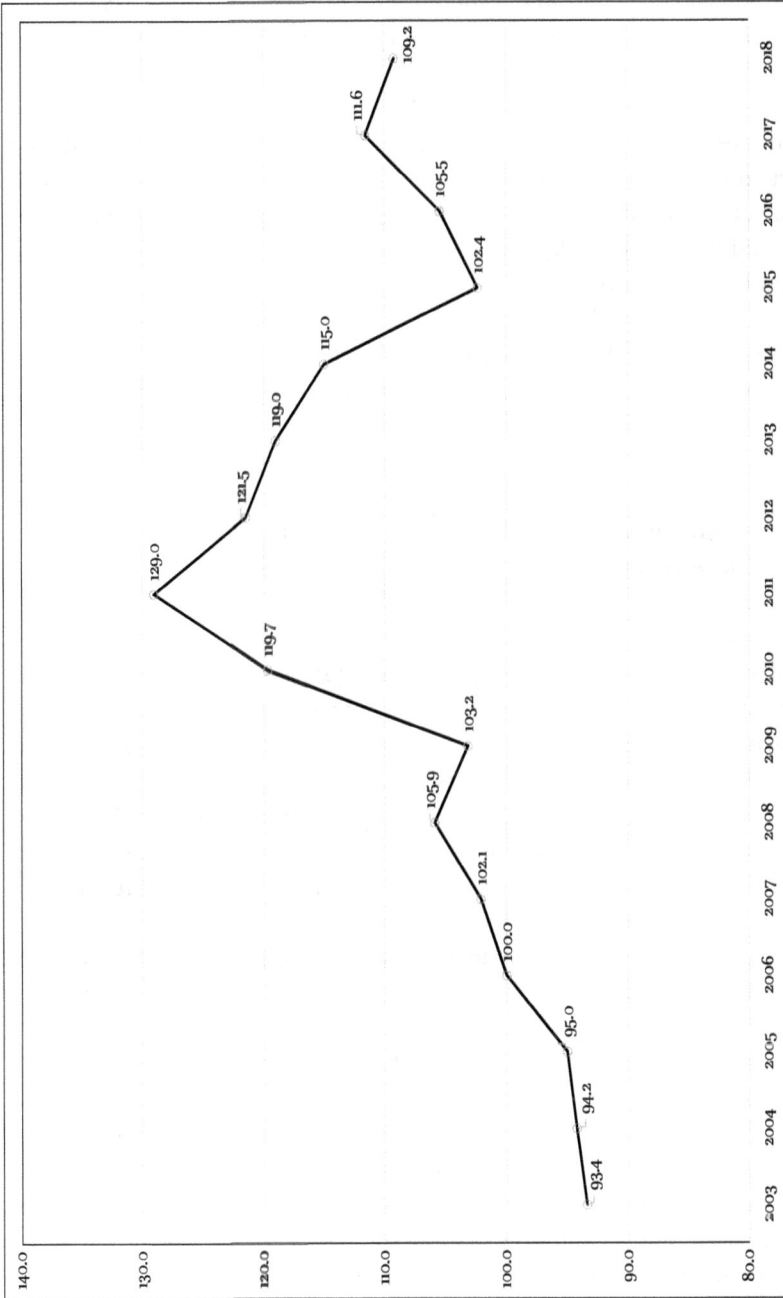

FIGURE 3.4 Terms of trade (average 2006 = 100), 2003–2018

DATA FROM BANCO CENTRAL DO BRAZIL, 2020

exchange reserves but also because of the reduction of the currency mismatch associated with a change in the composition of short-term gross foreign debt. This change stemmed from two simultaneous trends: a decrease in foreign debt and an increase in foreign portfolio investments in the domestic market (Biancarelli, Rosa, and Vergnhanini 2017). Further, the increasing current account deficit between 2009 and 2014 was financed almost fully by foreign direct investment, which in 2015–2018 was higher than the foreign deficit. Thus, in the short term, Brazil did not face external constraints, even if external liquidity indicators slightly deteriorated between 2016–18 due to a slowing down of foreign portfolio investment inflows in the domestic capital market and the halt in the policy of building up international reserves. This explains, along with the dirty floating exchange-rate regime, why a balance-of-payments crisis did not break out despite the huge outflow of those investments amid a deep economic and political crisis (Banco Central do Brasil 2017).

4   Economic and Social Policies under the PT and Temer Governments

4.1   *Macroeconomic Policies*
The first term of Lula da Silva's government (2003–2006), following a confidence crisis in 2002 with a massive speculative attack on the currency, was characterized by the continuity of the tripod of macroeconomic policies adopted after the 1999 currency crisis (inflation targeting, primary-surplus targets, and a dirty floating exchange-rate regime). Within this framework, fiscal and monetary policies remained mostly orthodox, characterized by a large primary surplus and the maintenance of a high (albeit decreasing) real interest rate, while the currency appreciated gradually (Figure 3.6).

In a positive external environment in terms of trade and capital flows (see Figure 3.4) the high interest rate stimulated speculative operations through portfolio investment and foreign exchange derivatives. These operations along with the current-account surplus resulted in significant currency appreciation. The interventions in the foreign exchange market of the monetary authority in 2005 did not curb this appreciation but resulted in the buildup of foreign exchange reserves. The so-called precautionary demand for reserves contributed to the decrease of net public foreign debt and improvement in the country's eternal liquidity. Moreover, in this period bank credit to the private sector recorded significant growth, stimulated, among other factors, by the implementation of payroll-deductible credit operations, which reduced bank risk and, consequently, the cost of loans to households. From 2006 on, credit from

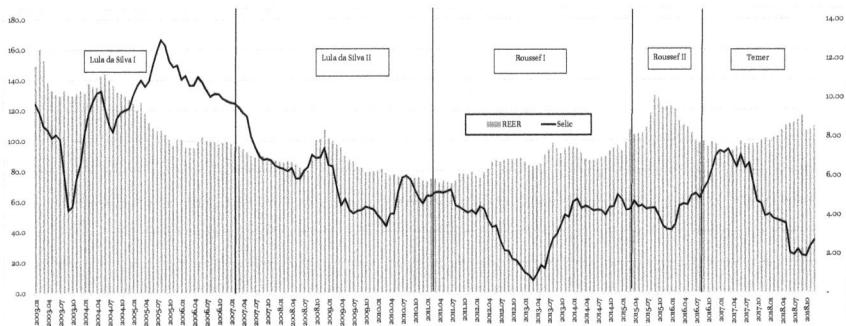

FIGURE 3.5 Policy rate (Selic interest rate [percent annually]) and real effective exchange rate
(June 1994 = 100)
DATA FROM BANCO CENTRAL DO BRASIL, 2020

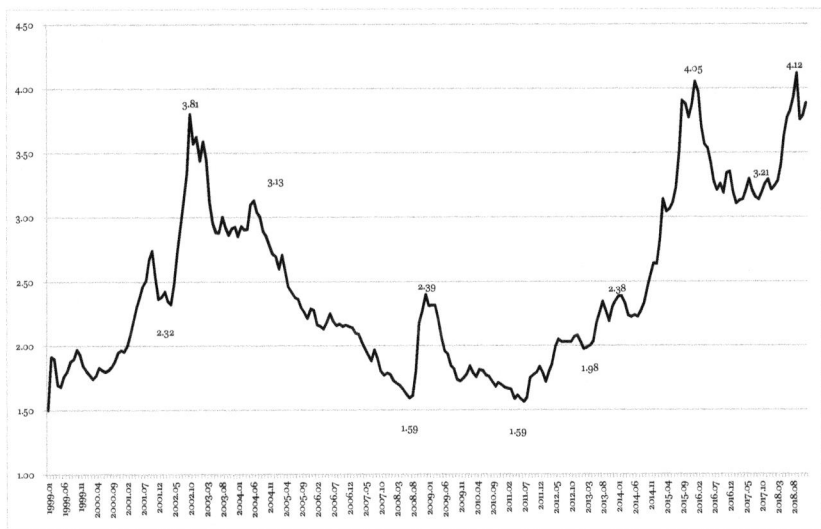

FIGURE 3.6 Exchange rate (R$/US$), January 1999–December 2020
DATA FROM BANCO CENTRAL DO BRASIL, 2020

state-owned banks to corporations also gained momentum, especially when
in 2007, the first year of Lula's second term, a huge program of public investment in infrastructure called the Growth Acceleration Program (*Programa de
Aceleração do Crescimento* – PAC, in Portuguese) was launched. Thus, even
before the contagion effect of the global financial crisis, this term was characterized by greater state activism (Singer 2015).

The Brazilian authorities responded to the global financial crisis by adopting a number of countercyclical measures (Barbosa 2010; Paula, Modenesi, and Pires 2015): (1) to avoid the spread of the credit crunch, the Central Bank of Brazil adopted a series of liquidity-enhancing measures and intervened in the foreign exchange markets; (2) the state-owned banks were encouraged to expand their credit operations to compensate for the deceleration in the credit supply by private banks (see Figure 3.2); and (3) the Ministry of Finance undertook fiscal measures to stimulate aggregate demand. The countercyclical reaction was possible, to a large extent, because of the policy space created by the government's shift toward a net creditor position in foreign currency. Consequently, the currency devaluation favored public finance.

In the context of the quick recovery of the economy and a new "twin boom", Brazil again faced huge short-term inflows boosted by a still high differential between domestic and foreign interest rates. As the Central Bank resumed the exchange-rate policy adopted before the crisis, Brazil's currency recorded a huge appreciation in 2009 (see Figure 3.5), the Ministry of Finance started imposing regulations on capital flows, starting with a tiny financial transaction tax on foreign portfolio investments in October 2009. Soon these regulations were strengthened with the first measure targeting foreign exchange derivative operations and administrative controls. Moreover, the Central Bank of Brazil adopted macroprudential regulations to curb the domestic credit boom (Paula, Modenesi, and Pires 2015; Prates and Fritz 2016).

In mid-2011, during Rousseff's first term, a gradual change was introduced for what the government itself called the "new macroeconomic matrix", a set of countercyclical measures for boosting growth in the context of the worsening of the euro crisis and increasing the competitiveness of the Brazilian industry damaged by years of currency appreciation and increased competition in the foreign markets after the global financial crisis. The regulatory toolkit for the spot and derivatives foreign exchange markets was broadened because the previous measures had only mitigated the currency appreciation trend underlying the deterioration in competitiveness of Brazil's manufacturing sector in both foreign and domestic markets (Prates and Fritz 2016). It was completed by a progressive reduction of the policy rate. At the same time, as a precondition for changing exchange-rate and monetary policy without jeopardizing price stability, fiscal policy was tightened in the first half of 2011 (Cagnin et al. 2013). The interplay of the new foreign exchange regulations, the relaxation of monetary policy, and the increase in the risk aversion of global investors resulted in the intended depreciation of the Brazilian currency (see Figure 3.6).

Besides the change in the interest and the exchange rate, the government launched a wide range of instruments that favored the domestic manufacturing sector and were intended to dampen inflationary pressures in face of the currency depreciation: a nominal freeze of relevant public tariffs (such as on energy and gasoline), the use of state-owned banks to reduce bank spreads, and tax exemptions. It is worth mentioning that in the first year these measures did not change the overall fiscal policy stance (Paula and Pires 2017; Mello and Rossi 2017).

In April 2013, however, because of an increasing inflation rate, the Central Bank began gradually increasing the policy rate (see Figure 3.5) and removed regulations on foreign exchange operations as a result of signaling by the Federal Reserve that its quantitative easing policy would soon be withdrawn. At the same time, the Brazilian government further increased tax exemptions and tried to intensify investment in infrastructure. Moreover, affected by the decline of oil prices and the first effects of Operation Car Wash,[8] Petrobras reduced its investments, and this had a strong impact on overall investment (Mello and Rossi 2017).

Compared with the policies launched to counter the contagion effect of the global financial crisis, the countercyclical fiscal policies implemented in 2012–2014, with the use of tax exemptions instead of public expenditures, were very limited and had little aggregate impact on production and employment. The same holds for public investment, which had been significantly higher in 2006–2010.

In 2015, after the reelection of Dilma Rousseff, the government shifted its economic policy somewhat radically toward a more orthodox stance. The main aim was fiscal adjustment mainly in public expenditures, which was understood as fundamental for restoring actors' confidence as a precondition for economic recovery. For this purpose, the government committed itself to a primary fiscal surplus of 1.2 percent of the GDP, implementing a set of measures to reduce public expenditures (mainly through the budget), and readjusted monitored prices (energy and oil), while the Central Bank further increased its policy rate from 10.92 percent annually in October 2014 to 14.14 percent in August 2015. As a result of the severe devaluation in 2015, the bank had to intervene in the foreign exchange market to reduce exchange-rate volatility and offer exchange-rate hedging to private actors through swap operations (Paula and Pires 2017; Carneiro 2017).

---

8 Operation Car Wash is an investigation conducted by the Federal Police of Brazil and the Court since March 17, 2014, of allegations of corruption at the state-controlled oil company Petrobras. For an analysis of the effects of the Operation Car Wash ("Lava-Jato" in Portuguese) on the Brazilian economy, see also Paula et al (in this volume).

These efforts at fiscal adjustment failed. Fiscal revenues dropped dramatically in 2015, and the Ministry of Finance had to revise its fiscal targets. As a result of the recession and increasing interest payments, the nominal public deficit increased even further in 2015. Net public debt over GDP, which had recorded its lowest level during the period under analysis in 2013 with 30.5 percent, again increased steeply (to 46 percent of GDP in 2016). Gross debt increased even more, from 51.5 percent to 69.6 percent over GDP in the same period. This means that the government's assets (mainly foreign reserves and loans to public banks) shrank in relative terms, in contrast to the situation in 2010–2014, when they rose significantly.

At the beginning of 2016, Nelson Barbosa, the new finance minister, announced his strategy of fiscal consolidation, which, among other things, was expected to reverse the upward trend of public spending that, contradictorily, compromised the capacity of the Brazilian state to implement public policies in the long term (Paula and Pires 2017). The spread of the political crisis virtually paralyzed the government, making impossible the adoption of any economic policy agenda until the impeachment of President Rousseff in 2016.

The Temer government, under the leadership of the Minister of Finance, Henrique Meirelles (who had been central bank president between 2003 and 2010), adopted significant economic policy changes. The so-called economic policy tripod (inflation targeting, primary-surplus targets, and a dirty floating exchange-rate regime) was strengthened. Therefore, a new liberal-orthodox agenda directed the economy towards a new development model, based on liberalizing reforms (labor reform, social security reform, etc.) and the reaffirmation of economic policies conducted in an orthodox way: a more conservative monetary policy, a contractionary fiscal policy (implementation spending ceiling based on the "expansionary fiscal contraction" argument), and a more passive exchange rate policy.

Under the new president of the BCB, Ilan Goldfajn, exchange rate policy moved closer to a clean fluctuation regime, and monetary policy became more conservative until the first quarter of 2017. Although 12-month accumulated inflation began to decline in June 2016, the central bank started cutting interest rates only in October and at a very slow pace, which resulted in a high level of real interest rate in the first semester of 2017, only declining since September 2017 (see Figure 3.5).

The main problem of the Brazilian economy in this period was the lack of demand and not an eventual supply-side problem, due to an "overkill" in terms of excessive conservatism of economic policy. The maintenance of a contractionary monetary policy for a very long period of time, under a context in which fiscal and, above all, financial policy (BNDES disbursements) were also contractionary, contributed greatly to the economy having a slow recovery with a tendency to stagnation. On the other hand, the high indebtedness of firms and families generated a "balance sheet recession", i.e., a drop in the level of economic activity and aggregate demand due to the deleveraging process of firms and families (Paula and Oreiro 2019).

At the end of 2016, the National Congress approved a labor reform, introducing a series of flexibilizations in the labor market: union contribution became optional; rules on dismissal, rest and holidays were loosened; working hours up to 12 hours allowed; term contract and intermittent work permitted, etc. Another important change in Temer's economic policy occurred in the field of fiscal policy: a rigid public spending ceiling was imposed through the Constitutional Amendment 95 (EC95), which cemented public spending in real terms, at limiting its increase to the inflation of the previous year (measured by the consumer price index IPCA). By this, any countercyclical fiscal policy in times of economic slowdown was made impossible to be adopted. But the EC95 had no short-term impact. The economic team, still in its provisional phase, significantly expanded the primary deficit target (from R$97 billion to R$170.5 billion), adopting what Biancarelli (2017) called "patronage Keynesianism". Notwithstanding, its objective was to reduce the role of the state in the economy and to cut back the social rights guaranteed by the 1988 constitution, one of the cornerstones of re-democratization (see also Dweck et al. 2018). Consistent with its fundamentals, the government did not envisage any tax reform.

4.2 *Industrial Policies*
After a long period of almost complete absence of industrial policies, three programs of industrial policy were launched during the period analyzed here. Industrial policy oscillated between two types of strategies: (1) prioritizing high-tech sectors and selecting "national champions" in industries with comparative international advantages such as agribusiness, steel, and mining; and (2) favoring the sectors damaged by strong foreign competition (see Almeida and Novais 2014; Kupfer 2013).

The first program, the Industrial, Technology, and Foreign Trade Policy, launched in 2004, aimed to address Brazil's vulnerability, emphasizing an active policy of adding to exports value based on innovation. To this end, three areas were identified: (1) incentives for strategic sectors (capital goods, software, semiconductors, and pharmaceuticals); (2) horizontal actions to stimulate innovation and technological development, international integration via exports, and modernization of the institutional environment; and (3) priority for biotechnology, nanotechnology, and renewable energy.

With the rapid and intensive improvement of Brazilian terms of trade from 2004 on, which resulted in substantial surpluses in the trade balance, priorities for industrial policy changed. The Productive Development Policy was launched in May 2008 in a context in which Brazil had received investment grade because of its sound economic fundamentals (low inflation, fiscal surplus, etc.). The main objective was to foster growth and productive investment in the domestic market. For this purpose, the program set ambitious investment goals (from 17.6 percent of GDP in 2007 to 21.0 percent in 2010) and an increased participation of Brazilian exports in world trade.

The changing global scenario led to the launch of a third program, the Greater Brazil Plan, in August 2011, continuously modified in the following years in view of the worsening global economic conditions. The initial objective of the plan was the productive and technological consolidation of value chains, but the intensification of foreign competition in domestic and foreign markets forced its direction toward the defense of the domestic market and the recovery of systemic competitiveness conditions. In line with the "new macroeconomic matrix," the government adopted compensatory measures to minimize the impact on domestic manufacturing output of the increasing penetration of imported goods into Brazil, including the expansion of subsidized credit by the Brazilian Development Bank and further tax and social security payment exemptions, causing significant fiscal costs with limited effects on industrial production.

In his assessment of industrial policies in the period analyzed, Kupfer (2013) concludes that these remained an auxiliary element of macroeconomic policy that was often in conflict with it, its effectiveness reduced by the strong currency appreciation until 2011 and very high interest rates.

This policy with dampened efficiency was substituted for the absence of any industrial policy during the Temer government. Additionally, in September 2017, the 'modus operandi' of BNDES underwent an important change: the TJLP, the long-term interest rate used by BNDES in its credit operations, which had generally been lower than the Selic rate over 2002–2016, was replaced by the a new long-term rate TLP, which automatically follows the risk rate charged by the market for 5-year National Treasury bonds, added to the IPCA.[9] This further contributed (besides the sharp decline in the investment rate) to the drastically shrinking of BNDES' lending volume for domestic firms, which

---

9   According to Torres Filho et al (2020), TLP surpassed the Selic rate in most months in 2018/ 2020, removing from the federal government a key instrument for the formation and application of industrial policy.

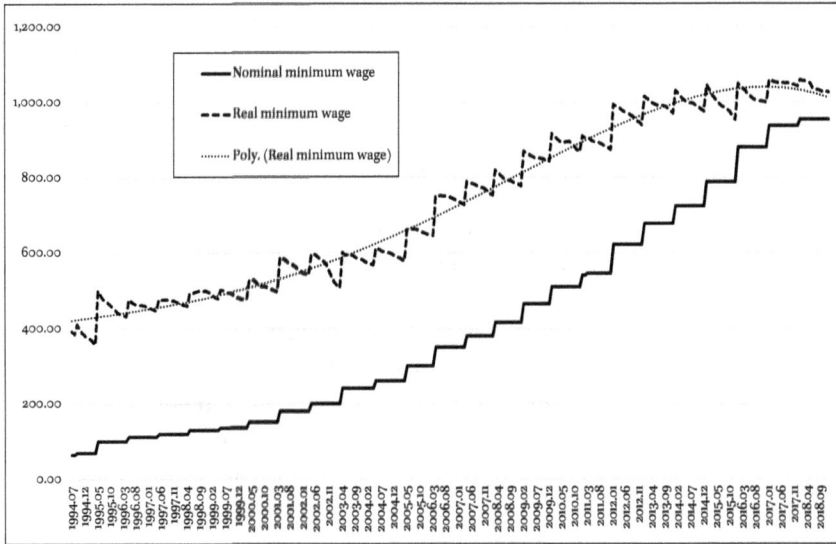

FIGURE 3.7   Minimum wage, nominal and real, deflated by national price index
            IPEA, 2020

is one of the main drivers of the reduction of state-owned banks' credit supply
in 2018 (Figure 3.2).

4.3   Social Policies

Highly active social policies were one of the major features of policy orientation
during the period examined. These policies were crucial for achieving the aim of
the income redistribution, which was to foster domestic consumption. The two
main factors that contributed to improving income distribution were the huge
increase in the minimum wage (66.9 percent in real terms from December 2003 to
December 2014) and income transfers in the form of an increase in pension benefits and the Bolsa Família program. However, one can see that the real minimum
wage has been stagnated since 2015, due to high inflation and low or negative
growth (Figure 3.7), which has contributed to the worsen in the social inequality
in this period, combined with the high level of unemployment.

The most important instrument was certainly the increase in the minimum
wage. The rule for adjusting that wage adopted during this period was to add
the inflation of the previous year and the GDP growth rate of the year before
that. In this way, high economic growth resulted in high real wage increases,
since the wages of low-skilled workers (both public and private, formal and

informal) and public pension payments were linked to the minimum wage.[10] In this institutional setting, minimum wage policy turned into a powerful redistributive tool.

Another social policy instrument that gained high national and international visibility was the conditional cash transfer program *Bolsa Família*. It was designed to combat extreme poverty and achieved almost complete coverage of very poor families with children of school age at very low cost.

Fiscal policy was completely absent in the area of redistribution policies. While in the Organization for Economic Cooperation and Development countries taxes are responsible for the bulk of public redistribution, in Brazil the tax system even had a slightly regressive effect (Lustig, Pessino, and Scott 2014).

In the Temer government, the minimum wage adjustment rule adopted since 2008 was maintained, but given the low or even negative growth rates, the real minimum wage ceased to increase. While the family allowance programme *Bolsa Familia* was maintained, harsh labor reforms allowed for a significant flexibilization of labor contracts. These orthodox reforms, together with the long and profound crisis, resulted in a partial reversal of the progressive income redistribution effects of the PT governments. Only the reform of the pension system, which aimed to add to this restorative agenda of regressive redistribution, did not get a vote in Congress in the period analyzed here.

5   Varieties of Developmentalism under the PT Governments

Assessing the policies adopted during the four PT governments, we find significant changes over time. Although for some aspects exact and uniform periodization is rather difficult, we also find that these changes were largely associated to the external context. We have earlier identified three phases in that context, and we use them here in developing a typology of the policies that helps to uncover the fundamental flaws of the macroeconomic foundation of redistributive policies for most of the period analyzed (Table 3.2).

The last phase (2011 to mid-2016) is split into two subperiods in view of the changes in economic policies in Rousseff's second term. These were largely shaped by domestic factors, especially the crisis of political confidence crisis initiated in her first term with the street protests of June 2013 and fostered in her second term by a mix of economic crisis and corruption scandal. Operation

---

10   According to Saboia and Hallak-Neto (2015), the minimum wage adjustment policy improved income distribution in 2004–2013 through the labour market as well through pensions and other public transfers.

Car Wash contributed to the loss of political majority and of voters' backing, leaving the government with little support to fend off a power grab by political rivals who impeached President Rousseff not on charges of corruption but on charges of manipulating the federal budget (the so-called creative accounting that also took place in former governments).

The first phase, from 2003 to September 2008, was marked by an orthodox macroeconomic policy. Moreover, following the path of other emerging economies, from 2005 on the favorable international context had enabled Brazil to adopt the precautionary strategy of accumulating foreign exchange reserves, which had a key role in reducing its vulnerability, being consistent with both varieties of developmentalism. This policy stance was mixed with increasing elements of social developmentalism, in particular the formation of a market of mass consumption that was boosted by increasing the minimum wage in real terms, stimulating private credit, and increasing households' purchasing power in a setting of lower prices of imported goods due to currency appreciation. However, since industrial policy was mostly oriented toward strengthening exports, this policy field can be characterized as new developmentalist.

A second phase, from October 2008 to 2010, was the time when "we were all Keynesians." In the context of the contagion effect of the global financial crisis, the Lula government in its second term launched a more flexible fiscal policy, including an increase in public investment that started in 2007 with the Growth Acceleration Program, promoted a countercyclical role of state-owned banks, and boosted social policies. These measures, consistent with social developmentalism, were taken with some pragmatism and departed from what we have called orthodox policies before the crisis. Once the economy had recovered, the government adopted price-based capital controls and macroprudential regulations on the credit market to curb, respectively, currency appreciation and the credit boom. Although these two types of financial regulation (Ocampo 2012) were to some degree part of the conventional toolkit of macroeconomic recommendations after the 2008 global crisis (Blanchard, Dell'Ariccia, and Mauro 2010), they fit within both new and social developmentalism (e.g., Rossi 2014).

The third phase was characterized by strong oscillation in macroeconomic policy between orthodoxy and developmentalism, and classification becomes especially difficult. One could interpret the so-called new macroeconomic matrix as influenced by new-developmentalist prescriptions because of the initial currency devaluation and the decreasing policy rate backed by fiscal austerity, but other elements of this approach were absent, especially with regard to fiscal policy in 2013–2014. This policy was not only increasingly expansive but also supply-side-oriented instead of focusing on the public demand side.

TABLE 3.2   Typology of policies by phase

	Lula before GFC, 2003–08/08	Lula during GFC, 09/08–10	Dilma 1, 2011–14	Dilma 2, 2015–05/16	Temer, 08/16–18
Macroeconomic policies					
Monetary	ORT	ORT; ND/SD; ORT	ND/SD; ORT	ORT	ORT
Exchange-rate	ORT	ORT; ND	ND; ORT	ORT	ORT
Fiscal	ORT	SD; ORT	ORT/ND; (SD)	ORT	ORT
Social policies	SD	SD	SD	SD	ORT
Public investment	SD	SD	(SD)	SD	ORT
Financial policies	SD	SD	SD	ORT	ORT
Industrial policies	(ND)	SD	SD	SD	ORT

Notes: ORT = orthodox; SD = social developmentalist; ND = new developmentalist. Parentheses indicate that the policy does not follow entirely a particular strategy, being only influenced by it.

Indeed, public investment decreased in 2010–2014. Then, they were even criticized by social developmentalists (Bastos 2015). However, from 2013 on, a more orthodox approach in terms of monetary and exchange-rate policies aimed at inflation stabilization was resumed. At the same time, in the first Rousseff government, the pillars of social developmentalism of the first two phases – minimum wage increases, stimulus to private credit, and an active role of public banks and of industrial policies – were maintained. Thus, this period was characterized by a mix of social and new developmentalism, as Singer (2015) also suggests.[11]

As we have pointed out, the second Rousseff government (2015–2016) was marked by a radical shift, with the implementation of orthodoxy mainly in the field of fiscal and monetary policies. The Central Bank implemented a strategy for reducing volatility and providing a hedge against exchange-rate risk but did not intend to be involved with the determination of the exchange rate. In terms of social policies there were no significant changes. As we have seen, the rule for minimum-wage readjustment remained in place, although high inflation in 2015–2016 and low growth in the years before limited real wage increases.

If President Rousseff's precociously interrupted second term had already reflected the pressures of the "renewed single bourgeois front around the neoliberal platform" (Singer 2018), the government of Temer represented the full restoration of this platform, with the adoption of orthodox and liberal policies in all fields considered here (see Table 3.2). The commitment to the three pillars of the macroeconomic tripod was reinforced and in the other areas the common denominator was the reduction of the role of the state: cutting public investment and social spending, making labor relations more flexible, resuming privatization, reducing BNDES loans and dismantling industrial policy instruments. Consequently, Temer's policy mix turned highly coherent, yet with a high price, as social and labor policies turned strictly regressive.

6   Conclusion

Our assessment of the policies of the PT-led governments in Brazil shows that we cannot label this period either completely orthodox or neoliberal or entirely developmentalist. Indeed, we find our first hypothesis confirmed: already at

---

11   As we have seen, according to Singer (2015) Rousseff's embrace in her first term of the agenda of the main industrial entities led to a "developmentalist experiment". Mello and Rossi (2017) make the same argument but call the strategy "industrialism".

the conceptual level we can identify more than one recent variety of developmentalism, the two most relevant to the economic debate being the social and the new. They share the aim of combining sustained economic growth with productive restructuring and income distribution by giving the state an active role. However, they diverge with regard to the priority given to policies for achieving this aim. The new-developmentalist approach centers on the management of a competitive exchange rate to achieve an export surplus in manufactured goods and job creation in the industrial sector. The social developmentalist variety favors redistributional policies to foster domestic demand and diversified domestic investment. Thus, answering the question whether the PT governments were developmentalist requires consideration of which variety of developmentalism is involved.

Our second hypothesis is also confirmed. Some of the policies applied were more explicitly social developmentalist, among them the social policies and such economic policies as public investment and such financial policies as access to credit for lower-income households and the outstanding role given to public banks. The core of new developmentalist policies – an undervalued currency supported by fiscal austerity, low interest rates, and capital controls – was applied only for a rather limited period of time during the first Rousseff government. Yet the macroeconomic policies applied followed the current orthodox prescription during the first phase. There is no clear pattern of macroeconomic policies' shifting toward a more developmentalist stance. Rather, the reaction to the spillovers of the global financial crisis was shaped by countercyclical policies that were the global standard in this context, and the third phase was characterized by a mixture of all types of policies. This, for instance, applies to monetary policy from the second half of 2012 on and especially to the policies of Rousseff's second term, which in its struggle against a widening and mutually nurturing economic and political crisis was dominated by orthodox policies.

This makes our third hypothesis more significant than we had expected. We encountered a number of difficulties in finding clear criteria in terms of both periodization and classification, since the changes especially in macroeconomic policies were very frequent. Certainly, policies should not be expected to be a simple result of theoretical considerations, but they are highly dependent on institutional path-dependency and concrete circumstances in interplay with specific interests. It is clear, however, that the international context shaped policy options over the period. In the third phase, the swift macroeconomic policy shifts certainly had to do with necessary adjustments to a volatile international environment. Beyond this, however, they may also reflect accumulating domestic conflicts among dominant economic actors over redistributional aims and outcomes of public policies, which grew acute with the growth of the political corruption scandal involving the governing parties.

Appendix

TABLE 3.3   Brazil: main economic indicators

Economic Indicator/Year	2003	2004	2005	2006	2007	2008
ECONOMIC ACTIVITY						
Inflation rate (IPCA[1]), %	9.3	7.6	5.7	3.1	4.5	5.9
GDP growth (%)	1.1	5.8	3.2	4.0	6.1	5.1
Agricultural	8.3	2.0	1.1	4.6	3.3	5.8
Industry	0.1	8.2	2.0	2.0	6.2	4.1
Services	1.0	5.0	3.7	4.3	5.8	4.8
Unemployment rate[2] (%)	12.4	11.0	9.7	9.7	8.6	7.9
Investment rate (% GDP)	16.6	17.3	17.1	17.2	18.0	19.4
MONETARY AND CREDIT INDICATORS						
Interest rate (Selic), average p.a. (%)	16.5	17.75	18.0	13.25	11.25	13.75
Domestic credit (% GDP)	24.4	25.5	28.0	30.4	34.7	34.7
Household credit (% GDP)	n.a.	n.a.	n.a.	n.a.	15.9	17.2
Corporate credit (% GDP)	n.a.	n.a.	n.a.	n.a.	18.8	22.5
EXTERNAL SECTOR						
Real effective exchange rate[3]	137.4	135.0	110.3	98.5	91.4	88.9
Commodity price index (% growth p.a.)	21.9	11.4	-8.3	2.7	-3.2	8.1
Brazil's terms of trade (% growth p.a.)	-1.4	0.9	0.8	5.3	2.1	3.7
Trade balance (US$ billion)	23.749	32.538	43.425	45.119	38.483	23.802
Net debt of public sector (US$ billion)	160	125	47	-47	-177	-295
Manufacturing import coeficient (%)[4]	10.5	10.8	11.4	11.1	11.4	11.6
Current account (% GDP)	0.67	1.70	1.52	1.18	0.03	-1.81
Foreign direct investment (% GDP)	1.81	2.71	1.73	1.75	3.19	3.00
Foreign reserves (US$ billion)	49,296	52,935	53,799	85,839	1,80,334	1,93,783
External solvency indicators[5]						
Net external liability/Total exports	3.65	2.91	2.52	2.54	3.08	1.23
Net external liability/ Manufacturing exports	4.66	3.71	3.25	3.33	4.17	1.77

009	2010	2011	2012	2013	2014	2015	2016	2017	2018
3	5.9	6.5	5.8	5.9	6.4	10.7	6.3	2.9	3.7
).1	7.5	4.0	1.9	3.0	0.5	-3.6	-3.3	1.3	1.8
3.7	6.7	5.6	-3.1	8.4	2.8	3.3	-5.2	14.2	1.3
4.7	10.2	4.1	-0.7	2.2	-1.5	-5.8	-4.6	-0.5	0.7
1	5.8	3.5	2.9	2.8	1.0	-2.7	-2.2	0.8	2.1
9	6.2	5.5	6.9	6.2	6.5	8.9	12.0	11.8	11.0
.1	20.5	20.6	20.7	20.9	19.9	17.8	15.5	14.6	15.1
75	10.75	11.0	7.25	10.0	11.75	14.25	13.75	7.00	6.50
2.6	44.1	46.5	49.2	50.9	52.2	53.9	49.7	47.2	34.7
3.8	20.0	21.1	22.4	23.4	24.5	25.3	25.0	25.2	17.2
3.8	24.1	25.4	26.8	27.4	27.7	28.5	24.7	22.0	22.5
8.4	77.1	75.0	84.1	89.9	91.2	111.5	105.7	96.3	108.0
2.6	7.8	20.9	3.0	4.3	9.3	18.6	2.6	-3.5	17.6
2.6	16.0	7.8	-5.8	-2.0	-3.4	-11.0	3.0	5.8	-2.1
4.958	18.491	27.625	17,420	389	-6,629	17,655	44,635	63,960	53,047
216	-220	-386	-437	-471	-484	-817	-677	-177	-295
.3	11.8	11.8	11.8	11.8	11.3	11.0	10.6	10.6	
.57	-3.58	-2.92	-3.4	-3.23	-4.13	-3.03	-1.35	-0.73	-2.0
88	3.73	3.92	3.76	3.05	3.57	3.60	4.13	3.35	4.18
38,520	2,88,575	3,52,012	3,73,147	3,58,808	3,63,551	3,56,464	3,65,016	3,73,972	3,74,715
65	4.49	3.20	3.32	3.06	3.44	2.50	3.77	2.56	2.16
49	7.27	5.54	5.59	5.07	5.81	3.98	5.73	4.85	4.31

TABLE 3.3   Brazil: main economic indicators (*cont.*)

Economic Indicator/Year	2003	2004	2005	2006	2007	2008
External liquidity indicators						
Standard&Poors indicator[6]	2.71	1.52	0.50	0.32	0.34	0.46
Standard&Poors + Portfolio in the country[7]	5.43	4.42	2.92	2.76	2.48	1.37
PUBLIC FINANCE[8]						
Primary fiscal result (% GDP)	3.2	3.7	3.7	3.2	3.2	3.3
Public debt service (% GDP)	-8.4	-6.6	-7.3	-6.7	-6.0	-5.3
Nominal fiscal result (% GDP)	-5.2	-2.9	-3.5	-3.6	-2.7	-2.0
Gross public debt (% GDP)[9]	n.a.	n.a.	n.a.	55.5	56.7	56.0
Net public debt (% GDP)	54.3	50.2	47.9	46.5	44.5	37.6
SOCIAL INDICATORS						
Gini index (%)[10]	0.583	0.572	0.570	0.563	0.556	0.546
Poverty index (% of population)	35.75	33.71	30.83	26.75	25.36	22.6
Wage share[11]	36.71	35.84	36.82	38.28	39.01	40.00

Notes: (1) Acumulated rate in 12 months; (2) Data is relative to December; methology to calcule unemployment changed since 2012.

(3) Yearly average, June 1994 = 100; (4) Ratio "total value of imports of industial sector" over "total value of domestic output of industrial sector";

(5) "Net external liability" refers to the "Net international investment position"; (6) Ratio "Gross External Financing Needs (GEFN)" over "External Reserves", where GEFN =

Current account + short term external debt + long term external debt repayment in the next 12 months; (7) Ratio "GEFN + portfolio investment in the country" over "External Reserves";

(8) Data is relative to December; (9) Data according to new metodology implemented in 2006; (10) Since 2015, data extracted from Barbosa et al. (2020).

(11) Salary mass (deflated by INPC) divided by GDP (deflated by the implicit deflator).

SOURCE: BANCO CENTRAL DO BRASIL (2020), EXCEPT INVESTMENT RATE, GINI INDEX AND PORVERTY INDEX (IPEADATA), MANUFACTURING IMPORT COEFFICIENT AND MANUFAC-TURING SECTOR AS SHARE OF GDP (CEMACRO), TERMS OF TRADE (FUNCEX) AND WAGE SHARE (BRUNO AND CAFFE 2018)

2009	2010	2011	2012	2013	2014	2015	2016	2017	2018
0.33	0.53	0.44	0.40	0.41	0.62	0.47	0.36	0.49	0.48
2.14	2.41	1.75	1.67	1.64	1.76	1.20	1.37	1.43	1.35
2.9	2.6	2.9	2.2	1.7	-0.6	1.9	-2.5	-1.7	-1.6
5.1	-5.0	-5.4	-4.4	-4.7	-5.4	-8.4	-6.5	6.1	5.5
3.2	-2.4	-2.5	-2.3	-3.0	-6.0	-10.2	-9.0	-7.8	-7.1
49.2	51.8	51.3	53.8	51.5	56.3	65.5	69.8	73.7	76.5
40.8	37.9	34.5	32.2	30.5	32.6	35.6	46.1	51.4	53.6
0.543	n.a.	0.531	0.530	0.527	0.518	0.525	0.538	0.539	0.545
21.41	n.a.	18.42	15.93	15.09	13.29	n.a.	n.a.	n.a.	n.a.
41.69	41.95	42.85	45.26	45.05	46.78	46.32	n.a.	n.a.	n.a.

References

Almeida, J.S., and Novais, L.F. (2014). Indústria e política industrial no contexto pós-crise. In: Novais, L.F. et al. (eds.), *A economia brasileira no contexto da crise global*, 193–221. São Paulo: FUNDAP.

Ban, C. (2012). Brazil's liberal neo-developmentalism: new paradigm or edited orthodoxy? *Review of International Political Economy* 20(2): 298–331.

Banco Central do Brasil. (2020). *Time series management system*. https://www3.bcb.gov.br/sgspub/localizarseries/localizarSeries.do?method=prepararTelaLocalizarSeries.

Barbosa, N. (2010). Latin America: Counter-cyclical policy in Brazil: 2008–09. *Journal of Globalization and Development* 1(1): 1–12.

Bastos, P.P. (2015). *Austeridade para quem? A crise global do capitalismo neoliberal e as alternativas no Brasil*. Instituto de Economia da UNICAMP, Texto para Discussão 257.

Bastos, P.P. (2012). A economia política do novo-desenvolvimentismo e do social desenvolvimentismo. *Economia e Sociedade* 21: 779–810.

Biancarelli, A., Rosa, R., and Vergnhanini, R. (2017). *O setor externo no governo Dilma e seu papel na crise*. Instituto de Economia da UNICAMP, Texto de Discussão 289.

Bielschowsky, R. (2012). Estratégia de desenvolvimento e as três frentes de expansão no Brasil. *Economia e Sociedade* 21: 729–748.

Bielschowsky, R. (2015). Structuralist reflections on current Latin American development. In: Barbara, F., and Lavinas, L. (eds.), *A Moment of Equality for Latin America? Challenges and Limits for Redistributive Policies*, 129–144. Burlington, VT: Ashgate.

Blanchard, O., Dell'Ariccia, G., and Mauro, P. (2010). *Rethinking Macroeconomic Policy*. IMF Staff Position Note SPN/10/03.

Boito, A., and Berringer, T. (2014). Social classes, neodevelopmentalism, and Brazilian foreign policy under Presidents Lula and Dilma. *Latin American Perspectives* 41: 94–109.

Boyer, R. (2002). Variété du capitalisme et théorie de la regulation. In: *L'Année de la regulation, No. 6 (2002–2003): Économie, institutions, pouvoirs*, 125–194. Paris: Presses de Sciences Po (P.F.N.S.P.).

Bresser-Pereira, L.C. (2011). From old to new developmentalism in Latin America. In: Ocampo, J.A., and Ros, J. (eds.), *The Oxford Handbook of Latin American Economics*, 108–130. Oxford: Oxford University Press.

Bresser-Pereira, L.C. (2015). *Reflecting on New Developmentalism and Classical Developmentalism*. FGV Working Paper 395. São Paulo: Fundação Getúlio Vargas.

Bruno, M.A.P., and Caffe, A.R.D. (2018). Determinantes das taxas de lucro e de acumulação no Brasil: os fatores estruturais da deterioração conjuntural de 2014-2015. *Revista de Economia Política* 38(2): 237–260.

Cagnin, R.F., Prates, D.M., De Freitas, M.C.P., and Novais, L.F. (2013). A gestão macroeconômica do governo Dilma (2011 e 2012). *Novos Estudos CEBRAP* 97: 169–185.

Carneiro, R. (2012). Velhos e novos desenvolvimentismos. *Economia e Sociedade* 21: 749–778.

Carneiro, R. (2017). *Navegando a contravento (Uma reflexão sobre o experimento desen-volvimentista do Governo Dilma Rousseff)*. Instituto de Economia da UNICAMP, Texto de Discussão 289.

Carvalho, C.E. (2004). Governo Lula, o triunfo espetacular do neoliberalismo. *Margem Esquerda* 3: 131–146.

Carvalho, L. (2018). *Valsa Brasileira: do boom ao caos econômico*. São Paulo: Todavia.

Cunha, A.M., and Ferrari, A. (2009). A Argentina depois da conversibilidade: um caso de novo-desenvolvimentismo? *Revista de Economia Política* 29(1): 3–23.

Dweck, E., Oliveira, A.L., and Rossi, P. (2018). *Austeridade e Retrocesso: impactos sociais da política fiscal no Brasil*. São Paulo: Brasil Debate e Fundação Friedrich Ebert.

Fonseca, P.D. (2014). Desenvolvimentismo: a construção do conceito. In: Calixtre, A.B., André, M.B., and Cintra, M.A. (eds.), *Presente e futuro do desenvolvimento brasileiro*, 29–78. Brasilia: IPEA.

Fritz, B., and Lavinas, L. (eds.). (2015). *A Moment of Equality for Latin America? Challenges and Limits for Redistributive Policies*. Burlington, VT: Ashgate.

Fritz, B., Paula, L.F., and Prates, D. (2017). *Developmentalism at the Periphery: Can Productive Change and Income Redistribution Be Compatible with Global Financial Asymmetries?*" desiguALdades Working Paper 101.

Gobetti, S.W., and Orair, R. (2015). *Progressividade tributária: A agenda esquecida*. Tesouro Nacional, Concurso de Monografia em Finanças Públicas 3, Tópicos especiais. Brasília: Tesouro Nacional.

Hall, P.A., and Soskice, D. (eds.). (2001). *Varieties of Capitalism: Institutional Sources of Comparative Advantage*. Oxford: Oxford University Press.

IBGE (Instituto Brasileiro de Geografia e Estatística). (2017). *Contas nacionais*. https://www.ibge.gov.br/estatisticas/economicas/contas-nacionais.html.

IMF (International Monetary Fund). (2017). *IMF Database*. https://www.imf.org/en/Data.

IPEA (Instituto de Pesquisa Econômica Aplicada). (2020). *IPEADATA*. http://www.ipeadata.gov.br/Default.aspx.

Kupfer, D. (2013). Dez anos de política industrial. *Valor Economico*, 7 August.

Lustig, N., Pessino, C., and Scott, J. (2014). The impact of taxes and social spending on inequality and poverty in Argentina, Bolivia, Brazil, Mexico, Peru, and Uruguay. *Public Finance Review* 42: 287–303.

Mello, G.S., and Rossi, P. (2017). *Do industrialismo à austeridade: a política macro dos governos Dilma*. Instituto de Economia da UNICAMP Texto para Discussão 309.

Ministério do Planejamento, Orçamento e Gestão. (2003). *Plano plurianual 2004–2007: Orientação estratégica de governo Um Brasil pra todos: Crescimento sustentável, emprego e inclusão social*. Brasília.

Morgan, M. (2017). *Extreme and Persistent Inequality: New Evidence for Brazil Combining National Accounts, Surveys, and Fiscal Data, 2001–2015.* WID. World Bank Working Paper Series 2017/12.

Ocampo, J.A. (2001). Raúl Prebisch and the development agenda at the dawn of the twenty-first century. *CEPAL Review* 75: 25–40.

Ocampo, J.A. (2012). The case for and experience with capital account regulations. In: Gallagher, K.P., Griffith-Jones, S., and Ocampo, J.A. (eds.), *Regulating Global Capital Flows for Long-Run Development*, 13–22. Boston, MA: Pardee Center Task Force Report.

Paula, L.F., Modenesi, A.M., and Pires, M.C. (2015). The tale of the contagion of two crises and policy responses in Brazil: a case of (Keynesian) policy coordination? *Journal of Post-Keynesian Economics* 37: 408–435.

Paula, L.F., and Oreiro, J.L. (2019). Macroeconomia da estagnação. Insight Inteligência n. 87: 90–99.

Paula, L.F., and Pires, M.C. (2017). Crise e perspectivas para a economia brasileira. *Estudos Avançados* 31(98): 125–144.

Prates, D.M., and Fritz, B. (2016). Beyond capital controls: regulation of foreign currency derivatives markets in the Republic of Korea and Brazil after the global financial crisis. *CEPAL Review* 118: 193–213.

Prebisch, R. (1950). "The economic development of Latin America and its principal problems. MS, United Nations Department of Economic Affairs.

Rossi, P. (2014). Regime macroeconômico e o projeto social-desenvolvimentista. In: Calixtre, A.B., Biancarelli, A.M., and Cintra, M.A. (eds.), *Presente e futuro do desenvolvimento brasileiro*, 195–226. Brasilia: IPEA.

Saboia, J., and Hallak-Neto, J. (2016). *Salário mínimo e distribuição de renda no Brasil a partir dos anos 2000.* IE/UFRJ Discussion Paper 002/2016.

Singer, A. (2018). *O Lulismo em crise (2018) – Um quebra-cabeça do período Dilma (2011-2016).* São Paulo: Companhia das Letras.

Singer, A. (2015). Cutucando onças com varas curtas: o ensaio desenvolvimentista no primeiro mandato de Dilma Rousseff (2011–2014). *Novos Estudos CEBRAP* 102: 39–67.

Torres, E., Macahyba, L., and Martins, N. (2020). BNDES: as debilidades da TLP. *Observatório da Economia Contemporânea / Le Monde Diplomatique*, July.

CHAPTER 4

Puzzles of Economic Growth and Crisis under the Workers' Party Governments

Pedro Cezar Dutra Fonseca, Marcelo Arend and Glaison Augusto Guerrero

1   Introduction[1,2]

The governments of Lula da Silva (2003–2010) and Dilma Rousseff (2011–2016), from their inception, generated controversy with regard to the focus of their economic policies. Lula's 2002 "Letter to Brazilians", launched during the presidential campaign in June 2002, was understood as a way of "calming the markets", but at the same time its ideas drew away from the historical principles of the Partido dos Trabalhadores (Workers' Party – PT). The economic policy of Antônio Palocci of the Ministry of Finance and Henrique Meirelles of the Central Bank confirmed the promises of the letter. The orthodox economic policy of the government of Fernando Henrique Cardoso, based on inflation targeting and characterized by high real interest rates, a positive primary result in public accounts, and an appreciated exchange rate, was maintained as a basic guideline for macroeconomic policy. This allowed several observers to stress the continuity of economic policy with a strong neoliberal focus between the two governments (Paulani 2003; 2005; 2007; Paula 2005; Assis 2005; Carvalho 2007). Others, pointing to the high growth rates of the Lula period and the decline of the Gini index, began to interpret the period, especially its second term, as a resumption of developmentalism (for example, Belluzzo 2009; Novy 2009a; 2009b; Nakano 2010; Cervo 2009; Herrlein 2011; Cardoso Jr. 2011; Anderson 2011; Bastos 2012; Costa 2015). Later works sought to overcome the polarization of orthodoxy and developmentalism. Erber (2011) pointed out that in Lula's government there were two "pacts" or worldviews, a more orthodox "strict institutionalist" view and one called "neodevelopmentalism", both with "distinct analytical hard cores ... [and] therefore ontologically

1   An earlier version of the arguments in this chapter appeared in Fonseca et al. (2019).
2   Patricia Fierro is an American Translators Association–certified translator living in Quito, Ecuador. The authors thank Leda Paulani for her suggestions and PIBIC/UFRGS/CNPq fellow César Prazeres Fraga Pereira for his collaboration.

conflicting". Morais and Saad-Filho (2011) similarly argued that Lula's policy was "hybrid" and even included policies that were close to the "new developmentalism" formulated by Bresser-Pereira (2011). Fonseca, Cunha, and Bichara (2013) argued that, although there were aspects of both rupture and continuity with Cardoso's policy, there was insufficient reason to interpret this as a return to developmentalism.

Regarding Dilma Rousseff's government, the controversy was no less intense. In August 2011 it abandoned policies that had been in place since the Cardoso administration, forcing the Central Bank to lower the interest rate and devalue the exchange rate. Our hypothesis is that this reorientation represented more than a mere change in economic policy. It was a point of inflection of these governments, since it meant the abandonment of the class-coalition pact signed by Lula with segments of the business elite. At the start of her second term, Rousseff sought to rebuild alliances established by Lula in 2002, but the conditions for doing so no longer existed. Regardless of economic policy choices, the lack of material, economic, and political foundations made the continuity of the alliance infeasible. The economic and political scenario from 2015 on made it impossible to reconcile orthodox economic policies with state redistributive interventionism.

The following questions arise: Can Rousseff's reorientation of economic policy, sometimes called the "new macroeconomic matrix", be considered as the abandonment of orthodoxy in favor of a developmentalist option? What were the reasons for it? Which bourgeois sectors supported the PT governments, and why did they move away?

2   Interventionism and Developmentalism

To examine whether the two governments' policies may be associated with developmentalism, we need to clarify what this means. "Developmentalism" is used in many senses, and this ambiguity fosters a certain conceptual confusion. Perhaps the biggest problem is the confusion of developmentalism with interventionism. The tendency has been established, especially among mainstream writers and the Brazilian media, to treat any state intervention as developmentalism and, by extension, pejoratively, as "economic populism". However, developmentalism is a particular form of interventionism, not to be confused with mere crisis-reactive policies aimed at stopping Keynesianism cycles. Additionally, it has historically represented a set of measures for overcoming underdevelopment and therefore a strategy or guide to action for overcoming a historical-structural condition. Thus, developmentalism, even with interventionist features (such as social democracy and a labor movement), must not be confused with either Keynesian countercyclical policies or socialism, since it is not aimed at overcoming capitalism and is an economic project based on industrialization within the institutional framework of this economic system or mode of production.

We adopt a portion of Fonseca's (2014: 60) definition: "Developmentalism is an economic policy formulated, deliberately or not, and/or implemented by governments (national or subnational) to transform society to achieve the desired ends, through the growth of production and productivity, under the leadership of the industrial sector, especially to overcome its economic and social problems, within the institutional frameworks of the capitalist system." This definition was developed through a method inspired by Sartori (1970; 1984) that is considered an alternative to the development of ideal models in that it requires that the attributes of a concept be extracted from the specialized literature itself – the use of theoretical terms by a community of scientists. Fonseca's examination of the application of the concept "developmentalism" to 34 governments in eight Latin American countries revealed that the core attributes – those common to all uses of it – were (a) the defense of a national project or a strategy aimed at overcoming underdevelopment, (b) deliberate state intervention, and (c) industrialization, which provides opportunities for a greater convergence of income, productivity, and technological stage with the richer and more developed countries. For an economic policy to be considered "developmentalist" it must have these three attributes. Concepts of course change over time, but this involves the inclusion or exclusion of attributes without affecting the core.

As used here, then, the term "developmentalism" applies to deliberate, consciously executed policies with a well-defined purpose, as anticipated by Latin American structuralist thinkers such as Raúl Prebisch and Celso Furtado. The redistributive attributes sometimes associated with developmentalism, such as income redistribution, reduction of inequalities, agrarian reform, and even democracy, vary with the country's historical experience, and research has shown that they seldom appear in Latin American developmentalist experiments. Several governments regarded as developmentalist not only have not redistributed income but have defended its concentration, and many of them have been dictatorships.

3   Deindustrialization and Income Distribution

Returning to Lula's government, the absence of a project that could be called "developmentalist" is now clear. The PT never programmatically defended protecting industrialization as a way to overcome underdevelopment. This proposal was, as a rule, regarded as outdated, associated either with the import-substitution-industrialization stage or populism or even the military regime and income concentration of the "miracle" of 1968–1973. Consequently, developmentalism produced an industrialized but excluding country that did not even establish an "autonomous national capitalism", since the rule was to associate with or submit to foreign capital. The PT from its foundation had its socialist currents and was averse to defending "reformist" or "social-democratic" economic proposals, and this made it difficult to formulate an economic project, developmentalist or otherwise. The meeting point of all these currents was the confrontation of social inequalities, from which proposals such as the expansion of democracy, popular participation, and agrarian reform were developed. Thus there was a project for the country that assumed that there were would be intervening economic policies to execute it, which included attributes (a) and (b) of the above-mentioned core, but this project did not address growth or development. Our hypothesis is that the absence of a project to reverse the deindustrialization of the country is the main obstacle to characterizing PT governments as "developmentalist". Although government documents expressed an awareness of both social inequalities and the decline in the position of industry, the measures actually taken were basically related to inequalities.[3]

Although three versions of a long-term industrial policy can be identified, the short-term priorities of macroeconomic policy and fluctuations in the international economy have always been shaped mainly by countercyclical policies, redistributive project aids, and past investment patterns in commodities and industrial sectors of low and medium technological intensity. In Lula's governments, two industrial policies were launched: the 2004 Industrial, Technological, and Foreign Trade Policy and the 2008 Productive Development Policy. Under Rousseff's government there was the 2011 Greater Brazil Plan. Deindustrialization had already begun in the 1980s and continued and intensified under the PT governments (Figure 4.1).

---

3 Nunes's (2018) thesis on this issue uses the same concept (Fonseca 2014) to analyze Lula's government and distinguishes between intended measures, those implemented, and actual results. It reveals that although there are documents that express awareness of industrial problems, no steps were taken to solve them.

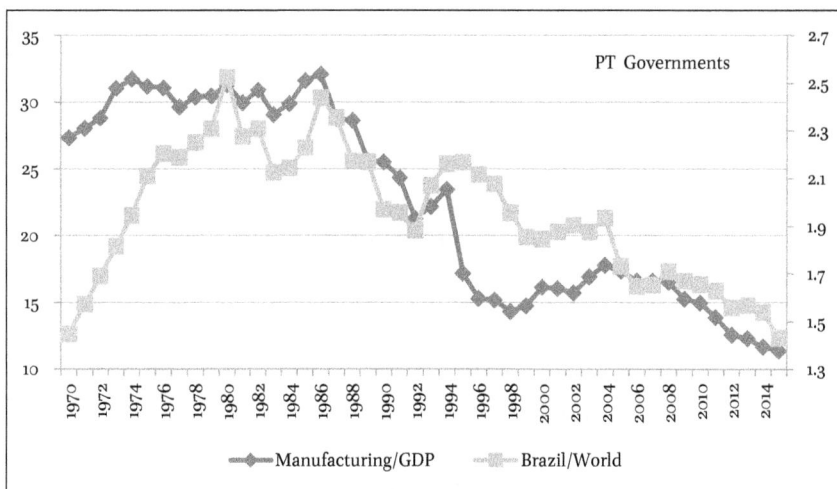

FIGURE 4.1   Percentage of manufacturing in Brazil's GDP (left axis) and proportion of world
industry (right axis) from 1970 to 2015
UNCTAD DATA

Lula started 2003 with industry representing 16.9 percent of the gross
domestic product (GDP), and Rousseff ended 2015 with industry representing
11.4 percent and a decline of 5.5 percentage points in GDP. Regarding the participation of Brazilian industry in global industry, the decline registered during
PT governments was greater than the one between 1990 and 2002, a period
usually connected with the hegemony of neoliberal ideas. In 1990 Brazilian
industry was 1.97 percent of world industry, and in 2002 it was 1.90 percent, but
in 2015 it was 1.43 percent. Under Rousseff's government, deindustrialization
was more pronounced than under the two Lula governments. The proportion
of the GDP represented by industry declined approximately 4 percent between
2011 and 2015, and its proportion of world industry was reduced to 0.2 percent.
Accordingly, it can be argued that the deindustrialization that started in the
mid-1980s and intensified in the 1990s maintained its continuity under the PT
governments and that the relative stagnation of Brazilian industry in international terms was even more striking than in the 1990s. The relative stagnation
of Brazilian manufacturing in international terms is apparent from its value
added between 2003 and 2015 in constant US dollars, which was 126 compared
with 167 for the world, 298 for Asia, and 742 for the BRICS (UNCTAD).

With regard to the redistribution of income, the governments of Lula and
Rousseff certainly had a project in this sense.

When Lula took office, he sought to honor the promise to reverse inequalities (not only of income but of gender and race) but lacked an actual economic project. The rejection of neoliberalism was agreed on by all, but there was no agreement on what would replace it. After several defeats, and seeking to expand its range of alliances, the business sector began by inviting José Alencar, an entrepreneur in the textile industry, to become a vice presidential candidate. This could be interpreted as an alliance with sectors of the local bourgeoisie in a pro-production, industrialist, developmentalist, and anti-neoliberalism agenda, but the "Letter to Brazilians" indicates the opposite: the commitment to maintain the economic policy guidelines of the Cardoso government reveals a recognition of the hegemony of financial capital and a willingness to include it in the power bloc. This meant nothing less than the abandonment of historical principles of the party such as aversion to the "Dutch disease" and rejection of internal and external debt. During his campaign Lula had said that he would audit such debts. That the letter was not just a list of intentions or the vain promises of a candidate is apparent from the fact that the economic team, including many orthodox economists, executed it faithfully, including maintaining the autonomy of the Central Bank (by political decision, since the Constitution did not guarantee it). The use in both the first and he second government of two indispensable instruments for the execution of development policies and for dealing with deindustrialization – exchange rates and interest rates – makes it impossible to interpret the relatively high growth rates of the latter as a result of a developmentalist project. A more reasonable hypothesis is a cyclical expansion after several years of low growth rates enabled by the favorable international situation (Chinese demand), the expansion of family loans (indebtedness), and the significant real growth of the minimum wage, which brought about an expansion of domestic demand for goods and services. The minimum wage as an index of pensions and social security played an important role in maintaining the historical commitment to income redistribution and opened the way for what Singer (2012) has called "Lulism".

In the evolution of the minimum wage and the unemployment rate we see again an inflection point from the beginning of Lula's administration in 2003 for four variables (Figure 4.2).

The minimum wage in the Cardoso government had increased from R$70 to R$200 between 1995 and 2002, and under the PT governments its growth was greater than that under previous governments, reaching R$788 in 2015. The US$100 mark for the minimum wage has always been emblematic and was achieved in Cardoso governments at the very beginning. In 2005, under Rousseff's government, it reached its highest historical value, US$333.The

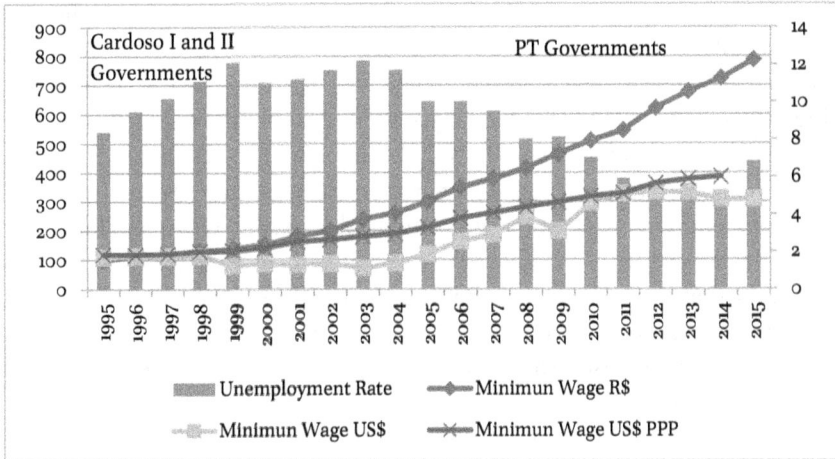

FIGURE 4.2   Evolution of the minimum wage in R$ and US$ (left axis) and of the
unemployment rate (right axis)
IPEADATA

purchasing power parity of the minimum wage approached US$400 in 2014,
evidencing the improvement in the consumption pattern achieved by the
working class under the PT governments. Along with this there was a sustained
drop in the unemployment rate until the end of 2014, when it reached its historically lowest level of 4.8 percent.

4   Rousseff's Government and the "New Macroeconomic Matrix"

With regard to the "new macroeconomic matrix" of Rousseff's government, the
initial question is whether it makes sense to interpret the change as overcoming neoliberalism and orthodoxy in favor of developmentalism. First, because
it represented the abandonment of the economic policy that had been implemented since the Cardoso administration, it meant limiting the Central Bank's
autonomy, and this was a major change. Second, much of the literature, both
favorable to and critical of the measures, defends its developmentalist character. The "new matrix" did not repeal the inflation targeting system, but it
did make it flexible. It forced the Central Bank, even when anticipating rising
inflation, to lower the interest rate and, consequently, raise the exchange rate.
The SELIC interest rate rose from 12.50 percent in August 2011 to 7.25 percent
at the beginning of 2012, reaching its lowest historical real value since the
1980s. No less relevant, the exchange rate, which was R$1.56 to the US dollar in

August 2011, underwent devaluation, reaching R\$2.63 to the dollar at the end of Rousseff's first term, in 2014 (Central Bank of Brazil 2018). It is reasonable to suppose that these measures combined were perceived by financial capital and the large domestic internationalized groups as not fulfilling commitments, especially those related to liabilities in dollars in their portfolios. At the same time, the Banco Nacional de Desenvolvimento Econômico e Social (Brazilian Development Bank – BNDES) was encouraged to expand credit and financing to particular sectors of the economy through vertical policies. Thus, there is no doubt that the measures of the "new matrix" altered the fixed directives approved by Lula and represented an increase in interventionism and a move away from neoliberalism. These measures cannot even be considered a variant of neoliberalism.

However, although some attributes associated with developmentalism and a reorientation of economic policy toward stimulating growth can be observed, once again we do not see a solid basis for describing this as "developmentalism". Contrary to the long-term strategy that marks developmental interventionism, the measures were adopted as a reaction to a crisis expressed by a slowdown in growth and as a way of confronting an international situation that had begun to reverse the commodities boom of Lula's golden years. Commodity prices increased until mid-2011 and then decreased, worsening the deficit of current-account transactions (Figure 4.3).

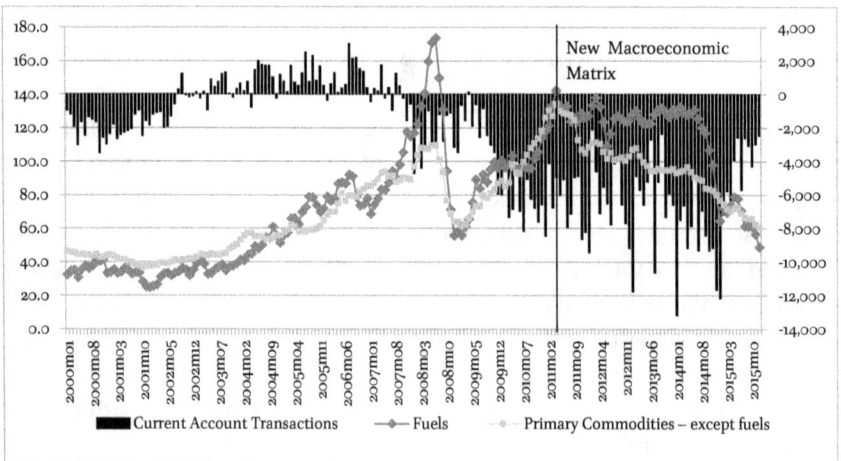

FIGURE 4.3   Index of international prices of fuels and primary commodities (2010 = 100), (left axis) and current-account balance in US\$ millions (right axis)
NETHERLANDS BUREAU OF POLICY ANALYSIS AND IPEADATA

It was this situation, from 2011 on, that forced the government to exert pressure on the Central Bank to lower interest rates and devalue the currency. There is no doubt that measures such as these could have reactivated the industrial sectors both by causing a relative price change that was favorable to domestic production and by fostering export-orientation, as in Bresser-Pereira's (2016) new developmentalism, but the exchange-rate devaluation also had a negative impact on industrial and financial companies whose costs depended on external suppliers and those that had loans in dollars (a condition that was widespread because of the appreciation of the real). Thus the effect of the new economic policy on some sectors of business was the trigger for eliminating others, chipping away at the alliance established by Lula in 2002. Most important, however, is that these changes in economic policy occurred as a reaction to the perceived cyclical deceleration rather than as a development strategy. Neither their motivation nor their results can be associated with developmentalism. They did not reverse deindustrialization or activate aggregate demand in accordance with the Keynesian model, the government stimulus being focused much more on the supply side than on the demand aspect (Fonseca 2016; Paulani 2017). The government concentrated not primarily on public expenditures (as Brazilian governments of the "developmentalism era" had historically done) but on lowering costs and stimulating private groups as a way of fostering growth. In a sort of "supply-side economics", energy tariffs decreased and particular sectors had abundant credit, reduced taxes, exemptions, and subsidies (later pejoratively termed "grants for businesses"). It seems to us premature to describe as developmentalist, as does Singer (2015: 44), programs such as Greater Brazil Plan, which opened lines of financing at the BNDES and reduced taxes on industrialized products of microentrepreneurs, and the Inovar-Auto program for the protection of the automobile industry. Both, on the contrary, seem more like responses to the pressure exerted by the sectors themselves (both entrepreneurs and workers, who felt threatened with losing their jobs).

The minimum requirement for being designated "developmentalism" would be that such interventionism start with a diagnosis of the low growth of the Brazilian economy in recent decades and its regressive specialization and deindustrialization and the formulation of a plan with goals and identification of the instruments to be applied.[4] For example, such a plan should at least point out ways to favor new branches of greater technological density, on the

---

4   Schapiro (2013) states that the policies adopted by the Greater Brazil Plan had a more corrective bias, with a profile more similar to neoclassical industrial policy theories. The strategies adopted by Dilma's government ended up maintaining the current Brazilian position in the

Schumpeterian model, so as to fill the gaps of Brazilian industry in emblematic manufacturing sectors of the technological revolution based on microelectronics or even link the choice of "national champions" to emerging sectors of the new advanced manufacture or "Industry 4.0". Programs like Inovar-Auto, on the contrary, ironically invoke a "national developmentalism inside-out", fostering polluting multinational industry and the technology of the past.

The policies of the new matrix that did correspond to a developmentalist strategy were not negligible, but they were sectoral, applying to the shipbuilding industry, the Pre-Salt, ports, and electric power, for which the government sought to establish regulatory frameworks with a long-term impact, both technological and institutional, that would protect areas for national capital and allow state control and supervision as part of a strategic vision. In tribute to the above-mentioned interpretation of Erber (2011), it was in these sectors that the "neodevelopmental convention" was able to assert itself and achieve a certain balance of forces with regard to a "limited institutionalism".

5   Financial Hegemony and Class Coalition: The Pact and Its Crisis

It is now appropriate to reply to the two questions asked earlier: what led the government to change its economic policy in 2011 and which sectors of capital back edit and then moved away. Initially, it is necessary to mention the difficulty of identifying the classes, groups of classes, and social sectors that constitute the bloc in power and determining which of them holds hegemony.[5] First, that state policy favors certain sectors of the bloc and plays a mediating role does not mean that it excludes others. There is no clear dividing line. Listing the measures implemented by the government in favor of a particular sector does not mean that that sector is hegemonic and participates in the bloc in power, since the game of politics is more complex in its formulations and results. (The saying that hegemony means strength and willingness to

---

international division of labor, since they mainly encouraged Brazil's traditional industrial activities.

5   The term "hegemony", although inspired by Gramsci, will be used in a more restricted sense in this chapter. Hegemony for Gramsci (1975) involved variables that are outside the scope of this chapter, such as intellectual structure, culture, and the pursuit of legitimation through mechanisms of ideological dissemination. In this chapter the categories "bloc in power" and "hegemony" are used as Poulantzas (1976) used them. The concept of bloc in power assumes the recognition of "internal differentiation of the ruling classes", and hegemony implies the possibility that some class group might impose its interests on others or have more relative power within that bloc to assert its interests.

compromise is applicable here.) Secondly, the reason for this is that bourgeois groups in current capitalism are quite heterogeneous, with varied portfolios in various branches. This diversification also applies to the working class (which cannot be confused with nineteenth-century workers because now there are new service segments, a public sector, informal markets, etc.). Thus, while in analyses at a higher level of abstraction one can still use categories such as "industrial capital", "banking", "agrarian", or "exporter", in concrete historical studies it is much more difficult to mark the dividing line between them when we are speaking not of capital but of the capitalists who personify it. Since manufacturing companies, and not just big ones, have financial investments that depend on real interest rates, measures such as lowering the interest rate are no longer a consensual measure for significant segments of industry. Similarly, financial conglomerates have agribusiness ventures, and therefore exchange rates and monetary policies may have diverse impacts according to the segment involved. In other words, a company or even an individual capitalist may belong to more than one group, and this hinders the clear demarcation between class groups in studies such as those that examine the association between their class interests and the policy options for a specific situation. The same is true for companies that produce for both domestic and foreign markets and whose costs are both in dollars and in reals, which in theory might make them, in principle, not favor either appreciated or depreciated exchange, since the weight of different cost items varies depending on each situation.

There are, however, two interpretations that have more fully dealt with these issues. Both recognize the complexity of clearly demarcating the interests of class groups in present-day Brazilian society. On the one hand, Singer (2015) detects in Lula's government a polarity between two currents that he calls "rentiers" and "productivists" – the former including financial capital and the traditional middle class and the latter consisting of industrial entrepreneurs associated with groups of the organized working class. Lula was the arbiter of the correlation of forces, "sometimes favoring one and other times favoring the competition". Rousseff's 2011 change is understood as a "developmental test" with a "firm brand: 'state activism' in the pursuit of reindustrialization". On the other hand, Boito Jr. (2005a; 2005b; 2012) and Boito Jr. and Saad-Filho (Boito Jr. and Saad-Filho 2016), citing Poulantzas (1976), believe that the basic polarity is between an internal bourgeoisie (including industry, banks, agribusiness, and civil construction) and a class that is more associated with foreign capital and mainly the international financial sector. With Singer, they accept that the dividing line between classes is subtle and that the two blocs are made up of diverse sectors, and they emphasize that a significant part of the bourgeoisie has always avoided getting close to the PT governments. However, they consider all the internal contradictions of this heterogeneous bloc secondary to "the contradiction represented by the dispute with big international capital" (Boito Jr. 2012: 77). The rationale for this thesis is well-established, showing the support of sectors of the bourgeoisie for Lula's government through articles and statements by leaders of the Federation of Industries of the State of São Paulo and laws, financing, and exemptions for companies of the bloc in power, mainly the "national champions" of the BNDES. More careful than Singer, Boito Jr. (2012: 69) treats economic policy as "neodevelopmentalism", creating a radial concept to justify its "hybridism".[6]

It is impossible to evaluate these arguments in detail here, but both see the debate as unfinished and recognize the need for more research to move forward on this topic. Lula's 2002 "Letter to Brazilians" fulfilled two functions in particular: it addressed the bourgeoisie as a class and promised the abandonment of the most radical PT principles with regard to debt moratoriums and audits of internal and external debt and property rights, and it emphasized the banking sector and all sectors with financial investments, not only large companies but smaller ones, the middle class, and even the unions through their pension funds (Oliveira 2003). The inclusion of the financial bourgeoisie and rentier sectors in the bloc in power and their hegemony was established. This commitment was confirmed through the maintenance of the inflation targeting system of the Cardoso government, which demanded high interest rates, appreciated exchange rates, and a primary surplus. The latter excluded interest from its calculation, and it was one of the pillars of the hegemony of the financial sector because it safeguarded such fractions of capital from any measures that might reduce public expenditures. Thus, although financial hegemony is not unique to Brazil, it is notable not only that interest rates in the country are consistently higher than those prevailing internationally but also that the treatment of the primary surplus as a fundamental clause in economic policy makes it unquestionable. This is a way to retain financial gains if any public-sector adjustment is implemented.

These policies for maintaining these sectors as the most important ones in the bloc in power eventually led to the main reward that was the promise of autonomy for the Central Bank (its president was Henrique Meirelles, who

---

6   Radial concepts are used to extend a concept to cover new facts. Generally, this is done with prefixes or adjectives, as with "neodevelopmentalism", "newdevelopmentalism", "socialdevelopmentalism", etc. One should be careful not to allow the traveling of a concept to cause a stretching of it that might lead to distortion (Weyland 2001), in this case making it too broad (for example, considering any interventionist measure or measure in favor of the industrial sector "developmentalist").

was linked to the Brazilian Social Democracy Party). In the Brazilian institutional framework, the Central Bank, through its monetary policy committee, is responsible for establishing monetary and exchange-rate policies. When it agreed to maintain its rule, Lula's government gave up a significant portion of its control over economic policy. What remained under its influence was only the fiscal policy of the Ministry of Finance (and an escape valve that would then be used to reward other bourgeois groups and workers in the conflict of the private banking sector with public banks).

One can speak of hegemony here because this class group was given, through two key instruments (exchange and interest rates), the option to determine its degree of autonomy from the government. Thus it was able to determine the profit rate not only of the financial sector but of all the capitalist classes. In a context of rising inflation such as that under Rousseff's government, the problem was the greater because to achieve a primary surplus it is necessary to reduce the expenditures of all the other sectors but the payment of public-sector interest rates is guaranteed. Furthermore, since the struggle against inflation usually produces higher interest rates, financial gains increase even more when the expenditures of other sectors are reduced. Paradoxically, the Central Bank had the freedom to carry out exactly the opposite policy: raising interest rates, which increased public spending, raised the nominal deficit, and neutralized the recessive fiscal policy.

Thus, Singer's interpretation that the conflict between rentier and productivist sectors was balanced by Lula's arbitration seems inappropriate. It is not that the correlation of forces did not change over that period, but it cannot be suggested that the two were of equivalent or even similar weight in the power bloc (and therefore that there was no hegemonic fraction). Our analysis reinforces the hypothesis that the balance was always tilted toward one side, an interpretation that coincides with those that support the idea that the productive sector was subordinate to financial capital in the bloc in power (e.g., Paulani 2003; 2017; Teixeira and Pinto 2012; Gonçalves 2012; and Filgueiras 2015). Even the reversal of deindustrialization, which in theory could have placed greater weight on the productivist side, was neither the focus of economic policy nor its result. In this regard, Boito Jr. (2012: 69) is right in arguing that the government coalition accepted a regressive specialization, thus revealing that there was no project for reversing Brazil's subordinate position in international capitalism.

Our interpretation, therefore, is that Lula's government, by colluding with the hegemonic financial sector, never abandoned this agreement (to the point of suggesting to Rousseff, in a *realpolitik* understanding just before her impeachment, that to avoid it the best formula for "calming the markets" would be to invite Meirelles to lead the economic area). To other social sectors, capital or labor, Lula responded with policies that can be called compensatory. Thus, the central thesis of our interpretation of Lula's economic policy is that the hegemony of national and international financial capital became the center of monetary and foreign-exchange policy and compensatory policies were applied to the other groups of capital and to the workers. This social pact was based on a formula that foresaw macroeconomic austerity along with the redistribution of income, but the government adopted policies for increasing the minimum wage, expanding programs such as Zero Hunger, Family Grant, My House, My Life, Electricity for Everyone, Consigned Credit, Science without Borders, and More Doctors, and increasing the number of available spots in public universities and adopting of a system of racial and socioeconomic quotas. The historical commitment to income redistribution and social inclusion was maintained by both PT governments, and this reduces the temptation to consider them neoliberal simply because they maintained the guidelines of a neoliberal macroeconomic policy and/or lacked the political power or will to confront the financial sector's hegemony. Consequently, social programs were broadened, and the Gini index and the poverty rate consistently improved.

Similarly, there is robust empirical support for the interpretation of Boito Jr. and Saad-Filho regarding measures that favored the "internal" sectors of capital. These sectors benefited most from BNDES policies through credit, subsidies, and exemptions. The same was true of national banks, which, as under the Cardoso administration, even in the crisis did not perceive any threat to their profits or the possibility of their being bought by foreign groups. At the same time, the expansion of the national agribusiness and contractors' sectors was guaranteed even when foreign policy favored the South-South axis, Mercosur, and the BRICS.

How are we to interpret the "new macroeconomic matrix" and the changes of the second half of 2011? In fact, they can only be understood as a reaction to a crisis rather than as a plan for resuming industrialization, and this makes it impossible to consider it a developmentalist shift. Why did the focus change? Our fundamental hypothesis is that the international crisis, combined with internal compensation policies, made it impossible to maintain the pact Lula had established. The adopted "formula" of class conciliation – austerity with increasing compensatory policies – assumed that the GDP and national income would also increase. It was possible to maintain this formula while there was (a) a balance-of-payments gap, hitherto ensured by favorable terms of trade of commodities and increasing external capital inflows either through direct foreign investment or financial speculation; (b) the opportunity to raise the minimum wage and salaries in the private sector, given the gap between such wages and productivity because of the wage tightening that had been in force since the end of the 1970s; and (c) a primary surplus, which allowed public expenditures and exemptions and capital subsidies to grow without increasing the tax burden. With the decline in production and unemployment, a primary deficit could no longer be avoided because of the greater inelasticity of expenditures in relation to revenues and the fact that some of these had a constitutional link, which aggravated the dispute over public resources for sectors that had hitherto coexisted with reasonable courtesy.

Rousseff's decision to implement changes, therefore, was not a simple choice but based on events that demanded them. The material basis of the agreement no longer existed, and her only option to avoid recession and thereby prevent the worsening of political conflict was a countercyclical policy. The question was with what instruments. This was only possible through the disruption of the coalition established by Lula – confrontation of the autonomy of the Central Bank and the easing of the system of inflation targets, which were not just symbolic but essential to the hegemony of the bloc in power. In making this decision Rousseff's government not only fully achieved the institutional framework that guaranteed hegemony for the financial sector but also gradually drove other bourgeois groups away from the government. Since it was impossible to increase the public deficit and the tax burden, the government opted for providing incentives for private investment to respond to the reactivation of the economy. In this connection, Carneiro (2017) posed the question (which deserves to be studied more closely) whether the Brazilian state really had the tools (public companies, banks, and planning capacity) to guide the rate of economic growth.[7]

As suggestions deserving further investigation, we list the following factors that would have contributed to driving the business sectors away:

---

[7]   In an interview with *Folha de São Paulo* on March 9, 2017, Dilma Rousseff, asked about the failure of her industrial policy, said, "What was not well matched was the reduction of taxes for the industry. We wanted to provide tax incentives so that employment would not decrease. What was proved that way? That for this sector, in Brazil, the first option is to increase the profit margin. The second may be to increase investments, but I did not see that this option was actually implemented." Here she admitted that the objective was the maintenance of the level of employment and that its "supply-side" policy was a mistake, but she attributed their failure to the behavior of the entrepreneurs who sought to increase profit margins when in fact the profit rate was dropping, and the reduction of taxes only counterbalanced the maintenance of the margin. On the problem of the decline in profit rates, see Marquetti, Hoff, and Miebach (2016) and Prado (2017).

- The public deficit exacerbated conflict among the sectors benefiting from compensatory policies; the business sectors had to divide the cuts between themselves and the workers.

- The government showed that it would not abandon the workers. In other words, the decrease of profits was not relieved by a reduction in wages (the solution classically applied by orthodox governments, which preferred a recession to a crisis). Government pressure took the form of significant investment in productivity, which made business itself responsible.

- The only alternative for continuing with expenditures without increasing the public deficit was tax increases. Entrepreneurs began to call for cuts in spending such as pension reform and the downsizing of the public sector and social programs. The risk was that the government would opt for progressive taxes on profits and property, further crippling the class coalition established by Lula in 2002.

- Vertical government policies that promoted "national champions", tax exemptions, and subsidies appealed to the sectors benefited but displeased others. The leaders of industrial and commercial associations gained support from disgruntled small and medium-sized businessmen with tax burdens and labor costs with a pro-austerity argument.[8]

- The internationalized sectors joined others to condemn interventionism when they were adversely affected by measures of a "nationalist" character in programs such as the Pre-Salt and shipbuilding, which protected some domestic capital investment. The media intensely explored the fact that Rousseff's "national-developmentalism" in these sectors resembled the Varguism that Cardoso had promised to eliminate forever. This is why we were not as surprised as Singer (2015: 59) (who considered it "ironic") that the industrialists of São Paulo Federation of Industries were aligned against the government even though the intervention responded to what he identified as "their own interests". This could have been part of the business resistance to interventionism pointed to by Rugitsky (2015), citing Kalecki (1943), but the other reason offered by Kalecki – the private sectors' fear that the government would occupy their role to reverse the cycle – is less likely. A different option was already assumed by their own economic policy, with its supply-side measures.

---

8   Carneiro (2017: 27) argues that BNDES financing fostered a more even distribution of income and that there was even deconcentration in the period. He acknowledges, however, that there was a "great negative publicity" about the "champions", and this is what we consider a persuasive element in criticizing the government.

Thus, for various reasons, the pact established by Lula was being undone, unifying all segments of the bourgeoisie against the government. Upon taking office for her second term, Rousseff realized this and set up a more orthodox team with Joaquim Levy, linked to the financial sector, as finance minister. In implementing the economic policy that had existed before 2011, he opposed the popular base that had led to the slim victory of the PT but showed that he would respect the commitments made to the hegemonic financial sector. In this situation the contradictions of the government were no longer with this sector, since the Central Bank had already pulled back from the policy of low interest and devalued exchange. Increased inflation justified the return to austerity. The center of the discussion of economic policy was once again the primary surplus. Once the continuity of financial hegemony was guaranteed, the focus was on compensatory policy, which increased uncertainty on several fronts. What primary spending would be cut? What taxes would be increased? Would subsidies and exemptions to entrepreneurs be maintained? Who would pay for the cost of adjustment? While entrepreneurial sectors such as the Federation of Industries were already leading the impeachment campaign, the last group of capitalists to join was the financial one. Not surprisingly, the minister of finance, Joaquim Levy, had emerged from its ranks and the sector was the only one that remained unaffected by the crisis. This was guaranteed by the prevailing economic policy. It was therefore the only sector that had a certain amount of uncertainty about what it could lose due from so risky and radical an act as overthrowing an elected government.

6   Conclusion

The economic policies of Lula's and Rousseff's governments deviate from neoliberalism, but they cannot be considered developmentalist either. It is impossible to conclude that they attempted to execute a steady long-term project with a strategy for reversing the deindustrialization of the country or advancing to a new technological paradigm, despite documents that proposed this and sectoral measures. Our analysis suggests that these governments, while lacking a structured economic development project, had a historical commitment to income redistribution whose policies were largely successfully implemented. The broad social pact proposed by Lula in the "Letter to Brazilians" acknowledged the hegemony of financial capital or "rentiers", which helps explain the continuity of Cardoso's economic policies. This pact was based on the inflation target system and on the independence of the Central Bank to manage it, and it was implemented through high interest rates, increased exchange rates, and a primary surplus. Its contradiction was that it protected the hegemonic group by means of monetary and fiscal policies while at the same time demanding constant intervention with compensatory policies that were made feasible only by fiscal policies (taxation, transfers, and subsidies). The primary surplus necessary to meet interest payments and public expenses could be maintained only while there was GDP growth, a favorable balance of payments, and a gap between wages and productivity.

As of 2011, the crisis, in addition to changes in the international situation, with slowing growth in China and other leading economies, that had a negative impact on the Brazilian trade balance, did not allow this to continue, and therefore the Rousseff government changed policies. The "new macroeconomic matrix" devalued the exchange rate and lowered interest rates, but it can hardly be interpreted as a "developmentalist turn". Although unorthodox, to a great extent it resembled countercyclical policies, whether Keynesian (supporting aggregate demand) or supply-side (seeking to secure growth with incentives for private investment). In any case, it represented a continuation of the proposal for social inclusion that had emerged in Lula's administration, in addition to an awareness that, with recessive policies, the phasing out of the pact was imminent, even with sectors of capitalists that had hitherto benefited. At the beginning of her second term Rousseff, under the pressure of inflation and macroeconomic imbalances, chose to return to austerity and, in this way, to mend the coalitions established by Lula in 2002. This option further intensified the conflict of the other bourgeois groups among themselves as well as with workers. The conditions no longer existed for the maintenance of the primary surplus and compensatory and income redistribution policies. It was not, therefore, a matter of correct or incorrect economic policy but a matter of the lack of the material, economic, and political grounds for their execution.

References

Anderson, P. (2011). Lula's Brazil. *London Review of Books* 5(1): 3–12.

Assis, J.C. (2005). A macroeconomia do pleno emprego. In: Sicsú, J., Paula, L.F.P., and Michel, R. (eds.), *Novo desenvolvimentismo: Um projeto nacional de crescimento com equidade social*, 77–93. Barueri: Manole.

Bastos, P.P.Z. (2012). A economia política do novo-desenvolvimentismo e do social desenvolvimentismo. *Economia e Sociedade* 21: 779–810.

Belluzzo, L.G. (2009). Um novo estado desenvolvimentista? *Le Monde Diplomatique* 3 (27): 4–5.

Boito Jr., A. (2005a). O governo Lula e a reforma do neoliberalismo. *Revista ADUSP* 34: 6–11.

Boito Jr., A. (2005b). A burguesia no governo Lula. *Crítica Marxista* 21: 52–77.

Boito Jr., A. (2012). Governos Lula: a nova burguesia nacional no poder. In: Boito Jr., A., and Galvão, A. (eds.), *Política e classes sociais no Brasil dos anos 2000*, 67–104. São Paulo: Alameda.

Boito Jr., A., and Saad-Filho, A. (2016). State, state institutions, and political power in Brazil. *Latin American Perspectives* 43(2): 190–206.

Bresser-Pereira, L.C. (2011). Crônica do novo-desenvolvimentismo e sua macroeconomia estruturalista. MS.

Bresser-Pereira, L.C. (2016). Reflexões sobre o novo desenvolvimentismo e o desenvolvimentismo clássico. *Revista de Economia Política* 36(2): 237–265.

Cardoso Jr., J.C. (2011). *Para a reconstrução do desenvolvimento no Brasil: Eixos estratégicos e diretrizes de política.* São Paulo: Hucitec.

Carneiro, R. (2017). *Navegando a contravento: uma reflexão sobre o experimento desenvolvimentista do Governo Dilma Rousseff.* Campinas: IE/UNICAMP, Texto para Discussão 289.

Carvalho, F.C. (2007). Lula's government in Brazil: a new left or the old populism? In: Arestis, P., and Saad-Filho, A. (eds.), *Political Economy of Brazil: Recent Economic Performance*, 24–41. London: Palgrave Macmillan.

Cervo, A.L. (2009). A construção do modelo industrialista brasileiro. *Diplomacia Estratégia Política* 10: 75–87.

Costa, L.B. (2015). Governo Lula: retorno ao desenvolvimentismo? Ph.D. diss., PPGE/UFRGS.

Erber, F.S. (2011). As convenções de desenvolvimento no governo Lula: um ensaio de economia política. *Revista de Economia Política* 31(1): 31–55.

Filgueiras, L. (2015). A natureza e os limites do desenvolvimentismo no capitalismo dependente brasileiro. *Margem Esquerda*, no. 23: 32–38.

Fonseca, P.C.D. (2014). Desenvolvimentismo: a construção do conceito. In: Calixtre, A.B., Biancarelli, A.M., and Cintra, M.A.M. (eds.), *Presente e futuro do desenvolvimento brasileiro*, 30–79. Brasília: IPEA.

Fonseca, P.C.D. (2016). Prejuízo conceitual: intervencionismo não é sinônimo de desenvolvimentismo. *Folha de São Paulo*, March 6.

Fonseca, P.C.D., Cunha, A.M., and Bichara, J.S. (2013). O Brasil na era Lula: retorno ao desenvolvimentismo? *Nova Economia* 23: 403–428.

Fonseca, P.C.D., Arend, M., and Guerrero, G.A. (2019). Growth, Distribution, and Crisis: The Workers' Party Administrations. *Latin American Perspectives* 47(1): 65–82.

Gonçalves, R. (2012). Governo Lula e o nacional-desenvolvimentismo às avessas. *Revista da Sociedade Brasileira de Economia Política* 31: 5–30.

Gramsci, A. (1975). *Quaderni del carcere.* Torino: Einaudi.

Herrlein, R. (2011). *Estado democrático e desenvolvimento no Brasil contemporâneo: Um ensaio de economia política*. Porto Alegre: Editora UFRGS.

Instituto de Pesquisa Econômica Aplicada (IPEADATA). Dados macroeconômicos. Disponível em: http://www.ipeadata.gov.br/Default.aspx.

Kalecki, M. (1943). Political aspects of full employment. *Political Quarterly* 14: 322–330.

Marquetti, A., Hoff, C., and Miebach, A. (2016). Lucratividade e distribuição: a origem econômica da crise política brasileira. Paper presented at the Twenty-second National Conference of Political Economy, Campinas.

Morais, L., and Saad-Filho, A. (2011). Da economia política à política econômica: o novo-desenvolvimentismo e o governo Lula. *Revista de Economia Política* 31: 507–527.

Nakano, Y. (2010). Catch up. *Folha de São Paulo*, January 24.

Novy, A. (2009a). O retorno do estado desenvolvimentista no Brasil. *Indicadores Econômicos FEE* 36(4): 121–128.

Novy, A. (2009b). Política e economia, outra vez articuladas. *Le Monde Diplomatique Brasil* 3(27): 6–7.

Nunes, W. (2018). Uma estratégia desenvolvimentista sem um 'estado desenvolvimentista': o caso dos governos Lula. Ph.D. diss., UFPR.

Oliveira, F. de. (2003). *Crítica à razão dualista: O ornitorrinco*. São Paulo: Boitempo.

Paula, J.A. (2005). *Adeus ao desenvolvimentismo: A opção do governo Lula*. Belo Horizonte: Autêntica.

Paulani, L. (2003). Brazil delivery: razões, contradições e limites da política econômica dos primeiros seis meses do governo Lula. In: Paula, J.A. de (ed.), *A economia política da mudança*, 58–73. Belo Horizonte: Autêntica.

Paulani, L. (2005). Sem esperança de ser país: o governo Lula 18 meses depois, In: João Sicsú, J., Paula, L.P. de, and Michel, R. (eds.), *Novo desenvolvimentismo: Um projeto nacional de crescimento com equidade social*, 49–76. Barueri: Manole.

Paulani, L. (2007). The real meaning of the economic policy of Lula's government. In: Philip, A., and Saad-Filho, A. (eds.), *Political Economy of Brazil: Recent Economic Performance*, 43–54. London: Palgrave Macmillan.

Paulani, L. (2017). A experiência brasileira entre 2003 e 2014: neoliberalismo? *Cadernos do Desenvolvimento* 12(20): 135–155.

Poulantzas, N. (1976). *A crise das ditaduras: Portugal, Grécia e Espanha*. Rio de Janeiro: Paz e Terra.

Prado, E.F.S. (2017). Das explicações para a quase estagnação da economia capitalista no Brasil. *Revista de Economia Política* 37: 478–503.

Rugitsky, F. (2015). Do ensaio desenvolvimentista à austeridade: uma leitura Kaleckiana. http://jornalggn.com.br/noticia/do-ensaio-desenvolvimentista-a-austeridade-por-fernando-rugitsky/ (accessed September 11, 2017).

Sartori, G. (1970). Concept misformation in comparative politics. *American Political Science Review* 64: 1.033–1.053.

Sartori, G. (1984). Guidelines for concept analysis. In: Sartori, G. (ed.), *Social Science Concepts: A Systematic Analysis*, 15–85. Beverly Hills: Sage.

Schapiro, M.G. (2013). *Ativismo estatal e industrialismo defensivo: instrumentos e capacidades na política industrial brasileira.* Texto para Discussão1856. Brasília: IPEA.

Singer, A. (2012). *Os sentidos do Lulismo: Reforma gradual e pacto conservador.* São Paulo: Cia. das Letras.

Singer, A. (2015). Cutucando onças com varas curtas: o ensaio desenvolvimentista no primeiro mandato de Dilma Rousseff (2011–2014). *Novos Estudos* 102: 39–67.

Teixeira, R.A., and Pinto, E.C. (2012). A economia política dos governos FHC, Lula e Dilma: dominância financeira, bloco no poder e desenvolvimento econômico. *Economia e Sociedade* 21: 909–941.

United Nations Conference on Trade and Development (Unctad). Unctadstat. https://unctadstat.unctad.org/EN/.

Weyland, K. (2001). Clarifying a contested concept: populism in the study of Latin American politics. *Comparative Politics* 34(1): 1–22.

CHAPTER 5

Sailing against the Wind: The Rise and Crisis of a Low-Conflict Progressivism

Gustavo Codas Friedmann and Claudio A. Castelo Branco Puty

1   Introduction[1]

We first wrote this chapter in September 2017 when signs that Brazil was heading to socio-economic disaster were clear, but it was hard to imagine what how bad things could get. Now we live in a context of a country that endured five years of deep economic recession, intervals of mediocre recovery combined with very high unemployment and rising rates of work force despondency. Poverty rates have boomed, with a decrease of the income of the poorest 40% (85 million people) of 1.4% per year since 2015. Inequality has also risen, with the Gini coefficient reaching 0.550 in 2018 from 0.525 in 2015 – the lowest in the country's recorded history (IBGE 2019). The current crisis goes back to the last year of the Partido dos Trabalhadores (Workers' Party – PT) government and then with the presidency in the hands of Michel Temer, the center-right former vice president who actively conspired to overthrow President Dilma Rousseff in May 2016. Temer promoted an unprecedented agenda of neoliberal reforms with the support of the Partido da Social Democracia Brasileira (Brazilian Social Democracy Party – PSDB), a party that was defeated by the Partido dos Trabalhadores in four consecutive elections. Lula's imprisonment (from April 2018 to November 2019) in a politically motivated process under false criminal charges blocked his possible candidacy for presidency when he was leading the opinion polls and drawing crowds to the streets of Brazilian cities in caravans organized by the PT. Finally, the election of Jair Bolsonaro as president – the far-right politician, associated with police militias, neo-pentecostal evangelical churches and a die-hard follower of Donald Trump policies – marks the apex of this neoliberal/neoconservative counter-revolution in Brazil. Amid the multiple layers of the crisis, an assessment of the PT governments is fundamental for the reconstruction of emancipatory paths for the Brazilian people.

---

1   An earlier version of the arguments in this chapter appeared in Friedmann and Puty, 2020.

Whom did the governments led by the PT represent? Would they have promoted the same neoliberalism of the 1990s, mitigated this time by compensatory social policies – a kind of "social neoliberalism"? Did they function as a
sort of indirect agent of neoliberalism by demobilizing the working class? Or
were they a true "post-neoliberal" experiment? And, after all, what comes
after neoliberalism on the periphery of world capitalism? We have reviewed
the PT's political trajectory in Brazil's recent history in an attempt to understand how the party has approached the task of governing Brazil since 2003.
We will critically address these governments, especially in their economic and
social dimensions, in the Latin American context and conclude with an effort
to characterize the PT experiment. The PT governments braved the turbulent
seas of the political struggle in Brazil and had good results while the economic
conditions allowed sufficient nautical speed. However, the incipient democratization that they promoted triggered reactions in which constraints that had
been latent for many years became open opposition. The ship slowed down
and, engulfed in the vortex, capsized, astonishingly, in the coup of 2016.

2   Progressivism in the Era of Programmatic Disorganization

The progressive cycle of governments in Brazil began in 2003 not as a result
of a linear programmatic and organizational accumulation of forces of the
Brazilian left in the previous period but because of the combination of the
neoliberal crisis and popular resistance that opened the way for the conquest
of the presidency. The trajectory of the PT embodies these contradictions.
Founded in 1980, in the following decade the PT passed through two very distinct phases. After its origin, growth, and implantation across much of the
national territory there was a period of resistance to the neoliberal reforms
of the 1990s, with a reduction of its strategic perspective to purely electoral
dynamics. Until the election of 1989, electoral dispute was for the PT part of a
strategy of democratic "rupture". In that year Lula came close to winning the
presidential election defending a popular-democratic, antilandowner, and
anti-imperialist platform in the wake of social struggles, including a two-day
general strike in March 1989. A few months before, the PT deputies had voted
against the approval of the final text of the 1988 Constitution in protest of what
was considered a restricted and conservative redemocratization.
    Beginning in the 1990s, with increasing institutional victories, elections
became more and more the PT's path to power. This was at a moment of
immense defeat of the left at the world level with an accelerated reversion
of the experiments in "real socialism" to savage capitalism that strengthened

neoliberal hegemony. We do not underestimate the importance of this ideological and theoretical retreat. In the "programmatic disorganization" of the
left[2] socialism disappeared from the strategic political perspective of the main
leftist parties that survived, and Cuba, which dared to maintain its socialist
experiment, was thrown into the difficult conditions of the "special period".

Two countertendencies illustrate efforts at resistance. In 1990, on the initiative of Lula and Fidel Castro, an open meeting of leftist and progressive parties was convened in São Paulo and developed into the Forum of São Paulo, a
broad area of convergence that remained alive throughout these decades. In
the following year, 1991, the PT held its first congress, in which it debated and
approved what would become "PT socialism" and asserted that it could not be
similar to the experiences of European social democracy or the "real socialism"
of the Soviet Union but instead was a general framework for the development
of a project of a democratic socialism. In this context, the idea became consolidated that governing meant reversing the priorities for the management of
the public machine in favor of the majority. It was about having a strategy for
improving the living conditions and income levels of the socially marginalized
popular sectors and depressed regions. In the 2002 campaign, two main ideas
were reinforced. The first was that Lula would feel fulfilled if, at the end of his
term, all Brazilians ate three meals a day. The second was that improvement in
the conditions of life of the majority would be achieved without causing losses
to the capitalists, the upper middle classes, and the more developed regions.
These goals not only were part of his campaign rhetoric but are still part of
Lula's defense of the legacy of his two governments.

3   A Brief History of the PT Governments

Lula's electoral victory in 2002 came after three failed attempts (1989, 1994, and
1998) and after the PT and its network of social movements had been the main
opponents of the implementation of the Washington Consensus agenda in
Brazil throughout the 1990s.

The liberalizing economic policy of the governments of Fernando Henrique
Cardoso had a repressive bias and concentrated income. It involved a period of
overvaluation of the real in the form of an exchange-rate anchor, mechanisms

---

2   "Programmatic disorganization" is a characterization of this period developed over the years
    by Miguel "Moro" Romero (1946–2014), editor of the Spanish magazine *Viento Sur*. For the
    record of the main party resolutions since its founding until 1998 see PT (1998). For an analy-
    sis of the PT's programmatic debates in the 1989, 1994, and 1998 elections, see Árabe (1998).

for attracting flows of foreign capital through the opening of the capital account, restrictive monetary policy and high interest rates, broad commercial liberalization, the privatization of state enterprises, an end to restrictions on foreign direct investment, severe fiscal tightening, reduction of the state's role in the economy and the provision of public services, and, last but not least, regressive tax reform with exemptions for capital gains and reduction of income tax rates for the richest.[3]

The rise of governments led by the PT to the central executive branch occurred in the context of the exhaustion of the model of macroeconomic adjustment that had limited growth in the years of President Fernando Henrique Cardoso. Added to this, the blackout of electricity service throughout the country caused in 2001–2002 by the lack of investment in this sector, leading to its privatization, further eroded neoliberal hegemony. This phenomenon had been appearing in most of the region, with Lula's victory being preceded by the election of Hugo Chávez in Venezuela in 1998, the intense crisis and dollarization in Ecuador, and the Argentine default of 2001.

The election of Lula did not, however, come without important political concessions. After pressing the party, Lula nominated as his vice president a businessman from the garment industry, José Alencar of the center-right Liberal Party. He then launched the "Letter to the Brazilian People"[4] of June 22, 2002, in which he guaranteed that the new economic model implemented by the PT would be based, "of course, on respect for the contracts and debts of the country".

In the assembling of his first cabinet, he gave another clear signal of adherence to the agreement with financial capital by naming to the presidency of the Central Bank Henrique Meirelles. a federal deputy newly elected by the PSDB (and, not coincidentally, currently the finance minister and the main guarantor together with the market of the government of Michel Temer). Clearly, this affirmed a political option for nonconfrontational coexistence with financial capital and the main characteristic of the PT cycle in government: a progressivism that sought to promote social inclusion and substantive improvements in the living and working conditions of the majorities through the solutions that caused the least friction with the ruling class.[5]

---

3 Before 1985, the income tax already had a maximum rate of 60 percent. In 1988 the personal income tax table included a maximum rate of 45 percent and 11 levels. Since then it has had a maximum rate of 25 percent and three levels. In addition, since 1996, the distribution of profits and dividends has been exempt from taxation (Law 9249/1995).

4 http://www1.folha.uol.com.br/folha/bra sil / ult96u33908.shtml.

5 For an analysis of the relationship of the PT governments with the popular sectors, see Singer (2017: 15), in which the author defends the thesis that the electoral discourse of "Lulism"

Given the characteristics of the Brazilian political system, the PT assumed the government with a minority in the National Congress and faced with various political crises that threatened to lead to impeachment and took refuge in the relative stability of the "coalition presidency". In this pattern of governability, inherited from the Cardoso years, the political center (at that moment the Partido Movimento Brasileiro [Brazilian Democratic Movement Party – PMDB]) played a central role in sustaining the government and, most important, the Senate. This parliamentary dynamic and its counterpart, the occupation of government posts and the subsequent determination of electoral alliances in the subnational elections, deeply marked the tactics of the PT in those years. Especially after the *mensalão* scandal, which almost destroyed Lula in 2005–2006, the PMDB became the anchor of governability and preferred ally of the majority of the PT as opposed to its leftmost sectors, even in internal party disputes. By adopting this pattern of governability, the PT and its allies on the left fit within the framework of the narrow Brazilian democratic-liberal institutionality, opening a fatal flank by not daring – by convening a constituent assembly – to make political reforms that altered the democratic bases of power.

Two other characteristics of the battlefield on which Lula's government was moving were the oligopolistic character of the media in Brazil and the siege on the government by the state. The media in Brazil are controlled by a few family or religious groups, and their integration with the financial sector both as owners and large advertisers is apparent. The dispute between these groups for the resources of official publicity generates the illusion that the government can guide them when, in fact, in the long run it is exactly the opposite that occurs. This illusion of control of the oligopolistic media through funding of advertising generated yet another political deficit of the PT governments, which did not even attempt to democratize the mass media. As if responding to a single editor, radio and television networks and print newspapers with a national circulation developed, from the *mensalão* case in 2005 until 2016, an efficient campaign for the political erosion of the PT, identifying it as the sole representative and beneficiary of corruption in the country.

What we call the siege on the government by the state refers both to the rules of its functioning and to its personnel composition, which were ill-suited to the purposes of a government committed to the democratization of power: laws and regulations that ultimately played a regressive role in the allocation of the

---

coincided with a certain "popular conservatism" of the "subproletariat" excited by the idea of "a state that is strong enough to reduce inequality without a threat to the established order".

public budget and Supreme Court justices, judges, prosecutors, public employees, and even holders of commissioned positions many of whom were resolute opponents by origin or class position of any left-wing project but holders of specialized knowledge, power, and ties to the high bureaucracy, not to mention the military and the state military police.

Therefore, Lula's victory had some important constraints: a center-left/left congressional minority, broadly hegemonic financial capital, a media oligopoly by private groups, and a state commitment to antiredistributive logic. The experience of the PT governments was therefore highly conciliatory toward big business – the media, agribusiness, financial capital, and some industrial groups. Justified in terms of the need to achieve a parliamentary majority and minimum conditions of governability, this ended up extending to the campaign finance dynamics of the PT and its allies, leading to scandals such as that of Petrobras. The enormous influence of the banks over the policies of the Treasury and the Central Bank and the formal presence of representatives of the private banking federations in the management of state and parafiscal funds are just a few examples of the direct power of finance over the Brazilian state.

Public policies also followed the path of least conflict/veiled compromise, increasing vacancies in higher education by purchasing vacancies in private schools with public money and thus allowing rapid expansion (since the private schools were idle) but placing a mass of young people under the ideological control of private education in addition to transferring large financial resources to private educational groups.

Under great pressure from capitalist agribusiness, the deconcentration of landownership through agrarian reform eventually disappeared, with the Dilma government's defense of a "rural middle class" and the "quality" of the settlements being a sign that new expropriations were no longer a priority. The government adopted in its official discourse the liberal vulgate that Brazil had created a "new middle class" – a mystifying thesis for at least two reasons: because the income of the alleged middle class was too low to constitute a stable middle stratum and because it overlooked their being part of the working class.

With regard to macroeconomic management, the PT governments were initially characterized by preservation of the tripartite framework, but after 2005 there was a clear change. The increase in central government revenues (Figure 5.1) had already guaranteed fiscal space for programs of social inclusion and reconstruction of state capacities.

After the global financial crisis this option became clearer when there was an undeclared abandonment of the bases of the tripod, deepening the

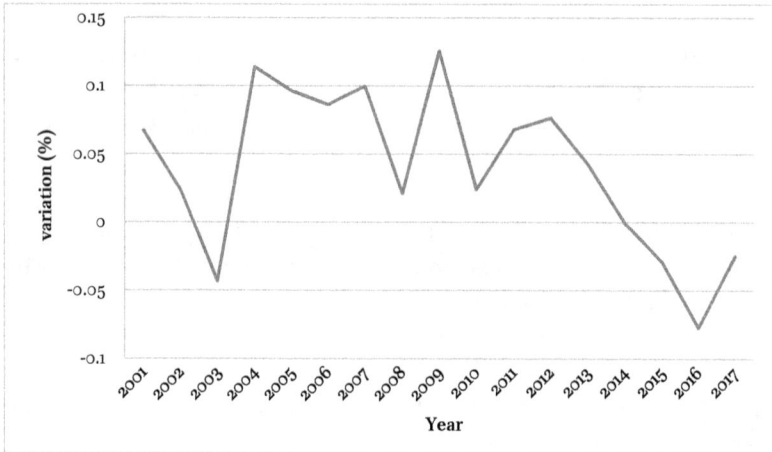

FIGURE 5.1   Annual variation of central government's net current revenues (%) in 2017 prices
AUTHOR'S ELABORATION WITH DATA FROM THE BRAZILIAN SECREATARY OF
TREASURY

conflicts between so-called developmentalist and neoliberal sectors within the government. The first Dilma government followed the path of Lula's second and began with the clearest attempt to break with the inherited principles of macroeconomic management, peaceful coexistence with financial capital, and congressional governance through bargaining. In a May 1, 2012 statement, the president argued that the banks had a "perverse logic" and mandated that state banks lower their interest rates to record levels. From then on and throughout 2012, the period was one of marked conflict. The distributive dispute between capital and labor in the context of a heated labor market began a moderate increase in inflation, which was at the "ceiling" of the annual inflation target. This triggered significant pressure from the press for the government to take tougher measures against inflation – to raise basic interest rates. Faced with the strong pressure of "published" opinion, the government backtracked and resumed a process of raising the Central Bank's basic rate, which had consequences for the exchange rate and for industrial competitiveness.[6] We consider this as having determined the future of Dilma Rousseff's government.[7]

---

6   https://www.noticiasagricolas.com.br/noticias/agronegocio/120795-banco-central-
    aumenta-a-selic-taxa-basica-de-juros-pela-1-vez-de-julho-de -2011.html.
7   Curiously, it was with the neoliberal turn in the conduct of the economic policy of the second
    Dilma government, with a price shock managed within the strategy of "fiscal austerity", that
    2015 inflation reached 10.67 percent, the highest since 2002.

Then we had the mobilizations of June 2013, an expression of the malaise felt by a significant part of the traditional middle class. Symbolically threatened by the social rise of the poorest and facing inflation in services, particularly domestic services, this middle class exploded into activism that was capitalized on by far-right groups funded by American think tanks and nongovernmental organizations such as those linked to the Koch brothers. The pattern of the demonstrations was diffuse, starting with municipal issues and as became clear, ending up being part of the international promotion of "color revolutions" by organizations linked to the United States, where legitimate discontent over particular issues became a political whirlwind of regressive bias. The corporate media clearly saw the opportunity to manipulate the sense of the mobilizations to combine this social discontent with its agenda against the macroeconomic management of the PT government and the struggle against PT corruption connected with what was called Operation Car Wash.

The government's response to the demonstrations was advanced by proposing to the Congress elements of a democratization of the Brazilian political system, but it had not created the conditions for confronting the new political moment. From that point on it was clear that with the end of the commodity cycle and the ensuing win-win period in the Brazilian economy, a change in the pattern of class struggle in Brazil was under way. In fact, several studies have shown that, beginning in 2011, there was both a contraction of the profit margins of Brazilian companies (Rocca and Santos Jr. 2015) and a decline in the aggregate profit rate (Marquetti, Hoff, and Miebach 2017). The consequence was a decline in aggregate saving, private investment, and economic growth. The Dilma government's attempts to stimulate investment with ever-increasing tax exemptions for industry and a shift from regulatory frameworks in the logistics area to facilitating private investment were insufficient and ineffective. The general phenomenon undermined the conditions of governability by eroding the PT executive's power of arbitration between classes.

Still, in 2014, after an ideologically polarized campaign, Dilma defeated by a narrow margin Aécio Neves, the neoliberal right-wing candidate, and was reelected. By the end of that year the country had the lowest unemployment rate in its historical series (4.8 percent), and opinion polls showed that one of the decisive factors in Dilma's candidacy was job and income outcomes. However, by the end of 2014 federal revenue was dropping. Associated with this, problems accumulated in the external accounts and paralysis in private investment. Added to this scenario were two other crises: Operation Car Wash, which revealed the extent of corruption at Petrobras and the involvement of almost all the heads of the Congress in kickback schemes, and the rise of Deputy Eduardo Cunha, who symbolized the toxic combination of business interests and politics, to the presidency of the Chamber. Faced with the free fall of revenues, the paralysis of Petrobras and the entire civil construction sector, and an uncontrolled Congress, the government opted for more concessions to financial capital, repeating the formula used by Lula in 2003: calling in a neoliberal economic team to manage a fiscal adjustment plan for a supposedly rapid recovery of the economy and thus have peace on one of the fronts of battle. Nothing could have been more misleading.

The idea of the adjustment plan was (1) to liberalize administered prices in an attempt to modify profit margins for the electric, oil, and gas sectors; (2) to substitute state investment for private investment from a concessions program in the infrastructure sector with readjusted rates of return and Banco Nacional de Desenvolvimento Econômico e Social (National Bank of Economic and Social Development – BNDES) support, this time for financing via debt instruments in the capital market such as infrastructure bonds; (3) to cut primary expenditures; and (4) to intensify the fight against inflation through successive increases in basic interest rates. The plan was a failure. The economy slowed still further, deepening the recession, generating a price shock, blowing up unemployment, and increasing the fiscal problem. The effect of the option for austerity was social demobilization and the further weakening of government ties with the working class. This was accentuated when, on the eve of her impeachment, Dilma announced a pension reform and measures that promoted the privatization of state-owned enterprises.

Meanwhile, the other two crises were getting worse. Operation Car Wash advanced on the PT and Lula and the Congress elected Eduardo Cunha, who immediately carried out a series of measures that sabotaged any initiative of the government toward economic recovery and used the receipt of a demand for the impeachment of Dilma as an instrument of blackmail. The government, under pressure from Lula, opened up more space for the PMDB, including giving the task of congressional articulation to Michel Temer himself.

In retrospect, the ill-fated adjustment of 2015 stemmed from the – largely political – standoff in economic management, with the decline in the policy of lowering interest rates and the intensification of disputes between the Treasury and the Central Bank. For a number of years there has been a dysfunctional relationship between moderate expansionism and relative price management and measures to ensure the latter's inflation target. At the heart of the problem was once again the macroeconomic tripod, since monetary policy kept the real overvalued – deepening current-account problems – as the government's reluctance to admit a primary deficit (until 2015 Brazil was the only country in Latin America to maintain a primary surplus) restricted fiscal policy, preventing the soft landing that occurred in other Latin American countries in the same period. While the anachronistic macroeconomic framework under-mined the prospects for confronting economic stagnation, political circum-stances led to the fatal error of a severe fiscal adjustment in the midst of a slowdown even though Brazil had absolutely reasonable debt indicators com-pared with the world standard. The combination of higher rate for electric-ity and fuel, interest rate increases, and reduction of the Growth Acceleration Program, as well as Operation Car Wash's blocking of the huge investments projected by Petrobras, generated a perfect storm that sank the country in the worst recession ever registered.

The story of the government's terminal crisis would not be complete with-out mentioning the role of state institutions such as the Federal Police, the Federal Court of Audit, and almost all of the judiciary in making the Dilma gov-ernment inviable. These institutions, increasingly articulated with the press, barred public policies (for example, the TCU embargo on changing the regu-latory framework of ports and the opposition of sectors of the judiciary to the More Doctors program), prevented the presence of Lula in the Dilma cabinet and called into question her accounts and her ministers in a process of con-stant obstruction that gradually paralyzed the government and led to its fall.

4   Neoliberal Governments?

The history of the PT governments suggests that many of the choices they made were not for the necessary ideological conversion or abandonment of a reformist program. In most cases they were the result of an evaluation – per-haps conservative – of the correlation of forces combined with an institutional illusion that led to the government's not creating the conditions for a change from social mobilization and effective democratization of the state and other "ideological apparatuses" as in the case of the oligopolized media. Even so, important innovations in public policy and politically significant outcomes occurred during this period.[8]

In foreign policy, Brazil had a global role unprecedented in its history through what was known as the "active and dignified" policy. Independence vis-à-vis the United States was central to the consolidation of the G20 in the struggle for reform of the International Monetary Fund and the World Bank and the establishment of the BRICS, signaling the need for a new post-Bretton

---

8   The three main parties of the Brazilian left have published assessments of the Lula and Dilma
    governments: Guerra et al. (2017) for the PT, Rabelo and Monteiro (2017) for the Communist
    Party of Brazil, and Maringoni and Medeiros (2017) for Socialism and Freedom.

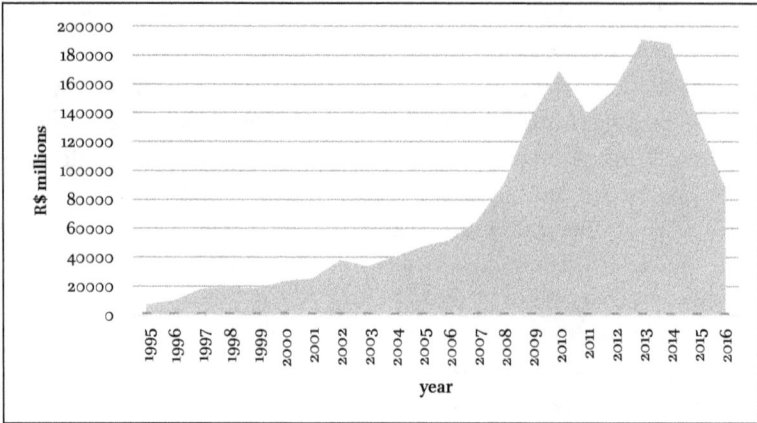

FIGURE 5.2   Evolution of BNDES disbursements, 1995–2016
BNDES, 2016. AUTHOR'S ELABORATION WITH DATA FROM BNDES

Woods global governance arrangement. Lula's presence in the Brazilian government was fundamental for burying the proposal of the Free Trade Area of the Americas, the main U.S. strategy for the region since 1994. The PT governments were decisive for the creation of regional institutions promoting political integration such as Unasur and CELAC and the strengthening of Mercosur. Finally, the presence of a progressive government in Brazil provided a level of political and economic protection to the other progressive experiments in the region.[9]

The recovery of the capacity for state intervention was remarkable. The BNDES exhibited an unprecedented increase in its support for industry and the strengthening of national business groups, with disbursements exceeding R$150 billion beginning in 2009. The repositioning of the state took various forms – public tenders, career structure, the creation of specific ministries – that allowed a strengthening of the action of the public sector. Robust investment programs in infrastructure and housing construction were also established (Figure 5.2).

There was a strengthening of universal public policies in terms of both increased budgets and coverage. The approval of a national education plan that included spending 10 percent of the GDP on education and the allocation of 50 percent of the resources from the Pre-Salt oilfields toward a social fund for

---

9   For the international dimension of the experience of the PT governments, see Maringoni, Schutte, and Berron (2014), Padula and Fiori (2016), and Pomar (2017).

education and 25 percent to health was a legacy of the political environment of that period. The opening of a record number of new public universities and increased funding for existing ones and the establishment of racial quotas for admissions changed the face of public higher education in Brazil. The More Doctors program, which enabled thousands of health professionals, including foreigners (a good number of Cubans) to be hired and mobilized to serve populations for which assistance was lacking, was also a milestone. The creation of ministries aimed at family agriculture and social development, respectively, allowed for a series of innovations in public policies for small farmers, agrarian reform settlers, and families in vulnerable situations that, together with real adjustments of the minimum wage in all the years of the government, allowed about 30 million people to escape poverty.

The strong infrastructure investment policy had multiplier effects, generating around 20 million jobs in the period before the crisis that led to the coup. A constitutional amendment guaranteed unprecedented labor and pension rights to domestic workers (Brazil has the world's largest contingent of women, mostly black, in domestic work). Public social security coverage increased and pension accounts, as a result of the boom in the labor market, became sustainable.

The discovery of oil in the Pre-Salt layer on the Brazilian coast led to an increase in investment in the oil and gas chain, with multiplier effects on shipbuilding thanks to the Lula government's policy of requiring national content in the company's large procurement contracts. Petrobras's share of the holding has grown, and so has the company, threatened with privatization in the 1990s. The Pre-Salt regulatory framework, to the dismay of private companies after a hard battle in the Congress, made the state the owner of the oil and placed a state-owned oil company, Petrosal, in control of production. A sovereign fund was set up to receive resources from the exploitation of the Pre-Salt layer. All these measures were the fruit of intense battles in the Congress, since the right was radically opposed to them.

The PT governments had a clearly redistributive character, as is apparent in the behavior of the Gini index, which declined steadily from .54 in 2004 to .49 in 2014 (Ministério do Desenvolvimento Social 2015). Despite persistent inequality in Brazil and increasing income concentration in the world, the poverty rate in 2014 had fallen by 70 percent in relation to 2004, and about 36 million people had risen above the extreme poverty line, generating a new working class. The significant decline in the proportion of the GDP represented by wages up till 2004 was reversed in 2005. The criticism of liberal sectors and some of the left that revenues in this period were due exclusively to the favorable conditions of international liquidity overlooks the unconventional and successful management of the crisis of 2007, when world orthodoxy advocated austerity and the government was decisively expansionist.

5   Brazil in the Latin American Progressive Cycle

The Brazilian experiment is better understood by looking at the rest of Latin America. With the electoral victory of Hugo Chávez in Venezuela in 1998, the region experienced the beginning of an unprecedented cycle of popular governments – electoral victories of progressive forces (Uruguay, Bolivia, Ecuador, Nicaragua, El Salvador), alliances led by progressives (Argentina, Brazil, Paraguay), and progressive reconversions of conservative governments (Honduras). Cuba went from the final phase of the "special period" begun in 1992 to the updating of its model with the assumption of the government's leadership by Raúl Castro in 2006 (on a provisional basis) and 2008. Within this synchrony there was significant heterogeneity in the characteristics and dynamics of the national processes. In three cases (Venezuela, Bolivia, and Ecuador) the new governments responded by convening constituent assemblies to reestablish the republics. In the others electoral victories occurred within constitutional continuities. In some countries (Venezuela, Bolivia, Ecuador, Paraguay) the victorious forces were relatively recent or unstructured, while in others (Brazil, Uruguay, Nicaragua, and El Salvador) they were the result of decades of construction. In three cases the governments were interrupted by coups (Honduras in 2009, Paraguay in 2012, Brazil in 2016).

Both the right and the left tried to classify these governments as "carnivorous" (revolutionary) or "vegetarian" (reformist), but these attempts greatly impoverish the analysis. For example, in the two processes considered most radical or revolutionary – those of Venezuela and Ecuador – the former approved the autonomy of the Central Bank and the latter maintained the dollarization of the economy, both clearly neoliberal measures adopted within an assessment of the correlation of forces in society and what the priorities of governments should be. In virtually every case of a progressive government we find (1) the urgency of removing the large human contingents that were below the poverty line, (2) the effort to strengthen the state as an actor in the country's economy by capturing larger portions of the extraordinary incomes resulting from the commodities boom and expanding its capacity to guide national development vis-à-vis the market, and (3) varying degrees of national sovereignty with regard to U.S. imperialism requiring our countries to deepen, for which it was understood that our countries needed to deepen regional integration.

In the beginning, the radical nature of some of these processes had a political dimension – a fierce effort to defeat the old oligarchies that had so far dominated these countries' political life. The three programmatic lines mentioned above served to forge alliances between the new governments and large majorities, beginning with the poorest. In no case did the government program approach the radicalness with which Salvador Allende won elections in Chile in 1970, which enunciated a peaceful transition to socialism through the electoral process. There were no "socialist" programs in the recent progressive cycle, although there were some unusual forms, such as "Amazonian capitalism" (Bolivia) and "serious capitalism" (Argentina). It was in an attempt to realize those basic programmatic axes that political dispute developed, and eventually there was programmatic deepening. The most emblematic case was the Venezuelan, which only in the seventh year of Chávez's government in January 2005 opened the discussion of twenty-first-century socialism and later proposed the reorganization of the state in terms of communes. Even there, the government had already gone through a coup in 2002 and an oil strike. Confronting political and economic difficulties of all kinds, however, it made little progress on the programmatic path indicated.

The trajectories of progressive governments had sharp contradictions with sectors of civil society in relation to environmental issues, since the financing of some public policies required a degree of intensification of primary export activities, which, in general, came into conflict with the traditional populations affected and with environmental concerns. In many national experiments, the basic program of the government was not free of contradictions within progressivism itself. There were problems in macroeconomic management; inflation, external constraints, and fiscal difficulties whose tax solution was blocked by the resistance of the very rich were common bottlenecks of these experiments. In short, the PT governments of Brazil were not fundamentally different from other progressive governments in Latin America. What seems to distinguish them is the dynamics of the political disputes that surrounded them.

6   The Nature of the PT's Experiments

Neoliberalism as a global system of domination by financial capital has lived several lives since the 1970s. It has gone from advocating a "minimal and strong state" to the promotion of dismantling nation-states. These contradictions lead Duménil and Levy (2017) and others to say that neoliberalism is already experiencing a transition toward a new social order on the right.[10] But what, after all, would characterize a neoliberal government in Latin America?

In the 1990s there was little doubt that Latin American peripheral capitalism was being reformatted by a neoliberal program. The menu included privatization of companies and public services, indiscriminate opening to international trade, deregulation of financial markets, and liberalization of the capital account of the balance of payments for the free international flow of capital. The consequences were a regime of low economic growth and social devastation: increase in structural unemployment with the growth of the informal market and deregulation of formal work; the dismantling of peripheral Fordism through the relocation and de-verticalization of companies and productive chains within countries ("fiscal warfare" between states in Brazil) and internationally a "race to the bottom" on social and labor rights. Latin American neoliberalism, in addition to the defense of values and policies aimed at the promotion of the free market and the implementation of mechanisms for the valorization of fictitious capital, was characterized by subordination to an economic and therefore political hierarchy that has in the United States undisputed leadership in the region. This hierarchy leads to resignation to specialization in the production low-complexity and primary products – the historical expression of interrupted development.

The pattern of state intervention, distributional outcomes, concern with the national question, and a history of political conflicts of the distributive function seem to clearly indicate that the PT governments were not a tropicalized neoliberal experiment. After all, why would financial capital, industrial confederations, and the wealthy in general overthrow a government that supposedly promoted a regime of neoliberal accumulation and domination? Indeed, in the Brazilian context, left-wing governments have promoted mostly progressive agendas without having overcome important contradictions in the structure and dynamics of their economies and a certain political ambiguity stemming from the aforementioned institutional conditions. There is certainly a big difference between being an active part of implementing a neoliberal program and political survival through the promotion of changes that respect the limits of the established international order. In fact, given the inherited political and institutional conditions, which remained unchanged, it is admirable that the governments lasted so long and managed to move forward in an

---

10   A kind of managed neoliberalism or neomanagerism characterized by greater state intervention, production reallocated in the national territory, less concern with so-called shareholder value, and therefore greater power for management.

absolutely inhospitable environment. But if the PT governments were not a type of neoliberalism, what were they?

The political debate on the left on Latin American progressivism seems to have revolved around three positions. In addition to the already discussed idea that they were a kind of social liberalism or a new type of neoliberalism, there is the idea that they were post-neoliberal (Sader 2007) and the idea that in the cases of Venezuela, Bolivia, and Ecuador they were postcapitalist (Borón 2017). The conceptual problem with the idea of post-neoliberalism is its indeterminacy: either it suggests a roadmap of rupture and solid transition that does not appear to have occurred or it simply adds to the set of forms of twenty-first-century progressivism. Most proponents of this idea see a return, under the direction of popular and leftist forces, to the national-developmentalist, industrialist, and statist program with a much stronger social and democratic dimension than in the period of import substitution. Hence the designation, which seems appropriate to the Brazilian case, "social developmentalism". However, it should be kept in mind that import substitution began in the period of interruption of foreign trade by the crisis that began in 1929. The recent period represents exactly the opposite, with high prices for exportable primary products that made possible a strategy for social development and the expansion of state capacities in the midst of deindustrialization and reprivatization of the economy, which makes social developmentalism an eminently political concept.

Sectors of the left close to environmentalism have insisted that the character of the experiment is a neoextractivist neoliberalism (Svampa 2017) – the continuation of the historically developed model in the region, this time with the use of extractive resources to finance social policies. The problem with this characterization is that, while in some national cases (Venezuela, for example) or sectors (agribusiness and minerals in Brazil), it does seem to correspond to the facts, it does not account for the model. In a few cases there have been efforts at economic diversification, industrialization, expansion of environmental stainability policies, and the recognition of the rights of indigenous and traditional peoples in terms totally contrary to traditional extractivism. The fact is that the experiments of the PT governments put great emphasis on the social "emergency" – the priority of service to those who are starving or in absolute poverty. This was expressed in stimulation of the expansion of the internal mass market (part of the party program since the 1990s), which resulted in a strategy of social inclusion by consumption.

Our notion of a low-conflict progressivism may correctly express the picture but not the dynamics of the period, since these governments began with a less progressive profile in 2003–2005 to reach a high point in 2011–2012 with the social mobility and deepening democracy that were interrupted by the 2016 coup. This characterization follows Singer's (2012) proposal of a "weak reformism" to describe the two Lula governments (2003–2010) but emphasizes that the program fell short of deep structural reforms. It distances itself, however, from Modonesi's (2017a) attempt, borrowing a concept from Gramsci, to frame the experiment as a "passive revolution". According to Modonesi himself (2017b), "Gramsci maintained that [the class profile of passive revolution] originated at the initiative of the ruling classes and ... this characteristic did not correspond to the Latin American cases." His attempt to dilute this concept, whether because the bourgeois sectors termporarily associated themselves with progressive governments or because they were favored by those governments' policies, modifies the concept and sterilizes it. In the Brazilian case, the right-wing counteroffensive launched since 2014 is proof of the progressive content of the experience and the bourgeois character of the opposition it suffered in its decisive moments.

As for postcapitalism, which is certainly not the case in Brazil or Argentina, we can recall cases in which an attempt to overcome peripheral capitalism was based on the notion of twenty-first-century socialism (in Venezuela) or some modality of "living well" (in Bolivia and Ecuador). The evaluation of these experiments in terms of that they actually did does not indicate effective efforts to go beyond the social relations of capitalist production or liberal democracy.

Finally, it is important to mention the meaning of leadership, charismatic and deeply popular as Lula's was, in the scenario of progressive governments. Descriptions of the relationship of these leaderships to the impoverished sectors of society identify so-called populism as a democratic and authoritarian anomaly, fundamentally a threat to the institutional order or, in its ambiguity, a betrayal of the "program of the revolution". From our perspective, the emergence of leaders with this profile in the Latin American left represents precisely the opposite – a progressive expression of unsatisfied demands found in the figure of the charismatic leader, a catalyst for the construction of a popular identity in the midst of preexisting social conflict. According to Laclau (2013), populism is not an ideology but a political construction that may assume ideological forms from right to left, as is the case here. It is no wonder that, in contrast to leaders of this type, more and more assert the need for technocratic governments in accordance with the dictates of an institutionality built for the financial market.

Therefore, in the light of the history of the PT governments and the comparison with the experiments of neighboring countries, it seems to us more prudent to view them as part of a long war of position on the political terrain between democracy and capital in our continent, which has shown little progress since the reclaiming, now by progressive forces, of the banners abandoned in the 1980s by the Latin American bourgeoisie.

7   Conclusion

The characterization of the PT experiment as low-conflict progressivism aims to capture the dynamics of the Lula government in 2003 and record its limitations. The PT's victory in 2002 was a result of criticism of Cardoso's neoliberal government (1995–2002) and the recognition of the PT as the main political force that opposed him over the years.

Lula's tactic, carried out on the periphery of capitalism, of implementing policies for the benefit of popular sectors, national sovereignty, and regional integration without prejudice to bourgeois economic interests was quickly confronted by U.S. imperialism. This became clear when Brazil, with the support of all of Mercosur and Venezuela, took up the rejection of the Free Trade Area of the Americas, negotiated since the mid-1990s as the U.S. priority hegemonic project for the region, at the Summit of the Americas in Mar del Plata, Argentina, in November 2005. The worldwide crisis of capitalism in 2008 and its repercussions throughout the world system over the following years narrowed the margins of operation of this tactic both within the country and in Brazil's relationship with the world market. The first term of President Dilma (2011–2014) was the scene of an increasingly intense dispute between big capital and the progressive government led by the PT.

There were glimpses of answers from the Dilma government, as in the speech that the president made on May 1, 2012, and the platform that responded to the mass demonstrations of June 2013 (which, however, was quickly blocked by its conservative allies), and the election campaign that gave her the fourth consecutive PT victory in October 2014 was in programmatic terms the party's most radical since 1989. Were these announcements of the passage from the slow war of position to embryonic forms of a war of maneuver? In fact, this seems to have been the reading given it by the right, given the intensity of the counteroffensive unleashed to overthrow the government from the day after the 2014 PT electoral victory. However, surprisingly, in programmatic terms the second Dilma government looked like an attempt to return to the 2003 tactic, now with the appointment as finance minister of an extreme neoliberal to implement a recessionary fiscal adjustment program. This did not soothe the forces of the right-wing coup but diffused the ability to resist of the popular sectors, since it was read as if the government had taken over the program that the Dilma candidacy had just defeated at the polls.

The path to the coup was open, with a powerful regrouping of conservative forces that undercut the alliances the PT had made with center-right parties to win the 2014 election and achieve governability in Congress. Attempts to correct course in 2016 were incomplete and late. The fall of the Dilma government occurred without great resistance on the part of the popular sectors, although there was at that time an unbroken confluence of left-wing forces around a common assessment of the conjuncture – that it was a reactionary coup that called for unified resistance that had not occurred since 2004, when the PT experienced the crisis and division that gave rise to the Socialism and Freedom Party.

In the midst of the backlash against the progressive governments, it is not yet clear that their cycle has ended. While the right-wing forces do not have a project with hegemonic capacity such as the neoliberalism they imposed in the 1990s, conservatism has gained space because of the economic or political difficulties the progressive governments encountered. It has expanded in a vacuum, not because it has a better program to offer Brazil and Latin America. Faced with this dilemma, the challenge for the left is not simple. In order for a new batch of electoral victories to have strategic meaning, it is necessary to overcome the impasse of the phase that has just ended. In this connection, an appreciation of the difficulties, advances, and defeats of progressivism is crucial, but it seems to us that the best method is not an abstract assessment, one that relegates history to the background or imagines that the best way of evaluating the construction of an emancipatory politics is in terms of variations on an ideal type, whether developmentalism, socialism, or neoliberalism. We have preferred in this chapter to try to construct a picture of the PT experience that arrives at different conclusions from the normative traditions, which, with their grand narratives, find comfort in denouncing the deviations and inadequacies of the experiments of the left in the government but may shed little light on the unfolding of the concrete political struggle. We have situated the PT governments historically in a broad spectrum of disputes between autonomous and democratic development a hierarchical economic order led by the United States.

References

Árabe, C.H. (1998). *Desenvolvimento nacional e poder político: o projeto do Partido dos Trabalhadores em um período de crise*. Master's thesis, Universidade de Campinas.

http://repositorio.unicamp.br/jspui/bitstream/REPOSIP/279229/1/Arabe_
CarlosHenriqueGoulart_M.pdf (accessed August 20, 2017).

Borón, A. (2017). Una reflexión sobre el progresismo latinoamericano. In: Gerardo
Szalkowicz and Pablo Solanas (eds.), *América latina: Huellas y retos del ciclo progresista*. Buenos Aires: Ed. Sudestada.

Duménil, G., and Dominique, L. (2017). A propósito da grande bifurcação. para acabar
com o neoliberalismo. Interview with Bruno Tiel. *Revista Democracia Socialista*, no.
5. http://democraciasocialista.org.br/wp-content/uploads/2017/06/revista5_web2.
pdf (accessed August 20, 2017).

Guerra, A., et al. (2017). *Brasil 2016: Recessão e golpe*. São Paulo: Fundação Perseu
Abramo. https://fpabramo.org.br/publicacoes/wp-content/uploads/sites/5/2017/
05/Recessao-Golpe-web.pdf (accessed September 6, 2017).

Friedmann, G.C., and Puty, C.C.B. (2020). Sailing against the wind. The rise and crisis
of a low-conflict progressivism. *Latin American Perspectives* 47(1) (January): 83–99.

IBGE. (2019). Síntese dos Indicadores Sociais. https://www.ibge.gov.br/estatisticas/sociais/protecao-social/9221-sintese-de-indicadores-sociais.html?edicao=25875&t=sobre (accessed December 13, 2020).

Laclau, E. (2013). *A razão populista*. São Paulo: Ed. Três Estrelas.

Maringoni, Gilberto, Giorgio Romano Schutte, and Gonzalo Berron (eds.). (2014).
2003–2013: Uma nova política externa. Tubarão, Santa Catarina: Ed. Copiart.

Maringoni, Gilberto, and Juliano Medeiros (eds.). (2017). *Cinco mil dias: O Brasil na era
do lulismo*. São Paulo: Boitempo/Fundação Lauro Campos.

Marquetti, A., Hoff, C., and Miebach, A. (2017). Profitability and distribution: the origin of the Brazilian political crisis. https://www.researchgate.net/publication/
316583351_Profitability_and_Distribution_the_origin_of_the_Brazilian_political_
crisis (accessed August 20, 2017).

Ministério do Desenvolvimento Social. (2015). Um país menos desigual: pobreza
extrema cai a 2,8% da população. http://www.brasil.gov.br/economia-e-emprego/
2015/11/um-pais-menos-desigual-pobreza-extrema-cai-a-2-8-da-populacao
(accessed September 8, 2017).

Modonesi, M. (2017a). Conversando sobre revoluções passivas. November 24. https://
desinformemonos.org/conversando-revoluciones-pasivas/ (accessed June 1, 2018).

Modonesi, M. (2017b). Revoluções passivas na América Latina. Paper presented at the
International Antonio Gramsci Colloquium, Universidade de Campinas, August.
http://outubrorevista.com.br/revolucoes-passivas-na-america-latina/ (accessed
June 1, 2018).

Padula, R., and Fiori, J.L. (2016). Brasil: geopolítica e abertura para o Pacífico. *Revista de
Economia Política* 36: 536–556.

PT (Partido dos Trabalhadores). (1998). *Resoluções de encontros e congressos, Partido
dos Trabalhadores 1979–1998*. São Paulo: Fundação Perseu Abramo.

Pomar, V. (ed.). (2017). *Brasil: Uma política externa altiva e ativa*. São Paulo: Fundação Perseu Abramo.

Rabelo, R., and Monteiro, A.A. (eds.). (2017). *Governos Lula e Dilma: O ciclo golpeado*. São Paulo: Anita Garibaldi.

Rocca, C.A., and Santos Jr., L.M. (2015). Redução da taxa de poupança e as empresas não financeiras, 2010–2014. IBMEC: Nota CMEC 01/2015. http://ibmec.org.br/instituto/wp-content/uploads/2014/10/NOTA-CEMEC-01-2015-.pdf (accessed September 8, 2017).

Sader, E. (2007). A América Latina pós neoliberal. Interview by Ricardo Azevedo. *Revista Teoria e Debate*, no. 74. http://csbh.fpabramo.org.br/o-que-fazemos/editora/teoria-e-debate/edicoes-anteriores/entrevista-emir-sader-america-latina-pos-ne (accessed September 12, 2019).

Singer, A. (2012). *Os sentidos do lulismo: Reforma gradual e pacto conservador*. São Paulo: Companhia das Letras.

Singer, A. (2017). A ideia do lulismo. In: Gilberto Maringoni and Josué Medeiros (eds.), *Cinco mil dias: O Brasil na era do lulismo*. São Paulo: Boitempo/Fundação Lauro Campos.

Svampa, M. (2017). Crítica a los progresismos realmente existentes. In: Gerardo Szalkowicz, and Pablo Solanas (eds.), *América latina: Huellas y retos del ciclo progresista*. Buenos Aires: Ed. Sudestada.

CHAPTER 6

The Growth Model of the PT Governments

A Furtadian View of the Limits of Recent Brazilian Development

Pedro Rossi, Guilherme Mello and Pedro Paulo Zahluth Bastos

1   Introduction[1]

The Partido dos Trabalhadores (Workers' Party – PT) government cycle ended dramatically, with a sharp contraction in economic activity in 2015 and 2016 after a few years of slowdown. In the context of political and institutional crisis, interpretations of the slowdown and the economic crisis are still affected by the lack of historical distance and by a fierce political dispute over the economic narrative. Although reflecting diverse theoretical positions, these interpretations focus mainly on possible errors in the conduct of economic policy.

Orthodox interpretations attribute the economic failure to the excesses of state interventionism and heterodox macroeconomic policies. In this interpretation, economic policy underwent an inflection of its previous orienting axis, the so-called macroeconomic tripod, with the adoption of policies aimed at promoting the growth of domestic demand. This new way of conducting economic policy, the "new economic matrix", was incompatible with the rules that had guided the traditional tripod (Barbosa 2015; Mesquita 2014).[2] The resumption of the old management of the so-called tripod that took place after 2015 (along with strong fiscal adjustment) is defended by the adherents of this school as a way of bringing inflation toward the center of the target and thus

---

1 An earlier version of the arguments in this chapter appeared in Rossi, Mello and Bastos, 2020. Luis Fierro is a translator living in the Miami area.

2 "The NME [new economic matrix] was characterized by an expansionary fiscal policy, the abandonment by the Central Bank of the protocol of the inflation-targeting regime setting low interest rates incompatible with the inflation target, the expansion of credit by the state banks, and the systematic intervention of the Central Bank (Bacen) in the foreign exchange market, leaving aside the flexible exchange system. In addition, price controls on petroleum products were introduced, and with the renewal of electric power concession contracts, there was an interest in reducing electricity tariffs" (Barbosa 2015: 53).

regaining the confidence and productivity growth undermined by the adoption of interventionist policies.[3]

In the heterodox camp, some interpretations identify the neoliberal management of the instruments of macroeconomic policy as a determinant of deceleration and economic recession. Bresser-Pereira (2016) points to the overvaluation of the Brazilian currency as a central element of the deterioration of the Brazilian structure of production and the consequent economic deceleration.[4] For Serrano and Summa (2012; 2015), the conservative management of the Dilma government's fiscal policy had recessive effects and became the main cause of the subsequent deceleration, since a set of investments scheduled before the imposition of this "brake" on the economy was disarticulated.[5] Others emphasize the failure of a set of economic policies of the first Dilma government aimed at stimulating aggregate supply in response to the structural deterioration of the Brazilian industrial complex and political pressure from business (Rossi and Biancarelli 2015).

In addition to the macroeconomic policies highlighted in most of these interpretations, this chapter presents an explanation for the economic slowdown centered on structural aspects of the Brazilian economy, showing that the Brazilian crisis was a reflection of contradictions of the growth model beyond macroeconomic management and the ambiguity of its hybrid developmentalist/neoliberal orientation. For this analysis, we make use of the structuralist development literature, particularly the work of Celso Furtado, to show how, under the PT governments, the Brazilian economy underwent a process of modernization and massification of consumption patterns without, however, modernizing the structure of production to the point of sustaining the development process and overcoming the structural obstacles typical of underdevelopment.

This work is divided into three sections. The first discusses aspects of Celso Furtado's view of underdevelopment that contribute to the understanding of recent Brazilian development. Based on the Furtadian approach and using

---

3 "One possible conjecture is that the huge public sector interventionism that began in the most extreme form in 2009 greatly reduced incremental capital productivity, probably because of poor resource allocation" (Barbosa and Pessoa 2014: 4).

4 "The main cause of the failure of the social developmental period was not high public deficits (the government missed that point only in 2013 and 2014) but the appreciated currency in the long run – an equally populist policy. The appreciation of the real was brutal during the Lula administration and made the Dilma government infeasible" (Bresser-Pereira 2016).

5 "Analysis of the data on the Brazilian economy shows that internal macroeconomic policy, both monetary and fiscal, was responsible for a good part of the sharp deceleration of product growth in Brazil as of 2011" (Serrano and Summa 2012: 199–200).

illustrative literature and statistics, the second section describes the model of growth of the PT governments – the stimulus to the so-called mass consumption market and its impact on the demand structure, the structure of production, and the labor market. The third section highlights the contradictions and limitations of the model, whose viability stemmed from the relaxation of external constraints and which was accompanied by increasing denationalization of the structure of production. Finally, we summarize the main arguments of the text.

2   Celso Furtado and Underdevelopment

Celso Furtado's greatest scientific contribution was probably incorporating the distinction between development and underdevelopment into the center-periphery model proposed by Raúl Prebisch and providing a broader and more comprehensive historical perspective to the analysis of Latin American structuralism (Furtado 1961). For Furtado, underdevelopment was not a stage through which countries moved toward a final stage of development that mimicked the economic structure of the central countries, but a structural situation characterized by the permanence of social heterogeneity, a restricted and unequal consumer market, and the prevalence of informality and underemployment in the labor market.

According to Oliveira (1972) and Bielschowsky (2006), Furtado revived the discussion of the work of Arthur Lewis (1954)[6] and introduced into the structuralist framework discussion of the difficulty that modern urban sectors face in absorbing the underemployed labor force of the subsistence sector. In his classic *Development and Underdevelopment*, Furtado (1961) argued that underdeveloped countries were not "developing", as Lewis assumed, because of the effects of importing patterns of production and consumption that were not suited to their "factor endowment": (1) technology that was intensive in capital and scale imported from the central and developed countries, which even when it was feasible saved on the abundant resource by not employing

---

6   For Lewis, development was guaranteed because the technologies mimicked would increase labor productivity without raising wages in the modern sector to a much higher level than that of the subsistence sector. The extraordinary profits earned by modern entrepreneurs under these circumstances would be reinvested in rapid capital accumulation until structural dualism was eliminated through the absorption of subsistence workers into the modern sector. For Lewis, simply raising real wages could delay development by stimulating consumption by workers and reducing capitalists' saving and investment.

enough workers, and (2) the adoption by an economic elite of foreign consumption patterns that allocated resources to superfluous imports and wasted
the resources needed to address supply bottlenecks. This income concentration limited markets and kept capacity in the modern sector idle, aborting new
investment and generating a tendency toward stagnation (Furtado 1966).

The resumption of Brazilian growth in the "economic miracle" of the 1970's
and a set of criticisms from Keynesian and Marxist authors that questioned his
adoption of neoclassical concepts led Furtado to deepen his critical analysis
of underdevelopment, leading to a new phase of his work[7] in which the key
pair was now development and modernization. While the developed countries
enjoyed technological autonomy to change their patterns of production and
consumption, the underdeveloped imitated the most superficial aspects – the
consumption patterns of minorities imitating lifestyles without mastering the
techniques for their production, thus reproducing the country's technological dependency (Furtado 1968; 1972; 1974). According to Furtado (1992), one
of the main causes of underdevelopment was the modernization of patterns
of consumption restricted to a richer population without technological modernization. In other words, assimilation of the technical progress generated in
the developed centers took place on the demand side of final consumer goods,
leading to a structural conformation that limited growth and, more important,
blocked the transition from growth to development.

Articulating the structure of demand and the structure of production,
Furtado argued that the concentration of income and the narrowness of the
domestic consumption market limited the scale of companies and the development of the production structure. This limitation tended to perpetuate itself
by generating a poor income distribution and the coexistence of modern sectors of the economy with sectors of low productivity that harbored underemployment and informality. Furtado also combined a critique of modernization
with an analysis of the tendency toward external bottlenecks, arguing that the
divergence between the modernization of consumption and production technology led to an imbalance since, as was the case in the period of external-
oriented growth in the peripheral countries, the income elasticity of exports
was less than that of imports. In other words, the partial modernization of

---

7 Oliveira (1972) and Tavares and Serra (2000 [1970]) criticize Furtado's thesis that the poor
   structural distribution of income generates a tendency toward stagnation of economic
   growth. They argue that capitalist accumulation can occur in spite of a limited consumer
   market and a large marginalized population in a concentrating and exclusionary kind of capitalist development.

structures of production did not eliminate the balance-of-payments crises of peripheral and industrialized countries.

At the same time, a situation of an abundance of foreign exchange reserves was not necessarily conducive to development. It is true that proper planning of the use of foreign exchange reserves and the growth of exports could facilitate the overcoming of productive bottlenecks by allowing the import of capital goods and inputs required by deepening import substitution itself. In the absence of adequate planning, however, export growth could generate currency appreciation and further stimulate the import of consumer goods, disrupting the modernization of production and, even more so, development. This was the central message of Furtado's (2008) studies of the Venezuelan economy: unless the modernization of consumption was controlled and the use of foreign exchange reserves planned, underdevelopment with an abundance of foreign exchange reserves was possible and even probable.

In the late 1970s, Furtado began to address the "new dependency" represented by the control over the production system of foreign affiliates and, to some extent, the cultural system of underdeveloped countries.[8] Given the "internalization of dependency", subsidiaries broke the connection between industrialization and national autonomy in underdeveloped countries: on the periphery, industrialization with dependency was the most likely pair. Under these circumstances, external constraints assumed financial characteristics through the transfer of profits, dividends, royalties, and interests abroad. The new dependency accentuated the tendency toward external disequilibrium unless two vectors stimulated by the foreign affiliates – the modernization of consumption and the accumulation of foreign debt – were controlled by national planning and compensated for by the diversification of exports.

In short, more than access to the modern technology typical of a "developed" economy, overcoming underdevelopment required identifying the purposes of development democratically and autonomously.[9] In contrast to the

---

8 In the 1970s, Furtado pioneered a critique of the neoclassical emphasis on the accumulation of "human capital" and the emphasis of the new institutional economy on education as a panacea for underdevelopment. Such arguments were widely employed in Brazil to legitimize the worsening income distribution under the military dictatorship and received a torrent of Keynesian, institutionalist, and Marxist critiques (Barone, Bastos, and Mattos 2017).

9 For Furtado (1978; 1984), a country was not autonomous that did not determine the objectives of its technical-productive development and its educational and scientific efforts but simply sought to adapt to the objectives determined by others. Appropriate control of the "instrumental reason" inherent in technologies originating in the developed countries – control that was difficult in itself – did not mean autonomy unless "substantive reason" were determined democratically rather than subject to the demands of the global corporations, including the diffusion and stimulation of private consumption aspirations.

omniscient technocrat, Furtado advocated democratically oriented development, in opposition to the global corporations, in the name of a domestically owned capitalism. Beyond the mere reduction of inequality of access to modern consumer goods, the development of technologies to meet basic needs, eliminate poverty, increase leisure time, and reduce dependency was at the heart of his concerns. Instead of attempting to generalize the style of imported consumption previously limited to the local elites and the middle classes, the objective should be universalizing the benefits of modern technology by expanding the supply of public goods and services to the point of changing the balance of private consumption. Without such a transformative aspiration, the various dimensions of underdevelopment would be reaffirmed as long-lasting structures beyond favorable conjunctures.

Furtado's approach can serve as a tool for analyzing the growth model adopted by the PT governments, which achieved structural changes on the demand side and in the labor market through the expansion of the consumer market and the modernization of consumption patterns of a large part of the population by incorporating a large contingent of workers into the formal labor market but failed to overcome the barriers to underdevelopment.

3   The Growth Model of the PT Governments

3.1   *The Mass Consumption Market*

According to Bielschowsky (2014) and Bastos (2012), the constitution of a mass consumer market was a deliberate economic strategy of the PT governments made explicit in the party's platform in 2002 and the Lula government's multiannual plans. The formation of this mass consumer market was based on two pillars: the distribution of income, promoted by monetary transfer policies and an increase in wages, and the stimulus to bank inclusion and credit for families.[10] Once established, this market was expected to stimulate the domestic structure of production to meet the expanding demand and, through

---

10   In practice, none of these policies directly opposes the core of neoliberal thinking. The Family Grant program, created by the first Lula administration, is fundamentally a focused social policy for combating poverty in line with the neoliberal notion of poverty reduction through conditional income transfers (Saad-Filho 2016). Payroll-deductible credit policies, which help broaden concessions and cheapen the credit supply, also find shelter in a neoliberal view of the economy as combating "market failures" derived from an asymmetry of information, in this case between borrowers and lenders, thus reducing the risk of default and, consequently, the final cost of credit. Besides, the set of universal social and welfare policies established in the 1988 Constitution saw their financing bases

economies of scale in domestic companies, to increase productivity and economic growth. As it turned out, the strategy of developing a mass consumer
market was not just on paper; there was political intentionality in (1) the policy of raising the minimum wage, which achieved real growth of 70 percent
throughout the PT governments and increased income from labor and contributed to the reduction of inequality;[11] (2) income transfer policies, both the
increase in the value of social security and social security benefits (linked to
a large extent to the minimum wage) and the creation of transfer programs
such as the Family Grants (the Bolsa Família);[12] (3) policies to facilitate credit
to families and companies, such as payroll loans, housing loans, and credit
from public banks, in particular after the 2008 crisis;[13] and (4) the increase of
public expenditures in the social area from 21.9 percent of the GDP in 2005 to
25.2 percent in 2010, which had a large multiplier effect and contributed to the
generation of formal and informal jobs (Castro 2012).

   Although it did not necessarily represent a break with neoliberalism, the
emphasis on the creation of a mass consumer market, stimulated by state
action, with a significant emphasis on the increase in the minimum wage
and social security transfers pointed to a new economic and political setup.
Economically, the state and workers' expenditures played a central role in the
dynamics of the new growth model. Politically, the government adopted a new
stance in its relationship with the power bloc. This new arrangement of forces,
called the "neodevelopmentalist" front by Boito and Saad-Filho (2016), may
have been responsible for making it possible to introduce measures rejected
by important portions of the bourgeoisie and the middle class such as the
increase in the minimum wage and in public participation in the decisions of

---

eroded by policy decisions on tax exemptions and the financialization of various public
services (Lavinas 2017).

11   According to Hoffmann (2013), because it represents the greater part of declared income,
salary improvement was the most important factor (40 percent) in explaining the reduction of the Gini index in the period.

12   The Family Grant program included 14 million families in 2012, according to the Ministry
of Social Development and Hunger Relief and contributed 16 percent of the improvement
in the Gini index between 2001 and 2011 (Hoffmann 2013), even though it represented less
of 1 percent of total declared income.

13   These measures, together with the increase in income and employment, accounted for
an increase in the credit-to-GDP ratio from 23.8 percent in 2003 to 55.8 percent in 2014
and from 32 percent of the total credit balance in 2008 to 44 percent in 2013, in particular
payroll loans (growth of 128.9 percent between January 2008 and December 2013) and
real estate credit (growth of 474.8 percent). (DIEESE 2014).

allocation of investment through the public banks and the state companies and through public purchases and the requirement of national content.[14]

3.2   Changes in Demand and the Labor Market

The impact of these policies was reflected in the reduction of poverty and income inequality as measured by the Gini index, which fell from 0.593 to 0.526 between 2001 and 2012.[15] According to Castro (2012), the proportion of the population living on less than half a minimum wage per month went from 46.6 percent in 2003 to 29.2 percent in 2009. According to Quadros (2015), between 2002 and 2013 there was a significant decrease in the number of poor people, from 45 million to 16 million, with a significant increase in the middle-income levels (the lower middle class, for example, went from 54 million in 2002 to 89 million in 2013). In addition to the income increase, the credit market also included a significant portion of the population. Loans to individuals increased at high rates between 2008 and 2013, increasing from R$712 million to R$1.46 billion in 2013 (DIEESE 2014).

With the increase in income and credit, the consumption of durable goods jumped, causing the proportion of the population with access to a set of durable goods (telephone, television, stove, refrigerator, radio, and washing machine) to increase from 28.2 percent in 2003 to 44.4 percent in 2012 (IPEA 2013). A broad modernization of the consumption pattern of the Brazilian population had a major impact on the labor market, in which there was a substantial reduction of underemployment – one of the classic characteristics of underdevelopment pointed out by Furtado. There was also a significant decline in the unemployment rate and an increase in formal employment.

---

14   At the same time, Loureiro and Saad-Filho (2017) show the limits of the kind of pragmatic political alliance necessary to put into practice the strategy of "conciliation" promoted by the PT governments, pointing to their inability to deal with the problems arising from the external scenario and the cooling of national economic growth and preventing the approval of deeper reforms of Brazilian capitalism.

15   It is important to note, however, that recent studies based on income tax declarations tend to minimize the distribution of income in the period, confirming an improvement in the distribution of income from labor (between the poor and the well-to-do salaried worker) but pointing to a certain stability in the distribution of total income as a result of capital income (Medeiros, Souza, and Castro 2015). Likewise, Dedecca (2014) shows that the proportion of the total income of the richest 1 percent remained unchanged, with redistribution only among the intermediate strata. This improvement in social stratification did not mean a better distribution of wealth, according to Carvalho and Rugitsky (2015), indicating the need for further study on the subject. It is noteworthy that the massive investments in the automotive sector are not incorporated in this historical series because they occurred after 2011.

The unemployment rate fell from 12 percent in 2002 to close to 5 percent in 2014 (IBGE, several years) which, together with the growth of formal employment (which grew by 10 percentage points, reaching 63 percent of the workforce) and the increase in average real wages (17 percent), helped explain the improvement in social indicators (Komatsu and Menezes Filho 2015). However, this reconfiguration of the labor market mainly benefited employment in the services sector, which rose 41.5 percent between 2004 and 2013, representing 79.6 percent of the nonagricultural jobs created (Baltar and Leone 2015). Between 2001 and 2008, growth in investment and industrial production was accompanied by significant growth in industrial employment, 2,747,000 new employees, but from the peak in 2008 until 2014 the manufacturing industry lost 1,083,000 (IBGE, PNAD, several years).

3.3   Changes in the Structure of Production

The profound changes in the structure of demand and the labor market were accompanied by supply-side changes, but the latter did not help to overcome the structural obstacles to development. According to Bielschowsky, Squeff, and Vasconcelos (2014), investment, measured by gross fixed capital formation, in sectors linked to the mass consumer market showed a sharp increase in the years of the strongest expansion of the Brazilian economy (2005–2008), with an average expansion of 13.2 percent per year, higher than the average aggregate investment growth rate (12.4 percent per year). However, this expansion occurred mainly in the services sector (14.4 percent per year) and in the nondurable consumer sector (12.9 percent per year), while investment in the durable consumer goods sector was close to zero (−0.1 percent per year).[16] According to Bielschowsky and colleagues, domestic production covered only 50.6 percent of the variation in consumer demand for durable goods during the period 2006–2008, 36.1 percent of which was attended by increased imports and 13.3 percent due to a drop in exports. In these same industrial sectors, the import penetration rate increased from 8.1 percent in 2005 to 17.3 percent in 2008, and the export ratio from 12.8 percent to 9.3 percent. Thus, concerning

---

16   For Santos et al. (2015: 6), imports were scantly influenced by changes in the exchange rate because they were concentrated in goods of high technological content and corresponded to productive chains that were not even effectively installed at the national level, such as fine chemicals, microchips, and semiconductors or products embedded in global value chains whose imports and exports depended primarily on the strategies of transnational corporations and on the way in which domestic firms were embedded in these chains.

the durable goods sector, mass consumption did not generate the expected dynamism in the supply of domestic products.

There are indications that the structure of production of the manufacturing industry and the ownership structure dominated by global corporations were determinants of the export ratio and the import penetration rates, with some degree of independence from the exchange rate and commodities prices.[17] While such leakage of domestic demand for imports was already important in the period in which Furtado had criticized Brazil's "new dependency", it was aggravated by the integration of the Brazilian industry into global production chains from the 1990s on. Especially in the industrial sectors with more foreign ownership, the result of the trade opening was the loss of density of the structure of production as the subsidiaries began to import more capital goods, parts, and components for assembly operations to meet the final demand (Sarti and Laplane 2003). Given this structure, when the mass market drove domestic demand in the 2000s, there was a substantial increase in the import penetration rates of both final goods and inputs and capital goods along the production chains. According to Morceiro (2016), the demand generated by the expansion of the mass market was mainly focused on high- and medium-technology goods controlled by global corporations – goods that typically materialize patented technological innovations and the demand for which has great income elasticity. Import penetration rates increased because the subsidiaries did not internalize the production technology.[18]

---

17   "From 2004 to 2013, Brazilian industrial production grew 33.9 percent, while total demand grew 55.3 percent. ... About 40 percent of the growth in demand leaked abroad in the form of imports. In some sectors, the demand spill was even more intense. ... Between 2003 and 2013, the import penetration rate doubled, increasing from 13.5 to 26.8 percent" (Morceiro 2016: 9–14). On the contemporary role of foreign affiliates in Brazilian technological dependence, see Fontaine and Cassiolato (2013).

18   In Sarti's (2017) words, "Although Brazil continues to rank among the ten largest global industries, its share of global MAV [manufacturing value added] has declined from 3.6 percent to 2.3 percent in the past two decades. ... According to CNI [National Confederation of Industry] data, the import penetration rate, given the proportion of imports in apparent consumption, increased from 14.1 percent to 21.7 percent between 2003 and 2015. The imported industrial input (CII) coefficient, the proportion of imported inputs in total inputs, jumped from 19.7 percent to 28.8 percent in the same period. The coefficient of exports (CX) was relatively stagnant, rising from 12.7 percent in 2003 to 14.3 percent in 2014. ... The increase in acquisitions and mergers in Brazil after the onset of the international crisis in 2008 was a consequence of cross-border (CB) operations, involving foreign capital companies and national capital companies ... primarily those in which foreign capital companies acquired national companies in Brazil." On the change in the geographical pattern of Brazilian industrial trade after the 2008 crisis, see Bastos and Hiratuka (2017).

This problem was aggravated by the global crisis of 2007–2009, with a decline of demand in the developed countries and an advance of Chinese exports that dislocated Brazilian products both in the local market and in Latin America. As a result, demand for industrial products continued to grow in Brazil after 2009, but industrial production stagnated (Bastos 2015; Bastos and Hiratuka 2017). The deterioration of the Brazilian industrial sector after 2009 occurred despite industrial policies, public purchases, and investment by state-owned companies such as Petrobras and credit policies led by BNDES. These policies led to gains in competitiveness and a reduction in the import penetration rate in sectors such as the petroleum and the automobile industry, but they coincided with the aforementioned general leakage of demand. Despite the specific problems of these policies (which are beyond the scope of this chapter), according to Rossi and Rocha (2016), there was also a lack of coherence in the interaction between industrial policies and macroeconomic policy.[19] This is because the pro-industry agenda was hampered by macroeconomic policies that posed challenges to the sector, such as exchange-rate and interest-rate volatility, currency appreciation (until 2011), and a structurally elevated interest rate compared with international standards. Thus, these policies were unable to protect the industrial sector in the context of the reduction of demand from the central countries and the increase in exports from the central countries and China.

The denationalization of the industrial structure also advanced, deepening the process of regressive specialization of the production and export agenda initiated in the 1990s and the export of industrial products of low technological intensity and dependence on imports of goods of medium and high technological intensity. According to Sarti (2017), there was a marked decline in the proportion of Brazilian manufacturing value added in global manufacturing value-added and the increase of the import penetration rate in final demand and inputs since the Brazilian industry specialized in the assembly of final goods. This resulted from the decisions of the large corporations that controlled the regional and global value chains and production networks that dominated the leading sectors of the Brazilian industry and expanded their control after 2008.

---

19 "Even the attempt to recreate some industrial policies in recent years lacks coherence since institutions have not been reestablished to define a long-term development path for domestic manufacturing with protection and incentive policies. Given the lack of a proper policy framework, two trends may continue unabated: large enterprises will prevail over small and medium-sized companies, and the ownership of Brazilian enterprises may continue to be transferred to foreign economic groups" (Rossi and Rocha 2016: 195).

Therefore, the growth cycle of the Lula governments was characterized by the broad modernization of the demand structure without equivalent modernization in the structure of production capable of supplying or even directing the demand. As is pointed out by Nogueira, Infante, and Mussi (2014), analysis of the productivity of various sectors of activity between 2000 and 2009 shows that the structure of production remained practically as heterogeneous as, historically, it had always been.

4   Contradictions and Limitations of the Model

4.1   *Relaxation of External Constraints*
As is highlighted by Medeiros (2015), the Brazilian growth cycle was made possible by the relaxation of external constraints due to the significant improvement in the terms of trade and the strong inflow of foreign capital as part of a global liquidity expansion before and after the crisis of 2008.[20] The improvement in the terms of trade played a dual and contradictory role. On the one hand, it contributed to the formation of the mass consumer market through the cheapening of industrial goods and the availability of foreign exchange for imports; on the other hand, it reinforced the reprimarization of exports. Between 2007 and 2010, the share of primary products jumped 10 percentage points, reaching 51 percent of exports (de Negri and Alvarenga 2011), while the composition of imports was relatively stable, with the proportion of industrial goods about 40 percent of imports in spite of the relative decline in the prices of industrial goods and the relative increase in numbers of imported industrial products (Santos et al. 2015; Cano 2012). Thus, there was no improvement in the composition of foreign trade that was considered central by Furtado (1971) and Pinto (1979); on the contrary, the asymmetry between imports and exports was reinforced.

One important contradiction of the model stands out: the cheapness of imported industrial goods and the productive surplus of the primary sector supported the mass consumption market but at the same time, contributed to the deterioration of the foreign trade agenda and the structure of production.

---

20   "In the past decade, the relaxation of external constraints due to the demand for commodities, the change in the terms of trade, and international liquidity enabled the country – and commodity-exporting countries in general – to grow and reduce poverty and income inequalities. ... With the increase of the minimum wage, income transfers, and credit expansion, there was a great massification of consumption patterns and strong penetration of imports" (Medeiros 2015: 168).

4.2   *Financial Opening and Macroeconomic Instability*

The movement of peripheral currencies against the liquidity cycle can be seen as a concomitant of underdevelopment, corresponding to the context of liberalization and financial openness. In contemporary capitalism, countries with peripheral currencies and broad financial openness are subject to a macroeconomic instability that is transmitted from the volatility of financial capital flows to key economic prices such as exchange and interest rates (de Conti, Biancarelli, and Rossi 2013). From this point of view, the PT governments did little to alter the reality of Brazil's financial openness, maintaining the preconditions of the neoliberal period except for a brief period during the first Rousseff government when it sought control measures to limit the currency appreciation driven by the excess liquidity typical of the post crisis period (Mello and Rossi 2017). In particular, the strong negative correlation between these currencies and commodities prices, which were also conditioned by the liquidity cycle, mitigated the inflationary impact of the fluctuation of these prices but reinforced the incorporation of these economies into the old division of labor. In other words, while the exchange rate absorbed commodities price shocks for the domestic economy, it also created increased uncertainty for the industrial entrepreneur, who had difficulty forming expectations about price, risk, and return.

In this context, the inflow of foreign capital stimulated by elevated interest rates in Brazil contributed to a strong appreciation of the R–US$ exchange rate,[21] which in turn contributed significantly to the operation of the mass consumer market by reducing the prices of tradable goods and alleviating the inflationary pressures arising from the redistributive process.[22] Concomitantly with the positive effects on the consumption cycle, the inflow of foreign capital through exchange-rate appreciation had effects on the industrial structure. Among them, the deconstruction of productive chains and the increase in the import penetration rate, which in the manufacturing industry, for example, increased from 10.2 percent in 2003 to 17.6 percent in 2014, and especially in industrial inputs, which went from 16.5 percent in 2003 to 25.8 percent in 2014 (CNI).

---

21   In reality, the currency appreciation cycles occur less because of capital flows and more because of speculation with foreign exchange derivatives, as shown by Rossi (2016).

22   Between 2004 and 2009, rising service prices pushed up the inflation index, but was offset by low tradable goods inflation. As shown by Summa (2014), the average in this period of food and industrialized inflation was respectively 4.9 and 3.9 percent, and was below the average IPCA (5.2 percent) and well below the inflation of services (6.5 percent).

Besides, the significant inflow of foreign capital allowed for greater absorption of imported products as well as affecting the structure of production. The increase in foreign direct investment in Brazil was especially significant, rising from US$108 billion in March 2003 to US$660 billion in March 2015 (BCB). While these investments propitiated technology transfers and modernization of the domestic structure of production, the increasing denationalization of the structure of production conditioned investment decisions to the global strategies of the multinationals. As is pointed out by Pinto (1971), an excessive inflow of foreign capital causes "foreignization" and technological dependency besides "the alienation of the decision centers".

5   Conclusion

This chapter has dealt with the growth model of the PT governments in terms of a structuralist reading following Celso Furtado. At the heart of this growth model was the mass consumer market driven by a set of economic policies. The dynamics of this model alleviated the typical characteristics of underdevelopment by modernizing the consumption patterns of a significant portion of the population and qualitatively improving the labor market by reducing unemployment and informality under conditions of relaxation of external constraints. However, the growth model was unable to modernize the structure of production to sustain demand-side transformations, increase employment in higher-productivity sectors, limit the control of foreign affiliates over the modernization of consumption patterns and the global distribution of the activities of the manufacturing industry, or reduce the structural vulnerability inherent in specialization in basic commodities exports. In other words, there was modernization and massification of consumption patterns without modernization of the structure of production to support development and overcome the structural obstacles characteristic of underdevelopment.

Also, the growth model was marked by inherent contradictions, since some elements that helped support the consumption cycle contributed to damaging the structure of production. The significant improvement in the terms of trade relaxed the external constraints and contributed to the currency appreciation, cheapening industrial goods and consolidating a broad consumer market. However, it also increased the fragility of the industrial sector with a great increase in imported inputs. Likewise, the strong inflow of foreign capital in the context of an expansion of global liquidity before and after the crisis of 2008 increased the capacity utilization of the economy but generated pressure for currency appreciation and denationalization of the domestic structure of production. Regarding this last aspect, it should be pointed out that the PT governments did not confront the vulnerability resulting from Brazil's financial openness with any structural measures.

Therefore, in addition to the errors in the conduct of economic policy throughout the PT period – in particular the continuation of certain neoliberal policies of the Cardoso government alongside developmentalist ones – the deceleration of the Brazilian economy must be understood in terms of the structural elements that constituted the formation of the consumer market and the production structure's difficulty in keeping pace with the changes in demand. Finally, to sustain a model of distributive growth in Brazil, it is necessary to consider the changes in production structure required to overcome the structural obstacles that conditioned Brazilian underdevelopment. According to Furtado, overcoming these obstacles depended on (1) more coherence between macroeconomic, industrial, and commercial policies, with greater control over the strategies of foreign subsidiaries; and (2) strategic planning of Brazilian development focused on providing public goods and services capable not only of boosting the economy, increasing its productivity, and generating skilled jobs but also of changing the balance between public and private consumption, mitigating the limitations imposed by imported consumption patterns.

References

Baltar, P., and Leone, E. (2015). O emprego assalariado nos anos 2000: mudanças de composição e de renda por idade e sexo. In: *Anais do XIV Encontro Nacional da ABET*. [ABET-Salvador].

Banco Central de Brasil (BCB). *Sistema de series temporais, setor externo, several years*. BCB: Brasília.

Barbosa, F. (2015). Crises econômicas e política de 2015: origens e consequências. *Revista Conjuntura Econômica* 69(9): 53.

Barbosa, F., and Pessoa, S. (2014). Desaceleração recente da economia. In: Centro de Debates de Políticas Públicas, *Sob a luz do sol, uma agenda para o Brasil*, 123–240. São Paulo: CDPP.

Barone, R.S., Bastos, P.P.Z., and Mattos, F.A.M. (2017). Capital humano ou capitalismo selvagem? Um balanço da controvérsia sobre distribuição de renda durante o 'Milagre' brasileiro. *Revista de Economia Contemporânea* 21(3): 1–25.

Bastos, P.P. (2012). A economia política do novo-desenvolvimentismo e do social desenvolvimentismo. *Economia e Sociedade* 21: 779–810.

Bastos, P.P. (2015). Austeridade permanente? a crise global do capitalismo neoliberal e as alternativas no Brasil. In: L.G. Belluzzo and P.P.Z. Bastos (eds.), *Austeridade para quem? Balanço e perspectivas do governo Dilma Rousseff.* São Paulo: Carta Maior/ Fundação Friedrich Ebert.

Bastos, P.P., and Hiratuka, C. (2017). *A política econômica externa do governo Dilma Rousseff: Comércio, cooperação e dependência.* Texto para Discussão 306.

Bielschowsky, R. (2006). Celso Furtado's contributions to structuralism and their relevance today. *CEPAL Review* 88: 7–14.

Bielschowsky, R. (2014). Estratégia de desenvolvimento e as três frentes de expansão no Brasil: um desenho conceitual. In: A. Calixtre, A. Biancarelli, and M.A. Cintra (eds.), *Presente e futuro do desenvolvimento brasileiro*, 195–225. Brasília: IPEA.

Bielschowsky, R., Squeff, G., and Vasconcelos, L. (2014). Evolução dos investimentos nas três frentes de expansão da economia brasileira na década de 2000. In A. Calixtre, A. Biancarelli, and M.A. Cintra (ed.), *Presente e futuro do desenvolvimento brasileiro*, 115–134. Brasilia: IPEA.

Boito, A., and Saad-Filho, A. (2016). State, state institutions, and political power in Brazil. *Latin American Perspectives* 43(2): 190–206. .

Bresser-Pereira, L. (2016). Onde foi que erramos? Quando e por que a economia saiu da rota. *Folha de S. Paulo*, March 27.

Cano, W. (2012). A desindustrialização no Brasil. *Economia e Sociedade* 21: 831–851.

Carvalho, L., and Rugitsky, F., (2015). *Growth and Distribution in Brazil the 21st Century: Revisiting the Wage-led versus Profit-led Debate.* Departamento de Economia da FEA-USP, Working Paper 2015-25.

Castro, J. (2012). Política social e desenvolvimento no Brasil. *Economia e Sociedade* 21: 1011–1042.

CNI (Confederação Nacional da Indústria). *Coeficientes de abertura comercial.* CNI: São Paulo. Available on the website: https://www.portaldaindustria.com.br/estatisticas/coeficientes-de-abertura-comercial/.

De Conti, B., Biancarelli, A., and Rossi, P. (2013). Currency hierarchy, liquidity preference and exchange rates: a Keynesian/Minskyan approach. Paper presented at the Congrès de l'Association Française d'Économie Politique, Bordeaux.

Dedecca, C. (2014). A queda da desigualdade de renda corrente e a participação do 1% de domicílios de maior renda, 2000–2010. *Revista de Economia Política* 34(2): 249–265.

de Negri, F., and Alvarenga, G. (2011). A primarização da pauta de exportações no Brasil: ainda um dilema. *Radar Tecnologia, Produção e Comercio Exterior*, no. 13: 7–14.

DIEESE (Departamento Intersindical de Estatística e Estudos Socioeconômicos). (2014). *A evolução do crédito na economia brasileira.* Nota Técnica 135.

Fontaine, P., and Cassiolato, J. (2013). O papel das empresas transnacionais no SNI num contexto de globalização financeira. Paper presented at the Conferência

Internacional LALICS 2013, "Sistemas nacionais de inovação e políticas de CTI para um desenvolvimento inclusivo e sustentável", Rio de Janeiro, November 11–12.

Furtado, C. (1961). *Desenvolvimento e subdesenvolvimento*. Rio de Janeiro: Fundo de Cultura.

Furtado, C. (1966). *Subdesenvolvimento e estagnação na América Latina*. Rio de Janeiro: Civilização Brasileira.

Furtado, C. (1968). *Um projeto para o Brasil*. Rio de Janeiro: Saga.

Furtado, C. (1971). *Teoria e política do desenvolvimento*. São Paulo: Nacional.

Furtado, C. (1972). *Análise do "modelo" brasileiro*. Rio de Janeiro: Civilização Brasileira.

Furtado, C. (1974). *O mito do desenvolvimento econômico*. Rio e Janeiro: Paz e Terra.

Furtado, C. (1978). Criatividade e dependência na civilização industrial. Rio de Janeiro: Paz e Terra.

Furtado, C. (1984). Cultura e desenvolvimento em época de crise. Rio de Janeiro: Paz e Terra.

Furtado, C. (1992). O subdesenvolvimento revisitado. *"Economia e Sociedade* 1(1): 1–167.

Furtado, C. (2008). *Ensaios sobre a Venezuela: Subdesenvolvimento com abundância de divisas*. Rio de Janeiro: Contraponto.

Hoffmann, R. (2013). Transferências de renda e desigualdade no Brasil (1995–2011). In: Tereza Campello and Marcelo Côrtes Neri (ed.), *Programa Bolsa Família: Uma década de inclusão e cidadania*, vol. 1, 207–226. Brasília: IPEA.

IBGE (Instituto Brasileiro de Geografia e Estatística). (2001–2015). Pesquisa Nacional de Amostra de Domicílios. Rio de Janeiro: IBGE. Available on the website https://www.ibge.gov.br/estatisticas/sociais/trabalho/9127-pesquisa-nacional-por-amostra-de-domicilios.html?=&t=o-que-e.

IBGE. (Several years). Pesquisa Mensal de Empregos (PME). Rio de Janeiro: IBGE. Available on the website: https://www.ibge.gov.br/estatisticas/sociais/trabalho/9180-pesquisa-mensal-de-emprego.html?=&t=o-que-e.

IPEA (Instituto de Pesquisa Econômica Aplicada). 2013. Duas décadas de desigualdade e pobreza no Brasil medidas pela PNAD/IBGE. *Comunicados do IPEA*, no. 159: 1–54.

Komatsu, B., and Menezes Filho, N. (2015). Salário-mínimo e desigualdade salarial: um estudo com densidades contrafactuais nas regiões metropolitanas brasileiras. *Revista Pesquisa e Planejamento Econômico* 45(3): 53–67.

Lavinas, L. (2017). *The Takeover of Social Policy by Financialization: The Brazilian Paradox*. London: Palgrave Macmillan.

Lewis, A. (1954). Economic development with unlimited supplies of labour. *Manchester School* 22(2): 139–191.

Loureiro, P.M., and Saad-Filho, A. (2017). The limits of pragmatism: the rise and fall of the Brazilian Workers' Party (2002–2016). *Latin American Perspectives* 46(1): 66–84.

Medeiros, C. (2015). *Inserção externa, crescimento e padrões de consumo na economia brasileira*. Brasília: IPEA.

Medeiros, M., Ferreira de Souza, P.H.G., and Castro, F.V. (2015). A estabilidade da desigualdade de renda no Brasil, 2006 a 2012: estimativa com dados do imposto de renda e pesquisas domiciliares. *Ciência e Saúde Coletiva* 20: 971–986.

Mello, G., and Rossi, P. (2017). *Do industrialismo à austeridade: A política macro dos governos Dilma*. Texto para Discussão 309.

Mesquita, M. (2014). A política econômica do governo Dilma: a volta ao experimentalismo. In: *Sob a luz do sol: Uma agenda para o Brasil*, 3–15. São Paulo: CDPP.

Morceiro, P.C. (2016). *Sectoral Demand Leakage and Competitiveness of the Brazilian Manufacturing Industry*. Department of Economics, FEA-USP, Working Paper 2016-12.

Nogueira, M., Infante, R., and Mussi, C. (2014). Produtividade do trabalho do trabalho e heterogeneidade. In: F. de Negri and L. Cavalcante (eds.), *Produtividade no Brasil: Desempenho e determinantes*, 337–372. Brasília: IPEA/ABDI.

Oliveira, Francisco. (2015[1972]). A economia brasileira: crítica à razão dualista. In: F. Oliveira, *Crítica à razão dualista: O ornitorrinco*, 19–80. São Paulo: Boitempo.

Pinto, A. (1979). Heterogeneidade estrutural e modelo de desenvolvimento recente. In: J. Serra (ed.), *América Latina: Ensaios de interpretação econômica* , 220–242. Rio de Janeiro: Paz e Terra.

Quadros, W. (2015). Paralisia econômica, retrocesso social e eleições. *Revista Plataforma de Política Social*, January 21: 4–17.

Rossi, P. (2016). *Taxa de câmbio e política cambial no Brasil: Teoria, institucionalidade, papel da arbitragem e da especulação*. Rio de Janeiro: Editora FGV.

Rossi, P., and Rocha, M. (2016). Industrialization and the growth model in Brazil: a historical overview. In: Rudolf Traub-Merz (ed.), *Economic Crisis and Industrial Policies: Policy Options for a Return to Growth in Russia*, 183–196. Moscow: ROSSPEN.

Rossi, P., Mello, G., Bastos, P.P.Z. (2020). The Growth Model of the PT Governments: A Furtadian View of the Limits of Recent Brazilian Development. *Latin American Perspectives* 47(1): 100–114.

Rossi, P., and Biancarelli, A. (2015). Do industrialismo ao financismo. *Revista Política Social e Desenvolvimento* (January 29): 14–17.

Saad-Filho, A. (2016). Social policy beyond neoliberalism: from conditional cash transfers to pro-poor growth. *Journal of Poverty Alleviation and International Development* 7(1): 67–94.

Santos, C., Cieplinski, A.G., Pimentel, D., and Bhering, G. (2015). *Por que a elasticidade-câmbio das importações é baixa no Brasil?* Texto para Discussão 2046.

Sarti, F., and Laplane, M. (2003). O investimento direto estrangeiro e a internacionalização da economia brasileira nos anos 90. In M. Laplane, L. Coutinho, and C. Hiratuka (eds.), *Internacionalização e desenvolvimento da indústria no Brasil*, 11–57. São Paulo and Campinas: UNESP/IE-UNICAMP.

Sarti, F. (2017). *Desnacionalização e desenvolvimento.* Revista Facto 11 (52). Abril/Maio/ Junho 2017. Access: http://www.abifina.org.br/revista_facto_materia.php?id=670.

Serrano, F., and Summa, R. (2012). A desaceleração rudimentar da economia brasileira desde 2011. *Oikos* 11(2): 166–202.

Serrano, F., and Summa, R. (2015). Aggregate demand and the slowdown of Brazilian economic growth from 2011–2014. *Center for Economic and Policy Research*, August.

Summa, R. (2014). *Uma nota sobre a relação entre salário-mínimo e inflação no Brasil a partir de um modelo de inflação de custo e conflito distributivo.* Texto para Discussão Instituto de Economia UFRJ 012.

Tavares, M.C., and Serra, J. (2000 [1970]). Além da estagnação: uma discussão sobre o estilo de desenvolvimento recente do Brasil. In: Bielschowsky, R. (org.), Cinquenta anos do pensamento da CEPAL, volume 2, 589–608. Rio de Janeiro: Editora Record.

CHAPTER 7

The Brazilian Crises: Profits, Distribution and Growth

Adalmir Antonio Marquetti, Cecilia Hoff and Alessandro Miebach

1 Introduction[1]

Neoliberalism is a phase of the capitalism originated from the crisis of the Golden Age. The declining profit rate in the middle 1960s drove a reaction of the capitalist class in order to restore the profitability. A series of institutional reforms favored the capital, particularly the finance capital. As these changes solidified, the financial sector became hegemonic, consolidating the basic tenets of neoliberalism. The reforms converted the market into the fundamental mechanism of resources allocation to raise the profit rate.

Neoliberalism succeeded in restoring profitability, however, it has its own contradictions. The financial sector profitability requires new spaces of unrestrained valorization in order to convert capital assets into other types of capital assets. This movement resulted in financial innovations and speculative bubbles in the developed and developing countries. Triggered by the defaults on the subprime mortgage loans, the financial crisis of 2008 reached rapidly the United States and the global financial system with enormous consequences to the productive sector. The 2008 crisis was the structural crisis of the neoliberal capitalism.

The structural crisis and the institutional framework changes of the world economy are fundamental for analyzing the Brazilian economic history. The international context gave the economic and ideological constraints and incentives for the Brazilian economic models: the developmentalism during the Golden Age from 1950 to 1980 and the neoliberal model from 1990 to 2002. After 2003, during the Workers' Party administration there was a combination of both models with a redistributive policy. The 2008 crisis impacted

---
1 An earlier version of the arguments in this chapter appeared in Marquetti et al. (2020). The authors are grateful for the comments of the referees and the editors of *Latin American Perspectives*. This study was partially financed by the Conselho Nacional de Desenvolvimento Científico e Tecnológico (CNPq), grant number 307310/2015-9.

the Brazilian economy with negative effects in the profit rate and economic growth.

The 1980s crisis opened the space for institutional reforms that gradually abandoned the import substitution model. In 1990, the first year of Fernando Collor's presidency, while maintaining some institutions from the developmentalism, Brazil adopted the neoliberal model (Amann and Baer 2002; Filgueiras 2006).

The renegotiation of the external debt made possible the accumulation of the foreign reserves to implement the Real Plan in 1994. The Plan succeeded in reducing the inflation and electing Fernando Henrique Cardoso as president in the 1994 elections. Neoliberalism increased the flow of international capital and the volatility of exchange rates. Following the path of financial crises in developing countries, Brazil devaluated the Real in early 1999, just after the reelection of Pres. Cardoso.

The authorities adopted an economic policy that combined inflation targeting, primary fiscal surplus and floating exchange rate based on a high interest rate and, therefore, a high rentability to the finance capital. Lula's government maintained this macroeconomic policy. The inefficacy of neoliberal economic policies to promote growth and employment played a role in the PT's victory in 2002. There was another reason for Lula's election: the organization of a class coalition supported by different social sector (Vianna 2007; Boito and Saad-Filho 2016). The candidate for vice president was José Alencar, a CEO of a large textile manufacturing company, representing the industrial bourgeoisie. In the "Letter to the Brazilians" published in July 2002, Lula informed the financial sectors that the future government would maintain some features of the neoliberal economic policy, in particular, the high real interest rate. In power, the Workers' Party economic policy combined contradictory elements of both developmental and neoliberal models.

The favorable international environment, with China's soaring demand for commodities, the adoption of elements of developmental state, and measures of social inclusion resulted in rising economic growth and falling unemployment. Lula was reelected in 2006. Early next year, there was the launching of the Programa de Aceleração do Crescimento (Growth Acceleration Program, PAC), consisting of a set of public and private investments under the coordination of the minister Dilma Rousseff. The Brazilian state returned to intervene in markets with a developmentalist policy.

By the late 2000s, it seemed that Brazil had recovered its growth dynamic lost in the 1980s. Between 2002 and 2010, the Brazilian economy expanded at four percent annually. In 2010, Dilma Rousseff was elected the first Brazilian woman president, it was the third consecutive victory of the Workers' Party.

The GDP growth rate declined to 2.4 percent per year between 2010 and 2014. Despite mounting economic problems, Pres. Rousseff was reelected in 2014. In the campaign, she argued against the return of reduced economic growth and high unemployment represented by the opposition candidate. However, Rousseff implemented austerity measures which associated with the cyclical downturn that had started in the second quarter of 2014 (CODACE 2017), and the decline in commodity prices drove a GDP fall of 3.8 percent in 2015, followed by a 3.6 percent fall in 2016. The economic crisis coupled with the impact of corruption allegations played a central role in the impeachment of Pres. Rousseff in 2016.

This chapter investigates the economic policy of the Workers' Party governments and the political crisis under the perspective of the profit rate and its determinants. The profit rate is central for the functioning of capitalist firms to various schools of economic thought. The decline of the profitability after the 2008 crisis played a key role in breaking the political coalition organized under Lula's leadership, opening the possibilities for the soft coup in 2016.

The paper is organized as follow. Section two investigates the profitability, distribution and economic growth between 2003 and 2010, the period of Lula's presidency. Section three reviews the economic policy and profitability in the first Rousseff's government between 2010 and 2014. Section four discusses the austerity measures implemented after the reelection and Pres. Rousseff and her impeachment. Section five concludes the paper. The Appendix discusses the profit rate, its determinants and its computation in the Brazilian economy.

2   Profitability and Functional Income Distribution in Brazil: 2003–2010

The profit rate is a key determinant of the expected profitability of new investments, playing a central role in the business cycle (Weisskopf 1979). The increase in profit rate rises the expected profit rate that drives up the investment which expands both production and employment. In a context of falling profit rate and expected profitability, the investment will decline and the economy will slowdown. Figure 7.1 shows that the investment and the GDP growth rates were strongly associated with the profit rate in Brazil between 2000 and 2016. Thus, the study of the profit rate and its components is fundamental to understand the Brazilian economic history.

The Figure 7.2 shows a decline in the profitability in Brazil between 2003 and 2015. However, there were two phases in the profit rate. First, between 2003 and 2007 the profit rate increased despite the fall in the profit share. It

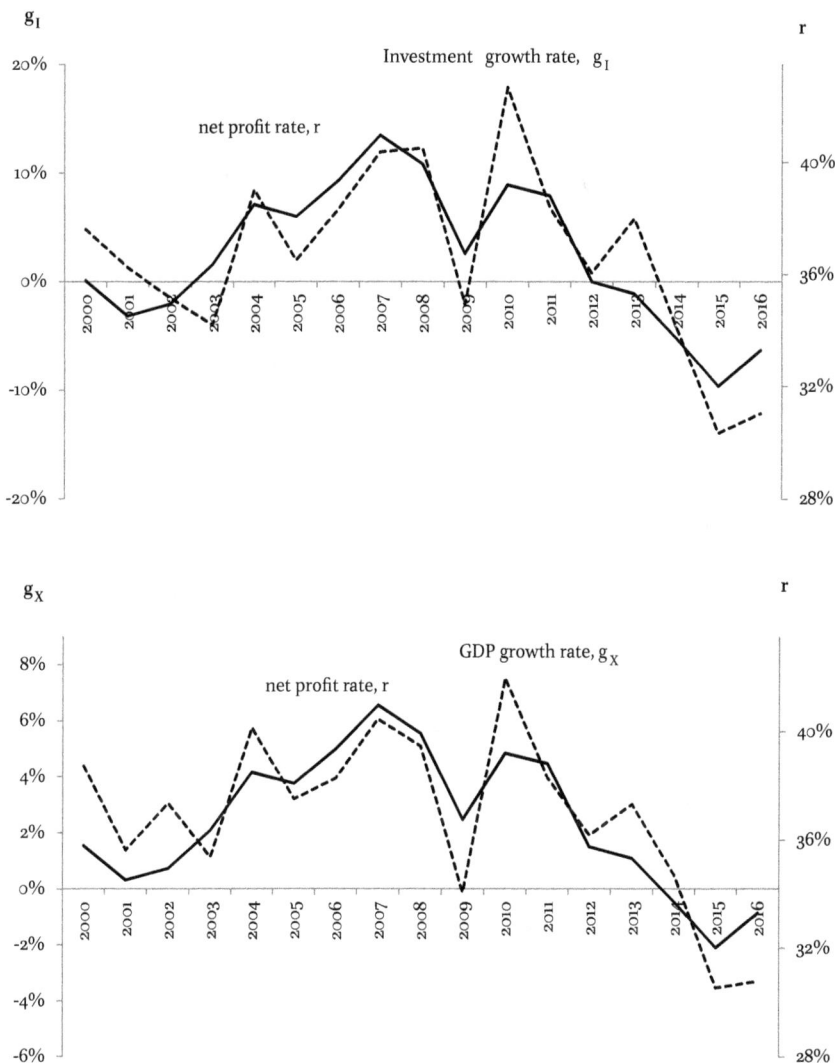

FIGURE 7.1   The relationship between the profit rate, r, the investment growth rate, g$_I$, and the GDP growth rate, g$_x$, Brazil, 2000–2016
SOURCE: IBGE (2017, 2016), MARQUETTI ET AL. (2019)

happened due to a raise in the level of capacity utilization and in the potential productivity of capital. Second, between 2007 and 2015, the profit rate declined due to an increase in the wage share and a fall in the potential productivity of capital. In 2010, the last year of Lula's government, the profit rate was higher than in the early 2000s.

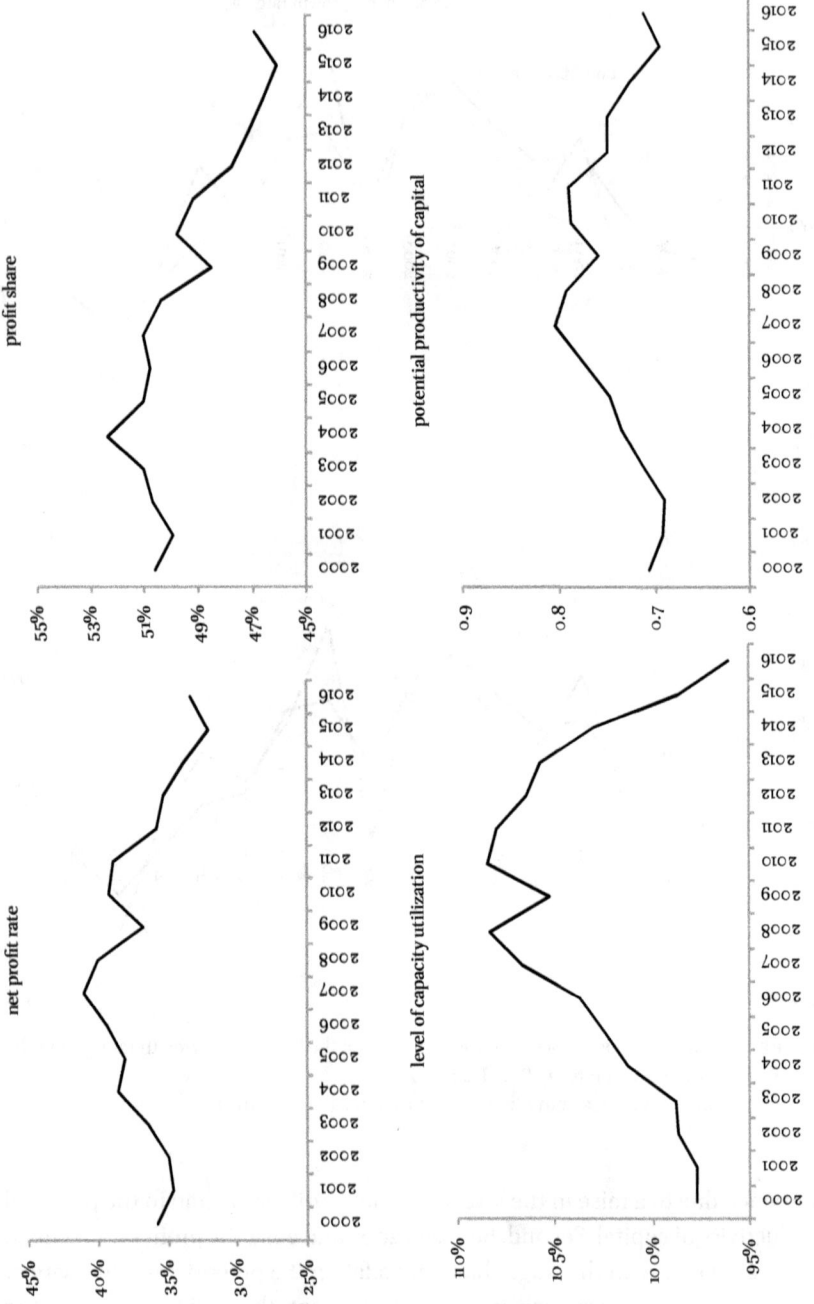

FIGURE 7.2   The profit rate and its components, Brazil, 2000–2016
SOURCE: IBGE (2017, 2016), MARQUETTI ET AL. (2019)

The 2002 electoral process was perceived by the financial bourgeoisie as a threat for neoliberalism in Brazil. There was a speculative attack with devaluation of the real in 2002, after the polls showed the probability of the Lula's victory, despite the "Letter to the Brazilians" and the presence of José Alencar as candidate to vice-president. Yet, there were discontentment in the popular sectors and in some industrial and agrarian capitalist sectors with the inefficacy of neoliberal economic policies to promote growth and employment that played a prominent role in the election.

In the first two years in power, despite the political dispute within the government, the Pres. Lula adopted an economic policy with a neoliberal hegemony.[2] There was the continuity of the inflation targeting policy and the commitment to maintain public finances under control with the adoption of primary surplus targets and the floating exchange rate. The key element of this policy was the high real interest rate on public debt. Henrique Meirelles, former CEO of international financial institutions, was the president of the Brazilian Central Bank. The benchmark Selic rate was set at 26.5 percent in 2003.[3] The government wanted to establish a coalition with the industrial, agrarian and financial fractions of capitalist sector.

The rising demand for commodities opened up the possibility to implement an economic policy that promoted economic growth and income redistribution. The Bolsa Família consolidated several conditional cash transfer programs directed towards the poor population. Under unions pressure, the minimum wage rose in real terms in 2004 and 2005. The increase in tax revenues and the growing labor market formalization allowed combining the expansion of income transfer programs with primary surpluses.

The developmental economic policy became hegemonic after the 2005 political crisis known as Mensalão, a monthly payment to congress members in exchange for government support, and the change of the finance minister Antonio Palocci Filho by Guido Mantega. The fiscal policy won preeminence to expand growth, while the monetary policy, under the control of the Central Bank, followed a conservative approach. The new minimum wage

---

2 Singer (2012: 10–11) argues that Lula "maintained the neoliberal order established in the mandates of Collor and FHC. Lula avoided the confrontation with capital and adopted a conservative economic policy". Sader (2011: 124) considered that the "leftist sectors that remained in the PT ... struggle in order to allow the government to change its route ... exerting pressure within the framework of recognized contradictions ... Especially after 2005 ... the Lula government moved to a new phase."

3 Bruno (2007) investigate the relationship between financialization and Selic rate in Brazil. Augustin Filho (2016) discuss the Selic's effects on private investment, public debt, fiscal variables, exchange rate and balance of payments.

policy came into force by late 2006, linking the minimum wage rise to past inflation and GDP growth, which enabled the income transfer to workers and expansion of household consumption. In January 2007 was launched the Growth Acceleration Program, PAC, under the coordination of minister Dilma Rousseff. It included a set of public and private sector investments with the aim of expanding economic growth.

In late 2006, the government built a new political alliance with the Brazilian Democratic Movement Party, PMDB. In order to pass their agenda in the congress, Brazilian governments organized political coalitions composed by many parties and interest. It constraints the agenda of the party in power in exchange for political stability. Despite the support of leftist political parties, the PT had the minority in congress. The PMDB controlled the Brazilian legislatures since the end of the military dictatorship, its main goal was to influence the government budget. In the early years of Lula's government, the PMDB lost political power and employed the Mensalão to restore its influence.

The Mensalão produced a large media coverage and a spectacular judgment, when Joaquim Barbosa, a Brazilian Supreme Court judge, achieved high popularity. The scandal resulted in the prison of some PT's leaders, including the minister José Dirceu. In the Brazilian history, there was a series of corruption scandals. However, for the first time the investigation resulted in the arrest of a minister, but it failed to reach Pres. Lula. The government had strong political support in an environment of economic growth with rising wages and profits. As stated by the former Pres. Cardoso a proposal of impeachment would open a social fracture in the country (Cunto 2011).

The international demand for commodities increased with the expansion of the world economy. The commodity prices rose 135 percent between 2002 and 2007 (IMF 2016). The exchange rate appreciated with the high interest rate and commodity prices. It allowed the increase in real wages and the control of the inflation rate, but reduced the manufacturing competitiveness. The cost was the deepening of the process of early deindustrialization (Nassif, Pereira, and Feijó 2017). Deindustrialization had an important political aspect: the increase of the influence of agribusiness in the economic policy and in the defense of conservative interests in congress and in the Brazilian society.

The political alliance that sustained the PT governments encompassed the agrarian ruling elite. Roberto Rodrigues, former chair of the Brazilian Agribusiness Association (Associação Brasileira do Agronegócio, ABAG) was ministry of agriculture between 2003 and 2006. The alliance was important for the government, despite representing the economic interests of large rural producers and supporting the right wing conservative policies, the rural caucus was one of the largest group in the parliament.

Sauer (2019) considers that the limits of PT's agrarian policies originated from the contradictory necessity to respond to the historical demands for land reform from popular sectors and to preserve the main interests of the agrarian elite and the agribusiness sectors. This dual compromise implied in a permanent mistrust of the agrarian elite sector towards the PT's governments.

The economic policy and the terms-of-trade increase allowed combining a raise in the profit rate with the increase in the wage share. As Table 7.1 shows, this combination was due to the expansion in the capacity utilization and in potential productivity of capital. The increase in profitability played a role in expanding the investment rate from 16.6 to 18 percent between 2003 and 2007, a 32 percent raise in investment at constant price. The GDP growth rate went from 1.1 percent in 2003 to 6.1 percent in 2007 (IBGE 2016).

Initially, the crisis of neoliberalism had a reduced effect in Brazil, despite the fall in commodity prices. The government employed fiscal and monetary expansionary policies to stimulate the demand for manufacturing goods after the collapse of Lehman Brothers in late 2008. The state-owned enterprises expanded their investments and the supply of credit. In 2010, the investment rate reached 20.5 percent of GDP and economic growth hit 7.5 percent. The economic and political expectations were optimistic, the statue of Christ the Redeemer, representing Brazil, took off on the cover of The Economist on November 12th, 2009.

The profit rate fell with the 2008 crisis, recovering partially in 2010. After declining in 2009, the level of capacity utilization increased with the economic policy, reaching its peak in 2010. For economic and political reasons, the wage share continued to expand. The government answered successfully the first effects of the crisis of neoliberalism. Pres. Lula referred which the crisis hit Brazil as a small wave, a "marola" in Portuguese. However, the long-term path of the profit rate started to decline after the crisis of neoliberalism.

The Lula's government, especially in his second term, broke two central tenets of neoliberalism. First, there was income transfer from capital to labor with the strengthening of workers bargaining power due to political and institutional changes and the decline in the unemployment rate from 12.3 percent in 2003 to 6.7 percent in 2010. Second, the government adopted a developmentalist policy. Conversely, the financial gains resulting from high real interest rates on the public debt were preserved. The stock market gains were astonishing, the Ibovespa, the main Brazilian stock market index, was multiplied by 6.4 between December 2002 and December 2010. Any attempt to reduce the financial gains would end the implicit agreement expressed in the "Letter to the Brazilians". The manufacturing production, despite deindustrialization, expanded by 27.4 percent between 2002 and 2010 (IBGE 2018). The land price increased after 2002 (Bacha et al. 2016).

There was a strengthening of the social alliance established in the 2002 election. The economic and political conditions allowed the policies of social inclusion and the increase of the real wage above labor productivity. The economic growth was the cohesive feature that unified the Brazilian social groups of interest. It allowed the Workers' Party to combine redistributive and developmental policies with some central tenets of neoliberalism.

3   Profitability and Income Distribution in Brazil: 2010–2014

In an optimistic environment, the Pres. Rousseff was elected in 2010. The real GDP expanded four percent annually between 2002 and 2010. However, after overcoming the first effects of the crisis, sustaining the growth would require changes in the economic policy to adjust to the dynamics that emerged in the world economy. Moreover, there was the exhaustion of the elements that contributed to the rising profit rate and the growth acceleration in Lula's administration.

The coalition that elected Rousseff changed in comparison with the Lula's period. The Vice President was Michel Temer, a politician with a long career in the PMDB, and the Central Bank president was Alexandre Tombini, a public servant. The Workers' Party, through the apparent success in overcoming the

TABLE 7.1   The decomposition of the net profit rate, r, into the profit share, π, in the level of capacity utilization, u, and the potential productivity of capital, ρ, Brazil, 2003–2016

Period	r	π	ρ	u
2003–2016	-0.67	-0.65	0.19	-0.22
2003–2014	-2.78	-1.31	-0.99	-0.49
2003–2007	2.99	-0.03	1.11	1.91
2007–2010	-1.48	-0.79	-1.24	0.56
2010–2014	-3.76	-1.69	-0.79	-1.28
2014–2015	-5.20	-1.06	0.17	-4.31
2014–2016	3.96	1.87	4.79	-2.70

SOURCE: IBGE (2017, 2016), MARQUETTI ET AL. (2019)

crisis of neoliberalism, sought to amplify its degrees of freedom for the elaboration of the economic policy. The approval rate above 70 percent allowed the Pres. Rousseff to promote changes in the economic policy.

The global capitalist economy imposed challenges to Brazil. Between 2010 and 2011, the downturn in world trade and aggressive monetary policy in the United States had two effects on the Brazilian economy. First, the decline in demand in the developed countries shifted global oversupply to countries with a growing internal market. Second, the real further appreciated by the influx of speculative capital in search for high interest rates.

Domestically, the high level of capacity utilization indicated that to maintain a four percent growth would require an expansion in the investment rate. In the government's view, a higher investment by the private sector would enhance the firms' competitiveness, expanding productivity and reducing costs.

Following Augustin Filho (2012), former deputy secretary of the finance ministry between 2007 and 2014, the basis for the expansion of private investment would be the change in both the interest rate and the exchange rate. A devalued exchange rate would restore the manufacturing competitiveness. This movement would be reinforced by infrastructure spending by the government through the PAC. Another element in the growth strategy would be the investment in the exploitation of large offshore oil reserves by Petrobras and the policy of national content on downstream activities related to petroleum production. Petrobras announced the discovered the pre-salt oil reserves in 2006, starting the production in these fields in 2010.

The condition for the depreciation was an interest rate fall and lower foreign capital inflows. The Central Bank cut the target of the Selic rate from 12.5 percent per year in August 2011 to 7.25 percent in October 2012 (Figure 7.3). Moreover, the public banks increased their competition with the private sector, expanding their market share to 40 percent of the credit operations in early 2010s.

The fall in the Selic started a dispute with the financial sector and the productive companies that had in the financial gains on public debt an important element of their profitability. There were strong criticisms in the national and international press. For Loyola (2011), former Central Bank president, the decline of the Selic broke fundamental principles of the inflation target regime and the independence of Central Bank. On May 10, 2012, Bloomberg published the article "In Dilma Versus Banks, Round One Goes to Government" about the dispute over the interest rate (Phillips 2012). The class coalition constructed by Lula's administration had started to fall apart. For the financial sector, the government had abandoned the "Letter to the Brazilians" (Vaccari and Perez 2017).

The economic measures produced some exchange rate depreciation as Figure 7.4 shows.[4] However, the measures did not avert lower economic growth. The Brazilian Institute of Geography and Statistics (IBGE) informed a GDP growth rate of 2.7 percent for 2011. It was a major decrease from the 7.5 percent of the previous year. The rapid slowdown induced further changes in the economic policy. A government member named of "new economic matrix" this economic policy. It included an increase in tax exemptions and subsidies; the use of public banks to reduce the spreads and lower interest rates; the use of sectoral measures to reduce costs, such as the intervention in the electricity industry by extending concession periods in exchange for lower prices on power; the exemption on payroll taxes; and, the offer of loans with subsidized interest rates by the National Bank for Economic and Social Development (BNDES) to firms.

Briefly, the government attempted to expand investment with two sets of measures. The first aimed to expand profitability thought fiscal and costs reduction. The second aimed to reduce the interest rate for productive investment. The higher economic growth would increase the fiscal revenues. However, the IBGE announced that the GDP growth rate in 2012 was 0.9 percent.[5] The reduced growth prompted further criticisms to the economic policy. For example, Goldfajn (2013), chief economist and partner of Itaú Bank, wrote that "it is necessary to temporarily slowdown both consumption, adjusting it to supply, and labor market, adjusting the wage increases to labor productivity growth. The tax exemptions only postpone the needed adjustments to the future".

The main result of the "new economic matrix" was to maintain the investment rate above 20 percent between 2011 and 2014. As shown in Figure 7.5, the capital accumulation, the growth rate of capital stock, though declining after 2011 with the falling profit rate, was higher than four percent between 2011 and 2013. The labor demand continued to expand, the unemployment rate reached 4.8 percent in 2014. The annual growth rate of the real wage, see Figure 7.6, was 2.1 percent, while the labor productivity increased at 0.53 percent between 2010 and 2014.

4　The real exchange rate was computed as the nominal exchange rate multiplied by the ratio between the United States Consumer Price Index computed by the Bureau of Labor Statistics and the Expanded Consumer Price Index computed by IBGE. The real exchange rate is expressed in prices of December 2016.

5　The IBGE published the Brazilian System of National Accounts Reference 2010 in 2015, the GDP growth rate for 2011 was revised from 2.7 to 3.9 percent and for 2012 from 0.9% to 1.9% (IBGE 2016).

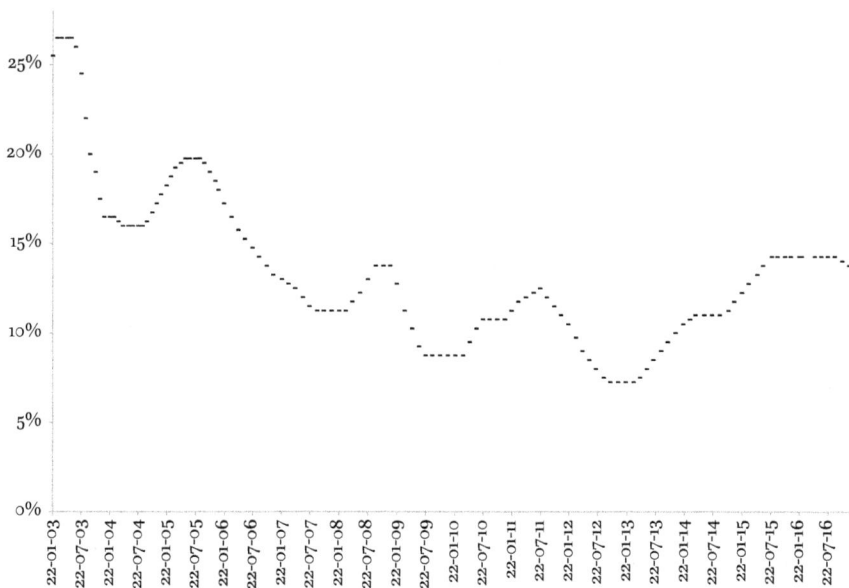

FIGURE 7.3   The benchmark Selic rate, 2003–2016
SOURCE: BANCO CENTRAL DO BRASIL (2017)

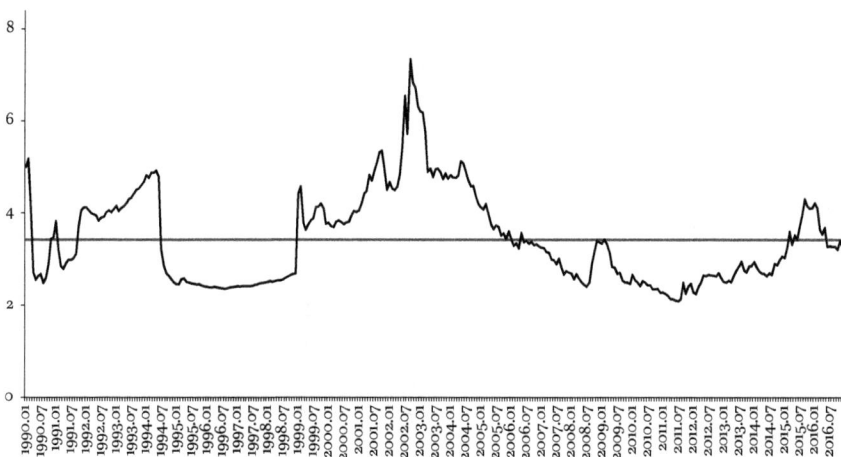

FIGURE 7.4   The monthly and the average real exchange rate, e, 1990–2016
Note: The exchange rate is defined as the price in reals of one dollar. It is expressed
in prices of December 2016.
SOURCE: IPEA (2019)

The profit rate plunged after 2011. The main factor, as Table 7.1 shows, was the declining share of net profits from 51 percent in 2003 to 49.2 in 2011, then to 46.5 percent in 2014. The capacity utilization and the potential productivity of capital also fell between 2011 and 2014. The simultaneous decline in the profit rate and financial profitability is at the origin of the end of the class coalition constructed by Lula's Government. Singer (2015) describes how segments of the industrial bourgeoisie went to the opposition in 2012 and 2013.

The new economic policy failed to maintain the GDP growth rate between 2011 and 2013. There were criticisms saying that the government abandoned the key macroeconomic fundamentals of the market. The expectations were of further decline of the profit rate as the workers strengthened their bargaining power. The number of strikes in the private sector skyrocketed in early 2010, rising from 264 in 2009 to 1106 in 2013 with the mobilization of categories with lower organizational tradition typical of periods of greater bargaining power of labor and their unions (DIEESE 2015).

In a context of reduced manufacturing competitiveness, global economic slowdown and appreciated exchange rate, the rise in workers' purchasing power increased the demand for imported and non-tradable goods. The manufacturing share in value added declined from 16.5 percent in 2008 to 12 percent in 2014. The manufacturing and the service sector were not prepared for the increase in demand originated by the higher income (Rugitsky 2016).

The tax incentives granted by Rousseff's government to the private sector went from R\$ 3.6 billion in 2011 to R\$ 100.6 billion in 2014. The primary surplus declined from 2.13 percent of GDP in 2011 to a deficit of 0.32 percent in 2014. Supposedly, the tax relief and the reduced financing cost would expand investment and economic growth. However, private companies lower their investments in periods of declining profitability. Despite, the subsidies, for many non-financial enterprises the cost of capital was superior to their actual profitability. The return on investment of the industrial enterprises listed on Bovespa declined from 10.2 percent in 2010 to 0.4 percent in 2015 (IEDI 2016: 20).

In 2013, social unrest emerges for the first time in the PT's governments. There were a series of public protests with diffuse goals. Initially, the protest organized by the Movimento Passe Livre (Free Fare Movement), a leftist group, against the rise in the public transport fares. The change of nature occurred when the conservative sectors of middle class started to participate, the protests encompassed other claims, such as the improvement in public services, the costs of organizing the World Cup, and against corruption. The protests grown in magnitude and there were reports of participants refusing any link with the political parties (Garcia and Pedersoli 2013). In June 20, 2013 more than one million people protested all over the country. The 2013 protests were

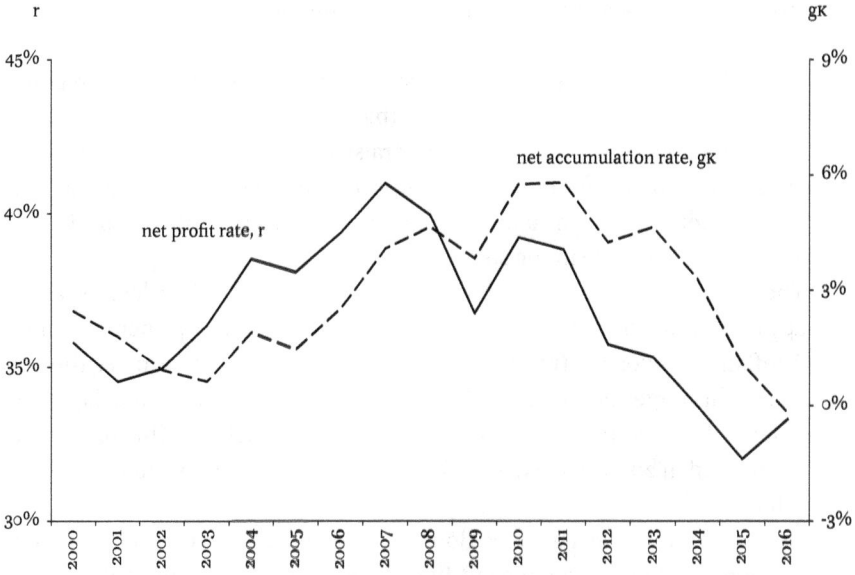

FIGURE 7.5   The net profit rate and the capital accumulation, Brazil, 2000–2016
SOURCE: IBGE (2017, 2016), MARQUETTI ET AL. (2019)

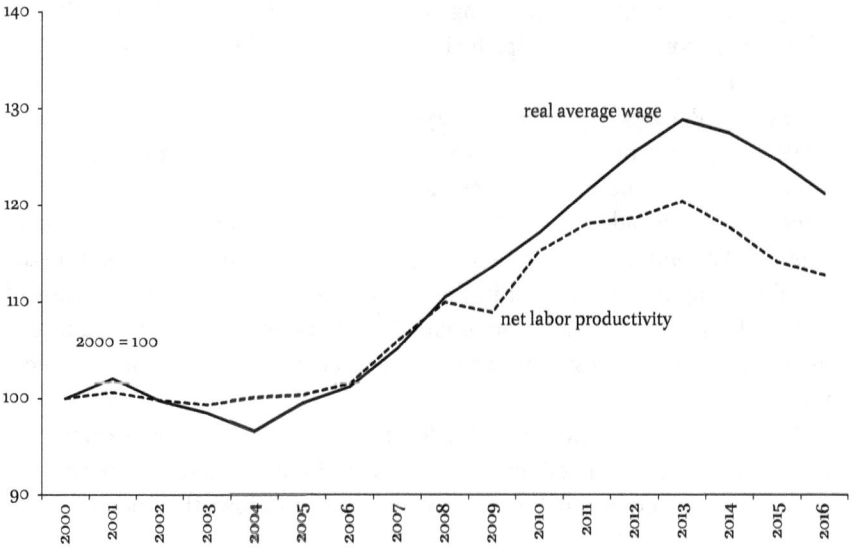

FIGURE 7.6   The real average wage and net labor productivity, Brazil, 2000–2016
SOURCE: IBGE (2017, 2016), MARQUETTI ET AL. (2019)

complex social phenomena, still attracting attempts to establish a coherent interpretation.

The massive protests required an answer from the government. The popularity of Pres. Rousseff suffered a major setback with the government's inability to make concrete proposals to the issues raised in the streets. Another consequence was the organization of rightwing groups for the first time after democratization. Some of them had connections with the far right in the United States and played a role in the soft coup.[6]

The government, then, sought to improve its approval ratings looking at the 2014 presidential election. The strategy was to maintain low unemployment and inflation under control. Given the growing difficulties to meet the primary surplus target set by the National Congress, the government delayed the transfer of funds to public banks to cover up budget deficits. This procedure, which started in 2000, was expanded in 2013 and 2014 with the mounting fiscal problems.

In the electoral campaign, Pres. Rousseff recognized the economic problems, the GDP expanded just 0.1 percent in 2014. She assured that the adjustments would be gradual to preserve employment and social achievements, central goals of her electorate. The narrow margin with which she was re-elected, with 51.6 percent of the votes, the great rejection in most industrialized regions, along with fierce opposition during the election campaign, indicated that, in addition to economic hardship, the Pres. Rousseff would face political difficulties in her second term.

The first Rousseff's government crystallizes some contradictions of the PT relationship with neoliberalism. The government assumed a more proactive role, stimulation the private investment through tax exemptions and lower interest rates instead of raising the public sector investments. There was a conception of a genuine cleavage between productive and financial capitals in the neoliberal capitalism. The fall in the interest rate would reduce the gains of financial capital and benefit the productive capital that would expand investments. The public investment would have a secondary role to stimulate economic growth.

These "new economic matrix" failed to stimulate growth and revealed a misconception about neoliberalism, in which the financialization permeates the entire productive structure. This misconception allows the understanding

---

6   Following Puty (2018) and Fiori and Nozaki (2019) there are many signs that the US government played a role in the Brazilian soft coup. The Brazilian approximation to China and the discovery of the pre-salt oil reserves were focus of attention from the White House. The combat of corruption became a tool for the United States to safeguard its interests.

of the contradictory position of the Rousseff's government in relation to neo-liberal policies, breaking with some while preserving others, and explains the limits of her economic policy to overcome the decline of growth associated with falling profit rates.

4   The Return to Neoliberal Hegemony: The Second Rousseff's
       Government

The Pres. Rousseff won the 2014 election with strong support from leftwing voters. During the campaign, there were accusations that an opposition victory would represent the return to neoliberal economic policy with negative effects on employment, real wages and social spending. Despite, the announcement of a replacement in the economic team in case of re-election, the social movements and leftist organizations reacted with surprise and criticism to the change in the economic policy signaled by the appointment of Joaquim Levy as finance minister. Levy, an economist trained at Chicago University, worked in the financial sector when his appointment was announced.

Pres. Rousseff was seeking a rapprochement with the sectors of the bourgeoise. Contrary to her promise during the campaign, Pres. Rousseff adopted an economic policy with a neoliberal hegemony. Apparently, the idea was to repeat the success of 2003, however there were limits of how much she could concede to recover the support of the bourgeoise.

The first fiscal measures announced in January 2015 restricted the workers' access to unemployment insurance and changed the rules for some social security benefits. There was a reduction of fiscal spending, the federal government investment declined 32 percent in 2015 in relation to 2014. Another measure was the revision of the pricing policy of public companies. The increase in public prices concomitant with the exchange rate devaluation expanded the inflation to 11.07 percent in 2015. The Central Bank increased the Selic in 300 points between October 2014 and July 2015. The changes in the Selic rate have a lag between two and four quarters to affect the GDP. Moreover, Petrobras reduced by one third its investments between 2013 and 2015.

The combination of contractionary fiscal and monetary policies with cyclical downturn and falling commodities prices led to a profound economic crisis. In 2015, there was a 14 percent fall in investment and a 3.8 percent decline in GDP. The unemployment rate rose to 6.8 percent and the average real wage declined. The profit rate plunged due to the fall in the level of capital utilization.

The "car wash operation", an investigation of money laundering and corruption, and its selective leaks to the press stimulated the climate of belligerence against the government. There were similarities and differences with the Mensalão. There was a large media coverage, and the judge Sérgio Moro was the new hero.[7] Instead of economic growth, now there is a recession with increasing unemployment and shrinking profits and wages. The economic crisis reinforced the political crisis and the links made by the press and the rightwing political parties between the economic crisis, corruption and the PT's governments.

A 2015 survey pointed out that 67 percent of Brazilians believed that corruption was the main reason for the economic crisis (Alencar 2015). The media associated the economic and political crises. In early 2016, O Globo (2016), a major newspaper, published the editorial entitled "The impeachment is an institutional way-out of the crisis." The media coverage of the car wash and the economic crisis allowed the organization of a large right-wing coalition composed by the far right, the agrarian, industrial and financial capitalists, the conservative sectors of the judiciary, and the corporate media.

Throughout the year, the streets were taken by right-wing sectors protesting against the government and calling for the impeachment of Pres. Rousseff who saw her approval rate to drop to 11 percent by late 2015. The right-wing coalition delegitimized the PT's government among the popular sectors through the association of the economic crisis with the corruption scandals, recovering the climate of the 2013 protests. Segments of the workers and the middle classes joined gradually the protesters against Rousseff and the PT.

In December 2015, Nelson Barbosa replaced Joaquim Levy as the finance ministry. For economic and political reasons there was limited room for change. The fiscal position had been compromised by the stimulus to private investment and the negative growth.

Barbosa proposed a soft austerity, combining higher fiscal expenses in the short term with change in the social security rules, and the return of the tax over financial transactions. These proposals were criticized by the opposition and sectors which supported the government. The political strength of the government in the congress declined after the adoption of the austerity measures. The rural caucus gradually moved into opposition as the government lost the popular support and did not comply with the demands of the agribusiness sector that traditionally relied in public credit and subsidies.

In December, 2015 the Federação das Indústrias do Estado de São Paulo (Federation of Industries of the State of São Paulo, FIESP) announced its

---

7 The Intercept published in 2019, using leaked Telegram messages, a series of reports denouncing that the Sérgio Moro acted as a judge and a prosecutor in the Car Wash operation (Greenwald et al. 2019).

support for the impeachment proceedings (G1 2015). This position was followed by other business organizations, including the Confederação Nacional da Agricultura e da Pecuária do Brasil (National Confederation of Agriculture and Livestock of Brazil, CNA) in April 2016 (CNA 2016).

These organizations pointed that the impeachment was the only way out of the economic and political crises. In their view, it was necessary a fiscal adjustment based on reduction of the public expenditure without any increase in taxes. The government would not regain the confidence of the "markets" and large wealth holders. The business sectors that had allied to the government in order to reap benefits in the bonanza period switched side in the crises. They never forget the leftist origin and the popular support of the PT's governments. Moreover, the financial sector always criticized the social democratic character of the Brazilian constitution. Goldfanj (2015) wrote that "the society has adopted a large "social contract" since the 1988 Constitution, whose benefits granted to various social groups no longer fit into GDP. The tax burden necessary to pay for this welfare state already paralyzes the economy ... you cannot waste a crisis to make the hard changes."

The PMDB, the party of Vice President Michel Temer, proposed the hard changes in October, 2015 through the document *A Bridge to the Future* (Uma Ponte para o Futuro). The proposals were a series of neoliberal measures aimed to expand the profitability and to control the fiscal deficit. The document suggested the reduction of labor costs, changing the minimum-wage indexation rule, reform in the labor law, a social-security reform, eliminating the constitutional spending in education and health, privatization and trading openness. The proposals were consistent with the "hard changes", a radical neoliberal turn, proposed by the bourgeoisie and were far beyond the political possibilities and the history of the Workers' Party. The document represented a manifesto for a government led by Temer.[8]

The neoliberal turn in the economic policy after the election was a fundamental mistake by a government that faced ferocious political opposition. The adoption of a program similar to the proposals of Aécio Neves, the PSDB's candidate, was a signal that the critiques from the opposition were correct. Moreover, this move raised criticisms and reduced the government political support among its popular sector constituents.

The growth strategy through subsidies and incentives to private investment in a period of declining profit rate and profit share was a mistake of the first

---

8   Several proposals of the neoliberal economic program present in the "*A Bridge to the Future*" were implemented by Temer's and Bolsonaro's governments.

Rousseff's government. The Instituto de Estudos para o Desenvolvimento Industrial (Institute of Study for Industrial Development, IEDI) a think-tank linked to large Brazilian industries, put in the tittle of its newsletter in July 2016 the reason why investment did not expanded: no profits, no investments. The subsidies and fiscal incentives resulted in large fiscal deficits after 2013.

The mistake in the second government was the adoption of a neoliberal economic policy. The neoliberal turn drove an increase of the profit rate in 2016 due to raising profit share and potential productivity of capital, despite falling capital utilization. The economic policy expanded the unemployment and reduced the real wage. As the political and economic crises deepened, Pres. Rousseff alienated herself from the capitalists and the popular sectors. The sharpening of the economic crisis opened the door for the impeachment.

5   Conclusion

Lula's election in 2002 was a victory of the social groups that were opponents or dissatisfied with neoliberalism. However, the PT's governments did not represent a rupture with neoliberalism. The strategy of the Workers' Party was pragmatic and moderate, combining elements of developmentalism and neoliberalism in a contradictory construction. There was a redistributive policy toward to poor population and the wage share expanded, but the profit rate increased initially and the high interest rate on the public debt was maintained most of the time. A neoliberal economic policy was hegemonic in the 2003–2005 and 2015–2016 years, while developmentalism was hegemonic between 2005 and 2014.[9]

Benefited by rising commodity price of and an economic policy that gradually abandoned some of the tenets of neoliberalism, the profit rate and the wage share raised between 2003 and 2007. There was an increase in the investment and the higher wage stimulated the family consumption. The economic growth consolidated the class coalition under Lula's leadership that combined different social sectors of the Brazilian society, from different segments of the capitalist class to industrial workers.

The favorable international conditions changed after the crisis of neoliberalism in 2008. Perhaps, in 2009 there was the possibility of implementing major economic reforms in order to reduce the power of financial sector.

---

9 Augustin Filho (2016) denominated the 2005–2014 period as the developmentalist essay, and the period 2015–2016 as the neoliberal shift.

However, between confrontation and composition, the path chosen was not that of confrontation with neoliberalism. Confrontation would tear down the political coalition that supported the government.

The 2008 crisis eliminated the conditions that allowed the concomitant growth of wages and profit rate. Pres. Rousseff had the task of preserving the class alliance that gave support to Lula's administration. Her government adopted a series of fiscal and financial stimulus for private investment in a period of declining profitability. The result was a decline in the GDP growth rate and fiscal imbalances. As the profit rate plunged and the economic policy maintained the gains in workers' income, the broad alliance with the capitalists' sectors began to collapse. As the political confrontation intensified, the expectations on profitability and on economic growth further declined.

Rousseff won the 2014 election with the support of the Brazil's poorest regions. In her second term, Rousseff attempted to restore the former alliance, adopting a neoliberal economic policy with a program of fiscal austerity that generated a 3.8 percent fall in GDP and an inflation rate of 11 percent in 2015. The recession provoked a sharp rise in unemployment and a deterioration of fiscal budget. The neoliberal turn did not restore the confidence of the capitalist class and reduce the political support among the leftist sectors of Brazilian society.

The car wash investigations provided fuel for the large political demonstrations against Rousseff, the former Pres. Lula and the Workers' Party. The manifestations produced a political amalgam of the right-wing groups that opposed the government. Moreover, the popular sectors had little reason to support a government that implemented an austerity program.

These developments reduce the capacity of the Workers' Party to fight against the impeachment process that overthrew Rousseff's government. Her impeachment enabled the restoration of central tenets of neoliberalism that were put on halt by the PT's governments, particularly the compression of the real wages.

The political stability achieved under Lula's leadership was derived from the conditions that enabled the rise in the profit rate concomitantly with a better income redistribution. It allowed the construction of an alliance between different social sectors. When these conditions changed, the political alliance lost support, resulting in a reaction from the capitalists' sectors in order to recover profitability with a resumption of full neoliberalism.

In this perspective, the Workers' Party governments did not confront the foundations of neoliberalism implanted in the 1990s. However, it opened up space for a set of policies that increased bargaining power of workers, reduced inequality and poverty. Policies that increase the power of workers in the class struggle are against the neoliberalism. The capitalist class did not perceive these policies as confrontational until the profit rate started to decline.

The Workers' Party lost power when the cycle of left-wing parties in government in most of the South America countries were also finishing. The crisis of neoliberalism with the end of the commodity boom limited the capability of the leftist governments to maintain economic gains to the different social classes. The PT's governments distributed some of the gains of the economy growth to workers and poor sectors of population. The crisis of neoliberalism, paradoxically, allowed the implementation of a deepened version of neoliberalism in Brazil with the impeachment of the Pres. Dilma Rousseff.

Appendix: The Profit Rate and Its Components

The goal of production and investment in the capitalist society is to produce profits, profitability is the driving force of capitalism. The profit rate is a key determinant of the expected profitability of new investments and plays a central role in the explanation of the economic crisis because it (Weisskopf 1979: 341). The decisions on new investments are based on the expected profitability of the capital. The decline in profit rate reduces the expected profit rate that diminishes the investment and the capital accumulation. A lower investment rate reduces the levels of production and employment. Economic policy may raise investment and capital accumulation in the short term. However, in a context of falling profit rate and expected profitability, the investment and capital accumulation will decline in the medium and long term.

The path of the profit rate, as suggested by Weisskopf (1979), can be explained by three factors which, in the Marxian perspective, are related to different sources of crisis in a capitalist economy. The first is the decline in the profit share due to higher bargaining power of workers. For political and economic reasons, wages can rise faster than labor productivity reducing the profit share. The second is the fall in potential productivity of capital due to rising organic composition of capital associated with technical change and capital accumulation. In an open economy, the change in terms of trade affects the profit rate through the profit share and the potential productivity of capital. The decline of the terms of trade increases the cost of production for a given share of imported wage goods, reducing the amount of profits per unit of output and the profit share. The decline of the terms of trade rises the cost of investment for a given share of imported capital goods, reducing the potential productivity of capital. The effect of declining terms of trade is similar to the fall of labor and capital productivities. The third is the decline in the level of capacity of utilization due to lack of aggregate demand. However, independent of its source, the fall in the profit rate results in declining investment and capital accumulation and, consequently, lower economic growth.

The profit rate is measured by the ratio between the total profits created during a period to total advanced capital. Weisskopf (1979) proposed a decomposition of the profit rate, r, that allows investigation of whether its change in time depends on the profit share, π, in the level of capacity utilization, u, and the potential productivity of capital, ρ. The profit rate is computed by:

$$r = \frac{Z}{K} = \frac{Z}{X} * \frac{X^p}{K} * \frac{X}{X^p} = \pi \rho u$$

where Z is net profit, K is the net capital stock, X is net output, and X^p is the net potential output.

The profit rate was computed as the ratio between the net operational surplus and the net stock of fixed capital. The net stock of fixed capital was estimated through the perpetual inventory method. The net profit is the net domestic product minus the compensation of employees. The compensation of employees includes part of the mixed income computed. It is assumed that the mixed income has the same share of capital and labor incomes of the rest of the economy. The potential productivity of capital is the ratio between the net domestic product trend and the net stock of fixed capital. The net domestic product trend was computed using the Hodrick-Prescott filter. The level of capacity utilization is the ratio between the net domestic product and its trend. For some years, this ratio can be greater than one. For further information on the construction of the variables see Marquetti et al. (2019).

References

Alencar, K. (2015). Para 67%, corrupção causou crise econômica, diz. Datapopular *Blog do Kennedy* November 24. https://www.blogdokennedy.com.br/para-67-corrupcao-causou-crise-economica-diz-datapopular/ (consulted May 26, 2017).

Amann, E., and Werner, B. (2002). Neoliberalism and its Consequences in Brazil. *Journal of Latin American Studies* 34(4): 945–959.

Augustin Filho, A. (2012). *As Bases do Crescimento de Longo Prazo: um Brasil de oportunidades*. [PowerPoint presentation]. Porto Alegre: Ministério da Fazenda. 12/10/2012.

Augustin Filho, A. (2016). Os fatos são teimosos. *Revista Democracia Socialista* 4: 67–94.

Bacha, C., Stege, A., and Harbs, R. (2016). Ciclos de preços de terras agrícolas no Brasil. *Revista de Política Agrícola* 18(4): 18–27.

Banco Central do Brasil. (2017). *Histórico das taxas de juros.* http://www.bcb.gov.br/Pec/Copom/Port/taxaSelic.asp (consulted May 30, 2017).

Boito Jr., A., and Saad-Filho, A. (2016). State, state institutions, and political power in Brazil. *Latin American Perspectives* 43(2): 190–206.

Bruno, M. (2007). Financiarisation et accumulation du capital productif au Brésil les obstacles macro-économiques à une croissance soutenue. *Revue Tiers Monde* 189(1): 65–92.

CODACE (Comitê de Datação de Ciclos Econômicos). (2017). *Comunicado de Datação de Ciclos Mensais Brasileiros.* October 31. https://portalibre.fgv.br/estudos-e-pesquisas/codace/ (consulted May 4, 2019).

CNA (Confederação Nacional da Agricultura e Pecuária do Brasil). (2016). *CNA decide apoiar o movimento em favor do Impeachment da Presidente Dilma Rousseff.* April 6. https://www.cnabrasil.org.br/notas-oficiais/cna-decide-apoiar-o-movimento-em-favor-do-impeachment-da-presidente-dilma-rousseff (consulted May 4, 2019).

Cunto, R. (2011). FHC: oposição evitou impeachment de Lula para não criar "fenda social". *Valor Econômico.* December 9. https://www.valor.com.br/politica/1132244/fhc-oposicao-evitou-impeachment-de-lula-para-nao-criar-fenda-social (consulted February 4, 2019).

DIEESE (Departamento Intersindical de Estatística e Estudos Socioeconômicos). (2015). Balanço das greves em 2013. *Estudos e Pesquisas n. 79.* https://www.dieese.org.br/balancodasgreves/2013/estPesq79balancogreves2013.html (consulted July 14, 2019).

Filgueiras, L. (2006). O neoliberalismo no Brasil: estrutura, dinâmica e ajuste do modelo econômico. In: Basualdo, Eduardo, and Enrique Arceo (eds.), *Neoliberalismo y sectores dominantes. Tendencias globales y experiencias nacionales*, 179–206. Buenos Aires: CLACSO.

Fiori, J.L., and Nozaki, W. (2019). Conspiração e corrupção: uma hipótese provável. July 25. *Jornal GGN.* https://jornalggn.com.br/artigos/conspiracao-e-corrupcao-uma-hipotese-provavel-por-jose-luis-fiori-e-william-nozaki/ (consulted July 26, 2019).

Fundação Ulisses Guimarães. (2015). *Uma Ponte para o futuro.* https://www.fundacaoulysses.org.br/wp-content/uploads/2016/11/UMA-PONTE-PARA-O-FUTURO.pdf (consulted July 15, 2019).

G1. (2015). *Fiesp declara apoio ao processo de impeachment da presidente.* December 12. http://g1.globo.com/hora1/noticia/2015/12/fiesp-declara-apoio-ao-processo-de-impeachment-da-presidente-dilma.html (consulted May 10, 2019).

Garcia, J., and Pedersoli, B. (2013). *"Sem partido!", gritam manifestantes contra uso de bandeiras em protesto em SP.* June, 17. Uol.https://noticias.uol.com.br/cotidiano/ultimas-noticias/2013/06/17/sem-partido-gritam-manifestantes-contra-uso-de-bandeiras-em-protesto-em-sp.htm (consulted May 11, 2019).

Greenwald, G., Reed, B., and Demori, L. (2019). *Como e por que o Intercept está publicando chats privados sobre a Lava Jato e Sérgio* Moro" The Intercept, June 9. https://theintercept.com/2019/06/09/editorial-chats-telegram-lava-jato-moro/.

Goldfajn, I. (2015). Qual é a alternativa? *O Globo*, September 1. https://oglobo.globo.com/opiniao/qual-a-alternativa-17364145 (consulted May 12, 2019).

Goldfajn, I. (2013). Combater a inflação, mexer no emprego. *O Globo*, March 5. https://oglobo.globo.com/opiniao/combater-inflacao-mexer-no-emprego-7738616 (consulted May 18, 2019).

IBGE (Instituto Brasileiro de Geografia e Estatística). (2016). *Sistema de contas nacionais: Brasil: 2010–2014*. Rio de Janeiro: IBGE.

IBGE (Instituto Brasileiro de Geografia e Estatística). (2017). *Contas Nacionais Trimestrais*. Rio de Janeiro: IBGE. https://www.ibge.gov.br/estatisticas-novoportal/economicas/contas-nacionais.html (consulted December 7, 2017).

IBGE (Instituto Brasileiro de Geografia e Estatística). (2018). *Pesquisa Industrial Mensal Produção Física – Brasil*. Rio de Janeiro: IBGE. https://www.ibge.gov.br/estatisticas-novoportal/economicas/industria.html (consulted November 18, 2018).

IEDI (Instituto de Estudos para o Desenvolvimento Industrial). (2016). Sem Lucro, Sem Investimento. *Carta IEDI* 738. https://iedi.org.br/cartas/carta_iedi_n_738.html (consulted January 21, 2019).

IMF (International Monetary Fund). (2016). *IMF Primary Commodity Prices*. http://www.imf.org/external/np/res/commod/index.aspx (consulted November 1, 2016).

IPEA (Instituto de Economia Aplicada). (2019). *Ipeadata. Dados macroeconômicos e regionais*. http://www.ipeadata.gov.br (consulted May, 2, 2019).

Loyola, G. (2011). Regime de metas para a inflação agoniza. *Valor Econômico*, September 5. https://www.valor.com.br/opiniao/997940/regime-de-metas-para-inflacao-agoniza (consulted May 2, 2019).

Marquetti, A., Morrone, H., Miebach, A., and Ourique, L. (2019). Measuring the Profit Rate in an Inflationary Context: The Case of Brazil, 1955–2008. *Review of Radical Political Economics* 51(1): 52–74.

Marquetti, A., Hoff, C., and Miebach, A. (2020). Profitability and Distribution: The Origin of the Brazilian Economic and Political Crisis. *Latin American Perspectives* 47(1): 115–133.

Mier, B. (2018). US DOJ and Operation Car Wash: Facts and Questions. *Brasil Wired*, August 20. http://www.brasilwire.com/us-doj-and-operation-car-wash-facts-and-questions (consulted May 10, 2019).

Nassif, A., Bresser-Pereira, L.C., and Feijó, C. (2017). The case for reindustrialization in developing countries: towards the connection between the macroeconomic regime and the industrial policy in Brazil. *Cambridge Journal of Economics* 42(2): 355–381.

O Globo. (2016). O impeachment é uma saída institucional da crise O Globo, March 3. https://oglobo.globo.com/opiniao/o-impeachment-uma-saida-institucional-da-crise-18912997 (consulted May 5, 2019).

Perez, R., and Vaccari, G. (2017). A doxa política das finanças: O discurso dos banqueiros diante da nova matriz econômica do governo Dilma Roussef (2011–14). *Revista Eletrônica de Ciência Política* 8(3): 2017.

Phillips, D. (2012). In Dilma versus banks round one goes to government. *Bloomberg*, May 10. https://www.bloomberg.com/opinion/articles/2012-05-10/in-dilma-versus-banks-round-one-goes-to-government (consulted May 2, 2019).

Puty, C. (2018). A estratégia de segurança nacional do EUA e o combate à corrupção na América Latina https://revistaforum.com.br/estrategia-de-seguranca-nacional-do-eua-e-o-combate-corrupcao-na-america-latina/ (consulted July 27, 2019).

Rugitsky, F. (2016). Milagre, miragem, antimilagre: a economia política dos governos Lula e as raízes da crise atual. *Revista Fevereiro* 9: 40–50.

Sader, E. (2011). Neoliberalismo versus pós-neoliberalismo: a disputa estratégica contemporânea. *Margem Esquerda* 16: 123–127.

Sauer, S. (2019). Rural Brazil in the Lula Administration: Agreements with agribusiness and disputes in agrarian policies. *Latin American Perspectives* 46(4): 103–121.

Singer, A. (2012). *Os sentidos do lulismo: reforma gradual e pacto conservador*. São Paulo: Cia. das Letras.

Singer, A. (2015). Cutucando onças com varas curtas – o ensaio desenvolvimentista no primeiro mandato de Dilma Rousseff (2011–2014). *Novos Estudos Cebrap* 102: 43–71.

Vianna, W. (2007). O estado novo do PT. *La Insignia*, July 13, 2007. www.lainsignia.org/2007/julio/ibe_007.htm (consulted May 5, 2019).

Weisskopf, T. (1979). Marxian crisis theory and the rate of profit in the postwar US economy. *Cambridge Journal of Economics* 3(4): 341–378.

CHAPTER 8

Why Bolsonarism Should Be Characterized as Neofascism

Armando Boito Jr.

1   Where Is Fascism in Brazil[1]

I have been characterizing the movement that supports Jair Bolsonaro and his administration as neofascist (Boito 2019). In this chapter, I intend to further present this case with perhaps sounder arguments and point out my differences with the literature that refutes such characterization.

May the reader note that I am referring to a neofascist movement and a neofascist government, not a fascist dictatorship. Some observers and analysts engaged in Brazilian politics have argued that characterizing Bolsonarism as fascism, either in general or as a variation of this political phenomenon, is not appropriate, because the country still holds elections and presents other elements that could characterize a democracy. Yes, we still live in a bourgeois, albeit deteriorated democracy in Brazil; however, a fascist social movement can evidently emerge in a democratic regime and – perhaps not so evidently – a fascist government may be formed without transitioning to a fascist dictatorship. While Adolf Hitler started a transition process into a dictatorship less than a month after he took office, Benito Mussolini remained within the boundaries of the bourgeois democratic regime during his first few years in power. Togliatti (1976) further analyzes the history of the latter, maintaining that the National Fascist Party (NFP) did not even have a "dictatorship project" set up when it first came to power. Togliatti argues that the implementation of the fascist dictatorship eventually became a goal and turned out feasible as a result of the evolution of the economic situation and class conflict in the early and mid-1920s.

It is a grave error to believe that fascism started out in 1920, or from the March of Rome, with a pre-established, predetermined plan for the

---

1 Published in the journal *Crítica Marxista* (2020), Brazil, No. 50: 111–119.

dictatorial regime, as this regime has been organized in the course of ten
years, and as we see it today. This would be a grave error.

TOGLIATTI 1976: 13–14

The fascist dictatorship has been driven to assume its current forms by
objective factors, by real factors – by the economic situation and the
mass movements this situation has brought into being.

TOGLIATTI 1976: 14

Between 1923 and 1926 [...] Totalitarianism was born. Fascism was not
born totalitarian; it became so [...].

TOGLIATTI 1976: 23–24[2]

Today in Brazil, we have a predominantly neofascist government, based on
a neofascist movement, but we still have, in regard to a political regime, a
bourgeois, albeit deteriorated democracy. Why is it a bourgeois democracy?
Because incumbent officials have been elected and the Brazilian Congress is
still in running order, effectively influencing decision-making processes – and
while its influence is limited by Brazil's hyperpresidential system, this limitation is not new to the current political situation. And why is it a deteriorated
democracy? Fundamentally for two reasons. First, because since the beginning of Operation Car Wash and thanks to the so-called Clean Slate Act (*Lei
da Ficha Limpa*), the Brazilian judicial apparatus has created a political screen-
ing process to challenge the candidacy of leftists or center-leftists who have a
real chance of winning elections; and secondly, because the country's political
institutions – including the Supreme Court (STF) – are being watched over by
the Armed Forces, particularly by the Army. Some examples of this include
the episode when General Eduardo Villas Bôas, then Army commander, publicly reprimanded the Supreme Court in April 2018, ordering the country's top
court to dismiss a petition for a writ of *habeas corpus* filed by ex-president Luiz
Inácio Lula da Silva's defense lawyers; and also, the fact that the Legislative
branch is not authorized to legislate the military pension system – the bill
currently under consideration was actually drafted by the Armed Forces. The
backsliding of the democratic organization of State institutions corresponds
to changes in the current political regime, a plan in which we find threats and

2   English translation: Togliatti, P. (1976). *Lectures on Fascism*. New York: International
    Publishers.

attacks against political freedoms, including censorship, attacks on the right to assembly, arbitrary detention, etc.

2   For a General and Theoretical Concept of Fascism

It is, therefore, a neofascist movement and a predominantly neofascist government, but it is not, up to this point in time at least, a fascist dictatorship. Now, we may ask a general question: why is it possible to talk about fascism or neofascism in the 21st century and in a country on the periphery of international capitalism? Isn't fascism a typical political phenomenon of the 20th century in imperialist countries? With regard to this matter, there are some answers that we believe are mistaken and should be criticized before we present our own definition.

The first mistake arises from a proposed approach according to which the fascist phenomenon is limited to 1919–1945 Italy or, at most, to Germany that same period. Gentile (2019), a prestigious historian of fascism, has recently published a book advocating for this restrictive thesis. It is a radical historicist approach, according to which, similarly to the concept of fascism, we should understand that other concepts, in general, could only stand for the phenomena of the period in which and/or for which they were originally created. Gentile sums up his thesis with the following statement: the concept of fascism is the history of fascism itself; it did not have predecessors in the 19th century, and it will not have successors in the 21st century (Gentile 2019: 126). Presenting an in-depth critique of this kind of approach would require more space than we have for this *Crítica Marxista* dossier. We may argue, however, that just as we generalize when we elaborate on and use the concepts of democracy, dictatorship, monarchy, republic, and other Political Science concepts, we must also generalize when we elaborate on and use the concept of fascism, which is a reactionary political movement of the intermediate strata of capitalist society, and a specific type of bourgeois dictatorship.

While Gentile is not a Marxist, historicism is also found in some Marxist traditions, including Italian Marxism. A Marxist author, Atilio Borón, has recently written about Bolsonaro by resorting to this same general idea: that fascism is a historical phenomenon that cannot be repeated (Borón 2019). Borón specifically argues that the hegemonic bourgeois fraction of the fascist dictatorship was a national bourgeoisie, a political group that has supposedly disappeared as a result of a new wave of internationalization of the capitalist economy. I have provided a detailed criticism of this thesis in my article mentioned above (Boito 2019). I have not explored the matter – and will not do it here – of whether or not the bourgeoisie from different capitalist countries has merged into one world bourgeoisie. But I do want to point out this: with respect to its political regime, fascism is a kind of dictatorship and, like other political regimes, it can accommodate, within certain limits, different makeups of the bloc in power – the contradictory unity of the bourgeois fractions that hold state power – with different hegemonic bourgeois fractions. The same political regime can accommodate different hegemonic forces, and the same bourgeois fraction may exercise its hegemony in different regimes – which is not necessarily simply the flip side of the coin. On the one hand, bourgeois democracy has availed the organization of the hegemony of middle business during the age of competitive capitalism and the organization of the hegemony of big monopoly business as of the 20th century. On the other hand, while big business has established its hegemony through fascism in Italy and Germany, that same fraction of the bourgeoisie reached a hegemonic position in England and the United States through bourgeois democracy. A fascist government or regime can, therefore, implement either: a) an interventionist economic policy, representing the interests of the national bourgeoisie of its country, or b) a neoliberal economic policy, representing the interests of the foreign imperialist capital and the fraction of the bourgeoisie of the dependent country subordinated to that capital. This is exactly the case in Brazil today, which combines neofascism with neoliberalism. While the relationship between the bloc in power and the political regime is not random, it is also not univocal.

The second mistake we intend to criticize is regarding the authors who, like us, work with a general concept of fascism, but with one we consider to be descriptive. We are going to refer to two authors who have published works that have made an impact. We are thinking about Eco (2018), with his little book *Il Fascismo Eterno*, which has thirty published editions, and Paxton (2004), with his important work *Anatomy of Fascism*. In these cases, we argue that fascism is defined descriptively, because these authors follow what may be the hugely dominant trend in research on the topic, which defines it by creating a list, whether bigger or smaller, of what would be its attributes as a political and ideological phenomenon. Eco (2018: 34–48) lists fourteen characteristics of fascism; at the end of his book, Paxton (2004: 218–220) resorts to as many as twenty attributes to define the fascist political behavior. This kind of definition should be regarded as descriptive because the authors do not elucidate the theoretical criteria based on which they selected the attributes of fascism. Through a radical empiricist approach, they believe they create the concept based solely and directly on empirical facts. They do not make a distinction between what is primary and what is secondary, they do not qualify the relationships between different attributes – that is, whether or not they constitute an organized whole –, and they also do not provide us insights on how to proceed in face of a historical phenomenon that may eventually present only part of the list of characteristics they compiled to characterize the concept.

3   A Reactionary Mass Movement and Dictatorial Regime

We understand that the concept of fascism is a general concept. We also understand that its definition should be theoretical, not descriptive. That means that, based both on historical facts and on a general theory of politics and State, it should situate what is essential to the phenomenon, offering a path to historical analysis. As we define capital as the value that values itself, the State as a specific institution that organizes class domination, and social classes as groups defined by their common position with respect to social production, by using these definitions we are indicating a path for analysis development, not presenting an exhaustive list of the characteristics of each of these phenomena – capital, State, social class. Similarly, when we present a theoretical definition of fascism, we then are able to find directions toward historical analysis.

Every historical type of State with exploitative ruling classes – slave societies, feudal and capitalist modes of production – historically occurs in dictatorial or democratic forms. Fascism, as a form of organization of the State apparatus and power, is one version of the dictatorial form of the capitalist State, which means it is a type of dictatorship that differs from a military dictatorship, for example. However, fascism, as we have pointed out earlier, is also the ideology that justifies such a dictatorship and the movement that, by finding cohesiveness through this ideology, can fight to implement or maintain this type of dictatorship. The works that support us are Marxist analyses of fascism. We are thinking about authors who were contemporary with the phenomenon, as well as others who are more recent. In one or the other case, we may mention Palmiro Togliatti and his *Corso Sugli Avversari – Le Lezioni Sul Fascismo*, which gathers lectures the Italian communist leader gave in 1935; Daniel Guérin and his 1936 book *Fascisme et Grand Capital*; and Nicos Poulantzas' 1970 work *Fascisme et Dictature*.

We define the fascist movement as a *reactionary mass movement* and, following Togliatti, the fascist dictatorship as a *reactionary mass regime*. This element distinguishes it from a military dictatorship, a topic that was extensively debated among the Brazilian left in the 1960s and 1970s. Fascism is, so to speak and borrowing a term from biology, the genus, while the original fascism and the Brazilian neofascism are two different species of the same genus to which they both belong. Each of these two species effectuates the qualities of the genus in a particular fashion. We provide an attempt to break down these general similarities and specific differences in Table 8.1.

The fact that it is a movement of the intermediate strata of capitalist society is an important aspect of it. Fascism is not a bourgeois movement, even though it comes to power by being co-opted by the bourgeoisie, and even though it ideologically relies, from its inception, on the bourgeoisie. It is a mass movement of a middle grouping and, therefore, presents short-term ideological elements and economic interests that may be at odds with the immediate ideology and economic interests of the bourgeoisie. Through its petty-bourgeoisie-like conservative critique of capitalism, the original fascist movement actually confused socialists and communists in several aspects – Poulantzas (1970) mentions a "*status quo* anti-capitalist" ideology. In Brazil, the reactionary mass movement originated in 2015 during the campaign conducted to oust Dilma Rousseff. From that movement, after a sifting process, a specifically neofascist movement unfolded: Bolsonarism. The criticisms of corruption and the so-called "exchange of favors" policy made by this movement and also by its surroundings – this latter also of middle class social composition – confused left and far-left parties. The hegemonic sector of the Workers' Party (PT) and even Rousseff's government officials were imbued by the ideology according to which the institutions of the bourgeois State are socially neutral (the so-called "republicanism") and believed that Operation Car Wash really aimed at fighting corruption, and not aimed at using the fight against corruption as a tool on behalf of the interests of international capital, meeting the ideological expectations of the upper middle class (Boito 2018). The Unified Workers' Socialist Party (PSTU) and one of the sectors of the Socialism and Freedom Party (PSOL), in turn, were drawn to Operation Car Wash, in this case driven by the political miscalculation of choosing the PT's reformism as the primary enemy they should fight. To a greater or lesser extent, part of the left and the center-left also failed to realize that the criticism against old politics was, and is, the criticism against parliamentary politics, that is, against the bourgeois democracy itself – the neofascist group aspires to rule by decree.

The mass base of the fascist movement creates a complex situation when it rises to power, which happens thanks to it being co-opted by the bourgeoisie, especially by one of the bourgeois fractions that fights for hegemony within the bloc in power. In order to fulfill their role in organizing the hegemony of big monopoly business, Hitler and Mussolini had to squirm free of the so-called plebeian segment of fascism, actually physically eliminating the leaders of that segment, as it is known. Also, they had to change (in Mussolini's case) or invalidate (in Hitler's case) the movement's original program (Guérin 1965; Poulantzas 1970; Shirer 2017; Togliatti 1976). On a smaller scale, to primarily yet

TABLE 8.1   Genus and species: Original fascism, neofascism

The fascist movement genus	Species: Original fascist movement (Italy, Germany)	Species: Neofascist movement (Bolsonaro's Brazil)
Reactionary mobilization of intermediate social strata of capitalist society.	Mainly petty bourgeoisie, with middle class elements.	Mainly middle class, with small owners.
Eliminate the left from the political process.	Eliminate the labor movement that organized in socialist and communist mass parties.	Eliminate bourgeois reformism with an unorganized popular base – workers of the marginal mass.
Conservative ideology, although superficially critical, connected to the social situation, values, and interests of intermediate social strata of society.	Anti-communism, cult of violence, criticism of big business and bourgeois democracy; political use of chauvinism, racism (systematically), and homophobia (diffusely).	Anti-communism, cult of violence, criticism against corruption and the old (democratic) politics; political use of chauvinism, racism (diffusely), and homophobia (systematically).
Base mobilization.	Mass party organizing with militia groups.	Loose organization through social media.

General process through which fascism rises to power	Species: Original Fascism	Species: Neofascism
Emergence during political crisis with polarizing class conflict and conflicts between State institutions.	Yes, with high polarization.	Yes, with mild polarization.

TABLE 8.1   Genus and species: Original fascism, neofascism (*cont.*)

General process through which fascism rises to power	Species: Original Fascism	Species: Neofascism
Crisis in traditional bourgeois parties.	Exhaustion of the bourgeois government's conciliation formula in Italy, Nazi Party's election *tsunami* in Germany.	Election decline of Brazilian Social Democracy Party (PSDB) and Brazilian Democratic Movement Party (PMDB). Abrupt increase in voting results favoring the right and far right in 2018 elections.
Political defeats for labor and people's organizations and power relations favorable to the bourgeoisie.	Defeat in the *Biennio Rosso* (Italy); defeats in the 1918 German Revolution.	Dilma Rousseff's ousting, Michel Temer's labor reform, conviction and imprisonment of Luiz Inácio Lula da Silva, challenge to Lula da Silva's candidacy, and Bolsonaro's election.
Bourgeois solution: co-optation of the fascist movement by a reactionary fraction of the bourgeoisie allows the movement to rise to power and establish a new bourgeois hegemony.	The fascist party (PNF, NSDAP) takes office and establishes the political hegemony of the bourgeois fraction of "big imperial, monopoly business"; middle capital moves to a subordinate position within the bloc in power.	The neofascist group takes over the Brazilian presidency and re-establishes the political hegemony of the bourgeois fractions of "big international capital" and "associated, dependent bourgeoisie" – internal big bourgeoisie moves to a subordinate position within the bloc in power.

TABLE 8.1   Genus and species: Original fascism, neofascism (*cont.*)

General process through which fascism rises to power	Species: Original Fascism	Species: Neofascism
Crisis dynamics: movement from the bottom co-opted by the top. A supporting class prevents the fascist government from being reduced to a passive tool in the hands of the bourgeoisie.	Yes, with a strong, organized movement from the bottom. Petty-bourgeoisie as a supporting class in the big business government leads to turmoil within the government support base.	Yes, with weak, poorly organized movement from the bottom. Middle class as supporting class for the government of international capital and associated bourgeoisie leads to turmoil within the government support base.

not exclusively serve the interests of international capital and its associated bourgeoisie, Bolsonaro is led to come into conflict with segments of the middle class aspiring to put an end to what they call "old politics", as well as with the movement of truck drivers, his supporters who feel betrayed because of his fuel pricing policy, which serves the interests of international investors.

The political crisis that created the original fascism is more severe than the Brazilian political crisis that created neofascism. Both have general common elements: they are connected to an economic crisis of capitalism; they expose a crisis of hegemony within the bloc in power – a contention between big and middle business, in one case, and a contention between the big internal bourgeoisie and the big bourgeoisie associated with international capital, in the other; they accommodate the bourgeoisie's aspirations to eliminate victories from the working class; they are aggravated by the abrupt establishment of a disruptive middle class or petty-bourgeois political movement; they can accommodate a crisis of bourgeois partisan representation; they are marked by the inability of labor and people's parties to present their own solution to the political crisis – socialists and communists were defeated before fascism rose to power (Poulantzas 1970) and the democratic and people's movement in

Brazil has been experiencing a number of setbacks since Dilma Rousseff's oust-
ing, showing an inability to react (Boito 2018; 2019). These similarities between
the two crises are very strong and extremely important to characterize fascism
and explain its origins in capitalist societies (Poulantzas 1970). There is, however, a key component that sets the political crisis in which the original fascism
emerged apart from the political crisis in which neofascism develops. And that
difference brings us back to the matter of the mass base of fascism.

The "left" that the original fascism opposed was a mass labor movement,
organized in socialist and communist parties, and because of what the political struggle then required, the original fascism then made an effort to replicate
that kind of organization, creating militias as a substitute for cells and sections. Its enemy was more threatening and powerful then. Meanwhile, neofascism is facing a "left" that is represented by bourgeois reformism – the neodevelopmentalism of the PT administrations – that relies on an unorganized
popular base. The enemy of neofascism is less threatening and politically more
fragile. In this situation, neofascism has organized fundamentally through
social media. In the case of the original fascism, actions by fascist groups pro-
liferated, as they carried out physical assaults and political killings, set labor
organizations' facilities on fire, and attacked communists and Roma and
Jewish communities, always counting on the lenient disposition of the court
system (Shirer 2017). In the case of neofascism, we have witnessed episodes
of verbal abuse and threats in public spaces or through social media, as well
as blatant expressions of discrimination against people from the Northeast of
Brazil, Black people, and lower-income people, with the cooperation of the
court and law enforcement systems to threaten crowds of democratic and people's movements and arrest their leaders.

Today, neofascism is displaying organizational incompetence. The two pro-
government demonstrations they called had a poor turnout. The government
itself hesitated to call the protests, and eventually flinched. The ideologist
behind this movement, Olavo de Carvalho, has realized this weakness and is
now calling his horde to organize in order to be able to stand up for the government. We do not rule out the hypothesis that this movement could decline,
and its ruling group may be absorbed by the deteriorated democracy they have
contributed to create in Brazil. We must bear Palmiro Togliatti's wise words in
mind: a fascist dictatorship may or may not arise from a certain economic situation and class struggle, and not only – nor especially – due to fascist authoritarian projects and ambitions. And we might add, the neofascist movement
may ultimately dissolve or moderate its own program, just like a left-wing party
may moderate its own program and mischaracterize itself by changing what
it must change to secure its own government power. And this is what must

change: the neofascist movement's obstacle is the form of the bourgeois democratic State, while a socialist movement's obstacle is the bourgeois State itself.

References

Boito Jr., A. (2019). O neofascismo no Brasil. *Boletim LIERI*, UFRRJ, No. 1, 1–11. Available at http://laboratorios.ufrrj.br/lieri/wp-content/uploads/sites/7/2019/05/Boletim-1-O-Neofascismo-no-Brasil.pdf (consulted October 15, 2019).

Boito Jr., A. (2018). *Reforma e crise política no Brasil: os conflitos de classe nos governos do PT*. São Paulo; Campinas: Unesp; Unicamp.

Borón, A. (2019). Caracterizar o governo Bolsonaro como fascista é um grave erro. *Brasil de Fato*. Available at https://www.brasildefato.com.br/2019/01/02/artigo-or-caracterizar-o-governo-de-jair-bolsonaro-como-fascista-e-um-erro-grave/ (consulted October 10, 2019).

Eco, U. (2018). *Il fascismo eterno*. Milan: La nave di Teseo.

Gentile, E. (2019). *Chi è fascista*. Roma-Bari: Editori Laterza.

Guérin, D. (1965 [1936]). *Fascisme et grand capital*. 2nd Edition. Paris: François Maspero.

Paxton, R.O. (2004). *The anatomy of fascism*. New York: Alfred A. Knopf.

Poulantzas, N. (1970). *Fascisme et dictature*. Paris: François Maspero.

Shirer, W. (2017). *Ascensão e Queda do Terceiro Reich*. 2nd Edition. Rio de Janeiro: Nova Fronteira.

Togliatti, P. (1976). *Lectures on Fascism*. New York: International Publishers.

CHAPTER 9

The Failure of Dilma Rousseff's Developmentalist Experiment

André Singer

Why did Dilma Rousseff's attempt to ensure sustainable growth with reindustrialization during her fist term (2011 and 2014) fail?[1] My hypothesis is that the president bet on a coalition between industrialists and workers to sustain a developmentalist turn, but in the midst of the effort the coalition disbanded as the industrialists changed their position, sinking the policy architecture that could have dealt with the shock waves generated by the recurrence of the world crisis that started in 2008. In place of a coalition between industrial capital and labor, a renewed bourgeois united front emerged around a neoliberal platform focused particularly on cuts in public expenditures and labor and social security reforms. What I want to investigate in this chapter is the political components of the failure of the developmentalist experiment, linked to the problem of class coalitions that support this or that economic orientation.

For a minimal definition of developmentalism, I'd use the definition offered by the economist Ricardo Bielschowsky (1995: 7):

> By 'developmentalism' we understand ... the ideology of the transformation of Brazilian society defined by an economic project that is composed of the following fundamental points: (*a*) full industrialization is the way to overcome poverty and underdevelopment in Brazil; (*b*) there is no way to achieve efficient and rational industrialization in Brazil through the spontaneous forces of the market; therefore, it is necessary for the state to plan it; (*c*) planning should identify the desired expansion of the economic sectors and the instruments to promote this expansion; and (*d*) the state must also direct the expansion, capture, and orientation of financial resources, promoting direct investments in those sectors where private initiative is insufficient.

---

1 An earlier version of the arguments in this chapter appeared in Singer (2020). The main ideas had already been published in articles since 2015 and consolidated in the book Singer, André. O lulismo em crise: um quebra-cabeça do período Dilma Rousseff (2011–2016). São Paulo, Companhia das Letras, 2018.

Examining the practical proposals of the "new economic matrix" of Dilma Rousseff in terms of Bielschowsky's criteria, one perceives their developmentalist bias. The clearing of paths for industrial recovery, the efforts at full industrialization, the belief in the indispensability of state planning, the distrust of spontaneous market forces, the decision by the state of which sectors to expand and the public role in its financing – all these factors were present during Rousseff's first term.

1   Advance, Peak, and Retreat

After a semester that was to a certain point typical of the beginning of a presidential term, with its budgetary constraints,[2] ministerial adjustments, and so on, in the Brazilian winter of 2011 the second phase of the global financial crisis interrupted Dilma Rousseff's routine. On August 4 and 5, markets around the globe revived the turbulence of 2008. Following the example of what had been done in 2008, the president sought to sustain the pace of local growth despite the generalized downturn. Calculations showed that to continue the reforms of Lulism it was necessary for the gross domestic product (GDP) to grow by about 5 percent a year (Singer 2012: 160). This was where the opportunity opened up for the new economic matrix that had been in preparation since the replacement of Henrique Meirelles by Alexandre Tombini as head of the Central Bank in November 2010.[3] In the anticyclical program adopted by Rousseff, interest rate reduction, intensive use of the Brazilian Development Bank, reindustrialization, deregulation, infrastructure projects, reform of the electrical energy sector, devaluation of the real, capital controls, and protection of national products were highlighted.[4]

Lulism was the strategy employed by Lula from 2003 on of maintaining economic orthodoxy (especially in his first term of office, between 2003 and 2006) and promoting the internal market for the less fortunate, which, added to the maintenance of stability, was nothing less than a complete class (or

---

2   For some economists budgetary constraint was excessive at this stage and determined the further course of the new economic matrix. Guido Mantega (2012), however, says that it "was very important to raise the 2011 primary result to support interest rate reduction".

3   "The relapse of the international crisis that occurred in the second half of 2011 had a severe impact on economic activity. In this context, the decline of interest rates opened up the opportunity for us to advance without risking inflation and while reducing the impacts of the foreign crisis on Brazil" (Mantega 2012).

4   This is a summary of the hundreds of initiatives taken by the government in the period. For more details, see Singer (2018).

class-fraction) program. This fraction was not the organized working class, whose movement had started in the late 1970s as a "break with the current economic model" (PT Diretório Nacional 2002: 15), but what Paul Singer (1981: 22, 83), analyzing the social structure of Brazil in the early 1980s, called the "subproletariat," those who "offer their labor force in the market without finding anybody who is willing to acquire it at a price that ensures their reproduction under normal conditions." Included in this category were "domestic servants, wage earners of small direct producers, and workers deprived of the minimum conditions of participation in the class struggle".

It fell to Rousseff, a cadre with experience in the developmentalism of the former governor of Rio Grande do Sul and Rio de Janeiro, Leonel Brizola, to move away from economic orthodoxy, adopting the systematic intervention of the state in the economy for the first time in almost 40 years. The former minister Luiz Carlos Bresser-Pereira, sensitive to the national question, soon noticed what was at stake, writing in the heat of the moment that the president was "certainly thinking of leading a national project with broad support from society" and willing to confront the Gordian knots of the situation, "high interest rates and overvalued exchange rates" (Bresser-Pereira 2013a: 10).

Given the domination since the 1980s of neoliberal theses, with their interdiction of state intervention, the program implemented by Rousseff was audacious but flawed. For example, according to Bresser-Pereira, an exponent of the "new developmentalism", the real would have had to be devalued even more to make Brazilian industry effectively competitive. He spoke at the time of pegging the dollar to R$2.75 when it had only reached R$2.00 in the minidevaluation promoted by the new economic matrix (Bresser-Pereira 2013a).[5] According to the economist Ricardo Carneiro (2018: 18), however, "a real effective devaluation on the order of 20 percent is not insignificant" (Carneiro 2018: 18). In tune with "social-developmentalism," the economist Pedro Paulo Bastos, in turn, criticized the lack of public investment in Rousseff's experiment: "A good countercyclical policy would be similar to 2009: imagine if the government had pursued a high primary surplus or merely increased subsidies in 2009! The countercyclical policy then depended on a strong acceleration of public spending and particularly of investment, which directly encourages effective demand" (quoted in Guimarães 2015). Carneiro notes, however, that "public investment as a whole widens slightly" between Lula's second term and Rousseff's first term, "ranging from 4.1 percent of GDP to 4.3 percent,

---

5 Later, because of worsening political and economic conditions, the dollar rose again, reaching R$3.40 at the end of July 2015, but by then the context was already different.

proportionally divided between state and public administration" (Carneiro 2018: 30). In other words, public investment may not have been enough to reorient production in an adverse period, but there had been no reversal of the previous policy.

These critics did not, however, deny that, in the context of a weak Lulista reformism, the new matrix implied picking new fights, since it confronted the political power of the financial sector (see Singer 2012: 4). It is as if, taking advantage of the previous political accumulation obtained, Dilma was trying to accelerate the pace of Lulism. With Guido Mantega's ascent to the Ministry of Finance in 2006, the creation of the conditions for greater state activism had begun. In 2007, through the Growth Acceleration Plan, the state began to awaken from the lethargy of the 1980s. Then, in 2008, public banks acquired a crucial role in the reorganization of production, representing powerful levers for the promotion of private initiative. In 2009 and 2010, the incorporation of selective fiscal incentives into the arsenal of available instruments gave the state access to levers previously blocked. Finally, the appointment of Alexandre Tombini, on the eve of 2011, incorporated the Central Bank into the preparations for a substantial policy leap.

While from this angle there was continuity between Lula and Rousseff, from the political point of view there was an inflection. Lula always operated on the margins, avoiding confrontation. Rousseff, in contrast, entered into combat. By reducing interest rates and forcing down spreads, she broke the détente with rentierism. In that moment (in 2012), the rupture was supported by the industrialists. "Finally", wrote the steel entrepreneur and vice president of the Federação das Indústrias do Estado de São Paulo (Federation of Industries of the State of São Paulo – FIESP) Benjamin Steinbruch (2012), Brazil entered "the era of civilized interests".

In addition to confronting the core of capital (the financial sector), Dilma decided to politicize the theme, again departing from the Lulista script. At the launch of the second national industry protection package in 2012, she said that it was difficult to technically justify the level of spreads being maintained by the country's private banks. Later she stated that the government possessed the "instruments" to allow companies "access to a lower cost of capital" (Mendes 2012) and, through Finance Minister Mantega, caused the public Bank of Brazil to reduce its own spreads. Threatened with losing markets, the private banks were forced to retreat. It was understood that from then on over-throwing Mantega was the goal of the financial sector. "The banks' diagnosis is that, if they do nothing to reduce rates, they will lose customers to public institutions, especially in service to companies," reported *Folha de S. Paulo* (D'Amorim and Sciarreta 2012). It was in this triumphal mood that Rousseff said on May 1 (worker's day in Brazil), 2012, "The financial sector ... cannot explain this perverse logic to Brazilians: the SELIC [prime rate] is low, inflation remains stable, but interest on bank overdrafts, loans, and credit cards does not diminish" (*Folha de S. Paulo* 2012).

In October 2012, with only a 4.6 percent unemployment rate and workers' income on the rise, the PT won the election in the city of São Paulo. Fernando Haddad – a young politician whose technical profile resembled that of Rousseff herself – had beaten the veteran José Serra of the Partido da Social Democracia Brasileira (Brazilian Social Democracy Party – PSDB). The PT's performance in the municipal elections made it seem as if Rousseff's shift was going well. The federal government then prepared to end 2012 with a flourish, reducing the price of electricity in connection with the campaign launched by the FIESP in 2011 and simultaneously making a gesture toward the poor, for whom the size of the energy bill was significant. It looked like the right strategy for the victory of the industrial-popular coalition. The developmentalist effort had reached its peak.

The climax, however, foreshadowed a painful decline. Adding the jewel of a reformed electrical sector to the crown destroyed the basis of the experiment. Taking advantage of a rise in prices in January 2013, the Central Bank president, in a conversation with a journalist on February 7, revealed that inflation was "showing strong resilience" and that the situation was "not comfortable" (Leitão 2013). It was enough for investors to start betting on interest rates. Using monetary policy to hold back inflation – the watchword of neoliberal leadership – just when the reduction of costs to the borrower was finally complete meant dismantling the developmentalist experiment.

Until the Central Bank started to raise interest rates, the developmentalists encouraged hopes of a resumption of the pace of GDP growth. The increase of only 1.8 percent (as calculated by the new method) in 2012 and the fact that investment did not increase despite all the measures taken agonized the advocates of the new economic matrix, but until the rise in interest rates in April 2013 there was hope that the countercyclical measures adopted from mid-2011 on would work. To some extent, the forecast was promising, since there was a 2.7 percent increase in GDP in 2013. While this growth rate was insufficient, it did help maintain the level of employment and the wage gains of workers. However, with the continuous increase in interest rates, whose contractionary effects usually appear only six months to a year after being enacted, the prospects for maintaining growth in 2014 were canceled out. In fact, in 2014 GDP increased only 0.5 percent.

At the same time, growing criticism of state activism by foreign banks, risk agencies, international institutions of economic control, multinational corporations, and multiple voices in the Brazilian mass media created the ideological climate needed to force a neoliberal turn. Countless articles and editorials, thousands of reports on domestic and foreign communication vehicles, and millions of minutes of radio and TV were devoted to showing how necessary it was to cut the government's inefficient and "uncontrolled" spending and let the market function to "reorder the country" and return to growth. The most effective pressure in favor of the neoliberal shock came, however, from where it was least expected and was therefore decisive. As the policy in their favor was being applied, the industrial entrepreneurs were paradoxically noncompliant. How is this enigma to be explained?

2   The Pendulum Swing

In order to account for the class articulations that characterized Lulism, I have formulated an interpretative scheme according to which, throughout Lula's two terms, two opposing coalitions, the "rentier" and the "productivist", were the chief protagonists. The rentier represented financial capital and the traditional middle class, while the productivist was composed of industrial entrepreneurs associated with the organized fraction of the working class. Leveraging the two with support from the subproletariat, the Lulista governments would arbitrate conflicts according to the correlation of forces, sometimes favoring one coalition and sometimes its competitor (Singer 2012: 155–168 and 200–221).[6]

The rentier program aimed to keep Brazil aligned with the neoliberal recipe and within the orbit of large international capital and U.S. geopolitical leadership. For the productivist coalition, the primary goal was to accelerate the growth rate through state intervention, leading to reindustrialization and allowing a faster distribution of income. It was assumed that the rentier coalition would find a privileged channel in the PSDB (Partido da Social Democracia Brasileira – Social Democratic Brazilian Party) because of the sympathy with the party of the financial sector and the traditional middle class. In the productivist camp, the PT remained close to the union movement and, in its Lulista version, the subproletariat, as well as having a friendly relationship with the industrial sector reflected in the presence of the textile entrepreneur José Alencar as Lula's vice president in 2002 and 2006. The Partido do Movimento Democrático Brasileiro (Brazilian Democratic Movement Party – PMDB, now

---

6   Bresser-Pereira (2013b) speaks of a "financial-rentier" coalition made up of "the high and middle rentier bourgeoisie and the financiers" whose objective would always be to maintain a high level of interest rates.

MDB), in turn, managed to put down roots in agrobusiness, a sector that, along with the PMDB itself, oscillated between the two main coalitions.

In the first half of 2011, the pact between industrialists and workers was intensified with a joint document signed by the FIESP, the two largest union centrals – the Central Única dos Trabalhadores (Workers' Central – CUT) and Força Sindical – as well as the Metalworkers' Unions of the ABC and São Paulo. The document, "Brazil for Dialogue, Production, and Employment", launched in May of that year, noted that the "growing reprimarization of the export agenda", the "replacement of domestic production by imported industrial products and inputs", and the "significant decline in national content in production" served as a warning and a call for joint action (Skaf, Henrique, and Silva 2011). The mystery is that, in spite of the evident convergences, the industrialists, instead of consolidating their support for the government, gradually moved away from Dilma Rousseff and aligned themselves with the rentier bloc. It was as if every move of the government to carry out the program they had proposed raised the fear of "interventionism", making investment infeasible and creating distrust. At first, the entrepreneurs' complaints were muted, but soon they publicly split from the 2011 agreement.

In April 2013 the FIESP released a study showing the advantages for Brazilian industries of settling in Paraguay (FIESP 2013): "We see a huge potential for integrating productive chains with Paraguay, with significant labor availability for the traditional manufacturing industry, which has been suffering and losing competitiveness in relation to the outside," the entity's director said at the seminar "Investment Opportunities in Paraguay". Among the advantages would be the 36 percent cheaper labor in the neighboring country because of the absence of labor benefits there.

One of the CUT signers of the pact of two years earlier responded harshly, "Perhaps this is the FIESP's great dream: a region where the tax burden is the smallest possible, one that can paternalistically offer only minimal service to those in extreme poverty and condemn various countries in the region, starting with Paraguay, to becoming maquiladoras for increasing the profits of the big companies" (Henrique 2013). When in June the FIESP illuminated the facade of its imposing building on Avenida Paulista (São Paulo) with the national flag in sympathy with the symbols adopted by the centrists and right-wingers who were demonstrating in the streets, it was clear that it had gone over to the opposition. Its president, Paulo Skaf (2013), who was present at one of the demonstrations that month, wrote that he had witnessed a "cry for renewal". The demonstrations in June, although far more than that, inaugurated the middle-class wave against Rousseff, which was to culminate in March 2016 with the definitive push to overthrow the president (Singer 2018: Chap. 3).

In response to the employers' offensive, the union centrals have tried ever since, with less success, to put labor-specific issues on the table (CUT 2013). The productivist coalition was thus undone, and the class struggle resumed its centrality.

At the same time, a bourgeois united front emerged in opposition to the developmentalist experiment. A columnist (Safatle 2013) exposed the situation on the front page of the economy newspaper *Valor*. The federal government had concluded that the policies demanded by the industrialists, such as the reduction of interest rates and payroll exemptions, had not produced the expected effects, generating, on the contrary, distrust in the business environment. Pressured by the situation, the executive branch began to make concessions, such as greater returns to the concessionaires of public utilities, but this did not help. At the end of 2013, at the national industrial summit promoted by the Confederação Nacional da Indústria (National Confederation of Industry – CNI), shortly after the president retired from the stage an associate took the floor to attack: "We went back on the side of growth and productivity." In August 2014 Steinbruch, now acting president of the FIESP, who had once welcomed Brazil's entry into the era of civilized interests, said, "Only a madman invests in Brazil." He also migrated to the defense of the flexibility of the Consolidation of Labor Laws as the CNI had done two years earlier.

With the support of industrialists, agrobusiness, commerce, and services to the proposals of the financial sector, capitalist unity around the cut in public expenditures, a decrease in the valuation of labor, and a reduction of protection for workers had become complete. Reflecting this, in November 2014 the president of the CNI, Robson Andrade, defended the fiscal adjustment and even an increase in interest rates (Branco 2014), which, in theory, would be detrimental to the interests of the productive sector. While Rousseff was leading the developmentalist advance from above, the industrial bourgeoisie took the floor from below.

3   A Stunning Zigzag

The zigzag of the entrepreneurs seems to have caught the president by surprise. "I ... never understood the history, except a posteriori, of the richer classes of Brazil in relation to interest rates, and I did not realize their degree of aversion to paying for any part of the crisis" (quoted in Piccin and Pomar 2017). Unprepared for the blow, Rousseff failed to react. To react from the left it would have been necessary to mobilize the organized working class and the popular movements, but since this was not part of the Lulist agenda Rousseff retreated point by point, trying to win back business support. In the protests of June 2013, she promoted a cut of R$10 billion in the 2013 budget, "in response, above all, to the financial market, which accuses [the government] of leniency with inflation" (Barrocal 2013: 37). Consistent with this effort to rebuild the productivist coalition, in early 2014 she again limited public spending, abandoning the legislative bill that reduced the debts of states and municipalities. As a result, the strategic city hall commanded by Haddad was strangled, endangering the future of the PT in São Paulo's administration (which would effectively be lost in the 2016 election). With contention over public expenditures and continually high interest rates, it is understandable that GDP growth in 2014 was virtually zero (UOL 2015). Contractionary monetary and fiscal policy, together with the deep distrust of the bourgeoisie, contributed to sinking investment, which dropped by 4.4 percent in the election year. The decline of economic activity, in turn, pulled down revenue, leaving the state vulnerable to new proposals for fiscal adjustment that become overwhelming from that point on. The neoliberal agenda, as a whole, gained momentum.

Finally, aware that the siege was ending, the president maintained the prevailing zigzag: she blinked to the left and turned to the right. She decided to keep the stimulus policies, such as payroll exemptions, reductions to the tax on industrialized products for durable goods, the investment support program, and the contribution to the "My House, My Life" program in order to guarantee employment stability and wage increases during the 2014 campaign. This allowed her to convince progressive sectors and the popular electorate that she was willing to avoid the neoliberal shock represented by the PSDB. "They ... want to bring back the recession, unemployment, wage tightening, increased inequality, and all Brazil's past submission to the International Monetary Fund," Rousseff said in the campaign, referring to the PSDB (Souza 2014). Once reelected, however, she made an abrupt turnaround, appointed a neoliberal finance minister, and opened the way for her impeachment.

4   Explanations

The concept of fractions of the capitalist class remains current in political science. In a recent note, the political scientist Sebastião Velasco e Cruz (2017: 4) points out that in several countries the possible "emergence of a transnational capitalist class" is being discussed. In Brazil, the political scientist Armando Boito Jr. (2012a) has defended the permanence, despite recent transformations, of important local bourgeoisies. For him, beyond the productive or rentier aspect of economic activity, the key element for understanding the position of each bourgeois segment is its national or international character. Companies controlled by the "internal great bourgeoisie", which "fears being swallowed up or destroyed by large foreign economic groups", need "the protective and active action of the Brazilian state" (Boito Jr. 2012a: 77). He stresses that the desire for protection by the state distinguishes national banks from foreign ones and national from international industry. The whole "internal bourgeoisie", which according to Poulantzas (1975: 77) "has its own economic foundation and accumulation base", wishes to be defended from foreign competition, which threatens to suffocate it, while foreign capitalists resist protectionism, favoring the opening up of markets. The Brazilian internal bourgeoisie, whether rentier or productive, has a number of common interests: customs protectionism for domestic products, limiting the inflow of foreign capital into the banking sector, stimulating domestic ethanol production, preference for national factories in state purchases, state policy abroad to assist Brazilian exports and heavy construction companies outside the country (Boito Jr. 2012a: 77), financing of national companies by the Brazilian Development Bank, support for the export of goods and capital of Brazilian companies, and maintenance of domestic demand and state investment in infrastructure (Boito Jr. 2012b).

Boito's view extends to coalitions. Instead of the struggle between productivists and rentiers that I have proposed he sees a struggle of the internal bourgeoisie, allied with the unions and the popular movements, against a bourgeoisie that is "perfectly integrated with and subordinated to foreign capital" (Boito Jr. 2012b: 69–70). According to this view, the internal bourgeoisie is hegemonic within the power bloc representing Lulism: "The PT governments do not arbitrate; in fact they prioritize the interests of this bourgeois fraction" (Boito Jr. 2013: 175). Herein lies the heart of our divergence. What is at stake is identifying the main contradiction, whether engagement in production versus rentier profits or national capital versus international capital. Boito Jr. (2013: 179) acknowledges that "the industrial sector has a conflict with national banking capital," just as I admit that there are interests that oppose firms with national capital in favor of international capital. Perhaps we both admit that in order to illuminate the totality, interbourgeois tensions must be taken into account.

The program established in "Brazil for Dialogue, Production, and Employment", representing the productivist coalition, coincides, in my view, with what Boito Jr. attributes to the internal bourgeoisie. The measures taken in the developmentalist experiment correspond to both the interests of the productive bourgeoisie and those of the internal bourgeoisie. As a consequence, the question posed about the internal bourgeoisie could be applied to the industrial bourgeoisie: Why did it not mobilize in defense of the developmentalist experiment when it was surrounded by the powerful armies of international financial capital? Why did it support a return to neoliberalism that in theory was not in its interest? Boito Jr. rightly points out that intercapitalist competition does not erase general bourgeois agreement on issues such as wage de-indexation, the deregulation of labor relations, and the reduction of social rights. It must also be considered that the fractions of capital may be more mixed than before. The imbrication of productive enterprises with rentier investments and the association of national capital with international capital blur boundaries that earlier were better established. Leda Paulani's suggestion (in discussion in São Paulo June 26, 2015) is that we think of capitalist interests as a "fractional continuum" in which constant tensions are perceived.

Among the profusion of possibilities to be considered in explaining the attitude of entrepreneurs in the period 2011–2014, I will highlight four:

1. *Imbrication of production and rentierism.* Certain structural features of the Brazilian industrial bourgeoisie made the productivist coalition fragile. On the one hand, the financialization of capitalism had led to a mixture of capital from industry and finance. Several production lines fell under the control of banks and investment funds. On the other hand, according to the economist Guilherme Mello (2013), "after decades of unrealistic interest rates, the Brazilian business community, whether productive or financial, is involved in purely rentier activities, taking advantage of the certainty of high gains in safe investments and high liquidity." Rousseff, herself, made a similar assessment *a posteriori*: "All Brazilian companies have a banking variant called treasury, in which the financial part is progressively more significant than the productive part" (quoted in Piccin and Pomar 2017: 8). A flagrant example of this overlap was the difficulties experienced by companies in the national productive sector during the 2008 financial bottleneck. Strongly committed to speculative operations, they found themselves in trouble when the markets went into turmoil.

The dual condition of industrialist and rentier restricted the degree of commitment to the productivist platform. As a captain of industry, the entrepreneur wants cheap credit and, therefore, interest rate reductions. However, as the owner of a conglomerate that is also financial, he aspires to high interest rates. The productive character of the activity in which this entrepreneur is engaged impels an alliance with the workers, but the link with the financial component of profits makes this impulse susceptible to reversal when the general environment changes. With a reduction in financial gain, the result will be a limited commitment to productivist aims. Once again, as Dilma argued, "This process is so hard that they are not interested, no" (quoted in Piccin and Pomar 2017: 9). Put another way: as the confrontation heats up, the industrialists recoil.

2. *The ideological factor.* For Bresser-Pereira (2013b), businesspeople in general, even productive ones, are sensitive to the arguments put forward by rentier thinking. As indicated above, the rentier coalition mobilized an extensive apparatus for formulating and disseminating criticisms of the developmentalist experiment. "Faced with the failure of industrial policy and the low growth caused by long-term exchange rate overvaluation in Brazil, the rentier bourgeoisie and its liberal economists sought to co-opt entrepreneurs, even though their interests were in conflict" (Bresser-Pereira 2013b). Under the umbrella of anti-interventionism, the Rousseff administration was accused of incompetence, arbitrariness, authoritarianism, and leniency with regard to corruption.

The worsening of objective conditions enhanced the ideological effect. The low GDP growth in 2012, some inflationary pressure and a reduction in profit margins provided fuel for antidevelopmentalist arguments. While the popular strata may have been less sensitive to the media bombardment of low growth and rising prices, since employment and income were preserved, it is reasonable to imagine that the traditional middle class and perhaps the industrialists close to them were influenced by the media. In the specific case of the industrialists, the element of most objective importance may have been the oscillation of profits. According to the CNI, there was a generalized fall in the profit margin in 2012, with some recovery in 2013 and a further decline in 2014 (Alegretti 2013).[7] According to Bresser-Pereira (2014: 369), as of 2012, with the "depreciation of the real far short of what was necessary for industry to reinvest, ... the importation of manufactured goods" increased, and consequently "there was a radical fall in the rate of profit of industrial enterprises, to much lower than the average SELIC interest rate." Discontented with the objective situation, industrialists were even more likely to join the neoliberal chorus.

3. *Class struggle.* The advance of state intervention led to the expansion of formal jobs. Unemployment rates in the Rousseff period were low, around 4.5 percent between 2011 and 2014. In such situations, as the economist Fernando Rugitsky (2015) recalled from the reasoning of Michal Kalecki (1943), entrepreneurs tend to distance themselves from government. Kalecki argued that the maintenance of full employment by the government withdraws a decisive element from the entrepreneur's domination of the political economy – the threat of unemployment. To overturn a state framework that sustains full employment, the bourgeoisie may use the investment strike, and in

---

7   See http://www.portaldaindustria.com.br/cni/imprensa/2014/03/1,34219/custos-sobem-menos-e-industria-recupera-em-2013-parte-da-reduction-of-profit-margin.html and http://www.portaldaindustria.com.br/cni/imprensa/2015/04/1,60059/industrial-model-in--2014-were-by-expenses-with-production-and-capital-of-giro.html (accessed January 28, 2019).

fact investment in Brazil stagnated from 2011 to 2013 and fell in 2014 (Rugitsky 2015).[8]

Full employment strengthened the unions, and this resulted in a continuous increase in the number of strikes from 2008 on. There were almost 87,000 strike hours in 2012, the highest rate since 1997 (DIEESE 2013a), and they continued to grow, hitting 111,000 hours in 2014 (DIEESE 2013b). There were 873 strikes in 2012 and 2,050 in 2013. The sociologist Ruy Braga had noted in internal discussions of the Centro de Estudos dos Direitos da Cidadania that the previous peak in the total annual strike level had occurred in 1989, with 1,962 strikes, and that the number of work stoppages in Rousseff's first term was sufficient reason to distance capital from labor, undoing the productivist coalition. The average real salary increased by 13 percent between 2011 and 2013 (my calculation from data of Villas Bôas 2015). In view of the cost pressure due to inflation and the exchange-rate devaluation, coupled with the slowdown of the economy, business segments began to complain about the increase in labor costs. This increase, which could not be passed on in prices because of the economic slowdown, would at least partly explain the reduction in profitability. It was thus understood in this context that the neoliberal perspective of lowering wages and entitlements became attractive. Combining the three factors – loss of control over economic policy with full employment, increasing strikes, and rising incomes – it makes sense to think that the opposition of industrial capitalists to the developmentalist experiment was directly linked to the internal class struggle.

4. *The external dimension.* International relations have changed since the 2008 crisis. According to former President Fernando Henrique Cardoso (2013), writing before Trump's rise, the result of the changes was a world dominated by the "competitive coexistence" of the United States and China; hence the option of U.S. leadership in which "Canada, Mexico, Argentina, and Brazil can have a place in the sun." But for this to happen, the country would have to clearly choose the United States and reject China (Cardoso 2014). Velasco e Cruz (2017: 16) stresses that in the second decade of the twenty-first century, liberated from the burden of the Iraq War, the United States began watching with "undisguised restlessness" the advance of China and Russia in Latin America and redesigning commercial mega-agreements to confront the situation.

---

8 Unemployment fell from 5.3 percent in 2010 to 4.7 percent in 2011, 4.6 percent in 2012, and 4.3 percent in 2013 and 2014 (as measured by the Instituto Brasileiro de Geografia e Estatística in December of each year). For a complete analysis of the investment question, it should be remembered that state owned Petrobras, a fundamental source of investment in the country, invested less in 2014.

Cardoso's analysis was then in line with what was being discussed in the Transatlantic Trade and Investment Partnership (TTIP) (Halimi 2014; Jennar and Lambert 2014). A "free-trade agreement negotiated since July 2013 by the United States and the European Union to create the world's largest market with more than 800 million consumers" (Jennar and Lambert 2014), this was the Western response to the irresistible rise of the China-India partnership.[9] A key point was its attempt to "subject existing legislation on both sides of the Atlantic to free-trade rules, which in most cases correspond to the preferences of large European and American companies" (Jennar and Lambert 2014). One can imagine which social groups would benefit from such "innovations" and which would be harmed. According to Wolf Jäcklein (2014) of France's Confédération Général du Travail, one of the threats of the agreement was the "lack of respect for fundamental labor rights".

The TTIP initiative was well-received in Brazilian industrial circles. Pedro Passos (2014), a former president of the Institute for Studies for Industrial Development, who had been fighting for Brazil's re-inclusion in global production chains, argued that "Brazil's international isolation may deepen if the country does not become part of the trend of mega-agreements launched in 2011 with the launch of the TPP (Trans-Pacific Partnership), which involves the United States and 11 other countries on three continents, and the Transatlantic Trade and Investment Partnership (TTIP), bringing together the United States and the European Union." Despite the victory of Donald Trump in the United States at the end of 2016, which cooled the U.S. enthusiasm for free-trade treaties, in Brazil the liberalizing agenda, as seen with the labor reform approved in July 2017, followed its course.

According to the Western view, Mercosur would leave Brazil isolated by its lack of alignment with the North American bloc. Not coincidentally, two of Rousseff's ministers in her second term, when the developmentalist experiment had already been shelved, issued declarations against Mercosur in 2015 and in favor of rapprochement with the United States. Roberto Mangabeira Unger of the Secretariat for Strategic Affairs called Mercosur "a body without spirit" and said that with the United States agreements on various aspects were possible (Oliveira 2015). Armando Monteiro (Brasil 247, 2015), minister of development and former president of the CNI, said that the United States represented "the greatest opportunity for increasing Brazilian exports" and defended not being tied only to Mercosur. The reorganization of international relations described

---

9   It is also worth noting the rapprochement between Russia and China in the context of global reordering.

here also coincided with the Chinese offensive in the Brazilian market for manufactured products, provoking an anti-Chinese defensive reaction in the affected sectors. In fact, there are reports that the Chinese threat mobilized industrial segments in the first half of the Rousseff governments.[10]

In 2003, sectors of Brazilian industry had supported the Lulista opposition to the Free Trade Area of the Americas and investment in the South-South relationship, creating a privileged link with Mercosur and China. By the end of 2013, however, the president of the CNI, Robson Andrade, speaking to U.S. businesspeople in Denver, Colorado, said that Brazil should conclude a free-trade agreement with the United States, leaving Mercosur out of the picture (Mello 2013). What had happened? According to the president of the Brazilian Electrical and Electronic Industry Association, Humberto Barbato, "We changed our position. Ten years ago we were recalcitrant. ... Now we are isolated. Brazil is out of the value chains. We will soon be similar to the countries of the old Iron Curtain" (quoted in Mello 2014). Expressing a diametrically opposed view but one that also privileges the external variable, Sampaio Jr. (2013) argues that Rousseff underestimated the strength of the international constraints. To compensate for the contraction of exports through the expansion of the domestic market as China did after 2008, Brazil would need to "break with the parameters of the global order" – to limit the movement of capital, forcing capitalists to invest in the national interest. In the absence of such control, investors would seek gainful platforms in "urban land and commercial speculation, fostering capital concentration and pushing the state toward new rounds of privatization of infrastructure and public services".

5   Conclusion

The four causes discussed above are complementary. The fact that the industrial sector has a rentier side at the same time makes it more sensitive to neoliberal ideology, although this orientation objectively prejudices productive activities. The same applies to the intensification of the class struggle: it makes the arguments of neoliberalism more attractive to the industrialists. The damage to the plurality of the business strata – external and internal, rentier and productive – during the developmentalist experiment explains the united reaction against it. Changes in the international environment may have consolidated the antidevelopmentalist united front. The fact is that these fractions, many

---

10   The political scientist Danilo Martuscelli had already warned of this factor.

of them fueled by abundant material in the press, both domestic and foreign, joined and then swallowed the new economic matrix.

As a result, the chronology of the period 2011–2014 reveals the occurrence of a hidden war from which the working class remained estranged because the president herself may not have understood the nature of the campaign to which she was being subjected. It is plausible to imagine that this occurred because Rousseff had been the victim of an optical illusion similar to that which engulfed the nationalism of the 1950s and 1960s. In responding to the demands of the industrial bourgeoisie, she imagined that she would have the backing of these industrialists when the opposition reacted. Faced with a similar situation in 1964, Fernando Henrique Cardoso, then a young professor and researcher at the São Paulo University, wrote that "to assert itself as a politically dominant class and to expand economically, the industrial bourgeoisie is forced to support reforms and measures that oppose the traditional dominant groups." However, such a movement puts (or seems to put) its future hegemony at risk, given the possibility of the ascent of the popular strata, causing a retreat "in the present so as to not lose everything in the future" (Cardoso 1964: 186).

The terms, of course, cannot be taken word for word. In 1963–1964 the Brazilian bourgeoisie felt threatened by the possibility of a socialist revolution, a fear that did not exist 50 years later. Nonetheless, the fear of confronting a project with popular support that wanted to expand the scope of the state, set prices, regulate and control private activity, and, in a distant projection, nationalize strategic sectors may have been enough to unify it in combating the developmentalist experiment, as had occurred half a century before.

The erratic character of Rousseff's performance after June 2013 opened an avenue for anti-Lulism that eventually brought her down. The gears that had been waiting for the opportunity since 2003, when Lula took over, were set in motion. An ambitious coalition led by the PMDB and the PSDB was being stitched together at least as early as August 2015. Resentful of its fourth successive defeat in presidential elections, the PSDB provided elements for the construction of the parliamentary coup of 2016. Although the final protagonist was the PMDB, which would organize the vote in the House on April 17 and take over the presidency on May 12, 2016, the legal formulation, the economic program, the bridge with business, and legitimization with the middle class occurred through the actions of the PSDB, not to mention the hundreds of votes that the party galvanized in the legislature. The Car Wash scandal, which mobilized the middle class through the media, also helped, covering Dilma Rousseff's impeachment with social support (Singer 2018: 31).

Thus, on a small scale, Rousseff's developmentalist experiment may have followed in the footsteps of that of 1964. At the outset, the industrial bourgeoisie called for a state offensive for growth with reindustrialization. In the second act of the tragedy, pressured by falling profits, rising strikes, and international hegemonic reorientation, industrialists "discovered" that, given the initial step, they were dealing with a power over which they feared to lose control and one that favored their class opponents (workers), occasional allies only. In the third episode, the industrial bourgeoisie turned against its own interests to avoid the greater evil: a sovereign national policy based on the unified popular strata. The industrialists then changed sides, joining the conservative bloc determined to stop the dangerous experiment.

References

Alegretti, L. (2013). Custo pressionou indústria em 2012 e reduziu margem de lucro. March 14. http://economia.estadao.com.br/noticias/geral,custo-pressionou-industria-em-2012-e-reduziu-margem-de-lucro,147198e (accessed May 29, 2015).

Barrocal, A. (2013). Arno não é mais uma Brastemp. *Carta Capital* 759 (July 31), 37.

Boito Jr., A. (2012a). Governo Lula: a nova burguesia nacional no poder. In: A. Boito Jr. and A. Galvão (eds.), *Política e classes sociais no Brasil dos anos 2000*, 67–104. São Paulo: Alameda.

Boito Jr., A. (2012b). As bases políticas do neodesenvolvimentismo. *Fórum Econômico da FGV*. https://bibliotecadigital.fgv.br/dspace/bitstream/handle/10438/16866/Painel%203%20-%20Novo%20Desenv%20BR%20-%20Boito%20-%20Bases%20Pol%20Neodesenv%20-%20PAPER.pdf (accessed August 6, 2018).

Boito Jr., A. (2013). O lulismo é um tipo de bonapartismo? Uma crítica às teses de André Singer. *Crítica Marxista* 37 (First Semester): 173–181.

Bielschowsky, R. (1995). *Pensamento econômico brasileiro: O ciclo ideológico do desenvolvimentismo*. Rio de Janeiro: Contraponto.

Branco, M. (2014). Presidente da CNI pede política econômica rumo à estabilidade. November 5. http://agenciabrasil.ebc.com.br/economia/noticia/2014-11/presidente-da-cni-pede-politica-economica-rumo-estabilidade (accessed June 21, 2015).

Brasil 247. (2015). Armando ao 247: 'EUA são grande oportunidade.' January 14. http://www.brasil247.com/pt/247/economia/166612/Armando-ao-247-%27EUA-s%C3%A3o-grande-oportunidade%27.htm (accessed June 6, 2015).

Bresser-Pereira, L.C. (2013a). O governo Dilma frente ao 'tripé macroeconômico' e à direita liberal e dependente. *Novos Estudos* 95 (March): 5–14.

Bresser-Pereira, L.C. (2013b). Governo, empresários e rentistas. *Folha de S. Paulo*, December 2.

Bresser-Pereira, L.C. (2014). *A construção política do Brasil*. São Paulo: Editora 34.

Cardoso, F.H. (1964). *Empresário industrial e desenvolvimento econômico no Brasil*. São Paulo: Difel.

Cardoso, F.H. (2013). Sem disfarce nem miopia. *O Estado de S. Paulo*, March 3.

Cardoso, F.H. (2014). Mudar o rumo. *O Globo*, February 5.

Carneiro, R. (2018). Navegando a contravento. In: Ricardo Carneiro, Paulo Baltar, and Fernando Sarti (eds.), *Para além da política econômica: Crescimento, desaceleração e crise no experimento desenvolvimentista*, 11–54. São Paulo: Unesp.

CUT (Central Única dos Trabalhadores). (2013). 11 de julho: manifestação nacional. July 8. http://cut.org.br/noticias/11-de-julho-manifestacao-nacional-1845/ (accessed August 9, 2015).

D'Amorim, S., and Sciarreta, T. (2012). Bancos recuam e preparam juro menor. *Folha de S. Paulo*, April 18.

DIEESE (Departamento Intersindical de Estatística e Estudos Socioeconômicos). (2013a). Balanço das greves em 2012. *Estudos e Pesquisas* 66 (May). http://www. dieese.org.br/balancodasgreves/2012/estPesq66balancogreves2012.pdf (accessed July 29, 2015).

DIEESE (Departamento Intersindical de Estatística e Estudos Socioeconômicos). (2013b). Balanço das greves em 2013. *Estudos e Pesquisas* 79 (December). https:// www.dieese.org.br/balancodasgreves/2013/estPesq79balancogreves2013.pdf (accessed August 6, 2018).

FIESP (Federação das Indústrias do Estado de São Paulo). (2013). Paraguai oferece vantagens competitivas para o setor têxtil, destaca diretor do Departamento de Relações Internacionais e Comércio Exterior da FIESP. April 3. http://www.fiesp. com.br/noticias/paraguai-oferece-vantagens-competitivas-para-setor-textil-destaca-diretor-do-departamento-de-relacoes-internacionais-e-comercio-exterior-da-fiesp/ (accessed July 30, 2015).

Folha de S. Paulo. (2012). Leia íntegra do discurso de Dilma pelo dia do Trabalho. April 30. https://www1.folha.uol.com.br/poder/1083760-leia-integra-do-discurso-de-dilma-pelo-dia-do-trabalho.shtml (accessed August 6, 2018).

Guimarães, L. (2015). Para professor da Unicamp, ajuste em meio à recessão é contraproducente. *Valor*, August 6. http://jornalggn.com.br/noticia/para-professor-da-unicamp-ajuste-em-meio-a-recessao-e-contraproducente (accessed August 15, 2015).

Halimi, S. (2014). As potências redesenham o mundo. *Le Monde Diplomatique Brasil*, 83, June.

Henrique, A. (2013). Os lucros, a ganância, a usura e a cegueira. May 1. http://www.cartacapital.com.br/politica/os-lucros-a-ganancia-a-usura-e-a-cegueira-3894.html (accessed July 29, 2015).

Jäcklein, W. (2014). ... e dez ameaças aos europeus. *Le Monde Diplomatique Brasil*, 84, July.

Jennar, R.M., and Lambert, R. (2014). Descobrindo o tratado. *Le Monde Diplomatique Brasil*, 84, July.

Kalecki, M. (1943). Political aspects of full employment. *Political Quarterly* 14(4).

Leitão, M. (2013). Alta desconfortável. February 7. http://blogs.oglobo.globo.com/miriam-leitao/post/alta-desconfortavel-485606.html (accessed February 28, 2015).

Mantega, G. (2012). O primeiro ano da nova matriz econômica. *Valor*, December 19.

Mello, G. (2013). *Percalços da transformação monetária e a nova contrarrevolução liberal conservadora*. MS, Fundação Perseu Abramo.

Mello, P.C. (2014). Indústria brasileira propõe firmar acordo de livre-comércio com os EUA. November 14. http://www1.folha.uol.com.br/mercado/2013/11/1371141-industria-brasileira-propoe-firmar-acordo-de-livre-comercio-com-eua.shtml (accessed August 13, 2015).

Mendes, P. (2012). Para facilitar crédito, Dilma defende diminuição do 'spread' bancário. April 3. http://g1.globo.com/economia/noticia/2012/04/para-facilitar-credito-dilma-defende-diminuicao-do-spread-bancario.html (accessed July 11, 2015).

Oliveira, E. (2015). Mercosul é 'corpo sem espírito' e foco deve ser EUA, diz Mangabeira Unger. May 9. http://oglobo.globo.com/economia/mercosul-corpo-sem-espirito-foco-deve-ser-eua-diz-mangabeira-unger-16105668 (accessed June 6, 2015).

Passos, P. (2014). O Brasil não pode ser uma ilha. *Folha de S. Paulo*, January 17. http://www1.folha.uol.com.br/colunas/pedropassos/2014/01/1398869-o-brasil-nao-pode-ser-uma-ilha.shtml (accessed June 6, 2015).

Piccin, M., and Pomar, V. (2017). Entrevista exclusiva: Dilma Rousseff sem censura, ou quase. *Esquerda Petista*, June 12, 9. http://www.pagina13.org.br/revista-esquerda-petista/entrevista-exclusiva-dilma-rousseff-sem-censura-ou-quase/#.WW4fi9QrJnI (accessed July 18, 2017).

Poulantzas, N. (1975). *As classes sociais no capitalismo de hoje*. Rio de Janeiro: Zahar.

PT Diretório Nacional. (2002). *Concepção e diretrizes do programa de governo do PT para o Brasil*. http://csbh.fpabramo.org.br/uploads/concepcaoediretrizesdoprog.pdf (accessed August 6, 2018).

Rugitsky, F. (2015). Do ensaio desenvolvimentista à austeridade: uma leitura Kaleckiana. *Carta Maior*, May 8. http://cartamaior.com.br/?/Editoria/Economia/Do-Ensaio-Desenvolvimentista-a-austeridade-uma-leitura-Kaleckiana/7/33448 (accessed June 6, 2015).

Safatle, C. (2013). Dilma agirá para abrandar a desconfiança de empresários. *Valor*, October 7.

Sampaio Jr., P.A. (2013). 2013: o gato subiu no telhado. *Jornal dos Economistas* 282, January. http://www.corecon-rj.org.br/documents/11827/13953/Janeiro+-+2013+(n%C2%BA282)/1da4d5eb-89ab-4c6a-a2a9-45d11cd1baef?version=1.1 (accessed August 7, 2015).

Singer, A. (2012). *Os sentidos do lulismo: Reforma gradual e pacto conservador.* São Paulo: Companhia das Letras.

Singer, A. (2015). Cutucando onças com varas curtas. *Novos Estudos* 102 (June): 43–71.

Singer, A. (2016). A (falta de) base política para o ensaio desenvolvimentista. In: André Singer and Isabel Loureiro (eds.), *As contradições do lulismo: A que ponto chegamos?*, 21–54. São Paulo: Boitempo.

Singer, A. (2017). The failure of the developmentalist experiment in three acts. *Critical Policy Studies* 11: 358–364.

Singer, A. (2018). *O lulismo em crise: Um quebra-cabeça do período Dilma (2011–2016).* São Paulo: Companhia das Letras.

Singer, A. (2020). The failure of Dilma Roussef's Developmentalist Experiment. *Latin American Perspectives* 47(1): 152–168.

Singer, P. (1981). *Dominação e desigualdade.* São Paulo: Paz e Terra.

Skaf, P. (2013). Do que o Brasil precisa. June 24. http://www.fiesp.com.br/noticias/no-diario-de-s-paulo-artigo-de-paulo-skaf-fala-sobre-as-manifestacoes-em-todo-o-pais/ (accessed July 30, 2015).

Skaf, P., Henrique, A., and Silva, P.P. (2011). Um acordo pela indústria brasileira. *Folha de S. Paulo*, May 26.

Souza, M.M. (2014). Dilma diz que PSDB quer 'trazer de volta recessão e desemprego. May 30. http://www.valor.com.br/politica/3569748/dilma-diz-que-psdb-quer-trazer-de-volta-recessao-e-desemprego (accessed August 29, 2015).

Steinbruch, B. (2012). País diferente. *Folha de S. Paulo*, October 9. http://www1.folha. uol.com.br/colunas/benjaminsteinbruch/2012/10/1166305-pais-diferente.shtml (accessed July 11, 2015).

UOL (Universo Online). (2015). Importante no PIB, investimento de empresas cai há 6 trimestres seguidos. March 27. http://economia.uol.com.br/noticias/redacao/2015/03/27/importante-no-pib-investimento-de-empresas-cai-ha-6-trimestres-seguidos. htm (accessed August 2, 2015).

Velasco e Cruz, S. (2017). *Burguesia e empresariado no Brasil: viagem a um passado distante e o caminho de volta.* MS.

Villas Bôas, B. (2015). Desemprego nas metrópoles sobe a 6,9% em junho, maior taxa desde 2010. July 23. http://www1.folha.uol.com.br/mercado/2015/07/1659358-desemprego-nas-metropoles-sobe-a-69-em-junho-maior-taxa-desde-2010.shtml (accessed February 27, 2016).

CHAPTER 10

The Political Economy of Lulism and Its Aftermath

Ruy Braga and Fabio Luis Barbosa dos Santos

1 Introduction[1]

As is widely argued in the literature that critically analyzes the development model of the Lulist governments (see, among others, Saad Filho and Morais 2018), the Partido dos Trabalhadores (Workers' Party – PT) presidencies (2003–2016) opted for class reconciliation as a method for reforming Brazilian capitalism. This was based on the premise, which is in fact reasonable, that much could be done to address the country's acute inequality without confronting the structures that reproduce it. The Zero Hunger program, which was initially led by a Catholic friar, epitomized this approach. After all, who would be opposed to ending hunger? But while bread would appease the poor, reconciliation with the rich required a commitment to so-called economic stability. Its founding milestone was the Real Plan, implemented by Minister of the Economy Fernando Henrique Cardoso in 1994, which completed a process that turned Brazil into a "platform for valuing international financial capital" (Paulani 2008).

At the same time that the country was becoming consolidated as a destination for speculative capital, the flow of these capitals became indispensable from the point of view of the so-called macroeconomic tripod. This was a situation that emerged from policies focused on fiscal targets, a floating exchange rate, and inflation targets. Fiscal adjustment, high interest rates, contractionary monetary policy, and free capital movement were the pillars of this macroeconomic strategy. It was this commitment that candidate Lula secured when he launched the "Letter to the Brazilian People" during the campaign in 2002. It was, in fact, a letter to capital, aimed at warding off the specter of capital flight that was looming on the verge of the election of the workers' president.

Once sworn in, the PT government was true to its commitment, espousing all aspects of neoliberal adjustment. The commitment to international credibility required deepening antisocial reforms such as the new Bankruptcy Law,

---

1 An earlier version of the arguments in this chapter appeared in Braga and Santos (2020) and a sequel to this text analyzing political developments since Bolsonaro's election with the provisional title of "From Lula to Bolsonaro: elective affinities" is forthcoming.

which placed workers on equal terms with other creditors, counteracting the premise that business risks burden the employer. But the main knot untied in Lula's first term was the reform of social security. The move from the social security model to the private pension system broke with the idea of generational solidarity, in which the contributions of young people ensure the pensions of the elderly, in favor of a model in which each worker has an individual account managed as a pension fund investment. Generational and class solidarity gave way to co-participation in the mechanisms and risks associated with financial capital (Marques and Mendes 2004).

This reform was emblematic for two reasons. First, it revealed the PT's functionality to the interests of the traditional ruling classes of the country, with the financial sector in the forefront. The president's prestige among workers was fundamental in enabling, in the first year of his term, a reform that his predecessor had not achieved because of the opposition he faced. Secondly, it transformed a social right into a financial product. Beyond the macroeconomic options that caused the first Lula government to be described as "the most complete incarnation" of neoliberalism (Paulani 2008: 10), it turned out that the party's civilizing perspective was in perfect harmony with the hegemonic neoliberal rationality (Dardot and Laval 2010).

However, it was never assumed that PT politics was neoliberal. On the contrary, in Lula's second term, when there was a growth spurt driven by rising commodity prices due to the Chinese expansion, the proposition that a "neodevelopmentalist" project was under way was championed by government cronies. After decades of stagnation, the slow recovery of wage-earning power, declining unemployment, a slight improvement in income distribution, the reduction of extreme poverty through targeted policies, and the expansion of consumption that accompanied the abundance of credit backed the discourse that Brazil was plunging into a period of development, whose parallel with post-World War II national-developmentalism justified the neologism.

The common denominator of the various neodevelopmentalist formulations was the diagnosis that the country should seek an alternative route between the financialization that characterized neoliberalism and the nationalism linked to developmentalism. Renewed emphasis on production to the detriment of rentierism without incurring inflation, fiscal populism, nationalism, and other elements of national developmentalism was proposed. Sampaio Jr. (2012: 46) synthesized the neodevelopmentalist agenda as follows:

> The challenge of neodevelopmentalism is therefore to reconcile the "positive" aspects of neoliberalism – unconditional commitment to currency stability, fiscal austerity, the pursuit of international competitiveness,

and the absence of any discrimination against international capital – and the "positive" aspects of old developmentalism – commitment to economic growth, industrialization, the regulatory role of the state, and social sensitivity.

The opportunity to reconcile "an external element, liberalism, with another internal element, Brazilian developmentalism" (Cervo 2003), materialized in the support for the internationalization of large companies with national capital or headquartered in the country, understood as vectors of national capitalist development. This was the "national champions" policy, whose main vehicles were the business diplomacy practiced by Itamaraty, especially in South America, and the credit policy of the Banco Nacional de Desenvolvimento Econômico e Social (National Bank for Economic and Social Development – BNDES). At its peak in 2010, the bank's lending for this purpose was more than two and a half times the sum of the funds handled by the World Bank and the Inter-American Development Bank (Leopoldo 2011).

The bank's action intensified the concentration of capital in sectors of the economy considered internationally competitive, notably primary exports and construction. It provided the JBS group with R$6 billion for acquisitions in Brazil and abroad, which made it the largest meat producer in the world; R$2.4 billion for Votorantim Celulose to acquire Aracruz Celulose, making it one of the world's largest pulp producers, Fibria; and more than R$1.5 billion for the merger of Sadia with Perdigão, making the Brasil Foods group the world's largest chicken exporter (Garcia 2012). However, the protagonist of Brazil's commercial expansion was construction, a sector that has done business in all the Latin American countries, from Colombia to Cuba, as well as in other parts of the world, especially Portuguese Africa. The sector also benefited at the domestic level from the Growth Acceleration Program, which foresaw an infrastructure works agenda, and the My House, My Life program, which extended housing loans to the popular classes. All in all, this internationalization of Brazilian corporations, mainly in South America, corresponded to a political project of regional leadership. The strategy anticipated that the economic expansion of Brazilian business would serve as the foundation for the country's political projection on the world stage (Santos 2018).

During the economic expansion cycle that lasted until Rousseff's first term, this proposal advanced with relative success. The expansion of Brazilian business corresponded to a recognition of the country's political role, embodied in the figure of President Lula, who was seen by Obama in 2009 as the most popular politician on Earth (*Newsweek* 2009). However, the conjunction of economic downturn and corruption scandals starting in 2014 put this project on the defensive. While the Brazilian economy was in recession, several reports described corruption schemes involving contractors and other national champions at home and abroad. These disclosures undermined the reliability of the government and its ruling party and jeopardized the foundations of the neodevelopmentalist project with which they identified.

Additionally, several indications called into question the effectiveness of the national champions strategy. In the first place, some companies that had received large contributions from the BNDES began to be controlled internationally. The Ambev beverage conglomerate merged with a Belgian corporation and had its headquarters moved to that country, and EBX partnered with Chinese and Korean capital companies after approving large volumes of public credit for their projects (Tautz et al. 2010). The Odebrecht operation in Peru became independent and registered as a local company; it no longer has projects supported by the BNDES, but neither does it participate in the export of Brazilian services and products. On the whole, there is little evidence that support for these businesses met neodevelopmentalist expectations. At the same time, there is evidence that national champions have used longterm credits to reduce capital costs or even to profit by manipulating interest rates in arbitrage transactions (Bonomo, Brito, and Martins 2014).

While the national-champions strategy bore doubtful fruit, the expected association between neodevelopmentalism and industrialization did not flourish. On the contrary, under the PT administrations the dismantling of Brazilian industry, a phenomenon that preceded it, was intensified. Since 1985 the participation of industry in the gross domestic product (GDP) decreased from 35.88 percent to 13.13 percent in 2013. Brazil's share of world industrial production fell from 2.8 percent to 1.7 percent in the 2000s, stabilizing at this level until 2010 (UNIDO 2011). That year, a report from the Ministry of Finance classified 64.6 percent of Brazilian exports as commodities, a figure that in 1994 had been around 50 percent (Esposito 2017). The dismantling of industry is suggested by indicators such as the increase in the participation of primary components in industrial production, the increase of imported inputs in the manufacture of industrial goods, and a greater concentration of value added in a few segments. These elements denote a weakening of the links that allowed industry to function as an organic whole (Carneiro 2008).

The percentage of imports and exports in relation to GDP increased under the PT administrations, reflecting a greater degree of openness of the economy and dependency. Equally significant, average capital mobility increased from 5 percent between 1986 and 1990 to 37 percent between 2006 and 2010, during which time external liabilities also multiplied, indicating an increase in the country's vulnerability to crises caused by capital flight (Sampaio Jr.

2012). In short, the convergence between the dismantling of the industrial system, the dislocation of the dynamic axis of the economy to a focus on foreign companies, and the erosion of internal decision-making centers in relation to international finance points to a remarkable deindustrialization of the country.

These results spell out the ideological character of the neodevelopmentalist proposal. By suggesting a contradictory association between the supposed salutary aspects of neoliberalism and the longing for the earlier developmentalism, the neodevelopmentalist pastiche ignored the links between the various dimensions inherent in the two ideas – for example, the antithetical relationship between restrictive monetary policy and economic growth that characterized neoliberalism and the protection of national capital that conditioned industrialization from a developmentalist perspective. Moreover, it abstracted from the historical conditions that supported the utopian national developmentalist project as a way of humanizing peripheral capitalism, since the possibilities for a national approach to development were quite limited (Santos 2018).

Under this rhetorical veneer, a conservative economic policy was followed that accepted macroeconomic parameters and the neoliberal landscape. In practice, the Brazilian economy continued to operate as a platform for increasing the value of international financial capital, largely focused on neoextractivist activists, an exporter of raw materials, and a backer of multinational corporations that exploited the domestic market but also exported (although exports of manufactured products have diminished). The prevailing economic trends – denationalization, deindustrialization, environmental devastation, overexploitation of labor, trade and financial openness, and vulnerability to crises and their counterpart, subjugation to international finance – intensified.

Disconnected from reality, this neodevelopmentalist ideology lent itself to an ideological purpose, "differentiat[ing] the Lula government from the Cardoso government, casting on the latter the label of 'neoliberal' " (Sampaio Jr. 2012). Neodevelopmentalist rhetoric restricted the economic debate to micro economics, thus limiting the breadth of political debate. By reducing social change to the parameters accepted by neoliberalism, the political debate was confined to a discussion of the pace and intensity of structural adjustment, distinguishing itself only in secondary aspects such as the intensity of the World Bank's money transfer policies, the strategy for dealing with social tensions, the role attributed to the regional environment, and marketing for internal and external consumption. The PT strategy related to issues of this kind was referred to as the Lulist mode of social conflict regulation.

2   The Lulist Mode of Social Conflict Regulation Coordination of
       Two Forms of Consent

The Lulist mode of social conflict regulation can be summarized as the combination of modest gains for the lowest levels of the Brazilian social pyramid and the expanded reproduction of the regime of financial accumulation supported by extractivism. This combination of small gains for the lowest levels with the usual profits for the upper ones supported the relative social pacification of the country until June 2013. Lulist hegemony was based on the coordination of two forms of consent. The first of these was the passive consent of the subordinate classes to the project of government embraced by a union bureaucracy that, during the period of economic growth, was able to guarantee modest but effective concessions to workers. In general, the semirural subproletariat in various areas of Brazil benefited from the Bolsa Família program, moving from extreme poverty to the official poverty line. The unstable urban class benefited from increases in the minimum wage above inflation and from the creation of formal jobs. Finally, in the context of a heated labor market, the proletariat, when organized in unions, achieved advantageous collective bargaining in terms of both wages and benefits (Braga 2014; 2015). In a country renowned for abysmal inequalities, these advances were enough to solidify the subordinates' consent to Lulist regulation. At the same time, the PT government concretely coordinated the interests of the union bureaucracy, the leaders of the social movements, and the intellectual middle classes, laying the groundwork for active consent to Lulism focused on the state apparatus. In addition, by occupying positions on the boards of pension funds and public banks, the high-level union bureaucracy merged its interests with those of financial capital (Oliveira 2003).

The acceptance by the Central Única dos Trabalhadores (Unified Workers' Central – CUT) of this project revealed the philosopher's stone of Lulism: the main social organizations that had once resisted the advance of neoliberalism now supported a government committed to the execution, albeit slightly modified, of neoliberal policies. The relationship of trust built over the years between the party and the social organizations was used to neutralize them. Lula's personal charisma was also manipulated to this end. As part of this regulation, public policies and instances of participation spread. They did nothing to modify social structures but were successful in confusing social activism. Activists became government project managers or sometimes simply government officials. Taken together, this arsenal of practices and strategies consolidated active consent to the PT project, weakening the autonomy of the popular field.

Initially, leaders and organizations justified their tacit support by arguing that the government was in dispute. However, the notion that it was possible to contest the government and try to shift it to the left failed before it was even applied. Ever since Lula's first victory, the party had never considered building a correlation of forces to modify the state. On the contrary, it focused on forging alliances to ensure governability, which in the Brazilian political system, characterized by a multiplicity of parties, meant agreements with forces that had historically opposed social change.

The political crises emphasized the disjuncture between the venality of the government and the loyalty of the movements. Since the first serious corruption crisis, the so-called "mensalão" in 2005, the PT's structural base had brandished the coup threat despite the consensus against impeachment among the bourgeoisie at the time. Instead of considering the possibility that the PT, whose policies in all spheres were conservative, could also maneuver the Congress in a conventional manner by resorting to bribery, the popular bases closed ranks with the government: 43 organizations signed a "Letter to the Brazilian People" (with the same name as the 2002 document) describing the allegations as coup maneuvers. Meanwhile the government responded by reinforcing the participation of the Movimento Democrático Brasileiro (Brazilian Democratic Movement – MDB) in government, financial capital commitments, and focused welfare policies that were mainly managed by social organizations controlled by the Evangelical churches (Georges and Santos 2016).

In short, the convergence between PT strategies for the neutralization of criticism and the inability of some activists to disengage from the party caused a kind of "hijacking" of the country's left political agenda. Paradoxically, the main legacy of the active consent to PT hegemony was inaction, which has had politically pernicious consequences ever since the Lulist peace plummeted.

3   Conservative Modernization

The Lulist mode of social conflict regulation was remarkably successful during Lula's presidencies and Rousseff's first term. To understand its subsequent exhaustion and the reaction that followed it is necessary to analyze the dynamics that underlay the passive consent of the subordinate classes. Specifically, job creation, the increase in the minimum wage, and the expansion of college education had touched the key players of the June 2013 protests, when the contradictions of Lulism surfaced. The failure of the urban reform encouraged by the first PT governments in the 1980s, which spread a "PT way of governing", and the retreat from land reform (an issue that mobilized the most powerful

Brazilian popular movement under neoliberalism) completed the panorama of a "conservative modernization" advanced in the period.

The exhaustion of passive consent to the Lulist pact became evident starting in June 2013, when the largest cycle of popular mobilization since the end of the dictatorship in 1985 took place. Field research indicates that the protests were led by young workers who were students. This segment was doubly affected by the PT project in that more than 60 percent of the jobs created during these administrations were occupied by young people between 18 and 24 years old, who were also the main clients for the expansion of higher education (Braga 2014). Contrary to the mythology surrounding a "new middle class", studies have shown that what happened under the PT governments was a broadening of the base of the Brazilian social pyramid. Of every 10 new jobs created during the 2000s, 9 paid less than one and a half minimum wages. In 2014, when the effects of the economic slowdown intensified, about 97.5 percent of the jobs created were in this salary range. The driver of the expansion was the service sector, spanning segments of society that had historically received lower wages and been discriminated against in the labor market: women, blacks, and young people (Braga 2014; Pochmann 2012).

From the point of view of economic dynamism, according to Marcio Pochmann (2012), "this expansion of low-paid jobs has been shown to be compatible with the absorption of the huge surplus of labor previously generated by neoliberalism." Reflecting on the impact of this movement on the social structure, he notes that "either by income level, by type of occupation, or by personal profile and attributes, the bulk of the emerging population does not match serious and objective criteria for its clear identification as middle class" (47). Instead, this group displays the characteristic profile of the popular sectors, which, in the face of rising incomes, do not save money but immediately increase consumption.

For this group, the recovery of the minimum wage was a crucial factor in the reproduction of its consent. Despite a slight increase in labor income participation over the overall amount of national income under the Lula governments, recovering the value of the minimum wage was a trend that predated the PT cycle. During the Cardoso governments, between 1994 and 2002, there was a 42 percent recovery of this value, while between 2003 and 2014 the appreciation recorded was 76.5 percent. The policy in force after 2008 linked wage increases to inflation and GDP variation during a period of economic growth. It had some effect during the commodities boom but had no effect during periods of economic recession (Krein, Manzano, and Santos 2015). Furthermore, the recent employment increase was based on a noticeably low level. The highest unemployment rates of the 1990s were around 12 percent.

Correspondingly, the increase in the real average salary of workers returned in 2013 only to a level similar to the beginning of the Real Plan, but its purchasing power remained lower than in the early 1980s, which in turn, reflected two decades of dictatorship.

While quantitative advances were negligible, qualitative data indicate a worsening of working conditions. The increase in outsourcing, flexibility in working hours, turnover, and accidents and deaths at work were all indications of a deterioration of those conditions. Considering that the driving forces of the economy in the period were construction, agribusiness, and the service sector, we could hardly have expected a different result. In summary, the situation of labor under the PT governments advanced in line with the global movement toward increased insecurity. Groups deprived of labor guarantees, subject to uncertain incomes, and lacking a collective identity entrenched in the labor world have grown (Braga 2015).

Many of these young people were in higher education, expecting to compete for jobs that pay more than one and a half minimum wages and correspond to the middle class. Thus, they became the main clients of the expansion of private universities that offered poor courses at low prices. While it is true that under the Federal Universities Restructuring and Expansion Plans Support, implemented from 2003 to 2012, 14 new federal universities and 100 new campuses were created. These new universities and campuses increased by around 60 percent the enrollment in public on-site undergraduate courses, although the precariousness of this expansion is well known. The deterioration of working and career conditions for technicians and teachers, compounded by violent cuts in education funding, produced two extended strikes, in 2012 and 2015.

In fact, higher-education expansion was brought about not by the public sector but by the private one. Between 2003 and 2014, the offer of undergraduate courses in the country spread from 282 to 792 municipalities, and in 2014 78.5 percent of the vacancies in higher education were new. However, of the 8 million vacancies, 90.2 percent were in private universities (Zagni 2016). Strictly speaking, this was a subsidized expansion, since the government operated through the Student Financing Fund and the University for All program – massive transfers of public resources to private education. The underlying logic was that it was cheaper for the state to subsidize university students in private colleges than to maintain and expand public institutions to educate them.

It turns out that when their college studies were over, many found that the path to social ascent was more limited than promised. Precarious work, originally envisioned as temporary, became a permanent reality; precariousness ceased to be a step and became a wall. Life became distressing – compressed,

narrow, stressful. For most of the population, this distressed and unstable existence took place in the city, between home, study, and work. Transportation
was at the center of life, and Brazilian cities collapsed and were no longer experiences of social life and places of civilization (Maricato 2011).

To understand this process, Pedro Arantes (2014) analyzes the trajectory of
the struggle for urban reform in Brazil and its connection with federal urban
policies. Drawing an analogy with the union movement, which little questioned the private ownership of the means of production, Arantes argues that
the housing movements never crossed the threshold of private landownership. Thus, to the extent that the "popular-democratic" urbanism practiced
by PT municipal administrations in the 1980s became exhausted, involving
the urbanization of slums, collective self-construction (*mutirão*) and self-
management, and participatory budgeting that characterized the "PT way of
governing", the conditions emerged for a consensus based on a mercantile
solution to the problem adopting the ideology of home ownership.

At the same time, the PT administrations viewed cities as a brand or a business, increasingly using international urban consultants, introducing post-
modern city privatization mechanisms such as urban operations, certificate
sales of additional building potential, big urban projects, and megaevents.
Depleted of their original transformative potential, the practices that characterized the "PT way of governing" became impoverished urban mass management technologies.

In line with the ideological inflection experienced by the PT, urban reform
was no longer seen as a whole and was even confused with "the real estate
practices of right-wing governments and of the World Bank", as Arantes (2014)
points out. Thus, substantive urban policies were abandoned – the very end
of urban reform. Mobility understood as a fundamental urban right because it
was a means of access to other rights was one of the dimensions buried along
with this problem. Just as landownership was not questioned, the turnstile was
not considered an issue even when it was at the heart of the cycle of urban
rebellion that began in 2013.

Once the presidency was reached, the main form of PT conciliation
between capital and labor with regard to popular housing was the My House,
My Life program. In the government's rationale, the challenge was to persuade
real estate capital to serve the poor, which meant turning the homeless into
housing consumers and popular housing into a profitable business. The era
of self-construction and joint efforts gave way to an alliance between workers and real estate interests backed by public funds. In this arrangement, all
dimensions of the construction process were controlled by the private sector,
from land policy to urbanization standards, construction sites, and technology.

The relationship between the right to housing and the right to property was sealed in a process that Arantes (2014) interprets as a "compensatory solution to urban reform that did not occur."

The agrarian question was similarly addressed with equally frustrating results. According to Ariovaldo Umbelino de Oliveira (2013: 122), it was evident from the beginning that land reform under Lula would be marked by two principles: "Don't do it where agribusiness is dominant, and do it only where it can 'help' agribusiness. In other words, land reform is definitely connected to the expansion of agribusiness in Brazil." A set of measures of PT governments solidified this antipopular orientation, among them the Biosafety Law, which regulated the production and marketing of transgenic seeds, the Legal Land program, which legalized land grabbing in the Amazon, the renegotiation of ruralist debt, the elimination of the Forestry Code, and the infrastructure works aimed at enhancing agribusiness referred to in the Growth Acceleration Program and the South American Regional Infrastructure Integration Initiative. This reality confronted rural organizations such as the Landless Rural Workers' Movement with a difficult situation. Support for the government contradicted the defense of land reform that was their raison d'être. At the same time, federal management beckoned with multiple possible links from the appointment of activists to low-level positions to the diffusion of welfare policies such as Bolsa Família at the base of the movement. This was a striking contrast to the repression of the previous administration.

At the level of production, the government multiplied the resources of the National Program for Strengthening Family Farming, emulated by the World Bank and implemented in the country under the Cardoso administration. More than just a line of credit, the program design entailed social engineering geared to turning family farming into a component of transnational agribusiness. From the political point of view, this incentive contemplated one of the bases of the movement, the families that were already settled, but the demand from this group was met at the expense of encamped landless families, impoverished farmers, and agricultural workers in general. As a rule, incentives for family farming tended to dismiss the mediation of social movements and almost always fostered monoculture. Half of the credits between 2003 and 2011 went to corn and soybean crops. As a result, in both the Northeast and the South, as Hilsenbeck (2013) points out, there were Landless Workers' settlements dedicated to castor bean or sunflower monocultures in initiatives mediated by agreements with Petrobras, to the detriment of the polyculture of foodstuffs.

The way the PT presidencies dealt with land reform and urban issues – problems that have mobilized the most combative popular movements in Brazil since the end of the dictatorship period – is indicative of the political econ-omy that was proposed. In the countryside, the contradiction between family farming and export monoculture has been blurred but at the expense of land reform. In the city, the contradiction between the right to housing and the city as a business was resolved but at the expense of urban reform.

Across the countryside and the city, the intention was to alleviate the con-tradiction between social integration and overexploitation of labor, replac-ing the struggle for rights with the capitalization of the poor. The expansion of family grants and low-paying jobs was linked to the expansion of popular credit and private higher education to forge a horizon of individual integration mediated by consumption. The dream of social mobility encouraged precari-ousness as a transitory condition that had family grants as its floor and private higher education as its higher ceiling. Popular credit fueled dreams of consum-erism and career advancement, as well as home ownership and commercial farming. While some families ate more, others were able to send their children to college for the first time. They all dreamed of getting out of the slave quar-ters (*senzala*), though not together.

In their efforts to alleviate the ills of colonial origin that afflict Brazilian soci-ety, the PT governments temporarily mitigated some of their symptoms, but their causes got worse. Modest progress corresponded to a deepening of struc-tural problems evidenced by the deterioration of working conditions and the setbacks of urban and agrarian issues against the backdrop of the return to an economy based on commodities. Politically, the focus on class reconciliation nurtured conservative business interests while accommodating through con-cessions and privileges many of those that had pushed for change in the past. However, in June 2013 this effort to circumvent the contradictions that strained Brazilian society, as if it were possible to eradicate the evils without disturbing their roots, began to crumble.

4   Lulism in Crisis

4.1   *From June 2013 to the Impeachment Mobilizations*
The contradictions associated with Lulism surfaced in the June 2013 pro-tests, although the government itself did not interpret events in this way. For those who saw Brazil through the glasses of Lulism, the popular revolt came like lightning in a blue sky. A multifaceted movement that generated diverse interpretations, mobilizations gravitated around three key issues: the democ-ratization of cities, universal public policies, and a reaction to parliamentary cretinism – the illusion that Congress represented the nation. All in all, the

rebellion challenged the conservative modernization deepened by the PT. For approximately three weeks in that month, a social earthquake shook the political scene. At its peak, an estimated 2 million people took to the streets in more than 120 cities (in other words, about 80 percent of Brazilians supported the protests). Initially, the protests reacted against the increase in public transport fares, but soon the agenda included other public services, notably health and education. The broadening of the original scope of the protests was summarized in the slogan "It's not for pennies, it's for rights!"

Coinciding with the Confederations Cup, a trial run for the World Cup facilities, the June protests captured a synthesis of conservative PT modernization based on FIFA's relations with the country. The parody "It was a very funny country; it had no schools, only stadiums" epitomized this malaise, in which sophisticated consumption patterns coexisted with a primitive social existence. Raised with public money at the cost of population removal and overexploitation of labor as part of international business that has enriched politicians and contractors and amused the few who could pay for tickets, the World Cup stadiums emerged as authentic monuments to underdevelopment (Santos 2016). While it is true that the demonstrations were not aimed at specific PT governments, it is also a fact that the party was perceived as part of the establishment targeted by protestors. It can be argued that the malaise on the streets was not directed at the federal government and the PT only if we consider that, 10 years after reaching the presidency, they had nothing to do with what the country had become. The opposite is more likely: that the demonstrations reflected, albeit diffusely, enormous frustration.

However, the government's reaction revealed that the frustration would continue. Although the protests succeeded in suspending fare adjustments throughout Brazil, the political agenda did not change. Pennies were earned but not rights. The Rousseff administration played a role in playing games and making rhetorical commitments, but it soon announced a new round of privatization, raised interest rates, and tightened fiscal adjustment further, cutting public spending and increasing the primary surplus. Instead of reflecting the demands of the protesters, it streamlined the enactment of an antiterrorism law to threaten them, aiming to keep the masses away from the 2014 World Cup and the 2016 Rio de Janeiro Olympics.

In the presidential elections of October 2014, the public agenda of the protesters of the previous year was ignored. Government priorities are illustrated by data from the Citizen Debt Audit indicating that, in that year, 45.11 percent of the budget was spent on public debt interest and amortization – 12 times the amount invested in education, 11 times the amount invested in health, and more than double the expenditure on social security (Fatorelli and Avila

2015). However, this election witnessed a political polarization that did not correspond to what was actually in dispute, which was the management of the looming crisis. A climate of visceral hostility intoxicated the electorate, and the country witnessed a reactionary radicalization. In this context, many of its best representatives have come to a passionate defense of the PT, stripped of any potential for change. At the same time, a ruling class always averse to popular protagonism felt that the Lulist momentum had passed and resumed the onslaught. With no programmatic alternatives to present, its critique quickly slipped into prejudice revealing intolerance of the existence of a workers' party, albeit one devoid of class autonomy.

Reelected by a narrow margin, Rousseff faced a different scenario in her second term. The reversal of the international commodity-friendly environment, inflationary pressures, rising unemployment, high interest rates, declining exports, plummeting industry – all amid a succession of corruption scandals – underlined a weakness of the executive branch that was exploited by a Congress whose profile reflected the degradation of the Brazilian social fabric. In this context, Rousseff immediately abandoned her campaign platform and adopted the losing candidate's agenda, implementing a draconian fiscal adjustment that entailed cuts in all socially focused ministries. Haunted by the specter of impeachment, the government was pressured to yield more and more, hoping to placate the voracity of the MDB and big business.

However, the economic slowdown, which resulted in negative growth rates in 2015 and 2016, undermined the government's bourgeois support. In turn, cuts in federal spending aggravated the effects of the recession on employment, harming workers. According to the Monthly Continuous Household Sample Survey, the unemployment rate for the quarter ending in November 2016 reached 12.1 million workers, compared with 9.1 million in the previous year. At the same time, the hostility of the traditional middle sectors resurfaced, disturbed by the increase in salaries for domestic work, the inflow of the popular classes in malls and airports, and the competition for jobs that paid more than one and a half times the minimum wage.

As allegations of corruption around Petrobras began to corner the news, the dissatisfaction of this middle class exploded in a wave of protests in favor of Rousseff's impeachment, with protests in major Brazilian cities, in March and April 2015. Marcelo Badaró (2015) highlights the difference in the social base of protesters compared with June 2013. In place of the workers who were students, in 2015 it was the adult population, between 30 and 50 years of age, white, with salaries of more than five minimum wages. Protesters from families earning up to three minimum wages did not exceed 20 percent. In addition, the protests were media-supported, led and funded by organizations with class ties, and some were linked to U.S. think tanks. Therefore, there was a turnaround rather than a linear continuity between the 2013 and 2015 cycles of protests.

However, there was at least one important relationship between the two waves of protest. In June, a new political conjuncture marked by the exhaustion of the Lulist mode of social conflict regulation was opened. The economic crisis then narrowed the scope for class reconciliation, leading to an update of the accumulation regime. The PT version of inclusive neoliberalism gave way to social plunder while conciliation slipped into class warfare. Although initiated under the Rousseff administration, this inflection was consumed by the impeachment process.

5   Impeachment

Framed in this way, the impeachment that toppled Rousseff reflected not a substantive dispute but a realignment of political forces and accumulation strategies in the context of the depletion of the Lulist social pacification process. Initially, the strategy of the anti-PT right wing did not contemplate a coup; instead, as was openly said, the idea was "to make the government bleed". However, as is often the case in history, politics acquired its own dynamism and the times became accelerated. When the PT launched a party candidate for the congressional presidency, the parliamentary base of the government cracked. First accused of Operation Car Wash, which investigated the corruption associated with Petrobras, the president of the Chamber of Deputies, Eduardo Cunha, soon became a ruthless enemy of the presidency, instigating the conspiracy initiated by his co-president, Vice President Michel Temer.

In April 2016, Rousseff was removed from office, and when the Olympic Games ended in August the deposition took place. The pretext was the so-called tax pedaling – postponing the transfer to public banks of the resources to be distributed in government programs such as Bolsa Família with the aim of minimizing imbalances in the state budget. In order not to delay the programs, banks used their own resources, which were then repaid by the federal government. According to the opinion of the Federal Court of Auditors, this practice constituted a loan, which was prohibited by the Fiscal Responsibility Law. It was, however, a common practice in Brazilian public management and one that had appealed to previous presidents (Cardoso and Lula) as well as 17 governors that same year. What followed was a political trial disguised as a judicial process: a coup d'état operated by the Congress in collusion with the judiciary and the mainstream press.

This coup was not, however, motivated by any fundamental programmatic contradiction. In fact, the government welcomed right-wing agendas such as pension reform, the freezing of public spending, and the denationalization of the Pre-Salt. The process was confined to a dispute within what Marx described as the "party of order", averse to popular protagonism. On this diapason, the government tried until the last moment to negotiate Rousseff's salvation with Cunha himself, always in the terms of antirepublican horse-trading politics.

The loss of command over the small politics that the PT had successfully handled for 13 years reflected the depletion of the Lulist mode of social conflict regulation. When the party took office in 2003, its prestige with the workers' organizations was instrumental in enabling pension reform that Cardoso had failed to achieve. In 2016, however, activism was passive, beset by dispersion and resignation. At the same time, the reduction in household consumption that was anticipated for the first time since 2004 suggested that the popular base of Lulism was at risk, while the economic downturn (-3.8 percent in 2015, -3.5 percent in 2016) undermined his bourgeois support. The political functionality of Lulism had been depleted. The right-wing branch of the establishment resumed the initiative and had no reason to be lenient with its rivals. Lula's arrest in April 2018, in a markedly persecutory process and without any consistent evidence of corruption, was a thorough demonstration of this offensive.

6   The Political Economy of the Temer Administration and the Popular Response

The Temer administration reflected the abandonment of the conciliatory strategy of the Brazilian bourgeoisie in favor of open confrontation with the working class. The combination of a 20-year cap on public spending, labor reform, and the projected pension reform pointed to a return of workers' living conditions to the nineteenth century. Deeply antipopular, this process was accompanied by the intensification of the repression and criminalization of social struggle, attacks on union organization and the right to strike, the gag law, the advance of the "nonpartisan school" law in many municipalities, and high-school reform, among other measures aimed at curbing the insurgency of the popular sectors, particularly among the young. It was the requiem of the "New Republic" founded on the "Citizen Constitution".

However, in contrast to the military coup in 1964, these measures did not reflect a turning point in history but pointed to an acceleration of the pace of prevailing politics. For example, the constitutional amendment that froze

public spending for 20 years radicalized the logic of structural adjustment practiced by the PT administrations. A month before being impeached, Rousseff
had surprised civil servants with Bill 257, which was more modest in scope
but had a similar rationale. The change in the Pre-Salt oil exploration regime,
deepened by Temer, had also been initiated by the deposed government, while
popular persecution was anchored in Rousseff's antiterrorist law on the eve of
her removal from office. The continuities are reflected by Henrique Meirelles,
Temer's finance minister, who had headed the Central Bank during Lula's terms
(2003–2010), having left the position of Brazilian Social Democracy Party deputy in the Congress to assume that office. From this point of view, Temer's
government can be seen as a metastasis of the PT administrations, since the
antipopular interests that they had never confronted now spread unimpeded.
In the same way, the corrupt professionals who had asserted PT governability
were no longer supportive, taking over command of the state. In short, the
breakdown of Lulism depleted mediations between the predatory aspirations
of the Brazilian bourgeoisie and the rights and aspirations of the workers.

The assault on workers' rights that ensued raises the question why the reactions of the popular classes have fallen short. This problem requires a brief
examination of the legacy of Lulism at the level of popular mobilization and
of PT politics after the coup. First of all, the ruling PT collaborated to confuse,
calm, and alienate the popular classes, by implementing a right-wing program
and practices but presenting itself as a left-wing government. The lack of differentiation between left and right fueled apathy, a form of depoliticization.
It is from this perspective that one understands the very high abstention rates
in the municipal elections in October 2016, which in the two largest cities surpassed the vote of the elected when added to the blank and null votes. The
other side of PT politics implied distancing itself from its popular bases. As we
have seen, rather than neglecting the organizations that had historically supported them the PT administrations sought to involve them in public management not to fulfill their historical demands but to neutralize them. Of course,
this was a two-way street: organized sectors of Brazilian workers identified
with this politics, either believing in the possible advances or for the material
and symbolic benefits they gained in the process.

The disjunctive between being a minority partner of power or opposing it
caused fractures in the union movement and the popular organizations. The
defense of a government that was antipopular but identified with the left
created ambiguous situations for activists at all levels. In the end, the contradictions distanced organizations from their bases. Only the groups most
committed to the PT politically or emotionally were able to turn a blind eye
to what was happening. Although these tensions did not converge in a leftist

opposition, disillusionment reinforced passivity and fragmentation. Finally, PT politics contributed to alienating the people rather than politicizing them in that it promoted popular consumption as a solution to social problems – an individual path that further commodified rights such as health, education, and social security. Rather than fostering class solutions for Brazilian problems, the party in the presidency fostered different versions of liberal ideology and practice: targeted policies, class reconciliation, and inclusion by consumption.

It is in the light of the promoted confusion, calming, and alienation that we understand the negligible popular reaction to critical events that followed: the impeachment, the antipopular assault led by Temer, and Lula's arrest. During these events, the PT position was ambiguous, since popular demonstrations were subordinated to electoral calculations, with plans for the return of its maximum leader. In this context, it is difficult to say whether the party failed to turn to the masses for fear of opening a Pandora's box or because it thought it would be a fiasco. The fact is that when the former president was taken to prison his eternal leadership in presidential polls did not turn into sympathy on the streets.

7   Conclusion

The PT was an extraordinary political construction of the Brazilian workers, who at the beginning of the twenty-first century elected for the first time in the Americas a workers' leader to the presidency. This feat in the last country to abolish slavery on the continent explains the party's identification with the left in the eyes of many, despite the party's unequivocal adaptation to the establishment. At the same time, those aiming for social change need to take stock of 40 years of PT hegemony, which ultimately means an assessment of the scope and limits of a strategy for change within that order. It is clear that this task will not be carried out by the party itself. Between the coup in August 2016 and Lula's arrest in April 2018, any expectation of self-criticism was thwarted. On the contrary, the gap between base indignation and party practice remained abysmal: two months after the impeachment, the PT allied itself with base parties that had supported the coup in the presentation of some 1,500 candidates for mayor. The former CUT president and former minister Luis Marinho justified this approach by arguing that "the majority of the people also supported impeachment, and we want to recover the majority of the people," while Lula spoke of "forgiving the coup backers who disgraced the country". In municipal elections, party candidates avoided talking about impeachment, among them the former mayor of São Paulo, Fernando Haddad, who considered the word "coup" "a bit harsh". Shyness affected popular protests. In the general strikes of the following year, many shouted "Temer get out!" but criticism of the austerity agenda, with which a reelected Lula would not break, was avoided.

Among the left, the notion that it was necessary to appeal to the PT in order to contrive a broad front, limited the scope of criticism. This dilemma was evident in the Socialism and Freedom Party (PSOL) internal dispute that preceded the presidential elections in 2018: either a broad-front candidacy gambling on a moralized PT or on transcending this perspective in the name of a radical project that could have little immediate resonance. In the internal dispute, the candidacy of the homeless leader Guilherme Boulos pointed to the first path, while the other pole was embodied by the economist Plínio Sampaio Jr., who was defeated.

The dilemma of a left struggling to break free of the magic lamp of Lulism was thus revived. In 2016 the challenge had been to oppose impeachment without endorsing the Rousseff government; in 2017 it was to build a "Temer get out!" campaign that did not endorse the PT, and in 2018 it was an electoral campaign not focused on Lula's release while condemning the injustice. In short, the Brazilian left still has accounts to settle with the PT – a necessary premise for a political landscape that overcomes it. Meanwhile, the country is plunging into the reactionary tide that characterizes world politics.

References

Arantes, P. (2014). Da (anti) reforma urbana brasileira a um novo ciclo de lutas nas cidades. In: Sampaio Jr., P. (ed.), *Jornadas de junho: A revolta popular em debate*, 129–151. São Paulo: ICP.

Badaró, M. (2015). Junho e nós: das jornadas de 2013 ao quadro atual. *Blog Junho*. http:// blogjunho.com. br/junho-e-nos-das-jornadas-de-2013-ao-quadro-atual/ (accessed July 2, 2015).

Bonomo, M., Brito, R., and Martins, B. (2014). *Macroeconomic and Financial Consequences of the After-Crisis Government-driven Credit Expansion in Brazil*. Banco Central do Brasil Working Paper 378. Rio de Janeiro: Banco Central do Brasil.

Braga, R. (2014). As jornadas de junho no Brasil: crônica de um mês inesquecível. In: Sampaio Jr, P. (ed.), *Jornadas de junho: A revolta popular em debate*, 53–78. São Paulo: ICP.

Braga, R. (2015). Conto.rnos do pós-lulismo. *Cult*, no. 206.

Braga, R., and Santos. (2020). The political Economy of Lulism and Its Aftermath. *Latin American Perspectives* 47(1): 169–186.

Carneiro, R.M. (2008). *Impasses do desenvolvimento brasileiro: A questão produtiva.* Textos para Discussão 153.

Cervo, A. (2003). Política exterior e relações internacionais do Brasil: enfoque. paradigmático. *Revista Brasleira de Política Internacional* 46(2): 43–64.

Dardot, P., and Laval, C. (2010). *La nouvelle raison du monde: Essai sur la societé neoliberal.* Paris: La Découverte.

Esposito, M. (2017). Desindustrialização do Brasil, uma análise a partir da perspectiva da formação nacional. *Revista da Sociedade Brasileira de Economia Política*, no. 46: 77–104.

Fatorelli, M.L., and Avila, R. (2015). Gastos com a dívida pública em 2014 superam 45% do orçamento federal executado. http://www.auditoriacidada.org.br/blog/2015/02/24/gastos-com-a-divida-publica-em-   2014-superaram-45-do-orcamento-federal-executado/ (accessed May 5, 2015).

Garcia, A.E.S. (2012). *A internacionalização de empresas brasileiras durante o governo Lula: uma análise crítica da relação entre capital e Estado no Brasil contemporâneo.* Ph.D. diss., Pontifícia Universidade Católica.

Georges, I., and Santos, I.G. (eds.). (2016). *As novas políticas sociais brasileiras na saúde e na assistência.* Belo Horizonte: Fino Traço.

Hilsenbeck, A. (2013). *O MST no fio da navalha: dilemas, desafios e potencialidades da luta de classes.* Ph.D. diss., Universidade Estadual de Campinas.

Krein, J.D., Manzano, M., and dos Santos, A.L. (2015). *A recente política de valorização do salário mínimo no Brasil.* MS, Universidade Estadual de Campinas.

Leopoldo, R. (2011). BNDES empresta 391% mais em 5 anos e supera em três vezes o Banco Mundial. *Estado de São Paulo*, March 10.

Maricato, H. (2011). *Impasse da política urbana no Brasil.* Petrópolis: Vozes.

Marques, R.M., and Mendes, A. (2004). O governo Lula e a contra-reforma previdenciária. *São Paulo em Perspectiva* 18(3): 115–134.

Newsweek. (2009). Brazil's Lula: the most popular politician on Earth. September 21. http://www.news-week.com/brazils-lula-most-popular-politician-earth-79355 (accessed July 5, 2018).

Oliveira, A.U. (2013). A questão agrária no Brasil: não reforma e contrarreforma agrária no governo Lula. In: Emir Sader (ed.), *10 anos de governos pós-neoliberais no Brasil: Lula e Dilma*, 145–166. São Paulo: Boitempo/FLACSO Brasil.

Oliveira, F. (2003). *Crítica à razão dualista: O ornitorrinco.* São Paulo: Boitempo.

Paulani, L. (2008). *Brasil Delivery.* São Paulo: Boitempo.

Pochmann, M. (2012). *Nova classe média? O trabalho na base da pirâmide social brasileira.* São Paulo: Boitempo.

Saad-Filho, A., and Morais, L. (2018). *Brasil: Neoliberalismo versus democracia.* São Paulo: Boitempo.

Sampaio Jr., P.A. (2012). Desenvolvimentismo e neodesenvolvimentismo: tragédia e farsa. *Serviço Social e Sociedade* 112: 32–57.

Santos, F.L.B. (2018). Neo-development of underdevelopment: Brazil and the political economy of South American integration under PT. *Globalizations* 16(2): 216–231.

Santos, F.L.B. (2016). *Além do PT: A crise da esquerda brasileira em perspectiva latino-americana.* São Paulo: Elefante.

Tautz, C.F., Siston, J.R.L., Pinto, and Badin, L. (2010). O BNDES e a reorganização do capitalismo brasileiro: um debate necessário. In: João Paulo de Almeida Magalhães (ed.), *Os anos Lula: Contribuições para um balanço crítico, 2003–2010,* 249–286. Rio de Janeiro: Garamond.

UNIDO (United Nations Industrial Development Organization). (2011). *Industrial and Development Report.* Vienna: UNIDO.

Zagni, R.M. (2016). Carta aos calouros ou bem-vindo à pátria educadora. *Boletim Adunifesp,* May. http:// www.adunifesp.org.br/artigo/carta-aos-calouros-ou-bem-vindos-patria-educadora-por-rodrigo-medina-zagni (accessed July 17, 2016).

CHAPTER 11

Assessing the Developmentalist Character of the Workers' Party Government Project

Luiz Fernando de Paula, Fabiano Santos and Rafael Moura

1   Introduction[1]

After the disappointment regarding the outcomes of the liberal reforms carried out in Latin America in the 1990s, the region witnessed, at the beginning of the new century, a strong renewal of the discussion on the viability of
developmentalist projects. In this context, two new theoretical perspectives
emerged: *social developmentalism* and *new developmentalism*, both updating the classical developmentalism formerly advanced by the Economic
Commission for Latin America and the Caribbean (ECLAC) but adding new
dimensions to the concept. Specifically, both supported a domestic strategy
whereby state activism was required for structural change focused on (re)
industrialization and a broad process of social transformation.

Although the renewal of the debate originated in academia, its transformation into an economic policy agenda took place under the governments of the
Partido dos Trabalhadores (Workers' Party – PT) starting in 2003. The central
objective of this chapter is to defend the plausibility of this *hypothesis*, to which
we add the following subsidiary questions: First, we refute the thesis of a lack
of differentiation between left-wing and right-wing parties on the ideological
spectrum of Brazil. Confirming the existence of a specific project concerning
PT, we argue that elections and the political system offer the society public
policy alternatives. Secondly, we briefly revisit the debate over *Lulism* (Singer
2009) by examining the extent to which this phenomenon differs from the
broader PT project. Supposing that a developmentalist inspiration was present
from the beginning of the Lula administration and culminated in more radical efforts by the first Dilma administration, Lulism can be interpreted, in line
with Samuels and Zucco (2018), as an epiphenomenon of PT rather than as
something ontologically distinct. This discussion brings us, finally, to whether
the developmentalist project of the PT governments was classical, social, or

---

1   An earlier version of this chapter appeared in Paula et al. (2020).

new developmentalist. Reflecting on the reasons that policy makers adopted different strategies at different times, we seek to shed light on the external or internal, political or economic constraints on the broader project of political differentiation of PT. From this perspective, we argue that two dimensions conditioned the dynamics of the project's advance or retreat: whether the constraints were exogenous or endogenous and whether they were political or economic.

In this study we will present, in the light of the available literature, a critical assessment of the PT's developmentalist project, identifying possible reasons for its peak and crisis. We divide the chapter into three major sections, besides this introduction. Section 2 deals with the nature and framing of the party's project: Social Developmentalism or New Developmentalism? PT project-versus-Lulism? Section 3 examines some conditioning factors of the performance of the PT governments: (1) financialization and the reduction of space for heterodoxy, (2) how external and internal factors, both economic and political, combined to favor or limit the implementation of developmentalist policies, (3) the pattern of interlocution between political and societal actors, and finally (4) the economic effects of Operation Car Wash ("Lava Jato"). Finally, section 4 concludes the chapter.

2   The Nature of the PT Governments' Developmentalist Project

2.1   *The Definition of Developmentalism*
The *concept of developmentalism* encompasses different premises depending on the author and the period. Two essential references are Bielschowsky (1988) and Fonseca (2014). Bielschowsky (1988: 247) defines developmentalism as a "planned and state-supported industrialization project". Its key concept is the transformation of Brazilian society according to an economic project including (1) comprehensive industrialization as a way of overcoming underdevelopment, (2) awareness that efficient and rational industrialization cannot be achieved through the spontaneous operation of market forces, (3) planning (identifying the desired expansion rates of economic sectors and instruments to promote that same expansion), and (4) state execution of the expansion, assembling the financial resources and promoting direct investment where private initiative is insufficient (Bielschowsky 1988: 7).

Fonseca (2014), in turn, considers two analytical keys for developmentalism – *ideas* and *political practice* – and seeks to determine the intersection of both these dimensions. His method has two stages: researching the "attributes used by various authors in expressing their understanding of what developmentalism is" and determining the attributes of the "historical experiments normally listed in the literature as examples of developmentalism" (Fonseca 2014: 7). From this examination, he extracts the *common core of the concept*: interventionism, industrialization, and a national project. *Industrialization* is understood as the only way to promote national development – "to accelerate economic growth, productivity, and technical progress" (13). *Interventionism* is the involvement of the state administrative apparatus as the coordinating entity of the project, an instrument of national development. *Nationalism* is the prioritization of the national interest instead of fragmentary interests.

2.2   The PT Project: Social Developmentalism or New Developmentalism?
Two questions arise in the discussion of the nature of the PT governments' project. *The first is whether it was actually developmentalist.* As we have seen, the canonical concept of developmentalism assumes a national project, state interventionism, and industrialization. From this perspective, therefore, there was no developmentalist project, since, although the first Dilma government did adopt an unsuccessful industrialist agenda (Mello and Rossi 2018), the party did not reverse or deepen the ongoing deindustrialization. The reasons for the failure of Dilma's industrialist agenda are subject of significant discussion, with some writers highlighting changes in the international scenario (Sarti and Hirakuta 2018) while others stress inconsistencies in the policies adopted by the PT governments, especially the first Dilma government (Paula et al. 2015; Carvalho 2018). As for social advances, there is some consensus on important gains in terms of reducing unemployment, moderate improvement in income distribution, and greater access for the lower-income segments to utilities and basic appliances. Thus, in terms of the canonical concept of developmentalism, it is doubtful that the PT's project was in fact developmentalist, but it can perhaps be identified as "social developmentalist".

This brings us to the second question, which is *what kind of developmentalism the project represented.* Because of the failure of neoliberal policies in the 1990s, neodevelopmentalist strands (new developmentalist and social developmentalist) have emerged to revive the discussion of developmentalism as part of the ECLAC structuralist tradition.[2] *Social developmentalism* (Bielschowsky 2012; Carneiro 2012) argues that the growth of the domestic mass market must be stimulated by both employment expansion and improved

---

2   A broad assessment of these development strategies is made by Ferrari-Filho and Paula (2016) and Fritz et al. (2017).

income distribution. Further, since a mass-consumption-based growth strategy loses momentum over time, expansion must be complemented by public investment in infrastructure. The advocated policies include: wage policies (minimum wages being powerful instruments for increasing demand and redistributing income), social transfers directed to the poorest segments of the population, promotion of consumer credit, public investment in infrastructure to create incentives for private investment, industrial policies, and financing subsidized by public banks. Therefore, this approach is a kind of wage-led growth strategy – pursuing growth through an increase in the proportion of wages in the national income, which induces investment and profit (Ferrari-Filho and Paula 2016).

New developmentalism (Bresser-Pereira 2011; Bresser-Pereira et al. 2016), on the other hand, emphasizes the two fundamental problems of middle-income economies: the tendency of wages to increase less than productivity because of the abundance of labor supply, and the tendency toward overvaluation of the exchange rate as a result of the combination of the "Dutch disease"[3] with abundant flows of foreign capital towards emerging economies, attracted by their generally higher profit and interest rates and also the policy of growth with foreign savings. This type of developmentalism advocates policies for *catching up*: an income policy that promotes wage increases in line with productivity and an exchange-rate policy that neutralizes exchange-rate overvaluation, aiming at a rate that allows domestic producers to compete in foreign markets with fair profit margins. The (re)industrialization process is, thus, directly linked to the goal of obtaining surpluses for the manufactured exports in order to stimulate new investments in this sector. Under this strategy, a developing economy must resort to an export-led growth strategy[4] for catching up in a short time.

Prates et al. (2019) have shown that the PT governments' developmentalist project combined elements of both social developmentalism and new developmentalism together with orthodox economic policies. In general, however, these governments sought to stimulate, by an actual increase in minimum wages, in social transfers and credit expansion, growth based on

---

3   The situation in which increased revenue from natural-resources exports overvalues the local currency and leads to the deindustrialization of the manufacturing sector, which is less competitive with foreign products.

4   A growth regime in which the dynamics of growth are primarily determined by the increase in net exports, which generates an increase in and the subsequent maintenance at a high level of the export coefficient.

mass consumption – a predominantly wage-led growth strategy[5] that was closer to the social developmentalist approach. The first Lula administration, because of the 2002 crisis of confidence, started with a very orthodox economic policy, with high interest rates and high primary surpluses (averaging 3.5 percent of the gross domestic product [GDP] in 2003–2006), to cope with external imbalances and rising inflation whose contractionary effects were felt less acutely because of the beginning of the commodities' boom that favored Brazilian exports.

After 2006 the government adopted a less conventional set of policies, among them the accumulation of foreign exchange reserves, an increase in the minimum wage and in disbursements from the National Bank for Economic and Social Development (BNDES), and a plan to accelerate economic growth through increased public and private investments in infrastructure. In response to the international financial crisis in September 2008, a set of countercyclical policies that included a credit policy via public banks, tax exemptions for consumption of durable goods, increases in public investment, expansion of credit through the Brazilian Development Bank, and the creation of the popular housing program My House, My Life ("*Minha Casa, Minha Vida*") was successful in addressing its impacts on the Brazilian economy.

In the first Dilma administration, there was a change in the direction of economic policy in the midst of the deterioration of the external scenario (the international crisis and deceleration of the Chinese economy). From mid-2011 on, the government adopted a set of measures called the "new macroeconomic matrix", which included a reduction in the SELIC interest rate by the Central Bank (from 12.5 percent in July 2011 to 7.5 percent in August 2012), devaluation of the currency (by 25 percent from August 2011 to May 2012), intensive use of BNDES in subsidizing credit lines to finance investments, the promotion of reindustrialization with the Greater Brazil Plan, tax exemptions (particularly for payrolls), an infrastructure plan (the Logistics Investment Program), a reform of the power sector, capital controls, a tightening of monitored prices (energy and oil), and protectionism (Singer 2018).

Finally, in 2015, at the very beginning of her second term, Dilma made a sharp turn, adopting a policy switch and the questionable discourse of "expansionist fiscal contraction",[6] with a set of measures that included fiscal adjustments in

---

5 According to Prates et al. (2019), the proportion of wages in the Gross Domestic Product (GDP) increased from 35.8 percent in 2004 to 46.8 percent in 2014.

6 According to Prates et al. (2019), the proportion of wages in the Gross Domestic Product (GDP) increased from 35.8 percent in 2004 to 46.8 percent in 2014.

public spending, even higher interest rates, accelerated adjustment of managed prices (energy and oil), and the elimination of subsidized credit.

Regarding *social policies*, these were active throughout the entire PT government, being key instruments for achieving the goals of income redistribution and the promotion of domestic consumption. The two main factors that contributed to improving the distribution profile were the significant increase in the minimum wage (66.9 percent in real terms from December 2003 to December 2014) and the income transfer policy anchored in the increase of social security benefits and the Bolsa Familia (family subsidy) program.

In summary, the PT governments adopted a social-developmentalist approach in both social policy (in particular, the minimum wage increase) and economic policy (public investment, credit to families, and the actions of public banks). The key instrument of new developmentalism – maintaining the exchange rate at a competitive level – was adopted only for a short period of time and in the context of a poorly coordinated economic policy.

2.3   *Implications for the "PT-versus-Lulism" Debate*

In an influential work, Singer (2009) traces the origin of *lulism* to the 2006 elections, which, according to him, triggered a deep and significant electoral realignment, a change in the boundaries of electoral loyalties in a long political cycle. In the context of a favorable international environment that allowed President Lula to promote redistributive and antipoverty policies, a distinction emerged between the bases of support for the president and those for his party. Lulism was characterized by the manifestation of support for Lula by the subproletariat, a class fraction that benefited from the public policies that were being implemented. This subproletariat, heavily concentrated in the North and Northeast, was highly vulnerable because of its low income, employment, and general subsistence conditions, but according to Singer nevertheless contributed to a change in the sociopolitical base of PT support, rearranging the class foundations of the existing power bloc.[7] In a sense it was stronger than the PT in that it configured a change in the social composition of voters for leftist presidential candidates, and it became the pivot of a pragmatic turn toward "weak reformism" – a gradual shift in the state's emphasis on social policy and the abandonment of any radical program or direct confrontation with capital (Singer 2009; see also Loureiro and Saad-Filho 2019).

---

7   This view is corroborated by Boito Jr. and Berringer (2013: 34), who refer to this subproletariat as a socially and politically disorganized "marginal mass" composed of unemployed, underemployed workers dependent on precarious work or self-employment, mainly in the peripheries of the great urban centers of the country and in the North and Northeast.

Samuels and Zucco (2018) adopt a different perspective. Analyzing the distinct socioeconomic underpinnings of lulism and PT supporting bases, they detect, as does Singer, a poorer, nonwhite, and less educated profile for supporters of the presidential candidate while the profile of the PT's declared militants and supporters remained that of a generally organized and activist middle class, mostly white, especially employees of the formal public sector. They declare that, despite the former president's capacity for political articulation and rhetorical eloquence, Lulism as a psychological and sociological phenomenon is considerably weaker than the PT and quite independent of it. They see Singer's argument as ambiguous in that it does not examine the ideological basis of lulism, which combines a progressive view of state interventionism with conservative attitudes toward social interests. Moreover, they argue, notions such as realignment are problematic in this context because they fail to take into account the executive's vote on legislative choices. Thus, the debate should include broader considerations of parliamentary results and party identification profiles beyond the presidential election.

Through surveys and experimental techniques, Samuels and Zucco show that the PT's predilection for Dilma Rousseff's election and reelection survived even troubled social episodes such as the street protests of June 2013.[8] Identification towards the party derived mainly, on the one hand, from its associative roots in civil society and, on the other hand, from the economic vote of government approval, characteristic of multiparty presidential systems anywhere in the world. They conclude that partisanship remained very important in helping to solidify long-term support for the PT. They attribute the success of the PT in building its identity to organizational efforts to put down roots in civil society with a more participatory approach to politics. Lulism, expressed in support of the former president and his style of government, will eventually be moderated, but PT partisanship will survive, drawing its strength from elements beyond Lula. Over time, they suggest, the legacies of Lula and the PT will converge in the ideals of greater democracy and socioeconomic equality.

What our working hypothesis allows us to consider regarding this debate is that programmatic motivation has never been absent from economic policy decisions. In other words, while developmentalism has always served as a horizon for actions of the PT governments, it does not seem to us credible that

---

8   Such a high degree of identification is even more impressive given the limited partisanship of the Brazilian voter in a scenario in which the national political system is characterized by low educational levels, patronage in political campaigns, party fragmentation, constant changes of acronyms that confuse voters, and the recent return to democracy (Samuels and Zucco 2018).

the actions of Lula and later Dilma were detached from an attempt to create a political identity different from the one that marked liberal center parties in Brazil such as the Brazilian Democratic Movement Party and the Brazilian Social Democratic Party. Thus Lulism, although very important for understanding the outcomes of particular elections, becomes less important than the attempt to construct PT's own brand in the context of macroeconomic choices.

3   The Heyday and Crisis of the PT Developmentalist Project

3.1   *Financialization, Rentierism, and the Limits of the Policy Space*
An important impact of contemporary capitalism on the degree of freedom for developmentalist and interventionist policies in developing countries has been the financialization of the economy – a worldwide trend in countries with some sophistication in their respective financial systems. As measured by various indicators, Brazil is widely regarded as a highly financialized economy but one with particular characteristics (Bruno et al. 2011). *Financialization* is understood as "the increasing role of financial motives, financial markets, financial actors and financial institutions in the operation of domestic and international economies" (Epstein 2005: 3) or "a pattern of accumulation in which profit-making occurs increasingly through financial channels rather than through trade and commodity production" (Krippner 2005: 174). Finance-led capitalism has spread around the world because of neoliberalism, promoting policies such as financial liberalization, labor market flexibility, and the draining of the social and developmental state.

An important issue for emerging economies is the asymmetric international financial integration with regard to the dynamics and magnitude of capital flows directed to peripheral countries experiencing globalization. These flows depend mainly on exogenous factors, making these countries permanently vulnerable to their reversal either because of changes in monetary conditions at the center or because of the increased preference for liquidity of global investors (Paula, Fritz, and Prates 2017). International studies show that financialization significantly reduces the autonomy of national states in formulating domestic economic policies independent of international or long-term conditions, consistent with the conditions of production and interests of domestic nonfinancial sectors (Becker et al. 2010).

Bresser-Pereira (2018: 27) argues that since the late 1980s we have seen the emergence of a financial-rentierist capitalism "in which capitalists are predominantly rentiers, while highly placed technobureaucrats are the top executives

of companies or financiers." Rentiers, most of them inheritors, replace entrepreneurs in the ownership of big firms and leave the management of companies to financiers. Financialization in Brazil since 1994 has been brought about
by the replacement of a monetary regime characterized by inflationary gains
to one based on gains from interest. This process was spurred by the increasing
liberalization of capital accounts, given the speculative nature of capital flows
from both residents and nonresidents. Under the new regime the government
has sought to reconcile the interests of rentierist-based accumulation with
redistributive social policies favoring segments whose income derives from
interest and other financial gains. Thus financialization has been stimulated
by two interrelated factors – high actual interest rates and an "overnight" circuit in the Brazilian economy inherited from the period of high inflation but
maintained in the post-real period – into which high-yield investments of economic agents are channeled[9] (Bresser-Pereira et al. 2020). Some of the detrimental effects of this process in Brazil are worth mentioning. On the one hand,
financialization converts into a paroxysm the capitalists' (including industrial
entrepreneurs-turned-rentiers') preference for liquidity, reducing gross fixed
capital formation in favor of short-term financial investments that compete
with investments in capital assets by increasing the liquidity premium (Bruno
et al. 2011). On the other hand, it has had clear concentrating effects on high-
income segments, considering that financial income, dividend income, and
inheritance and gifts represent almost 40 percent of the country's income
(Menezes Filho 2017).

3.2   Internal and External Economic Constraints

The Brazilian economy is highly integrated into the international system
in terms of capital flows and partially dependent on commodity exports.
Although the significance of commodity exports is less pronounced than in
other Latin American economies, their direct (the income effect) and indirect (through financial conditions, country risk, exchange rate, inflation, and
monetary policy) impacts are considerable. In addition, the form of its international financial integration is crucial in terms of policy space for the implementation of developmentalist and interventionist policies. The Brazilian
economy has undergone an intense liberalization of its capital account and

---

9   In fact, the real interest rate (discounted by the Consumer Price Index) averaged 5.0 percent
    per year in 2007–2016 (as compared with 12.5 percent in 2002–2006). On the other hand,
    SELIC-indexed short-term financial operations – including treasury bills and repurchase
    agreements – increased from 35.4 percent of GDP in December 2006 to 40.7 percent of GDP
    in April 2015 (Salto and Ribeiro 2015).

balance of payments since the early 1990s becoming quite integrated from this perspective (Paula 2011). The Lula administration was complaisant regarding these flows, which increased considerably after 2004 and, with a brief gap at the height of the international financial crisis, returned strongly starting in 2009 in the absence of any effective measures to moderate them. The Dilma administration, in contrast, faced an avalanche of external resources resulting from the quantitative easing of the Federal Reserve and began regulating capital flows, even on the derivatives market, which contributed to the Central Bank's devaluing of the exchange rate in August 2011. However, when the flow of capital began to reverse, it eliminated those controls.

In this context of strong international financial integration and dependence on commodities' exports, Campello (2015) describes a "confidence game" in which emerging countries, especially in Latin America, vulnerable to global liquidity and price cycles, are required to adjust their domestic policies to changing external conditions, especially in downturn periods. In good times of abundant financial flows and high prices, governments have some leeway to implement an agenda of income distribution. However, during times of reversal in financial flows and/or commodity prices, governments, regardless of their political orientation, are exposed to pressures to reverse market conditions and curb resource leakage. Thus, the imposition of supply-side policies and the general convergence toward orthodoxy are based not on autonomous decisions but on exposure to global market volatility.

Lula's government was pressured to adopt orthodox policies at the beginning of its first administration in 2003, and since international conditions (the commodities boom) were favorable it implemented a more interventionist and distributive agenda while maintaining an orthodox macroeconomic policy. However, in the first Dilma administration, given a less favorable international scenario with a sharp deterioration in the country's terms of trade, policies moved away from more conventional measures, thus breaking away from the confidence game. In her second term Dilma tried rather desperately to regain market confidence through an orthodox adjustment, but it turned out to be counterproductive in a recession that was already under way and in a quite adverse international and domestic context.

Undoubtedly, the Lula administration was favored by the international economic context, but discretionary domestic policies played an important role in increasing the autonomy of its economic policy, in particular the combination of a policy of accumulating international reserves starting in 2005 (from US$28 billion in 2004 to US$352 billion in 2011) and the reduction of the external public debt (from US$136 billion in 2003 to US$86 billion in 2006), which made the Brazilian government a creditor in dollars starting in 2007. In contrast,

domestic policy during the Dilma administration was faltering. Initially orthodox, it later combined orthodoxy with heterodox policies and finally returned
to strongly contractionary policies in 2015. The countercyclical policies
adopted by the first Dilma administration were poorly conceived on the fiscal
issue – with ambitious targets being maintained through nonrecurring budget
operations and exemption-oriented fiscal expansionism and excessive intervention in regulated markets (energy and oil), among other things.[10]

Although it is common to attribute the deceleration of the Brazilian economy starting in 2011 and the recession from mid-2014 on to policy errors
and particularly to the new macroeconomic matrix, Borges (2017) has asked
whether the crisis was a consequence of *bad luck* or *bad policy*. He concludes
that, despite mistakes made (especially in the fiscal area), exogenous factors
played an important role in slowing growth. Using varied methodologies, he
estimates that between 40 and 60 percent of the 2012–2016 GDP growth slowdown was brought about by exogenous factors (both international and domestic). He highlights four factors: (1) the water crisis between 2013 and 2015,
(2) the impact of Operation Car Wash on the economy, particularly the civil
construction and oil and gas sectors, (3) a sharp drop in commodity prices,
and (4) the virtual insolvency of Petrobras in 2015–2016. Usually attributed to
corruption, accumulated losses between 2011 and 2014 with the sale of gasoline and diesel in the domestic market at prices below those paid on imports,
and the ambitious program of investments implemented after the discovery of
the Pre-Salt oil layer in 2007, the Petrobras situation was, according to Borges,
mainly the result of "the strong and highly unexpected collapse of international oil prices starting at the end of 2014". The second Dilma government
faced a "perfect storm", caused by a set of exogenous shocks. While her management was marked in part by bad policy, there was also a lot of bad luck.

3.3 *From Societal Corporatism to the Crisis: Conspiracy and the Return to the Neoliberal Route*

The 2002 elections significantly changed the correlation of political forces
between representatives of capital – particularly financial capital, until then
hegemonic – and labor, with the rise of previously marginalized sectors (Boito
Jr. and Berringer 2013). The difficulties of the Washington Consensus–inspired
policies in leveraging industrial growth favored a partial degree of convergence between some domestic businesses and wage earners (Ianoni 2018).
This "productivist" coalition was responsible for the gradual flexibilization of

---

10 For a more in-depth analysis, see Paula, Modenesi, and Pires (2015) and Carvalho (2018).

the macroeconomic tripod via the mediation platform created by segments of Brazil's political, business, and civil society actors (Bresser-Pereira 2014; Ianoni 2018). The result of easing measures was a mix of policies now including actions focused on the productive sector and fight against poverty.

From a path-dependence perspective, the Lula administration was marked by both advances and concessions reflecting the difficulties of maintaining a capital-labor consensus in the framework of financial globalization and the power of the financial-rentier sectors. Still, growth was the guarantor of the support for the PT from the "center", an eclectic coalition enlisting new actors and reflecting the influence of the financial sector, productive-sector entrepreneurs, and workers on government policy making (Ianoni 2018). Other significant changes were the creation of broad forums for civil society sectors to participate in public policy formulation, the assignment of key positions in the executive branch and in large state-owned companies to leaders drawn from the union movement or heterodox economic thinkers, and, finally, greater participation of labor representatives in the dynamics of development through pension funds (Boito Jr. and Berringer 2013; Boschi 2014).

In the first Dilma administration, Lula's political consensus was maintained; and, from 2011 onwards, there was an inflection with the new macroeconomic matrix (Ianoni 2018; Carvalho 2018).[11] The new matrix proved controversial and sparked debate about future tensions that would lead to the collapse of the government's supporting coalition. By bringing about changes in interest and exchange rate policies, with a drastic reduction in the SELIC rate and bank spreads, Dilma eventually strained the relationship with representatives of this financial-rentier segment (Singer 2018).

In addition to the strife with the very own Brazilian Federation of Banks (FEBRABAN), in June 2013 erupted widespread protests in the country's capitals that produced a fundamental cleavage in the Dilma government (Singer 2018: 99). The political climate of the country was rattled by the episode. The drop in the president's popularity put the federal government in a defensive stance, with setbacks such as the restoration of higher interest rates by the Central Bank in mid-2013 and "the beginning of the mobilization of the middle class, which would eventually play a decisive role in the fall of Dilma" (Singer 2018: 103). This new window of opportunity caused much of business representatives and actors to detach themselves definitively from the governing coalition and protest against the prevailing economic policy (Singer 2018). Still,

---

11   According to former Finance Minister Guido Mantega (2012), the new macroeconomic matrix was a government offensive against three major obstacles to the Brazilian productive regime: high interest rates, appreciated exchange rates, and high costs.

Dilma won the 2014 elections, albeit by a narrow margin (51.8 percent against 48.2 percent for Aécio Neves). The opposition began to enjoy a more favorable margin of support and number of representatives, displaying and intensifying the same regional and income polarization hinted at in the 2006 and 2010 elections. Partisan fractionalization in Congress increased (with a considerable increase in small parties and a reduction of the deputies of PT), bringing about a correlation of forces that was more complex and heterogeneous and showing the future difficulties regarding the conciliation of the legislative and executive branches (Santos and Canello 2015; Miguel and Assis 2016).

Reelected after harsh campaigning with strong criticism to Neves and his orthodox-liberal agenda, Dilma then announced a financial-sector representative (Joaquim Levy) as minister of economics and adopted the defeated program. This change led to the accusation of "electoral swindle", with mass protests intensifying in the streets concomitant with the deepening recession and dissatisfaction with the president, whose rejection rate jumped from 30 percent to 70 percent from September 2014 to September 2015 (Datafolha 2018; Carvalho 2018). The erosion of middle-class support for the PT was marked, as was the own middle-class which backed the protests together with right-wing political actors, movements, and business entities (Singer 2018). The liberal rhetoric critical of interventionism ascribed to the PT – holding it responsible for the mistakes that had led the country to the crisis – gained momentum.

At the political level, the concatenation of a more conservative Congress and a new president of the Chamber of Deputies (Deputy Eduardo Cunha) colliding directly with the executive branch hindered any consensus on a common agenda between the two powers. It is in this context that Vice President Michel Temer gained strength. Given the president's lack of popularity and communication problems, he became a relevant political coordinator, mediating with the Congress and specifically with his party Brazilian Democratic Movement – increasingly detached from Dilma – for the approval of liberalizing and austerity measures.[12]

3.4   *Economic Consequences of Operation Car Wash*

Operation Car Wash was closely intertwined with all this turbulence in the country, and the investigation of it, which began in 2014, had a great impact on both the political and the economic crisis and in particular on two powerful and interconnected national production chains: oil and gas, and construction

---

12   For example, increased working time to obtain the right to unemployment insurance, restrictions on sick leave, and the approval of outsourcing of core business activities.

(Belluzzo 2018; Campos 2019). Officially launched with the arrests of the Petrobras director Paulo Roberto Costa and the black-market banker Alberto Youssef in April 2014, it quickly resulted in an investigation of several Petrobras contracts with other companies and the blocking of hundreds of accounts totaling more than US$400 million. The investigation culminated in October 2014 with the leaking of Youssef's unveiling of the scheme to the Federal Prosecutor's Office and the "Doomsday Operation" (within Car Wash) that led to the arrest of top executives of major construction firms.

It is no easy task to estimate the aggregate impact of Operation Car Wash on the economy. Consulting companies such as GO Associados e Tendências, for example, attribute around a 2 to 2.5 percent contribution, respectively, to the 2015 and 2016 GDP contractions to impacts on the metalworking, naval, construction, and heavy engineering sectors, whose losses may amount to R$142 billion (BBC 2015; *Valor Econômico* 2016). The main effects of the crisis were concentrated in the construction industry, which was paralyzed by the sharp downturn of state investment. Between 2014 and 2017 it registered a negative balance between hiring and dismissals of 991,734 formal vacancies (predominantly in the Southeast of Brazil). Between 2014 and 2016, this balance was 1,115,223 out of 5,110,284 (or 21.8 percent) of the total job loss of the period, and from the second quarter of 2014 until the last quarter of 2018 there was a strong downturn.[13]

The dismantling and decapitalization of major construction firms are also noticeable. Data collected by the maganize *O Empreiteiro*, made available by the Brazilian Chamber of the Construction Industry (CBIC), show that between 2015 and 2016, for example, the gross revenues of Queiroz Galvão, Andrade Gutierrez, and Camargo Corrêa dropped by 37, 31 and 39 percent, respectively. Odebrecht, the largest national construction company, had, in 2014, gross revenues of R$107 billion, with 168,000 employees and operations in 27 countries. By 2017 – less than four years after the outbreak of the scandal and after its president had been arrested – they were R$82 billion, with 58,000 employees and activities in only 14 countries. Other industry giants – Queiroz Galvão, OAS, Andrade Gutierrez, and Camargo Corrêa – also saw their consolidated financial assets melt from around R$25.77 billion in 2014 to approximately R$8.041 billion in 2017,a loss of 68.6 percent (CBIC 2019). Many firms, forced to carry out divestment plans to fit the new scenario of fewer projects and comply with heavy leniency agreements, also sold many assets to foreign groups. Odebrecht

---

13   The survey carried out by *Valor Econômico* (2019) based on data from the National Heavy
      Construction Industry Employers' Association corroborates that from 2014 to 2019 the
      sector witnessed the elimination of over 1 million jobs.

initiated the sale of its subsidiary Braskem – until then the largest petrochemical company in Latin America, producer of biopolymers with significant participation from Petrobras – to the Dutch group LyondellBasell; Andrade Gutierrez sold its control over OI to Dutch and Portuguese shareholders, and Camargo Corrêa sold CPFL to State Grid, a Chinese company (Campos 2019).

With regard to the oil sector, the scandal involving the cartel made up of state and other companies occurred in the context of a sharp drop in the price of the commodity, costing Petrobras net losses of R$26.6 billion in the last quarter of 2014 and R$36.9 billion in the last quarter of 2015 (Petrobras 2018a). The crisis required the company to reduce its investment volume from approximately US$48.8 billion in 2013 to US$15.1 billion in 2017, a decrease of almost 70 percent (Petrobras 2018b). Its investments fell from 1.97 percent of GDP in 2013 to 0.73 percent of GDP in 2017 and from 9.44 percent of total investment to 4.69 percent in the same period, and its share of public investments declined from 49.3 percent in 2013 to 36.5 percent in 2017. This sharp downturn affected staff and numerous projects with other firms, contributing to a reduction in the number of formal employees in the Petrobras system from 86,108 to 68,829 between 2013 and 2016 and from 360,180 to 117,555 among outsourced workers for the same period. Within four years the company's direct production chain lost nearly 260,000 formal and informal jobs (DIEESE 2017). The crisis due to the Petrobras scandal, coupled with the Temer government's new liberalizing program, led to a radical policy reversal for the oil sector and the massive sale of refineries and state-owned assets. Petrobras transferred 90 percent of its assets related to a Southeast pipeline network, the Nova Transportadora Sudeste (NTS), to the Canadian group Brookfield; and also, the gas pipeline and transport network in the North and Northeast, (TAG), to the French group ENGIE (Valor Econômico 2017; Carta Capital 2019).

In summary, the oil and gas segment was the spearhead of the dismantling of Brazil's engineering and infrastructure, accentuating a serious trend toward denationalization of the country's productive activities ongoing since the Real Plan, with serious impacts on employment and income.[14] The disruption of these two sectors – civil construction, and oil and gas – greatly contributed, on one hand, to the deepening of the economic crisis from 2015 onwards and, on the other hand, to the disruption of some of the few sectors that had substantial domestic capital and were internationally competitive.

---

14 Pinto et al. (2019) support the connection of Operation Car Wash with leaks to the mainstream media that exposed the relationship between the state (and its bureaucracy) and part of the bloc in power of Brazilian capitalism, which contributed to the disruption of the existing rules (expressed and tacit) governing the accumulation of capital.

4   Conclusion

In this chapter we have highlighted the existence of a political-economic project of the PT that we characterize as rather close to social developmentalism.
This project was different from those of previous governments and their liberal
centrist tendencies. In addition, we have described how the financialization
of the economy in Brazil has, at various times, imposed policies in favor of
the interests of financiers/rentiers, dramatically limiting the state's scope for
adopting measures to stimulate growth. Finally, we have discussed the internal and external constraints on deepening the developmentalist project in
Brazil: financially integrated and commodity-dependent emerging countries
are subject to a confidence game in which leftist governments with distributive aims are exposed to the ups and downs of global cycles of liquidity and
commodity markets and therefore required to adjust their domestic policies to
these global conditions.

The first Lula administration faced the problem of a crisis of confidence
and adopted orthodox policies but was able, with the improvement of international conditions, to launch policies that were more interventionist and distributive. Dilma Rousseff, facing a downright unfavorable international context, explicitly broke with the confidence game by applying the policies of the
new macroeconomic matrix. In the transition to her second term, she radically
reversed the policy orientation, moving toward strong fiscal adjustment and
monetary orthodoxy, and this eventually undermined her few sources of political support. The political conspiracy that produced her impeachment ended
up occurring with surprising ease, fueled by the effects of Operation Car Wash
and the erratic trajectory of economic policies once the government became
aware of continuing difficulties regarding the new macroeconomic matrix.
The economic crisis from the second half of 2014 on undoubtedly contributed
to the political crisis, which in turn made infeasible any attempt to implement
policies in order to reverse the situation. Dilma's impeachment finally interrupted the PT's developmentalist project, with its mistakes and successes,
allowing the emergence of new political actors.

References

BBC. (2015). *Escândalo da Petrobras "engoliu 2,5% da economia em 2015"*. Available
at: https://www.bbc.com/portuguese/noticias/2015/12/151201_lavajato_ru   (consulted December 2, 2015).

Becker, J., et al. (2010). Peripheral financialization and vulnerability to crisis: a regulationist perspective. *Competition and Change* 14(3–4): 225–247.

Belluzzo, L.G. (2018). As consequências econômicas da Lava Jato. In: Kerche, F., and Feres Júnior, J. (eds.), *Operação Lava Jato e a democracia brasileira*, 21–35. São Paulo: Contracorrente.

Bielschowsky, R. (1988). *Pensamento econômico brasileiro: o ciclo ideológico do desenvolvimentismo*. Rio de Janeiro: Contraponto.

Bielschowsky, R. (2012). Estratégia de desenvolvimento e as três frentes de expansão no Brasil. *Economia e Sociedade* 21: 729–748.

Boito Júnior, A., and Berringer, T. (2013). Brasil: classes sociais, neodesenvolvimentismo e política externa nos governos Lula e Dilma. *Revista de Sociologia e Política* 21(47): 31–38.

Borges, B. (2017). Impacto dos erros (reais) da Nova Matriz tem sido muito exagerado. *Blog do Ibre*, September 8. Available at: https://blogdoibre.fgv.br/posts/impacto-dos-erros-reais-da-nova-matriz-tem-sido-muito-exagerado (consulted June 22, 2019).

Boschi, R.R. (2014). Politics and trajectory in Brazilian capitalist development. In: Becker, U. (ed.), *The BRICS and Emerging Economies in Comparative Perspective: Political Economy, Liberalisation and Institutional Change*, 123–143. London: Routledge.

Bresser-Pereira, L.C. (2011). From old to new developmentalism in Latin America In: Ocampo, J., and Ros, J. (eds.), *The Oxford Handbook of Latin American Economics*, 108–130. Oxford: Oxford University Press.

Bresser-Pereira, L.C. (2014). *A construção política do Brasil: Sociedade, economia e estado desde a Independência*. São Paulo: Editora 34.

Bresser-Pereira, L.C. (2018). Capitalismo financeiro-rentista. *Estudos Avançados* 32 (92): 17–28.

Bresser-Pereira, L.C., Oreiro, J.L., and Marconi, N. (2016). *Macroeconomia desenvolvimentista*. Rio de Janeiro: Elsevier.

Bresser-Pereira, L.C., Paula, L.F. de, and Bruno, M. (2020). Financialization, coalition of interests and interest rate in Brazil. *Revue de la régulation* 27 (1st semester), 1–24.

Bruno, M., Diawara, H., Araújo, E., Reis, A.C., and Rubens, M. (2011). Finance-led growth regime no Brasil: estatuto teórico, evidências empíricas e consequências macroeconômicas. *Revista de Economia Política* 31: 730–750.

CBIC. (2019). Banco de Dados. Available at: http://www.cbicdados.com.br/menu/empresas-de-construcao/maiores-empresas-de-construcao (consulted September 21, 2019).

Campello, D. (2015). *The Politics of Market Discipline in Latin America: Globalization and Democracy*. Cambridge: Cambridge University Press.

Campos, P.H. (2019). Os efeitos da crise econômica e da operação Lava Jato sobre a indústria da construção pesada no Brasil: falências, desnacionalização e desestruturação produtiva. *Mediações* 24(1): 127–153.

Carneiro, R. (2012). Velhos e novos desenvolvimentismos. *Economia e Sociedade* 21: 749–778.

Carta Capital. (2019). *Venda de refinarias aprofunda desmonte da Petrobras.* Available at: https://www.cartacapital.com.br/economia/venda-de-refinarias-aprofunda-o-desmonte-da-petrobras/amp/?__twitter_impression=true&fbclid=IwAR3F8x5hMzubSwuzkQw1G62MudJYUEjW8sj8pS_KXjQMofbMgNWLqj178eg (consulted July 13, 2019).

Carvalho, L. (2018). *Valsa brasileira: Do boom ao caos econômico.* São Paulo: Editora Todavia.

Datafolha. (2018). *Avaliação Datafolha da Presidente Dilma.* Available at: https://www1.folha.uol.com.br/paywall/signup.shtml?https://www1.folha.uol.com.br/infograficos/2015/02/118652-avaliacao-datafolha-da-presidente-dilma.shtml (consulted December 10, 2018).

DIEESE. (2017). *Conjuntura econômica, indicadores do setor de petróleo, da Petrobras e outros números de interesse para os trabalhadores.* Available at: https://sindipetro.org.br/wpcontent/uploads/2017/09/DIEESE_Subs%C3%ADdios_SINDIPETRO_RJ.pdf (consulted June 19, 2019).

Epstein, G. (ed.). (2005). *Financialisation and the World Economy.* Cheltenham, UK: Edward Elgar.

Ferrari-Filho, Fernando, and Luiz Fernando de Paula. (2016). Padrões de crescimento e desenvolvimentismo: uma análise keynesiano-estruturalista. *Nova Economia* 26: 775–807.

Fonseca, P.C.D. (2014). Desenvolvimentismo: a construção do conceito. In: Calixtre, A.B., Biancarelli, A.M., and Cintra, M.A. (eds.), *Presente e futuro do desenvolvimento brasileiro,* 29–78. Brasília: IPEA.

Fritz, B., Paula, L.F. de, and Prates, D. (2017). Developmentalism at the Periphery: Can Productive Change and Income Redistribution Be Compatible with Global Financial Asymmetries? *desiguALdades Working Paper 101.*

Ianoni, M. (2018). *Estado e coalizões no Brasil (2003–2016): Social-desenvolvimentismo e neoliberalismo.* Rio de Janeiro: Contraponto.

Krippner, G. (2005). The financialisation of the American economy. *Socio-Economic Review* 3(2): 173–208.

Loureiro, P., and Saad-Filho, A. (2019). The limits of pragmatism: the rise and fall of the Brazilian Workers' Party (2002–2016). *Latin American Perspectives* 46(1): 66–84.

Mantega, G. (2012). O primeiro ano da nova matriz econômica. *Valor Econômico,* December 19. Available at: http://www.valor.com.br/brasil/2945092/o-primeiro-ano-da-nova-matriz-economica (consulted June 19, 2019).

Mello, G., and Rossi, P. (2018). Do industrialismo à austeridade: a política macro dos governos Dilma. In: Carneiro, R., Baltar, P., and Sarti, F. (orgs.), *Para além da política econômica,* 245–282. São Paulo: Editora UNESP.

Menezes Filho, N. (2017). A desigualdade caiu no Brasil? *Valor Econômico*, September 22. Available at: https://www.valor.com.br/opiniao/5129416/desigualdade-caiu-no-brasil (consulted June 19, 2019).

Miguel, L.F., and Assis, P.P. (2016). Coligações eleitorais e fragmentação das bancadas parlamentares no Brasil: simulações a partir das eleições de 2014. *Revista de Sociologia e Política* 24(60): 29–46.

Paula, L.F. de. (2011). *Financial Liberalization and Economic Performance: Brazil at the Crossroads*. London: Routledge.

Paula, L.F., Modenesi, A., and Pires, M. (2015). The tale of the contagion of two crises and policy responses in Brazil: a case of (Keynesian) policy coordination. *Journal of Post-Keynesian Economics* 37: 408–435.

Paula, L.F., Fritz, B., and Prates, D. (2017). Keynes at the periphery: currency hierarchy and challenges for economic policy in emerging economies. *Journal of Post-Keynesian Economics* 40(2): 183–202.

Paula, L.F., Santos, F., and Moura, R. (2020). The developmentalist project of the PT governments: An economic and political assessment. *Latin American Perspectives* 47(2): 8–24.

Petrobras. (2018a). *Resultados financeiros – holding*. Available at: http://www.investidorpetrobras.com.br/pt/resultados-financeiros/holding (consulted October 16, 2018).

Petrobras. (2018b). *Destaques operacionais – investimentos*. Available at: http://www.investidorpetrobras.com.br/pt/destaques-operacionais/investimentos (consulted October 19, 2018).

Pinto, E.C., et al. (2019). A guerra de todos contra todos e a Lava Jato: A crise brasileira e a vitória do capitão Jair Bolsonaro. *Revista da Sociedade Brasileira de Economia Política* 47: 107–147.

Prates, D., Fritz, B., and Paula, L.F. (2019). *O desenvolvimentismo pode ser culpado pela crise? Uma classificação das políticas econômica e social dos governos do PT ao governo Temer*. Texto para Discussão IE/UFRJ 9.

Salto, F., and Ribeiro, L. (2015). Operações compromissadas, gosto de subdesenvolvimento. *Valor Econômico*, June 8. Available at: https://www.valor.com.br/opiniao/4083296/operacoes-compromissadas-gosto-de subdesenvolvimento (consulted June 22, 2019).

Samuels, D., and Zucco, C. (2018). *Partisans, Antipartisans, and Nonpartisans: Voting Behavior in Brazil*. Berkeley and Los Angeles: University of California Press.

Santos, F., and Canello, J. (2015). Brazilian Congress, 2014 elections and governability challenges. *Brazilian Political Science Review* 9(1): 115–134.

Sarti, F., and Hiratuka, C. (2018). Desempenho recente da indústria brasileira no contexto de mudanças estruturais domésticas e globais. In: Carneiro, R., Baltar, P., and Sarti, F. (eds.), *Para além da política econômica*, 127–170. São Paulo: Editora UNESP.

Singer, A. (2009). *Os sentidos do Lulismo: Reforma gradual e pacto conservador*. São Paulo: Cia das Letras.

Singer, A. (2018). *O Lulismo em crise: Um quebra-cabeça do período Dilma (2011–2016)*. São Paulo: Cia das Letras.

Valor Econômico. (2016). *"O efeito da Lava-Jato no PIB se confirmou", diz Gesner Oliveira*. September 15. Available at: https://www.valor.com.br/valor-investe/casa-das-caldeiras/4672327/o-efeito-da-lava-jato-no-pib-se-confirmou-diz-gesner-olivei (consulted July 13, 2019).

Valor Econômico. (2017). *Estatal fecha venda de 90% da NTS para Brookfield*. April 5. Available at: https://www.valor.com.br/empresas/4927334/estatal-fecha-venda-de-90-da-nts-para-brookfield (consulted July 13, 2019).

Valor Econômico. (2019). *Construtoras encolhem 85% em 3 anos*. July 1. Available at: https://www.valor.com.br/empresas/6326143/construtoras-encolhem-85-em-3-anos (consulted July 13, 2019).

CHAPTER 12

The Limits of Dependency: The Foreign Policy of Rousseff's Administration

Pedro Paulo Zahluth Bastos and Célio Hiratuka

1 Introduction[1]

There is some consensus among experts that the foreign economic policy of Dilma Rousseff's government continued that of the government of Luís Inácio Lula da Silva but that the president, to say the least, was less concerned with its issues. Engagement with foreign policy is sometimes assessed by the number of international trips made by the head of state. Lula made 160 trips in his second term, while Rousseff made only 63 in her first (Souza 2016). The consensus is that Lula was more involved with foreign policy and made a point of capitalizing domestically on his international projection. Rousseff originally questioned the point of attending the India–Brazil–South-Africa (IBSA) summit and attended it only once. It is alleged that she less frequently participated in forums and that her foreign ministers lacked the status or the international visibility of Celso Amorim, who was considered by the *Foreign Policy* editor David Rothkopf (2009) "the best foreign minister in the world".[2]

Lula's foreign-policy chiefs reinforced the chorus of criticism. Before taking over the Defense Ministry, Amorim opposed the government's shift on human rights in Iran in March 2011, seen as a departure from South-South diplomacy and a rapprochement with the United States. In a meeting with Rousseff, Lula is said to have commented, "And Africa, Dilminha? It is abandoned" (Pinheiro 2014). The strongest demonstration came from the ambassador and former minister Samuel Pinheiro Guimarães when he resigned as Mercosur high representative in June 2012. His complaints involved both Brazil's lack of financial investment in economic cooperation in Mercosur and the lack of political support from the president (Bonis 2012a, 2012b). In 2015, when both Armando Monteiro, Ministry of Development, Industry, and Trade and Roberto Mangabeira Unger, head of the Secretariat for Strategic Affairs,

---

1 An earlier version of the arguments in this chapter appeared in Bastos and Hiratuka (2020).
2 In an interview with Bandeira (2016), Rothkopf contributed to the chorus of critics of Rousseff.

criticized the South-South project and praised the rapprochement with the United States, tensions with the nationalist wing of Itamaraty (as the Brazilian Ministry of Foreign Affairs is called) increased to such a degree that Guimarães strongly criticized the president: "There is a lack of personal participation of the president ... Itamaraty is not an NGO [nongovernmental organization] that offers mere hints ... The one that promoted Brazil abroad in Lula's government was Itamaraty" (Barrocal 2015).[3]

This chapter relativizes the consensus on Rousseff's foreign economic policy. Without denying the president's lesser involvement and political capacity compared with Lula, we address the problem by emphasizing the radical change in the international and local context. This difference in perspective is necessary first because the literature gives so much importance to the presidency and so little to the international context, which is inappropriate for the analysis of a country that is incapable of shaping the scenario in which it operates. Although the theoretical framework of these analyses is not explicit, the differences from that time when dependency theory influenced research on the international position of underdeveloped Latin American countries like Brazil are striking.[4]

It is true that there was no complete agreement among the different versions of dependency theory. Discussing their differences in depth is beyond the scope of this chapter, but it is important to stress that there was a marked difference between the theorists who considered capitalist development impossible for dependent countries and those who criticized the style of dependent development but did not anticipate their enduring economic stagnation's being a prelude to the socialist revolution.[5]

---

3 Guimarães's explanation for the lack of involvement is biographical: "Before the presidency, Lula made 110 international trips. Being a Northeastern and a metalworker, he knew in his skin the importance of relations with the underdeveloped and racially mixed countries of South America and Africa. His successor has hardly been abroad, even when she was a minister. As the daughter of a middle-class family and having studied at a nun's college that formed part of Belo Horizonte's elite, where it was customary to say 'good morning' in French, she had a more theoretical view of certain things in life" (Barrocal 2015). Cervo and Lessa (2014: 135–136) believed that the causes "of Brazil's decline on the international scene can be detected in internal politics. ... Internal causes are only slightly aggravated by the international financial and economic crisis."

4 Disregard for dependency is not new. The article at the beginning of the first issue of *Latin American Perspectives* stated that the repercussions of dependency theory "provoked the editors of the present journal to reassess its importance in the face of determined efforts on the part of many scholars to disregard it altogether" (Chilcote 1974: 5).

5 Among the former were Baran (1957), Frank (1966; 1967), Marini (1969), and Bambirra (1972). The latter included Cardoso and Faletto (1970), Tavares and Serra (1972), Furtado (1973), Mello (1982), and Evans (1979). Santos (1968; 1973) and Amin (1974) are more difficult to classify.

Among the former, Andre Gunder Frank (1966; 1967) considered capitalism infeasible in dependent economies and in particular in Latin America. According to him world capitalism developed in the context of growing polarization between the metropolitan center and its peripheral satellites. Since the essence of the relationship was the extraction of economic surplus from the satellites, the underdeveloped regions were those that maintained closer ties with the world economy. The relationship was not only external; the influence of the center penetrated and structured the particular features of the economic and political lives of the satellites. The exporting latifundium, for example, was not an archaic transplant of feudalism but the other side of capitalist development in the center. In general, the expansion of capitalism on a world scale reproduced a tendency toward uneven development, with progress in the major centers and underdevelopment and stagnation in the satellites. Development in the satellites was possible only through the overcoming of capitalism by popular revolutionary groups opposed to any conciliation with imperialism and national bourgeoisies.

Among the latter theorists, Cardoso and Faletto (1970) considered the relationship between development and dependency less deterministic and more elastic, allowing dependent societies various forms of integration and participation in the world economy. Dependency was understood as a fundamental concept for an "integrated analysis of development" that the concept of underdevelopment could not provide. While the concept of underdevelopment covered the limitation of the diversification of structure of production associated with a subordinate position in the international division of labor, the concept of dependency focused on the power relations that allowed certain domestic social groups to guide the national system toward a particular form of international economic coupling and political alliance with foreign countries and groups. Although full autonomy was out of the question as long as the underdeveloped country was integrated into and occupied a subordinate position in the global structure of the capitalist system, forms of incorporation and dependency varied historically. Ultimately, transformations in the international system might change the forms of dependency by modifying the context, creating constraints or opening up opportunities for capitalist development in dependent regions. The incorporation of different regions

---

They were socialists like the former but emphasized internal factors and the possibility of dependent development, which brought them closer to the latter. For analyses and classifications that focus on the nuances of dependency theories, see Chilcote (1974; 1984; 2009) and Mantega (1984; 1997). For a recent reassessment of dependency theory, see Kufakurinani et al. (2017).

and countries, however, varied with the ways in which the local economic and political system reacted to new constraints. The reaction might be to tighten restrictions or exploit opportunities.

For a dependent country to advance in the process of industrialization, it was not sufficient for the international system to allow, for example, the arrival of new forms of foreign investment. Cardoso and Faletto wrote of foreign capital that was not restricted to reaffirming the primary-exporting specialization of underdeveloped countries but might contribute to their industrialization through the so-called internationalization of the internal market. They argued that it was also necessary for local groups that perceived industrialization as the threat of loss of status and wealth to be overtaken by favorable coalitions, among them not only fractions of the bourgeoisie, workers, and the middle classes but also, in cases of dependent development, foreign capital and its local representatives.

Thus, stagnation and even structural regression was not an inevitable result of dependency but only the effect of one of the forms it might assume. Dependency might even bring about the development of the forces of production directed toward industrialization and thus have some political support from the middle and popular classes. It was therefore necessary to analyze different dependency situations taking into account the specific features of the constraints and the economic structure and local power relations involved. The product of these forces was in each national situation of dependency a certain potential for development of the forces of production and a repositioning in the international scenario that would distinguish each case of dependent development.[6]

All the versions of the theory of dependency recognized that the international context confronted by dependent countries has a fundamental role in shaping their development trajectory. Although Cardoso and Faletto's version of dependency theory gave greater weight to local initiatives and predicted a greater probability of development's being associated with dependency, it also conferred veto power, ultimately, on structural transformations of the international system. Ultimately, no version of dependency theory (or analysis of dependency situations) allowed for the underdeveloped country's ascent inside the international hierarchy if the international situation were to block

---

6 On the correlation of forces between classes and class fractions, Evans (1979) added the degree of autonomy of government leadership and state bureaucracy as an important constraint on the potential of dependent development, taking the Brazilian case as illustrative. Evans (1995) developed the theoretical model and extended the comparison of the Brazilian case to South Korea and Zaire.

it.[7] This common conclusion of dependency theories is the fundamental theoretical reason that international changes cannot be omitted from an assessment of the success or failure of the foreign policy of Rousseff's government.

A second reason for relativizing the antidependency consensus on Rousseff's
foreign policy is empirical. Rousseff does not appear to have altered the foreign
policy objectives and tactics of Lula's administration. On the contrary, there
are indications that she even extended them to cover some domestic politics.
In other words, even if we admit that, in the first instance, foreign policy influenced the results achieved, this independent variable did not vary in the opposite direction to that of Lula to the point of explaining its inferior results.

Thirdly, if the discontinuity between Lula and Rousseff is not radical, then
it is probable that the shortcomings of the economic results were due to
changes in the international context that favored gains (including prestige)
under Lula's government and then began to restrict them. Dependency may
have been stronger than the analyses that emphasize differences in Brazilian
foreign policy under Lula's and Rousseff's governments seem to assume. Thus,
some of the favorable results achieved by Lula, especially in South America,
may have had as their necessary but insufficient condition a favorable international context that began to change in the last years of his administration and
shifted profoundly in the next one.

We will argue that there was no change in the objectives of foreign economic policy under Rousseff's government but at most their adaptation to a
more hostile context and even that the typical objectives of Itamaraty became
more important under Rousseff. Although the new government did not radically reverse trade or financial liberalization, it pursued a relatively successful
policy for inducing foreign direct investment in the main industrial sector (the

---

7   The attack by Cardoso and Faletto was influential to the point of contributing to the aban-
    donment of the hypothesis of stagnation and stimulating the study of peripheral and depen-
    dent development styles in the face of the novelty of the "internationalization of the internal
    market". Additionally, the importance given to foreign affiliates in the "new dependency"
    was the fundamental contribution of Santos (1968; 1973). Under the impact of these anal-
    yses, one of the classic thinkers of the Economic Commission for Latin America and the
    Caribbean, Celso Furtado (1973; 1998), would abandon its classical perspective and move
    toward dependency theory in the 1970s. Compared with Cardoso and Faletto, Furtado, how-
    ever, more incisively criticized the irrationalities, vulnerabilities, and injustices of a depen-
    dent development model characterized by the control of decision centers over the allocation
    of surplus and even the styles of consumption by multinational corporations. Furtado also
    seems to have advanced analytically in relation to Santos. We do not have room here to dis-
    cuss Furtado's interpretation and how his interpretative model can be used to understand
    the growth pattern of the Brazilian economy in the 2000s. For details, we refer the reader to
    Rossi, Mello, and Bastos (in this book).

automobile industry) and altered neoliberal orientations in the management of foreign exchange policy to cause a competitive currency depreciation. This inevitably increased conflict in Mercosur, given the changes in the international and regional scenario and even in Argentine economic policy.

We will also argue that the limitations of the government's "active and haughty" foreign policy were structurally related to the dependency associated with the control of global corporations over the international insertion of the local affiliates that dominated the main industrial sectors. Of course, in line with dependency theory, the correlation of local forces also mattered. Although we cannot develop this issue here, the gradual rejection of South-South politics by many industrial entrepreneurs who had supported it also indicates an internal limit to Lula's foreign policy. If this analysis is correct, the existence of the structural limits described requires that the struggle to achieve an independent foreign policy involve deeper political and ideological battles and a more radical questioning of neoliberal capitalism.

To develop these ideas, the chapter has three sections in addition to this introduction. The first deals with the main changes in Lula's foreign policy in relation to Cardoso's. The second addresses the Dilma Rousseff period and highlights its history, developing the main arguments of the article. The third presents final considerations, reviewing the discussion of the structural limits of a more independent foreign policy.

2   Lula's Foreign Economic Policy Compared with Cardoso's

The governments of Cardoso and Lula represented different alternatives for international engagement that expressed very different interests and views of Brazilian foreign policy. Given the structural differences between the Lula and Cardoso administrations, the changes in Rousseff's foreign policy may seem almost irrelevant, related to different forms of conducting the same strategy rather than the interests, guidelines, views, and foreign policy concepts. Cardoso's foreign policy was explicitly stated and then openly criticized by Lula's intellectuals. Rousseff did not return to the alternative it represented by Cardoso but deepened Lula's guidelines.[8]

---

8   Our method is to emphasize the foreign policy strategies as presented by their own executors, since in general they corresponded to the policies implemented (although they did not produce the expected results). It is unquestionable, however, that diplomatic rhetoric does not explain the deep determining factors of public policy. In any case, our giving voice to foreign policy actors in this chapter does not supplant but complements studies of their sociological

What inspired and legitimized Cardoso's foreign policy was the doctrine of "autonomy through integration" of Foreign Minister Felipe Lampréia. It resembled Cardoso and Faletto's (1970) hypothesis that international dependency might lead not to regression but to development provided that the peripheral country attracted with conducive business environments, creating a model of dependent and associated development (Cruz 1999). This meant overcoming autonomist and Third Worldist perspectives that counterposed the South to the North and sought theoretically to "increase autonomy through greater self-sufficiency" (Lampréia 1998: 10). After all, "the 'globalized world' increasingly functioned on the basis of reliability and, conversely, risk assessments" (Lampréia 1998: 13). Therefore, it was preferable for Brazil (since it had no "surplus power") to abandon the pursuit of self-sufficiency and become a country with "external credibility". This meant adapting institutionally to new international regimes to integrate a wave of modernizing transnationalization led by foreign affiliates of Transnational Corporations from the developed countries.[9]

Argentine foreign policy underwent a similar reformulation, calling itself "peripheral realism", under Carlos Menem's government. According to Escudé (1992), since they did not make the "rules of the game", peripheral countries should avoid the cost of confronting the hegemonic power, concentrating on gaining credibility with that power and its enterprises. Rather than the typical "naive realism" of the military or the "idealistic confrontationism" of Raúl Alfonsín's administration, adaptation to the "rules of the game" and alignment with the hegemonic power were the viable path to peripheral development. Those responsible for Brazilian foreign policy did not go so far as to describe the Brazilian relationship with the United States as did the Argentine minister Guido di Tella – as "carnal relations". They agreed with him, however, to change the proposed direction of the Brazil-Argentina integration of Sarney's and Alfonsín's governments, replacing a program aimed at complementing industrial productive chains with regional economies of scale, for the so-called

---

determinants. Boito and Saad-Filho (2016a; 2016b) stress the changes in the power blocs that are the social bases of governments and channel the material interests that are given priority attention by economic policy in general and by foreign policy in particular. Overall, such studies identify the hegemony of the associated bourgeoisie and foreign capital in the economic policy of the Fernando Henrique Cardoso administration, and the hegemony of the internal bourgeoisie (in the terms of Nicos Poulantzas [1974]) in the governments of Lula and Rousseff. For a critique of the use of the concept of the internal bourgeoisie, see Abu-El-Haj (2016), and for a sympathetic view that emphasizes the structural power of financial capital, see Bastos (2017).

9 Lampréia (1998; 1999) and Corrêa (1999). For an academic evaluation, see Vigevani and Oliveira (2007).

open regionalism. This was consistent with the neoliberal economists' argument under Cardoso and Menem, which was to increase the efficiency of resource allocation through competitive import pressure, thus making the system of production more capable of capturing export opportunities in the global economy. This is why the Mercosur quickly became a customs union whose common external tariff was much lower than national tariffs, especially in the Brazilian case (Sarti 2001). Criticism of this strategy in Brazil came from key players in Lula's future government such as Samuel Pinheiro Guimarães (1999) and Marco Aurélio Garcia (1996), who proposed a strategy that would be called "active and haughty foreign policy" and followed even by Rousseff's government.[10]

The critique of "autonomy through integration" was that Cardoso's government had rejected a development project defined and coordinated by the national state, transferring decisions to international organizations, multinational groups, and financial speculators, by adhering to neoliberalism. As a result, the space for diplomacy was diminishing, limiting itself to defending particular interests affected by the strategy of openness rather than questioning the asymmetric international order that developed countries were trying to institutionalize through multilateral treaties and the dissemination of favorable ideologies. The historical mission of a new government was reversing the loss of autonomy – recovering the state's capacity for intervention and seeking forms of international participation less susceptible to crises – in the name of economic and social development. The role of diplomacy, then, was not only to defend the interests impaired by the inevitable economic opening but to negotiate the opening of opportunities for development policies and, in general, strive for the political construction of a less asymmetric international order.

It was essential to deconstruct the ideology that globalization was a neutral process that would homogeneously reduce states' capacity for the benefit of the international division of labor and punish only those unable to abide by the international regulations that provided the right incentives to the private sector. On the contrary, the globalization of markets involved crises and accentuated asymmetries. The multilateral standardization effort of international relations, led by the United States, was anything but neutral. It strengthened asymmetries by reducing protection to developing areas and by limiting

---

10   Members of Lula's government confirmed central aspects of this view of foreign policy
       (Amorim 2004; 2015; Guimarães 2006; 2009; 2010; and Garcia 2010). For the origins of the
       strategy, refer to Cruz and Stuart (2010). For criticism by members of Cardoso's govern-
       ment, see Barbosa (2010) and Ricupero (2010). For the discussion of criticism of neoliber-
       alism, we rely on Bastos (2012a).

development policies so as to preserve the central countries' control over tech-nology and capital-intensive industries, which in turn created greater pros-pects for growth and value added.[11]

The developed countries tried to induce developing countries to enter into asymmetric agreements threatening to signing agreements only with countries that were willing to accept new conditions in exchange for preferential access to Northern markets (Bastos 2004a). To avoid isolation, it was necessary for developing countries to pursue alliances with large peripheral states that were not interested in giving up development and hence to encourage the diversi-fication of allies on a South-South axis. South-South political cooperation and trade integration had to go hand in hand.

The threat to development was greater in the proposal of the Free Trade Area of the Americas (FTAA), which offered a timid opening to products of South American interest (sugar, soy, cotton, ethanol, corn, meats, orange juice, textiles, footwear, steel, tobacco, dairy products, cocoa products, etc.) and refused to limit subsidies or trade protections of the United States. In addi-tion, it proposed restrictions on development policies greater than those of the WTO (called "WTO-plus") for government procurement, intellectual property rights, investment incentives, and regulation of foreign capital, among other clauses. In the Doha Round, the opening-up of agricultural markets and sub-sidy restrictions in developed countries remained limited, although restrictive corrections of "unfair" development policies were required.

Broadly speaking, foreign policy in Lula's government adopted this critical view of neoliberalism. According to Bastos (2004b), the priority given to pre-serving development policy opportunities and South-South relations was evi-dent when, in July 2003, Amorim responded to the U.S. tariff reduction offer

---

11   A similar movement occurred in the attempt to broaden the UN Security Council's "humanitarian" agenda without significant participation by peripheral countries (Guimarães 1999). The WTO was the main institutional creation that completed the so-called Washington Consensus, in line with the shift in the orientation of the Bretton Woods institutions (the International Monetary Fund and the World Bank) toward radi-cal neoliberalism (Panitch and Gindin 2012: Chapter 9). By opening markets and changing the rules of the game for development policy, it has contributed to deepening the inter-national asymmetries characteristic of neoliberal globalization. Thus, it is representative of what Stephen Gill (1998) called "new constitutionalism", a set of neoliberal norms regulated by international treaties that constrain national sovereignty and democracy in signatory countries to promote the international freedom of capital. More than that, it has created rules that constrain underdeveloped countries much more than developed ones (Chang 2002; Weiss 2005). Lula's foreign policy at the WTO's Doha Round sought to overhaul some of the WTO asymmetries without abandoning them, since it also limited the unilateralism of the major powers.

(which sliced the FTAA into four regions, discriminating against Mercosur) with the "three rails" approach. The multilateral rail would address sensitive issues such as government procurement, investment policy, and respect for patents that would not be covered by the FTAA. The FTAA rail would establish basic commitments in several areas but leave market access negotiations in the 4 + 1 framework, linking Mercosur with third countries or blocs (Amorim 2003). Thus, agreements with Latin American countries would depend not on the success of a treaty involving North America but, on the preferences, accepted by the Associación Latino-Americana de Integración (Latin American Integration Association – ALADI).

South-South alliances were to avoid adapting to the rules of the game preferred by the developed countries. Already in 2003, a Brazilian-led coalition, the G20 Trade Coalition, blocked a WTO-friendly agreement and redirected the agenda to priority issues for developing countries (Blustein 2009). Meanwhile, the alliance between Brazil, Argentina, and Venezuela barred the FTAA. Contrary to George W. Bush's prediction, countries that had bilateral agreements with the United States negotiated with Mercosur in the ALADI environment toward a free-trade zone in the area of the South American Community of Nations that became the embryo of the Union of South American Nations (UNASUR). At the same time, political, cultural, and defense initiatives introduced, sometimes more rhetorically than in practice, new spheres of cooperation in the region in which, from the Latin American Free Trade Association in the 1960s to the regionalism that emerged in the 1990s, initiatives have always focused on economic and, above all, commercial issues. Politically, the mediation of Brazil and, later, of UNASUR were essential for resolving political crises and attempted coups in South America. The convulsion resulted from the reaction of conservative social groups to the electoral victories of the so-called pink tide, the new governments to the left of the political center that paralyzed or reversed some neoliberal reforms and influenced the distribution of income, including renegotiating the distribution of the income obtained from increased sales of natural resources (Natanson 2008; Sader 2016).

The first significant initiative of foreign relations of Lula's government was to create a Group of Friends of Venezuela, in January 2003, that concluded a first pacification agreement in May 2003. UNASUR contributed to the Morales government to battle against the attempted secession in Bolivia in 2008 as well as denouncing the attempted coup in Ecuador and supporting Rafael Correa in 2010. It did not achieve the same success in Honduras in 2009 or in Paraguay in 2012. In the case of Honduras, Brazil and Venezuela led a rejection that came to isolate the United States in the Organization of American States (OAS) (Bandeira 2008; Weisbrot 2015).

The weakening of the OAS reflected South America's greater independence from the United States, as was intended by "active and haughty" diplomacy. This involved new institutions from which the United States was absent, such as the UNASUR, the South American Defense Council, and the Community of Latin American and Caribbean States. In Brazil's defense policy, independence was reflected in the 2008 military agreement with France, which included the construction of a nuclear submarine as the United States announced the re-creation of the Fourth Fleet in the South Atlantic after the oil discovery in the Pre-Salt region.

3   Foreign Economic Policy under Dilma Rousseff

The trouble with the consensus that the poor results of foreign policy under Dilma Rousseff's administration resulted from policy changes themselves is that, first, it underestimates transformations in the international context and, second, there are no signs that Rousseff reversed the policy inherited from Lula. First, the multilateral path was not replaced by bilateral agreements. In contrast to the so-called Pacific Alliance of South American countries, Brazil didn't join the Transpacific Partnership that the United States negotiated with the Asian countries, with a view at isolating China and imposing WTO-plus conditions. Rousseff continued the expansion of Mercosur toward "Bolivarian countries" such as Venezuela and Bolivia even though this cost it Paraguay's suspension after a coup endorsed by the United States. She supported the con-solidation of UNASUR and its role as mediator of conflicts and privileged South-South alliances that questioned the control of multilateral financial institu-tions based in Washington. Her government also sought to take advantage of the opportunities for development policies that still existed after neoliberal policies and conventions had been implemented. In other words, it conferred more substance on the nationalist and developmentalist goals of Itamaraty.[12]

The success of initiatives is another issue, since it may depend on variables beyond the control of the state. The global financial crisis, for example, con-tributed to transforming the international division of labor that generated favorable trade results of South-South diplomacy (Bastos and Hiratuka 2017). The international context also changed in that it diminished the protagonism

---

12   For an analysis of the foreign policy of Rousseff's government, see Cervo and Lessa (2014), Cornetet (2014), and Souza (2016); writers who emphasize continuity without neglecting change are Berringer (2017), Lima (2011; 2013; 2014a; 2014b), Saraiva (2014), and Saraiva and Gomes (2016).

of the WTO, where Lula's government had a wager aimed at the reformulation of multilateral order. The impasse in the Doha Round, which occurred when Lula was still president, and the reaction of the Obama administration towards the negotiation of regional mega-agreements reduced Brazil's visibility regardless of any change in policy stance. In other words, they changed the context that gave visibility to the WTO and Brazil, although this visibility did not bring real gains (besides the symbolic ones) given the existing impasse.

The same can be said about the geopolitical change brought about by the Arab Spring and the wars in Libya and Syria, as well as the war in Ukraine and the tension over sovereignty in the Pacific islands. In conjunction with the refugee crisis, this new scenario diminished the importance of economic issues in which Brazil was a key player and gave centrality to the policy of the military powers, involving Russia and China directly. The possibility of Brazilian prominence in the Middle East had already been diminished when the Obama administration rejected the proposed agreement with Iran under Brazilian and Turkish mediation in 2010, only to negotiate a very similar agreement five years later.[13] It is difficult to imagine that, in the light of these changes, any amount of greater physical presence (or charisma) of Dilma Rousseff would compensate for Brazil's tendency to lose projection. In addition, previous successes had made it less necessary to travel to play a leading role. The Rio + 20 conference in 2012, the 2014 World Cup, and the 2016 Olympic Games led to the mass influx of heads of state, ministers, and businessmen to Brazil.

Notwithstanding the paralysis of the WTO, Rousseff also did not abandon the emphasis on the multilateral path to negotiate bilateral or plurilateral WTO-plus agreements at any cost, under the pretext of the threat of isolation alleged by Lula's and Rousseff's neoliberal critics. This means that her government did not move toward a concrete alternative to "active and haughty" diplomacy, which was some version of the "autonomy through integration" that Michel Temer and Jair Bolsonaro would undertake. In terms of relations with the United States, Rousseff cannot be reproached on the issue of independence. Faced with the revelation by Edward Snowden of espionage in the presidency and Petrobras in 2013, her reaction was to cancel the presidential trip to the U.S. and, with the support of Angela Merkel, present to the United Nations the issue of digital privacy protection. In addition, the choice of the Swedish Gripen as the military jet of the Brazilian Air Force had advantages associated with the transfer of technology, but it was regarded as a position of

---

13   The doctrine proposed by Brazil at the UN in 2011 to regulate humanitarian interventions, "Responsibility to Protect", did not advance because it did not find support from any of the great powers. For a brief analysis of the new scenario, see Cruz (2014).

independence in confrontation with the United States or even retaliation for the breach of trust generated by the espionage.[14] More important, the core of regional policy persisted. Mercosur expanded with the addition of Venezuela in 2012, after the suspension of Paraguay in view of the impeachment of Fernando Lugo. Having overcome the veto of Paraguay, Venezuela placed the bloc farther to the left and away from the United States and from agreements with neoliberal conditions. The same thing happened when Bolivia joined as a full member in 2015. It is noteworthy that Suriname and Guyana were incorporated as associate members in 2013 and 2015.

The extraregional dimension of South-South diplomacy was strengthened with the expansion of the BRICS (Brazil–Russia–India–China–South Africa) to South Africa in 2011, although one of the reasons was that the IBSA (India–Brazil–South Africa) had lost relevance. More than the IBSA, the BRICS had the power to reduce the importance of control by the developed countries, particularly the United States, of institutions of the Washington Consensus, the International Monetary Fund (IMF), and the World Bank. In 2014 the BRICS entered into a contingent reserve arrangement that created an alternative to the need for exchange reserves to cover balance-of-payments emergencies. The supply of reserves was not only the main function of the IMF but also the channel through which neoliberal reforms were imposed in the form of conditionalities. To obtain exchange reserves under the arrangement, unless countries had agreements with the IMF there was 30 percent limit on the amount of foreign currency supplied. In any case, it opened up an alternative channel to the IMF that could grow over time without a U.S. veto (Batista Jr. 2015). The BRICS's New Development Bank entered the sphere of the World Bank to offer loans for infrastructure investment that were not restricted to the geographical area of the BRICs and had the potential to weaken Washington's multilateral institutions and strengthen South-South cooperation as proposed by the diplomacy of Lula's government. Whether this constituted a threat to the multilateral institutions under U.S. hegemony only time will tell, but the first concrete step was taken by Rousseff's government.[15]

The continuity of these governments' objectives is also apparent in their influence on the rest of economic policy. If the pursuit of development with

---

14   The episode was essential to the proposal of the Brazilian Civil Rights Framework for the Internet, which ensures so-called net neutrality – less control by access providers and large content providers (usually U.S.) over user access to the network.

15   On the BRICS, Panitch (2015) and Stuenkel (2015) limit its importance regarding challenging U.S. hegemony, while Desai (2013), Rostowska (2013), and Smith (2014) discuss its considerable significance in the long run. On the BRICS and Brazil, see Guimarães (2015).

national autonomy was the central objective of Itamaraty under Lula's government, one might argue, contrary to the consensus, that it became even more important in the management of economic policy under Rousseff's. The agreement that Amorim attempted to negotiate in 2005 to conclude the Doha Round was criticized by the Indians and the Argentines because of the acceptance of the "big bargain" proposed by the developed countries – exchanging agricultural openness in the developed ones for industrial opening in the developing ones. If industrial diversification and the rejection of a model focused on the export of commodities are among the criteria for development, Rousseff could be said to have defended the industry even more, including increasing antidumping actions against a preferential policy partner of Lula, China (Araújo Jr. 2017). In addition, her government used the degree of freedom negotiated by Itamaraty against the conditions of neoliberal treaties in a different way from Lula's. While Itamaraty struggled to secure policy opportunities to induce development and protect investment, Lula's government increased the value of the real (BRL), which cheapened imports and threatened the profitability of industrial investments (Bastos 2004c).

The change in exchange-rate policy under Rousseff's government was preceded by a diplomatic effort to legitimize capital controls and policies favorable to currency depreciation. This occurred in the wake of Guido Mantega's keynote speech in September 2010, which accused the developed countries of waging a "currency war" in an effort to escape from the economic crisis through exports and import substitution. The term and theme went viral in the international debate. Before that, the Brazilian position had been presented at the financial G20, where the country had aligned itself with China to demand a change in the composition of quotas and votes in the IMF to reflect the weight of the developing countries. Small changes in quotas were celebrated in November 2010 (still under Lula's administration) in conjunction with the commitment to consider non-U.S. and European representatives for the leadership of the multilateral financial organizations, as was already done in the WTO and the UN (Scandiucci 2018). More important was diplomatically broadening the scope for economic policy and, this time, using it. The other side of the charge that the developed countries had resorted to quantitative easing to depreciate currencies was, from the point of view of the developing countries, the authorization of capital controls to protect them from currency appreciation and global excess liquidity, breaking with the neoliberal mantra of full financial liberalization. At the G20 meeting in April 2011, Brazil was able to have removed any mention of limits on capital controls (Alexander 2011).

Judging that the intensification of international competition demanded a change in exchange policy, the government modified it after Henrique

Meirelles was replaced by Alexandre Tombini at the Central Bank. In mid-2011 the combination of limits on speculation in the future foreign exchange market and interest-rate reduction began a process of exchange-rate correction that might improve industrial competitiveness (Rossi 2016). The change in exchange-rate policy met the developmentalist objectives that guided foreign policy but increased trade conflicts with Argentina. For domestic reasons, Argentina began to seek appreciation of the peso, and as a result it sacrificed industrial competitiveness but ensured cheap imports of capital goods that it could not replace for domestic production in the short term. It also limited the acceleration of inflation resulting from production bottlenecks due to the pace of growth of demand.[16] It was inevitable that policy divergence would be reflected in exchange rates to undermine Argentina's competitiveness. The response, as predicted by Bastos (2012a), was the expansion of Argentine protectionism, which involved the nonautomatic licensing of imports. Contrary to what Brazilian businessmen demanded, Rousseff's government maintained an accommodative policy that placed long-term political goals above particularistic demands, avoiding a punitive protectionist escalation.

Despite not having suffered retaliation, Argentine industry experienced diminished ability to diversify because of Brazil's ability to attract foreign direct investment in the region's market. The industrial policies that increased the attractiveness of the Brazilian market limited import substitution in Argentine industry. Rousseff's government enforced trade barriers and domestic-content requirements as a counterpart of access to state subsidies and fees in order to stimulate foreign direct investment in the oil, military, communications, hospital, electronics, and automotive sectors (Bastos 2012b). In the region's main industrial branch, the automotive industry, the Inovar-Auto program used the size of the Brazilian market to contribute to an investment boom through subsidies and higher prices of imported final goods and inputs. As a result, the installed capacity of the automotive industry in Brazil was twice the local demand in 2014, the fourth-largest market in the world. In this case, Rousseff's government not only used the opportunities for development policies negotiated by diplomats in multilateral institutions but exploited them with policies more advanced than the bargaining power of the diplomats might have authorized. The Inovar-Auto program was judged illegitimate by the WTO in November 2016. In addition, several old industrial policy programs,

---

16   For an assessment of Argentine economic policy and, in particular, exchange policy, see especially Weisbrot (2015) and Pont (2016).

TABLE 12.1   Brazilian trade balance (US$ millions) in manufacturing goods, 2003–2014

Region	2003	2008	2014
World	2.235	-35.193	-89.010
Developed countries	-5.287	-31.581	-46.363
Developed countries: North America	3.330	-6.094	-10.447
United States	3.228	-4.612	-8.917
Developed countries: Asia	-2.297	-6.680	-5.621
Japan	-2.051	-5.593	-4.838
Developed countries: Europe	-6.496	-19.526	-30.227
Developing countries	8.115	-258	-39.680

SOURCE: UNCTAD (HTTPS://UNCTAD.ORG/EN/PAGES/STATISTICS.ASPX)

such as the Software Law, were denounced in the same arbitration decision (Marques 2017).

It is true that the lack of cooperation for complementation in production contributed to the fact that the attraction of foreign direct investment to Brazil stifled import substitution in Argentina. Rousseff's government cannot, however, be blamed for this characteristic of Mercosur, since it was promoted by the bloc and was not modified by Lula's government (Bastos 2012a). One could argue that Rousseff did not advance in the energy integration plan with Venezuela alluded to by Lula's government. Given the problems with Venezuela's participation in the Abreu and Lima refinery, however, it is difficult to argue that her prudence was unwelcome, especially considering the priority given to the Pre-Salt oil deposits, which were discovered after the beginning of the ultimately failed cooperation in Abreu and Lima.

In the light of all this, how can it be said that Rousseff's government reversed the foreign policy objectives that had existed since 2003? If it did not, it is likely that its different results arose from changes in the context in which the policies were implemented. That the results were different there is no doubt. From 2008 to 2014, for example, the Brazilian trade deficit in manufactured goods with developed countries increased by 47 percent (Table 12.1) but by no less than 15,280 percent with the developing countries, which was the essential objective of South-South policy (Table 12.2).

After the great recession, in a context of intense international competition for foreign markets, industrial production lost market share to exports from

TABLE 12.2 Brazilian trade balance (US$ millions) in manufacturing goods, developing countries, 2003–2014

Regions	2003	2008	2014
Developing countries	8.115	-258	-39.680
Latin America	8.517	22.737	10.890
Mexico	2.045	942	-1.675
Argentina	1.720	7.182	1.796
Bolivia	296	957	1.347
Chile	1.181	2.293	1.366
Colombia	564	1.610	1.376
Ecuador	321	819	713
Paraguay	580	1.743	1.944
Peru	417	1.732	1.379
Uruguay	88	694	362
Venezuela	397	2.656	1.333
Developing Asia	-1.289	-25.263	-51.575
China	-251	-17.010	-33.506
Taiwan	-192	-1.938	-2.548
India	-130	-1.317	-2.386
South Korea	-561	-3.884	-7.612
Malaysia	-281	-1.202	-1.596
Singapore	-238	137	1.165
Thailand	58	-492	-1.540
Africa	882	2.257	1.001
Developing Oceania	5	10	4
Economies in transition	-592	-3.352	-2.492
Russia	-374	-1.601	-1.755

SOURCE: UNCTAD (HTTPS://UNCTAD.ORG/EN/PAGES/STATISTICS.ASPX)

developed countries or foreign affiliates based in Mexico and to Asian exports, mainly from China. This increased the deficit in manufactured goods and broke up the regional division of labor that had favored Brazilian industry. None of this was brought about directly by decisions related to Rousseff's foreign policy. It was much more related to changes in the global scenario in which the synchronized growth of the world economy in the postcrisis period was replaced by fierce conflict caused by imbalances between relatively stagnant world demand and a supply of manufactured goods that continued to grow.

China was the country that most affected the domestic market, threatened more manufacturing exports, and limited the expansion of intraregional trade. About one-third of the market share losses of the Mercosur countries in the region are explained by Chinese increasing marke share (Hiratuka 2016). While on the one hand the commodity boom and exports to China were crucial to explain the growth of domestic demand from several Latin American countries, which somehow stimulated intraregional industrial exports, on the other hand imports from China became the biggest obstacle to regional intraindustrial trade and the preservation of several manufacturing sectors in Brazil and the region. This was not a result of decisions by Rousseff's government.

4   Conclusion: Successes and Structural Limits of Brazilian Foreign Policy

It seems undeniable that the "active and haughty" foreign policy maintained by Rousseff's government had some positive results:

1.   It helped to curb the integration under United States-led global neoliberalism that was about to establish international regimes even more unfavorable for developing countries than the WTO Marrakesh Treaty. It also consolidated the importance of development support on the multilateral agenda, thus inducing the United States to seek asymmetric plurilateral and bilateral agreements.

2.   It created new institutions in South America that increased the political autonomy of each of those countries against U.S. intervention, which almost always favored conservative groups and often coup plotters in the region and increased economic, political, and cultural cooperation with nations so close, but that have always been far apart.

3.   It established the BRICS group, which was fundamental for ensuring exchange reserves and offer more options for financing infrastructure projects in Brazil while creating an alternative to the multilateral institutions that continued to disseminate neoliberal reforms.

4.   It provided Brazil with prestige, visibility, and influence through the defense of peace and cultural diversity and the fight against international discrimination and inequality.

5.   It expanded or consolidated trade agreements and investment projects that supported intraindustry trade in Mercosur and in Latin America and

the global South and increased Brazilian exports despite the worsening trade balance.

The most ambitious long-term economic objective of this policy was to change Brazil's position in the international division of labor, reversing the loss of autonomy generated by the foreign debt crisis in the 1980s and the deindustrialization brought about by neoliberalism. This objective, outlined by Lula's government, became even more important in Rousseff's. However, the success of foreign policy was not simply dependent on the resources that the government enjoyed; rather, in the terms of Cardoso and Faletto's classic *Dependency and Development in Latin America*, even though development depended on internal constraints, it was ultimately subject to external variables beyond the control of the state, particularly when, as was the case in Brazil, the dependency was internalized because of control by global corporations on the international insertion of the main manufacturing sectors.

The problem is that acknowledging the existence of dependency should not led to praising it, under the argument that offering a "business environment" that maximizes the freedom of action of foreign affiliates will attract investment that will better position Brazilian manufacturing industry in international trade controlled by intrafirm transactions or indirectly through the corporate networks that dominate global productive chains. As in the 1990s, the "dependentist" hope that characterized the Michel Temer government (2016–2018) and now characterizes the government of Jair Bolsonaro is that such corporations will be drawn to invest here and reexport provided that wage and tax costs are reduced through neoliberal reforms, regardless of the fact that these measures limit the growth of the domestic market that has always been the main factor of attraction for foreign direct investment in industrial Brazil. Foreign investment should be attracted also by cutting tariff and nontariff costs through WTO-plus bilateral agreements that shield neoliberalism with international treaties. Hence the urgency of removing Brazil from the South-South axis of countries that challenge the globalization defended by Washington and returning it to the U.S. orbit.[17]

Without focusing on the idea that the victory of Donald Trump buried the rebirth of the FTAA and the termination of the Trans-Pacific Partnership and the Transatlantic Trade and Investment Partnership, it should be remembered that when a precedented project of open trade was carried out in the 1990s by Brazil and Argentina, imports of inputs, parts, and components by foreign

---

17   Ironically, it was the former Marxist sociologist Fernando Henrique Cardoso (2014) who set the tone for the neoliberal attack. On the reasons for the adherence of business to the neoliberal critique of foreign policy, see Berringer (2017).

affiliates increased but the subsidiaries remained mainly interested in domestic markets. When competitive pressure increased after the crisis of 2008, the same type of import integration into global value chains occurred – the import penetration rate increased in industrial production chains but again without leading to increased exports in these chains. An aggravating factor was that replacement with imports began to affect the final goods produced by subsidiaries even more strongly. In this context, the importance of the protection of the regional market by tariff preferences is apparent in the fact that, while the Brazilian trade surplus with the regions of origin of the industrial subsidiaries was reversed, it was in Mercosur, apart from China, that the trade surplus decreased the least from 2007 to 2014. This occurred in spite of the structural vulnerability of regional countries to the deflation of commodities and the deterioration of the terms of trade, which hindered the growth and import capacity of the main Brazilian partners in the region, Argentina and Venezuela.

Considering this experience, one can agree with Celso Furtado (1973; 1998), that the main structural limit of a peripheral development policy is the structure of capital ownership in industrial production. The economic decision-making system controlled by the multinational corporations reproduces the limited technological autonomy of industry in the industrialized periphery, its subordinate role in global value chains, and its commercial and financial vulnerability. To summarize, dependency may allow some degree of development of production forces, but it limits the country's rise in the technological hierarchy of the international division of labor and subjects its participation to conjunctural changes and harmful structural variations like those after the crisis of 2008. On the one hand, if an "active and haughty" policy was unable to limit all the effects of this structural dependency and was subject to the impacts of the financial crisis, overcapacity, and the intensification of global competition, how could we imagine that a policy that did not even seek to protect itself from their regressive effects would have more favorable results? On the other hand, how can we blame Rousseff's foreign policy for the worsening of commercial results in the period?

While Itamaraty was struggling to secure autonomous space for policy to induce economic development and to protect local investments, Lula's government implemented an exchange-rate policy characterized by the appreciation of the real, which cheapened imports and thus threatened the profitability of industrial investments in competitive sectors (and not complementary ones) due to imports (Bastos 2004c). This exchange-rate policy had anti-inflationary objectives and served the interests of foreign investors and local agents with debts in foreign currency. Its institutional framework was the commercial and financial opening produced by neoliberal reforms of the 1990s that Lula's government did not reverse. According to Diegues (2015), the coexistence of currency appreciation with trade liberalization produced a "Brazilian disease" characterized by the structural adaptation of local productive units to the international division of industrial labor developed since the 1980s, with the redistribution of industry into regional or global production chains that began to import capital goods, parts and specialized components for industrial assembly of final goods in Brazil. Given that high import penetration rate, a sudden currency devaluation might severely depress industrial profitability in Brazil by increasing the costs of irreplaceable imports and foreign liabilities, even though it would reduce the unit labor cost in dollars, without leading to any structural diversification in Brazilian industry. In the same direction, as Hiratuka (2015a, 2015b) has documented, microeconomic adaptation to currency appreciation and declining international prices of manufactured goods involved not only increasing the import penetration rate but also importing and distributing final products.

We have seen that, in the face of these tendencies, the reaction of Rousseff's government was to interrupt the trend toward currency appreciation and, at the same time, to negotiate with foreign affiliates an increase in the national content in global production chains. This can be seen as a partial questioning of the neoliberal framework that had marked such policies in Lula's governments. What is regrettable is that such changes had not occurred before. When they occurred in 2012, it may already have been too little, too late to reverse the production and trade decisions made by the command centers of the multinational corporations after the global crisis.[18]

At the same time, some industrial entrepreneurs complaining about high interest rate and an overpriced real were increasingly opposed to the approach to the so-called Bolivarian countries of South America while others complained of both Third Worldism and the changes in monetary and exchange-rate policy that, in theory, would favor industry. To explain this behavior, in addition to the rejection of a regional bloc whose rationale seemed more political than economic, we have to factor in the loss of attractiveness of the region as the ability to import from the main partners was impaired by the deterioration of the terms of trade. Also, one cannot dismiss business attraction to the internal benefits of neoliberal criticism of Rousseff's economic policy. After all, this criticism, as expressed in the Social Democrat Party platform in 2014 and the Brazilian Democratic Movement document (*A Bridge to the Future*) in 2015,

---

18   According to Morceiro (2016), the increase in import penetration rates in several industrial sectors was concentrated in the period up to 2012, being slightly reversed thereafter in some cases, such as automobile production (but not auto parts) and oil refining.

promised not only the business environment supposedly necessary for better integration into global value chains, but also austerity in social spending and the "flexibilization" of labor contracts (Bastos 2014; 2015).

In short, a fundamental limitation of "active and haughty" diplomacy was that dependency was internalized in the production and financial structure, in the interests, and perhaps even in the culture of most Brazilian entrepreneurs. The future struggle to achieve an independent foreign policy cannot be restricted primarily to international diplomacy and must involve internal political and ideological struggles to transform or modify structures that are as resistant or stronger than those found in the multilateral forums.

References

Abu-El-Haj, Jawdat. (2016). Brazilian left Bonapartism and the rise of finance capital: a critique of the internal-bourgeoisie thesis. *Latin American Perspectives* 43(2): 207–216.

Alexander, N. (2011). O G20, a América Latina, e o futuro da integração regional. *Heinrich Böll Stiftung*, June.

Amin, S. (1974). *Accumulation on a World Scale: A Critique of the Theory of Underdevelopment*. New York: Monthly Review Press.

Amorim, C. (2003). A ALCA possível. *Folha de São Paulo*, July 8.

Amorim, C. (2004). Conceitos e estratégias da diplomacia do governo Lula. *Diplomacia, Estratégia e Política* 1(1): 41–48.

Amorim, C. (2015). *Teerã, Ramalá e Doha: Memórias da política externa ativa e altiva*. São Paulo: Saraiva.

Araújo Jr., J.T. (2017). Um virtual cartão de fidelidade antidumping. *Valor*, February 10.

Bambirra, V. (1972). *El capitalismo dependiente latinoamericano*. Santiago: Prensa Latinoamericana.

Bandeira, L.M. (2008). A importância geopolítica da América do Sul na estratégia dos Estados Unidos. *Espaço Acadêmico*, no. 89: 1–21.

Bandeira, L.M. (2016). Desfazer o que Lula fez em política externa não é bom para o Brasil. *BBC Brasil*, May 20.

Baran, P. (1957). *The Political Economy of Growth*. New York: Monthly Review Press.

Barbosa, R. (2010). *Mercosul e a integração regional*. São Paulo: Imprensa Oficial.

Barrocal, A. (2015). As recomendações de Samuel Pinheiro. *Carta Capital*, January 25.

Bastos, P.P.Z. (2004a). A política comercial estadunidense: a estratégia de liberalização competitiva, os acordos bilaterais e a ALCA. *Economia Política Internacional*, no. 1: 1–9.

Bastos, P.P.Z. (2004b). A ALCA entre a Rodada do Desenvolvimento da OMC e o regionalismo unilateral dos Estados Unidos. *Economia Política Internacional*, no. 2: 34–42.

Bastos, P.P.Z. (2004c). Análise do passado e projeto regional: qual comunidade sul-americana das nações é viável? *Economia Política Internacional*, no. 3: 25–37.

Bastos, P.P.Z. (2012a). Economia política da integração da América do Sul no mundo pós crise. *Observatório da Economia Global*, n. 10: 1–82.

Bastos, P.P.Z. (2012b). A economia política do novo-desenvolvimentismo e do social desenvolvimentismo. *Economia e Sociedade* 21: 779–810.

Bastos, P.P.Z. (2014). Retomada da ALCA e o fim do Mercosul. de novo? *Brasil Debate*, October 23.

Bastos, P.P.Z. (2015). O impeachment de Dilma Rousseff e o programa do novo PMDB. *Carta Maior*. http://www.cartamaior.com.br./.

Bastos, P.P.Z. (2017). Ascensão e crise do governo Dilma Rousseff e o golpe de 2016: poder estrutural, contradição e ideologia. *Revista de Economia Contemporânea* 21(2): 1–63.

Bastos, P.P.Z., and Hiratuka, C. (2020). The Foreign Economic Policy of Dilma Rousseff's Government and the Limits of Dependency. *Latin America Perspectives* 47(2): 25–46.

Bastos, P., and Hiratuka, C. (2017). A política econômica externa do governo Dilma Rousseff: comércio, cooperação e dependência. *Textos para discussão* 306. Instituto de Economia (Unicamp).

Batista Jr., P.N. (2015). BRICS: um novo fundo monetário e um novo banco de desenvolvimento. Carta Maior. http://www.cartamaior.com.br/.

Berringer, T. (2017). A burguesia interna brasileira e a integração regional da América do Sul (1991–2016). *Oikos* 16(1): 15–29.

Blustein, P. (2009). *Misadventures of the Most Favored Nations*. New York: Public affairs.

Boito, A., and Saad-Filho, A. (2016a). State, state institutions, and political power in Brazil. *Latin American Perspectives* 43(2): 190–206. .

Boito, A., and Saad-Filho, A. (2016b). Rejoinder. *Latin American Perspectives* 43(2): 217–219.

Bonis, G. (2012a). Brasileiro deixa cargo de Alto Representante Geral do Mercosul. *Carta Capital*, June 28.

Bonis, G. (2012b). Brasil deve ser 'firme' e 'prudente' com Paraguai. *Carta Capital*, February 27.

Cardoso, F.H., and Falletto, E. (1970). *Dependência e desenvolvimento na América Latina*. Rio de Janeiro: LTC.

Cardoso, F.H. (2014). Mudar o rumo. *O Globo*, January 5.

Cervo, A., and Lessa, A. (2014). O declínio: inserção internacional do Brasil (2011–2014). *Revista Brasileira de Política Internacional* 57(2): 133–151.

Chang, H.J. (2002). *Kicking Away the Ladder: Development Strategy in Historical Perspective*. London: Anthem Press.

Chilcote,   R.H.   (1984).   *Theories   of   Development   and   Underdevelopment.* Boulder: Westview Press.

Chilcote, R.H. (2009). Trotsky and development theory in Latin America. *Critical Sociology* 35: 719–741.

Chilcote, R.H. (1974). Dependency: a critical synthesis of the literature. *Latin American Perspectives* 1(1): 4–29.

Cornetet, J.C. (2014). A política externa de Dilma Rousseff: contenção na continuidade. *Revista Conjuntura Austral* 5(24): 111–150.

Corrêa, L.S. (1999). O Brasil e o mundo no limiar do novo século: diplomacia e desenvolvimento. *Revista Brasileira de Política Internacional* 42(1): 5–29.

Cruz, S.V. (1999). Ideias do poder: dependência e globalização em F. H. Cardoso. *Estudos Avançados* 13(37): 225–247.

Cruz, S.V. (2014). O futuro da política externa brasileira: desafios e perspectivas. In: Maringoni, G., Schutte, G., and Berron, G. (eds.), *Uma nova política externa,* 159–164. Tubarão: Editora Copiart.

Cruz, S.V., and Stuart, A.M. (2010). Mudando de rumo: a política externa do governo Lula. In: Cruz, S.V. (ed.), *O Brasil no mundo,* 71–86. São Paulo: Ed. UNESP.

Desai, R. (2013). The BRICS are building a challenge to Western economic supremacy. *Guardian,* April 2.

Diegues, A.C. (2015). As transformações no padrão de organização e acumulação da indústria: da desindustrialização à 'Doença Brasileira. In: Belluzzo, L.G., and Bastos, P.P. (eds.), *Austeridade para quem? Balanço e perspectivas do Governo Dilma,* 67–73. São Paulo: Carta Maior/Friedrich Ebert Stiftung.

Escudé, C. (1992). *Realismo periférico: Fundamentos para nueva política exterior argentina.* Buenos Aires: Planeta.

Evans, P.B. (1979). *Dependent Development: The Alliance of Multinational, State, and Local Capital in Brazil.* Princeton: Princeton University Press.

Evans, P.B. (1995). *Embedded Autonomy: States and Industrial Transformation.* Princeton: Princeton University Press.

Frank, A.G. (1966). The development of underdevelopment. *Monthly Review* 17 (September): 17–31.

Frank, A.G. (1967). *Capitalism and Underdevelopment in Latin America: Historical Studies of Chile and Brazil.* New York: Monthly Review Press.

Furtado, C (1973) *A hegemonia dos Estados Unidos e o subdesenvolvimento da América Latina.* Rio de Janeiro: Civilização Brasileira.

Furtado, C. (1998). *O capitalismo global.* São Paulo: Paz e Terra.

Garcia, M.A. (1996). Notas sobre a política externa. *Boletim. Secretaria de Relações Internacionais – Partido dos Trabalhadores,* jun./dez.: 2–10.

Garcia, M.A. (2010). O lugar do Brasil no mundo: a política externa em um momento de transição. In: Sader, E., and Garcia, M.A. (eds.), *Brasil, entre o passado e o futuro*, 153–176. São Paulo: Boitempo.

Gill, S. (1998). New constitutionalism, democratization, and global political economy. *Pacifica Review* 10(1): 23–38.

Guimarães, S.P. (1999). *Quinhentos anos de periferia.* Porto Alegre: Ed. UFRGS.

Guimarães, S.P. (2006). *Desafios brasileiros na era dos gigantes.* Rio de Janeiro: Contraponto.

Guimarães, S.P. (2009). Uma política externa para enfrentar as vulnerabilidades e disparidades. In: Jakobsen, K. (ed.), *A nova política externa*, 13–24. São Paulo: Perseu Abramo.

Guimarães, S.P. (2010). A América do Sul em 2022. *Carta Maior*, July 28.

Guimarães, S.P. (2015). O Brasil e os BRICS. In: Belluzzo, L.G., and Bastos, P.P.Z. (eds.), *Austeridade para quem? Balanço e perspectivas do Governo Dilma*, 55–66. São Paulo: Carta Maior/Friedrich Ebert Stiftung.

Hiratuka, C. (2015a). Mudanças na estrutura produtiva global e a inserção brasileira: desafios no cenário pós-crise. *Revista Política Social e Desenvolvimento*, vol. 24: 14–24.

Hiratuka, C. (2015b). Inserção comercial brasileira frente às transformações na economia global: desafios pós-crise. In: Barbosa, N.H., Marconi, N., Pinheiro, M.C., and Carvalho, L.B. (eds.), *Indústria e desenvolvimento produtivo no Brasil*, 295–334. Rio de Janeiro: Elsevier.

Hiratuka, C. (2016). Impactos de China sobre el proceso de integración regional de Mercosur. In: Dussel Peters (ed.), *La nueva relación comercial de America Latina y el Caribe con China:¿ Integración o desintegración regional?*, 195–244. Mexico City: Unión de Universidades de América Latina y el Caribe.

Kufakurinani, U., Kvangraven, I., Harvold, S., Dyveke, M., and Santanta, F. (2017). Dialogues on Development. Vol. 1. *On Dependency.* New York: Institute for New Economic Thinking.

Lampréia, L.F. (1998). A política externa do governo FHC: continuidade e renovação. *Revista Brasileira de Política Internacional* 42(2): 5–17.

Lampréia, L.F. (1999). Diplomacia, jogo duro. *Folha de São Paulo*, March 7.

Lima, M.R.S. (2011). Os primeiros cem dias do governo Dilma. *Boletim OPSA*, no. 1, 1–4.

Lima, M.R.S. (2013). Eleições e espionagem eletrônica na América do Sul. *Boletim OPSA*, no. 3: 2–5.

Lima, M.R.S. (2014a). A política sul-americana do governo do PT. In: G. Maringoni, G. Schutte, and G. Berron (eds.), *Uma nova política externa*, 81–96. Tubarão: Editora Copiart.

Lima, M.R.S. (2014b). Ortodoxia na economia e heterodoxia na política externa? *Boletim OPSA*, no. 3: 2–6.

Mantega, G. (1984). *A economia política brasileira.* Rio de Janeiro: Polis/Vozes.

Mantega, G. (1997). *Teoria da dependência revisitada: Um balanço crítico.* Relatório de Pesquisa 27. São Paulo: EASP/FGV.

Marini, R.M. (1969). *Subdesarrollo y revolución.* Mexico City: Siglo Veintiuno Editores.

Marques, F. (2017). Política industrial em xeque. *Pesquisa FAPESP*, no. 251.

Mello, J.M.C. (1982). *O capitalismo tardio.* São Paulo: Brasiliense.

Morceiro, P. (2016). *Vazamento de demanda setorial e competitividade da indústria de transformação brasileira.* FEA-USP Working Paper, no. 2016-12.

Natanson, J. (2008). *La nueva izquierda.* Buenos Aires: Editorial Sudamericana.

Panitch, L. (2015). BRICS, the G20, and the American Empire. In: Bond and Garcia (eds.), *BRICS: An Anti-Capitalist Critique*, 61–69. London: Pluto Press.

Panitch, L., and Gindin, S. (2012). *The Making of Global Capitalism: The Political Economy of American Empire.* New York: Verso.

Pinheiro, D. (2014). A afilhada rebelde. *Piauí*, no. 97: 2–13.

Pont, M. (2016). Cómo resurgir de las cenizas del modelo neoliberal: los límites de la restricción externa al proceso de desarrollo independiente. In: Daniel Filmus (ed.), *Pensar el Kirchnerismo*, 59–82. Buenos Aires: Siglo Veintiuno.

Poulantzas, N. (1974). *Les classes sociales dans le capitalisme d'aujourd'hui.* Paris: Seuil.

Ricupero, R. (2010). Carisma e prestígio: a diplomacia do período Lula de 2003 a 2010. *Política Externa* 19(1): 27–42.

Rossi, P. (2016). *Taxa de câmbio e política cambial no Brasil.* São Paulo: FGV Editora.

Rostowska, M. (2013). *BRICS and Global Economic Governance: The Case of the BRICS.* New Development Bank. Bulletin PISM 41 (494).

Rothkopf, D. (2009). The world's best foreign minister. *Foreign Policy*, October 7.

Sader, E. (2016). *Las vías abiertas de América Latina.* Buenos Aires: Editorial Octubre.

Santos, T. (1973). *Socialismo e fascismo: El nuevo carácter de dependencia y el dilemma latinoamericano.* Buenos Aires: Periferia.

Santos, T. (1968). El nuevo carácter de la dependência. *Cuadernos del Centro de Estudios Sociológicos*, no. 10: 1–25.

Saraiva, M.G. (2014). Balanço da política externa de Dilma Rousseff: perspectivas futuras? *Relações Internacionais*, no. 44: 25–35.

Saraiva, M.G., and Zimmer, B.G. (2016). Os limites da política externa de Dilma Rousseff para a América do Sul. *Relaciones Internacionales*, no. 50: 81–97.

Sarti, F. (2001). *Internacionalização comercial e produtiva no Mercosul nos anos 90.* Campinas: IE–UNICAMP.

Scandiucci, J.G. (2018). O Brasil e o G20 (2008–2015). In: Florencio, S.A.L., Neto, W.A.D., Ramanzini Jr., H., and Filho, E.S. (eds.), *Política externa brasileira em debate*, 135–166. Brasília: IPEA.

Smith, Y. (2014). Michael Hudson and Leo Panitch on BRICS Development Bank salvo v. the dollar. http://www.nakedcapitalism.com. Acessed on 02/02/2017.

Souza, V. (2016). Análise comparativa da política externa do primeiro governo Dilma Rousseff e dos governos Lula: níveis e fatores de mudança na condução. *Revista Fronteiras* 12 (24): 162–181.

Stuenkel, O. (2015). *The BRICS and the Future of Global Order.* Lanham, MD: Lexington Books.

Tavares, M.C., and Serra, J. (1972). Além da estagnação. In: M.C. Tavares (ed.), *Da substituição de importações ao capitalismo financeiro*, 153–207. Rio de Janeiro: Zahar.

Vigevani, T., and Oliveira, M. (2007). Brazilian foreign policy in the Cardoso era: the search for autonomy through integration. *Latin American Perspectives* 34 (5): 58–80.

Weisbrot, M. (2015). *Failed: What the Experts Got Wrong about the Global Economy.* New York: Oxford University Press.

Weiss, L. (2005). Global governance, national strategies: how industrialized states make room to move under the WTO. *Review of International Political Economy* 12: 723–749.

CHAPTER 13

Brazilian Labor Market: From the Workers' Party Administrations to the Bolsonaro Government

Ana Paula Fregnani Colombi and José Dari Krein

1 Introduction[1]

The bias of the economic policies they adopted and their impacts on the generation of employment and income, the character of their social policy, and the composition of the bourgeois fractions that made up the governments of the Partido dos Trabalhadores (Workers' Party – PT) have provoked intense debate in Brazilian society, both academic and political, over the degree of departure of this experience from the neoliberal paradigm. Under these governments, this discussion was constituted as an attempt to dispute the directions of the economic policy to be adopted. Today it is aimed at politically disputing the significance of the PT legacy and explaining the abrupt interruption of the second government of President Dilma Rousseff. It also continues to be fundamental to highlighting the reasons for the subsequent and rapid adoption of a strongly austerity-based agenda.

This debate is composed of various attempts to characterize the PT governments. Among them is the approach of Boito (2012), for whom the Lula and Dilma governments were *neodevelopmentalist*, supported by the ruling bourgeoisie and the working classes in order to apply the developmentalism possible within neoliberalism. Bielschowsky (2012) locates the Lula governments on the *social developmentalist* spectrum, since the expansion of the mass consumption market through the redistribution of income and the increase of public investment and social expenditures made the "social" the structuring axis of economic policy. According to Bresser-Pereira (2011; 2014), the Dilma governments could be considered *new developmentalist* for their attempt to stimulate private investment and change macroeconomic prices (exchange-rate depreciation and interest-rate reduction) with the aim of strengthening the market and making the country more competitive on the international stage. Filgueiras (2014) argues that the Lula and Dilma governments revealed traces of

---

1 An earlier version of the arguments in this chapter appeared in Colombi and Krein (2019).

continuity with the Fernando Henrique Cardoso administration in their trade and financial opening and their passive and regressive incorporation into the international division of labor, thus following a *liberal-peripheral model*. Finally, Martuscelli (2014) argues that the PT governments represented only a *reformed neoliberalism* that served the interests of subordinate fractions of the ruling bloc (the grande bourgeoisie) while making concessions to the popular sectors. Ranging from theses in the field of developmentalism to formulations on the arrangements and variations of neoliberal policies, these approaches reveal the hybridism of the PT governments and the differences between the Lula and Dilma periods. In these models the center of debate is the economic arena, with political disputes between the various fractions of capital dominating government decision making. The range of nomenclatures they present makes it difficult to examine the impact on the labor market and labor relations of the economic and social policies adopted in connection with the more general challenges present in the periphery of contemporary capitalism.

Emphasizing the labor aspects of the debate, this chapter examines the challenges presented by financial capitalism under neoliberal hegemony, relating them to the historical aspects of national capitalist formation and the consequent structural problems of the Brazilian labor market. In the next section we analyze how the transformations in the labor market and labor relations during the PT governments between 2003 and 2014 relate to the economic, political, and ideological characteristics prevailing since the 1980s. We show that economic growth through a mass consumer market reduced unemployment and generated formal jobs without overcoming the structural problems of the Brazilian labor market, as the permanence – even if at a slower pace than in the 1990s – of the trend of flexibility of labor relations. The hypothesis is that in 12 years of government the PT promoted a model of inclusion through the labor market and consumption with an increase in labor flexibility whose guidelines are linked to the characteristics of contemporary capitalism. In the third section, we point out that in a scenario of economic crisis and the rise of ultraneoliberal governments, the deterioration of employment indicators and the deconstruction of labor rights agenda gain new impulses.

2   Labor Trends in Contemporary Capitalism: Challenges to the
       Periphery

The developmentalist period (1930–1980) in Brazil was informed by a relational perspective[2] based on the effort to catch up with the productive structure of

---

2 Discussion of the possibilities for national development from a relational perspective refers
   to an eighteenth-century idea of progress that was enriched in the following century. The

the central countries. This perspective was based on the idea that industrialization would allow the underdeveloped countries to reach the level of economic and social development of the central ones. At the same time, public
regulation of labor would become part of a virtuous process of homogenization of the jobs generated, reflecting the reduction of social inequalities and
the lifestyles of workers. Although national industry has managed to consolidate the installation of technologically more advanced sectors and variations
in the social structure have provided upward social mobility (Mello and Novais
2009), a fluid regime of labor relations has become established. Despite the
extraordinary increase in salaried work between 1940 and 1980 and the existence of a model of labor relations regulated by law,[3] this regime is marked
by a large structural surplus of labor power, instability in employment, low
wages, a wide range of remuneration, and extreme informality, heterogeneity,
and turnover. In this disorganized labor market (Silva 1991), the freedom of
employers to establish the conditions of the use, hiring, and remuneration of
labor gives the Brazilian labor market a flexible character that, together with
the aforementioned characteristics, leads to predatory competition among
workers (Barbosa de Oliveira 1998; Baltar and Proni 1996; Krein 2013).

These historical characteristics intersect with the new trends imposed on
labor by contemporary capitalism. Since the 1970s, changes in the mode of capital accumulation under the hegemony of financial globalization have limited
the possibilities for economic development and the structuring and regulation
of the labor market in the Latin American periphery. Thus an understanding
of the evolution of the development of the labor market and labor relations
under the PT governments and the governments that followed it includes the
historical characteristics of a peripheral capitalist country that has failed to
structure its labor market and the consequences of a subordinate incorporation into financial globalization, including the adoption of neoliberal ideology
and orthodox economic policies that contribute to the flexibilization of labor
relations and the reduction of social protection of employees.

The political construction of a global financial system changed the model
of corporate competition associated with a rigidly hierarchical bureaucratic
organizational structure. According to Belluzzo (2013), the financialization

---

"impulse for comparison in terms of progress came from the observation that peoples, states,
continents, sciences, corporations, or classes were advanced relative to one another, with the
result that, from the eighteenth century on, it was possible to postulate acceleration or, in the
case of those who had lagged behind, achieving or exceeding" (Koselleck 2006: 284).

3   Cardoso (2003) and Noronha (1998) identify the Brazilian model as legislated, given the predominance of state regulation.

of capital accumulation allowed a new stage of centralization of property through an increase in mergers and acquisitions and the outsourcing of functions considered nonessential to the core business of a company. In addition, in the process of valuing securities independent of productive capital, financial accumulation became a source of profit for companies to the detriment of effective demand. Thus, the capacity for long-term productive investment emerged only in the face of a severe reduction of current costs, among them labor costs, accentuating the tendency toward precarization of the positions that remained and weakening the unions. This trend points to a scenario of difficulties for the achievement of full employment and for the survival of social and economic rights, which are considered an obstacle to the operation of the laws of competition and to the creation of protected occupations not only in peripheral countries but also in countries that had already experienced successful capitalist development (ILO 2015; Kalleberg 2011; Rodgers 1989; Belluzzo and Galípolo 2017).

The production of goods and services on an international scale impacted the distribution of production and had consequences for national labor markets. Asia became a producer of cheap manufactures, forming a large manufacturing area that pulsated around China and becoming a major importer of raw materials. Brazil and Latin America were practically excluded from the restructuring of global value chains. In Brazil, flows of financial capital predominated. In the productive sphere, the country participated only marginally in global value chains; national industry's main characteristic was the increase in the participation of sectors that depended heavily on natural resources and a loss of importance of segments of greater technological intensity (Arend 2014; Belluzzo 2013; Carneiro 2017). With regard to employment, this entailed the reduction of the proportion of jobs in manufacturing with the shift of jobs from large industrial enterprises to smaller establishments and the increase in the proportion of jobs in commerce and support services and in social activities such as education, health, welfare, and social assistance (Baltar and Krein 2013).

The consequences of a logic of accumulation dominated by financial capital with more internationalized production of goods and services also included the relaxation of labor relations and the reduction of social protection (Baltar and Krein 2013: 289):

Financial globalization and the internationalization of the production of goods and services are at the heart of contemporary transformations in capitalism. The organization of production changed, with a trend toward decentralization and flexibility of work. The political framework created by the predominance of neoliberalism not only promoted these changes but also helped to broaden the unfavorable impact on the public regulation of labor, which, instead of shaping the changes to limit the precariousness of employment relations, reinforced these effects, supporting the freedom of action of employers in adapting to the competitive environment.

Changes in the pattern of use, hiring, and remuneration of the workforce were also linked, as pointed out by Belluzzo (2013), to changes in the organization of companies associated with the spread of outsourcing and subcontracting, with their consequences for characteristics demanded of workers such as polyvalence and permanent training. For Boltanski and Chiapello (2009: 239) this was a transition from the 1970s that marked the building of a new spirit of capitalism based on the pursuit of collaboration among wage earners for the achievement of capitalist profit not by "the collective and political integration of workers into the social order through a form of the spirit of capitalism that linked economic and technological progress to a vision of social justice" but by the "development of a self-realization project that link[ed] the cult of individual performance and exaltation of mobility with reticular conceptions of the social bond."

The pressure on labor regulation systems was not only in the business sphere but also in that of the state. According to Dardot and Laval (2016), while under Keynesianism these interventions followed the principles of solidarity with the creation of a network of social protection, in neoliberalism they made up a new order that aimed to extend the incorporation of the market into social life through public policies that protected and supported the development of capitalist enterprises. The intervention of the state thus had a contrary meaning to that of the previous period: "It is not a question of limiting the market by an act of correction or compensation by the state but one of developing and purifying the competitive market with a carefully adjusted legal framework" (Dardot and Laval 2016: 69). For these writers this legal framework in the labor sphere involved changes in social legislation to the detriment of social protection and in favor of employers, whose general orientation was toward the dismantling of systems that protected wage earners against cyclical variations in economic activity and their replacement with new forms of flexibility. The promotion of flexibility was in this sense a mechanism for promoting competition.

The general trends of this economic order, however, had national specificities, since, as Silver (2005) points out, the differentiation of geographical areas of capital also determined the periodic oscillation of capitalism between phases that tended toward the "commodification" and others that tended toward the "decommodification" of work (see Polanyi 2000). The "constant dispute not only over the definition of the 'rights' of the working class but also over the type and number of workers with access to these rights" was determined by spatial strategies with regard to who would enjoy the rights and who would be left out (Silver 2005: 36).

The structural barriers to economic development in the periphery had an impact on the quantity, quality, and standard of regulation of the occupations generated in Brazil. Viewed from the outside, the marginal inclusion of the country in global production chains confirmed its subordinate role in capital accumulation and the valuation of financial wealth. Viewed from the inside, the "position of resisting passive incorporation into globalization ... was overcome by the position that exalted the effects of a sudden and indiscriminate opening to intensify competition and promote efficiency in the use of existing resources" (Baltar and Krein 2013: 274). The consequence of this pattern for employment was the spread of low-wage, high-turnover, and low-skill occupations, especially since the 1990s, in a labor market that was already very disorganized and flexible. Thus, while the 1990s were not the beginning of the precariousness and flexibilization of labor relations in the country, they did intensify the deterioration of jobs (Krein 2013) that in any case were never considered good and regulated (Cardoso 2013; Guimarães and Paugam 2016). It is not that working conditions in Brazil have not improved throughout the process of capitalist development but rather that industrialization has not guaranteed formal jobs with a broad pattern of protection in a flexible labor market and that shifting between formal and informal positions is intense. Disputes over labor regulation and the rights attached to it today are the more pronounced in countries of late-capitalist development and unstructured labor markets such as that of Brazil. Since the characteristics of contemporary capitalism are largely unfavorable to labor, the periphery poses an additional challenge in that it has not experienced either public regulation of labor or a broad system of social protection. With this in mind, we ask whether the dynamics of economic growth with job creation and income experienced by the country in the 2000s were running against the more general tendencies of contemporary capitalism. At the same time, we wonder why the positive trend on employment indicators was quickly and intensely reversed at the end of PT governments. The focus is on the possibilities for structuring and regulating the labor market of a country such as Brazil, which has its historical problems and is confronting the unfavorable tendencies for labor of contemporary capitalism.

3   The Dynamics of Labor Market and Labor Relations under Lula and
       Dilma Governments

The years in which the PT held the presidency were marked by increased economic growth achieved mainly by the promotion of the internal market with
the expansion of the "mass consumer society" (Medeiros 2015). This trajectory
was initially driven by a favorable export cycle and the adoption, especially
since 2006, of policies for increasing income and boosting credit and consumption with consequences for investment and employment growth. This
cycle began to be reversed with the change of focus of economic policy and the
expansion of fiscal adjustment as of 2011 and despite attempts to reduce financial gains and incentives for private investment. The expansion of the domestic market was at the core of the growth strategy of the period, since after the
commodity boom a series of consumption-promoting policies enabled the
economy to grow. The broad massification of durable and semidurable consumer goods present throughout the cycle was due, as Medeiros (2015) points
out, to the increase in the minimum wage and formal wage employment, the
expansion of credit, and the appreciation of the exchange rate.

    The increase in consumption and the expectation of continuity in the ele-
ments that favored it stimulated investment induced by current demand (Sarti
and Hiratuka 2011), but investment supported directly by state action and
based mainly on increased investment in infrastructure showed only modest
growth (Carneiro 2017). Only in 2010 did the contribution of investment to GDP
growth exceed that of consumption. This reduction of the role of investment
in economic growth was linked to the asymmetric way in which the country
had become part of the global value chains and economic policy options of
the period, since the "solvency conditions of a developing country depend as
much on the economic order ... as on macroeconomic and industrial policies"
(Medeiros 2015: 146). One reflection of the marginal position of the country
in the more internationalized production of goods and services and the consequent development of a national productive structure that was specialized
and low-technology was the limited effect on investment of the increase in
consumption (Carneiro 2017); part of the demand for machinery, equipment,
and intermediate inputs created by the expansion of consumption ended up
leaking abroad, resulting in increased imports (Sarti and Hiratuka 2017; Baltar
2014). Regarding the governmental options, "there was little or no progress in
Brazilian industrial policy," a fundamental condition for repairing the leakage
from the expansion of the domestic market (Medeiros 2015: 165). The extensive
growth of industry without progress in the high-technology sectors and activities and without an industrial policy aimed at increasing industrial exports

resulted in the maintenance of the supply structure. The result of this growth model, based on an increase in domestic consumption and the maintenance of the macroeconomic tripod (based on the upward revision of inflation rates, an increase in the basic interest rate, the primary-surplus target, and the maintenance of a floating exchange rate), was the absence of structural change in the economy. Although consumption continued to grow until 2014, industrial output remained stagnant from 2001 to 2013 and declined sharply thereafter (Sarti and Hiratuka 2017).

Following this dynamic, the growth trajectory of the Brazilian economy had its best moment between 2004 and 2008, when the average economic growth rate was 4.8 percent. After the effects of the international crisis hit the country, the maintenance of consumption levels was achieved through a set of measures taken to prevent the slowdown in economic growth. As a result, in 2009 the economy declined by only 0.1 percent, recovering rapidly to 7.5 percent in 2010. Starting in the following year, the effects of the slowdown resulting from the international crisis and the exhaustion of the consumption cycle due to the deceleration of the improvement of the income distribution and the increasing indebtedness of households called for a new direction. In 2012 the government's intention was to implement a "new economic matrix" based on stimulating private investment, but this did not produce the expected results despite the depreciation of the exchange rate, the reduction of interest rates, the tax exemptions provided, and concessions to increase the role of the private sector in the area of infrastructure. As a result, the GDP growth rate reached 3 percent in 2013, mainly because of the performance of consumption, and in 2014 stood at 0.1 percent. Between 2011 and 2014, the average growth rate of the economy was only 2.2 percent (IBGE).

The higher level of economic growth between 2003 and 2014 had positive effects on the labor market, with a consistent drop in the unemployment rate. The unemployment rate fell from 9.7% in 2003 to 6.9% in 2014 (PNAD, IBGE). At the same time, there was a deepening of the process of formalization, with a decrease in employment without a formal contract and in unpaid employment and self-employment. The formalization rate increased from 40.1% in 2003 to 50.1% in 2014 (IBGE, PNAD).[4] Low unemployment rates, even after the international crisis and at a time when the economy was slowing down, are fundamentally related to the decline of the growth rate of the economically active population expressed mainly in the decrease in participation of the under-25 age-group in the labor market. At the same time, formalization was

---

4 Formalization rate: formal workers/total occupied without considering employers. Formal workers: employees with a formal contract, civil servant and domestic worker with a formal contract.

mainly linked, as Krein et al. (2018) have shown, to policies aimed at the formalization of sectors with low access to social security (the self-employed and micro and small businesses) and the strengthening of the public institutions responsible for the enforcement of rights.

Another impact of this growth dynamic is that, although there was a generalized increase in employment in all sectors except agriculture and in all the pay ranges except half a minimum wage, it was the sectors linked to consumption and encouraged by government action that generated most of the jobs. The activity groups with the greatest dynamism in terms of new jobs were those promoted by income and credit facilitation for the poorest – housing, food, transport, commerce, storage, and communication. For example, the construction sector, which had the highest employment growth, benefited from the increase in real estate credit and the My House, My Life program. These sectors of activity are precisely the ones with the most low-wage jobs (Baltar, Souen, and Campos 2017). This explains why jobs increased sharply in low-paid activities. At the same time, the increase in these jobs was accompanied by the valorization of the minimum wage, triggering a significant reduction in income inequality.[5]

The experience of manufacturing, in which employment growth was modest and began to decline in absolute numbers from 2008 on, reveals the relationship between the marginal incorporation of the country into global value chains and the difficulty of promoting structural changes in the economy.[6] However, in terms of wages manufacturing contains half of the formal jobs, with an average wage of 1.9 minimum wages, taking 2013 as a reference (Baltar, Souen, and Campos 2017). This shows that the deindustrialization of the past three decades (Sarti and Hiratuka 2017) has had an impact not only on the number of jobs generated in manufacturing but also on the low level of remuneration of these jobs. Thus, the absence of structural change under this growth model therefore has two aspects: despite its ability to generate jobs in an economy with a vast internal market, the structural characteristics of labor have not changed, and public regulation is an important condition structuring the labor market and expanding the social protection of wage earners.

Regarding labor relations, flexibilization continued to advance both in collective bargaining and in labor legislation but at a slower pace than in the

---

5   The reduction is expressed in a Gini coefficient that fell from 0.58 in 2003 and 0.52 in 2014 (IPEADATA).

6   Between 2003 and 2014, employment grew by 12% in the manufacturing sector. In civil construction the growth was 73% and, in the sector related to housing and food, the growth was about 59% (PNAD, IBGE).

1990s (Krein 2013). Despite advances in labor market indicators, the tendency to make labor relations more flexible was expressed in the heterogeneity of the labor market and the persistence of precarious conditions in many occupations (Guimarães and Paugam 2016). While formal employment relations guarantee access to social rights, they cannot be understood as synonymous with quality jobs. By "flexibilization" we mean the increasing freedom of companies to determine the conditions of the use, hiring, and remuneration of work according to their needs, leaving the workers in a condition of increasing insecurity in that their contracts are subject to oscillations of the level of activity (Baltar and Krein 2013). The legislative measures adopted overlapped with the existing legal framework but did not supplant the Consolidation of Labor Laws, the norm regulating labor law in Brazil. They fell far short of what was wanted by the business sectors, which sought to restrict the possibility of state and union interference in labor regulation – a goal achieved with the labor reform adopted in 2017, as discussed in the next section. In addition, while the measures introduced tended toward labor flexibilization, in some respects they expanded social protection (Krein and Biavaschi 2015).[7]

The flexibilization of the 2000s was expressed in three central aspects of the employment relation: forms of hiring, remuneration, and working hours. With regard to the forms of hiring, there was an increase in subcontracting or outsourcing, "the form of labor contracting that has best conformed to the neoliberal format imposed on labor markets, giving companies a series of benefits, such as the flexibility of managing labor power at a reduced economic and political cost" (Filgueiras and Cavalcanti 2015: 1). A method developed by the Interunion Department of Statistics and Socioeconomic Studies (DIEESE 2017) based on data from the *Annual Report on Social Information* shows that between 2007 and 2014 the total number of formal links in these activities increased from 8.5 to 12.5 million. In 2014, typically outsourced activities accounted for a quarter of total formal employment. At the same time, there was an increase in disguised employment relations[8] expressed in internships and the hiring of independent contractors and individual microentrepreneurs. According to Krein (2013), internships sharply increased between 1995 and 2005. It is difficult to estimate the

---

7 Between 2003 and 2014, 15 measures of expansion of social protection were introduced, among them a minimum wage and regulation of domestic employment and 21 measures to increase flexibilization such as special contracts.
8 This growth would have been greater, as Krein and Castro (2015) point out, except for the counterposition of inspection institutions that declared such practices illegal and the presidential veto of an amendment that would have rendered infeasible the supervision of disguised employment relationships.

increase in hiring of independent contractors, but it is reflected in the number of companies without employees, which went from approximately 3,6000,000 in 2003 to 4,300,000 in 2013. Finally, there was an explosion of individual micro-entrepreneurs.[9] Alongside the Simple and Super Simple tax forms[10] created in 2007, the individual-microentrepreneur category both generated formalization and stimulated hiring in disguise. According to data presented by Krein et al. (2018), after the law was passed the number of individual microentrepreneurs formalized jumped from 44,000 in December 2009 to 5.5 million in December 2015. The initial purpose of the individual-microentrepreneur category was to ensure access to social security and credit for self-employed workers, but it ended up opening a formal space for the replacement of employment contracts with service delivery contracts – which, since the wage relationship persisted, constituted fraud. In addition, the creation of the category placed entrepreneurship at the level of "job and income generation policy" (Castro 2013: 46), and therefore it must be analyzed in terms of flexible working relationships. In this respect it both creates the possibility of replacing formal employment and/or formalizing labor with a lower level of rights and allows workers to transcend the passive status of wage earner and to view their jobs as business activities (Dardot and Laval 2016). The other expression of flexibility in forms of hiring was the indefinite contract, since the employer was free to withdraw it without justification, simply paying a fine if the contract period had not expired. This helps explain why atypical forms of contracting increased less than indefinite contracts (Krein and Castro 2015).

The second aspect in which the flexibilization of labor relations was reflected was the increasing trend toward variable remuneration. Krein and Teixeira (2014) show that advances in collective bargaining in the 2000s focused on salary adjustments and profit-sharing programs for companies in the private sector that were more economically structured and had unions. Perossi (2017), researching wages of factory workers in 217 large and medium-sized companies, has shown that 9 percent of annual compensation was variable, and 20 percent was indirect (benefits). In the automotive sector, the variable part amounted to 16 percent of total annual remuneration. Thus, while, as we have seen, the valorization of the minimum wage and the readjustment

---

9   Complementary Law 128 of 2008 created the category, stimulating the self-employed to become "formal".

10 The National Simple or Super Simple tax form was created by Complementary Law 123/06 with the objective of unifying the collection of taxes and contributions from micro and small companies, expanding the possibility of framing new service providers and professionals.

of categories above inflation allowed an increase in the purchasing power of wages, the flexibility of remuneration was associated with profit-sharing programs and indirect wages (benefits).

The third aspect in which flexibilization of labor relations was apparent was the flexibilization of the workday (Dal Rosso 2008; DIEESE 2009), despite the decline of the number of people working more than 44 hours per week in the 2000s (Krein and Biavaschi 2015). To the traditional means of making the workday more flexible (overtime, shift work, night work, group holidays) were added new forms such as the modulation of the annual work period, the liberalization of work on Sundays, a variety of arrangements tailored to each economic segment, and part-time work (Gibb 2017). As Gibb (2017) shows, the emergence of fragmented and special workdays in different economic sectors and even different jobs also occurred, and technological progress has enabled mechanisms of control of the workday such as the home office. Thus, the workday was tended to adjust the distribution of hours worked according to the interests of companies through the introduction of new modes of labor control (Rao 2013).

The valorization of variable remuneration, the flexibilization of the workday, and the promotion of disguised employment (with emphasis on outsourcing and the stimulation of entrepreneurship) indicate that formal employment is not necessarily secure, stable, and well-paid employment. Increasing flexibility means, on the contrary, that companies can manage the workforce according to their needs and with lower costs. The growth of employment in historically unstructured sectors with low wages and low capacity for collective organization also corroborates the persistence of precariousness in times of the formalization of employment, showing that the two can walk side by side. The increase in flexibilization combined with the creation of an increasingly heterogeneous and segmented labor market indicates that risk in the labor market is no longer suppressed by the existence of a formal employment relationship. Insecure and unstable forms of employment, even formal ones, serve to increase "cultural tolerance for uncertainty" (Streeck 2013) and naturalize the market as a locus of the pursuit of social welfare, placing the handling of the risks of their existence in workers' own hands (Dardot and Laval 2016).

4   Unemployment and Flexibility under Temer and Bolsonaro
       Governments

Even though it was shrouded in contradictions, the PT governments managed to reinstate the debate on the need to structure the labor market in Brazil.

However, since the economic crisis of 2015, when the policies of fiscal adjustments and reforms to make labor relations more flexible began in the second
Dilma administration, there was a rapid reversal of the indicators, with a significant advance in the disorganization of the labor market.

The neoliberal agenda, which has gained strength since 2015 during the
second Dilma administration, is characterized by the promotion of the fiscal
adjustment policy in response to the economic crisis, with an increase of 1.75
pp in the primary surplus, contingency in budgetary authorization and suspension of contracts for new public positions (Dweck, Silveira, and Rossi 2018); the
approval of provisional measures[11] that restricted access to illness aid benefits,
the restriction in pensions awarded to dependent spouses of deceased workers
(MP 664/2015), unemployment insurance and salary allowance (MP 665/2015);
and the launch of the Employment Protection Program (PPE), which made
it possible to reduce the workload with reduced wages. After the President's
impeachment, this agenda takes shape, driving an intense and rapid deterioration in employment indicators and creating a favorable climate for the
approval of the labor law reform in 2017.

The Constitutional Amendment[12] 95 (EC 95), which was approved in 2016
under Michel Temer's government, defined a New Tax Regime. In this new
regime, a constitutional limit was established for the annual growth of the
Federal Government's primary expenditure, which corresponds, at most, to
the inflation of the previous year, with a term of 20 years and with the possibility of revising the rule only after ten years. Rossi and Dweck (2016) explain
that, in practice, this New Tax Regime implies a real freeze in the total federal
government expenses so that public spending will not keep pace with popula-
tional growth. It is, the authors clarify, the institutionalization of a situation of
fiscal austerity for the next 20 years (Krein and Colombi 2019).

The Brazilian economy has been facing a drop in growth since 2015, when
the government of Dilma Rousseff bet on fiscal adjustment as a way to balance
public accounts and regain support from the private sector. The Temer government deepened this strategy with EC 95, which implied a negative growth trajectory in the country between the years 2015 and 2016. As shown in Figure 13.1,

---

11   A Provisional Measure (MP) is a legal act by the President of the Republic, that is enforced
      into law. It is edited without the participation of the Legislative Branch, which will only
      be called upon to discuss and approve it at a later time.
12   A constitutional amendment is a modification of the constitution, resulting in spe-
      cific changes to the constitutional text. In the phase prior to approval, a constitutional
      amendment must appear as a proposal, being called a Constitutional Amendment
      Proposal (PEC).

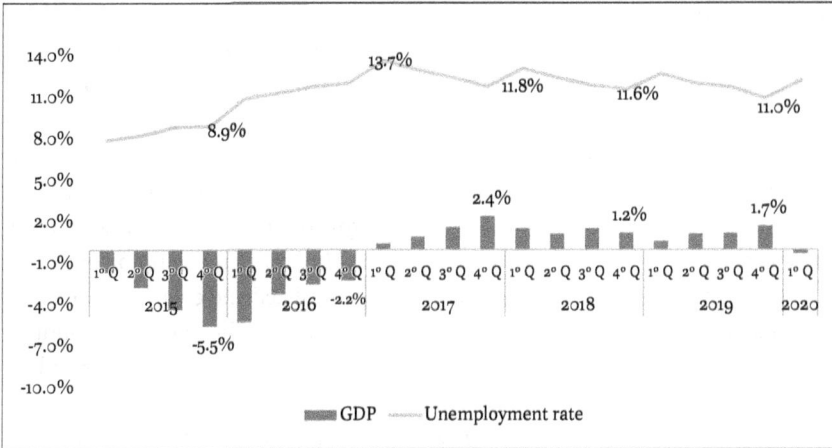

FIGURE 13.1 GDP growth and unemployment rate, 2015–2020 (% per quarter)
SOURCE: DESIGNED BY THE AUTHORS BASED ON DATA FROM THE SYSTEM
OF NATIONAL ACCOUNTS (SNC – GDP: VARIATION IN VOLUME IN RELATION
TO THE SAME QUARTER OF THE PREVIOUS YEAR) AND THE CONTINUOUS
NATIONAL HOUSEHOLD SURVEY (PNAD CONTÍNUA/IBGE)

the unemployment rate has assumed an upward trend since 2015. In the first quarter of 2017, after two consecutive years of negative GDP growth, unemployment reached 14.1 million people. The unemployment rate remained high and in double digits throughout the analyzed historical series.[13]

The 2015/2016 crisis, in addition to reversing the process of systematically reducing the unemployment rate, was used to justify the approval of labor law reform by conservative and neoliberal forces, as it would be, according to their defenders arguments, the condition for resumption of economic activity and employment. However, after 2017 the country was unable to resume economic activity and the labor market continued to undergo a process of disruption.

The labor law reform came into effect in November 2017 under the 13.467/2017 and 13.429/2017 laws. It created a series of rules that provide greater freedom for employers to adjust demand and the way in which the workforce is used according

---

13 The labor market data for the 2003–2014 period were taken from the National Household Sample Survey (PNAD). The data for the 2015–2019 period correspond to the CONTINUOUS National Household Sample Survey. The big difference is that the Continuous PNAD follows a scheme of household rotation, in other words, each selected household will be interviewed five times, once every quarter, for five consecutive quarters, making it possible to analyze their development and evolution on different aspects. Therefore, the Continuous PNAD contains quarterly data while PNAD is annual.

to their needs, in line with current standard labor regulations in contemporary capitalism (Krein 2018). Its objective was to create devices that remove protection and make the worker responsible for raising the requirements demanded by the market and for planning his life among occupations that remunerate him at a level that is sufficient to provide for his existence in the short term. The reform is quite extensive and is based on three pillars that cover: 1) the expansion of devices that allow the flexible use of working time, forms of hiring and remuneration in favor of the employer; 2) the weakening of public institutions and union organization, stimulating the definition of rules in a decentralized and even individualized manner; and 3) the individualization of risks, advancing the logic of instilling in workers the notion of employability and responsibility for the risks that are inherent to working life (Krein and Colombi 2019).

After three years from its approval, the issue that stands out is that the mediocre performance of the economic activity brought negative effects on employment without the counter-reform being able to reverse them. The result is a clear perception of worsening living conditions for those who live off their own labor. This aspect is confirmed by an explosion in the unemployment rate from 2015 onwards. The significant increase in these negative indicators occurred in 2016, as a result of the sharp drop in the GDP in this and the previous year, since the approval of the reforms was unable to change neither the economic growth nor the unemployment trajectories.

As shown in Figure 13.2, the small drop in the unemployment rate over 2017 was due to the increase in informal employment (with emphasis on self-employment) and the underutilization of the workforce. Unemployment remained at a stable and high rate. It did not rise since many people had to adopt their own strategies to be able to carry out some form of activity and earn income. For example, the occupations that grew the most were: door-to-door salesmen, food vendors and private drivers.

Considering that informal workers comprise workers without a formal contract, such as domestic workers, auxiliary family workers and those who are self-employed, the graph shows a growth trend in rates, even before the reform was approved, which does not reverse itself after 2017.[14] Informality has grown not only in service activities in which it is already more prevalent, but also in sectors historically recognized for the greater incidence of formal work and better structuring. This is the case for the industrial sector, that according to

---

14   The informality rate falls again in 2020 due to the impact of the health crisis on the labor market in the country. It is not a movement that indicates an improvement. On the contrary, many workers were prevented from carrying out their activities in the context of the pandemic and therefore left the workforce, causing a drop in the informality rate.

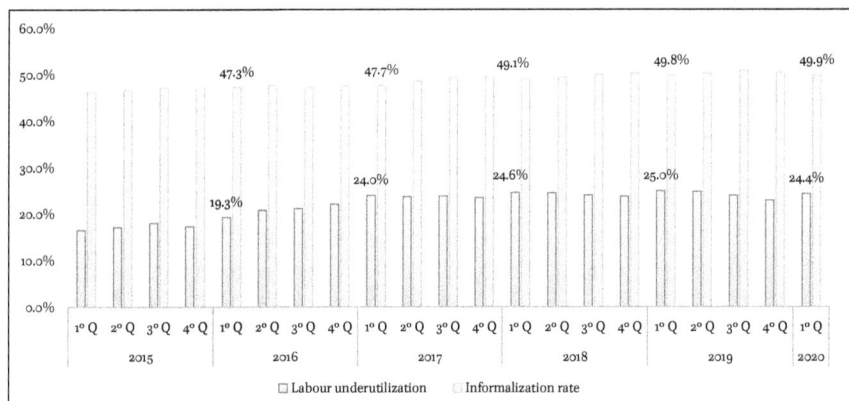

FIGURE 13.2 Labor underutilization rate and informalization rate, 2015–2020 (% per quarter)
SOURCE: CONTINUOUS NATIONAL HOUSEHOLD SAMPLE SURVEY (PNAD
CONTÍNUA/IBGE)

PNADC, presented an increase of 5.6% of informal workers between the last quarter of 2012 and at the same period in 2018. It is also important to highlight that, during the same period, informality grows more among workers with higher education.

Evidence of a worsening in the labor market also appears in the behavior of the underutilization rate of the labor force, which encompasses not only open unemployment, but also those who are currently employed but wished to work more hours, but cannot (the underoccupied workers), discouraged workers[15] and those who are available for work, but are unable to do so for some reason. To exemplify this precariousness, underoccupied people work an average of 19 hours a week and earn an average monthly income of R$734.00. While those who are regularly employed work an average of 38 hours a week and their average income is R$2,187.00.[16] In other words, underoccupied people work, on average, half of the hours and receive a third of the income from work compared to the total of those who are regularly employed. Adding the total of the underoccupied, unemployed workers and the potential workforce,[17] we reach a level of workforce underutilization that reaches a contingent of more than

---

15 People who want to work but are not seeking work because they believe no suitable job is available for them. Under current international statistical standards, discouraged workers are counted as not economically active and outside the labor force.

16 In November 2018 rates.

17 This corresponds to the sum of those who worked less than 40 hours a week and would like to work more; the unemployed who sought employment in the past 30 days and were

27.6 million people, considering the first quarter of 2020, with the unemployed corresponding to 12.9 million.

In sum, the data show that, after the reform, the generation of occupations was concentrated in more precarious activities, with the growth of informality and underutilization. On the one hand, this indicates that low economic growth is a key variable for job creation. Without it, the change in legislation does not have the strength to enhance the dynamics of the labor market. On the other hand, the reform itself has only shown its potential to lower the legal framework with the introduction of atypical and precarious contracts, which can spread with greater or lesser intensity, depending on the pace of growth. In this sense, the evidence is for the continuity of the trends started since the crisis of 2015 without an ultra-neoliberal agenda having been able to reverse the economic dynamics, job creation and the trend of increasing informality, which reinforces the movement for the destruction of rights and wage earning as channels for access to social citizenship.

From a labor relations perspective, outsourcing – which was already a reality in the Brazilian labor market, as discussed in the previous section – continues to grow. The data extracted from RAIS,[18] based on a methodology developed by DIEESE (2017), in the period between 2014 and 2019, show that the total of formal employees fell by more than 2 million, but in some typically outsourced activities there was a strong expansion of occupations, such as clerical services, management positions in the health sector, facilities management and support, supply chain and human resources management. In them, the growth rate varied between 140% and 260%. Druck and Franco (2008: 101) state that in the last fifteen years, "there has been a strong growth in outsourcing in all directions," both in the public and private sectors.

The creation of a more unfavorable situation for workers can also be seen when analyzing what is happening with working time. Regarding working hours, the first phenomenon is the interruption of the drop – which had been ongoing since the beginning of the decade – in the average hours usually worked per week since the 2015 crisis. As of 2017, it is possible to notice an increase in the number of people who work more than 49 hours a week and a small increase in the number of people who work up to 14 hours a week, considered insufficient to guarantee survival, but an expression of the crisis. If the

---

availabel to start working immediately; and people outside the workforce who would like to work and who have not sought employment in the past 30 days or were not available to work at the time of the survey.

18   Annual List of Social Information (Relação Anual de Informações Sociais).

trend persists, there may be a process of increasing polarization of the working hours journey, in which the two extremes will rise again, those who work
insufficient hours and those who work excessively. This trend can be explained
both by the maintenance of jobs of those who are currently in the market and
by the growth of self-employed workers, mainly due to precarious insertion in
the labor market.

As for the distribution of working hours, the trend to standardize the use of
working time has been occurring since the 1990s, especially since the introduction of the hour bank and the release of work on Sundays. In the post-reform
years, the indication is that this movement continues to increase. Based on the
analysis of the results of collective bargaining and surveys with union leaders,
with digital platform workers, it is possible to perceive workday re-composition
in the perspective of expanding the company's freedom to manage the use of
time (Galvão 2019). It is a movement that seeks to adjust working hours distribution to the needs of each economic segment and even sectors within the
same company. The generalization of the 12 by 36 journey for many categories,
especially in the service sector and commerce, was an example of an aspect of
the reform that advanced.

The working hours topic, which is essential in controlling the time between
capital and work, gains even more centrality in collective negotiations. It
stands out as one of the main points of employers' demands, in the initial
surveys with union leaders and the results of collective bargaining. Given the
situation of union weakening and unfavorable employment context, many of
these demands begin to take effect in the normative instruments, especially
the hour bank, the home office, the 12 by 36 working shift and/or other composition arrangements, the lunch break, work on Sundays and holiday installments. In addition, the reform also left the union with no option, as it allowed
individualized negotiation of compensation for the working hours. In other
words, flexibilization is still ongoing both because of the employer's discretionary increase and because of the unions the weakness in collective bargaining processes.

Little time has passed since the approval of the labor law reform and since
2015 the scenario of economic crisis has not been reversed, having intensified with the pandemic instead. The degradation of labor market indicators is
mainly due to the economic crisis. This scenario finds in the labor law reform
a point of deepening in the process of making labor relations more flexible,
which takes shape with the maintenance of the outsourcing process and the
intensification of the power of determination and control of working time by
employers. The fundamental movement, which runs through the most recent
transformations, is a strengthening of the business vision and its legitimation

in the form of the law. It is an impulse to the "tendency to weaken public regulation in favor of private regulation, in which workers are more exposed to market mechanisms in determining their conditions of survival" (Krein 2018: 79).

All of these impacts on the market and on labor relations highlighted above need to be understood within the context of the country, the economic crisis and the strengthening of ultraliberal governments. As a result, a scenario of growth of labor precariousness presents itself, with the expansion of heterogeneity in the composition of the working classes as well as the expansion of insecurity and vulnerability of those who need to work. The lives of most workers have become more complicated after the economic crisis and the approval of the labor law reform, a scenario that has become dramatic in the context of the pandemic.

5   Conclusion

The tendency toward flexibilization and reduction of social protection that has prevailed in the central countries in the past four decades is expressed in a particular way in each country according to the specificities of the historically constructed system of labor relations. In the case of Brazil, which has not been able to structure its labor market or create a comprehensive system of social protection, the effects of this logic were apparent as early as the 1990s, when the country chose passive participation in financial globalization. The countermovement under the PT governments was the continuation of flexibilization (although at a slower pace) alongside of an increase in employment and income. This countermovement was related to the decision to promote inclusion through the labor market and consumption, a process that did not alter the economic structure, overcome the labor market's historical problems, or alter the course of labor flexibilization. Although the legislative changes did not deconstruct the labor code, the dynamics of the labor market and the correlation of forces in the relation between labor and capital resulted in the deepening of the condition of the insecurity and vulnerability of workers.

During the PT governments, the dynamics of flexibilization expanded in the central elements of the employment relationship, creating pressure to change the legal framework. Starting in 2013, when the economic and political crisis intensified, this labor agenda gained greater visibility and the pressure to revise the labor code was exacerbated. This process culminated in a deep and substantive labor law reform that legalized the existing flexibilization and enabled new options for capital to manage the workforce according to its needs. It substantively changed labor law and weakened both the public institutions responsible for enforcing the law and union organizing and action.

Thus, the flexibilization of labor relations began in the 1990s, persisted under the PT governments, and deepened profoundly with the passage of the labor law reform in 2017 under the government of President Michel Temer.

The Temer and Bolsonaro governments have failed to overcome the economic crisis, with negative impacts on the number of jobs and the quality of occupations. In addition to the evident neoliberal orientation of the government, the increase in unemployment and informality – with a reversal of the gains that had been achieved in PT governments – only shows that its confrontation will require structural changes, which are outside the perspectives of the current political orientation.

In addition, the current government has also intensified the flexibilization agenda, as the actions to combat the pandemic have shown. From the approval of the labor law reform in 2017 to the Covid-19 pandemic crisis, numerous interim labor measures have been put forward. Only in the Bolsonaro government, there were more than 17 provisional measures dealing with the theme, among them: MP 905/2019 of the Green and Yellow Contract, revoked in 2020, which proposed to reduce costs for employers who hired young people in their first job as well as workers over 55 years of age who were outside the formal job market. This MP was not approved, but it is still on the agenda. In addition to this MP, there were others such as MPs 927 and 936 approved in the context of the pandemic. In all of them, the logic that flexibilization would be the way to combat unemployment and informality prevailed, showing that the process is indeed one of a wide labor counter-reform that has not yet ended. It is not without reason that Streeck's (2013) claim that the implementation of an ultraliberal agenda means the liberation of market justice from social justice through a State that guarantees the implementation of reforms and neutralizes the interventions of mass democracy. In the perspective of consolidating this agenda, capital sees no problem in supporting authoritarian governments, as shown by the Brazilian experience at the present time.

References

Arend, M. (2014). A industrialização do Brasil frente a nova divisão internacional do trabalho. In: André Bojikian Calixtre, André Martins Biancarelli, and Marcos Antonio Macedo Cintra (eds.), *Presente e futuro do desenvolvimento brasileiro*, 375–422. Brasília: IPEA.

Baltar, P. (2014). Crescimento da economia e mercado de trabalho no Brasil. In: André Bojikian Calixtre, André Martins Biancarelli, and Marcos Antonio Macedo Cintra (eds.), *Presente e futuro do desenvolvimento brasileiro*, 423–468. Brasília: IPEA.

Baltar, P., Souen, J., and Campos, G.C. (2017). *Emprego e distribuição da renda*. Texto de Discussão 298.

Baltar, P., and Krein, J.D. (2013). A retomada do desenvolvimento e a regulação do mercado de trabalho no Brasil. *Caderno CRH* 26(68): 273–292.

Baltar, P., and Proni, M. (1996). Sobre o regime de trabalho no Brasil: rotatividade da mão-de-obra, emprego formal e estrutura salarial. In: C.A. Barbosa de Oliveira and J. Mattoso (eds.), *Crise e trabalho no Brasil: Modernidade ou volta ao passado*, 109–150. São Paulo: Scritta.

Barbosa de Oliveira, Carlos Alonso. (1998). Formação do mercado de trabalho no Brasil. In: Marco Antonio de Oliveira (ed.), *Economia e trabalho*, 113–127. Campinas: Ministerio do Trabalho/UNICAMP.

Belluzzo, Luiz Gonzaga. (2013). A internacionalização recente do regime do capital *XII Cátedra Raúl Prebisch no Seminário sobre neoestruturalismo e economia heterodoxa*, 2–15. Santiago do Chile: CEPAL Disponível em: http://cesit.net.br/wp/wp-content/uploads/2014/11/Carta-Social-e-do-Trabalho-27.pdf. Accessed Feb. 2017.

Belluzzo, Luiz Gonzaga, and Gabriel Galípolo. (2017). *Manda quem pode, obedece quem tem prejuízo*. São Paulo: Editora Contracorrente.

Bielschowsky, Ricardo. (2012). Estratégia de desenvolvimento e as três frentes de expansão no Brasil: um desenho conceitual. *Economia e Sociedade* 21 (special): 729–748.

Boito Jr., Armando. (2012). As bases políticas do neodesenvolvimentismo. *Fórum Econômico da FGV*. https://bibliotecadigital.fgv.br/dspace/bitstream/handle/10438/16866/Painel%203%20-%20Novo%20Desenv%20BR%20-%20Boito%20-%20Bases%20Pol%20Neodesenv%20-%20PAPER.pdf. Accessed Jan. 2016.

Boltanski, L., and Chiapello, E. (2009). *O novo espírito do capitalismo*. São Paulo: Martins Fontes.

Bresser-Pereira, L.C. (2011). An account of new developmentalism and its structuralist macroeconomics. *Brazilian Journal of Political Economy* 31(3 [123]): 493–502.

Bresser-Pereira, L.C. (2014). *A construção política do Brasil*. São Paulo: Editora 34.

Cardoso, A. (2003). *A década neoliberal e crise dos sindicatos no Brasil*. São Paulo: Boitempo.

Cardoso, A. (2013). *Ensaios de sociologia do mercado de trabalho brasileiro*. Rio de Janeiro: Editora da FGV.

Carneiro, R. (2017). *Navegando a contravento (Uma reflexão sobre o experimento desenvolvimentista do Governo Dilma Rousseff)*. Texto de Discussão 289.

Castro, B.G. (2013). *Afogados em contratos: o impacto da flexibilização do trabalho nas trajetórias dos profissionais de TI*. Ph.D. diss., Universidade Estadual de Campinas.

Colombi, A.P.F., and Krein, J.D. (2019). Labor Market and Labor Relations under the PT Governments. *Latin American Perspectives*, vol. 47.

Dal Rosso, Sadi (2008). *Mais trabalho: A intensificação do labor na sociedade contemporânea.* São Paulo: Boitempo.

Dardot, P., and Laval, C. (2016). *A nova razão do mundo.* São Paulo: Boitempo.

DIEESE. (2009). As razões para a jornada de trabalho ser de 40 horas. https://cut.org.br/system/uploads/action_file_version/a7f895967045463o8668d1fab3d712e1/file/nt-2085-20set-202009-20argumentosreduzirjornada.pdf. Accessed Jan. 2016.

DIEESE. (2017). Terceirização e precarização das condições de trabalho. *Nota Técninca,* no. 172. https://www.dieese.org.br/notatecnica/2017/notaTec172Terceirizacao.pdf. Accessed Dec. 2017.

Dweck, E., Silveira, F., and Rossi, P. (2018). Austeridade e desigualdade social no Brasil. In: Rossi, P., Dweck, E., and Oliveira, A. (eds.), *Economia Para Poucos: impactos sociais da austeridade e alternativas para o Brasil.* São Paulo: Autonomia Literária.

Filgueiras, L. (2014). A natureza e os limites do desenvolvimentismo no capitalismo dependente brasileiro. *Margem Esquerda,* no. 23: 32–38.

Filgueiras, V., and Cavalcanti, S.M. (2015). Terceirização: um problema conceitual e político. *Le Monde Diplomatique Brasil.* http://www.diplomatique.org.br/artigo.php?id=1799. Accessed Jan. 2017.

Galvão, A. (2019). Um ano de vigência da reforma trabalhista: efeitos e perspectivas para os sindicatos. In: Krein, J.D., Filgueiras, V., and Véras, R.O. (eds.), *Reforma trabalhista no Brasil: promessas e realidade.* Campinas/Brasilia: Curt Nimuendajú.

Gibb, L.S.F. (2017). *A tendência de despadronização da jornada de trabalho.* Ph.D. diss., Universidade Estadual de Campinas.

Guimarães, N.A., and Paugam, S. (2016). Work and employment precariousness: a transnational concept? *Sociologia del Lavoro,* no. 144: 55–84.

ILO (Interntional Labor Organization). (2015). Perspectivas sociales y del empleo en el mundo: el empleo en plena mutación. http://www.ilo.org/global/research/global-reports/weso/2015-changing-nature-of-jobs/WCMS_368643/lang--es/index.htm. Accessed Jan. 2016.

Kalleberg, A.J. (2011). *Good Jobs, Bad Jobs. The Rise of Polarized and Precarious Employment Systems in the United States, 1970s to 2000s.* New York: Russell Sage Foundation.

Koselleck, R. (2006). *Futuro passado: Contribuição à semântica dos tempos históricos.* Rio de Janeiro: Contraponto/PUC-Rio.

Krein, J.D. (2013). *As relações de trabalho na era do neoliberalismo no Brasil.* Campinas: Editora LTr.

Krein, J.D. (2018). O desmonte dos direitos, as novas configurações do trabalho e o esvaziamento da ação coletiva. *Tempo Social: Revista de Sociologia da USP* 30(1): 77–104.

Krein, J.D., and Biavaschi, M. (2015). Brasil: os movimentos contraditórios da regulação do trabalho dos anos 2000. *Cadernos del CENDES* 32(89): 47–82.

Krein, J.D., and Castro, B.G. (2015). As formas flexíveis de contratação e a divisão sexual do trabalho. *Análise. Friedrich Ebert Stiftung*, no. 6: 5–24.

Krein, J.D., and Colombi, A.P.F. (2019). A Reforma Trabalhista em Foco: desconstrução da proteção social em tempos de neoliberalismo autoritário. *Educ. Soc.*, Campinas, vol. 40. .

Krein, J.D., Manzano, M., Santos, A.L., and Duarte, C. (2018). Projeto BRA102. Relatório final de Pesquisa. Adopción y fortalecimiento de políticas públicas para la formalización de trabajadores/as, de manera inclusiva y con atención especial a las/os trabajadoras/es domésticas/os y otros grupos vulnerables. Genebra: CESIT/OIT.

Krein, J.D., and Teixeira, M. (2014). As controvérsias das negociações coletivas no anos 2000 no Brasil. In: Roberto Véras de Oliveira , Maria Aparecida Bridi, and Marcos Ferraz (eds.), *O sindicalismo na era Lula: entre paradoxos e novas perspectivas*, 213–246. Belo Horizonte: Fino Traço.

Martuscelli, D.E. (2014). Social-liberalismo, classes dominantes e os desafios da esquerda socialista na conjuntura atual. *Blog Marxismo 21: Dossiê esquerdas, eleições e transformações estruturais da sociedade brasileira.* https://marxismo21.org/. Accessed Nov. 2016.

Medeiros, Carlos Aguiar de. (2015). *Inserção externa, crescimento e padrões de consumo na economia brasileira.* Brasília: IPEA.

Mello, João Manoel Cardoso, and Fernando Novais. (2009). *Capitalismo tardio e sociabilidade moderna.* 2nd edition. Campinas: Editora UNESP/FACAMP.

Noronha, Eduardo G. (1998). *O modelo legislado de relações de trabalho e seus espaços normativos.* Ph.D. diss., Universidade de São Paulo.

Perossi, M. (2017). *A composiçãoda remuneração do trabalhador nas grandes empresas.* Ph.D. diss., Universidade de Campinas.

Polanyi, K. (2000) *A grande transformação: As origens da nossa época.* 2nd edition. São Paulo: Editora Compus.

Rao, E. (2013). *Tempo de trabalho no Brasil Contemporâneo: a duração da jornada de trabalho (1990–2009).* Ph.D. diss., Universidade Estadual de Campinas.

Rodgers, J. (1989). Precarious work in Western Europe: the state of the debate. In: Jerry Rodgers and Janine Rodgers, *Precarious Jobs in Labour Market Regulation*, 1–16. Geneva: ILO.

Rossi, P., and Dweck, E. (2016). Impactos do novo regime fiscal na saúde e na educação. *Cadernos de Saúde Pública* 32(12).

Sarti, F., and Hiratuka, C. (2011). *Desenvolvimento industrial: Oportunidades e desafios futuros.* Texto de Discussão 187.

Sarti, F., and Hiratuka, C. (2017). *Desempenho recente da indústria brasileira no contexto de mudanças estruturais domésticas e globais.* Texto de Discussão 290.

Silva, L.A.M. (1991). Sobre a (des)organização do trabalho no Brasil urbano. *São Paulo em Perspectiva* 4(3–4): 2–5.

Silver, B.J. (2005). *Forças do trabalho: Movimentos de trabalhadores e globalização desde 1870*. São Paulo: Boitempo.

Singer, A. (2015). Cutucando onças com vara curta: o ensaio desenvolvimentista no primeiro mandato de Dilma Rousseff (2011–2014). *Novos Estudos*, no. 102: 43–71.

Streeck, W. (2013). *Tempo comprado: A crise do capitalismo democrático*. Coimbra: Conjuntura Atual.

CHAPTER 14

A Poverty-Reducing Variety of Neoliberalism?: The Workers' Party Distributive Policies

Pedro Mendes Loureiro

1 Introduction[1]

Brazil underwent a period of growth and redistribution during the largest part of the Workers Party (*Partido dos Trabalhadores* – PT) administrations (2003–2016), which allowed for the inclusion of large sections of the population into the market as consumers.[2] Between 2003 and 2013, per capita income grew about 56%, the extreme poverty headcount decreased from 12.7% to 4.9% of the population and the Gini index of household per capita income fell from 0.58 to 0.53.[3] Several other pieces of information report the same phenomenon, indicating it was not a statistical fluke, but rather a wide-ranging process of raising the monetary income of the bottom of the social pyramid. In this vein, poverty declined from 33.9% to 13.9% of the population, whereas the Palma ratio – or the ratio between share of income appropriated by the top 10% and the bottom 40% – fell from 5.2 to 3.8. Meanwhile, GDP grew on average by 3.8% per year, including a rapid rebound from the world economic crisis of 2008, compared to an average rate of 2.5% during the 1990s.

This growth and redistribution process was part of a larger Latin American trend, which, importantly, swam against the current of global developments.

---

1   I am gratefully indebted to the several friends and colleagues who have helped me develop these arguments. In particular, I extend my thanks to Alfredo Saad-Filho, Ana Paula Colombi, Juan Grigera and the other participants of the seminar 'The nature of the PT governments', as well as to Aiko Ikemura Amaral, Angus McNelly and the members of the Latin Americanist discussion group. This research has benefitted from a grant by Capes (BEX 0840/14-9).

2   The arguments in this chapter were originally presented in Loureiro (2020a). The present chapter updates some of the discussions, in particular by indicating, in the fifth section, how changes since 2013 have affected the provision of key goods and services in Brazil through the implementation of austerity and regressive reforms.

3   Per capita income calculated in constant 2011 purchasing-power-parity (PPP) International Dollars; extreme poverty is defined as households with a per capita income below $1.90 per day (2011 International Dollars), and poverty as below $4.00 per day. Except for GDP growth figures, which are based on IBGE (2016), all data in this paragraph were extracted from the PovcalNet platform (World Bank).

Between 2002 and 2013, extreme poverty in the region[4] declined from 13.0% to 5.4% of the population, whereas the median Gini coefficient of household per capita income declined from about 0.53 to about 0.48 (World Bank 2017b). Inequality within most countries of the world, on the other hand, was on the rise since at least the late 1980s. According to Lakner and Milanovic (2016), almost all regions of the world experienced continually rising income inequality between 1988 and 2008, including an 8% increase of the Gini coefficient for 'mature economies' and a 9% hike for Sub-Saharan Africa.[5]

This markedly different trajectory of Latin American countries with regards to the world gives rise to the question of whether a break with neoliberalism occurred during the 2000s. There are two dimensions to this question. The first regards the durability of this different trajectory, i.e. its long-term feasibility. A short-term deviation from the dynamics of neoliberalism does not constitute an anti-neoliberal alternative, however much certain social indicators might improve during such a spell. Associated to this, the second dimension regards whether Latin American countries were able to explore fortuitously favourable conditions during a period of time to manoeuvre *within* the confines of neoliberalism, or whether, on the other hand, the pattern of accumulation was changed at a deeper level. It is only by transforming the bases of neoliberalism with the goal of establishing sufficiently coherent foundations for different economic and social dynamics, rather than finding wiggle-room in particular conditions, that a substantive rupture obtains.

This chapter addresses the question of whether Brazil broke with neoliberalism during the PT administrations, exploring it through the country's social structure and associated distributive policies. The focus throughout is on how and to which extent the main policies related to the distribution of income, the labour market, and the provision of key services transformed the country's social structure.

More specifically, this article explores whether the PT governments, from the point-of-view of their impact on Brazil's social structure, can be seen as a form of 'mature' (Fine and Saad-Filho 2017), 'roll-out' (Peck and Tickell 2002)

---

4 The countries included in the calculation are: Argentina, Belize, Bolivia, Brazil, Chile, Colombia, Costa Rica, the Dominican Republic, Ecuador, El Salvador, Guatemala, Guyana, Haiti, Honduras, Jamaica, Mexico, Nicaragua, Panama, Paraguay, Peru, St Lucia, Suriname, Trinidad and Tobago, Uruguay and Venezuela.

5 There are no post-2008 updates for the authors' calculations with the same level of reliability, hence a strict comparison of Latin America and the rest of the world for the 2002–2013 period is not possible. For a detailed examination of developing countries, see Simson and Savage (2020), and for Latin America see Cornia (2015).

or 'roll-forward' (Jessop 2002) neoliberalism. These three terms are used inter-changeably to indicate a second – logical, if sometimes also temporal – phase of neoliberalism characterised by the development of *specifically neoliberal* forms of participation of state power in social and economic reproduction, as opposed to the roll-back of forms that obtains during the transition into neo-liberalism.[6] For the purposes at hand, this means the development of policies that *actively* spur the *commodification* of social reproduction. This stands in contrast both to the first phase of neoliberalism, characterised by state power *dismantling* previous systems of social provisioning, and to non-neoliberal capitalist state forms, in which state power supports the circuit of capital by *de-commodifying* key aspects of social reproduction. Thus, mature neoliberal-ism simultaneously reasserts that social reproduction is growingly mediated by the market, as non-commodified forms of provisioning are forestalled, and that some measure of social inclusion will obtain, through policies that facil-itate the entry of individuals as producers and consumers of commodified goods and services (as opposed to their simple exclusion from such processes).

The main argument presented is that the PT governments did not depart from neoliberalism, but rather implemented a poverty-reducing variant of mature neoliberalism. It was poverty-reducing not only in light of the posi-tive social outcomes indicated above, but because the latter were, as argued in the text, the result of key policy decisions and their implications. Centrally, rising minimum wages (MWs), conditional cash transfers (CCTs) and greater pension coverage aimed at reducing poverty, and were effective in doing so. As knock-on effects, faster growth led to lower unemployment and labour formal-isation, also with a positive impact across the lower segments of the income distribution.

In spite of these gains for low-income households, the PT governments were nevertheless still a variety of neoliberalism, as the horizon of change was cir-cumscribed to including individuals as consumers in privatised and commodi-fied systems of provision. No clear option was made in favour of public health, education or housing, but, on the other hand, sizeable subsidies and diverse stimuli were offered so that the private sector was leading provider of the latter.

---

6   'This ("third wayist") phase focuses on the stabilization of the social relations imposed in the earlier [transition] period, the consolidation and continued expansion of the financial sector's interventions in economic and social reproduction, state management of the new modalities of international economic integration, and the introduction of specifically neo-liberal social policies both to manage the deprivations and dysfunctions created by neolib-eralism and to consolidate and reconstitute social and individual agents along neoliberal lines'(Fine and Saad-Filho 2017: 695).

Which is to say, the government actively sought to commodify the access to key services. Furthermore, this was underpinned by a state-sponsored process of financial inclusion, a dimension of commodification in its own right, which led to growing indebtedness for the population. As a result, individuals and households were further subjected to market imperatives in order to reproduce themselves.

The chapter is structured as follows. After this introduction, the second section presents the main changes to the distribution of income from a class perspective, highlighting the formalisation of low-skilled labour and the stability of top capitalist income.[7] The third section explores the drivers of these changes, showing how key policies reduced poverty. The fourth section shows how the labour market improvements were incapable of driving a substantially different pattern of accumulation. This focuses on the precarious nature of the jobs created, concentrated as they were in low-productivity, low-wage services sectors. The fifth section looks at changes in the pattern of consumption, indicating the concerted efforts to commodify the provision of health, education and housing, supported by rising household indebtedness. The sixth section concludes.

2 Changes to the Brazilian Class Structure: Redistribution amongst Workers without Affecting Capitalist Income

There were substantial policy-driven income gains for the lower sections of the income distribution in Brazil during the PT administrations. This section details these gains throughout the Brazilian social structure, approached through a typology of seven class positions. This typology is based on the command over capital (and conversely the need to sell one's labour power), the command over scarce skills, and protection by the prevailing labour laws (i.e. the formality or not of the employment relation).[8] Those not in active employment arc classified as unemployed/inactive or pensioners, as appropriate. Based on this, households can be classified into one of the following seven categories (see Table 14.2 in the Appendix for precise classification procedures).

---

7 This section has a more detailed discussion of the class typology adopted than that present in Loureiro (2020a).
8 For analyses based on similar, but more complex typologies, see Figueiredo Santos (2015) and Souza and Carvalhaes (2014). See Saad-Filho (2014) for an analysis of the political and social features of the Brazilian class structure following a similar typology.

1. Large employers: those who employ more than 10 workers. This is the most privileged position, based on profiting over large amounts of labour, and is consequently the one most concentrated at the top of the income distribution. Even if the data used severely underreport their income, as household surveys are known to do, large employers can nevertheless still be found at the very top of the distribution.

2. Small employers: employers of 10 or less employees, this is an intermediate position based on commanding a smaller amount of labour. In practice, they mostly receive mixed income, due to their own work as supervisors or managers and due to profiting from the labour of others.

3. Professional workers: employees or self-employed workers in high-skilled occupations. They are also in an intermediate position, as they still have to sell their labour power but can do so at relatively more advantageous conditions given their command over scarce skills. Professional workers, and to a lesser extent small employer, are the middle-class in Brazilian society.

4. Low-skilled, formal workers: formal employees or self-employed workers that contribute to social security, in low-skilled occupations. This group have to sell their labour power for a living without the bargaining power that scarce skills offer but are covered by basic labour laws and social protection. Although there is considerable fluidity between formal and informal positions, given that individuals frequently shift between them, the key distinguishing element is that formal workers are paid at least the minimum wage.

5. Low-skilled, informal workers: informal employees or self-employed workers that do not contribute to social security, in low-skilled occupations. These are the most precarious workers, as they do not command scarce skills and are not even covered by the prevailing labour legislation. Together with their formal counterpart, these two groups are the backbone of the Brazilian social structure, responding for about 80% of the population and contributing with the largest part of labour-power sold.

6. The unemployed or inactive: those classified as looking for jobs but unable to find them during the reference period, or households without any members in the labour market. This is the most destitute group, incapable of entering into paid employment and relying, when available, on social security and cash transfers.

7. Pensioners: former workers who receive private or state pensions.

Table 14.1 shows the size and the relative per capita income of these seven class positions in the beginning of the PT administrations (2003–2005) and towards the end of their successful phase (2011–2013). The information presented is based on data from the National Household Sample Survey (*Pesquisa Nacional por Amostra de Domicílios* – PNAD). 2013 is taken as the final year of the analysis because it is the last moment when the growth and redistribution process was arguably still in place. After this year, GDP growth declined to less than 1% per year in 2014 and was in steep decline until then-president Dilma Rousseff was impeached in 2016 (IBGE). Therefore, the analysis is restricted to the successful growth and redistribution phase.

Table 14.1 shows both changes and continuities, with high levels of inequality prevailing throughout. At the end of the growth and redistribution phase, the Brazilian social structure had more than a third of households in the considerably vulnerable situation of low-skilled, informal workers, with an income about 40% less than the average. Professional workers grew by 1.9 percentage points, a substantial relative increase of nearly 30% over eight years. Combined to small employers, this amounted, however, to a middle-class only slightly larger than 10% of the population in the end of the period. These positions, if not plentiful, were considerably privileged: their relative income was about two and a half times the average. Naturally, this was a far shot from the top layer of large employers, who at 0.6% of the population displayed a mostly constant relative income of about five and a half times the average.[9]

If stark inequalities and vulnerability continued to prevail, there were nevertheless two sizeable changes over the analysed decade. First and foremost, the formalisation of low-skilled labour guaranteed a higher income and access to basic labour rights for about 8% more households. Formal workers became more numerous than their informal counterpart, an important process insofar as their income was about a third higher. Second, the relative income of professional workers decreased by about 16%, reducing the privilege of this group. This can be equated to a fall in the social ladder for the traditional middle-class, the only position who really lost in relative terms.[10]

These results, pointing to a redistribution of income amongst workers whilst preserving the position of capitalists, are reinforced by recent studies using tax

---

9   Given that the Palma ratio of income inequality decreased, as stated in the introduction, and that the relative income of large employers was stable, this indicates that it was the relative fall of high salaries for the professional middle-class that drove the decrease of the Palma ratio. This is further supported by tax data, discussed below.

10   Figueiredo Santos (2015) furthermore shows that, over a similar period, certain middle-class positions – such as non-managerial professionals – also lost in absolute terms. See also Loureiro (2020b).

TABLE 14.1   Composition and relative income of the Brazilian class structure in two periods, 2003–2005 and 2011–2013

Class position	Population-share			Relative per capita income* (multiples of average household per capita income)		
	2003–2005 average	2011–2013 average	Absolute change	2003–2005 average	2011–2013 average	Relative change
Large employers	0.6%	0.6%	-0.1%	5.77	5.45	-5.7%
Small employers	4.6%	3.4%	-1.2%	2.34	2.31	-1.3%
Professional workers	6.6%	8.5%	1.9%	2.99	2.51	-16.1%
Low-skilled, formal workers	36.4%	42.0%	5.6%	0.93	0.91	-2.3%
Low-skilled, informal workers	43.1%	35.1%	-8.1%	0.55	0.60	9.0%
Unemployed or inactive	2.1%	2.7%	0.6%	0.23	0.15	-35.5%
Pensioners	6.5%	7.8%	1.3%	1.19	1.05	-12.2%

Note: * = relative per capita income is the mean household per capita income of the group in question divided by the whole population's per capita income. In 2003–2005, for example, a household of professional workers on average had an income of 2.99 times that of all households taken together.
SOURCE: PREPARED BY THE AUTHOR BASED ON DATA FROM PNAD, IBGE

data (Gobetti and Orair 2016; M. Medeiros and Castro 2018).[11] Two key results
are relevant for the purposes at hand. First, the decrease of inequality might
have been much smaller than that measured by the PNAD. Although there is
uncertainty surrounding these estimates, Morgan (2017) calculates that the
top 1% in Brazil appropriated a somewhat stable share of national income
throughout the 2000s, about 27%. Second, capital was the main factor behind
the rise at the top, as income derived from it (profits, interest, dividends ...)
responded for an increasing share of top incomes. In sum, the highest-income
households in Brazil managed to maintain their position through the control
over capital.

Overall, the data point to a limited distribution between different categories of workers, without affecting the position of capital. The distribution was
limited insofar as it still left major vulnerabilities in the social structure, particularly as regards the sizeable share of informal workers. It was based on distributing income between categories of workers, given that the only sizeable
group to have lost in relative terms were professional workers, to the benefit
of informal, low-skilled ones. Furthermore, it did not imply losses for capital,
since the income of employers, large and small, was basically stable over the
whole period. Therefore, the Brazilian social structure was not transformed in
a way that consistently empowered workers, and neither were key sources of
vulnerability eliminated. On the other hand, what did take place was a certain
inclusion of low-skilled workers into formal labour markets, the maintenance
of the position of capitalists at the very top, and a decrease of middle-class
privilege.

3   Drivers of Redistribution: Minimum Wage Hikes, Labour
       Formalisation and Social Security Benefits

The drivers of the processes presented above can be explained with the help
of Figure 14.1 and Figure 14.2, which show the contribution of different sources
of income along the distribution of income. Both figures order households by
their per capita income in the X-axis, from lowest to highest, and display on
the Y-axis the average composition of income for that percentile of the distribution. Figure 14.1 refers to the beginning of the PT administrations (2003),
whereas Figure 14.2 brings the same information for 2013. Eight income sources

---

11   Data from tax returns are better able to capture the income at the very top of the distri-
      bution, whereas household surveys are generally better for the lower parts of the distribu-
      tion. Neither source is without its problems, so they should be taken as complementary.

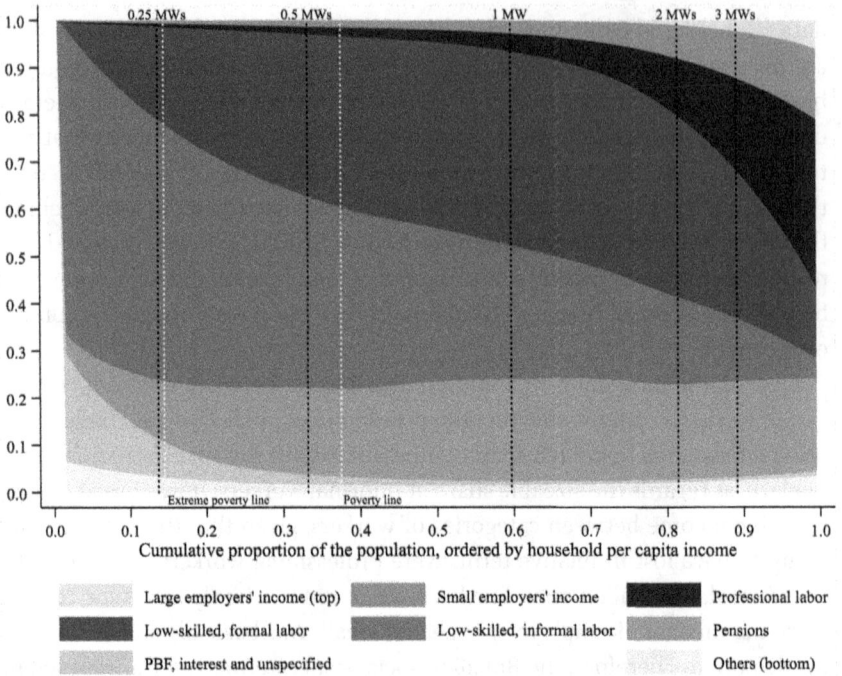

FIGURE 14.1 Contribution of different sources of income along the household per capita
income distribution in Brazil, 2003, and (extreme) poverty incidence
Notes: Large employers' income is the income reported by employers with more
than 10 employees; small employers' income is the income reported by employers
with 10 or less employees; professional labour income is the income of workers
in occupations that require higher education; low-skilled, formal (informal)
labour income is the income of workers in occupations that do not require higher
education and are in formal (informal) working arrangements; pensions are state
and private pension income; PBF, interest and unspecified is the income from
government benefits, savings accounts and other unspecified sources (see note
12); and others is the income from all other sources (such as rent and donations).
The (extreme) poverty line corresponds to a household per capita income of
(US$1.90) US$4.00 per day, converted according to the World Bank's estimate
of the constant 2011 purchasing-power-parity exchange rate. Lowess smoothing
applied to the curves.
SOURCE: PREPARED BY THE AUTHOR BASED ON DATA FROM PNAD, IBGE

are accounted for, six of which are associated to the revenues of the class positions presented above (e.g. the wages of low-skilled, formal occupations, and
the profits and mixed income of small employers). Beyond the income associated to these positions, the figures also present the contribution of social

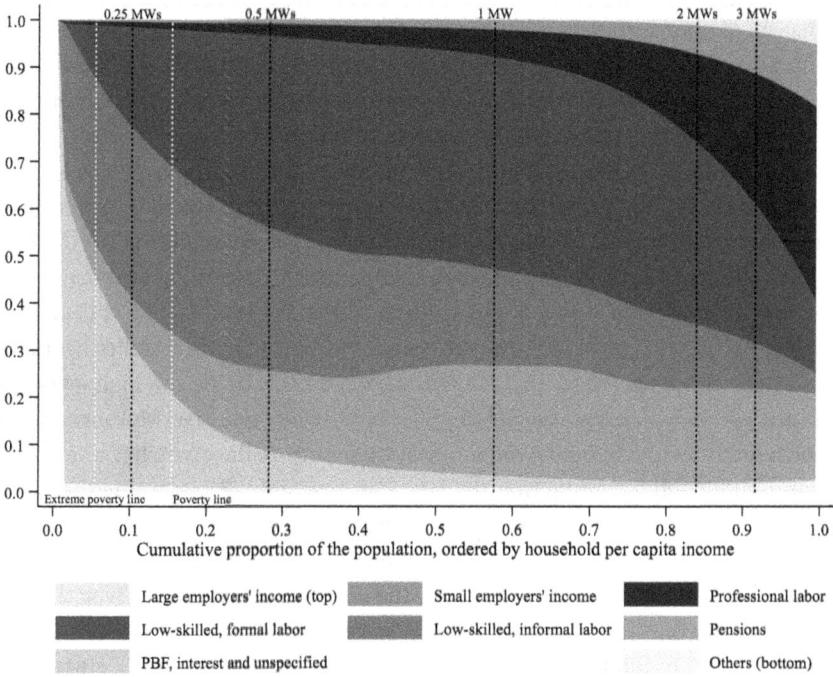

FIGURE 14.2 Contribution of different income sources along the household per capita income
distribution in Brazil, 2013, and (extreme) poverty incidence
Notes: see definitions in the note to Figure 14.1.
SOURCE: PREPARED BY THE AUTHOR BASED ON DATA FROM PNAD, IBGE

security benefits, in particular the CCT programme *Programa Bolsa Família*
(PBF, Family Allowance Programme),[12] and a small remainder category for all
other forms of income.

Figure 14.1 shows how, in 2003, government benefits (excluding pensions)
accounted for a very small share of the income of all households. To a very large
extent, most households relied on low-skilled, informal labour. For the bottom
40% of households, the latter was the main source of income, above which it
was superseded by low-skilled, formal wages. Professional occupations in turn
started to be relevant really only for the top 10% of households, at a per capita

---

12   The household survey used (PNAD) reports the income of social security benefits (exclud-
       ing pensions) together with that of interest from savings accounts and other unspecified
       sources of income. This is far from ideal, but it can be safely assumed that PBF and other
       low-value benefits, such as the Continued Assistance Programme (*Benefício de Prestação
       Continuada* – BPC), respond for the largest share of this income source, particularly
       towards the end of the analysed period. See Hoffmann (2013) for a detailed discussion.

income of approximately three MWs. Finally, pensions were relevant through-out most of the distribution, which highlights both the large spread in pension benefits – from one MW for most former workers, to the salaries of top civil servants – and their centrality for household budgets throughout Brazil.[13]

The position in the distribution of fractions and multiples of the MW is particularly telling about the structure of inequality in Brazil.[14] A per cap-ita income of one MW would already have put a household amongst the top 40% (which, as seen below, did not change much), revealing striking levels of inequality. Importantly, about a third of the population had an income below half a MW (representative of households with two low-skilled workers and two school-age children), the reason behind this being the high levels of informality – which are associated to incomes below one MW. Moreover, such households would be below the international poverty line, which is a very low standard indeed, meaning that the MW was incapable of sustaining the basic needs of a person and a dependent. Even more striking, a per capita income of a quarter of the MW – representative of a four-person household with one low-skilled, formal worker – was below the extreme poverty line. Given the lat-ter's definition as the minimum income necessary to buy a sufficient amount of food, it is not too far off the mark to say that the 2003 MW was a starvation wage for a family of four.

The major changes that occurred during the decade were in the bottom half of the distribution, particularly rising PBF transfers and low-skilled labour for-malisation. If benefits were a small portion of household income in 2003, ten years later they were the major source for the bottom 10% and were relevant for all of the lowest quartile.[15] The big change for the second quartile was in turn labour formalisation, as low-skilled formal wages became the largest form of income for this quarter of the population. The share of pensions did not increase substantially at any percentile, meaning that they grew at approx-imately the same level throughout the whole distribution. Hence, given the overall decrease of inequality, pensions were a contributing factor in this. The top half was much more stable, however, highlighting that distributional gains were concentrated in the bottom half.

---

13   For the impact of different kinds of pensions, see Hoffmann (2009).

14   The reason for fractions being relevant is that, although full-time formal workers always receive at least the MW, its translation into household per capita income will depend on the size and number of active workers in the household. The most representative values are for a quarter and half of the MW.

15   For an analysis of how CCTs are the key form of social policy in neoliberalism, see Saad-Filho (2015).

Two of the main distributive processes discussed above – labour formalisation and rising MWs – can be seen in the position of the MW in the distribution. The MW rose in real terms by about 70% between 2003 and 2013, deflated by the National Price Index for Consumers (*Índice Nacional de Preços ao Consumidor* – INPC), whilst, as indicated above, the share of low-skilled, formal workers' households increased by eight percentage points. The combination of these two processes multiplied their individual effects, as more workers began to receive at least the MW (through formalisation) and their income was increased further by rising real MWs. Rising MWs also affected informal workers being paid close to the MW, through what is known as the 'lighthouse effect', as well as employees whose wages were indexed to (low) multiples of the MW and thus got readjusted (see Maurizio and Vázquez 2016). Furthermore, in Brazil a series of social benefits and low-value public pensions are indexed to the MW, increasing the latter's impact on the economy (Orair and Gobetti 2010).

Labour formalisation and rising MWs thus decreased the percentage of the population receiving less than certain fractions of the MW and raised their real income. There was a substantial fall of five percentage points in the population with a per capita income below half a MW, whose rising value shifted it in relation to the poverty lines. In a process of qualitative import, one MW became capable of putting a worker and a dependent considerably above the poverty line in 2013. The latter is a very low standard, unrepresentative of the level above which individuals are not deprived of key goods but rising above it does mean that individuals can enter the market as consumers for more than very basic necessities. In other words, rising MWs alongside labour formalisation made large sections of the population consumers of a much broader and more sophisticated array of goods, as they escaped the lowest levels of destitution.

At this point, it should be noted that raising the MW – if not accompanied by growing non-compliance with the relevant legislation – might seem antithetical to neoliberal policymaking, as it implies a broad increase in the value of (simple) labour-power. However, if the *rise* of the MW was substantial during the PT governments, which does nuance their characterisation as neoliberal, looking at it from a longer-term perspective shows the MW did not reach historically high *levels*. In fact, in 2013 it was some 15% below the average real MW of the 1955–1964 period, and just 20% above the 1982 value.[16] What the PT did in terms of the MW, therefore, was to revert the direst aspects of the 1980s debt crisis and neoliberalism, but not move beyond the latter.

---

16   Data from Ipeadata. After 1964, the MW decreased and was roughly stable during most of the military dictatorship (1964–1985), as from 1964 until 1982 it was on average some 17% below the 2013 value. It lost nearly half its value from 1982 until its nadir in 1994, coming

In sum, this section has shown how the Brazilian social structure under the PT governments saw a change between categories of workers, whilst the position of capital was much more stable. Low-skilled workers gained the most, whilst professional workers as a group lost in relative and, in some cases, even in absolute terms. The drivers behind this were CCTs, rising MWs, labour formalisation and greater pension coverage. These processes had a large impact on the bottom half of the distribution but were ineffective in changing top incomes. Schematically, CCTs affected the very bottom, formalisation the first quartile, and rising MWs and pensions the second – and to an extent the third – quartile. Together, they reduced poverty substantially and, through the relative stability that formal employment offers, inserted millions of individuals into the market as consumers of a broader swathe of goods and services.

4   Formalisation without Quality Jobs: Limitations of the Gains in the Labour Market

This section explores how the labour market improvements were limited insofar as, if there were indeed gains from the formalisation of low-skilled labour, the formal jobs created were of low quality. In particular, the sectors that increased their employment the most were low-paid, low-productivity services, especially sales and construction, leading to a growing concentration of posts paying between one and three MWs. If this was an improvement compared to the preceding period, it does not amount to a transformation of the productive and social structure capable of either challenging the ingrained inequalities of the Brazilian economy or driving a development process. Which is to say, it could not break with neoliberalism, but only manoeuvred within it.

Data from National Accounts show that, between 2003 and 2013, construction and sales alone accounted for a third of net jobs created (IBGE). By adding transportation and storage, lodging and personal services, and for-profit health and education, this value reaches about 60%. These sectors share three characteristics that make them incapable of being the motors of an inclusive, high-wage process of development. They are all low-paid, with average wages about 30% below the national average; low-productivity, with labour productivity (value added per worker) also about 30% below average; and they are services for personal consumption, which imply low linkages with the rest of

to represent but 40% of what it would in 2013. Before the rise under the PT governments, the MW recovered by about 30% until 2002.

the productive structure and few opportunities for dynamic productivity gains. The employment they created might have improved the living conditions of workers, but they are incapable of driving a different pattern of accumulation with long-term perspectives of rapid growth and social inclusion.[17]

An effect of this shift of employment towards sectors with low dynamism was to increase the number of low-paid occupations. Between 2003 and 2013, the share of paid employees – excluding therefore self-employed and employers – that received between one and three MWs increased by ten percentage points (PNAD). On the lower end, this is explained by labour formalisation, with which the share of workers getting less than a MW fell by some four percentage points.[18] There was, however, a curtailing of the other end, as the number of jobs paying more than three MWs decreased by six percentage points, or about one million posts (PNAD). In this, it is important to notice that three key sectors whose employment-share grew by five percentage points – construction, wholesale and retail trade, and food and lodging – had very few high-paying jobs (13% of jobs in the sectors paid more than 3 MWs, against 20% for the whole economy in 2003, according to the PNAD). In other words, with the rise of low-paid, low-productivity sectors, fewer good-quality jobs were created.[19]

Two further processes negatively impacted the quality of the jobs created during the PT governments: outsourcing and high churning rates. The Interunion Department of Statistics and Socioeconomic Studies (*Departamento Intersindical de Estatística e Estudos Econômicos* – DIEESE) estimates that approximately 26% of formal workers were outsourced in 2014, up from 24% in 2007 (DIEESE 2017). Outsourced workers have lower wages, fewer benefits, less stable jobs, and face a harder task to organise themselves in trade unions, even when they are formal employees (Antunes and Druck 2013). Representatively,

---

17 Rugitsky (2016) shows how regressive structural change (i.e. the shift of labour to low-value-added sectors with few opportunities for dynamic productivity gains) and income redistribution were connected during this period, as rising incomes at the bottom of the distribution led to higher demand for wage goods and hence low-skilled workers to produce them, increasing wages and reinitiating the process. See also Rugitsky (2019).

18 Almost half of low-skilled, informal employees received less than a MW in 2003 and in 2013 (PNAD), hence one of the main features of becoming a formal employee is to receive at least a MW.

19 The decrease of high-paying jobs is also partially due to the rising real value of the MW, which implies using a moving target. Nevertheless, the MW is the legal reference for the remuneration of simple labour, hence its multiples are a better proxy for complex occupations than is a standard of real income. Excluding the self-employed, in 2003 about 20% of low-skilled, formal workers and 65% of professional workers received more than three MWs, decreasing, respectively, to 10% and to 50% in 2013 (PNAD). For informal, low-skilled workers these numbers were 5% and 3%.

in 2013, formal employees in outsourcing-intensive sectors had average wages a quarter below those in other sectors (excluding agriculture) and half the average job tenure (DIEESE and CUT 2014: 14). Likewise, the labour market churning rate for formal private employees[20] was not only extremely high in 2013, with forty-four dismissals for every one hundred outstanding jobs, but it was higher than in 2003, when there were forty-one dismissals to one hundred active jobs (DIEESE 2016). Formal jobs might have been created, but they were precarious and without stability, further blurring the distinction between formal and informal jobs that began with neoliberalism.

5   Consumption Patterns: State-Sponsored Commodification of Health Services, Education and Housing

CCTs, labour formalisation and higher MWs raised income above near-subsistence levels, whilst also partially integrating workers into formal circuits of commodity production, with the flipside of enabling access to a range of more sophisticated goods. This did not happen mainly through public provision, however, but rather through growing circuits for the private supply of commodified goods and services. In particular, through several state subsidies and growing indebtedness these workers became the consumers of private health, education and housing. This section thus shows how the PT's policies also acted on the consumption side to enlarge the circuit of capital and incorporate into it growing masses of workers-as-consumers – i.e. how the government policies had interconnecting effects that spurred the commodification of social reproduction.[21]

---

20   The churning rate is defined here as the number of jobs shed in a year at the employers' initiative divided by the outstanding stock of jobs at the end of the year. It thus excludes the cases where the employee asked for the work contract to be terminated, and only considers formal, private jobs.

21   Rossi et al. (2019a) argue, based on the works of Celso Furtado, that limitations of the changes in the productive structure during the analysed period made the PT's growth model incapable of driving a long-lasting and inclusive process of development. The arguments of this section are complementary to the authors' analyses, adding an investigation into the provision and consumption of key goods and services, specifically as regards their state-sponsored and state-subsidised commodification. Although an explicit 'Furtadian' viewpoint is not adopted here, Furtado's later works (e.g. 2021a, 2021b) are closely aligned to the arguments presented, as in this stage he integrates circuits of consumption and production into the analysis and is more critical of 'standard' notions of development,

5.1   The Commodification of Health Services

The provision of health services in Brazil occurs through the public and private sphere, but with several public subsidies for the latter. The country has got a universal healthcare system (*Sistema Único de Saúde* – SUS), free at the point of access, which was modelled after the British National Health Service (NHS). It has been, however, chronically underfunded (Mendes and Weiller 2015). At the same time, there are four main channels through which public money subsidises the private, commodified provision of healthcare: personal income tax exemptions for health expenditures; tax exemptions for companies' expenditures on health services for employees (which usually means offering health insurance at subsidised prices); tax exemptions for medicines and their inputs; and tax exemptions for charitable hospitals (Ocké-Reis and Gama 2016).

During the analysed period, the PT did not revert this two-pronged approach in which an underfunded public system coexisted with a subsidised private one. Ocké-Reis and Gama (2016) estimate that health-related tax exemptions amounted to about R$25 billion in 2013, with a real increase of about 70% since 2003. These exemptions were, moreover, a constant share of the Health Ministry budget, just under a third. Instead of strengthening the provision of public healthcare, therefore, what the PT's policies did was to offer subsidies so formalised workers could opt out of the public system. Consequently, out-of-pocket expenditures on health was the item that increased the most in household budgets between 2002 and 2009 (C.A. Medeiros 2015; Posenato Garcia et al. 2015), while the profits of private health insurance providers nearly tripled in real terms between 2003 and 2011 (Ocké-Reis 2014). Thus, the commodification of health services continued hand-in-hand with its public counterpart, underpinned by rising demand for private healthcare (through higher income) and public support (through fiscal incentives) for its commodified, for-profit provision.[22]

5.2   The Commodification of Education

A similar situation obtains with education, where a public and free system, extending from childcare to post-graduate degrees but with a severe shortage of vacancies, coexists with a subsidised private system. Focusing on higher

---

explicitly calling for a reconsideration of the meaning and goals of development (see also Loureiro et al. 2021).

22   Since the turn to austerity in Brazil, which began in 2015 but massively increased under Michel Temer's (2016–2018) government, access to healthcare has being made more precarious and commodified in the country, but with a greater weight of underfunding as a driver of this process (Menezes et al. 2020).

education institutions (HEI), the private sector has for decades enrolled the majority of students (Chaves and Amaral 2016). In order to enable the private sector to be the main provider of higher education, however, different subsidies were in place. Three main mechanisms are relevant in this regard: personal income tax exemptions for expenditures on education; the University for Everyone Programme (*Programa Universidade para Todos* – ProUni), which offers full or half tuition-fees waivers for low-income students in private HEIs (via tax exemptions for the HEIs in which they are enrolled); and the federal, subsidised student-loan programme Student Financing Fund (*Fundo de Financiamento Estudantil* – FIES).

The policies of the PT governments for higher education focused predominantly on expanding the for-profit, commodified segment of the private sector, albeit tempered by a simultaneous increase of funding for the public sector (Carvalho 2014). Tellingly, although enrolment in public HEIs increased by two thirds between 2003 and 2014 – a massive expansion by any account – *their share of total higher-education enrolment fell from 31% to 25%* over the same period (Chaves and Amaral 2016). Another important initiative, whose impact extends far beyond the scope of this chapter, was the introduction of racial and income-based quotas for students in HEI since 2012, which, if they did not revert the broad privatising trend, have mitigated the stratified access to higher education in Brazil (see Lehmann 2018).

Subsidies to private HEIs and loans to student-consumers allowed for this increased dominance of the private sector in the provision of higher education. In 2015, some R$15 billion went to the FIES programme and around R$1 billion to ProUni (Chaves and Amaral 2016), both of which directly or indirectly guaranteed the solvency of providing higher education as a commodity. Overall, it is estimated that in 2014 over R$30 billion of public money was destined to the private education sector in its different levels (Rezende Pinto 2016). One of the effects of this process is that Kroton, a Brazilian company founded in 1966, became the largest private education company in the world in 2014, reporting a revenue of US$2.5 billion and a net income of US$0.64 billion in 2016.[23] Access to higher education thus expanded tremendously during the period, including efforts to reduce its racialised and class-based segregation, under the aegis of expanding commodification.[24]

---

23   On the business strategies of for-profit HEI institutions, see Carvalho (2013).
24   Similar to the case of access to healthcare, austerity has led to a substantial and probably long-lasting underfunding of public education in recent years, changing the drivers of the commodification education at different levels (Rossi et al. 2019b).

5.3   *The Commodification of Housing*

In the provision of housing, the PT governments likewise shifted towards state-subsidised commodification. In the 1980s and 1990s, Brazil's housing policies were dismantled, leading to two decades with no substantial public investment in social housing, but rather a series of small-scale, market-enabling initiatives that sought to assert the primacy of private provision and financing for the sector (Valença and Bonates 2010). After this 'transition-phase' into neoliberalism, the government launched the programme My House, My Life (*Minha Casa, Minha Vida* – MCMV) in 2009. Differently from the previous model, MCMV directed vast public resources to stimulate the market-provision of housing for low- and middle-income households, attempting to mitigate deprivation by promoting commodification (Sengupta 2019).

MCMV was indeed capable of expanding the housing stock and homeownership, simultaneously creating profitable income streams for private companies and increasing household indebtedness. It involved the state, private construction companies and the state-owned bank Caixa Econômica Federal, with different arrangements depending on the income levels of the consumers.[25] Lowest-income consumers received a discount of up to 90% on the value of the housing unit, which the state paid directly to the construction companies, whereas other groups were offered subsidised credit. In all cases, the remaining value of the properties was to be paid through a mortgage provided by Caixa Econômica Federal. Official data indicate that about two million housing units were delivered until 2014, at a cost of R$88 billion in subsidies and generating debt obligations of R$131 billion.[26]

Differently from health and education, to which access increased under the PT administration, the overall effects on housing were more ambiguous. The estimated housing shortage in the country fluctuated around six million units from 2009 until 2014, largely due to a sharp rise in households paying excessive rent, i.e. low-income households paying over 30% of their monthly income as rent (Viana et al. 2019: 292). Rising rents were in turn caused by a heated real estate market, ripe with speculation, which resulted from the overall commodified approach of the housing policy (Maricato 2013; Rolnik et al. 2015). The housing policy of the PT governments thus included certain low-income households as consumers, subjected others to excessive rent in a speculative real estate market and created profit-streams in the state-subsidised, expanding circuits of production and consumption of housing as a commodity.

---

25   For details of the rules of the programme, see Krause et al. (2013).

26   Data for MCMV until December 2014 can be found in http://dados.gov.br/dataset/minha-casa-minha-vida.

6   Financial Underpinnings of the Commodification of
        Social Reproduction

The commodification of social reproduction was underpinned and accelerated by the insertion of lower-income groups into formal financial circuits (i.e.
financial inclusion), in itself a dimension of commodification, which, furthermore, carried attendant chains of debt. Data from the Findex database (World
Bank 2017a) show that from 2011 (the earliest available year) until 2014 several indicators of financial inclusion increased in Brazil: the ownership of an
account with a financial institution increased from 56% to 68% of the population, debit card ownership rose from 41% to 59%, and credit card ownership
rose from 29% to 32%. For the lowest-earning 40% of the population, these
changes were respectively from 38% to 57%, from 24% to 42%, and from 15%
to 20%, indicating *faster relative and absolute rises* for lower-income groups.
Indebtedness followed suit, although the available data are not disaggregated
by income level: between 2005 and 2014, the ratio of household indebtedness
to yearly income grew from 18% to 46%, whilst the share of income used to pay
interest and principal on loans increased from 16% to 22% (BCB).[27]

The connections between growing indebtedness and the commodification
of education (student loans) and of housing (subsidised mortgages) have been
presented above, but one final key policy must be discussed: the financial
innovation of *crédito consignado*, or payroll loans (for the connection between
CCTs and financialisation, see Lavinas 2017). Instituted through a specific
legislation in 2003, this modality of personal credit is characterised by debt
repayments being directly deducted from (formal employment) wages or state
pensions.[28] This is in effect a sort of insurance for the lender, which, in the case
of state pensions or civil servants, is offered by the government. This greatly
reduces the risks of default and allows for comparatively lower interest rates
for the borrowers, their main attractive.

The central element about payroll loans is how they fit in with the overall
pattern of accumulation, given their strict association with formal employment and pensions – and, as shown above, both increased substantially. With
this, acceding to formal employment came with the added benefit of accessing

---

27   The results of the rise of MCMV-related debts can be seen in that private indebtedness
      (outstanding debt in relation to yearly income) excluding mortgages stabilised after 2010
      and decreased after 2011, whereas if one includes mortgages it rose by some further ten
      percentage points until 2015 (BCB 2017).
28   For details of the successive regulatory changes and incentives given to payroll loans, see
      Oliveira and Wolf (2016).

credit at better rates. The rise of payroll loans was thus an endogenous result of the pattern of accumulation, accelerating growth as a central element of the overall macroeconomic scenario (Oliveira and Wolf 2016). Consequently, payroll loans were the fastest-growing modality of personal credit, jumping from a nominal stock of R$10 billion to R$220 billion between January 2004 and December 2013, whereas non-payroll loans went from R$20 billion to R$98 billion (BCB).

In sum, this section has explored how the PT governments operated at different junctures to stimulate the commodification of key services, underpinned by the extension of subsidised finance. From legislative innovations to subsidies and tax exemptions, different stimuli enabled the private sector to take the leading role in provisioning. On the one hand, this alleviated deprivation across different dimensions, such as by extending higher education to broader swathes of the population and reducing financial exclusion. This side of the equation allows the characterisation of the PT governments as poverty-reducing. They were a mature variety of neoliberalism; however, insofar as multi-dimensional deprivation was reduced by furthering the state-sponsored commodification of these dimensions. In the process, public money increasingly became the guarantor of financial rents and of the profits of firms in different sectors. The policies of the PT acted therefore not only to increase the income of those at the bottom (and the very top) of the ladder, but also to guarantee that, as these individuals improved their conditions, they could consume goods and services provided by private companies in highly lucrative conditions.

7   Final Remarks

This chapter has analysed changes in the distribution of income and in the provisioning of key services in Brazil, particularly health, education and housing, to argue that the PT governments constituted a poverty-reducing variety of neoliberalism. State power was used to include individuals into ever-expanding formal circuits of commodity production and consumption, as the government provided income to the poorest, drove wage gains in the labour market, passed legislation to allow for financial innovations, and subsidised the provision of privately provided services. Deprivation in multiple dimensions was thus reduced, but through further commodification of social reproduction and deepening chains of debt. This is broadly in line with 'mature' neoliberalism, where state power is directed not to dissemble previous patterns of accumulation and modes of societalisation, as happens during the transition into neoliberalism, but rather to lay down a specifically neoliberal state and its particular forms of social and economic policy. The upshot, in Brazil, was that social mobility did occur, but it came to mean exiting poverty, getting a formal, low-skilled job and accessing credit at lower interest rates to pay for state-subsidised private health, education and housing.

Although it is beyond this chapter to offer an in-depth explanation of *why* the PT governments implemented a poverty-reducing variety of neoliberalism, it is worth pointing out its place in the party's broader strategy for social change. Whether seen as centred on the combination of gradual reforms and a conservative pact (Singer 2012), or as a government for the internal bourgeoisie but supported by formal and informal workers (Boito Jr. and Galvão 2012), there is widespread agreement that large domestic capitalists and those at the bottom of the social ladder (unequally) shared in the gains during the PT governments. Fundamentally, the PT adopted a strategy whose legitimacy was anchored on guaranteeing growth and income redistribution, predicated on these goals being reachable without social confrontation (Loureiro and Saad-Filho 2019). Catering to the bottom and the very top through pragmatism and class conciliation is the expression, at the level of political strategies, of poverty-reducing neoliberalism: it is the attempt to use state power to manoeuvre *within* the dominant pattern of accumulation by *reducing deprivation through the expanded commodification of social reproduction*. Consequently, this strategy for reducing deprivation was only viable insofar as the conditions for class-conciliatory politics were present.

Ultimately, the intellectual purchase of deeming the PT governments neoliberal is to indicate the *limits* of what they represented and what could be achieved through them. If the characterisation is correct, it means that the party's project under Lula and Dilma was not an alternative *to* neoliberalism, potentially efficacious over a longer period of time and capable of, at different levels, implementing a durable new pattern of accumulation, altering deep structures of social inequality and stratification, prioritising the de-commodification of social reproduction and so on. The PT's projected represented, on the other hand, a comparatively more inclusive variety *of* neoliberalism, hence only viable under particular and restrictive circumstances. With the closing of this window of opportunity, progressive politics in Brazil have to look beyond the strategy the PT implemented in order to confront the enduring forms of neoliberalism and successfully promote social justice.

Appendix: Definitions of the Class Typology

TABLE 14.2   Definitions of class positions

Class position	Position in the occupation	Occupational category	Size of the company	Access to social security (pensions)
Large employer	Employer	Irrelevant	> 10 employees	Irrelevant
Small employer	Employer	Irrelevant	≤ 10 employees	Irrelevant
Professional workers	Self-employed, Formal employee, Informal employee	High-skilled*	Irrelevant	Irrelevant
Low-skilled, formal workers	Self-employed, Formal employee	Low-skilled**	Irrelevant	Yes
Low-skilled, informal workers	Self-employed, Informal employee, Unpaid worker	Low-skilled**	Irrelevant	No
Unemployed/Inactive	Unemployed or inactive	—	—	Irrelevant
Pensioners	—	—	—	Yes

Notes: * = major group in the International Standard Classification of Occupations (ISCO-08) equal to 1 (legislators, senior officials and managers) and 2 (professionals). ** = major group in ISCO-88 different from 1 or 2. Armed forces personnel are excluded from calculations.
SOURCE: PREPARED BY THE AUTHOR

References

Antunes, R., and Druck, G. (2013). A terceirização como regra? *Revista do TST* 79(4): 214–231.

BCB. (2017). Séries Temporais, *SGS*. https://www3.bcb.gov.br/sgspub/, accessed 21/10/2016.

Boito Jr., A., and Galvão, A. (eds.). (2012). *Política e classes sociais no Brasil dos anos 2000*. São Paulo: Alameda.

Carvalho, C.H.A. (2013). A mercantilização da educação superior brasileira e as estratégias de mercado das instituições lucrativas. *Revista Brasileira de Educação* 18(54): 761–776.

Carvalho, C.H.A. (2014). Política para a educação superior no governo Lula: expansão e financiamento. *Revista do Instituto de Estudos Brasileiros* 58: 209–244.

Chaves, V.L.J., and Amaral, N.C. (2016). Política de expansão da educação superior no Brasil – o ProUni e o FIES como financiadores do setor privado. *Educação em Revista* 32(4): 49–72.

Cornia, G.A. (2015). Income inequality in Latin America: Recent decline and prospects for its further reduction, *WIDER Working Papers*, 2015(20): 1–29. https://www.wider.unu.edu/sites/default/files/wp2015-020.pdf.

DIEESE. (2016). *Rotatividade no mercado de trabalho brasileiro: 2002 a 2014*. São Paulo: DIEESE.

DIEESE. (2017). Terceirização e precarização das condições de trabalho: condições de trabalho e remuneração em atividades tipicamente terceirizadas e contratantes. *Nota Técnica do DIEESE* 172: 1–25.

DIEESE and CUT. (2014). *Terceirização e desenvolvimento: uma conta que não fecha. Dossiê acerca do impacto da terceirização sobre os trabalhadores e propostas para garantir a igualdade de direitos*. São Paulo: CUT.

Figueiredo Santos, J.A. (2015). Classe Social e Deslocamentos de Renda no Brasil. *Dados* 58(1): 79–110.

Fine, B., and Saad-Filho, A. (2017). Thirteen Things You Need to Know About Neoliberalism. *Critical Sociology* 43(4–5): 685–706.

Furtado, C. (2021a). The Myth of Economic Development and the Future of the Third World. *Review of Political Economy* 33(1): 16–27.

Furtado, C. (2021b). Underdevelopment and Dependence: The Fundamental Connections. *Review of Political Economy* 33(1): 7–15.

Gobetti, S.W., and Orair, R. (2016). Tributação e distribuição da renda no Brasil: novas evidências a partir das declarações tributárias das pessoas físicas. *IPC-IG Working Papers* 136: 1–23.

Hoffmann, R. (2009). Desigualdade da distribuição da renda no Brasil: a contribuição de aposentadorias e pensões e de outras parcelas do rendimento domiciliar per capita. *Economia e Sociedade* 18(1): 213–31.

Hoffmann, R. (2013). Transferências de Renda e Desigualdade no Brasil (1995–2011). In: T. Campello and M. Neri (eds.), *Programa Bolsa Família: uma década de inclusão e cidadania*, 207–216. Brasília: IPEA.

IBGE. (2016). *Sistemas de Contas Nacionais – Brasil – referência 2010*. Brasília: IBGE.

Jessop, B. (2002). *The future of the capitalist state*. Cambridge: Polity Press.

Krause, C., et al. (2013). Minha casa minha vida, nosso crescimento: Onde fica a política habitacional? *Textos para discussão do IPEA* 1853: 1–50.

Lakner, C., and Milanovic, B. (2016). Global Income Distribution: From the Fall of the Berlin Wall to the Great Recession. *The World Bank Economic Review* 30(2): 203–232.

Lavinas, L. (2017). How Social Developmentalism Reframed Social Policy in Brazil. *New Political Economy* 22(6): 628–644.

Lehmann, D. (2018). *The Prism of Race: The Politics and Ideology of Affirmative Action in Brazil*. Ann Arbor: University of Michigan Press.

Loureiro, P.M. (2020a). Social structure and distributive policies in Brazil under the PT governments: a poverty-reducing variety of neoliberalism. *Latin American Perspectives* 47(2): 65–83.

Loureiro, P.M. (2020b). Class inequality and capital accumulation in Brazil, 1992–2013. *Cambridge Journal of Economics* 44(1): 181–206.

Loureiro, P.M., and Saad-Filho, A. (2019). The Limits of Pragmatism: The Rise and Fall of the Brazilian Workers' Party (2002–2016). *Latin American Perspectives* 46(1): 66–84.

Loureiro, P.M., et al. (2021). Celso Furtado and the Myth of Economic Development: Rethinking Development from Exile. *Review of Political Economy* 33(1): 28–43.

Maricato, E. (2013). Vulnerability and Risk in the Metropolis of the Periphery: Everyday Life in Brazil's Cities. *Progressive Planning* 196(Summer): 28–30.

Maurizio, R., and Vázquez, G. (2016). Distribution effects of the minimum wage in four Latin American countries: Argentina, Brazil, Chile and Uruguay. *International Labour Review* 155(1): 97–131.

Medeiros, C.A. (2015). *Inserção externa, crescimento e padrões de consumo na economia brasileira*. Brasília: IPEA.

Medeiros, M., and Castro, F.A. (2018). A composição da renda no topo da distribuição. *Economia e Sociedade* 27(2): 577–605.

Mendes, Á., and Weiller, J.A.B. (2015). Renúncia fiscal (gasto tributário) em saúde: repercussões sobre o financiamento do SUS. *Saúde em Debate* 39(105): 491–505.

Menezes, A.P. d. R., et al. (2020). O futuro do SUS: impactos das reformas neoliberais na saúde pública–austeridade versus universalidade. *Saúde em Debate* 43(spe5): 58–70.

Morgan, M. (2017). Extreme and Persistent Inequality: New Evidence for Brazil Combining National Accounts, Surveys and Fiscal Data, 2001–2015. *WID.world Working Paper Series* 2017(12): 1–50.

Ocké-Reis, C.O. (2014). Qual é a Magnitude do Gasto Tributário em Saúde? *Boletim de Análise Político-Institucional do IPEA* 5: 71–76.

Ocké-Reis, C.O., and Gama, F.N. (2016). Radiografia do gasto tributário em saúde – 2003-2013. *Notas Técnicas do DIEST/IPEA* 19(May): 1–35.

Oliveira, G.C., and Wolf, P.J.W. (2016). A dinâmica do mercado de crédito no Brasil no período recente (2007-2015). *Textos para discussão do IPEA* 2243: 1–132.

Orair, R.O., and Gobetti, S.W. (2010). Governo gastador ou transferidor? Um macrodiagnóstico das despesas federais no período 2002 a 2010. In: IPEA (ed.), *Brasil em Desenvolvimento,* vol. 1, 87–111. Brasília: IPEA.

Peck, J., and Tickell, A. (2002). Neoliberalizing Space. *Antipode* 34(3): 380–404.

Posenato Garcia, L., et al. (2015). Gastos com planos de saúde das famílias brasileiras: estudo descritivo com dados das Pesquisas de Orçamentos Familiares 2002-2003 e 2008–2009, *Ciência & Saúde Coletiva,* 20. http://www.redalyc.org/articulo.oa?id=63038239012, accessed 15/10/2017.

Rezende Pinto, J.M. (2016). Uma análise da destinação dos recursos públicos, direta ou indiretamente, ao setor privado de ensino no Brasil, *Educação e Sociedade,* 37. http://www.redalyc.org/articulo.oa?id=87346374009, accessed 15/10/2017.

Rolnik, R., et al. (2015). O programa Minha Casa Minha Vida nas Regiões Metropolitanas de São Paulo e Campinas: aspectos socioespaciais e segregação. *Cadernos Metrópole* 17(33): 127–154.

Rossi, P., et al. (2019a). The Growth Model of the PT Governments: A Furtadian View of the Limits of Recent Brazilian Development. *Latin American Perspectives* 47(1): 100–114.

Rossi, P., et al. (2019b). Austeridade fiscal e o financiamento da educação no Brasil. *Educação & Sociedade* 40(e0223456): 1–20.

Rugitsky, F. (2016). Milagre, miragem, antimilagre: A economia política dos governos Lula e as raízes da crise atual, *Fevereiro,* 9. http://www.revistafevereiro.com/pag.php?r=09&t=03, accessed 30/11/2016.

Rugitsky, F. (2019). Questão de estilo: a mudança estrutural para a igualdade e seus desafios. In: M.V. Chiliatto-Leite (ed.), *Alternativas para o desenvolvimento brasileiro: novos horizontes para a mudança estrutural com igualdade,* 75–95. Santiago: CEPAL.

Saad-Filho, A. (2014). Brazil: development strategies and social change from import-substitution to the "events of June". *Studies in Political Economy* 94(Autumn): 3–29.

Saad-Filho, A. (2015). Social Policy for Neoliberalism: The Bolsa Família Programme in Brazil. *Development and Change* 46(6): 1227–1252.

Sengupta, U. (2019). State-led housing development in Brazil and India: a machinery for enabling strategy? *International Journal of Housing Policy* (online first): 1–27.

Simson, R., and Savage, M. (2020). The global significance of national inequality decline. *Third World Quarterly* 41(1): 20–41.

Singer, A. (2012). *Os sentidos do lulismo: reforma gradual e pacto conservador*. São Paulo: Companhia das Letras.

Souza, P.H.G.F., and Carvalhaes, F.A.O. (2014). Estrutura de classes, educação e queda da desigualdade de renda (2002-2011). *Dados* 57(1): 101–128.

Valença, M.M., and Bonates, M.F. (2010). The trajectory of social housing policy in Brazil: From the National Housing Bank to the Ministry of the Cities. *Habitat International* 34(2): 165–173.

Viana, R.M., et al. (2019). Carências Habitacionais no Brasil e na América Latina: o papel do ônus excessivo com aluguel urbano. *Caderno de Geografia* 29(56): 287–305.

World Bank. (2017a). *The Global Findex Database* [online text], https://globalfindex.worldbank.org.

World Bank. (2017b). PovcalNet. http://iresearch.worldbank.org/PovcalNet/, accessed 01/10/2017.

CHAPTER 15

Brazilian Unions in the Twenty-First Century

Andréia Galvão and Paula Marcelino

1 Introduction[1]

Brazil today is in the midst of a dual crisis, economic and political, that has had a negative impact on the working and living conditions of the working classes. The economic crisis is related to the process unleashed at the international level in 2008, whose effects (albeit delayed) had an impact on the national economy. The political crisis is expressed in the dismantling of Dilma Rousseff's government support base, the loss of popular support, the process of institutional rupture that culminated in the impeachment of the president in August 2016. The economic crisis affected gross domestic product (GDP) growth. In 2015 and 2016, economic activity shrank 3.8 percent and 3.6 percent respectively, confirming the worst recession in the country's history. The GDP stopped falling in the first quarter of 2017, registering since then an insufficient growth to enable an economic recovery. Unemployment of the economically active population rose from 6.8 percent in 2014 to 12.8 percent in 2017 and dropped insignificantly in subsequent years, reaching 11.8 percent in 2019. Informality, which was on a downward trajectory until 2013, also increased. Added to this negative economic scenario for workers, after the reelection of Dilma Rousseff in 2014 political instability fostered by the mainstream press and the judiciary resulted in an institutional coup perpetrated by the National Congress. This situation worsened with the election of Jair Bolsonaro in October 2018 whose government, in addition to promoting the dismantling of social and labor policies, permanently threatens social movements and democratic institutions.

This dual crisis has made evident the contradictions accumulated throughout the PT governments, governments sustained by a broad but heterogeneous political-partisan and social coalition. This coalition included, on the one hand, centrist and right-wing parties and sectors of the bourgeoisie and, on the other, left-wing parties, unions, and social movements. Disagreements

---

[1] This text is an updated version of the article of the same title published by Latin American Perspectives, v. 47, pp. 84–100, 2020. Translated by Luis Fierro. Revised by Stephanie Weatherbee.

within the neodevelopmentalist policy front (Boito 2012; Boito and Saad-Filho 2016: 190) and the intensification of distributive conflict strengthened opposition to the government and criticism of the socially progressive policies it had implemented. The change in the correlation of social forces contributed to the resumption of the neoliberal agenda of the 1990s as early as at the beginning of Dilma Rousseff's second term. The social movements on the right, strongly upper-middle-class (Cavalcante 2015), took to the streets, and political conservatism intensified (Velasco e Cruz, Kaysel, and Codas 2015; Saad-Filho and Boito 2016). The "productivist coalition", founded on defending state intervention to promote industrialization, economic growth, and income distribution, dissolved, giving rise to a "bourgeois antidevelopmentalist united front" (Singer 2015: 67) or what Magalhães (2015) has called the "domination of a social bloc and an antidistributive pact". Thus the conditions under which Brazilian unionism operates are changing.

How do unions fit into this conjuncture? How are they affected by and how do they intervene in the crisis? What are the differences from the period when the government was under Partido dos Trabalhadores (Workers' Party – PT) command? These are the questions that this chapter proposes to discuss. To do so, we will first review the main characteristics of union action under the PT with regard to both joint institutional action with the state and sponsorship of collective mobilizations, with special emphasis on strikes. Next we will discuss the mobilizations between 2013 and 2016 and go on to indicate the more general changes in the recent political-economic conjuncture, discussing how unionism is reacting to the advance of the right and the austerity policies implemented by Temer and Bolsonaro governments.

2   Unionism under the PT Governments

The activity of the union movement between 2003 and 2014 has been called a "new phase" (Boito, Galvão, and Marcelino 2015) marked by the support of the great majority of union members for the PT governments, the growing participation of union centrals in state institutions, the achievements of the economic plan, and the resumption of strike activism. These features contrast sharply with the situation in the 1990s (Noronha 2009: 136), when

> (...) the Collor government, the Real Plan in the Itamar [Franco] government, and the Fernando Henrique Cardoso governments changed the signals for the union movement: the opening of the Brazilian economy and its consequences for the adjustment of companies; the mass layoffs

that have occurred since 1990, pointing to the rising trend of unemployment rates; and the control of inflation, which ended with the premature
aging of collective contracts such as occurred when high and unpredict-
able inflation rates eroded wages before the one-year period provided for
the renewal of collective agreements.

Saying that the union movement was going through a new phase, especially
from 2004 to 2013, is also justified by the increase in the legitimacy of union
activity from the point of view of public life in the country. Whereas Fernando
Henrique Cardoso had inaugurated a shock-treatment phase for unionism –
following Margaret Thatcher's model of the historic year-long strike of British
miners – including massive fines for unions and military repression against
strikers (Romão 2009), Lula appointed unionists to important positions in his
government: the Ministry of Labor, the presidencies of state-owned enterprises,
and the administration of the pension funds linked to them. In addition, the
Lula government in its first term expanded the participation of unions in government agencies – a possibility opened up by the 1988 Constitution and put
into practice during the 1990s – through the creation of two tripartite bodies,
the National Labor Forum and the Economic and Social Development Council,
to discuss the reforms it intended to implement. It also promoted a series of
conferences to discuss public policies in different areas, creating new opportunities for the intervention of workers through their union organizations and
social movements (Galvão 2014).

The results of the change in the economic, political, and ideological conjuncture under the PT governments can be identified in several ways. One of
them is that until 2013 all six officially recognized union centrals or federations, of which the most important were the Central Única dos Trabalhadores
(Unified Workers' Central – CUT) and Força Sindical (Union Power – FS),
supported the government of Dilma Rousseff (Galvão, Marcelino, and Trópia
2015). This support did not guarantee the fulfillment of union demands, nor
did it prevent the implementation of policies unfavorable to workers, but it
did make the union picture more complex. Achievements such as the revalu-
ation of the minimum wage, associated with positive labor market indicators,
and the results obtained through collective bargaining and strikes explain the
union position vis-à-vis the PT governments.

The relationship between the unions and the PT governments is widely
debated in the Brazilian literature. Some writers argue that the tendency
toward bureaucratization resulting from the corporatist union structure intensified under the governments of Lula and Dilma, which sought to integrate
the unions more organically into the state. They oppose bureaucratization

to union autonomy, pointing out (1) the co-optation of unionism by the state (Druck 2006; Antunes 2011), (2) the transformation of the high union bureaucracy associated primarily with the pension funds (Coutinho 2010; Bianchi and Braga 2011; Braga 2012; Soares 2013); (3) the passivity of the leadership (Mattos 2014), and (4) the passive consent of the masses to the governments of Lula and Dilma (Braga 2016). There is a point of convergence between our analysis and the ones we are referring to: there was, in fact, a connection between unionism and government that resulted in political moderation at the union top bodies. This moderation coexisted, however, with the resumption of union activity and the success of the struggle for union demands. In our view, it is impossible to understand the unionism of this period without taking into account the strong impact of the economic policies of governments on union bases with regard to both their disposition to the pursuit of demands at the level of occupational categories and their diffuse support for the PT governments (Boito, Galvão, and Marcelino 2015). This support sustained the candidates of that party in four consecutive elections and seems to have been only marginally in doubt with regard to the demonstrations of June 2013, given that Dilma was reelected in 2014.

In our assessment, from 2004 until at least 2012 the country experienced a cycle of strikes[2] whose characteristics allow us to group them together, the main one being that they were offensive strikes – strikes in which workers' demands for better wages and the expansion of labor benefits were on the agenda and very largely won through negotiations between workers and employers. The data of the Departamento Intersindical de Estatísticas e Estudos Socioeconômicos (Interunion Department of Statistics and Socioeconomic Studies – DIEESE) on which we base this analysis also allow us to highlight a certain stability in the number of strikes and strikers and the proximity in this regard of the public and private sectors.[3]

Brazilian unionism has traditionally mobilized over wage issues rather than the demands of particular occupational categories. This characteristic is not unique to it but has certainly been reinforced by the way it has been structured

---

2   We will not address the debate over the definition of "cycle of strikes" (see Noronha 2009; Marcelino 2017). The analysis of the strikes that follows is a modified version of Marcelino's text.

3   We do not have official data produced by state institutions on strikes. The Inter-Union Department of Statistics and Socioeconomic Studies is maintained by the contributions of approximately 700 unions and union federations. The information in its strike-tracking system "is obtained through news in print or electronic newspapers of the mainstream media and the union press" (DIEESE 2015: 2).

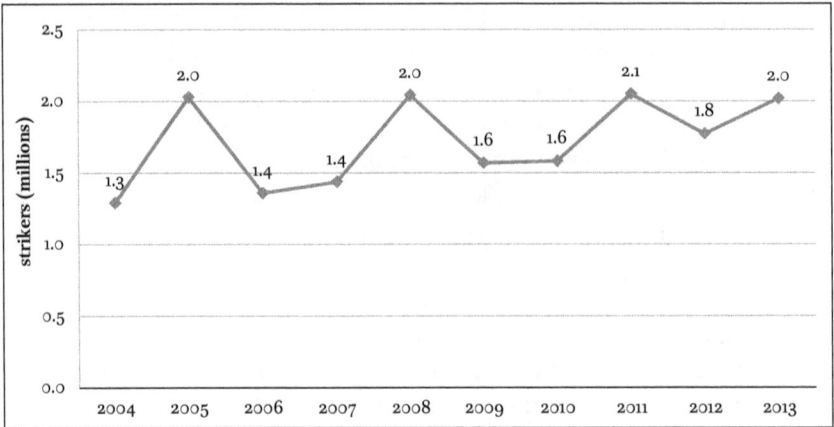

FIGURE 15.1 Numbers of strikers (in millions), 2004–2013
DATA FROM DIEESE, 2006; 2007; 2012; 2015; PREPARED BY DANILO TORINI

for more than 80 years (Boito Jr. 1991; Marcelino and Boito Jr. 2011; Martins 1989; Almeida 1975; Weffort 1973). Suffice it to mention, for example, that strikes in Brazil have a predictable date – the month in which the terms of their collective bargaining agreements are renegotiated. The data on wage adjustments for the past two decades are a clear indication of a new political and economic conjuncture that is more favorable to workers. In 2003, the first year of President Lula's administration, only 18.8 percent of the collective agreements to which the DIEESE had access achieved an adjustment above inflation. Most of the wage agreements of that year, 58.4 percent, sustained real losses; only 22.8 percent of the occupational categories experienced no loss in real terms (DIEESE 2016a; 2016b). The 1990s, as indicated by Noronha (2009), had been quite unfavorable for workers. In the years following 2003, we clearly see an improvement in the wages of Brazilian workers who were formally hired in the labor market and unionized. In 2012, 95 percent of the wage agreements signed were above the inflation index. Even in the year of the economic crisis, 2008, there was the prospect of growth in the Brazilian labor market that sustained the increase in the income of unionized workers. Krein and Teixeira (2014) show that, in the period under discussion, some occupational categories accumulated significant wage gains: metalworkers in São Paulo had their wages increased by 33 percent, and among bank tellers in São Paulo the appreciation was less but still significant, 11 percent.

The number of strikers remained relatively stable between 2004 and 2013, having passed 1.3 million in 2004.

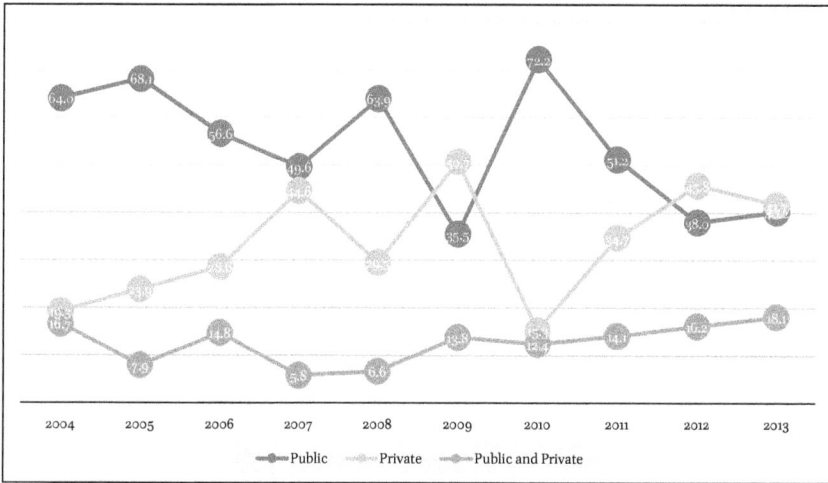

FIGURE 15.2 Distribution of strikers (%) between public and private sector, 2004–2013
DATA FROM DIEESE, 2006; 2007; 2012; 2015; PREPARED BY DANILO TORINI

In 2005, 2008, and 2011, the peaks in number of strikers were due to the numbers of strikes in the public sector. Because civil servants outnumber workers in private companies, enjoy more social protection, and are less subject to dismissal, strikes in the public sector tend to involve more workers and last longer around the world (Noronha 2009: 136). However, except in 2010, strikes in the private sector increased in number throughout this period, demonstrating increased confidence on the part of workers in their capacity to put pressure on management without risking dismissal. Furthermore, the total numbers of strikers was not directly related to the distribution of these strikers between the public and the private sphere. In both 2008 and 2010, the numbers of strikers in the public sphere significantly exceeded the numbers in the private sector. In 2008, however, the number of strikes was greater among private sector workers (54.5 percent of the total) while in 2010 the majority of strikes were in the public sector (60.3 percent of the total). The data show that what determines the number of strikers and the duration of strikes is the occupational category involved and the context. In 2008, workers benefited from the economic growth experienced in the last three quarters of the previous year, and only at the end of the year did the economic crisis begin to exert some moderating effect on the number of strikers through the decline in the availability of jobs.

The type of demand involved is important in characterizing the strikes of this period (Figure 15.3).

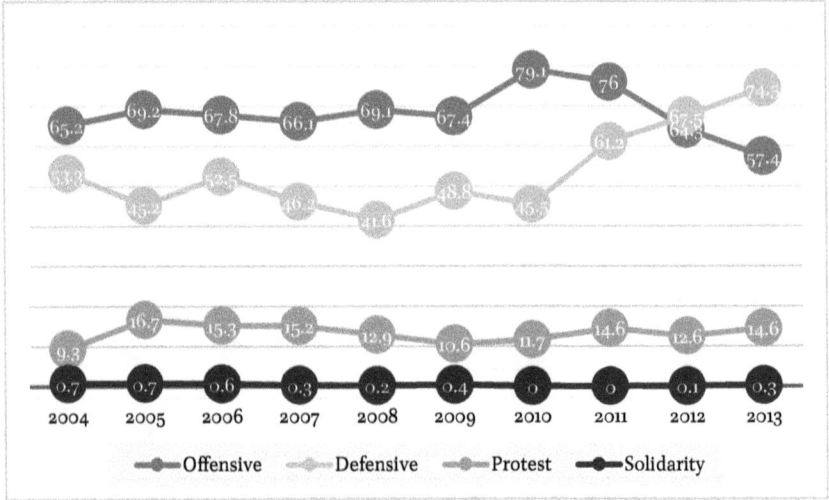

FIGURE 15.3 Types of demands in strikes (%), 2004–2013
Note: Because strikes may be motivated by more than one type of demand, percentages will not always add up to 100.
DATA FROM DIEESE, 2006; 2007; 2012; 2015; PREPARED BY DANILO TORINI

The number of strikes involving defensive demands such as late payment of wages and respect for norms and contractual clauses decreased. There was variation among sectors with regard to claims: traditionally organized sectors such as metalworkers, bank tellers, and oil workers, which tend to produce more strikes, also had more strikes over offensive demands, whereas for the services and trade sectors there were more strikes making defensive ones. These more ambitious strikes result from an economic, political, and ideological conjuncture more favorable to workers and made possible more achievements for the unionized workers. Strikes with offensive demands in the years in question were 68.2 percent of the total. (In contrast, under Fernando Henrique Cardoso in 1995–2002, 71 percent of strikes had involved defensive demands [DIEESE 2006: 19].) Between 2011 and 2013, however, the number of strikes increased from 800 to 2,050, and in 2013 74.5 percent of them involved defensive demands.

The data on strikes help to explain why from the end of Lula's second term unionism was a major support for the Lula and Dilma governments. Contrary to what might at first appear, there is no contradiction here. Striking does not necessarily mean opposition to the government, among other reasons because its immediate target is the company owner and only in the public sector is this figure the government. Nor is it possible to establish a correlation between increase in strikes and workers' dissatisfaction with the development model implemented by the PT governments, as Braga (2016) asserts, because this increase preceded the deterioration of economic indicators; for reasons that remain to be explained, there was a significant jump in 2013. Moreover, in contrast to the situation in the 1980s, there were no general strikes against the economic and social policies of the Lula and Dilma governments. The unions associated themselves with the employers' organizations around development policies (demanding from the government especially a reduction of interest rates and supporting it in this decision). Thus, the reinvigoration of economic demands expressed through strikes between 2004 and 2013 was associated with the unions' support of these neodevelopmentalist governments.

In the light of this support, how are we to explain the high incidence of strikes in the period and their favorable results for workers? In our view, the strikes between 2004 and 2013 were offensive and victorious because (1) they benefited from a favorable economic environment, (2) in contrast to the governments of Itamar, Collor, and Cardoso, the Lula and Dilma governments made unionism a legitimate interlocutor on the political scene and repressed it much less; (3) the most active sectors from the standpoint of strikes were those that had part of their leadership in second- and third-level government positions or in state or semi-state enterprises (the participation of these leaders in political institutions did not prevent strikes or eliminate the sources of conflict and mobilization); and, finally, as a hypothesis to be better investigated, (4) sectors that traditionally were not very active found room for strikes in this new conjuncture not because of discontent with the government but because of a perception of improvement in the conditions of struggle.

The relationship between unionism and the PT governments was permeated by difficulties and contradictions. The PT governments during Lula's two terms and Dilma's first made "contradictory movements in relation to social regulation" (Krein and Biavaschi 2015: 47), introducing certain rights (for example, the extension of social security to domestic workers and the extension of maternity leave) and eliminating others through the recognition of precarious employment contracts. Historical and more generally demands of the union movement such as the reduction of the work week from 44 to 40 hours without salary reduction, the end of dismissal without justified reasons, and the signing of International Labor Organization Convention 151 instituting obligatory collective bargaining in the public sector did not advance in the negotiation process. Thus, contrary to Cardoso (2014), the union movement did not become the government, since it failed to approve most of its agenda.

The difficulty of approving union demands was, in our view, due to three factors: (1) the heterogeneity of the political coalition,[4] which turned gains for workers into limits for the interests of another component of the neodevelopmentalist political front, the internal bourgeoisie, of which industrialists and agribusiness entrepreneurs were part (Boito Jr. 2012); (2) the difficulty of mobilizing workers around a broader range of rights in a context of economic growth, since the reduction of unemployment and the improvement in the distribution of income, along with the gains achieved through collective bargaining and strikes, satisfied the more immediate interests of many workers; and (3) the characteristics of the main tripartite advisory forums created by the Lula government, which did not allow the unions decisive influence on the development of public policy.[5]

Despite these limitations, most of the union movement, as we have said, supported the Lula and Dilma governments, and this, in our view, led to a moderation of the political struggle. Rather than questioning the development model adopted by the government, the union centrals sought to improve it. Thus they restricted themselves to fighting for economic growth and income distribution within this project, accepting the "weak reformism" and "the failure to confront capital" that characterized the PT governments (Singer 2012). One exception was the strategy adopted by Central Sindical e Popular (CSP) Conlutas and Intersindical, leftist and the minorities organizations that had emerged from a CUT split and did not meet the representativeness requirements for official recognition. They opposed the PT governments, pointing out that the contradictions and limitations of the neodevelopmentalist project made it impossible to meet most union demands. However, their criticism of a government that enjoyed broad popular support and the characteristics of these organizations made it difficult for them to establish roots in their bases.

Brazilian unionism continued under the PT governments to be marked by state corporatism, a unionism of leaders little rooted in the workplace. Several strikes were in fact started on the margins of the unions and sometimes against

---

4   The heterogeneity of the government coalition can be observed by examination of some of the measures under consideration in the National Congress. Of a set of 27 bills opposing the interests of workers and unions, 20 were proposed by allied parties (Galvão 2016). The two main parties of the allied base (the Republic, PR and the Brazilian Democratic Movement, MDB, which held the vice presidency in 2003–2010 and 2011–2016) were respectively responsible for the presentation of 3 and 7 bills contrary to workers' interests.

5   In addition, union participation in these bodies was restricted to representative union federations, excluding certain union positions. Finally, in the case of Economic and Social Development Council, the overrepresentation of employers provoked criticism from the union movement.

their leaders, among them those of the workers constructing the hydroelectric plants of Belo Monte, Jirau, and Santo Antonio, the petrochemical workers of the State of Rio de Janeiro (Comperj), the street cleaners of Rio, and the bus drivers of several state capitals (Mattos 2014; Véras 2014; Linhares 2015; Campos 2016). The effectiveness of unionism in mobilizing workers in the name of economic-corporative demands contrasted with its limited ability to mobilize around broader demands for changes in legislation and public policies. This is evident when we compare the "working-class" national marches held between 2004 and 2014 in defense of the increase in the minimum wage and of social rights with the demonstrations of June 2013 triggered by the Free Fare Movement, which assembled millions on the streets of Brazil's large and medium-sized cities.

The demonstrations in June brought out dissatisfaction with the PT governments that the unions shared, but except for the FS, which supported the Brazilian Social Democracy Party candidate, the officially recognized union centrals (despite some internal dissent) and the most important social movements supported Dilma Rousseff in the 2014 presidential elections. Although this support was instrumental in ensuring her reelection, Dilma chose to face the economic and political crisis through fiscal adjustment and a program focused on austerity, contrary to the commitment made in the inaugural address of her second term, "No right to less". This option undermined the social movements' relationship with the government and cost it a significant portion of its popular support. With the economic and political crisis that has been evident since 2015, there has been an increase in the difficulty for the union centrals to voice their demands on the institutional level, since opposition to the recognition and achievement of new rights has increased and part of the union movement has even agreed to waive some of its rights.

3 Unionism and the Streets from 2013 to 2016

The Brazilian workers organized in the country's thousands unions did not mobilize in a forceful way either against or in favor of the impeachment of Dilma, just as they had not played a leading role in the mobilizations since the demonstrations of June 2013. We have already mentioned that the preference for institutional action did not eliminate labor conflicts and strikes, but social protests generally took on new dynamics and intensity in June 2013, and it is necessary to reflect on the role that unions played in those demonstrations. At that juncture, the unions were replaced by social movements such as the Free Fare Movement, the homeless movements, and those opposed to the displacements caused by the construction of hydroelectric power plants, ports, and soccer stadiums, which assumed the leadership of large demonstrations, especially those that preceded the 2014 World Cup. Although, as Cardoso (2014) argues, it is inappropriate to compare these different movements, it seems possible to say that the two national days of struggle and work stoppage called for unions in July and August 2013 with the goal of "advancing the workers' agenda in the Congress" did not match the June demonstrations in terms of number of participants despite the wide range of demands presented and their success in temporarily halting important branches of production.

The demonstrations of June 2013 were heterogeneous in terms of both the demands presented and the actors involved. Left and right sectors criticizing the PT governments for different reasons met on the streets. Critics on the right sought to displace the meaning of the demonstrations, initially opposed to the increase in fares and the poor quality of public transport, to target the federal government as inefficient and corrupt. These sectors included people dissatisfied with social policies of income redistribution such as the Family Grant and My House, My Life programs and affirmative action such as ethnic-racial quotas for university entrance and public service and the public spending assigned to them (Saad-Filho and Boito 2016). Left critics denounced the Lula administration for its lack of structural reforms and maintenance of a conservative economic policy based on high interest rates, an overvalued exchange rate, and a fiscal policy that limited resources for social policies compared with the amount earmarked for the payment of the public debt. They were opposed to tax exemptions for the industrial sectors, the resumption of major infrastructure works (mainly hydroelectric power and ports), and the concessions and public-private partnerships that they considered privatizations in disguise. At the union level, this position was voiced by CSP Conlutas and Intersindical, whose mobilization capacity was limited.

In 2015 the sectors on the right gained prominence over the other sociopolitical groups with which they were disputing the streets. Taking advantage of the allegations of corruption involving state companies and PT politicians, they called for several demonstrations for the impeachment of Dilma, demonstrations that had a middle-class profile (Cavalcante 2015). The popular sectors participated in the demonstrations for impeachment but did not constitute their majority. Data on the demonstrations favorable and contrary to impeachment indicate a clear social and ethnic contrast between their participants (Datafolha 2015a; 2015b; Fundação Perseu Abramo 2016).

Despite the unions' criticism of the Dilma government, which stemmed largely from the austerity measures it adopted, the imminence of a coup led to a realignment of the positions held by the union centrals, which was a novelty in the postelection political scenario.[6] With the worsening of the political crisis in 2015, part of the leftist opposition once again approached the PT's closest movements in the name of defending democracy. Only the FS, the second-largest of the unions, located to the right on the political spectrum, despite the opposition of some of its leaders, joined the movement for the dismissal of Dilma, blaming her for the economic crisis and claiming the loss of the conditions for governance. Even this, however, did not translate into the mobilization of its unions in the streets.

The CUT and the Central dos Trabalhadores e Trabalhadoras do Brazil (Workers' Central of Brazil – CTB), a split-off from the CUT linked to the PT's political ally the Communist Party of Brazil, participated in the creation of two initiatives in 2015: the Popular Brazil Front, made up of the Landless Movement and others, and the Fearless People's Front, composed of the Intersindical and the Homeless Movement. Both sought to combine resistance to the dismantling of rights with the fight for democratic freedoms and structural reforms (democratization of the political system, the judiciary, and communications, tax reform, urban and agrarian reform), but the participation of movements linked to the Socialism and Freedom Party, which opposed the PT, in the Fearless People's Front led to tougher criticism by this front of the policy of the second Dilma government. CSP Conlutas did not join either of these fronts, considering that the defense of democratic institutions was no more than a pretext for the defense of the Dilma government. Thus it organized its own demonstrations, pronouncing at once against the government and against the opposition on the right under the banner "Everyone Must Go."

While the CUT, the CTB, and Intersindical, as top bodies of the union movement, played an important role in the articulation of resistance against the coup, at the base the union movement was not mobilized around the slogans "No Coup!" and "Temer Must Go!" seen in two large demonstrations in 2015 and another two in 2016. Admittedly, there were balloons, exhibit stands, and pamphlets of the unions at the demonstrations, and their leaders spoke through loudspeakers, but the unions affiliated with these federations (such as the ABC Metalworkers' Union, the Bank Tellers' Union, and the Teachers' Union/Apeoesp) were not present. The bulk of the protesters came from the landless, homeless, and women's movements, which Dilma

---

6 Some of the proposals made by Dilma in her first term already signaled the possibility of loss of rights: the discussion on the reform of the Consolidation of Labor Laws, the prevalence of the negotiated over the legislated, and the creation of new labor contracts (occasional, per hour worked) under the guise of ensuring a minimum level of rights for precarious workers. These measures would be introduced in the reform implemented by Temer in 2017.

approached in the months in which she was seeking to defend her mandate. There were also many demonstrators not organized into parties, unions, or movements.

The impeachment left the union movement in a defensive position both at the national policy level and in its negotiations with management, given the overlap of the political and economic crises. We do not yet have consolidated data on strikes that occurred in 2014 and 2015, but the situation had become quite unfavorable for workers. Unemployment increased from 6.8 percent in 2014 (the last year of Dilma Rousseff's first term and her reelection) to 8.5 percent in 2015 and 11.5 percent in 2016 (IBGE 2016). Social mobility had assumed a downward trend as early as 2013, showing a setback in living conditions for the lower middle class, precisely the sector that had risen the most in the previous period (Quadros 2015). For the first time in 11 years, the average income from work in all social classes declined: between 2014 and 2015 the average remuneration of the Brazilian worker fell by 5 percent. The GDP fell by 4.4 percent in relation to the same period of 2015 (Drummond 2016: 26). In addition to recession and unemployment, a conservative wave brought with it distrust of politicians and politics (Velasco e Cruz, Kaysel, and Codas 2015) that also affected the legitimacy of union activity.

Assessments of the collective bargaining negotiations for 2015 and 2016 clearly show the deterioration of the economic gains of unionized workers. According to the DIEESE (2016a: 2), not since 2004 had a result as unfavorable for workers as that of 2015 been observed; only 52 percent of workers had some real gain above inflation, while 30 percent succeeded only in keeping up with inflation and 18 percent faced wage losses. The sector most affected by the crisis was the industrial sector, in which 55 percent of wage negotiations resulted in an adjustment equal to or below inflation (DIEESE 2015: 3). In the first half of 2016 all these indicators worsened: only 24 percent of wage negotiations resulted in real gains above inflation; 37 percent obtained only inflationary replacement, and 39 percent produced wage losses. There was also a significant increase in staggered wage adjustments. While in the first half of 2012 the number of collective bargaining negotiations that resulted in a staggered wage increase was 4.8 percent, in the first half of 2016 this rate rose to 25.3 percent (DIEESE 2016a: 7).

About 81 percent of the strikes in 2016 included items of a defensive nature on the demand agenda (DIEESE 2017), while offensive demands were involved in only 34 percent of strikes. With this, we return to the typical scenario of the 1990s: an even higher frequency of strikes than in that decade (when they averaged 900 a year) aimed at defending what had already had been achieved. Workers were spending a lot of effort to stay where they were.

How did the union centrals respond to this scenario of losses? Even before this general worsening was perceived, the CUT – the largest union federation and traditionally considered left-wing and organically linked to the PT – had taken up certain controversial proposals, presenting them directly to the government without the mediation of the tripartite institutions.[7] Formulated by the ABC Metalworkers' Union, these proposals, such as the Employment Protection Plan (proposed in 2014), which would establish a reduction of the workday in exchange for a reduction in wages, promoted the flexibilization of labor relations. Employers, for their part, took advantage of the economic stagnation and the political instability to improve operating conditions and restore their profit margins. In this connection, they reinstated Law 4330/2004, which authorized outsourcing for all types of activity. This measure provoked a great union reaction: in 2015 alone three days of struggle were called whose main goal was the denunciation of this project, with massive demonstrations and work stoppages in some categories (such as metalworkers and public transport workers) on all of them. This example shows that when it comes to resisting measures that are contrary to social and labor rights, the union centrals can mobilize workers and build a movement that includes the left-wing unions. The FS was the only central absent from these demonstrations. Resuming, in part, the arguments for the flexibilization of rights that had marked its position in the 1990s, it was isolated in its defense of the project on the ground that it was necessary to regulate (and supposedly protect) the 12 million outsourced workers not covered by the regulation then in force (which prohibited outsourcing in a company's main activities). The FS's stance generated protests on the part of some of its member unions and a modification of its strategy, with the central deciding to offer amendments to the project. This resistance had not been enough to prevent an earlier proposal authorizing the outsourcing of activities (PL 4302/1998, under Cardoso) from being adopted.

4   The Temer Government's Offensive against Social and Labor Rights

Between August 2016, when Michel Temer was confirmed in the presidency, until the end of his term in December 2018, attacks on social and labor rights were constant. The Temer government adopted a set of policies that were very harmful to Brazilian workers. Three of them were particularly important in

---

7   The National Labor Forum ceased to operate after 2005, and under the Dilma government the Economic and Social Development Council met only a few times.

promoting the dismantling of social protection at work: (1) a social security reform proposal that established the minimum retirement age of 65 for men and 62 for women and eliminated the indexation of social security benefits for the minimum wage (Constitutional Amendment 287/2016); (2) the elimination of legal barriers to the outsourcing of any business activity (Law 13429/2017); and (3) a broad labor reform that authorized the waiver of the law through collective bargaining, expanded the modalities of precarious employment, and limited the possibilities of recourse to the Labor Court (Law 13467/17).

In contrast to what had been happening under the PT governments, these measures were not negotiated with the unions either through the tripartite institutions or directly with the heads of the representative union centrals. It is true that just before the reform was adopted in July 2017 the Temer government had established one of these institutions, the National Labor Council, with the participation of the six recognized union centrals, but this council did not participate in the discussions of labor reform. Although the focus of the reform was labor legislation, several of its aspects directly affected unionism by decentralizing collective bargaining, deepening the fragmentation of union representation bases with the expansion of forms of precarious employment, and introducing the possibility of individual negotiation of important aspects of the employment relationship, the possibility of contractual termination without union intermediation, and the representation of workers in the workplace outside the unions. In addition to eliminating union prerogatives, the reform had an impact on their finances, conditioning the levying of the union tax on the worker's prior consent (Cesit 2017).

In the face of these attacks, the unions took action. A general strike on April 28, 2017, convened by all the politically relevant union centrals including those taking different positions on the impeachment such as FS and the CSP Conlutas, went down in history as the largest general strike ever to take place in the country, with 35 million workers stopping work in 26 states and the Federal District. Another general strike was held on June 30, with lower participation, including categories with great strike traditions such as the subway workers of São Paulo. Some unions even replaced the term "general strike" with "mobilization and work stoppage".[8] Although union and popular

---

8   There are several hypotheses, not mutually exclusive, for explaining the lower numbers involved in this general strike: (1) division within the union centrals about whether to try to negotiate a provisional measure with the government; (2) assimilation by part of the union movement of the discourse of the modernization of labor relations and the fact that some trade unions even exist only because of outsourcing; and (3) the wage losses for strikers and fines imposed on the unions as a result of the strike on April 28 and the resulting absence from the action of the subway workers' union of São Paulo (without a transportation

demonstrations multiplied, they were unable to stop the labor reform.[9] In addition to the demonstrations, the six recognized union centrals presented a denunciation of the labor reform to the International Labor Organization. The CUT began to collect signatures for a popular initiative annulling the reform supported by the other union centrals. In 2017 the Workers' Union Forum, which included 22 confederations of the official structure and was chaired by the vice president of the New Workers' Union Central, launched the Resistance Movement for a Better Brazil to combat the setbacks imposed by the Temer reforms.

On another front, all the recognized union centrals except the CUT negotiated with the São Paulo Federation of Industries a proposal for promoting economic growth and job creation that included the resumption of credit and interrupted public works, incentives for civil construction through the resumption of infrastructure projects and popular housing, renewal of the fleet of vehicles and industrial machinery, compliance with the content standards placed on the oil and gas sectors, and additional mechanisms for unemployment insurance. This was therefore a development agenda quite similar to that of the PT governments, but it did not have the participation of the CUT, which refused to submite any proposal to a government it considered illegitimate. These same union centrals discussed the formulation of a provisional measure to revise the clauses of the labor reform they considered most harmful, such as the elimination of the union tax and the authorization of unhealthy work for pregnant women and infants, intermittent work, contract termination without union monitoring, and individual negotiation of working conditions. The CUT, again, did not participate in this discussion, and neither did the CSP Conlutas and Intersindical. Finally, the union centrals defended the need to elect workers' representatives to the National Congress in the 2018 elections as a way to stop and reverse the reforms.

However, Bolsonaro's election thwarted that possibility. In addition to not reversing the neoliberal reforms already carried out, his government has been intensifying the process of dismantling rights, as we will see below.

---

shutdown, a general strike is less effective); and (4) the proximity of the vote on the reforms (on July 11) and exhaustion due to the extensive schedule of mobilizations.

9 There were five national mobilization days in 2016 against Temer and the reforms and three in 2017, in addition to the two general strikes mentioned, and work stoppages were called by all of the union centrals except the FS. Eventually, faced with the extent of the damage to workers' rights, especially from the reforms to social security and labor, the FS began to participate in some of the demonstrations.

5   Neofacism and Neoliberal Orthodoxy: The Bolsonaro Government
         and the Outlook for Brazilian Labor

There are many dimensions to the policies that were introduced by the
Bolsonaro government in order to dismantle rights. We will highlight two of
them here, due to their impact on workers: pension reform and the deepening
of the labor reform, specifically a set of measures that we will address below.[10]

The pension reform approved by Bolsonaro was even more damaging to
workers than the one that was designed as a proposal in the Temer government. In practice, the reform established the minimum age as a general condition for the right to retirement and changed the calculation rule in order to
reduce the amount of benefits to be received in the future. Still, the reform is
especially harmful to the poorest and most vulnerable workers, who enter the
labor market earlier and will be forced to contribute longer, until they reach
the minimum age required for retirement. This is the case for rural workers,
who work from a young age and in strenuous conditions. In addition, informality and precarious employment contracts, expanded by the 2017 labor reform,
mean that a significant number of workers do not contribute to social security or are unable to contribute uninterruptedly. Finally, the reform penalizes
women, who are already burdened with the double hours of work that the sexual division of labor imposes on them, most of the time without reaching the
necessary contribution time to apply for retirement.

The union centrals organized several mobilizations against the pension
reform, expressing opposition to the capitalization regime,which would break
intergenerational solidarity for the benefit of the financial market. This and
other points were raised in the manifesto signed by all of the union centrals
(with the exception of UGT), launched in the National Assembly of the Working
Class: "In defense of public pensions and against the end of retirement".[11] The
assembly established a calendar of struggles that led to four national days of
action in defense of social security (three of which combined with specific

10   We resume here the arguments developed in Marcelino and Galvão (2020).
11   Available at: http://cspconlutas.org.br/wp-content/uploads/2019/02/Manifesto-
      unificado-das-centrais-sindicais-erca-Reforma-da-Previd%C3%AAncia.pdf.   Consulted
      on 02/02/2020. A new note would be released less than two months, this time with the
      signature of UGT, but without the adhesion of CGTB, Conlutas and Intersindical. This
      absence does not seem to signal a division or a disagreement, since the centrals would
      make May 1 unified a few days later. Cf. Note from the union centrals about the Social
      Security reform proposal https://fsindical.org.br/forca/nota-das-centrais-sindicais-sobre-
      a-proposta-de-reforma-da-previdencia. Consulted on 02/02/2020.

stoppages by students and teachers, due to cuts in education resources) and a general strike.

These events may have contributed to modifying some controversial aspects of the reform, such as the afore mentioned capitalization regime and the increase in the age and contribution time for rural retirement, including the preservation of the pay-as-you-go system.[12] Union centrals estimate the number of workers involved in the general strike against pension reform at 45 million, with the participation of civil servants, teachers, students, metal workers, bank workers, oil workers and transport workers from several state capitals.[13] Unlike labor rights, which affect a small part of the working population, social security rights are a fundamental element for the subsistence of entire families, both in terms of guaranteeing income and reducing social inequalities as well as combating poverty (Fagnani 2018), so that it may have caused a greater commotion and engagement of workers in defense of public retirement.[14]

In July 2019, the number of workers employed in the informal labor market broke a record and reached 41.3%, 38.683 million male and female workers in absolute numbers.[15] Despite the small reduction in the unemployment rate from 12.8 to 11.8 between 2017 and 2019, the 2017 labor reform did not generate the volume of promised jobs. Instead, it created precarious, informal, intermittent, outsourced, and part-time jobs, not chosen by workers (Filgueiras 2019; Teixeira 2019; Krein et al. 2019). Even so, the government sought further labor reforms through the law of economic freedom (Law 13.874/2019), which exempts companies of up to 20 employees from maintaining records of hours worked, as well as by proposing other measures that contribute

---

12   The president of UGT declared that "the general feeling is that it is not as bad as it once was." Available at: https://www1.folha.uol.com.br/mercado/2019/06/centrais-veem-avancos-em-relatorio-da-previdencia-mas-ainda-reclamam-de-idade-minima.shtml. Consulted on 02/02/2020.

13   Avaible at: https://oglobo.globo.com/economia/sindicatos-estimam-que-45-milhoes-de-trabalhadores-aderiram-greve-geral-1-23740014. Consulted on 05/03/2020.

14   The idea of working until death and, with that, of being prevented from enjoying a right if the reform was approved, was widely propagated and had an effect in several categories of workers. The use of black T-shirts with an indication of the age at which teachers could retire was a strategy that generated empathy and solidarity. At the same time, however, the theses according to which the alleged "pension deficit" and the increase in life expectancy justify the reform were also assimilated by workers and, certainly, contributed to the widespread perception that the reform was inevitable.

15   Avaible at: https://g1.globo.com/economia/noticia/2019/08/30/trabalho-informal-avanca-para-413percent-da-populacao-ocupada-e-atinge-nivel-recorde-diz-ibge.ghtml. Consulted on 02/02/2020.

to informalization or precarization of work,[16] such as Provisional Measure 905. Although this measure has expired, it comprises several proposals that remain on the government's horizon, such as: the creation of the Green and Yellow program, which establishes a fixed-term contract for young people with reduced contribution rates from the employer to the Fundo de Garantia Por Tempo de Serviço (FGTS),[17] the liberalization of work on Sundays without union authorization or additional payment per hour worked, and the authorization to open banks on Saturdays and thus the increase in hours of work for bank workers. Furthermore, it tries to weaken the role of unions and to make labor inspection difficult, even in situations of imminent risk for workers.

The context for the resistance of unionized workers is very adverse, either due to the pressure that unemployment and informality exert on the labor market, or due to the large-scale attacks directed at the left wing in general and to unionism in particular, which has contributed to many authors characterizing the government as neo-fascist (Boito Jr. 2020; Filgueiras and Druck 2020). The forces behind Bolsonaro have the elimination of the left and the defense of traditional patriarchy as clear goals, guided by a vision of a reactionary utopia. For the middle classes that are mobilized in defense of the government, economic policy is not as important as the ideological aspects of the government's discourse, and the persecution of social movements and the left as a whole. So, in Brazil, as well as in other countries around the world (such as the United States, India, Hungary and the Philippines), neoliberalism and neo-fascism have gone hand in hand. The government has sought to appeal to the most impoverished strata of the working classes with insufficient social policies, such as the emergency aid implemented due to the Coronavirus pandemic – 600 reais a month for three months, followed by another 300 for more three months – and with the recent attempts to replace Bolsa Família by a new income transfer program, Renda Brasil. Emergency aid has been responsible for securing the Bolsonaro government's approval ratings – currently, around

---

16   This is the objective assumed by Bolsonaro: to bring labor contracts closer and closer to the absence of legal contracts, that is, informality. Available at: https://exame.abril.com.br/economia/bolsonaro-diz-que-lei-trabalhista-no-brasil-deve-beirar-a-informalidade/. Consulted on 29/02/2020.

17   The FGTS is a fund to which employers contribute. Fines for unjustified terminations are based on the amount accumulated in this fund. Under certain conditions employees can gain access to the amount which accumulates into this fund in their name upon release from employment.

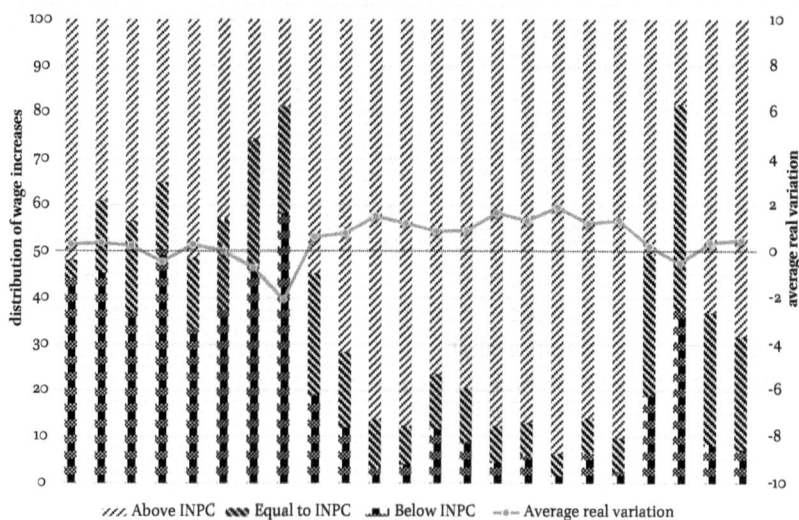

FIGURE 15.4 Distribution of wage increases compared to the inflation index (INPC–IBGE) and average real variation of wage increases in Brazil between 2003 and 2019
DATA FROM DIEESE, 2017

40%[18] – in a context characterized by economic crisis and alarming rates of unemployment.[19]

This political, economic and ideological conjuncture negatively impacted workers' ability to mobilize, as we can see from the strike indicators: 2018, the year following the labor reform, 2019, the first year of Bolsonaro's government and the first half of 2020, when the coronavirus pandemic began, have been difficult years for the struggle of formally employed unionized workers. The number of strikes remained significant, although declining: 1453 in 2018 and 1118 in 2019. However, the presence of defensive demands – those, as already mentioned, related to late payments and non-compliance with rights or clauses of collective bargaining agreements – became the major motivation behind

18   Avaible at: https://noticias.uol.com.br/politica/ultimas-noticias/2020/09/24/aprovacao-ibope-governo-bolsonaro-setembro.htm. Consulted on: 06/11/2020.
19   PNAD 2020 data indicates that between the second quarter of 2019 and the second quarter of 2020, about 10 million workers left the category of "employed". Most of these workers do not even make up official unemployment rates, because, due to the pandemic, they were not looking for a job the week the survey was conducted. It is estimated that, with the end of emergency aid and if the situation of the pandemic is stabilized or resolved, these workers will seek to return to the labor market. In this case, we will see an explosion in the unemployment rate and an even greater retraction of the country's GDP.

the strikes. In 2018, 81.8% of strikes had defensive claims on their agenda; this number increased to 82.4% in 2019 and in the first half of 2020 they were present in 89.6% of strikes (DIEESE 2019; 2020; 2020a).

Figure 15.4 above shows a clear movement towards an almost continuous increase in real wage gains during the PT governments. The first year of Dilma Rousseff's second term changes the course of that movement, starting a downward trend. This process, marked by the 2015 economic and political crisis, was even more accentuated in 2016, the year of the coup. Although wage readjustment rates above inflation have partly recovered in the years 2017 and 2018 (the last year for which there is available data), they are far from those reached at the peak of the neodevelopmentalist period (2010–2014).[20]

6   Conclusion

Unionism, an allied, albeit subordinate, force in the neodevelopmentalist political front of the governments of Lula da Silva and Dilma Rousseff, was relatively absent from the mobilizations against or in favor of Dilma's impeachment compared with other social movements. However, it sought to resist and, in a way, realign itself to counter the counterreforms of Michel Temer's and Bolsonaro's governments.

The deterioration of economic and social conditions observed even before the impeachment left the union movement in a defensive position. The labor force suffers from rising unemployment rates, and the overall outcome of collective bargaining shows a scaling back of economic gains achieved by unionized workers as well as a tendency toward strikes motivated by defensive demands. Although union and popular demonstrations have multiplied, the absence of a unified strategy in the face of the coup and the reforms have weakened the possibilities of union resistance, and losses for workers have accumulated since then.

Therefore, the pandemic of the new coronavirus has impacted an already precarious labor market and a unionism weakened by a restorative neoliberal offensive. The characteristics of the Bolsonaro government, which combine neoliberalism and neo-fascism, indicate that the trends are not favorable for workers and unions. Unionism's survival as a relevant political actor is threatened; together with the existence of the mass of workers that it has represented so far in our country, formally employed workers. The future of Brazilian

---

20   We thank DIEESE, specially to Luís Augusto Ribeiro da Costa, for the data provided.

unionism depends on its ability to face the challenge of representing precarious and informal workers. Only then will it be able to withstand the process of continuous and deep deterioration in working conditions and labor rights.

References

Almeida, M.H.T. (1975). Sindicatos no Brasil: novos problemas, velhas estruturas. *Debate Crítica* 6: 49–74.

Antunes, R. (2011). A 'engenharia da cooptação' e os sindicatos no Brasil recente. *Jornal dos Economistas* 268: 5–6.

Bianchi, A., and Braga, R. (2011). A financeirização da burocracia sindical no Brasil. Available at: http://www.correiocidadania.com.br/index (consulted December 10, 2016).

Boito Jr., A. (1991). *O sindicalismo de Estado no Brasil: Uma análise crítica da estrutura sindical*. São Paulo and Campinas: Hucitec/Unicamp.

Boito Jr., A. (2012). As bases políticas do neodesenvolvimentismo. Available at: http://eesp.fgv.br/sites /eesp.fgv.br/files/file/Painel%203%20-20Novo%20Desenv%20 BR%20-20Boito%2020Bases%20Pol%20Neodesenv%20 -%20PAPER.pdf (consulted April 11, 2013).

Boito Jr., A., Galvão, A., and Marcelino, P. (2015). La nouvelle phase du syndicalisme brésilien. *Cahiers des Amériques Latines* 80: 147–167.

Boito Jr., A., and Saad-Filho, A. (2016). State, state institutions, and political power in Brazil *Latin American Perspectives* 43(2): 190–206.

Boito Jr., A. (2020). Neofascismo e neoliberalismo no Brasil sob Bolsonaro. *Revista Observatorio Latinoamericano y Caribeño* (OLAC), prelo.

Braga, R. (2016). Terra em transe: o fim do lulismo e o retorno da luta de classes. In: André Singer and Isabel Loureiro (eds.), *As contradições do lulismo: A que ponto chegamos?*, 55–92. São Paulo: Boitempo.

Braga, R. (2012). *A política do precariado: Do populismo à hegemonia lulista*. São Paulo: Boitempo.

Campos, C.V. (2016). *Conflitos trabalhistas nas obras do PAC: o caso das Usinas Hidrelétricas de Jirau, Santo Antônio e Belo Monte*. Unpublished thesis Universidade de Campinas, Campinas.

Cardoso, A.M. (2014). Sindicatos no Brasil: passado, presente e future. In: Cattani A.D. (ed.), *Trabalho: Horizonte 2021*, 121 145. Porto Alegre: Escritos.

Cavalcante, S. (2015). Classe média e conservadorismo liberal. In: Velasco e Cruz, S., et al. (eds.), *Direita, volver! O retorno da direita e o ciclo político brasileiro*, 177–196. São Paulo: Editora Fundação.

CESIT (Centro de Estudos Sindicais e Economia do Trabalho). (2017). Subsídios para a discussão sobre a reforma trabalhista no Brasil: movimento sindical e negociação coletiva. Available at: http://www.cesit.net.br/wp-content/uploads/2017/11/Texto-de-discuss%C3%A30-5-Negociacao-coletiva-e-sindicalismo-1.pdf (consulted January 11, 2018).

Coutinho, C.N. (2010). A hegemonia da pequena política. In: Oliveira, F., et al. (ed.), *Hegemonia às avessas*, 29–43. São Paulo: Boitempo.

Datafolha. (2015a). Manifestação na Avenida Paulista, survey com participantes de 15/3/2015. Available at: http://datafolha.folha.uol.com.br/opiniaopublica/2015/03/1604284-47-foram-a-avenida-paulista-em-15-de-marco-protestar-contra-a-corrupcao.shtml (consulted April 5, 2016).

Datafolha. (2015b). Manifestação na Avenida Paulista, survey com participantes de 16/8/2015. Available at: http://datafolha.folha.uol.com.br/opiniaopublica/2015/08/1669735-135-mil-vao-a-protesto-na-paulista.shtml (consulted March 2, 2017).

DIEESE (Departamento Intersindical de Estatísticas e Estudos Socioeconômicos). (2006). Estudos e Pesquisas, ano 2, no. 20: as greves em 2005. Available at: http://portal.mte.gov.br/data/files/FF8080812BA5F4B7012BAB0B8EFD6AF8/Prod03_2006.pdf (consulted July 20, 2012).

DIEESE (Departamento Intersindical de Estatísticas e Estudos Socioeconômicos). (2015). Estudos e Pesquisas, no. 79: balanço das greves em 2013. Available at: http://www.dieese.org.br/balancodasgreves/2013/estPesq79balancogreves2013.pdf (consulted July 7, 2016).

DIEESE (Departamento Intersindical de Estatísticas e Estudos Socioeconômicos). (2016a). Estudos e Pesquisas, no. 81: balanço das negociações salariais no primeiro semestre de 2016. Available at: http://www.dieese.org.br/balancodosreajustes/2016/estPesq81balancoReajustes1semestre2016.pdf (consulted December 15, 2016).

DIEESE (Departamento Intersindical de Estatísticas e Estudos Socioeconômicos). (2016b). Estudos e Pesquisas, no. 80: Balanço das negociações salariais em 2015. Available at: http://www.dieese.org.br/ balancodosreajustes/2016/estPesq80balancoReajustes2015.pdf (consulted October 26, 2016).

DIEESE (Departamento Intersindical de Estatísticas e Estudos Socioeconômicos). (2017). Estudos e Pesquisas, no. 84: Balanço das greves em 2016. Available at: https://www.dieese.org.br/balancodasgreves/2016/estPesq84balancoGreves2016.html (consulted September 16, 2017).

DIEESE (Departamento Intersindical de Estatísticas e Estudos Socioeconômicos). (2019). Estudos e Pesquisas, no. 90: Balanço das greves em 2018. Available at: https://www.dieese.org.br/balancodosreajustes/2018/estPesq90BalancoReajuste2018.html (consulted November 6, 2020).

DIEESE (Departamento Intersindical de Estatísticas e Estudos Socioeconômicos). (2020). Estudos e Pesquisas, no. 93: Balanço das greves em 2019. Available at: https://www.dieese.org.br/balancodasgreves/2019/estPesq93balancoGreves2019 (consulted November 6, 2020).

DIEESE (Departamento Intersindical de Estatísticas e Estudos Socioeconômicos). (2020a). Boletim: De olho nas negociações, no. 1. Available at: https://www.dieese. org.br/boletimnegociacao/2020/boletimnegociacao001.html (consulted November 6, 2020).

Druck, G. (2006). Os sindicatos, os movimentos sociais e o governo Lula: cooptação e resistência. *Observatório Social da América Latina* 19: 330–331.

Drummond, C. (2016). O abismo que nos separa. *Revista Carta Capital* 22(930): 26–29.

Fagnani, E. (2018). Austeridade e Seguridade: a destruição do marco civilizatório brasileiro. In: Rossi, P., et al. (eds.), *Economia para poucos: impactos sociais da austeridade e alternativas para o Brasil*, 57–82. São Paulo: Autonomia Literária.

Filgueiras, V. (2019). As promessas da reforma trabalhista: combate ao desemprego e redução da informalidade. In: Krein, J.D., et al. (eds.), *Reforma trabalhista no Brasil: promessas e realidade*, 13–52. Campinas: Curt Nimuendajú.

Filgueiras, L., and Druck, G. (2020). O governo Bolsonaro, o neofascismo e a resistência democrática. In: Filgueiras, Luiz, and Druck, Graça. *O Brasil nas trevas (2013-2013-2020): do golpe neoliberal ao neofascismo*. São Paulo: Boitempo, e-book.

Fundação Perseu Abramo. (2016). Projeto – Manifestações de março, survey comparativo de 13 e 18, 2015/2016. Available at: http://novo.fpabramo.org.br/sites/default/files/FPA-Pesquisa-Manifestacoes-Comparativa-2015-2016-SITE-042016-ok.pdf (consulted April 20, 2016).

Galvão, A. (2016). Political action of the Brazilian labour movement: issues and contradictions facing PT governments. *Studies in Political Economy* 96: 1–15.

Galvão, A. (2014). The Brazilian labor movement under PT governments. *Latin American Perspectives* 41(5): 184–199.

Galvão, A., Marcelino, P., and Trópia, P.V. (2015). *As bases sociais das novas centrais sindicais*. Curitiba: Appris.

IBGE (Instituto Brasileiro de Geografia e Estatística). (2016). Taxa de desocupação das pessoas de 14 anos ou mais de idade, na semana de referência (em %). Available at: http://www.ibge.gov.br/home/estatistica/indicadores/trabalhoerendimento/pnad_continua/default_novos_indicadores.shtm (consulted November 20, 2016).

Krein, J.D., et al. (eds.). (2019). *Reforma trabalhista no Brasil: promessas e realidade*. Campinas: Curt Nimuendajú.

Krein, J.D., and Biavaschi, M. (2015). Brasil: os movimentos contraditórios da regulação do trabalho nos anos 2000. *Cuadernos del Cendes* 89: 47–82.

Krein, J.D., and Teixeira, M.O. (2014). As controvérsias das negociações coletivas nos anos 2000 no Brasil. In: Véras, R., et al. (eds.). *O sindicalismo na era Lula: Paradoxos, perspectivas e olhares*, 213–245. Belo Horizonte: Fino Traço.

Linhares, R. (2015). As greves de 2011 a 2013. *Revista Ciências do Trabalho* 5: 97–112.

Magalhães, J.C.G. (2015). Crescimento, emprego e distribuição de renda: o desempenho econômico do primeiro governo Dilma e o ressurgimento do pacto antidistributivista no Brasil. Available at: http://www.ifibe.edu.br/arq/201507272109076316364 87.pdf (consulted October 5, 2016).

Marcelino, P. (2017). Sindicalismo e neodesenvolvimentismo: analisando as greves entre 2003 e 2013 no Brasil. *Tempo Social* 29(3): 201–227.

Marcelino, P., and Galvão, A. (2020). O sindicalismo brasileiro frente à ofensiva neoliberal restauradora. *Tempo Social* 32: 157–182.

Marcelino, P., and Boito Jr., A. (2011). Novo operariado, velhos desafios: o sindicalismo de trabalhadores terceirizados. *Estudos de Sociologia* 31: 341–362.

Martins, H.T.S. (1989). *O Estado e a burocratização do sindicato no Brasil.* São Paulo: Hucitec.

Mattos, M.B. (2014). As lutas da classe trabalhadores no Brasil dos mega-eventos. *Observatório Social da América Latina* 36: 215–226.

Noronha, E G (2009) Ciclo de greves, transição política e estabilização: Brasil, 1978–2007. *Lua Nova* 76: 119–168.

Quadros, W. (2015). Paralisia econômica, retrocesso social e eleições. *Texto para Discussão* 249. Available at: http://plataformapoliticasocial.com.br/wp-content/uploads/2015/01/TD_WaldirQuadros012015.pdf (consulted January 10, 2017).

Romão, F.L. (2009). *Óleo da terra, homens e mulheres da luta: Petroleiros de Getúlio a FHC.* São Paulo: Expressão Popular.

Saad-Filho, A., and Boito Jr., A. (2016). Brazil: the failure of the PT and the rise of the "New Right", *Socialist Register*, 213–230. London: Merlin Press.

Singer, A. (2012). *Os sentidos do lulismo: Reforma gradual e pacto conservador.* São Paulo: Companhia das Letras.

Singer, A. (2015). Cutucando onças com varas curtas: o ensaio desenvolvimentista no primeiro mandato de Dilma Rousseff (2011–2014). *Novos Estudos CEBRAP* 102: 42–71.

Soares, J.L. (2013). As centrais sindicais e o fenômeno do transformismo no governo Lula. *Revista Sociedade e Estado* 13: 541–564.

Teixeira, M.O. (2019). Os efeitos econômicos da reforma trabalhista. In: Krein, J.D. et al. (eds.), *Reforma trabalhista no Brasil: promessas e realidade*, 53–80. Campinas: Curt Nimuendajú.

Velasco e Cruz, S., Kaysel, A., and Codas, G. (eds.). (2015). *Direita, volver! O retorno da direita e o ciclo político brasileiro.* São Paulo: Editora Fundação Perseu Abramo.

Véras, R. (2014). Brasil em obras, peões em luta, sindicatos surpreendidos. *Revista Crítica de Ciências Sociais* 103: 111–136.

Weffort, F. (1973). Origens do sindicalismo populista no Brasil. *Estudos CEBRAP* 4: 66–105.

CHAPTER 16

Social Policy since Rousseff: Misrepresentation and Marginalization

Lena Lavinas and Denise Gentil

1   Introduction[1]

In the first two decades of the twenty-first century, social policy in Brazil underwent important transformations both in terms of the scope of the programs and policies and in terms of the population coverage achieved.

The most remarkable accomplishment was undoubtedly the welfare policy, which was previously nonexistent. The 1988 Constitution established the Continuous Cash Benefit program,[2] a major institutional innovation, but it covered only a portion of the most vulnerable groups – the elderly and disabled living in extreme poverty –, and leaving out the large mass of the poor, made up of adults and children. With the creation of Bolsa Família (Family Grant program)[3] in 2004, this serious failure of coverage was finally remedied by extending to the entire population the right to claim a safety net.

This expansion, however, did not entail an alignment of all parameters applied to anti-poverty policy in order to avoid horizontal inequalities for the target audience. Poverty lines, eligibility criteria, and benefit values often vary depending on the clientele and the program. Thus, while the Continuous Cash Benefit program guarantees a minimum wage equivalent to R$998[4] without conditions, the average value of the Bolsa Familia is R$187,[5] and it imposes conditionalities on children and work requirements on other family members. Anti-poverty policy therefore lacks unity and uniformity.

---

1   An earlier version of the arguments in this chapter appeared in Lavinas L and Gentil D (2020) Social policy since Rousseff. Misrepresentation and marginalization. *Latin American Perspectives* 47(2): 101–116. The authors thank Ana Carolina Cordilha and Leonardo Oliveira for their valuable assistance in producing data.

2   Poverty line equivalent to a per capita household income below a quarter of the current minimum wage.

3   Bolsa Família defines indigence as below R$85 and poverty as below R$185 per capita monthly income.

4   In July 2019 the national minimum wage corresponded to about US$250.

5   Around US$50.

Moreover, except in 2010, social policy maintained its pro-cyclical profile of low effectiveness. This means that during periods of economic slowdown and increase in poverty rates (post-2012), the Bolsa Família program, for example, has not extended its coverage to mitigate the effects of the economy's loss of dynamism, failing to serve the neediest.

As has been widely highlighted (Saboia 2015; Lavinas 2017), what contributed most to the reduction of poverty and inequality in the years marked by economic growth (2003–2013) was less the direct impact of social policies but rather the recovery of formal jobs and an increase in the real earnings, especially the minimum wage.

Anchored in the legal notion of Social Security as a product of the 1988 Constitution, this phase also contributed to the strengthening of public provision: it gained more density. Despite significant tax exemptions and advantages granted to numerous business sectors, the Social Security budget had grown significantly, backed by the sharp rise in formal employment, with positive rebates of social insurance contributions, and the rapidly expanding mass consumption. Both are linked to the exclusive funding sources for Social Security. As a result, the pension system was running a surplus, with rising revenues and growing coverage (Gentil et al. 2017).

At the same time, the period also recorded an accelerated progression of pro-market mechanisms that, associated with new financial products, directly and indirectly broadened their links with the social protection system.

The fast-paced proliferation of highly segmented private health plans is the most acute and paradoxical expression of a path marked by ambiguity and disengagement (Lavinas and Gentil 2018) from a set of individual and collective rights established in the social contract drafted in the transition to democracy. It is worth remembering that a major innovation of the 1988 Constitution was the creation of the Unified Health System (SUS), with universal, free and full coverage. However, alongside the expansion of the public system, a spectacular development of the supplementary (private) health care sector took place at an even more intense pace. The latter benefited from numerous incentives for private medicine, including the maintenance of unlimited tax credits related to health expenses on the personal and corporate income tax, and the loosening of the criteria for granting philanthropy certificates to private entities in the medical-laboratory-hospital area.

Federal health spending as a proportion of GDP[6] remained virtually unchanged under the PT governments, although real spending did increase

---

6   The biggest contradiction of public health in Brazil is that private spending (5 percent of the GDP) prevails over public spending (4.5 percent).

at subnational levels. This trend did not reverse, however, the chronic under-funding imposed on a strategic area in which universal coverage would have decisively contributed to a sharp reduction in inequality rates.

Progress was made through the inclusion of ethnic minorities and low-income-earning groups in higher education, which had previously had a strongly exclusionary profile. Two programs – Univeristy Restructuring and Expansion (REUNI) and University for All (PROUNI) – opened the doors of universities to underprivileged young people and historically discriminated-against social groups. Strikingly, it was a student loan program, the Student Financing Fund (FIES), which experienced rapid expansion and popularity in those years.

In 2015, FIES was responsible for the enrollment of 49.5 percent of students in private colleges and universities. After the 2009 reform, public loans jumped from R\$1 billion to R\$15 billion in 2015, corresponding to 44 percent of total federal spending on public higher education (the overall federal budget for public higher education that year was R\$34 billion). FIES exponentially enlarged not only the number of student loans and, as a result, the almost unpayable amount of student debt – a new phenomenon in Brazil – but also the net worth of the large private corporations that benefited from the easing of access to credit.[7] This maneuver transferred the default risk to the state (Lavinas 2017). More than half (57 percent, around 500,000) of the students who have taken out a loan since 2009 are still in default. Overdue payments in 2018 amounted to some R\$20 billion, according to the National Education Development Fund (*O Estado de São Paulo*, 26 September 2018), as compared to R\$627 million in 2015.

With regard to asset appreciation of the big firms that loomed in higher education also driven by mergers and acquisitions mechanisms, it is sufficient to point to the remarkable rise in Kroton and Estácio share prices. While the Ibovespa index increased by 28.4 percent from 2009 to 2017, Kroton shares rose by 769 percent and Estácio shares by 238 percent (Lavinas and Gentil 2018).

Investment fund managers and foreign investors gradually and indirectly became managers of social policy by becoming the bulk shareholders of large companies in the health and higher education sector. According to Lavinas and Gentil (2018: 204), the majority of private equity funds that bought stakes in publicly traded companies in Brazil after 2009 were foreign: "Once again,

---

7　Elimination of the guarantor and the extended payment period, and an extension of the grace period.

this proves that the process of financialization is also a mechanism for the internationalization of welfare regimes."

The other side of mass financialization (Lavinas, Araújo and Bruno 2019) was access to consumer credit – unsecured credit with no strings attached regarding its use and approved almost instantaneously. Between 2003 and 2012, this credit line registered the highest growth rate (over 300 percent, while that of total wages only doubled). It gained momentum in virtue of being driven by a third organizational innovation: consigned credit, implemented as of 2003, with lower interest rates due to automatic payroll or pension benefit discounts (Lavinas 2017).

This ended up having as its preferential clients those dependent on government payments and transfers, such as civil servants and pensioners. In 2015 these two categories represented more than 93 percent of consigned credit borrowers (Banco Central do Brasil [BCB] 2016), and this remains the main profile. In other words, payments made by the state have become the collateral (Lavinas 2018) that practically eliminates moral hazard for banks besides ensuring considerable profits: while nominal interest rates on consumer credit averaged 140 percent per year in December 2015 (Associação Nacional dos Executivos de Finanças, Administração e Contabilidade 2016), zero-risk payroll-deductible loans still charged 30.7 percent per year (BCB 2016). The largest number of consumer borrowers in Brazil are still families earning up to three minimum wages. According to the Brazilian Central Bank (BCB 2015), they accounted for 61 percent of new loans in 2014 alone. That same year, this income bracket allocated 73 percent of disposable household income to debt repayments to the financial sector.

The strong expansion of consumer credit served to finance needs not met by public policies, which fell short in guaranteeing the new constitutional rights. Contrary to common knowledge, consumer credit was not only meant to purchase durable goods and other wage goods which, in fact, should be accessible through valued and adequate wages, and a fair tax system. The research on default rates carried out regularly by the Credit Protection Service and the National Confederation of Retailers (*Veja*, 12 February 2019) makes this clear. By the end of 2018, 63 million adults were in arrears with banks and financial companies for more than 90 days. Ninety-three percent belonged to classes C, D, and E (the lowest income brackets, including those living below the poverty line). The two most heavily delinquent items were clothing and food. Debt has become a mechanism of social reproduction in Brazil during the 2000s.

Market inclusion through consumption occurred, but at the price of a substantial indebtedness of a significant share of the population, which, in addition, repeatedly extends the list of very high default rates. The ambiguity of social policy was the hallmark of PT administrations. This ambivalence gradually changed the welfare regime designed in 1988, paving the way for the enhancement of the commodification process, announced by the pension and labor market "reforms" of the post-impeachment phase (2016).

The aim of this introduction was to provide a brief background to reflect on the events that followed the impeachment of President Dilma Rousseff, which utterly changed the political, economic, cultural, and social directions of the country. Thus the objectives of this chapter are (1) to characterize the social framework in the pre- and post-impeachment stages and to interpret the direction of the so-called Temer reforms and their impact on deepening and generalizing the financialization of the Brazilian economy and the takeover of social policy; (2) to highlight the low complementarity between macroeconomic policy and social policy in these two periods; and (3) to envision potential scenarios with the election of a right-wing government, ultra-liberal regarding the economy, and ultra-conservative regarding values and morals, pointing out redistribution challenges.

2   An Overview of Social Indicators on the Crisis

Following the sharpest recession ever experienced by the Brazilian economy, with a negative real product growth of 7.2 percent in 2015–2016, and a slight recovery in 2017 and 2018 when annual GDP (backed once again by agribusiness performance) increased by 1.1 percent (Instituto Brasileiro de Geografia e Estatística [IBGE] 2018), many social indicators collapsed.

Extreme poverty returned to levels prevailing at the beginning of the millennium, prior to the creation of the Bolsa Família program. By the end of 2018 there were around 15 million people, 7.5 percent of the population, living in extreme poverty, a similar percentage as in 2004 (Instituto de Pesquisa Econômica Aplicada [IPEA] 2018), and double that observed in 2014. Poverty now decimates the daily life of more than 24 million people.

The World Bank poverty cutoff line adopted in 2017 for middle-income countries corresponds to US$ 5.5 PPP/day,[8] more than double the poverty line considered by Bolsa Familia. According to this metrics, 55 million Brazilians (PNADc 2017), or ¼ of the population, have fallen below the poverty line. The

---

8 This poverty line corresponds to the median of the poverty lines of upper-middle-income countries such as Brazil. This line is then added to the existing one, which has a cutoff value of US$1.90 PPP (purchasing power parity) per day.

picture is dramatic, since nearly half of all Brazilian children under 14, according to this same indicator, are poor.

Different estimates of the percentage of poor and indigent in Brazil reveal profound imbalances regarding the degrees of destitution. This means that our view of poverty reinforces patterns of inequality with which we become accustomed to. Moreover, it still serves all sorts of assessments, from the most rigorous to the most lenient ones when it comes to measuring the real drop in poverty rates and the success of the welfare programs implemented. The most appropriate poverty threshold – for it is associated with the average standard of living of the Brazilian population –, is the one that adopts the metric of 50% below the median income, which increases to 30.1% the number of people living in poverty. Using common sense, it can be said that the magnitude of poverty is high in Brazil starting at the crisis, as it affects between 10% and 30% of Brazilians, or somewhere between 20 and 60 million people depending on the cutoff criterion chosen.

The corollary of this situation is the inflection, in the trajectory, of indicators that had shown constant improvement since the mid-1990s and were cause for celebration.

Unemployment remained above 12 percent (corresponding to approximately 13 million people) in the last quarter of 2018, well above all annual averages compiled since 1991 (IPEA 2018). Half of the unemployed are young (16–29), and the number of individuals neither studying nor working in this age-group has continued to rise and now exceeds 11 million (one in five).

Together, the unemployment and underemployment rates reached 18.6 percent, revealing the damaging and predictable consequences of the Temer-era labor reforms, a major promoter of job insecurity and a brake on wage recovery. Therefore, the Gini index[9] resumed an upward trend, albeit at a slow pace. A recent study by Daniel Duque (*O Estado de São Paulo*, 22 February 2018) on the evolution of the Gini index as measured by per capita household income revealed that by the end of 2018 it had reached 0.62, its highest level since the first quarter of 2012, when the Continuous National Household Sample series started. In other words, Brazil has returned to a level of inequality that prevailed in times of economic miracle under an authoritarian regime, when growth was brought about through strengthening the concentration of income. But now Brazilians have more inequality, with no prosperity.

---

9   According to the IBGE, the percentage of Brazilian families living in severe food insecurity was 6.5 percent in 2004 and dropped to 3.2 percent in 2013.

The recession, which led to an abrupt shrinkage of the labor market, had immediate effects on inequality, which in those years of relative prosperity, due to the ineffectiveness of tax policy, never decreased as expected. Having registered a modest drop in its inequality ranking during the commodity boom, Brazil saw its relative position deteriorate again, becoming, by the end of 2018, the ninth-most-unequal country on the planet, and number one in Latin America.

Surprisingly, the income estimates of the National Household Sample Survey show that between 2015 and 2017 there was no decline in average monthly labor income in constant values (IBGE 2017). Actually, there was a slight increase, to R$2,247 from R$2,197, which is a paradox considering the high level of unemployment. It is plausible to suppose, therefore, that the sharp increase in poverty and indigence rates is correlated with the complete exclusion of most of the working-age population from the labor market, most likely the groups favored in the recent growth phase (2003–2014) by the expansion of formal employment in the range of up to two minimum wages (Lavinas 2017). This corresponded to 82% of the balance of formal job creation in the period (Lavinas, Cordilha, and Cruz 2016). This means that the increase in real income, in a situation characterized by such high levels of unemployment, informality, and precarious employment, may be conveying that windows of opportunity have been closed to those with low skills and little experience at the bottom of the occupational pyramid.

It is a fact that employment and income indicators are the most sensitive to a serious and resilient economic crisis. But what do education indicators that capture longer-term outcomes display regarding the learning capacity of Brazilian youth over time? According to the Basic Education Assessment System (SAEB reference?), only 1.6 percent of young people enrolled in the last grade of high school in 2017 showed adequate performance in Portuguese (the percentage in Mathematics rose to 4.5 percent.) In addition, no state reached the Basic Education Development Index (IDEB reference?) target of 4.7 expected for high school; the index went from 3.7 in 2015 to 3.8 in 2017 (Instituto Nacional de Estudos e Pesquisas Educacionais 2017). As if the poor performance were not enough, it should be stressed that in 2017, according to the IBGE, 1.5 million young people aged 15–17 have dropped-out of school.

Finally, data from the Ministry of Health indicate that for the first time since 1990 the infant mortality rate reversed its downward trend. There were 14 deaths per 1,000 live births in 2016, an increase of 4.8 percent over 2015. Data from the Food and Nutrition Surveillance System compiled by the Abrinq Foundation reveal that from 2016 to 2017 the percentage of malnourished children under

5 years increased from 12.6 percent to 13.1 percent.[10] At the same time, Brazil plummeted 17 positions in the United Nations Development Program's Human Development Index ranking (*Valor Econômico*, 18 September 2018).

This demeaning scenario of drastically reduced future opportunities and even life expectancy for new generations is a direct consequence of austerity policies that did not spare social programs by the end of the second Dilma administration.

3 Macroeconomics Constraining Social Policy: The Dilma Rousseff Administration

It is no simple task to identify the social and political forces that aligned to promote the dismantling of the so-called social-developmentalist project during the second mandate of President Dilma Rousseff. However, over a period of five years (2011–2015), various factors cemented a distance between the PT government and its traditional political support base. At the same time, an elite union center was invigorated and reorganized to oppose the PT government. The conservative macroeconomic regime inherited from the Fernando Henrique Cardoso government (1999–2002), shaped by floating exchange rates, strict inflation targets, contractionary fiscal targets and a strongly regressive tax system, was once again assumed by President Dilma Rousseff as a condition for governability.

This wide party coalition demanded that these orthodox pillars remain untouched for the sake of achieving "peaceful coexistence" in the Congress. The novelty of the alliance lied in the alleged reconciliation of this strategy with broader low-cost welfare policies, maintaining the logic of targeting and conditionalities, in line with the neoliberal precepts of multilateral organizations. The fight against poverty prevailed over the consolidation of a sustainable and effective social protection system. The Rousseff administration, instead of reversing this path, unveiled a phase that deepened the conservative dimension of both economic and social policy.

In fact, the economic policy of the Rousseff administration was popularly known as the "New Macroeconomic Matrix". It was intended to replace the mass-consumption-based-growth model, exhausted after 2010,[11] with a new

---

10   According to the IBGE, the percentage of Brazilian families living in severe food insecurity was 6.5 percent in 2004 and dropped to 3.2 percent in 2013.

11   The dynamics of growth driven by consumption generated leaks; an important part of the demand was met by an import increase of 103.4 percent between the end of 2005 and the end of 2010. Between 2003 and 2009, the growth rate of imports of consumer

growth engine based on private investment and exports (Serrano and Summa 2014; Carvalho 2018). Lower interest rates and depreciated nominal exchange rates were priorities. Fiscal policy would be amended to amplify tax exemptions and cut spending (including social spending but especially public investment), thus offsetting the price increase produced by the devaluation of the real and lower interest rates.[12] Macroprudential credit restraint measures were also devised to discourage consumption but, albeit more slowly, credit continued with its upward trend.

The strategy of Dilma's government encompassed stimulus to private investment through extensive privatization of the infrastructure sector, lower energy rates, fuel price controls, and boosts to oil and gas sector development. It, however, did fail. The "New Matrix" managed to temporarily accelerate the pace of economic growth from the third quarter of 2012 to the first quarter of 2014 at an annualized growth rate of over 2.5 percent, but thereafter it collapsed (Oreiro 2017). It would be a mistake to consider this simply bad economic policy. For the purposes of this chapter, only the data, events, and mechanisms linked to social policy are highlighted.

From the point of view of fiscal policy, two factors produced ambiguous effects in the social arena, thus contributing to the subsequent political ruin of Dilma's government: a) the allocation of public spending, which focused on two pillars: monetary transfers to households (via pension and welfare benefits) and financial expenses, and b) the expenditure-financing structure, which involved the strongly regressive profile of the tax burden and the rapid growth of public debt starting in 2013, along with a steady increase in household indebtedness. These features were more important in slowing GDP growth, the ineffectiveness of income distribution, the fight against poverty, and the loss of decisive support for coping with political adversity than the level of social spending itself.

---

electronics increased by 33 percent per year (Lavinas 2017). It became increasingly evident that the growth phase of the 2004–2010 period had brought about the reprimarization of the Brazilian economy, the hypertrophy of the services sector, and major weaknesses in the industrial sector (Carvalho 2018). The rapid increase in social spending, credit, and the minimum wage generated fragile growth because there was no guarantee in domestic production.

12 In fact, the basic interest rate (SELIC) started to fall after August 2011, but this policy was short-lived. It rose again from March 2013 on as the inflation-targeting regime imposed increases in interest rates due to the symptoms of rising inflation. In fact, in 2013 inflation as measured by the IPCA (Broad Consumer Price Index) rose to 5.91 percent, very close to the upper limit of the inflation range.

Regarding the surge of social spending at the federal level,[13] there was a slight expansion as a percentage of GDP in the health, education, and social assistance sectors between 2011 and 2015. Nevertheless, this positive result was partly misleading because it stems from the deceleration of the GDP growth[14] in the same period (Table 16.1). The same table 16.1 also indicates that there were declining annual rates from 2011 until reaching negative rates in 2015. This is a clear demonstration that social policy in the Dilma Rousseff period was abandoned instead of gaining new momentum, acting countercyclically to rekindle consumption and preserve government legitimacy based on its traditional political support foundation.

Importantly, cash transfers accounted for half of federal government primary spending. Gobetti and Orair (2017) concluded that the average annual growth rate of social spending on transfers alone[15] for the Cardoso government was 7.5 percent per year. In both Lula governments, the rates were higher, reaching 8.7 percent per year, while in the Dilma period (2011–2014) the rate was 5.8 percent per year. In 2015, when a very strong fiscal adjustment took place, social spending fell to –0.7 percent per year. There is no doubt that social policy suffered a sharp contraction of resources.

It must be recognized, however, that reducing poverty and income inequality depends only partially on the level of social spending. An important part of this process relies on the structure of tax expenditures (Barr 2004), which contributes to broadening or restricting the redistributive effects of social policy. Another part is conditioned by the macroeconomic environment in which social policies are implemented. Thus, for the period analyzed, the redistributive effects of social spending responded to two major constraints. First, the design of means-test targeted programs, which excluded a large number of potential beneficiaries, and second, the recessionary economic environment that derived from the more conservative macroeconomic policy and the decline of commodity prices. Therefore, although social spending was selectively preserved (especially social insurance spending, to the detriment of healthcare and education, for instance), there were considerable limits to its compensatory effects.

---

13   There was an increase in social spending at the subnational level as states and municipalities increased their education and health spending in accordance with the Constitution.

14   Spending measured against GDP is influenced by the cyclical and structural conditions of the economy and is not a good indicator, especially in a strongly recessive period.

15   This value includes welfare expenses, social security, unemployment insurance, and salary bonuses.

TABLE 16.1 Settled federal social expenditures, annual real growth rate at 2017 prices (%) and % of GDP

Year	Social welfare		Pension plan[a]		Health		Education	
	%	% of GDP	%	% of GDP	%	% of GDP	%	% of GDP
2003	5.2	0.5	−3.8	8.5	−3.0	1.6	−2.4	0.8
2004	50.6	0.7	4.0	8.4	10.9	1.7	−6.6	0.7
2005	7.6	0.7	7.5	8.7	4.4	1.7	5.1	0.7
2006	34.0	0.9	10.8	8.8	7.1	1.6	5.3	0.7
2007	8.8	0.9	4.4	8.6	−5.6	1.5	3.7	0.7
2008	4.5	0.9	−0.9	8.3	−0.5	1.4	4.3	0.7
2009	13.5	1.0	10.7	8.7	9.6	1.5	27.5	0.9
2010	11.0	1.0	6.4	8.4	6.1	1.4	27.5	1.0
2011	7.3	1.0	1.7	8.2	5.9	1.4	4.6	1.0
2012	15.1	1.2	4.3	8.5	5.3	1.5	13.1	1.1
2013	6.1	1.2	4.8	8.6	1.6	1.5	13.0	1.2
2014	4.1	1.2	5.5	8.9	6.6	1.5	10.4	1.3
2015	−8.5	1.2	−5.9	9.1	−2.2	1.6	−3.2	1.4
2016	5.5	1.2	6.1	9.2	0.6	1.6	1.7	1.4
2017	5.3	0.3	9.9	10.0	0.0	1.6	1.7	1.4

a Includes RGPS and RPPS expenses (RGPS – PAYG general scheme; RPPS: civil servants PAYG scheme).
SOURCE: SIAFI-STN/CCONT/GEINC, MINISTRY OF ECONOMY; OWN ELABORATION

Table 16.1 confirms the relative stagnation of federal spending as a percentage of GDP in health, education and social assistance as of 2014. In the 2003–2017 period there was a significant increase in welfare benefits spending; a rise in federal spending on education; a more modest growth in pensions; and health care maintained its stagnant participation as a percentage of GDP over those 14 years.

4 Productive Structure and Social Policy

The interests of financial capital (expressed in public debt interest expenses and the rampant growth of debt) imposed a well-defined social policy, one in which money transfers predominated over the provision of decommodified public services (especially health, housing, transportation, and education). The latter are more costly and inhibit the expansion of private capital into highly profitable sectors.

The expansion of different modalities of income transfers to families allowed, as noted earlier, the incorporation of the poorer population in the mass consumption market, a target of the Lula-Dilma governments' legitimation strategy. However, the rampant shortage of essential public services forced the purchase of private services and drove families into the credit and insurance markets, squeezing income from wages and social benefits, leading to mounting indebtedness, and shifting workers' income to the financial sector, fueling interest-bearing capital. The combination of deficits in the public provision of decommodified goods and services along with insufficient benefits and wages led to turn income transfers – the bulk of social policy – into collateral to access the financial market (Lavinas 2018), which became the ultimate provider of wellbeing.

Inclusion in the labor market, although undisputed until 2014, was insufficient to hinder the growing share of family income devoted to debt repayments to the financial sector or capable of significantly augmenting the wage share in GDP. Total wages went from 38.9 percent of GDP in 2002 to 43.1 percent in 2013 (IBGE 2013). Credit went from approximately 21 percent to 54 percent of GDP in that same period.

A second key factor in explaining the intensification of struggles for redistribution derived from the combination of an upward trend in labor incomes with only modest improvements in productivity levels. The average variation of productivity remained around 1 percent per year between 2001 and 2013, even though it was significant in the agricultural sector (growing at 4.9 percent per year) alone, once again driven by the commodity boom (Table 16.2).

Saramago (2016) shows that real wages grew at an average rate of 3.5 percent per year in the 2009–2013 period while real productivity set the pace at 1.4 percent per year in the same period.

Given the arrangement supported by high interest rates, a powerful stimulus to nonproductive activities, companies and government did not prioritize technological innovation, expansion of labor productivity, or improvement of the educational level and technical skills of the workforce, which would have entailed long-term investment. There was therefore no pressure on the business sector – which depended on the state for their financial income – to allocate capital to productive accumulation, with potential impacts on productivity growth. This deepened the conflict for redistribution by creating a fierce dispute between social spending and financial spending within the public

TABLE 16.2   Variation in real labor productivity (% per year), 2001–2013

	2001–2004	2004–2009	2009–2013	Total
Total	0.0	0.8	1.9	1.0
Farming	2.2	4.6	7.2	4.9
Mining	0.7	1.7	–2.9	–0.1
Manufacturing	–0.8	–2.0	0.4	–0.9
Construction	0.4	–0.7	2.1	0.5
Trade	–1.3	1.4	0.7	0.5
Services	–0.5	0.8	3.1	1.2

SOURCE: SARAMAGO 2016: 80

budget. The scenario ended up characterized by unsustainability and a permanent contradiction between rent-seeking activities and low labor productivity, on the one hand, and universal public provision, on the other.

The state became all the more incapable of sustaining growth and well-being. With the end of the commodity boom and the slowdown of the world economy from 2012 on, this contradiction exploded.

A third factor was the heavy tax exemptions that marked President Rousseff's mandates. The labor market showed great dynamism between 2011 and 2014, maintaining significant levels of formal employment, which helped foster revenues linked to social protection policies (income from pensions and the social security system as a whole). But devastating tax cuts undermined the social security budget, reflecting attempts to rebuild the profit margins damaged by wage increases well above productivity and the appreciated exchange rate that intensified competition with imported goods.

Table 16.3 shows the steady growth in real values of income waivers and their equivalent as a proportion of GDP globally, but also referring exclusively to the social security budget. Between 2007 and 2016 (year of the impeachment), the value of tax exemptions increased and remained above 4 percent of GDP throughout most of Dilma's administration, with more than half being withdrawn from the social security budget.

The mismatch between revenues and expenditures of the social security system strengthened those who were calling for reforms in order to curb social rights. Dilma's government gave in to conservative appeals from its coalition in Congress, inevitably creating friction with its support base of unions, social organizations, and middle-income segments. Social policy narrowed as

TABLE 16.3   Tax exemptions in current R$ millions and % of GDP, 2007–2017

Year	Total exemptions	% of GDP	Social contribution exemptions				Total social security exemptions	% of GDP
			Contribution to pension funds	COFINS	CSLL	PIS/PASEP		
2007	102,673	3.95	n.a.	13,351	2,958	2,377	18,686	0.81
2008	114,755	3.78	n.a.	20,058	4,525	3,732	28,315	1.03
2009	116,098	3.65	17,905	29,418	6,087	5,651	59,061	1.85
2010	113,861	3.60	18,183	33,883	8,333	6,955	67,354	2.02
2011	152,406	3.68	21,156	34,618	5,830	6,542	68,146	1.75
2012	182,410	4.15	24,412	41,376	6,976	8,145	80,909	1.78
2013	225,630	4.66	33,743	46,142	8,788	9,060	97,733	1.97
2014	253,902	4.92	57,012	58,510	9,301	11,639	136,462	2.60
2015	282,437	4.93	62,519	70,538	10,490	14,100	157,647	2.75
2016	271,006	4.33	54,349	64,558	11,171	12,887	142,965	2.29
2017	284,846	4.19	62,493	64,023	11,792	12,720	151,028	2.22

Note: Data from 2015 to 2017 are estimates. COFINS, Contributions for the Financing of Social Security; CSLL, Social Contributions on Net Corporate Profits; PIS/PASEP, Program of Social Integration/Program for Public Servants' Endowment.
SOURCE: INTERNAL REVENUE SERVICE, MINISTRY OF FINANCE (2007–) PLOA (PROPOSAL FOR THE ANNUAL BUDGET LAW, PROJECTIONS) AND REAL BASES REPORT. OWN ELABORATION

rentism advanced with the use of budget resources at the same pace as interest rate climbed.[16] These exclusionary dynamics were already visible in the 2013 June protests but were underestimated by the PT government, which would only come to realize the existing impasse when it lacked the support of protesters during President Dilma's impeachment process.

Examination of the income tax statements filed with the Internal Revenue Service reveals the social setting that was being outlined. Medeiros et al. (2015) and Morgan (2017) showed that the reduction of income inequality under the PT rule was not what was imagined when reviewing only household survey data that essentially registered labor income, pensions and welfare transfers. Their analysis showed no fall in the income share of the richest 1 percent in the 2000s, and although wages at the bottom of the pyramid augmented their participation, capital income increased much more and remained highly concentrated among the wealthiest individuals.[17] The financial elite had no reason to complain. Additionally, there were many reasons for dissatisfaction in middle-income segments for they experienced a severe deterioration of their standard of living as the cost of essential basic services such as education and health rose many times above average inflation (Lavinas 2017).

In a period of falling profits for companies in the productive sector, soaring income from financial and real estate assets was responsible for the resilience of inequality. Examining the evolution of the return on equity rate of Brazilian publicly traded nonfinancial companies and the largest nonfinancial private companies, Rocca (2015, cited in Oreiro 2017) reported a trend toward reduction from 2011 on, reaching 4.3 percent per year in 2014, lower than the observed inflation, and therefore negative in real terms. Oreiro (2017) points out that the main factor in declining return rates was the drop in the profit margins of nonfinancial corporations, especially industry. At the same time, the stock of nonmonetary financial assets increased at an average annual rate of 7.9 percent between 2011 and 2014 (Lavinas, Araújo, and Bruno 2017), showing that financialization had invaded the logic of the private sector, rescuing the losses of nonfinancial corporations.

---

16   Reforms of varying degrees have been constant in the past 18 years, particularly in social security. The most important reforms of the PT governments were Constitutional Amendments 41/2003, 47/2005, and 70/2012, Law 12.618/12, and Law 13.134/15.

17   Morgan's (2017) data (cited in Carvalho 2018) suggest that while the poorest 50 percent increased their share of total income from 11 percent to 12 percent between 2001 and 2015, the richest 10 percent increased their share from 25 percent to 28 percent. The class that lost most in the growth of the period was the middle-income range, around 40 percent, whose share of income decreased from 34 percent to 2 percent in those years, creating the "squeezed middle" (Carvalho 2018).

5   The Temer Government: Radicalizing Neoliberal Policies
        (2016–2018)

From May 2016, with the removal of Dilma Rousseff, the federal government turned out to be controlled by the most profound conservatism in macroeconomic policy, which meant major changes in the management of social policy as well.

Immediately after his inauguration, President Michel Temer implemented an administrative reform of the ministries, removing the Ministry of Social Security, whose main responsibilities were transferred to the Ministry of Social Development and the Ministry of Finance. The Special Secretariat of Women was also terminated, and the Ministry of Science and Technology was incorporated into Communication, reducing both its social and technological strategic importance and relevance to the country's development. These initiatives unfolded the rebuilding of the new government's political base, hand in hand with the post-impeachment Congress. In so doing, they turned away from the most vulnerable social groups that, under the PT rule, had gained political visibility.

In a short time, a sequence of attacks on social rights took place. In December 2016, a constitutional amendment (95/2016) capped federal expenditures for 20 years, limiting the real growth of primary spending while leaving financial spending intact. Until then the government had to mandatorily allocate to health at least the amount spent in the previous year plus the GDP growth rate, and states and municipalities had to invest 12 percent and 15 percent, respectively, of their net tax revenue. Whereas the 2014–2024 National Education Plan had anticipated raising spending to 10 percent of GDP (from an average of 5 percent), under the new tax regime federal agencies were freed from the constitutional obligation to guarantee minimum percentages of their fiscal revenues for health and education. Thus the goals of the 2014–2024 education plan became worthless pieces of paper, aggravating the chronic underfunding faced by SUS and public universities over the years.

A new blow to social rights came with the Outsourcing Law (Law 13,429 of March 31, 2017), which dealt with temporary work and companies providing services to third parties. Now companies can outsource all activities – including their end activities. The measure deepens the precarious nature of work: wages tend to decrease (according to the Departamento Intersindical de Estatísticas e Estudos Socioeconômicos ([DIEESE] 2018), 2018, 30 percent lower than with direct hiring) and unions have been weakened (outsourcers are represented by different categories, demobilizing the strongest unions that had negotiated higher minimum wages).

Continuing the dismantling of Brazilian worker protection legislation, the Temer administration also implemented the Labor Reform that annulled constitutional rights that society had imagined almost impossible to be overruled. The main losses are as follows: the possibility of salary reduction by collective dismissal and rehiring through outsourcing or individual agreements; the prevalence of individual agreements over labor legislation; the division of holidays into up to three periods according to company preference; regulation of telecommuting by task rather than by work schedule; travel time to work no longer being considered time worked; work hours of up to 12 hours per 36 hours of rest; and the termination of equal pay for equal work in the same company.

The Congress, run by a majority whose many members are investigated on charges of corruption, money laundering, gangsterism, obstruction of justice, and other political crimes, approved the disruption of labor and worker protection. In the face of a demobilized and discouraged society, the democratic advances protected by the 88 Constitution were demolished without resistance.

Pension reform was left out. Nevertheless, on the revenue side, the Temer government implemented a providential dismantling, granting favors to companies with debt in installments and relief of fines and interest to tax evaders through the Fiscal Recovery Program. States and municipalities, as well as big individual and corporate farmers, did also benefit from debt relief. More than healthy finances, what was sought with the fiscal adjustment achieved through the loss of social rights was to make room for the advancement of private medicine and education, and private pension funds – in other words, the defense of the interests of large banks and investment funds.

Major cuts in social programs were adding up. The My House, My Life program suffered a 53 percent reduction in its budget in the first six months of 2017, reaching only R$1.4 billion compared with R$2.99 billion for the same period in 2016. The IBGE estimated the housing deficit at over 7 million homes. Between June and July 2017, about 543,000 Bolsa Família beneficiary families were removed from the program. Added to this list of exclusionary measures was the end of the Popular Pharmacy program, which had provided medicine for some 9 million people with chronic diseases.

President Temer was not only attacking social rights. His intervention was also fostering denationalization and deindustrialization. In the field of monetary policy, despite successive drops of the SELIC (the basic interest rate), banks and nonfinancial corporations continued to enjoy extremely high real interest rates (DIEESE 2018). Despite a totally adverse scenario, banks were able to expand their assets and profits, breaking records every quarter. They continued to invest in public securities and in the transfer of customer operations to virtual channels at very low cost to institutions reducing, by the same token, their physical and functional service structures. But their biggest source of profit came from the expansion of credit, reinforcing the logic of interest-bearing capital.

6   Conclusion

In 2018, the ballot boxes showed that the Brazil of the first two decades of the new millennium no longer existed. A candidate without a clear program of government won the presidential election. Averse to discussing ideas, he presented himself as ultraconservative in his social customs and values and ultraliberal in economic policy. He promised to take the dismantling of the state further, to such an extent that he envisions privatizing public security by making citizens' physical protection the responsibility of individuals and families rather than the monopoly and inherent attribute of a modern state. To this end, he proposed to allow the free possession and carrying of weapons. He emphasized that labor market deregulation must be deepened, creating a new green-and-yellow work card that does not link worker status to rights.

Reforming social security, particularly pensions, was one of his favorite topics for making people believe that the "fight against privilege" was his motto and line of action. The pay-as-you-go public system was to be sacrificed to balance public accounts without any mention of tackling the acute deindustrialization that is mortgaging the country's future and condemning Brazilians to live with a manufacturing sector with the lowest share of GDP since 1947 (11.3 percent by the end of 2018).

His approach to the "ruralist bench" (the agribusiness lobby), which was fundamental to his victory in the presidential elections, indicated that the Brazilian economy would once again focus on commodities, strengthening the old extractivist model with high costs either through the total liberalization of the use of pesticides and mining or by challenging the environmental reserves, particularly those managed by indigenous communities. These measures will bring about a rise of environmental crime – more murders of environmental leaders and repression of those who defend opportunities and incentives for family organic agriculture, a mechanism for the deconcentration of land and wealth. The liberalization of gun ownership in rural areas will be complete, bringing the risk of legitimate executions.

Without an ambitious and competent project for stimulating long-term growth with innovation and redistribution of income and wealth (aspects missing from the presidential candidate's platform in 2019), government action continues to focus on promoting additional cuts in public spending through the deconstitutionalization of rights and the dismantling of institutions. Such a dismantling will have the effect of offering devastated land to the market, which can then reshape the country in terms of its own interests without anchors or foundation.

It is premature to say what will happen to social policy as a whole. Prevention in the fight against poverty, food insecurity and violence, and in favor of universal and free health care and education, and good housing provision will very likely continue to lose budget shares as public policies tend to be disconnected from their preventive dimension. The logic of privatization is reinforced, leading to increasing shrinkage of the public sector. The financial players – pension funds, private equity funds, and investment funds – that already dominate these sectors will certainly benefit and be strengthened by mergers and acquisitions trends, sharpening the denationalization of the very profitable services sector. This means that the old Brazilian structural heterogeneity will persist, generating more inequality and exclusion.

References

Associação Nacional dos Executivos de Finanças, Administração e Contabilidade. (2016). Base de dados. Rio de Janeiro.

Banco Central do Brasil. (2016). Base de dados sobre crédito. Brasília.

Banco Central do Brasil. (2015). Relatório de inclusão financeira 2014. Brasília.

Barr, N. (2004). *Economics of the Welfare State*. London: Oxford University Press.

Carvalho, L. (2018). *A Valsa Brasileira: do Boom ao Caos Econômico*. São Paulo: Todavia.

Departamento Intersindical de Estatísticas e Estudos Socioeconômicos. (2018). Desempenho dos bancos. https://www.dieese.org.br/desempenhodosbancos/2018/desempenhoDosBancos1semestre2018.html (accessed as of 4 March 2019).

Gentil, D., Araújo, E., Puty, C., and Silma, C. (2017). *Uma análise não convencional para o problema da previdência social no Brasil: aspectos teóricos e evidência empírica*. Brasília: ANFIP/DIEESE and Plataforma Política Social.

Gobetti, S., and Orair, R. (2017). *Resultado primário e contabilidade criativa: Reconstruindo as estatísticas fiscais "acima da linha" do governo geral*. Discussion Text 2288. Brasília: Ipea.

Instituto Brasileiro de Geografia e Estatística. (2013). *Contas nacionais*. Brasília.

Instituto Brasileiro de Geografia e Estatística. (2012). *Pesquisa nacional por amostra de domicílios*. Brasília.

Instituto de Pesquisa Econômica. (2018). *Indicadores sociais, mercado de trabalho, taxa de desemprego, população acima de 10 anos*. Brasília.

Instituto Nacional de Estudos e Pesquisas Educacionais. (2016). *Sistema de avaliação da educação básica.* Brasília.

Lavinas, L. (2018). The collateralisation of social policy under financialized capitalism. *Development and Change* 49: 502–517.

Lavinas, L. (2017). *The Takeover of Social Policy by Financialization: The Brazilian Paradox.* New York: Palgrave Macmillan.

Lavinas, L., Araújo, E., and Bruno, M. (2019). Brazil: from eliticized to mass-based financialization. *Revue de la Régulation* 25(1) (accessed as of 7 June 2019).

Lavinas, L., and Gentil, D. (2018). Brasil anos 2000: A política social sob regência da financeirização. *Novos Estudos* 37(2): 191–211.

Lavinas, L., Cordilha, A.C., and Cruz, G. (2016). Assimetrias de gênero no mercado de trabalho no Brasil: rumos da formalização. In: Abreu, A.R.P., Hirata, H., and Lombardi, M.R. (eds.), *Gênero e Trabalho no Brasil e na França: Perspectivas Interseccionais*, 93–109. São Paulo: Boitempo.

Medeiros, M., Souza, P.F., and Castro, F.A. (2015). O topo da distribuição de renda no Brasil: primeiras estimativas com dados tributários e comparação com pesquisas domiciliares, 2006–2012. *Dados – Revista de Ciências Sociais* 58(1): 7–36.

Ministry of Finance. (2007). *Receita Federal.* Brasília.

Morgan, M. (2017). *Extreme and persistent inequality: New evidence for Brazil combining national accounts, surveys, and fiscal data, 2001–2015.* WID Working Paper 2017/12.

Oreiro, J.L. (2017). A grande recessão brasileira: diagnóstico e uma agenda de política econômica. *Estudos Avançados* 31(89): 75–88. .

Saramago, H.A. (2016). *Trajetória da parcela dos salários na renda no Brasil: análise de decomposição a partir do salário real e da produtividade (1990–2013).* Master's thesis, Universidade Federal do Rio de Janeiro.

Saboia, J.M. (2015). Salário mínimo e distribuição de renda no Brasil: potencial e limites. In: Barbosa, N., Pessoa, S., and Moura, R. (eds.), *Política de Salário Mínimo para 2015–18.* São Paulo: Elsevier-FGV, 65–82.

Serrano, F., and Summa, R. (2014). Notas sobre a desaceleração rudimentar da economia brasileira. In: Earp, F.S., Bastian, E., and Modenesi, A. (eds.), *Como Vai o Brasil? A Economia Brasileira no Terceiro Milênio*, 85–113. Rio de Janeiro: Imã Editorial.

CHAPTER 17

The Reform of Pensions under the Workers' Party

Shades of Commodification

Lucas Salvador Andrietta, Patrícia Rocha Lemos and Eduardo Fagnani

1 Introduction[1]

The Partido dos Trabalhadores (Workers' Party – PT) governments have long been the subject of polemics and reflections on the meaning of their policies. Among these, however, the prevailing understanding appears to be that they were characterized from the outset by the maintenance of a neoliberal economic policy (Morais and Saad-Filho 2011; Paulani 2003; Singer 2012) imposed by a political arrangement that encompassed a coalition of the most diverse interests. This strategy not only frustrated the execution of structural reforms but also increased the constraints of the combination of neoliberal macroeconomic policy and poverty reduction through the activation of the domestic market. Further, the strategy of "serving two masters" (Marques and Mendes 2007: 16)[2] often reached critical moments such as the global economic crisis of 2008 and the resulting slowdown of international trade. As the major sporting events and the elections approached, political conflict intensified in the demonstrations of 2013. The capture of some of these demands by sectors of the opposition, the economic "terrorism" of the 2014 elections, and the decisions made at the start of the second Dilma Rousseff administration created the context for the crisis that culminated in her impeachment in 2016. These events threatened the "weak reformism" that had started in Lula's second term (Singer 2012).[3]

---

1 An earlier version of this chapter appeared in Andrietta et al. (2020).

2 For the authors, the idea of "serving two masters" indicates that the first Lula administration favored, through economic policy, the interests of financial capital and agribusiness, while at the same time implementing a series of programs aimed at the poorer segment of the population (Marques and Mendes 2007: 16).

3 This is these authors' term for the idea that the first Lula administration favored the interests of financial capital and agribusiness while at the same time implementing a series of programs aimed at the poorer segment of the population.

These governments, although maintaining the essentials of the neoliberal macroeconomic policy of their predecessors, differed from them mainly by the extension of policies of income transfer to the poorest, such as Bolsa Família, the increase in the minimum wage (from 2006 on), the generation of formal jobs, and a set of public policies of limited scope and budget but significant social impact.[4] However, the social dimension of the political project – a fundamental component of the structure identified by Singer (2012) – did not allow the strengthening of universal social policies such as those on social security inherited from the 1988 Constitution. The trends observed in the areas of health and welfare,[5] for example, are very different from the stimulus and the positive and patriotic propaganda of focused policies such as the income transfers and the antipoverty programs (Lavinas 2015). Thus, an analysis of the social security issue can contribute to an understanding of the nature of the PT governments at a time when the dispute over the maintenance of social rights in the country has become more intense. Not only is social security, by its magnitude, a privileged target of austerity policies but the social security issue reveals political interests fundamental to an understanding of the underlying political structure of Lulism.[6]

The social security issue is understood in this chapter as a problem that involves the three parts of the Brazilian social security system,[7] which mobilizes the interests of various groups regarding the identification of its access rules, the calculation of benefits, its regulation of public and private institutions, its financing, and its implications for the national economy, especially the labor market and sectors that offer private alternatives. The hybrid nature of the system is the result of the historical path of the Brazilian social security issue, which consolidated a system in which different regimes coexisted, each functioning according to its own conception and dynamics (Delgado 2001). The struggle for redemocratization in Brazil was an important milestone on this path, since it disseminated a new social agenda founded on the principles of social security. In this sense, the formal definition of social rights of the 1988 Constitution suggested the structuring of policies inspired by the values of the

---

4   In describing the PT governments as weak reformist, Singer also highlighted the tension within the party itself between what were characterized as the "two souls of the PT". This dispute was expressed by Fagnani (2011: 45) as the coexistence within the government of forces that defended the paradigm of the minimal state those that defended universal rights.

5   For example, the Light for All program, the More Doctors plan, and the expansion of federal universities.

6   That could still be extended to education, housing, and other sectors (see Sestelo et al. 2017).

7   Inspired by Singer's concept, "Lulism" is understood here as an expression of a weak reformism that contains tensions between "two souls."

postwar European welfare state – a concept of social security as a public right guaranteed by the state to all citizens, with the possibility of its acting as a mechanism for the redistribution of income (Fagnani 2011).

The 1990s posed a threat to the maintenance of this concept with the implementation of reforms that advocated the reduction of the state's role in guaranteeing social rights, replacing the notion of rights with the idea of inclusion through a labor market. Universal social policies were rejected, restricting the social agenda to focused policies combined with the provision of services by the private sector. Economic opening, privatization, and the advance of the logic of financialization strengthened the commodification of social rights (Lavinas 2013). "Commodification" is understood here as the expansion of individual and capitalized modes of access to social security benefits in response to the flatness of the public modes. Therefore, it represents the increasing importance of the commercial logic of guaranteeing this type of income, concurrent with the deterioration of a concept of social security based on principles such as the socialization of risk, universality, and the redistribution of income. The current commodification may encompass a more comprehensive movement to dismantle social rights that is a fundamental aspect of the neoliberal agenda. The deterioration of public services and universal social policies affects a number of sectors – health, social assistance, education, and housing, for example. It can also take many different forms – scrapping, under financing, direct privatization, outsourcing of management, and financialization, among others (Salvador 2010; Sestelo et al. 2017).

This chapter analyzes the social security issue under the PT governments in terms of four main themes: fiscal adjustment, payroll tax exemptions, the expansion of supplementary pension plans, and the shift of public employees to pension funds. The argument is that despite the significant social impact of policies such as the increase in the minimum wage, the commodification of the social security system was not reversed. The following sections discuss the themes mentioned on two levels: the way they reveal that social security was no longer considered a social right and the practical consequences for the system. The final section shows how the changes and continuities in the above four areas support the hypothesis that the commodification of social security persisted in the period analyzed.

2   Tax Adjustments and the Deconstruction of Social Security Rights

A comprehensive social protection system such as was proposed by the 1988 Constitution jeopardized a considerable proportion of government spending and suggested a direction that was diametrically opposed to the liberalizing project, and thus it became an important focus of the reform strategy of the PT governments. Because they represented the majority of expenditures, public pensions were the prime target of austerity policies. The official perspective that addressed public accounts primarily from the point of view of the economic viability of spending rather than a guarantee of rights was unveiled under President Fernando Collor (1990–1992), and the social security debate has since been guided by the perspective of fiscal adjustment and focused on arguments that represent the so-called deficit myth (Gentil 2006). Since then, there has been persistent pressure to reduce social security expenditures and to examine the financial sustainability of the system. This pressure is what anchors the great majority of items on the reform agenda: the idea that expenditures are "high", the removal of the minimum wage floor, the ceiling for contributions and benefits, the expansion of deposit periods, the elimination of retirement based on length of service, the adoption of a minimum retirement age, and the removal of special regimes for public employees, as well as criticisms of specific rules for special retirement pensions, pensions, and insurance such as rural retirement (Araújo 2004). In the way it is generally presented, the argument considers pensions only from the actuarial point of view, as a balance between contributions and benefits, ignoring the existence of other sources of financing established to sustain the system with a more comprehensive perspective.

Throughout the 1990s, the idea of incompatibility between macroeconomic policy and public and universal social security was reinforced by the stabilization strategy of the Real Plan and the proposal for pension reform of the government of Fernando Henrique Cardoso.[8] Attempts at social security reform in this period faced strong resistance from society. The actions of social movements were fundamental in persuading the government to slow down the reforms. Thus, a striking feature of the Brazilian case was that instead of a radical structural reform along the lines of the World Bank project, pension reform was fragmented into a sequence of smaller incremental changes (Galvão 2003). The purpose of the reform, however, remained the same. The largest block of changes since 1988 was concentrated on Constitutional Amendment 20. The main change was the deconstitutionalization of the pension calculation rule, which created mechanisms for increasingly linking the value of

---

8   The general social security regime, which is public and compulsory for employees of the private sector and based on an intergenerational distribution system; the special social security regime, for public employees; and the supplementary pension schemes, which are voluntary and built upon a capitalization system.

benefits to contributions based on the argument that social security should seek "financial and actuarial balance" (Vianna 1998).The idea that was consolidated by openly neoliberal governments limited the options of using the social security system as an instrument of income redistribution and brought it even closer to an individualized actuarial approach. This restricted the possibility for lower-income beneficiaries to receive more than the amount contributed and neglected the fiscal regime created in 1988, which included taxation on corporate income and profits.

The orientation of the state toward the reduction of social spending in the1990s continued under the PT governments. The so-called fiscal adjustment, concealed in speeches as an indisputable technical question, was imposed as a supposed necessity on all governments regardless of their political-ideological orientation. In the 2000s, arguments justifying fiscal adjustment continued to constitute the core of the federal government's official communications on social security. The threat of cuts was ever-present, along with the realization of other measures that had been secondary for the previous government (Fagnani 2011). In addition to the limits on social spending, the fiscal adjustment regime subjected social security to the systematic reduction of its constitutionally established financing through the mechanism called the "unbundling of Union revenues", which emerged with the Real Plan in 1994 and was later made law. The mechanism allowed 20 percent of the amount collected from social security contributions to be used by the government for current expenditures. This mechanism became essential for the management of public accounts and, although "temporary", has continued ever since. It is estimated that between 2006 and 2015 about R$500 billion in revenues were deducted in this way (ANFIP and DIEESE 2017: 19).[9]

The continuity of the rules established by previous governments shows that universal social policies have been insignificant on the agendas of the PT governments. Although the increase in the minimum wage and the growth of the formal labor market may have had a positive effect on the cash flow of the Social Security Institute, social security law has remained under constant threat. Moreover, the government's notion of the social security issue shows

---

9 This reform proposal had among its main points the adoption of a minimum retirement age of 60 years, the elimination of many noncontributory benefits, special retirement rules, and the elimination of the lifelong minimum wage. At the same time, the deconstruction of the public system gained strength with the expansion of private supplementary pension plans and the idea that the market would be able to meet the demand for this service better than the state (Salvador 2010).

that options for universal social policies remained limited and subordinated to other determinants in terms of income and expenditures.

3   Payroll Tax Exemptions for Employers

Another concern that affected the direction of the social security system and appeared repeatedly on the national political agenda was the financing structure of the General Regime of Social Security. The system was designed to operate on payroll taxes (paid by both employers and employees) and taxes on companies' profits.[10] There was, as we have seen, constant pressure for pensions to be funded by contributions alone, and even payroll taxes were controversial. Specifically, the idea of exempting employers was often used to gain the political support of relevant national business sectors. In a globalized and competitive economy, social burdens were perceived as interfering with the level of efficiency needed to remain competitive (see Giambiagi 2007). Pressures for reducing or completely abolishing social burdens on businesses were part of the liberalizing agenda (Gentil 2006).

Despite being on the business agenda for many years,[11] the payroll tax exemption was not employed by the governments of Collor, Cardoso, and Lula. Only the 2008 crisis was capable of triggering this approach through measures to "prevent and combat a decline in the level of economic activity", mainly related to industrial production (IEDI 2011). Although the government's measures initially focused on the attempt to maintain household consumption and on monetary and fiscal stabilization, the spread of policies for coping with the crisis eventually reached the pension system (Ansiliero et al. 2008). Most of these measures were carried out within the framework of the Greater Brazil Plan under the first Dilma Rousseff government. This plan, launched in 2011, consisted of a coordinated set of policies at various levels – industrial, technological, and foreign trade, among others – with the primary objective of sustaining inclusive economic growth in an adverse economic context.[12]

The plan focused on the ideas of competitiveness and growth. Its approach sought to confront an "adverse international context" by prioritizing the increase of the competitiveness of national companies to ensure growth and

---

10   In 2016, shortly after the impeachment of President Dilma Rousseff, the mechanism was extended until 2023 and its limit increased to 30 percent.

11   Paiva and Ansiliero (2009) point out that a payroll tax exemption was part of at least four tax reform proposals in 2009.

12   http://www.brasilmaior.mdic.gov.br (accessed April 30, 2016, and now unavailable).

secondarily maintaining the level of employment. Among the axes of the plan was the "investment exemption", with emphasis on export sectors. The most significant of this set of tax exemptions were the reduction of the industrialized products tax and the exemption of social security taxes on wages for employers. The so-called payroll tax exemption changed the base of the pension fund contribution, replacing the 20 percent rate with a rate of 1.5 percent on gross revenue[13] for selected sectors. The government did not advocate or officially foresee a reduction of the tax burden in general terms. On the contrary, the idea was that pension fund income is not to be "in any way impaired".[14]

The government's analysis of the early stages of the plan highlighted the importance of exemptions to the productive sector and praised the measures for expanding them (see Mattos 2013: 20). From a business point of view, payroll tax exemptions were (in a favorable analysis) "a pioneering contribution" (IEDI 2011) or (in a more critical analysis) "meritorious but of limited scope" (Zanghelini et al. 2013). The plan did not address the possible negative effects of the measures adopted on the social protection system or even the budget. As we have seen, the tax reforms assumed that tax collection would not be impaired, but the results showed the opposite.

Since its launch, several critical voices have expressed their views on the threat that tax exemptions would pose to social protection (see Zanghelini et al. 2013). According to data from the Federal Revenue Service, the annual tax waiver resulting from tax exemptions after 2010 was R$75–80 billion, representing 7–8 percent of total taxes collected. Considering only payroll exemptions, the tax waiver was R$12.3 billion in 2013 and R$23.79 billion in 2014 (Leal 2015). In the last weeks of 2014, the government announced that such exemptions were strategies adopted to meet the demands of business. After the approval of Law 12.546 of December 14, 2014, the temporary and restricted exemption of 11 industrial sectors was extended by Congress on a permanent basis to 56 sectors.

At the beginning of Dilma Rousseff's second term, both Central Bank President Alexandre Tombini and Finance Minister Joaquim Levy publicly admitted that one of the mistakes of the previous administration was not to have dismantled the measures taken after the 2008 crisis. Despite the overt

---

13   This rate, created in 2011 for some sectors, was replaced by a range of rates, varying by sector, between 1 and 2.5 percent.

14   This was pointed out even by supporters of a wider exemption. For example, Werneck (2013, cited by Mattos 2013: 20): "The problem is that the government appears to be unprepared to deal with the challenges of an effective and substantial reduction of the tax burden."

goal of removing subsidies and stimulating production because of the "threat" of inflation, there was no evidence that the tax exemption for employers would be reversed or replaced. Only small changes occurred, such as in the rate charged on billing, with the explicit objective of guaranteeing a primary surplus both by the end of 2014 and in 2015.[15] These parameters are important indications of the correlation of forces among the business sectors, as well as of the hierarchy that was established by the tax exemptions, which favored the more organized business sectors, and the need to promote fiscal adjustment at any price.[16]

Federal Revenue Service estimates indicated that, in 2015, tax exemptions stemming only from the modification of the employers' social security contribution may have reached R$34.8 billion. If we take into account that the deficit of the General Regime, disclosed by the Social Security Institute itself, was aroundR$40 billion, the exemptions had a dramatic effect. Even so, at no time was this concern announced by the government, and no replacement was presented. This measure seems to have been instrumental in ensuring the cohesion of the bloc in power during the second Lula government and the first Dilma government, but it does not seem to have been enough if we consider the intensification of austerity after the 2014 elections and the process that culminated in the impeachment in 2016. The data available indicate that exemption impacts were not insignificant. In 2015 alone, about R$158 billion were not collected for social security (ANFIP and DIEESE 2017: 19). Besides, reserving space for universal social policy was secondary to the satisfying the interests that sustained the coalition.

4   Expansion of Supplementary Pension Plans

A key component of the arrangement that made governance feasible for the PT was satisfying the interests in the financial sphere. This took the form of expansion of supplementary pensions stemming from the stagnation of the public-employee regimes and the promotion of private pension funds. The

---

15   At the end of 2015 and the beginning of 2016, with the worsening of primary deficit expectations, some exemptions were reversed. This fact, while not appearing to have been crucial, certainly contributed to the slow process of "unloading" businesses from the central government, a key element in the political crisis that ended with the president's impeachment. The subject remained a concern after Michel Temer became president.

16   On the centrality of interest to the equilibrium of the political arrangement of that moment, see Singer (2015).

stagnation of the private social security regimes was based on Constitutional Amendment 41/2003 (see Morhy 2003). Officials at all levels of the public sector were entitled to their own rules of access to retirement, which had hitherto guaranteed a generally more favorable condition than the General Regime.[17] To justify the reform, the image, widespread throughout the 1990s, of public employees as privileged was revived as part of the rhetoric on the privatization of state-owned enterprises (Gentil 2006).[18] Following the parameters outlined in Constitutional Amendment 20/1998, Amendment 41/2003 eliminated the earlier schemes for civil servants and replaced them with the rules of access and calculation of benefits practiced in the General Regime while maintaining them in a regime of their own. At the same time, it allowed these employees to contribute to supplementary pension funds to be organized by each public agency (Granemann 2006). In practice, this reform began to be applied only in 2012, and the main milestone was the creation of the Federal Public Employee Supplementary Pension Foundation, which would become one of the largest pension funds in Latin America. According to the Association of Closed Entities of Supplementary Social Security (ABRAPP 2015: 2), the amount managed by these funds was around 14 percent of the GDP, R$718 billion in 2015 (12.2 percent). Consolidated statistics also show that the predominant profile of funds was public securities and fixed-income funds, which had greater exposure to risk and were restricted to larger entities. In the pension fund sector, only 10 entities accounted for 60 percent of its equity.

Despite the growth of its equity, the data of the National Office of Supplementary Social Security (PREVIC 2013) show that the number of closed supplementary pension plans (pension funds restricted to employees of particular companies, public or private) remains stable at about 300. This shows that the majority of agencies – especially at the municipal level – cannot meet the conditions for the organization of this type of institution. The funds are

---

17 However, not all federal agencies implemented their own pension schemes. According to the Social Security Statistical Yearbook, for example, in 2013 only 35 percent of the agencies in Brazil that offered some type of pension to their employees had distinctive regimes. The officials of 61 percent of such agencies were included in the general regime.

18 The idea involved an image of the highest-paid categories in the public sector that was very different from the average Brazilian labor market and did not correspond to the reality of most professionals in the sector. The majority of public employees at various levels have wages and working conditions equivalent to those of other participants in the labor market such as teachers, health professionals, social workers, police officers, and clerks. The above-mentioned distorted view also hides the fact that, in the private sector, professions with the same level of qualification and responsibility earn incomes equal to or greater than those in the public sector.

therefore located at federal and state levels and in some state capitals. It is apparent that the stagnation of the private social security plans fostered the expansion of supplementary pension schemes, but this was mainly because of the channeling of the best salaries to a few agencies and not the generalization of the capitalization regime to all public sector employees.

At the same time, an expansion of open supplementary pension plans (pension plans offered by financial institutions to anyone) is also notable. These plans establish a market for financial products that can be sold by banks, insurers, and even pension funds that may create parallel pension plans with differentiated rules to complement their portfolios. Whereas the assets managed by these plans in 2002 amounted to only R$10 billion, they reached almost R$300 billion in 2012, about 7 percent of the GDP for that year (CVM 2013: 29). Although they represent a smaller volume of investment than the closed pension plans, they have experienced faster growth, representing the fastest-growing component of the Brazilian social security sector for the past 10 years. Despite this, they are just beginning to accumulate collateral assets, whereas the pension funds are more fully developed (CVM 2013).

The expansion of private pensions was the result of pension reform. The flattening of public pensions increased the migration of large numbers of workers to pension funds and private pension market (Andrietta 2015), and the regulation of the private pension market – especially income tax exemptions for expenses incurred with contributions to supplementary pension funds – stimulated the sector in comparison with other forms of social security (Granemann 2006).[19]

The interest of financial institutions in the expansion of supplementary pensions can be measured, of course, by the direct revenue obtained through administrative fees and intermediation in private pension plans. However, the volume of funds in circulation in both open and closed pension plans indicates that the interest goes far beyond this. Granemann (2006) has shown that, through strategies such as cross-selling,[20] the viability and leverage of accumulation in the financial sphere make social security funds – in political economic terms, workers' indirect salaries – a great attraction. The central point of the expansion of supplementary pension plans is the capacity to control

---

19   A similar process can be observed in the health sector, where the expansion of private plans – one of the dimensions of the commodification of the sector – was favored by income tax exemptions for expenses related to supplementary health insurance (CEBES 2014).

20   The selling by a financial conglomerate of several different products (credit, insurance, supplementary pension, fleet outsourcing, etc.) to the same economic group.

this stock of wealth and have it flow through these institutions, strengthening a great diversity of businesses. In this sense, the existence of a simple distribution system that channels part of the indirect salary for the payment of social security benefits in a universal and redistributive manner, besides restricting the demand for new private pension plans, prevents these flows from being channeled into capitalization circuits. The commodified forms of social security are the gateway to these capitalization circuits. There is, therefore, a contradiction between these interests and the maintenance of a concept of social security as a public and universal social right.

5 Pension Funds and Union Strategies

The expansion of supplementary pension plans has one aspect that deserves to be addressed separately. The development of closed supplementary pension plans presents new contradictions for the objective of resisting the dismantling of public social security. Specifically, the active participation of union representatives in the management of large funds – especially in important public companies such as Petrobrás and the Bank of Brazil – introduces to the context of the union movement an agenda that is opposed to the commodification of social security. Pension funds, the so-called closed supplementary pension schemes that are restricted to employees of certain private companies or public enterprises, have been regulated since the 1960s as part of the reforms that structured the national financial system, but their specific regulations were established only with the passage of Law 6.435/77 of July 15, 1977. The expansion of pension funds accentuates the commodification of social security in that the benefits are directly linked to the conditions for the financial recovery of the amount collected by the fund. This means that access to this right changes according to the performance of an asset portfolio in the financial market and may be threatened in times of crisis (Sória 2014).

The interest in pension funds also links employees to the immediate concern of keeping interest rates attractive, which goes in the opposite direction from a macroeconomic investment policy aimed at consolidating rights and maintaining jobs. In this process, short-term strategies that increase labor market stability are reinforced and a negative impact on the public system is generated in that it removes higher-income workers from the distribution system (Granemann 2006). The expansion of pension funds reinforces the individual and individualistic approach, weakening solidarity among categories of workers and among generations and thus damaging the potentially redistributive role of the pension system (see Jardim 2009).

As mentioned earlier, under the PT governments pension funds were stimulated, mainly after the passage of Constitutional Amendment 41/2003, which consolidated the elimination of the public sector employees' regimes and the migration of these workers to the new funds managed with the participation of union leaders. In this sense, the development of pension funds during the PT governments was strongly related to changes in the discourse and practice of the Central Única dos Trabalhadores (Workers' Central – CUT). The CUT was the main union base in support of the government, and the expansion of pension funds was driven especially by leaders linked to the São Paulo Bank Clerks' Union. Contributing to this were changes in strategy from criticism of the myth of the social security deficit and the defense of a strongly social and redistributive system to more substantive and conciliatory formulations that made room for models and regimes once vehemently opposed (Andrietta and Lemos 2016: 513–514). As the resistance to the PT governments on this issue cooled down, there was increasing participation of private pension plans in the context of collective bargaining.[21]

The relationship between unionism and government was decisive for the approval of the constitutional amendment. Despite the CUT's declared commitment to public welfare, the success of the 2003 pension reform was favored if not made possible by the approval of the government's arguments by a significant portion of the country's union leaders. This factor is one of the results – and, at the same time, a symptom – of the Central Bank's long process of strategic changes (Andrietta and Lemos 2016: 511–513). These contradictions facilitated the approval of reforms and called into question the strength of the resistance to the commodification of social security. The CUT was the largest union central in the country, so its contradictory stance was a stabilizing element for the arrangement of interests of the period and made it difficult to reverse the general appreciation of the reforms.

6   Conclusion

In the early 2000s, with the ascent of the PT to the executive branch, there was a strong expectation of the recovery of the agenda developed in the 1980s,which called for reform that would lead to "decentralization, the participation of beneficiaries in decisions, the struggle against the clientelistic use of

---

21   Although there are no precise data on collective bargaining, National Federation of
      Private Pension Funds statistics indicate that by 2015 12 percent of private pension plans
      belonged to companies.

initiatives in the social area, streamlining and increased efficiency of spending, universal availability, and the pursuit of equity in the provision of social benefits and services" (De Almeida 2004: 8). However, tensions and reformulations of the PT project embodied in the interests created to guarantee governance produced continuity with the previous governments regarding social policy. As De Almeida (2004: 8) pointed out, the priority of transfers of income to the poorest was, from the beginning of the Lula administration, a striking feature of its social policy, whose aim was to create "a notion of social protection and a type of social policy that dismissed diffuse expectations about the PT's performance as reformer."

Lulism and the PT governments in general conciliated many contradictions. One was related to the inclusion of entrepreneurs in their social base and was strengthened by discussions aimed at minimizing the tensions of the capital labor relationship. Another was the combination of representing social demands and defending production with fulfilling the demands of the banking-financial sector. Yet another was dealing with the pressures of the physiological sectors of Brazilian politics (Araújo and Véras 2014: 37).[22]

Although the PT governments employed the discourse of more social dialogue and put the need for social policy on their agendas, the results were inconsistent with the expansion of social rights. While stimulating domestic consumption and income distribution increased the availability of credit and enabled mass consumption, this "inclusion by consumption", which removed thousands of people from poverty, simultaneously increased the vulnerability of families through debt and expanded the private and privatized market for social services such as health and education. This privatization was accompanied by the disorganization, precarization, and underfinancing of these services (Lavinas 2015). It caused the deterioration of the social security law and created problems in maintaining and strengthening universal and redistributive public access to benefits and at the same time promoted individual and commercialized access for a limited group of workers that in fact was not part of the labor market. Their "inclusion" and "poverty reduction" did not differ from those of the previous – openly neoliberal – governments, although they may have adapted them differently. Social dimensions advanced when they served business interests.[23] Furthermore, many of the social policies implemented (especially the Bolsa Família, in the forefront of government

---

22   Although Araújo and Oliveira refer only to Lula's administration, the tensions they identify persisted throughout the period analyzed here.

23   For a review of examples of the expression of this trend in several social policy sectors, see Sestelo et al. (2017).

propaganda) lacked any guarantee of continuity if the government's orientation, the available resources, or the target audience should change (Lavinas 2015; Marques and Mendes 2007).

The continuity of "neoliberalism" was also apparent in the persistence of cost-benefit notions with regard to the tax revenues that guaranteed the provision of services. With the justification of stimulating economic activity and promoting competitiveness and employment, exemptions, debt relief, and tax waivers were promoted that channeled public money to the private sector, exacerbating the chronic underfunding of social expenditures (Salvador 2010). The handling of the social security issue revealed tensions resulting from different interests that contributed to the commodification initiated under previous governments. The reforms begun in the 1990s were maintained under the PT governments along with the social policy that supported them. The development of several important social policies coexisted with the policy of fiscal adjustment. The continuity of neoliberal macroeconomic policy set rigid limits on the strengthening of a universal and comprehensive system of social protection. Public social security became an issue that the government could not avoid. The Collor government's notion of "economic viability" prevailed in the official speeches of the PT governments. The political structure that supported their governance heavily influenced the operations of the social security system in a different way from that of previous governments, but the development of the system remained unchanged. Thus the commodification of social security persisted as a basic component of the state's neoliberal reform project.

In addition, our analysis of the political economy of the social security issue shows that threats to this social right occur at several levels. The spending of social security revenues on other items, along with recurrent funding reductions, tax exemptions, and tax evasion, threatens its funding base. The inflection of union strategy reduces the possibility of resistance to reforms. Finally, the expansion of supplementary pensions intensifies inequalities in the labor market as resources are transferred from indirect wages to individual capitalization schemes.

Currently, whenever Brazil faces a political crisis, a new pension reform is announced in the midst of a number of unpopular measures for dealing with it. The speed and aggressiveness of government in approving changes are troubling. The elements covered by this chapter help to identify the magnitude and depth of the social security issue with the purpose of contributing to the debate on the subject and to the struggle for the continuity and expansion of social rights.

References

Associação Brasileira das Entidades Fechadas de Previdência Complementar (ABRAPP). (2015). *Consolidado estatístico (Dez/2015)*. São Paulo: ABRAPP. Available at: https://www.abrapp.org.br/wp-content/uploads/2020/09/Consolidado-Estati%CC%81stico_12_2015.pdf.

Andrietta, L.S. (2015). *A mercantilização do sistema previdenciário brasileiro (1988-2014)*. Ph.D. dissertation, Universidade Estadual de Campinas, Campinas, Brazil.

Andrietta, L.S., and Lemos, P.R. (2016). O sindicalismo da CUT e a mercantilização do Sistema Previdenciário Brasileiro (2003–2014). *SER Social* 18(39): 501–519.

Andrietta, L.S., et al. (2020). Pensions and Commodification under the PT Governments (2003–2015). *Latin American Perspectives* 47(2): 117–130.

Associação Nacional dos Auditores Fiscais da Receita Federal do Brasil and Departamento Intersindical de Estatística e Estudos Socioeconômicos. (2017). *Previdência: Reformar para excluir*. Brasília: ANFIP and DIEESE.

Ansiliero, G., et al. (eds.). (2008). *A desoneração da folha de pagamentos e sua relação com a formalidade no mercado de trabalho*. Brasília: IPEA.

Araújo, Â., and De Oliveira, R.V. (2014). O sindicalismo na era Lula: entre paradoxos e novas perspectivas. In: De Oliveira, R.V., et al. (eds.), *O sindicalismo na era lula: Paradoxos, perspectivas e olhares*, 29–59. Belo Horizonte: Fino Traço.

Centro Brasileiro de Estudos de Saúde – CEBES. (2014). Em defesa do direito universal à saúde: saúde é direito e não negócio. *Saúde em Debate* 38: 194–196.

Comissão de Valores Mobiliários. (2013). *Tendências demográficas e econômicas e o mercado de capitais*. São Paulo: CVM.

De Almeida, M.H. (2004). A política social no governo Lula. *Novos Estudos* 70: 7–18.

De Araújo, O. (2004). *A reforma da previdência social brasileira no contexto das reformas do estado, 1988 a 1998*. Natal: UFRN.

Delgado, I.G. (2001). *Previdência social e mercado no Brasil: A presença empresarial na trajetória da política social brasileira*. São Paulo: LTr.

Fagnani, E. (2011). A política social do Governo Lula (2003–2010): perspectiva histórica. *SER Social* 13(28): 41–80.

Galvão, A. (2003). *Neoliberalismo e reforma trabalhista no Brasil*. Ph.D. diss., Universidade Estadual de Campinas, Campinas, Brazil.

Gentil, D.L. (2006). *A política fiscal e a falsa crise da seguridade social brasileira*. Ph.D. diss., Universidade Federal do Rio de Janeiro, Rio de Janeiro, Brazil.

Giambiagi, F. (2007). *Reforma da previdência: encontro marcado*. Rio de Janeiro: Elsevier.

Granemann, S. (2006). *Para uma interpretação marxista da previdência privada*. Ph.D. diss., Universidade Federal do Rio de Janeiro, Rio de Janeiro, Brazil.

Instituto de Estudos para o Desenvolvimento Industrial. (2011). *Uma análise do Plano Brasil Maior*. São Paulo: IEDI.

Jardim, M.C. (2009). Nova' elite no Brasil? Sindicalistas e ex-sindicalistas no mercado financeiro. *Sociedade e Estado* 24: 363–399.

Lavinas, L. (2013). 21st-century welfare. *New Left Review* 84: 5–40.

Lavinas, L. (2015). A financeirização da política social: o caso brasileiro. *Politika* 1(2): 35–51.

Leal, L. (2015). As desonerações tributárias concedidas ao setor privado e seus impactos sobre os trabalhadores. *Brasil de Fato*, 15 Jan.

Marques, R., and Mendes, Á. (2007). Servindo a dois senhores: as políticas sociais no governo Lula. *Revista Katálysis* 10: 15–23.

Mattos, C. (2013). *Análise do Plano Brasil Maior*. Brasília: Consultoria Legislativa.

Morais, L., and Saad-Filho, A. (2011). Da economia política à política econômica: o novo-desenvolvimentismo e o governo Lula. *Revista de Economia Política* 31: 507–527.

Morhy, L. (org.). (2003). *Reforma da previdência em questão*. Brasília: UnB.

Paiva, L.H., and Ansiliero, G. (2009). A desoneração da contribuição patronal sobre a folha de pagamentos: uma solução à procura de problemas. *Planejamento e Políticas Públicas* (IPEA) 32: 9–36.

Paulani, L. (2003). Brasil *Delivery*: a política econômica do Governo Lula. *Revista de Economia Política* 23(4): 58–73.

Superintendência Nacional de Previdência Complementar (PREVIC). (2013). *Estatística trimestral, Dezembro/2013*. Brasília: PREVIC. Available at: https://www.gov.br/economia/pt-br/orgaos/entidades-vinculadas/autarquias/previc/centrais-de-conteudo/publicacoes/informe-estatistico-trimestral/informes-de-2013/40-trimestre.pdf/view.

Salvador, E. (2010). *Fundo público e seguridade social no Brasil*. São Paulo: Cortez.

Sestelo, J., et al. (2017). A financeirização das políticas sociais e da saúde no Brasil do século XXI: elementos para uma aproximação inicial. *Economia e Sociedade* 26: 1097–1126.

Singer, A. (2012). *Os sentidos do Lulismo*. São Paulo: Companhia das Letras.

Singer, A. (2015). Cutucando onças com varas curtas. *Novos Estudos* 102: 39–67.

Soria, S. (2014). As relações entre sindicalismo e fundos de pensão no governo Lula. In: De Oliveira, R.V., et al. (eds.), *O sindicalismo na era lula: paradoxos, perspectivas e olhares*, 149–181. Belo Horizonte: Fino Traço.

Vianna, M.L.T.W. (1998). *A americanização (perversa) da seguridade social no Brasil*. Rio de Janeiro: REVAN/UCAM/IUPERJ.

Werneck, R.L. (2013). *Abertura, competitividade e desoneração fiscal*. Rio de Janeiro: PUC.

Zanghelini, A., et al. (2013). *Desoneração da folha de pagamentos: Oportunidade ou ameaça*. Brasília: ANFIP.

CHAPTER 18

The Housing Policy under the PT Governments

Between the Social Inclusion and the Commodification

Cristhiane Falchetti

1   Introduction[1]

Brazil has recently undergone a political cycle of economic growth and poverty reduction driven by the commodities boom and strengthened by policies for income distribution among the working classes. The development model prioritized the incorporation into the international market of certain economic sectors, favoring mergers and the opening up of capital while stimulating domestic consumption through salary appreciation, the facilitation of consumer credit, and an increase in spending through income transfer programs. All these while preserving the pillars of neoliberal macroeconomic policy (inflation targets based on high interest rates, floating exchange rates, and primary-surplus targets) and maintaining the hegemony of the banking-financial fraction. There was no change in the productive structure, which was based on commodity export sectors, nor were there structural reforms that significantly altered the distribution of wealth (Cavalcante 2015). In the social sphere, Singer (2012: 195) considers the impossibility of Lulism's confronting big capital resulted in a "weak reformism" whose achievements in reducing poverty and inequality were limited.[2]

This scenario opened up a debate about the character of PT governments and the meaning of their policies in relation to neoliberalism.[3] Despite the differences between the PT government cycle and the previous one, the nature of the continuities with it leads us to consider an adaptation of neoliberalism

---

1   An earlier version of the arguments in this chapter appeared in Falchetti 2019, translated by Luis Fierro. The author introduced minor changes to the text and its organization in order to better adapt it to the proposal of this collection.

2   Singer associates "Lulism" with the changes that occurred under the PT and the constitution of a political project aimed at social change, albeit in conservative terms, describing it as based on the mass of the excluded and seeking to overcome poverty without confronting the privileges of the elite.

3   For review of example, see: Boito Jr. 2012; Moraes and Saad-Filho 2011; Singer 2012; Singer and Loureiro 2016.

rather than the "inflection" of it, as the notion of "neodevelopmentism" suggested.[4] In order to contribute with debate, this chapter directs attention to social policy with a focus on the housing program My house My Life (Minha Casa Minha Vida), seeking to point out the character of redefinitions in the form of state action. The purpose is not to classify governments and their policies but to offer an analysis that contributes to understand the dynamics of neoliberalism in its various contexts.

As already indicated by several analysts, the past decade has demonstrated the resilience of neoliberalism as a mode of hegemonic regulation. Even after the crisis of 2008, when its premises were compromised, the political machinery disciplined by the market remains intact, as do the social and economic political agendas devoted to the maintenance of investment confidence. Despite the varied experiences of regulatory restructuring, the limits of social welfare in each context and the material possibilities within which all must contend to achieve their political objectives are established. This scenario differs from the original analysis of neoliberalism and its impacts on social policy in revealing that neoliberalism is not static and homogeneous but, like all social processes, dynamic and varied.

The initial studies of neoliberalism under the Washington Consensus focused on the role of the state in social policy – fiscal adjustment, reduction of social spending, privatization of public services, and flexibilization of social rights – and produced the thesis of the minimal state. As the historical processes unfolded in space and time, neoliberalism was reformulated, and a second generation of reforms turned to poverty reduction strategies. The state began to be reoriented as complementary to the market, "fundamental for the process of economic and social development not as a direct agent of growth but as a partner, a catalyst and driver of this process" (World Bank 1997: 9).

Social policy studies then proceeded to investigate the degree of change brought about by reforms in social protection regimes. According to Draibe (2003: 65), some studies argued that these regimes were of two types: the "inclusive", based on universalistic social programs that maintained their social imperatives and deepened democracy, and the "selective", which stimulated growth but limited their actions to the poor. However, despite this

---

4 In Boito Jr.'s reading, neodevelopmentalism is a development perspective that aims at economic growth with some income distribution and that was supported under the Lula and Dilma governments by a "neodevelopmentalist front" that prioritized the repositioning of the Brazilian internal grande bourgeoisie in the bloc in power, promoting it internationally, while seeking concessions with countercyclical measures and consumption for the popular classes.

interpretation associating social policy with developmental strategy, the social policy develops under other historical conditions, which do not alienate them from neoliberal frameworks. Rather than representing a departure, the reappearance of the social question on the neoliberal agenda points to a rearrangement of neoliberalism. In its report "Building Institutions for the Market", the World Bank (2002) pointed to the centrality of markets in the lives of the poorest people and encouraged the promotion of institutions focused on economic growth and poverty reduction with the market as protagonist.

Understanding the dynamic of neoliberalism requires a analysis the role of the State in this reconfiguration of social policy and how its institutional architecture adjusts to the new patterns of accumulation at specific context. The housing policy of the Partido dos Trabalhadores (Workers' Party – PT) governments offers important elements for this investigation because it involves a combination of economic growth policy and social inclusion via the market. Although the housing policy is not representing the social system as a whole, I am based on the premise that housing acquires crucial importance in cities as capital accumulation comes to dominate the production of urban space (Harvey 2005), becoming an important element of social insecurity. In view of this, and in the context of Brazilian urban formation, housing policy is now a central component of social protection.

This chapter analyzes the My House, My Life program, observing the interaction between state and market and its implications for the orientation of social policy – its definition, decision processes, objectives, and impacts. Institutional documents, secondary data, and a review of the literature were its sources. The hypothesis developed is that the PMCMV has conformed to the process of commodification of social policy, as it mobilizes public fund as an instrument of capital accumulation, intensifies the financialization of the real estate sector and the commercializes housing. It therefore points to a reconfiguration of social policy under neoliberalism in the form of the commodification of the social, which displaces some understandings about citizenship. From that point of view, the recent political cycle associated with Lulism was not an inflection of neoliberalism but an updating of it to the specific context.

2 The Neoliberalization and Housing Policy in Brazil

Returning to Foucault's concepts, Dardot and Laval (2016: 17) argue that "neoliberalism can be defined as the set of discourses, practices and devices that determine a new mode of government for men according to the universal principle of competition." In this new governamentality, the financial market

is one of the main disciplinary agents and the state act developing and purifying the competitive market with a carefully adjusted legal framework.[5] The
juridical-institutional system is not an emanation of the economic structure
but "it immediately belongs to the relations of production, insofar as it shapes
the economic from within" (Dardot and Laval 2016: 24). Therefore, the mode of
production is not independent of the legal order and the originality of neoliberalism would be the creation of a new order, whose meaning is the commodification of all life.

However, the spread of neoliberalism and its generalization beyond the
economic field needs to be articulated concretely with the different dynamics
of capital accumulation and legitimation of national political life in specific
contexts. Thus, the process of neoliberalization is spatially unequal, tempo-
rally discontinuous and permeated by hybrid and contradictory experiments,
as proposed by Brenner et al. (2010):

> On the most general level, we conceptualize neoliberalization as one
> among several tendencies of regulatory change that have been unleashed
> across the global capitalist system since the 1970s: it priorizes market-
> based, market-oriented, or market-disciplinary responses to regulatory
> problems; it strives to intensify commodification in all realms of social
> life; and it often mobilizes financial instruments to open up new are-
> nas for capitalist profitmaking. (…) we view neoliberalization as a var-
> iegated form of regulatory restructuring: it produces geo-institutional
> differentiation across places, territories, and scales; but it does this sys-
> temically, as a pervasive, endemic feature of its basic operational logic.
> Concomitantly, we emphasize the profound path-dependency of neo-
> liberalization processes: in so far as they necessarily collide with diverse
> regulatory landscapes inherited from earlier rounds of regulatory forma-
> tion and contestation (including Fordism, nationaldevelopmentalism,
> and state socialism), their forms of articulation and institutionalization
> are quite heterogeneous. Thus, rather than expecting some pure, proto-
> typical form of neoliberalization to obtain across divergent contexts, we
> view variegation – systemic geo-institutional differentiation – as one of
> its essential, enduring features.
>
> BRENNER, ET AL. 2010: 329–330

---

5   The notion of governmentality is created by Foucault to describe the rationality that cross the
     multiple forms of government, not only the administrative and state practices, but also the
     government of the conducts (which includes the counter-conducts). See: Foucault (2008).

In order to better understand the variants of neoliberalization in Brazil, I examine housing policy, showing how the institutional arrangements among the state, the real estate market, and financial capital converged toward the commodification of housing policy.

In general, the intensification of commodification is associated with financialization, since it involves the accumulation of capital in pursuit of new sources of profit and income extraction. The large volume of capital accumulated through financial assets and the economic growth of emerging countries between the 1980s and the 2000s has spatialized and overcome the physical limits of its original markets of accumulation, driving the globalization of finance.[6] As a striking feature of the current development dynamics of neoliberal capitalism, financialization is understood as "the growing dominance of actors, markets, practices, and financial narratives at various scales, which results in the structural transformation of economies, enterprises (including financial institutions), the state, and family groups" (Aalbers 2016: 241).

As explored by the literature, urban expansion in Brazil between the 1950s and 1970s was accentuated by the concentration of income by industrialization, creating a peripheral and segregated pattern in which popular housing was characterized by informality in land ownership and self-construction (Holston 2013; Kowarick 1981). Housing policy was never sufficient to resolve the existing problems. The real estate market, in turn, was segmented and stratified and did not participate in the economic liberalization of the 1990s with the same intensity as other sectors of the economy: "Interest-bearing capital faced barriers to the freeing of urban land to circulate in the form of financial bonds. Real estate remained predominantly a reserved orbit of Brazilian companies structured like families, exempt from the denationalization that characterized the Brazilian economy at the time" [the 1990s] (Fix 2011: 217). Thus, although the production of urban space is one of the main fields of absorption of capital overaccumulation (Harvey 2005), in Brazil it is a process still under construction.

From the point of view of social policy, while, on the one hand, twentieth-century Brazilian developmentalism did not produce a full social welfare system similar to that of the central countries of Europe, on the other hand, the political-organizational assembly of society against the military regime made the democratization process an agenda of struggle for social rights. Thus the Constitution of 1988 established obstacles to neoliberalism by consolidating

---

6   In this period, the value of stocks, debentures, debt securities, and financial investments increased 16.2 times while the world gross domestic product (GDP) increased less than 5 times (Paulani 2010).

an institutional framework based on universalist social policies. However, the introduction of the neoliberal agenda had an impact on public investment capacity and on Keynesian-type regulatory arrangements. The liberalizing reforms of the 1990s restructured the institutional apparatus, reduced the state structure, decentralized policies, and instituted market regulations. Although states and municipalities gained greater autonomy and a more democratic structure as anticipated by the constitution, the economic contingency did not allow going beyond institutionality, and some provisions of the constitution converged toward an institutional reconfiguration guided by the neoliberal agenda.

The reconfiguration of the urban planning apparatus generated some convergences with the strategies of reproduction of capital in urban space. While constitutional regulation was oriented, on the one hand, toward the formalization of land structures, urban planning, and the management of housing policy and expanded the right to property and housing; on the other hand, it viewed legality and formality as a paradigm of legitimacy. With this it restricted access to urban land and met the requirements of the formal market. The 2001 City Statute and its urban intervention instruments, while equipping the state for the urban reform agenda demanded by the social movements, also paved the way for the strategic planning of global cities, with their "revitalization" projects, historical centers, removal of deactivated areas, financial investment in new centralities, urban operations, urban concessions, etc. Thus strategies were created for the establishment and valorization of real estate assets whose operating instruments would be regulated in the 1990s.

Housing policy moved from "a model focused on the financing of new housing production and based on a network of public providers toward a model focused on the financing of the final borrower and, particularly, the acquisition of used real estate." Associated with this, "market mechanisms were introduced to the management of urban development policies" (Arretche 2002: 442). With the end of the National Housing Bank – which had managed the Housing Finance System (consisting of the Brazilian Savings and Loan System and the Severance Indemnity Fund) and coordinated the investments of the Metropolitan Housing Company – and the transfer of its tasks to the National Monetary Council and its technical apparatus to the Federal Savings Bank, housing policy took on a monetarist character and was diluted in financial operations.

In addition, the increase in unemployment and the reduction in the level of income weakened the Housing Finance System, thus restricting financing for housing. A new regulatory framework more or less on the North American model was constructed for real estate credit. To expand the supply of credit in the real estate sector, the Financial Real Estate System was created in 1997 to raise funds in the secondary securities market, transforming real estate credit concessions into investments with security and liquidity. This was a modification of the traditional model of financial intermediation, since it transformed real estate credits into negotiable real estate securities in the financial and capital markets. Here there were two innovations, real estate receivables certificates[7] and certificates of additional building potential.[8] This institutional reorientation of housing finance stimulated the operationalization of financial capital in the real estate sector.

Initially, the Financial Real Estate System faced operating difficulties related to the regulatory environment. During the Lula administration a more secure legal framework was created for the operation of the market. In addition to the regularization of fiduciary alienation, other measures favored the financial market, such as Law 10.931/2004, which created a special tax on real estate development, expansion of the the issuance of real estate credit bills (bonds issued by financial institutions to raise funds to finance real estate loans), and the establishment of the real estate credit certificate and the bank credit certificate.

Securitization of real estate assets was a recommendation of the international agencies for leveraging investments, since it would distribute the risks and thus, by reducing the interest rate, increase liquidity (World Bank 2002). The expectation was that the development of the capital market and the expansion of long-term credit would reduce housing costs by expanding housing supply for the low-income population. However, according to Royer (2009: 16), while the Financial Real Estate System succeeded in establishing an institutional mortgage-lending system based on market principles and private agents, because of the specificity of Brazilian urbanization it was unable to cope with the housing deficit concentrated in the low-income sectors or meet Brazil's housing needs. Real estate operations focused on commercial and non-residential building finance certificates, since the percentage of income limited the market, and housing investment was restricted to the commercialization

---

7 Real estate receivables certificates are identified in Article 6 of the law that instituted the Financial Real Estate System as involving nominative credit title, freely negotiatable, backed by real estate credits and constituting a promise of payment in cash. They are generally compared to U.S. mortgage-backed securities, although there are differences.

8 Additional building potential is an authorization to build a particular project beyond the limits allowed by the legislation – in other words, the sale of created land. These securities may be invested in the venture or traded on the secondary market with gains through appreciation of the region.

rather than the production of real estate because of the better interest rates with the final contractor. The stratification and segmentation of the real estate sector, income inequality, and the high interest rates of public bonds were some of the obstacles to capital flows in the real estate circuit.

Some of these obstacles were removed or circumvented by state action in the past decade through urban and housing policies. During the Lula and Dilma governments, a set of measures expanded real estate credit and extended housing investment to lower-income sectors. Thus, housing policy combined the social demand for popular housing with the expansion of the real estate market. The 2004 policy divided the Housing Finance System according to the demand profile and the sources of financing, creating Social Interest Housing and Market Housing Subsystems. The Social Interest Housing Subsystem's programs were to be financed by the Severance Indemnity Fund, the related Leasing Fund, the Social Development Fund, the federal government, and the Financial Real Estate System. In practice, the two systems were interpermeable, since the real estate market had access to both (Shimbo 2010: 82). While the Social Interest Housing Subsystem complicated the institutional dispute as a source of funding, the Market Housing Subsystem captured most of the resources.[9]

With the resumption of economic growth and the expansion of formal employment, the Housing Finance System was strengthened, and the government redirected funds from the Savings and Loan System and the Severance Indemnity Fund toward housing financing. Between 2003 and 2008, the total amount of financing contracted by these two sources increased from R$5 billion to R$40 billion (Shimbo 2010). The amount of financing for existing real estate multiplied by 10 and new units increased from 14,088 to 140,164, triggering the so-called real estate boom (Royer 2009: 73). In addition to the increase in resources there was an easing of credit conditions, with the adoption of fiduciary security for real estate, an improvement in loan terms (interest rates, maturities, down payments, percentage financed) and an increase in subsidies. As a result of social pressure, the National Social Interest Fund was created, and this injected about R$1.3 billion a year into the financing and subsidizing of low-income housing (Rolnik 2015). Resolution 460/2004 of the Severance Indemnity Fund board allocated 60 percent of the agency's investments to

---

9   The Social Interest Housing Subsystem was created in 2005 by Law 11.124 and implemented in 2006 under Finance Minister Mantega. There was a lot of resistance from the economic team to the identification of resources to fund this system, and it was aggravated by changes in the Ministry of Cities team and the weakening of the PT after the allegations of corruption involving the mensalão.

popular housing, increasing housing allowances for lower-income families. This measure did not directly affect the metropolitan regions, where real estate valuation was more consolidated, but had an impact through national diffusion.

The resumption of real estate credit strengthened the real estate circuit by stimulating the financialization of the sector through investment in the partial acquisition of real estate companies and the subsequent entry of capital into the stock exchange. Since the early 2000s, the real estate industry has intensified the concentration and centralization of capital through mergers and acquisitions of construction companies and developers. Starting in 2005, companies such as Gafisa, Even, Cyrela, MRV, PDG, and 20 others began participating in the stock exchange, connecting to the financial market.[10] Among the main modalities of international capital inflow were investment funds, equity funds, and private equity, which circulated among builders and developers around the world (Fix 2011; Rolnik 2015).

By leveraging the housing market, even in the lower income brackets, real estate companies capitalized on stock exchanges adjusted their strategies, decentralized their geographic performance, stockpiled land, and created brands and products aimed at the lower-income "economic segment". Between 2007 and 2008, for example, 40 percent of residential launches came from publicly traded companies; in 2009, of the 14 publicly traded companies on the Bovespa, 9 began to operate in this segment after 2004 (Shimbo 2010: 338). Thus the obstacle posed by income inequality to the expansion of the housing market and the entry of financial capital began to be circumvented. The companies were planning to launch 200,000 units in the lower-middle-income segment when the real estate crisis broke out in the United States. With the crisis of 2008, the relationship between housing policy and the financialized real estate market took on new contours through the My House, My Life program.

3 My House, My Life: Between the Social Inclusion and the Commodification

The My House, My Life program was launched in 2009 by the federal government and represented the resumption of public investment in housing production after more than 20 years of stagnation. During the Dilma government

---

10   According to Fix (2011: 136), between 2005 and 2008 a total of R$8 billion was raised for companies (primary offers) and R$3 billion for controlling shareholders (in secondary offers), about 75 percent of it from foreign investors.

(2011–2014) it was one of the main components of the Growth Acceleration Program, which aimed at reactivating the economy through sectoral public investments, almost all involving the production of space. The establishment of the My House, My Life program points to a disarticulation of housing policy defined in terms of social rights and guarantees and their mode of legitimization. The proposal took the form of a housing package demanded by private real estate agents in the context of the 2008 mortgage-financial crisis (Rolnik 2015). As we have seen, the real estate sector emerged from a process of financialization and expansion driven by an increase in real estate credit. Given the risk of bankrupcy with the decline in stock prices and the withdrawal of investment, industry representatives asked the government for funding subsidies and a loan guarantee fund to enable the sale of the units produced. The government proposed to buy some of the shares through the Federal Savings Bank, but the private agents refused, considering this a nationalization of the sector (Fix 2011: 135).

Initial negotiations were conducted between the real estate sector and the Ministry of Finance, without the Ministry of Cities and in parallel with the National Housing Plan, which had been formulated with social participation through forums and councils. Since the beginning of the Lula administration, the institutional structure of housing policy had followed constitutional precepts. The 2004 Nacional Housing Policy established that all public resources destined for housing would be subject to the National Housing Plan. In the end, all the difficulties faced by the Social Interest Housing Subsystem in establishing financing were quickly resolved by the emergence of the financialized real estate sector. The social demand accumulated for decades on the urban reform agenda of the social movements 'converged' with the immediate economic interests and the need to expand the market, resulting in My House, My Life. However, its definition carried only the proposal of an endowment fund in the Social Interest Housing Subsystem as a form of subsidy to the low-income strata, leaving aside the institutional framework of the National Housing Plan. My House, My Life would restore the Residential Lease program, which had existed since 2001 as a housing program aimed at the low-income population. In practice, the change was an increase in public funds invested in the program.[11]

---

11   Residential Lease Program is a program of the Ministry of Cities operated by the Federal Savings Bank and financed. by the Residential Leasing Fund that aims to reduce the housing deficit in municipalities with more than 100,000 inhabitants, enabling home ownership by families with incomes of up to R$1,800.

In view of this situation, the housing movements and the National Forum for Urban Reform promoted a broad social mobilization and presented proposals for inclusion in the My House, My Life program, requiring a portion of the investment for self-construction, better finance conditions, and land viabilization through the acquisition, legal expropriation, or adaptation of public land (Rolnik 2015: 302). As a result, two components aimed at low-income families and organized by housing cooperatives, associations, and other private non profit organizations were added to the program, My House, My Life (Plan Associations) and the National Housing (Plan Rural). However, only 3 percent of the were earmarked for these modalities (Rolnik 2015: 302).

The housing program was structured in terms of income brackets for which the value and type of property, the percentage of the subsidy, and the interest rate varied (Table 18.1). In the case of Brackets 2 and 3, the builders were responsible for the production and marketing of the units. For Bracket 1 they produced the units but the beneficiaries of the subsidy were determined by the municipalities. In addition to the subsidies in Brackets 1 and 2 (20–90 percent of the value of the property), interest rates for all brackets were below the market and guaranteed by a public fund.

TABLE 18.1   Income brackets of the my house, my life program and financial conditions

Monthly family income*	Brackets	Conditions of financing
Up to R$1,800	Bracket 1	Up to 90 percent subsidy of the value of the property, which varied according to the city. Payment in up to 120 installments of maximum R$270 without interest
Up to R$2,350	Bracket 1.5**	Up to R$45,000 in subsidy, with 5 percent annual interest rate
Up to R$3,600	Bracket 2	Up to R$27,500 in subsidy, with 5.5–7 percent annual interest
Up to R$6,500	Bracket 3	Financing with an annual interest rate of 8.16 percent annual interest

Notes: * For farmers and rural workers, annual household income must be under R$78,000.

** Created in the second phase of program.

SOURCE: DATA FROM BRASIL (2016A)

The initial package proposed to facilitate the construction of 200,000 units in the "economic segment" (income from four to ten minimum wages), which corresponded to the developers' reserve for serving a social segment favored by economic improvement and the expansion of credit. However, the Lula government expanded the scale to a million units, increasing the percentage allocated to low-income people and including Bracket 1, a social stratum not previously addressed by a housing program. This was the largest amount of subsidies directed to low-income housing in the history of the country and the first use of the federal budget to finance housing. The remainder went to My House, My Life–Builders, which handled about 97 percent of the resources allocated to the program. Under this part of the program companies presented a housing project, received financing for it, and sold the units to buyers who had themselves received financing for the purpose. Thus the My House, My Life program linked economic growth and social inclusion in a countercyclical economic measure guided by civil construction, making possible investment by economic agents facing a crisis and expanding the consumer market (Brasil 2009):

> The urgency and relevance of the proposed measure is justified by the need for the implementation of structured governmental actions capable of moderating the impacts of the world crisis on the Brazilian economy in order to promote the conditions for resumption of economic growth and the generation of jobs and income and to reduce the housing deficit by expanding access to housing for low-income families.

Since the level of income was a limit to financing and, consequently, to the market, the state began to create financing for the low-income social strata that did not meet the demands of the market. In other words, the inclusion formula for consumption via the market implied the state's acting as financial guarantor (Brasil 2009):

> Current credit restrictions, even for a short period of time, can generate problems in the productive sector, with damaging consequences for the national economy. Therefore, it is appropriate to create a mechanism to reduce the credit risk associated with housing finance operations, encourage the repayment of loans, and enable the continuity of investment, especially in the construction sector, a great generator of employment and income for the segments with lower purchasing power.
>
> Associated with this is the diagnosis that the housing deficit is concentrated in the low-income population segment because of the difficulty

this population experiences in obtaining financing and demonstrating regularity and sufficiency of income, the decay of the Housing Finance System in the 1980s, and the very rapid urbanization of the past decade.

With a view to remedying a market failure and facilitating the access of the population with incomes of up to 10 minimum wages to new lines of real estate financing, we propose that the Union participate in a private fund that:

(a) guarantees payment to financing agents of the monthly installments of housing finance not paid by the final borrower whether because of unemployment or because of temporarily reduced ability to pay (...).

(b) assumes the debtor balance of real estate financing in cases of death and permanent disability or arising from the recovery expenses related to physical damage to the property.

Thus the developmentalist strategy of public investment and the social demand for housing subsidies converged in inclusion through consumption. However, there was a repositioning of state action in social policy: at the same time as the state became fundamental to making housing accessible, its action was centered on its financing, and the technical-institutional decision making, planning, and execution of housing policy became disarticulated, limited to creating the conditions for operationalization of the market. The most important change was the commodification of public funds, since the resources assigned to social policy become part of the circuit of capital valorization, abandoning its condition of "antivalue", as has called by Oliveira (2013). In this sense, the My House, My Life program was an instrument of the mercantilization of social policy.

This redefinition of state action occurred within the regulatory frameworks of neoliberalism. As noted by Brenner, Peck, and Theodore (2012: 330), "Neoliberalization is a particular form of regulatory reorganization: it involves the recalibration of institutionalized and collectively linked modes of governance and, more generally, economic state relations to impose, amplify or consolidate mercantilized and commodified forms of social life." This rearrangement also assumed its own format. In contrast to the National Housing Bank, which was responsible for the planning, regulation, supervision, and control of the construction of housing units, the Federal Savings Bank is responsible only for project approval and construction supervision. The builders determine the site and the project (with the approval of the appropriate authorities) and have the sale of the housing units guaranteed by the bank without bidding. There is no risk of vacancy or delinquency, and there are no incorporation or marketing expense, increasing profit margins to real estate.

The guidelines for the My House, My Life program and general production conditions are set by the Ministry of Cities, but it has little influence over the destination of resources. The municipalities determined the demand, which means a reduced role in relation to their importance in urban planning under the 1988 Constitution, separating housing policy from urban policy and housing from land. Thus, the production of the urban space resulting from the My House, My Life program benefited private agents and was outside the scope of the main public agent responsible for its regulation. There was no connection between housing construction and land-use regulation; on the contrary, while the promotion of the federal government's housing construction stimulated land appreciation, local governments did not use the instruments of land-use regulation to reduce speculation in real estate. Thus the production of housing units was guided by the calculation of economic profitability. According to the literature, the housing units produced under the Builders division for the low-income segment are built to low standards.[12] The problems range from failure to complete projects to lack of urban infrastructure, the homogenization of space, and the reproduction of socio-spatial segregation. In other words, market-mediated politics have resulted in the commodification of housing and land. According to Lefebvre (2001), exchange value has taken precedence over use value and "habitat" over "dwelling".[13]

The projects of the Corporations division of My House, My Life[14] were of higher quality and value because, through cooperation between the housing movement and the local authorities, their construction was oriented to the use value of real estate, involving partnerships in which the profit margins of the contractors were reduced and thus, with the same amount of financial resources, larger and better-located housing units could be produced. This also allowed the beneficiaries to participate in the design and construction of their homes. Despite this, the division had its limits, ranging from the limited resources allocated to it (about 3 percent of the budget) to the political

---

12   Camargo (2016), Danoso and Queiroga (2014), Fix (2011), Marques and Rodrigues (2013), Shimbo (2010), Rizek (2018), Rolnik et al. (2015), Rolnik (2015), TCU (2014).

13   For Lefebvre (2001), "dwelling" refers to "living", participating in social life in all its diversity and heterogeneity and collectively appropriating and modifying space, while "habitat" is something "conceived" and is imposed by homogenizing state and economic rationality. reducing living to the everyday functions of the dominant order.

14   A modality in which resources are managed by cooperatives or nonprofit associations undertaking projects through joint effort or hire companies to do so.

dilemmas faced by social movements defending a different conception of housing policy. The My House, My Life program did not result from a participatory process, did not constitute a housing policy, and was not linked to urban reform as the movement had hoped.

Despite the program's achievements in social outreach, the disproportion of investment to the housing deficit reveals that its goals were determined more by the market crisis than by the housing problem. About 83 percent of the country's housing deficit was concentrated in the social segment of up to three minimum wages (Fundação João Pinheiro 2015: 38), for which about 50 percent of the housing units produced were destined. According to a survey by Marques and Rodrigues (2013) comparing the housing deficit of each bracket with the My House, My Life deliveries up to June 2013, the program had met 7 percent of the deficit in Bracket 1, 50 percent of that in Bracket 2, and 100 percent of that in Bracket 3. In the Metropolitan Region of São Paulo, where the real estate is more valuable, more housing units were produced for Bracket 2 than for Bracket 1, which contained 83 percent of the housing deficit (Rolnik et al. 2015). Data for 2012 from the Fundação João Pinheiro (2015) show that, despite the construction of new units through the My House, My Life program, the housing deficit in the bracket of up to three minimum wages continued to increase.

Between 2009 and 2015, R$244.5 billion were invested in the program, contracting for around 3.7 million housing units, serving more than 10 million people (Brasil 2016b). There was a real estate boom in the main Brazilian cities. In São Paulo, real estate launches almost doubled between 2009 and 2011 (Secovi 2012). The construction sector registered record growth (15.3 percent) between 2009 and 2010, higher than the GDP and represented 9.8 percent of the new formal jobs in 2012 (Sinduscon 2012).[15] However, the economic gains resulting from state promotion of the private sector did not translate into collective gains. The increase in real estate prices was much greater than the increase in production costs and income. Between 2008 and 2014, while real estate prices increased by up to 250 percent, construction costs rose 61 percent and real per capita income 18 percent. In the cities of São Paulo and Rio de Janeiro, real estate prices increased 88 percent above the general price index. Thus, the subsidies and state incentives invested in the My House, My Life program were transformed into capital transfers through increasing prices and valorization of real estate.

---

15   See data on public investments, construction performance and employment in Sinduscon, *Conjuntura da Construção*, 2 (June 2012). https://sindusconsp.com.br/wp-content/uploads/2015/06/2012-jun.pdf (accessed 8, November, 2018).

Inter-American Development Bank data indicate that Brazil had one of the highest real estate valuation rates in the world between 2009 and 2015, about 121 percent. Examining the variables that affect real estate prices, Brando and Barbedo (2016) found that international enthusiasm about Brazil had the greatest impact, from which they concluded that the My House, My Life program and the increase in the limit for the use of the Severance Indemnity Fund contributed to the cycle of rising prices. With the launch of the program, companies recovered the value of their shares on the stock exchange, and announcements of the purchase of shares of the real estate sector increased (Fix 2011).

The financialization of the real estate sector not only makes the housing area more dependent on market fluctuations but also changes the logic of operationalization of the companies. According to Rolnik (2015: 292):

> The injection of financial capital [into the real estate sector] meant increasing power and control of its credit subsidiaries, transforming them into securitizers and subjecting the strategies of the construction companies to the logic of their financial arms. In many cases, the CEOs of the funds have also assumed command positions within the companies by combining boards of directors and management positions.

Once financial capital fuses with productive and commercial capital, real estate credit becomes a product to be exploited in the financial market, and this excludes the state from this activity. In a recent interview, the new president of Banco Bradesco, the second-largest private bank in Brazil, defending larger-scale loans rather than restrictive interest rates, identified real estate financing at the bottom of the pyramid as a promising market for the bank.[16]

When the residential real estate market showed signs of exhaustion, investors began to redirect their capital to real estate funds in segments of real estate destined for income extraction (offices, malls, industrial buildings, etc.), withdrawing investment from the housing sector. Indeed, after the announcement of the World Cup (2014) and Olympics (2015) mega-events, real estate funds went up, as can be seen in the continued growth of the IFIX (the index of the average performance of real estate funds shares on the Bovespa).[17] In addition, there were various government incentives, especially in the form of tax relief, for this type of operation.

---

16   See the interview Folha/UOL: https://bityli.com/hljLUW (accessed October 10, 2021).
17   Between 2014 and 2019, IFIX accumulated an appreciation of 91 percent.

Finally, although the My House, My Life program made significant progress with regard to housing inequality and absorbed much of the housing deficit in its second phase, the volume of investment could have inaugurated another paradigm in housing policy and incorporated the knowledge and organization accumulated by society in the past few decades. Based as it was on the market and never consolidated as social policy, its political support was fragile and subject to the economic contingency of the market, which was aggravated in the context of the financialization of the housing sector.

After the interruption of Dilma Rousseff's term in 2016, the Temer government (Partido do Movimento Democrático Brasileiro [Brazilian Democratic Movement Party] – PMDB) reduced the goals for Brackets 1 and 1.5, suspended the Corporations division projects, and raised the maximum value of real estate for financing by the Severance Indemnity Fund. As a result, it neutralized the positive aspects of the program, fueling real estate valorization and redirecting resources to the middle classes to the detriment of low-income groups.

4 Considerations on Market-Mediated Social Policy

Starting from the understanding that the key aspect of neoliberalism is the commodification of the whole of social life and that neoliberalization consists of the different ways in which specific experiences are connected to this trend, I have sought in this chapter to trace the neoliberalization of Brazilian social policy. I have identified a correlation between the dynamics of capital and the displacement of social policy, showing that, beyond the "minimal state", neoliberalism finds other paths toward commodification, cutting across governments and establishing new state arrangements. From this perspective, the recent political cycle associated with Lulism was not an inflection of neoliberalism but an adaptation of it to the specific conditions of the context.

The confluence of the measures adopted in the process of democratization with strategies for the commodification of urban space are evidence of the financialization of the real estate sector, which overcame the urban reform movement and, in a sense, benefited from it. The institutional reformulation established market variables in the regulation and financing of housing policy, which meant a repositioning of state performance. The analysis of the My House, My Life program makes it clear that this rearrangement, while it restricts the state's agency with regard to urban and housing policy and, consequently, the maintenance of the democratic decision-making processes established by housing policy, is critical to market expansion and financing. The preponderance of private agents in the orientation of social policy and the submission of the social public fund to the logic of valorization of capital are facets of the commodification of social policy.

As the developmentalism, the My House, My Life program meant public investment to boost economic growth, strengthening the private sector. However, the inclusive approach and the historical conditions under which the economic and social agents involved operated gave the program its own character. Under developmentalism, especially during the military regime, housing policy was used to promote the private productive sector, and this accentuated the concentration of income. The My House, My Life program has transformed the exclusionary consequences of the previous social formation into an opportunity for expansion of the market through social inclusion, as well as contributing to the financialization of real estate capital. Since the market cannot promote social justice and confronts barriers to its expansion in social inequality, social policy is mobilized as an instrument for including the low-income social strata in the consumer market. Thus policies of inclusion function as an adjustment to market primacy. Rather than fostering democratization of access to material goods, it commodifies social policy.

What I question about social inclusion through the market is not access to material goods but the dominance of the market over the social, the commodification of public funds, and the mercantilized mediation of citizenship. When social policy is employed as an economic and market-oriented instrument, its public character is dissolved and it abandons its distributive function. Housing policy based on homeownership and mortgage credit resulted in the standardization of social housing, an increase in the prices of real estate, and the displacement of the low-income population to the periphery, reinforcing the old pattern of unequal urbanization.

While this form of state action does not correspond to the developmentalist strategy, neither it is identified with that presupposed by the welfare state, in which the rights of citizenship are guided by social justice. Contrary to the view that associates neoliberalism with the minimal state, the state plays a key part in the neoliberalization process, whose meaning is the commodification of all life.

References

Aalbers, M. (2016). Corporate financialization. In: Castree, N., et al. (eds.), *The International Encyclopedia of Geography: People, the Earth, Environment, and Technology*, 1–11. Oxford: Wiley.

Arretche, M. (2002). Federalismo e relações intergovernamentais no Brasil: a reforma dos programas sociais. *Dados* 45: 431–458.

Boito Jr., A. (2012). Governo Lula: a nova burguesia nacional no poder. In: Boito Jr., A., and Galvão, A. (eds.), *Política e classes sociais no Brasil dos anos 2000*, 69–106. São Paulo: Alameda.

Brando, L., and Barbedo, C.H. (2016). Há fatores não econômicos na formação de preços de imóveis? *Revista de Administração Contemporânea* 20(1): 106–130.

Brasil, R.F. (2009). *Exposição de Motivos Interministerial 33/2009* (MF/MJ/MP/MMA/ MCidades), de 24 de março de 2009. http://www.planalto.gov.br/ccivil_03/_ato2007-2010/2009/Exm/EMI-33-MF-MJ-MP-MMA-Mcidades-09-Mpv-459.htm (accessed October 11, 2021).

Brasil, R.F. (2016a). Portaria Interministerial N.96, de 30 de marco de 2016. *Diário Oficial da União* 61: 52. https://www.in.gov.br/materia/-/asset_publisher/KujrwoTZC2Mb/content/id/22559076/do1-2016-03-31-portaria-interministerial-n-96-de-30-de-marco-de-2016-22558953 (accessed October 11, 2021).

Brasil, R.F. (2016b). Minha casa, minha vida. *Portal Brasileiro de dados abertos.* https:// dados.gov.br/dataset/minha-casa-minha-vida/resource/78c022bf-3e56-4743-afbd-c94be37a235b (accessed October 10, 2021).

Brenner, N., et al. (2010). After neoliberalization? *Globalizations* 7 (September): 327–345.

Camargo, C.M. (2016). *Minha Casa Minha Vida Entidades: entre os direitos, as urgências e os negócios.* Unpublished doctoral thesis, University of São Paulo, São Carlos, São Paulo, Brasil.

Cavalcante, S. (2015). *Reprodução social e revolta política da classe média no Brasil recente.* Paper presented at the Thirty-ninth Annual Meeting of ANPOCS, December, Caxambu, MG, Brasil.

Dardot, P., and Laval, C. (2016). *A nova razão do mundo: Ensaio sobre a sociedade neoliberal.* Translated by Mariana Echalar. São Paulo: Boitempo.

Donoso, V.G., and Queiroga, E. (2014). *Produção habitacional social: o programa minha casa minha vida na Região Metropolitana de São Paulo.* Paper presented at the Ninth Quapá-Sel Colloquium, August, Universidade Federal do Espírito Santo, ES, Brasil.

Draibe, S. (2003). A política social no período FHC e o sistema de proteção social. *Tempo Social* 15 (November): 63–101.

Falchetti, C. (2019). Social Policy and the Dynamics of Neoliberalism, The My House, My Life Program and the Commodified Mediation of Housing. *Latin American Perspectives* 20(30): 1–16 (accessed 20 December 2019).

Fix, M. (2011). *Financeirização e transformações recentes no circuito imobiliário no Brasil.* Unpublished doctoral thesis, University of Campinas, Campinas, São Paulo, Brasil.

Fundação João Pinheiro. (2015). Deficit habitacional no Brasil 2011–2012. *Centro de Estatísticas e Informações.* Belo Horizonte, MG. http://www.fjp.mg.gov.br/index. php/docman/cei/559-deficit-habitacional-2011-2012/file (accessed May 26, 2017).

Foucault, M. (2008). *Segurança, Território, População – Curso dado ao Collège de France (1977–1978)*. São Paulo: Martins Fontes.

Harvey, D. (2005). *A produção capitalista do espaço*. São Paulo: Annablune.

Holston, J. (2013). *Cidadania insurgente: Disjunções da democracia e da modernidade no Brasil*. São Paulo: Companhia das Letras.

Kowarick, L. (1981). *A espoliação urbana*. São Paulo: Paz e Terra.

Lefebvre, H. (2001). *O direito à cidade*. Translated by Rubens Eduardo Frias. São Paulo: Centauro.

Marques, E., and Rodrigues, L. (2013). O Programa Minha Casa Minha Vida na metrópole paulistana: atendimento habitacional e padrões de segregação. *Revista Brasileira de Estudos Urbanos e Regionais* 15 (November): 159–177.

Moraes, L., and Saad-Filho, A. (2011). Da economia política à política econômica: o novo-desenvolvimentismo e o governo Lula. *Revista de Economia Política* 31: 507–527.

Oliveira, F. (2013). *Crítica à razão dualista: O ornitorrinco*. São Paulo: Boitempo.

Paulani, L.M. (2010). *O Brasil na crise da acumulação financeirizada*. Paper presented at the Fourth International Symposium on the Economy, Politics, and Human Rights, 9–11 September, Buenos Aires, Argentina. http://www.madres.org/documentos/doc20100924143515.pdf (accessed February 18, 2017).

Rizek, C.S. (2018). Produção de moradia e produção urbana: políticas sociais, consensos, desmanches e violência de Estado. In: Barros, J., et al. (eds.), *Os limites da acumulação, movimentos e resistência nos territórios*, 13–25. São Carlos: IAU/USP.

Rolnik, R. (2015). *Guerra dos lugares: A colonização da terra e da moradia na era das finanças*. São Paulo: Boitempo.

Rolnik, R., et al. (2015). O Programa Minha Casa Minha Vida nas regiões metropolitanas de São Paulo e Campinas: aspectos socioespaciais e segregação. *Cadernos Metrópole* 17 (May): 127–154.

Royer, L.O. (2009). *Financeirização da política habitacional: limites e perspectivas*. Unpublished doctoral thesis, Universidade de São Paulo, São Paulo, Brasil.

SECOVI. (2012). Balanço imobiliário. http://www.secovi.com.br/files/Downloads/balaco-mercado-imobiliario-2012pdf.pdf (accessed February 20, 2016).

Singer, A. (2012). *Os sentidos do lulismo: Reforma gradual e pacto conservador*. São Paulo: Companhia das Letras.

Shimbo, L.Z. (2010). *Habitação social, habitação de mercado: a confluência entre Estado, empresas construtoras e capital financeiro*. Unpublished doctoral thesis, University of São Paulo, São Paulo, Brasil.

Tribunal de Contas da União – TCU. (2014). *Relatório de auditoria: Minha Casa, Minha Vida*. Brasília: Brasil. https://portal.tcu.gov.br/biblioteca-digital/auditoria-operacional-no-programa-minha-casa-minha-vida.htm (accessed October 11, 2021).

World Bank. (1997). *Informe sobre el desarrollo mundial.* http://documentos.bancomundial.org/curated/es/701691468153541519/pdf/173000WDR0SPANISH0Box128708B00PUBLIC0.pdf (accessed January 10, 2017).

World Bank. (2002). *World development report 2002: building institutions for markets.* https://openknowledge.worldbank.org/handle/10986/5984.

CHAPTER 19

Tackling Regional Inequalities under the Workers' Party

Advances and Limitations

Soraia Aparecida Cardozo and Humberto Martins

0 Introduction[1]

This chapter aims at analyzing the advances and limitations of the implementation of regional development policies in Brazil under the Lula and Dilma governments. Developmentalism and developmentalist policy discussions need to address the issue of regional inequalities, since the mitigation of this problem involves long-term structural changes. The main argument here is that during these governments, despite an interesting attempt to restructure instruments aimed at reducing regional inequalities, this process was partial and incomplete. From the first Lula government there was a trend toward greater state involvement based on planning and the implementation of policies to improve income distribution, but the commitment to neoliberal policies persisted. The difficulty in abandoning neoliberalism had to do with the fundamental characteristics of the current phase of capitalist accumulation, among them a high degree of transnational productive integration, significant trade liberalization, a high level of financialization, strong deregulation, and the flexibilization of labor markets. Thus the Workers' Party governments adjusted their policies to two axes: greater state participation and the characteristics of the system of accumulation. In this connection, this chapter asks the following questions: What was the nature of these governments? and Does their treatment of regional issues reveal advances and limitations that help to explain their development strategies?

In relation to Cardozo and Martins (2020), this chapter presents three new contributions. First, it brings new ideas and fresh insights into the matter, benefiting from the evolution of the theoretical debate on New Developmentalism. In this respect, we discuss some recent titles that feature

---

1 An earlier version of the arguments and ideas at this chapter appeared in Cardozo and Martins (2020).

an interesting exchange between Bresser-Pereira and Medeiros in Review of Keynesian Economics, 2020. Second, we explore new literature on the experience of Workers' Party governments, which generally confirms the core ideas of the chapter, but also contribute with a more thorough analysis of the subject and make an overall balance as the left-wing government cycle was interrupted in 2016. Finally, we update the data up to 2016, using the database that is now available.

The text has three sections in addition to this introduction and the final considerations. In the first section, aspects of new developmentalism are presented and the meaning of the Lula and Dilma governments is discussed in terms of this interpretation. In the second section, the limitations of the implementation of the National Policy for Regional Development and other policies (social, sectoral, infrastructure, educational, and credit) and their regional impacts are examined. The third section offers a brief review of the evolution of regional inequalities under the Lula and Dilma governments.

1   New Developmentalism and the Lula and Dilma Governments

1.1   *New Developmentalism*

With Bresser-Pereira (2001; 2006) as its pioneer, new developmentalism is a set of theoretical statements and economic policy proposals focused on growth and development. Based on Keynesian (and Kaleckian) economic theory and giving an important role in economic dynamics to the state and public investment, the proposals of new developmentalism largely reject neoliberal precepts (Bresser-Pereira 2016a; 2016b; Bresser-Pereira, and Gala 2010). From this perspective, growth must be stimulated by exports and the exchange rate must be competitive for manufacturing industry. New developmentalism is characterized by an assertive state along with a strong market, macroeconomic policies aimed at sustainable economic growth, and national development projects that combine economic growth (fast and sustainable development) with income distribution and reduction of inequality (Sicsú, de Paula, and Michel 2007). It differs from neoliberalism (conventional orthodoxy) both in its theoretical matrix and in its economic policy proposals.

At the same time, new developmentalism differs from classical developmentalism. Although it draws heavily on the formulations developed in the Economic Commission for Latin America and the Caribbean, it seeks a renewal of this theoretical field with innovative ideas. It rejects the strategy of growth with external indebtedness and is aimed at industrialized middle-income countries.[2] In addition, it defends a level playing field for competitive international integration, especially in connection with exports of processed goods (Bresser-Pereira 2016b; Bresser-Pereira and Gala 2010). Thus new developmentalism has three essential aspects: (1) it inherits from classical developmentalism the idea of development as structural change; (2) influenced by Keynes and Kalecki, it emphasizes demand-driven growth; and (3) it advocates policies that neutralize the tendency toward cyclical and chronic overvaluation of the exchange rate and consequently promotes the industrial sector and exports of processed products (Bresser-Pereira 2016b).

More recently, Bresser-Pereira (2020a) reaffirmed the idea of New Developmentalism as a "second moment" of Latin American structuralism, which is identified as part of Classical Developmentalism (Bresser-Pereira 2016a; 2016b). In this "second moment", the emphasis shifts from supply to demand. According to the author, while structuralist authors focused on the internal insufficiency of demand due to an unlimited supply of labor, New Developmentalism focuses on external factors. As postulated by its theoretical basis, i.e., the new "Structuralist Macroeconomics of Development", the emphasis is on the deprivation of external demand caused by a cyclical tendency to overvalue the exchange rate. Thus, the exchange rate acquires a major role in the economic dynamics and this centrality is claimed as an original contribution from New Developmentalism (Bresser-Pereira 2020a: 12).

The critic to this centrality is one of the main points provided by Medeiros in his assessment of New Developmentalism (2020). According to him, New Developmentalism has correctly identified that "Classical Developmentalism underestimated and insufficiently considered the role of demand as a motor of growth" (Medeiros 2020: 152). But its focus on external demand, which seems to respond automatically to macroeconomic prices, in particular to the exchange rate, is also insufficient. Medeiros (2020) states that this is a reductionist view of the economic dynamics and a simplification that can situate this interpretation closer to a "market failure" approach, moving away from structuralist tradition and other heterodox views. On the other hand, other approaches have recognized a broad range of relevant issues to the development process. From this perspective, they have fully considered the role of institutions, structural

---

2 According to the World Bank classification, middle-income countries are those with a gross national income per capita, calculated by the World Bank Atlas method, from US$996 to US$12,055 (in current prices) in 2017, divided into low–middle (from US$996 to US$3,895) and medium–high (from US$3,896 to US$12,055). With a gross national income per capita of US$8,580 in 2017, Brazil is classified as a medium–high-income country.

change and industrial policies that provide a better international insertion and stimulate the development process (Medeiros 2020: 159–160).

In response, Bresser-Pereira (2020b) argues that New Developmentalism does not give exchange rate too much importance, but the "right" amount of importance as it is considered the most strategic of the five macroeconomic prices (profit rate, exchange rate, interest rate, wage rate, and inflation rate). According to him, this importance is actually underestimated in economic theory as both the United Kingdom and the United States, the main countries of origin of economic theory, historically and sequentially had their own currency as the dominant reserve currency. In this perspective, New Developmentalism cannot be seen as an "expression of market failure approach", as it relies on Keynesian tradition and consequently adopts "the historical-deductive method that searches for regularities and tendencies which assume that economic agents are neither fully rational nor have full knowledge of the causes and consequences of their economic decisions" (Bresser-Pereira 2020b: 172). Accordingly, the author stresses that "the real adversary of New Developmentalism is Neoclassical economics, not Classical Developmentalism." In this sense, New Developmentalism is an heir of development economics and Classical Developmentalism (Bresser-Pereira 2020b: 177).

According to Mollo and Amado (2015) and Mollo (2016), to the developmentalist debate of the 2000s can be added the social-developmentalist proposal of an economic policy that stimulates domestic demand through mass consumption and investment. In this view, an increase in real wages stimulates demand and, consequently, intervenes positively in investment decisions. At the same time, it is important for reducing inequalities. Another aspect that is highlighted by this approach is that, while the crisis after 2008 would not support growth through exports, growth brought about by internal consumption would promote business interests and make possible a new social pact (Mollo 2016). To what extent can the economic and social policies of the Lula and Dilma governments be classified as "new developmentalist"?

1.2   *The Lula and Dilma Governments: A Limited Developmentalism*

In the first Lula administration, there was a clear choice of macroeconomic policies based on the macroeconomic tripod that had been employed since the 1999 foreign-exchange crisis: restrictive fiscal and monetary policy, inflation targets and floating exchange-rate goals, and free capital mobility. Agreements with the International Monetary Fund were also maintained. At the same time, the government implemented an industrial and technological policy and embarked on an increase of the minimum wage and the expansion of social benefits, mainly through the Bolsa Família (Family Grant) (Oliveira 2012). Beginning in 2006 there was a shift in government orientation reinforced by the response to the 2008 subprime crisis. Thus the second Lula government was defined by a new phase of economic policy with emphasis on measures for expanding credit through public banks and fiscal measures for stimulating aggregate demand. In the same period, the Growth Acceleration Program was implemented with the objective of expanding and improving the country's infrastructure. There was also a continuation of the actual appreciation of the minimum wage and an expansion of social benefits, among other territorial, agrarian, and educational public policies (Oliveira 2012).

Analyzing these policies, Morais and Saad-Filho (2011; 2012) point out that economic policy combined neoliberal characteristics and elements of the new developmentalist agenda. Especially in Lula's second term (2007–2010), there was an expansion of the state's economic activity that reinforced the application of new developmentalist theses.

Despite the effects of the subprime crisis of 2008 on credit, commodity prices, foreign capital flows and foreign exchange rates, the country achieved a rapid economic recovery, observed in 2010. This recovery can be explained by factors including: increases in transfer of resources within the scope of social policies, increases in the minimum wage, investments by PETROBRAS, the Growth Acceleration Program, programs related to tax exemption and credit expansion, and the My House, My Life program.

There was a strengthening of public policies and a greater coordination of the State on economic activities. However, despite being closer to new developmentalist policies, aspects like the lack of protagonism of the industry, the effects of the appreciation of the national currency over industrial activity, and the need for greater articulation between the expansion of the domestic market and the diversification of the industry, limited the possibilities of economic policies aimed at economic development.

At the end of 2010, according to Corrêa and Hamilton (2015), a contraction adjustment was implemented involving credit control, interest rate increases, and measures for reaching the target primary surplus. These measures affected public and state investments, considered important drivers of economic growth.

The growth model implemented from 2004 to 2010, which was mainly based on the dynamism of consumption, which, to a large extent, was a result of improvements in income and credit distribution, began to face a series of limitations.

In August 2011 the gradual macroeconomic policy changes known as the new macroeconomic matrix were introduced (Prates, Fritz, and Paula 2017).

Part of this new matrix was the regulation of capital flows in an attempt to contain the great appreciation of the national currency, the progressive reduction of interest rates, and the primary surplus. At the same time, an industrial and technological policy based on an increase in Banco Nacional de Desenvolvimento Econômico e Social (National Economic and Social Development Bank – BNDES) credits and tax exemptions was implemented. The expansion of public policies and social security continued. While incentives to private investment through concessions, exemptions, and credit lines were intensified, public investments were reduced.

Bresser-Pereira (2016b) debates the economic policies of Lula's and Dilma's governments in relation to the new developmentalism proposals. According to him, Lula's administration competently increased the minimum wage and implemented distributive policies, which contributed to strengthen the internal market and reduce inequality. However, as the government let the exchange rate become increasingly overvalued over the period of 2003–2010, the expansion of the domestic market was fully captured by imports (Bresser-Pereira 2016b: 340). According to the author, the reduction in the interest rates and the devaluation of the Real in the beginning of Dilma's government was not sufficient to make the economy react. The attempt to implement an industrial policy based on fiscal incentives also failed and, as the political and economic instability rose, the government was forced to retreat and increase the interest rate. In this adverse context, the economic policy in the second term began with an orthodox orientation and under austerity measures such as fiscal adjustments, which amplified the economic slowdown and crisis. Thus, the author concludes that the Workers' Party administrations did not follow the new developmentalism economic proposals, particularly regarding the centrality of a competitive exchange rate (Bresser-Pereira 2016b).

Analyzing the first Dilma government (2011–2014), Curado (2017) proposes assessing the extent to which its economic policy can be classified as developmentalist or new developmentalist and argues that no national development strategy or growth path based on internal savings – both important elements of the new developmentalist agenda – was established. In addition, the economic policy was incompatible with the new developmentalist agenda in that fiscal policy led to a deterioration of public accounts, monetary policy oscillated considerably, and exchange-rate policy did not produce an intentional change toward the devaluation of the real. Thus he concludes that "new developmentalist proposals did not match the concrete actions of the Dilma government" (Curado 2017: 143).

The policies that made up the new macroeconomic matrix began to lose their impetus in 2013. As of mid-2013, a wave of protests with general claims were triggered by an increase in the price of public transportation. In 2014, an election year, the protests – then against the government – grew, but Dilma was still reelected. In the same period, the international economy, the flexibilization of the North American monetary policy, the deflation in the Eurozone, and the slowdown in China made the external context unfavourable to the Brazilian economy. The economic policy assumed a hibrid character that aimed, on the one hand, to contain the devaluation of the real and, on the other, to expand social programs and fiscal stimulus.

As of 2015, the Dilma government abandoned developmental attempts when it implemented an agenda based on strict fiscal adjustments. In addition, the political crisis, the Lava Jato operation and its effects on civil construction and oil increasingly lead the country into a situation of reduced economic dynamism.

Carneiro (2018) highlights three types of crucial problems when analysing the Brazilian economy in the 2010s: (1) the high interest rate allowed a larger inflow of capital in the post-crisis period of 2008, but with an increase in the share of more volatile liabilities; (2) the trend towards greater capital centralization on a global scale and the structuring of Global Value Chains directly influenced the national productive structure and intensified the evidence of deindustrialization after 2011; and (3) in 2010 it was even more difficult to reconcile the financing of social spending with a regressive tax system, which generated a series of distributive conflicts.

According to Carneiro (2018), the operationalization of the economic policy and the low support received by the projects implemented in the first Dilma government from different social classes and interest groups are among the factors that explain the failure of the government's developmentalist experience.

Dilma began her second term with largely restrictive macroeconomic policies and a decline in public investment, although she continued the implementation of social and industrial policies. The economic crisis worsened along with the political crisis that finally brought about her impeachment in 2016.

Examining the period in which the Workers' Party leaders were president, Rossi and Mello (2016) draw on the theoretical framework of Celso Furtado in an attempt to introduce structural constraints to the debate. They argue that the cycle of economic growth of the past decade was largely centered on the creation of a mass consumption market. Indeed, economic policy in this period broadened the consumption patterns of the population and improved the labor market quantitatively and qualitatively, contributing to the reduction of poverty and inequality. However, this growth model was incapable of modernizing the structure of production or including the labor force in its higher-productivity sectors. While several factors contributed positively to the creation of a mass consumption market, others such as the exchange-rate appreciation negatively affected the structure of production.

The strategy of these governments, according to Fonseca (2016), cannot be considered developmentalist because it was a response to a crisis rather than established proactively. Added to this was the fact that the restructuring policies, the reduction of interest rates, and the devaluation of the real were not part of a long-term national development strategy. From this we can conclude that the Lula and Dilma governments were not basically developmentalist, although they differed substantially from the policies of Fernando Henrique Cardoso, which were in essence neoliberal.

During the second Lula government and the first Dilma government, public policies were strengthened. There were incentives to develop and expand infrastructure, and the state extended its role in guiding growth and reducing inequalities (including spatial disparities). However, the tripod of macroeconomic policy was not completely abandoned. The Brazilian economy presented evidence of deindustrialization and reprimarization of exports. There was no break with the pillars of neoliberalism as the degree of financialization deepened, and trade liberalization remained unchanged.

The new developmentalist proposals influenced the expansion of the role of the state and the Lula and Dilma governments from 2006 to 2013. The implementation of a primarily developmentalist program was limited mainly by the continuation of neoliberal policies. As Boito Jr. and Berringer (2013: 31) point out, the implementation of measures that can be called developmentalist without breaking with the neoliberal model was supported by a broad, heterogeneous political front. However, these measures introduced many contradictions. The Lula and Dilma governments implemented macroeconomic measures considered more orthodox along with social and productive policies that can be called new developmentalist. The two orientations of economic policy overlapped. Thus, the strategy of these governments can be considered a limited developmentalism. According to Boito Jr. and Berringer (2013), there was a political front that supported a set of development policies such as an increase in the minimum wage, the transfer of income, an increase in BNDES budget allocations, a foreign policy that sought to strengthen large national companies abroad and aimed to get closer to Africa, Asia, and the Middle East, and the strengthening of domestic demand in response to the crisis. In addition to these measures there was an attempt to implement a regional development policy of national scope, but it was constrained by the maintenance of the broad outlines of an orthodox macroeconomic policy, with developmentalist policies overlapping with macroeconomic policies and hindering de facto national development projects. In addition, there was a reversal of the favorable international situation with (albeit delayed) repercussions for Brazil. It was increasingly complicated, especially after 2013, to establish a social pact between the upper and the lower classes that would support a proposal of structural reform.

2   Public Policies and Regional Development under the Lula and Dilma Governments

2.1   *Regional Development Planning and Policies in a New Developmentalist Scenario*

Analyses of the Brazilian economy guided by the new developmentalist framework do not usually consider territorial diversity and the differentiated way in which the reproduction of capital expands. A sound understanding of the advances and limitations of regional policies helps to establish the features and the significance of the Lula and Dilma governments, and this understanding is possible only when they are linked to a more general framework of public policies and macroeconomic strategy. The economic policies implemented throughout the post-redemocratization period in Brazil have been discussed and their theoretical and political bases identified. Following a period of neoliberalism and privatization (especially after 1990), the Lula administration attempted to rescue government planning and promotion of national and regional development. In this context, the meaning and the scope of these actions have been debated.

Analyses of regional development policies add a fundamental structural element to this debate. These policies constitute a structural point par excellence, linked to long-term transformations and a process of inequality reduction that was considered a qualitative change. The renewed debate on the importance of the reduction of spatial inequalities in Brazil in the 2000s can be interpreted as part of a strategy to broaden the participation of the state in the implementation of policies aimed at reducing inequalities. However, regional policies were limited by the hybrid character of the economic strategies.

Since 2003, the federal government has had the goal of reorganizing regional planning in terms of a national policy. In a document released in that year by the Ministry of National Integration, the general outlines of the National Policy for Regional Development were presented as "a proposal for discussion". The need for a national-level policy, although one aligned with other levels of government coordinated by the ministry, was stressed. State action in the framework of a "development strategy for Brazil" and including a reduction of regional disparities was emphasized. From the outset, the policy was considered in the context of the new generation of regional strategies represented by the policy of the European Union. A typology at the microregional level with a range of priorities for action was developed. From data on household income and gross domestic product (GDP) growth on a microregional scale, 556 micro-regions were classified into four types: high-income, dynamic, stagnant, and low-income. The latter was considered the highest-priority and the focus of government action.

Two sources of funding were established. The first was the funds established by the Constitution of 1988, while the second was a national fund similar to the regional development fund of the European Union. The latter fund was not created, however, and this prevented the emergence of new sources of financing of the program's priority projects.

The regional development policy was implemented in 2007 in a context in which economic policy was more flexible. A positive international scenario with a favorable impact on Brazilian exports and the reduction of indicators of vulnerability due to growing trade surpluses contributed to this change. At the same time, initiatives sometimes classified as new developmentalist were implemented while, as we have seen, the macroeconomic policy tripod remained practically unchanged. Thus, in the second Lula term, there was a hybrid growth model in which neoliberal macroeconomic policies coexisted with policies for increasing investment and the minimum wage and transferring income to the lower classes. Along with these policies, progress was made in the formulation of a regional policy as another development initiative. The high growth rates of 2006, 2007, and 2008 were influenced by the strengthening of the domestic market (Oliveira 2012), and in this context the implementation of public policies for growth acceleration and regional development was emphasized. The "Citizenship Territories" policy, aimed at rural development and the reduction of regional inequalities, was implemented in 2007. The typology of the National Policy for Regional Development was adopted in public policies such as the grant and loan policies of the BNDES. The criteria for the use of the constitutional funds were modified to meet the objectives established by this policy (Macedo, Pires, and Sampaio 2017).

Describing the 2003–2010 period, Coêlho (2017) says that the prospects for the implementation of the regional development policy were promising in the beginning but gradually revealed their limitations in the context of a government policy whose developmentalist character was unchanged. In the first Dilma government, as part of the intensification of the new developmentalist agenda, the National Policy for Regional Development underwent reformulation to broaden its operations. The reference document of the 2012 National Conference for Regional Development advocated the so-called National Policy for Regional Development II, a proposal aimed at overcoming various difficulties in the implementation of the regional policy. It emphasized the need for ample and stable financing sources and proposed mechanisms for enhancing coordination. The conditions for the implementation of regional strategies as state policy, especially with regard to their developmentalist potential, became even more adverse as of 2013, largely because of the deepening of the international crisis of the European Union and the changes in the implementation of macroeconomic policy in Brazil.

Ever since the first Lula administration, regional matters have been considered a strategic axis. The attempt to implement the National Policy for Regional Development consisted of a broad initiative to structure a regional policy with national scope and a participatory character. For Castro (2014), it made the regional issue a matter of national concern that was critical for the implementation of a new developmentalist project. The roadblocks in the implementation of the national policy can be seen as arising from the pursuit of social inclusion and developmentalism without breaking with neoliberalism. Difficulties arose in implementing a policy aimed at regional development that was constrained by alliances within the power bloc that did not prioritize the regional issue. In addition, the lack of a long-term development project limited the opportunities for political negotiation in the creation of a national regional development fund. Thus the regional policy became secondary and was not fully implemented. The first Lula government failed to create the conditions for doing so, and when those conditions existed, in 2007, it was only in part. The national policy became more visible with the second Lula government. In the first Dilma government, National Policy for Regional Development II was launched with the implementation of a new macroeconomic matrix and the intensification of the application of incentives. When the government began to face economic and political difficulties, it was practically abandoned.

The advances and setbacks in the implementation of a national regional policy were also related to the problems linked to the restructuring of the institutions that would have implemented that policy. The Ministry of National Integration, established in 1999 under Cardoso, was in charge of proposing and conducting the National Policy for Regional Development. It was assigned the powers of a Regional Policies Secretariat and came to include the Department of Drought Works, the São Francisco and Paranaíba Valley Development Company, and the Northeast and Amazon Development Superintendencies (later eliminated). It was placed in charge of the administration of the constitutional funds for regional development and the available tax incentives. It had three operational areas: civil defense, water infrastructure, and regional development.

In the first Lula term (2003–2006), the ministry emphasized water infrastructure and civil defense projects at the expense of regional development. Coêlho (2017: 80) shows that, while more than 20 percent of the resources it managed in 2005 and 2006 were allocated to regional development projects, in 2007 this figure was less than 10 percent. Among the projects classified as regional development, the financing of those related to regional policy management and territorial planning accounted for around 1 percent or less (in 2005, 2007, and 2008) except in 2006, when it reached 8 percent. In 2007 there was a restructuring of the regional development superintendencies that had been abandoned under the Cardoso government, which, according to Coêlho (2017: 66), "were emptied of their historical role related to regional development planning". Thus regional policy was not transformed into state policy under the Lula and Dilma governments, and several factors prevented it from becoming the focus of government attention. As Brandão (2013: 341) points out, legitimizing regional matters as state policy remains the challenge. It is not enough to "reinforce the territorial dimension in the main federal policies and plans of a sectoral nature".

This point is strengthened by Brandão (2020), who made an assessment of the National Policy for Regional Development (NPRD) considering the whole period. The author highlights the interesting objectives presented in the NPRD 2, which were also criteria to establish the priority of the actions. Additionally, the author states that the governance proposals set by the NPRD 2 could stimulate a broad and democratic decision environment regarding the regional policy. Indeed, these objectives, criteria and governance proposals were established during a vast and participative elaboration process. However, they did not receive priority under Dilma's government. For instance, the Pluri(Multi) Annual Plan (PPA 2012–2015) was very imprecise regarding regional inequalities and the issue only appeared generally among a long list of 65 thematic programs (Brandão 2020).

This view is close to Macedo and Porto (2020a), who emphasized questions of governance and priorities, arguing that the regional policy did not achieve a relevant position in the government agenda and did not become a "state policy". Although they recognize that funding is a central question, the authors do not consider the absence of funding, especially the fact that a national fund was not created, a major obstacle to run the regional policy (Macedo and Porto 2020a: 254). Differently, in this work we state that the creation of this national fund is crucial to advance the regional policy. On the other hand, since 2017, these authors have proposed a useful update of the typology by using new data and criteria. In another study, the authors highlight how important it is for the regional development policy not to be assimilated by a market logic (Macedo and Porto 2020b).

The institutional and political aspects of Brazilian regional policies are highlighted by Randolph (2020), who discusses the experience of the National Policy for Regional Development in the 2000s from another theoretical view. This view is associated with the theoretical notion of "scheduling", which questions the real (sincere) priority of some themes listed in public policies. In his analysis, the author emphasizes the institutional aspects and "sociopolitical arenas", concluding that the implementation of the National Policy for Regional Development was marked by vulnerable institutional formats and political fragilities in the arenas.

The structuring of a regional development policy for national implementation and of the institutions assigned to sustaining it was marked by advances and limitations within the logic of the limited developmentalism. Therefore, the regional dynamics of this period cannot be explained in terms of the National Policy for Regional Development. On the one hand, the spatial impacts of social, sectoral, credit, and logistical infrastructure policies that are considered the marks of new developmentalist operations in these governments must be emphasized. On the other hand, the effect of the commodities boom on regions whose productive structures are closely linked to the production of primary goods and mineral extraction should also be highlighted.

2.2   The Regional Dimension of Social and Sectoral Policies

The fact that no funding was created for the regional development policy made it impossible to direct public resources to the subnational units with the lowest spending capacity. This problem impaired the creation of public mechanisms for funding or encouraging private investment that did not follow market logic and operated in the poorest regions, which needed more effective public operations to induce economic growth (Brandão 2013). Furthermore, federative connections were needed for multiscalar actions. As Brandão points out, non-reimbursable sources might finance small infrastructure works and allow connections between the policies of Brazil and those of its federative units. The National Policy for Regional Development relied on the traditional sources of financing guaranteed in the 1988 Constitution, funds made up of 3 percent of the revenues from the industrialized products tax and the income tax. These funds were managed by public banks and became lines of credit for entrepreneurs interested in investing in the North, the Northeast, and the Central-West. Macedo, Pires, and Sampaio (2017) have analyzed 25 years of constitutional-fund operations, comparing their use with the performance of economic indicators, and report that both the number of operations and the amount of resources increased significantly after 2003. Another change occurred in 2007 with the implementation of the national policy and the modification of the criteria for targeting these resources. These researchers conclude that, while the funds were important for proactive operations in the territory with the support of development banks, the level of intra- and interregional disparity remained high (Macedo, Pires, and Sampaio 2017: 274). They point out that the increase in the use of the funds can be explained in terms of an increase in average income and greater formalization of the labor market, along with increased public spending, the increase in the minimum wage above inflation, and the expansion of social programs. Starting in 2007, the National Policy for Regional Development's rules became an important factor in the greater demand for credit linked to resources from the constitutional funds. This process reveals the trend toward the strengthening under the Lula and Dilma governments of public banks, especially the Bank of the Northeast and the Bank of Amazonia, which were in charge of the administration of the constitutional funds for those regions. In the Central-West, the constitutional fund was managed by the Bank of Brazil. Public banks played an important role in places that were unattractive to private banks, which were concentrated in the economically more dynamic regions.

The explanation for the greater use of constitutional funds was linked to public policies that were the pillars of growth and income distribution in the period reviewed – social, sectoral, infrastructure, and productive financing policies such as the Bolsa Família, the Growth Acceleration Program, My House, My Life, and the expansion of federal higher education – and made significant contributions to regional development. Most of the resources of the Bolsa Família program were directed to the Northeast, which had the largest percentage of poverty. The Bolsa Família program, the minimum wage increase, and the expansion of social security were extremely important for the Northeast and the North in raising the income level of families at the bottom of the social pyramid. The domestic market was strengthened, and household consumption and living conditions were improved (Morais and Saad-Filho 2012). However, these policies did not bring about structural change in asset ownership or become established as state policies. Other policies needed to be implemented to drive changes in the structure of production and reduce regional inequalities.

Araújo (2013) points out that despite the positive effects of growth and income distribution policies on the poorest regions, socioeconomic indicators still reflect a high degree of spatial inequality. The concentration of high infant mortality and illiteracy rates among people aged 10 years and over in the North and Northeast and the disparities between urban and rural Brazil remain strong. The greater allocation of funds from the Bolsa Família program to the Northeast did not overcome regional disparities. Extreme poverty was reduced in all of the country's federative units, but the North and the Northeast continued to have the most (Figure 19.1).[3] This trend reinforces the importance of income transfer policies for the improvement of the living conditions of these regions, which have always had a high level of poverty. However, the goal of income transfer policies is not to solve regional problems, and they will succeed only if they are implemented along with other policies, especially asset redistribution, and permanent state policies. As Souza (2013) points out, actions considered developmentalist such as the Growth Acceleration Program and My House, My Life and the major projects related to the World Cup and the Olympics had important territorial impacts but were not proposed as broad state policies for regional development. The Growth Acceleration Program has been considered deconcentrative, its budget for the less-developed regions being greater than their percentage of the GDP. The North and the Northeast received 26.7 percent of total investment in 2007–2010 and 32.2 percent in 2011–2014 (Macedo, Pires, and Sampaio 2017), and therefore investment in infrastructure increased in those regions. However, Silva et al. (2016) show that, although historically infrastructure investments are highly correlated with the economic growth of states and regions, this had no significant impact on GDP dispersion among regions and states. Although relevant to sustain growth in national terms, especially in a context of international crisis, the program did not contribute significantly to reducing regional inequalities.

Rolnik and Klink (2011) argue that federal policies such as the Growth Acceleration Program have accentuated the divisions of the national territory, consolidating productive arrangements and export hubs with greater connectivity with the foreign market instead of focusing on the domestic market. Under the My House, My Life program, the increase in housing credit was centered on the lower classes and the housing sector. The loans granted led to major development of the real estate sector (through speculation and rapid appreciation of properties) that increased the challenge for cities to confront the demands of this development for better urban living conditions. Thus, despite the expansion of consumption and economic dynamism, these policies were not coordinated with a regional development policy for the whole country. In addition, they failed to change the pattern of regional development in a structural and consistent way, which is a fundamental feature of

---

3   This indicator refers to the percentage of individuals with per capita household income equal to or less than R$70 per month in August 2010, corresponding to approximately US$40.

the country's underdevelopment. The importance of these policies in reducing social inequalities and improving living conditions and the consumption capacity of peripheral regions is undeniable. They played a strategic role given the difficulty of implementing a regional policy, but, as Castro (2014) emphasizes, the absence of a territorial vision and of integration with other instruments as part of a national development project may produce contradictory results.

The family agriculture financing programs that began to include the low-income classes and a significant number of farmers in the poorest regions of the country also had a significant impact on the production and consumption systems of those regions. The minimum-wage increase produced greater dynamism of consumption in the poorer regions because of the improved wages and their effects on pensions and other social security programs.

The policy of higher-education expansion produced important spatial transformations through regional deconcentration as a result of the increase in funding credit for students in private institutions and the expansion of public institutions. From 2002 to 2014 total enrollment in undergraduate courses in public and private higher-education institutions increased by 86.4 percent, to 6,486,171, and expanded in all regions. The proportions of the Southeast and South were reduced, respectively, from 50.2 to 47.0 percent and from 19.5 to 15.4 percent. The Central-West remained stable at around 9.4 percent, while the North (5.5 to 7.0 percent) and especially the Northeast (15.6 to 21.3 percent) increased their proportions (INEP 2014). Enrollment growth in federal institutions was 103.8 percent. The participation of institutions located in the interior (outside the capitals of the respective federative units) went from 34.3 percent

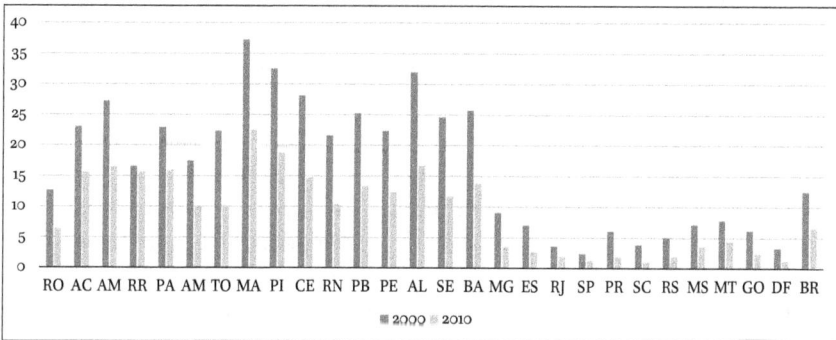

Source: (UNDP/IPEA/FJP, 2016

FIGURE 19.1 Proportion of populations of Brazilian federative units living in extreme poverty (2000 and 2010)
SOURCE: UNDP/IPEA/FJP, 2016

in 2002 to 49.9 percent in 2014. In federal institutions, the proportions of the Northeast (around 30 percent) and the North (around 13 percent) were higher than in all other institutions.

Despite some changes, the public policies under Dilma's first term continued and even amplified many of these non-territorial based initiatives. In the productive sector, although the plan "Bigger Brazil" launched in 2011 did not manage to coordinate the public and private investment, many assets have impacting Brazilian productive structure. Also launched in the first year of Dilma's first term (2011) the plan "Brazil without misery", devoted to eradicate extreme poverty, encompassed a mechanism of "active search" in order to include more people into social programs. The programs to increase access to higher-education also continued (Brandão 2020).

However, under a context of economic crisis amplified by the contractionary monetary policy, social expenses had a decrease in Dilma's second term. Expenditures in social protection, which grew in the first term (2011–2014), declined in 2015–2016. This was also observed in the total expenditure by the Ministry of Education, which fell 17.1% between 2014 and 2016 (IPEA 2018). This decrease in public policies led to poorer social, educational and productive indicators, or at least to their stagnation.

The interruption of the growth and distributional trajectories from 2015 was also identified by Brandão (2019). According to him, over a ten-year period (2004–2014), corresponding to the major part of Lula's two governments and Dilma's first term, Brazil achieved both economic growth and social inclusion. In this period, productive and infrastructural policies, as well as social protection and educational programs were very relevant. Social policies associated with internal market growth and with the formalization of labour relations played a crucial role in this process (Brandão 2019: 368).

This set of actions reflecting greater state activism and a more developmentalist character of the Lula and Dilma governments had important effects on the poorer regions of the country, but it could not replace a regional development policy of long-term structural change. Furthermore, these were measures that ultimately sought the expansion of the number of consumers through income increases, without any changes in property structure or transformations of the production system and social structure. Therefore, the treatment of the regional situation by the Lula and Dilma governments reveals the obstacles to the new developmentalism under the neoliberal model. The difficulty of implementing policies of substantial resumption of investment, restructuring of basic public services, and asset redistribution hindered changes that could have substantially modified regional disparities.

3   The Evolution of Regional Disparities under the Lula and Dilma
         Governments

The emergence since 2003 of issues that in the late 1980s were not prominent
on the government agenda is undeniable. At the same time, there were no
structural reforms or improvements in asset distribution, and therefore the
great gains of financial capital were maintained and even linked to the management of the public debt. Regional economic dynamics under the Lula and
Dilma governments involved a certain devolution of production. This deconcentration, according to Castro (2014), can be understood in terms of social
policies, Growth Acceleration Program projects, BNDES expenditures, and
the commodities boom. In other words, broadening public policies aimed at
growth and income distribution created a virtuous circle that brought about
considerable growth in the more peripheral regions. These policies, however, were not established according to any spatial logic, and "in the absence
of an explicit regional policy linked to a clear national development project,
deconcentration moved very slowly and presented disturbing trends" (Castro
2014: 513).

     The per capita GDP of the five Brazilian macroregions for the period reveals
that there was no significant change in the pattern of interregional income
distribution. For the Northeast this indicator remained below 50 percent of the
national average, going from 46 to 48 percent of per capita GDP from 1998 to
2011. The North had slightly better results, with its per capita GDP rising from
60 to 64 percent of the national per capita GDP. The improvement of this indicator compared with that of the Northeast can be explained by the impact
of the commodities boom in the North, which became the main exporter of
iron ore. The regions that historically had a per capita GDP greater than the
national average remained in their same positions, with a slight decrease in
the gap between the South and Southeast and the Central-West, with above-
average increases. The particularity of the latter was related to the impacts of
the commodities boom and the attraction of investments in industrial sectors
such as food and beverages, pharmaceuticals, and automobiles (the latter two
were concentrated in Goiás). The two regions that showed gains in per capita
GDP were the ones that benefited the most from an environment favorable to
exports of products derived from mineral extraction and agriculture (Cardozo
2018). Thus it is apparent that the policies implemented were important in
improving income levels but insufficient to reduce the interregional gap with
regard to per capita GDP.

     The assessment of the regional distribution of the GDP shows the continu-
ity of the slow and limited regional deconcentration process that has marked

the country since the 1980s, as the analyses of Diniz (1994) and Cano (2011) point out. The deconcentration of the GDP has intensified slightly since 2007 (Table 19.1). The regions that most increased their shares of the national GDP were the Northeast and the Central-West, followed by the North and the South. The Southeast was the only one whose share systematically decreased from 2007.

Data on manufacturing (Table 19.2) show an important deconcentrating trend. Extractive industry became more significant in the productive structure of the North and in Southeastern states such as Espírito Santo and Rio de Janeiro. The deconcentrated base of natural resources influenced the targets of investment, and the areas where natural resources exploration was predominant showed a significant connection to the international market (Cardozo 2018). From 2007 to 2016, the Southeast lost 6.4 points of its share of national manufacturing. The greatest gains were for the South (+2.5) and the Midwest (+3), followed by the Northeast (+1.3). The North lost 0.5 point due to the impacts of the crises on the manufacturing industry in the Industrial Polo of Manaus, which saw a drop in production from 2015.

The economic concentration that benefited the Southeast and the South in the twentieth century, although attenuated, is still a very strong trend in Brazilian regional development, especially industrial concentration. In 2016, the Southeast accounted for about 55.3 percent of the national manufacturing. There are several explanations for this, among them the country's growth dynamics, in which a set of public investments and incentives for private investment and social, sectoral, and territorial policies (including the National Policy for Regional Development) had a stronger impact on the poorer regions. In addition, territorial undercurrents were strongly affected by the commodities boom, which incorporated new fractions of the territory into the accumulation process and intensified the use of areas traditionally focused on extractive and agricultural activities (Cardozo 2018). This regional growth was largely a reflection of Brazil's growth pattern from 2003 to 2012, supported by the increase of commodities exports (which partly explain the improvements in North and the Central-West) and of the domestic market, to which the policies mentioned above contributed significantly (to explain the growth of the Central-West and the Northeast).

Thus, in a context of low priority for regional policies, public policies implemented by the Lula and Dilma governments contributed to important spatial impacts but did not produce a significant change in Brazilian regional development marked by significant interregional disparities.

TABLE 19.1 Relative proportions of the national GDP of Brazilian macroregions, 2002–2016

	2002	2003	2004	2005	2006	2007	2008	2009	2010	2011	2012	2013	2014	2015	2016
North	4.7	4.7	5.0	4.9	5.0	5.0	5.0	5.0	5.3	5.5	5.4	5.5	5.3	5.3	5.4
Northeast	13.1	12.8	12.9	13.0	13.2	13.0	13.1	13.6	13.5	13.3	13.6	13.6	13.9	14.2	14.3
Southeast	57.4	56.5	56.5	57.5	57.7	57.4	57.0	56.3	56.1	56.1	55.9	55.3	54.9	54.0	53.2
South	16.2	17.1	16.8	15.9	15.6	16.1	16.0	15.9	16.0	15.9	15.9	16.5	16.4	16.8	17.0
Central-West	8.6	8.9	8.9	8.6	8.4	8.6	8.9	9.3	9.1	9.1	9.2	9.1	9.4	9.7	10.1

SOURCE: IBGE 2002–2017

TABLE 19.2 Proportions of VTI (Industrial Transformation Value) of manufacturing industry in Brazilian microregions, 2007–2016

	2007	2008	2009	2010	2011	2012	2013	2014	2015	2016
North	5.5	5.3	5.2	4.9	4.7	4.4	4.7	5.0	5.1	5.0
Northeast	9.5	9.6	9.4	9.5	9.5	9.6	9.6	10.2	10.9	10.8
Southeast	61.7	61.2	59.8	60.1	59.7	58.6	57.5	56.2	55.6	55.3
South	19.9	20.1	20.9	20.7	21.2	21.6	22.4	22.6	22.1	22.4
Central-West	3.5	3.8	4.7	4.8	5.0	5.7	5.8	5.9	6.3	6.5

SOURCE: IBGE (2007–2017)

4   Conclusion

This chapter has analyzed the advances and limitations of the implementation of regional development policies in Brazil during the Lula and Dilma governments. To varying degrees, these governments combined policies linked to
greater state performance with more orthodox macroeconomic policies, and
therefore they can be characterized as limited developmentalist, a description
that reflects their hybrid character. Regional matters are as important as income
distribution policies to strategies for development and must be included in
any analysis of policies aimed at reducing inequalities. The National Policy for
Regional Development can consequently be interpreted as an advance toward
the implementation of new development policies. The obstacles to the implementation of this policy reflected the difficulty of executing de facto develop-
mentist policies combined with neoliberal macroeconomic measures.

For the first time since redemocratization, regional disparities were widely
debated under the Lula and Dilma governments, and a regional development
policy covering the country as a whole was formulated. However, in spite of the
institutional advance and the clarification of the Brazilian regional problem,
this policy was not implemented in its entirety, and after 2013 it was practically
abandoned. These governments' social and sectoral public policies achieved
satisfactory results in terms of labor market and income distribution improvements and had significant regional repercussions, but they were insufficient
for the structural change that might contribute to national development.

Thus, despite the attempt to implement a regional development policy and
the positive territorial impacts of nonterritorialized policies, Brazil still has
significant spatial disparities in income, living conditions, and the structure
of production. These differences are apparent in a comparison of social and
production indicators for the five macroregions. Intraregional inequalities are
also significant. While the policies which were typical of the Workers' Party
national governments were essential to reduce poverty and increase consumption in the poorest regions, they did not substantially modify the historically
high levels of regional disparity. The persistence of this problem reflects the
limitations of these administrations with regard to the implementation of a
national development strategy based on specific structural reforms, and this is
what is expressed by what we call a limited developmentalism.

With the end of the Dilma administration in 2016, limited developmentalism (which had already been undermined by the economic policy of 2015) was
replaced by policies that deepened economic deregulation, as an agenda of
labor, social security, and administrative reforms, among others, was implemented. In this sense, both the planning of regional policies and sectoral and

social policies that contributed to the reduction of social inequalities and had important territorial effects during the Lula government and the first Dilma government were also jeopardized.

References

Araújo, T. (2013). Tendências do desenvolvimento regional recente no Brasil. In: Brandão, C., and Siqueira, H. (eds.), *Pacto Federativo, integração nacional e desenvolvimento regional*, 39–51. São Paulo: Editora Fundação Perseu Abramo.

Boito Jr., A., and Berringer, T. (2013). Classes sociais, neodesenvolvimentismo e política externa nos governos Lula e Dilma. *Revista de Sociologia e Política* 21(47): 31–38.

Brandão, C. (2013). Pacto Federativo, reescalonamento do Estado e desafios para integração e coesão regionais e para legitimar políticas de desenvolvimento regional no Brasil. In: Brandão, C., and Siqueira, H. (eds.), *Pacto Federativo, integração nacional e desenvolvimento regional*, 163–174. São Paulo: Editora Perseu Abramo.

Brandão, C. (2019). Productive and economic changes and territorial reconfiguration in Brazil at the beginning of the 21st century. *Revista Brasileira de Estudos Urbanos e Regionais* 21(2): 258–279.

Brandão, C. (2020). Dinâmicas e transformações territoriais recentes: o papel da PNDR e das políticas públicas não regionais com impacto territorial. In: Monteiro Neto, A. (ed.), *Desenvolvimento Regional no Brasil – Políticas, estratégias e perspectivas*, vol. 2, 151–188. Rio de Janeiro: IPEA.

Bresser-Pereira, L.C. (2001). Decisões estratégicas e 'overlapping consensus' na América Latina. *Revista de Economia Política* 21(4): 3–29.

Bresser-Pereira, L.C. (2006). O novo desenvolvimentismo e a ortodoxia convencional. *São Paulo em Perspectiva* 20(3): 5–24.

Bresser-Pereira, L.C. (2016a). Teoria novo-desenvolvimentista: uma síntese. *Cadernos do Desenvolvimento* 11(19): 145–165.

Bresser-Pereira, L.C. (2016b). Reflecting on new developmentalism and classical developmentalism. *Review of Keynesian Economics* 4(3): 331–352.

Bresser-Pereira, L.C. (2020a). Novo Desenvolvimentismo – Um segundo momento do estruturalismo latino-americano. *Revista de Economia Contemporânea* 24(1): 1–20.

Bresser-Pereira, L.C. (2020b). New and Classical Developmentalism compared: a response to Medeiros. *Review of Keynesian Economics* 8(2): 168–177.

Bresser-Pereira, L.C., and Gala, P. (2010). Macroeconomia estruturalista do desenvolvimento. *Revista de Economia Política* 30(4): 663–686.

Cano, W. (2011). Novas determinações sobre as questões regional e urbana após 1980. *Revista Brasileira de Estudos Urbanos e Regionais* 13(2): 27–53.

Carneiro, R. (2018). Navegando a contravento: Uma reflexão sobre o experimento desenvolvimentista do governo Dilma Rousseff. In Carneiro, R., Baltar, P., and Sarti, F. (eds.), *Para além da política econômica*. São Paulo: Editora UNESP Digital.

Cardozo, S. (2018). Foreign trade, production structures, employment, and income in the Brazilian macroregions (2004–2014). *Revista Brasileira de Estudos Urbanos e Regionais* 20(2): 401–420.

Cardozo, S., and Martins, H. (2020). New Developmentalism, Public Policies and Regional Inequalities in Brazil: The Advances and Limitations of Lula's and Dilma's Governments. *Latin American Perspectives* 47(2): 147–162.

Castro, S. (2014). Política regional e desenvolvimento: caminhos para o Brasil e para o Nordeste. In: Guimarães, P., Aguiar, R., Lastres, H., and Silva, M. (eds.), *Um olhar territorial para o desenvolvimento*, 502–539. Rio de Janeiro: BNDES.

Coêlho, V. (2017). Política regional do governo Lula (2003–2010). In: Monteiro Neto, A., Castro, C., and Brandão, C. (eds.), *Desenvolvimento regional no Brasil: Políticas, estratégias e perspectivas*, 65–98. Rio de Janeiro: IPEA.

Corrêa, V.P., and Hamilton, V. (2015). Modelo de crescimento brasileiro e mudança estrutural: avanços e limites. In: Corrêa, V.P. (ed.), *Padrão de acumulação e desenvolvimento brasileiro*, 17–55. São Paulo: Editora Fundação Perseu Abramo.

Curado, M. (2017). Por que o governo Dilma não pode ser classificado como novo desenvolvimentista? *Revista de Economia Política* 37(1): 130–146.

Diniz, C. (1994). Polygonized development in Brazil: neither decentralization nor continued polarization. *International Journal of Urban and Regional Research* 18(2): 293–314.

Fonseca, P. (2016). O projeto desenvolvimentista no Brasil: histórico e desafios da atualidade. *Cadernos do Desenvolvimento* 11(19): 117–128.

IBGE (Instituto Brasileiro de Geografia e Estatística). 2002–2017. *Contas Regionais*. Brasília: IBGE.

IBGE (Instituto Brasileiro de Geografia e Estatística). 2007–2017. *Pesquisa Industrial Anual (PIA)*. Brasília: IBGE.

INEP (Instituto Nacional de Estudos e Pesquisas Educacionais). 2014. *Sinopse estatística da educação superior*. Brasília: INEP.

IPEA (Instituto de Pesquisa Economia Aplicada). (2018). *Políticas sociais: acompanhamento e análise*. Brasília: IPEA.

Macedo, F., Pires, M., and Sampaio, D. (2017). 25 anos de fundos constitucionais de financiamento no Brasil: avanços e desafios à luz da Política Nacional de Desenvolvimento Regional. *Revista Latino Americana de Estudios Urbanos e Regionales* 43(129): 257–277.

Macedo, F., and Porto, L. (2020a). Proposta de atualização das tipologias da Política Nacional de Desenvolvimento Regional (PNDR): nota metodológica e mapas de referência. In: Monteiro Neto, A. (ed.), *Desenvolvimento Regional no Brasil – Políticas, estratégias e perspectivas*, vol. 2, 245–304. Rio de Janeiro: IPEA.

Macedo, F., and Porto, L. (2020b). Existe uma Política Nacional de Desenvolvimento Regional no Brasil? In: Freitas, T., Deponti, C., and Silveira, R. (eds.), *Políticas públicas e desenvolvimento regional: atores e estratégias em regiões do Brasil*, 193–223. São Carlos: Pedro & João Editores.

Medeiros, C. (2020). A Structuralist and Institutionalist developmental assessment of and reaction to New Developmentalism. *Review of Keynesian Economics* 8(2): 147–167.

Mollo, M.L.R. (2016). Desenvolvimentismos, inclusão social e papel do Estado. *Cadernos do Desenvolvimento* 11(19): 131–143.

Mollo, M.L.R., and Amado, A.M. (2015). O debate desenvolvimentista no Brasil: tomando partido. *Revista Economia e Sociedade* 24(1): 1–28.

Morais, L., and Saad-Filho, A. (2011). Da economia política à política econômica: o novo-desenvolvimentismo e o governo Lula. *Revista de Economia Política* 31(4): 507–527.

Morais, L., and Saad-Filho, A. (2012). Neo-developmentalism and the challenges of economic policy-making under Dilma Rousseff. *Critical Sociology* 38(6): 789–798.

Oliveira, F. (2012). *Política econômica, estagnação e crise mundial: Brasil, 1980–2010*. Rio de Janeiro: Editora Beco do Azougue.

Portugal, R., and Silva, S. (2020). *História das políticas regionais no Brasil*. Brasília: IPEA.

Prates, D., Fritz, B., and Paula, L.F. (2017). Brazil at the crossroads: a critical assessment of developmentalist policies. In: Arestis, P., Baltar, C., and Prates, D. (eds.), *The Brazilian Economy since the Great Financial Crisis of 2007/2008*, 9–38. London: Palgrave Macmillan.

Randolph, R. (2020). Agendamentos políticos, arenas sociopolíticas e formatos institucionais de desenvolvimento regional a nível federal: duas experiências brasileiras. In: Silveira, R., and Deponti, C. (eds.), *Desenvolvimento regional: processos, políticas e transformações territoriais*, 161–202. São Carlos: Pedro & João Editores.

Rolnik, R., and Klink, J. (2011). Crescimento econômico e desenvolvimento urbano: por que nossas cidades continuam tão precárias? *Novos Estudos* 89 (March): 89–109.

Rossi, P., and Mello, G. (2016). Componentes macroeconômicos e estruturais da crise brasileira: o subdesenvolvimento revisitado. *Brazilian Keynesian Review* 2(2): 252–263.

Sicsú, J., Paula, L.F., and Michel, R. (2007). Por que novo-desenvolvimentismo? *Revista de Economia Política* 27(4): 507–524.

Silva, G., Martins, H., and Neder, H. (2016). Investimento em infraestrutura de transportes e desigualdades regionais no Brasil: uma análise dos impactos do Programa de Aceleração do Crescimento (PAC). *Revista de Economia Política* 36(4): 840–863.

Souza, M.B. (2013). *Variedades de capitalismo e reescalonamento espacial do estado no Brasil*. Campinas: Universidade Estadual de Campinas.

UNDP (United Nations Development Program)/IPEA (Instituto de Pesquisa Econômica Aplicada)/FJP (Fundação João Pinheiro). (2016). *Atlas do desenvolvimento humano no Brasil.* Brasília: UNDP.

Index

CPSIA information can be obtained
at www.ICGtesting.com
Printed in the USA
JSHW050005050123
35747JS00002B/2

9 781642 598100